A HISTORY OF VIOLENCE

DC COMICS

Dan DiDio VP-Editorial

Andrew Helfer Group Editor

Jim Higgins Assistant Editor

Robbin Brosterman Senior Art Director

Paul Levitz President & Publisher

Georg Brewer VP-Design & Retail Product Development

Richard Bruning Senior VP-Creative Director

Patrick Caldon Senior VP-Finance & Operations

Chris Caramalis VP-Finance

Terri Cunningham VP-Managing Editor

Alison Gill VP-Manufacturing

Rich Johnson VP-Book Trade Sales

Hank Kanalz VP-General Manager, WildStorm

Lillian Laserson Senior VP & General Counsel

Jim Lee Editorial Director-WildStorm

David McKillips VP-Advertising & Custom Publishing

John Nee VP-Business Development

Gregory Noveck Senior VP-Creative Affairs

Cheryl Rubin Senior VP-Brand Management

Bob Wayne VP-Sales & Marketing

A HISTORY OF VIOLENCE

WRITTEN BY **JOHN WAGNER**

ART BY **VINCE LOCKE**

LETTERING BY **BOB LAPPAN**

PARADOX PRESS

NEW YORK

To Blossom, who has her own
history of violence.

—JOHN WAGNER—

For Khrysta, without whose love
and support I would be lost.

—VINCE LOCKE—

INTRODUCTION

BY JOHN WAGNER

Picture this: a man goes berserk with an automatic rifle on a crowded street. People are falling, screaming, lying in their own blood, dead or dying. A cop runs onto the scene and is slammed back by a spray of bullets. He comes to rest close to a doorway where you've taken cover, his gun dropping from his dead hand, only inches away. The gunman is shouting incoherently, firing at random into the crowd. He pauses to reload. His back is to you, you'd have a clear shot. Even you couldn't miss from this range. And you know — you just know — if you don't drop this crazy sucker more people are going to die.

But what if you do miss? What if the madman turns on you — you're dead for certain then. And there's a way out. Slip away and even if more people do die, at least you won't be among them. What do you do? Hurry, time's running out. He's pushing a fresh magazine home — he's turning — he's seen you —

Too late.

Try this: you go to your car one morning and notice the engine's warm. Not only that, there's an extra three hundred miles on the clock. Unless you've been driving in your sleep, you know you didn't do it. When you return that evening all the lights are on in your apartment. There's the remains of a fried bacon sandwich in the kitchen. The bedclothes have been disturbed and there's a pervasive smell of after-shave. You live alone, you're a vegetarian, no one else has access to your life. What do you do? Call the police?

"Bacon sandwich, huh...? Right, lady, that sounds real serious, we'll have a squad car down there by two weeks next Tuesday."

During the night you come awake with an uneasy feeling. Gradually you begin to realize there's someone in your bed. A man. He reeks repulsively of stale sweat and Brüt and he's wearing that nice pink nightdress you got from Sears mail order. When you gasp and recoil from him, he sits up, solicitous: "Having another one of your nightmares, dear?"

The man claims to be your husband Ernie but you've never seen him before. Or have you? Is Ernie for real? Are you merely suffering from the delusion that he does not exist? Either way, you've got problems.

Or...you're an ex—marine, say, running a little car spares business in Phoenix. You get a call one morning. A man's voice: "We're going to kill you."

Huh?

"We hear you're a real hard man to kill. We're going to put you to the test."

"Who is this?"

"Better run.   It's your only chance."

Naturally, being a likable guy without an enemy in the world, you take this with a hefty pinch of salt. Even when later someone standing next to you at a lunch counter is shot through the head from a passing car — a single shot, right on the button — it doesn't quite connect. But that night you get another call...

"That was just a warning to show you we're serious."

"Who is this?" you manage to stammer.

"It could have been you. You wanna die?"

"What the hell do you want?"

"You got two choices. You can stay, or you can run. It's more fun when you run, though…"

What if you don't run? What if you go to the police — and the detective you speak to has the unmistakable twang of the voice on the phone? What if next they burn your house down…?

Ordinary people caught up in extraordinary situations. No muscled Arnies, no dirtied Harries, just normal people — you and me. The guy next door. That's the fascination. Put yourself in their place, wonder what you'd do, how you'd react — and be grateful that particular bombshell didn't fall your way. But it could have. Don't kid yourself, it could happen to you, anytime. Right out of the blue.

None of these scenarios, I hasten to add, appears in the story you are about to read, though the final storyline was originally submitted to Paradox, and I can see now that *A History of Violence* in some part stemmed out of it. There is that same sense of claustrophobic terror, of powerful, sinister, unstoppable forces closing in, crushing.

I met Paradox Press Editor Andrew Helfer at a convention in Scotland. Andy had been my editor on another project some years earlier. He was totally exasperating to work with but I had a lot of respect for his ability to produce good stories.   He outlined his plans for Paradox Press and, despite his incredibly low page rates (I didn't believe you till the first check came through, Andy!), I was interested. Real stories about real people. It was different. And it wasn't super-heroes. I've been writing comic strips for twenty-five years now, but I still can't force my brain (not willingly, at least) round super-heroes. Something missing in my upbringing, perhaps.

Months passed, as they do. I outlined the aforementioned idea for Andy, but he felt it was too close to another story of mine, *Button Man* (now available at all good comic shops!).   Could I come up with something else — something even better?   Time was running out. The phone calls from New York were growing more and more urgent.

"Mr. Waaagner." I dreaded the singsong greeting coming down the line. "I'm still waiting for that storr—ry." They'd filled all their slots, he was holding one open for me, but he needed the story NOW.

"You'd have it, sir, honest," I bleated, "if it wasn't for the dry rot."

Dry rot. A miserable, cold, wet April. Builders ripping the house apart, stripping down walls, knocking out foundations, hammers thudding, drills screaming, me confined to one room above it all. Constant interruptions, carrying what seemed like the whole house out to the bonfire, barrowing in rubble, shoveling concrete, weeping inside.

And then it came to me. A story about a man's life. What would happen if...? Not quite fully formed, but there in much of the essential detail. Damn, I wouldn't like to be in his spot...

Within two weeks of acceptance the first chapter was written. That was well over two years ago, and for that I must take the blame. I little realized the full implications of that first, shocking act of violence.

My sincere thanks to all the staff at Paradox who have worked and suffered on this book and especially to Joel Rose and Andy Helfer for supplying the idea, based on a true story, that provided the final, brutal twist of the knife. And of course to Vince Locke, who has labored long and hard for many months and whose fine art you can now appreciate. Let it draw you into the story. Picture yourself...

You may have realized by now that I have told you next to nothing about *A History of Violence*. This is deliberate. How I hate introductions that give away half the story, like reading the last page first. I want the events described to come as much of a surprise to you as they are to my characters.

Disturbing. Terrifying. Life-shattering.

Right out of the blue.

CHAPTER 1

A SMALL TOWN KILLING

"Beware of desp'rate steps.

The darkest day

(Live till tomorrow)

will have passed away."

-WILLIAM COWPER 'THE NEEDLESS ALARM'

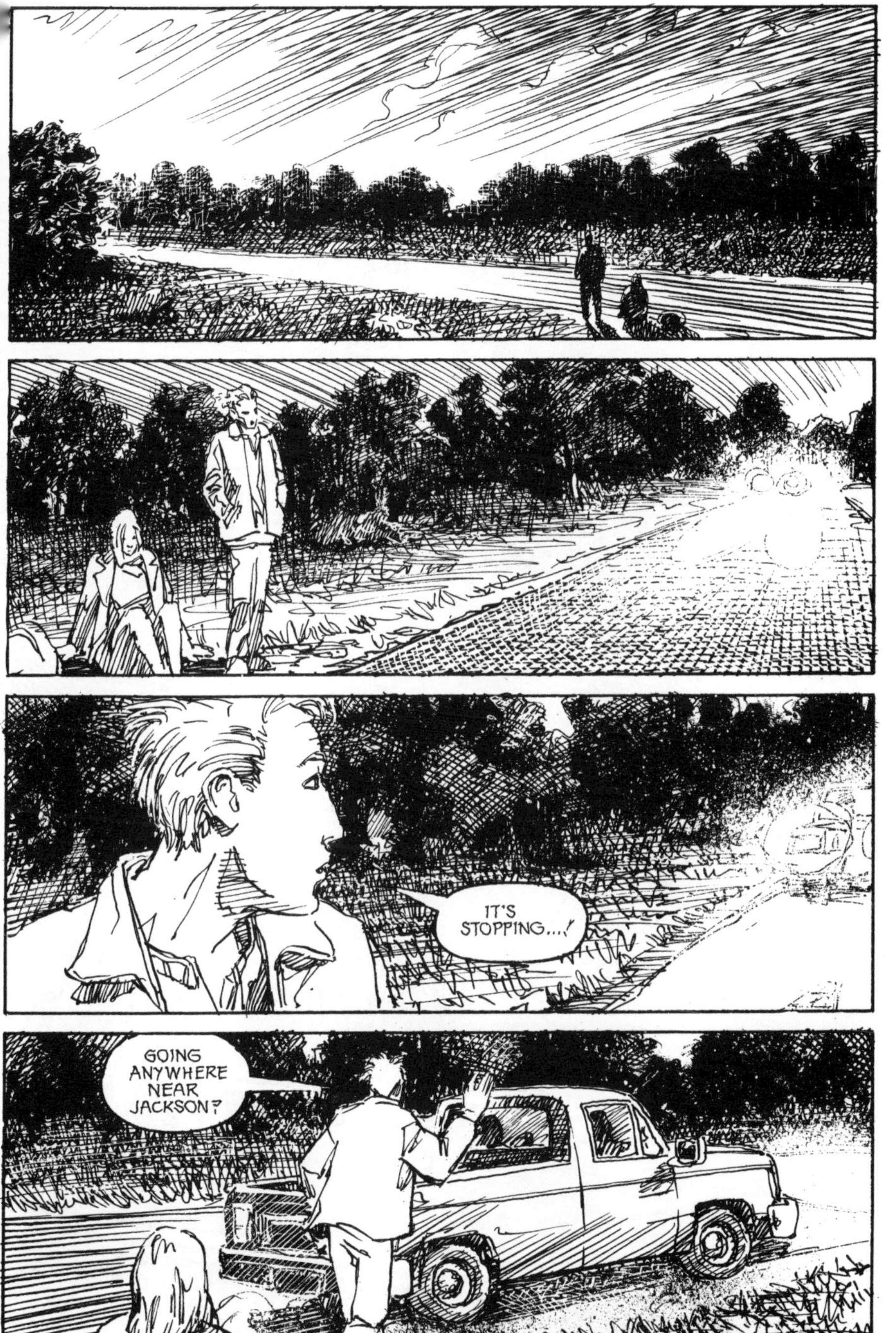

IT'S STOPPING...!
GOING ANYWHERE NEAR JACKSON?

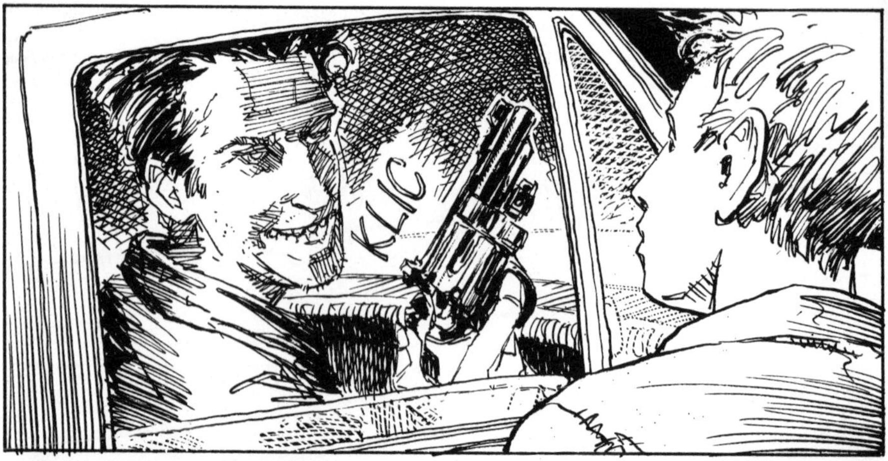
KLIC

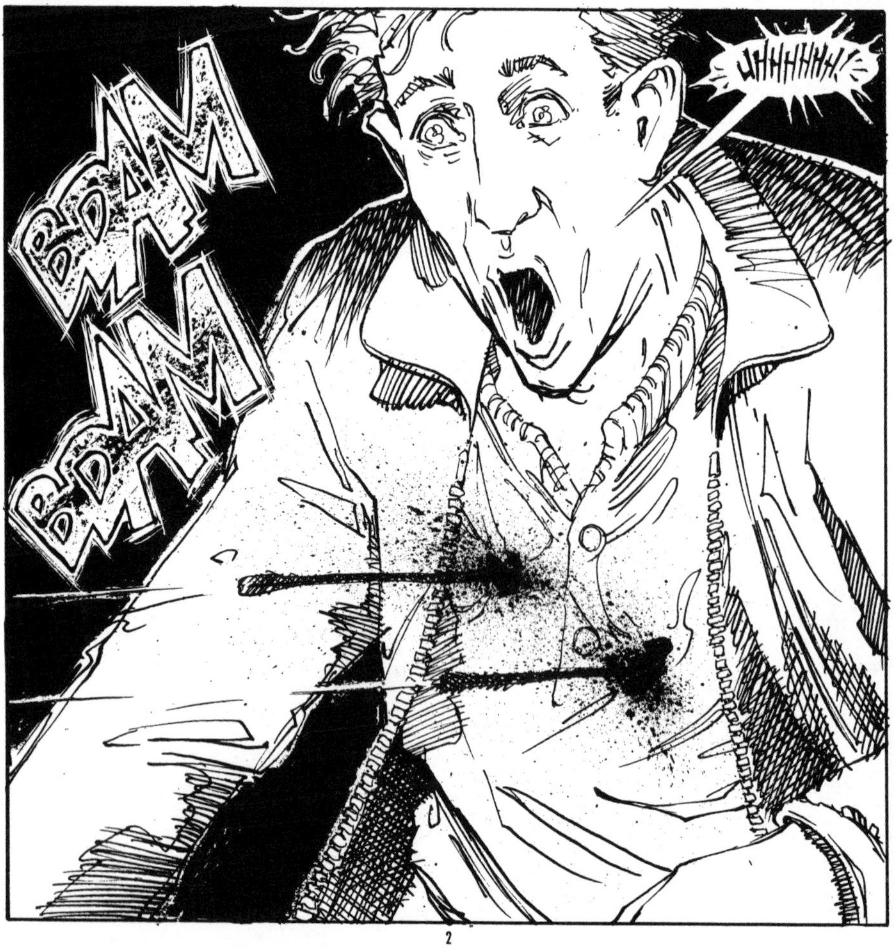
BDAM
BDAM
UHHHHHH!

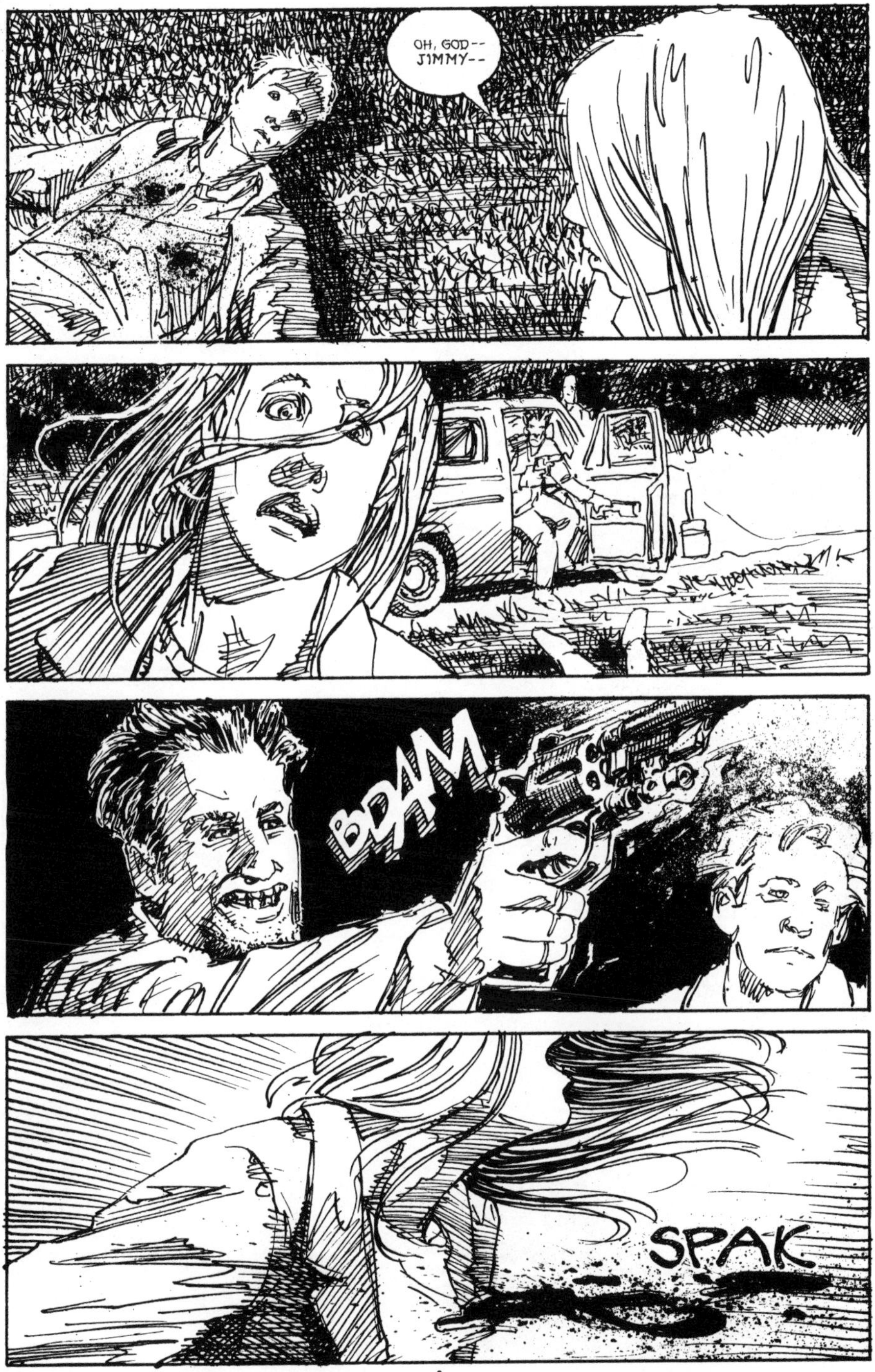
OH, GOD--
JIMMY--
BDAM
SPAK

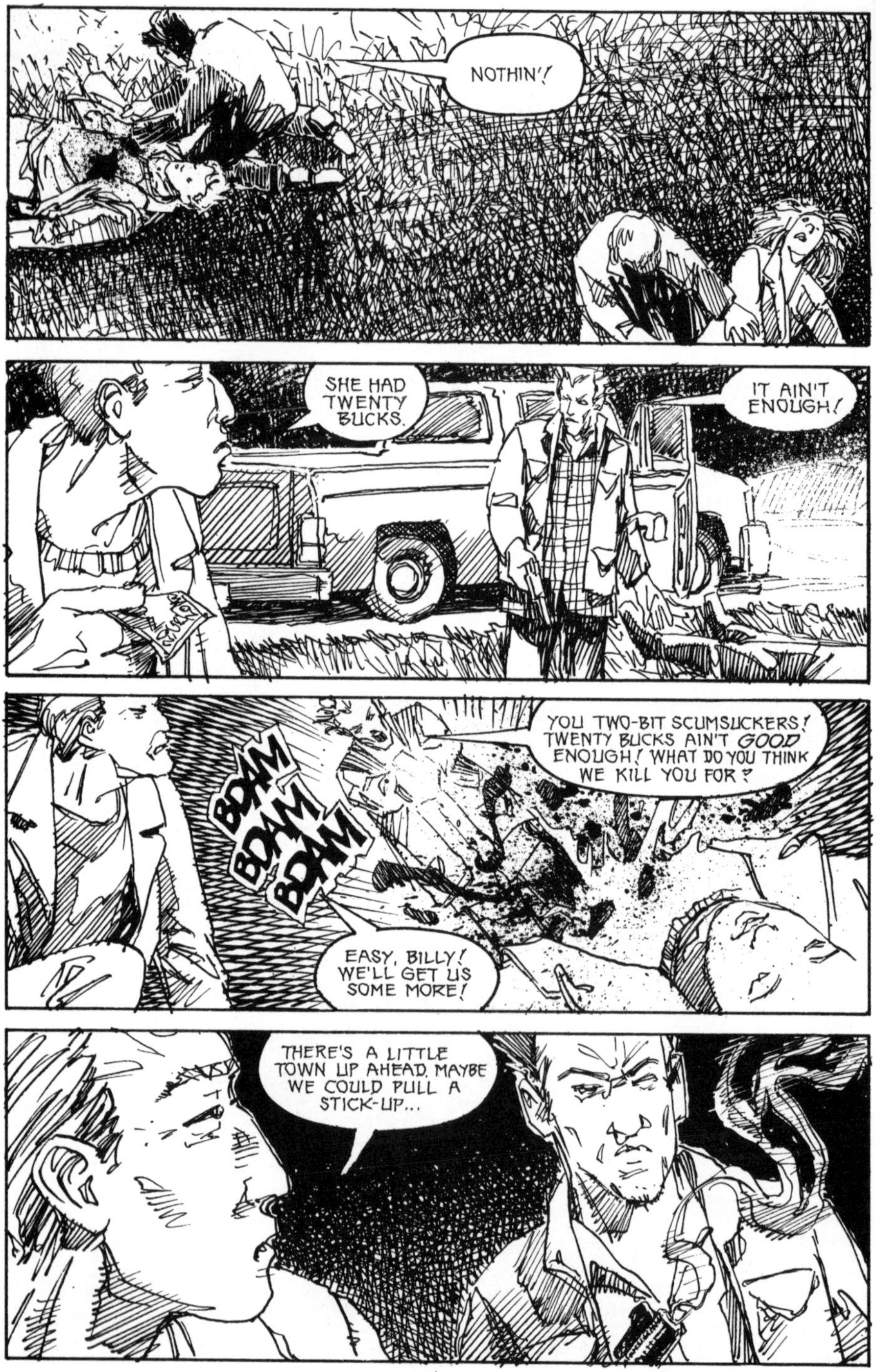
NOTHIN'!
SHE HAD TWENTY BUCKS.
IT AIN'T ENOUGH!
BDAM BDAM BDAM
YOU TWO-BIT SCUMSUCKERS! TWENTY BUCKS AIN'T GOOD ENOUGH! WHAT DO YOU THINK WE KILL YOU FOR?
EASY, BILLY! WE'LL GET US SOME MORE!
THERE'S A LITTLE TOWN UP AHEAD. MAYBE WE COULD PULL A STICK-UP...

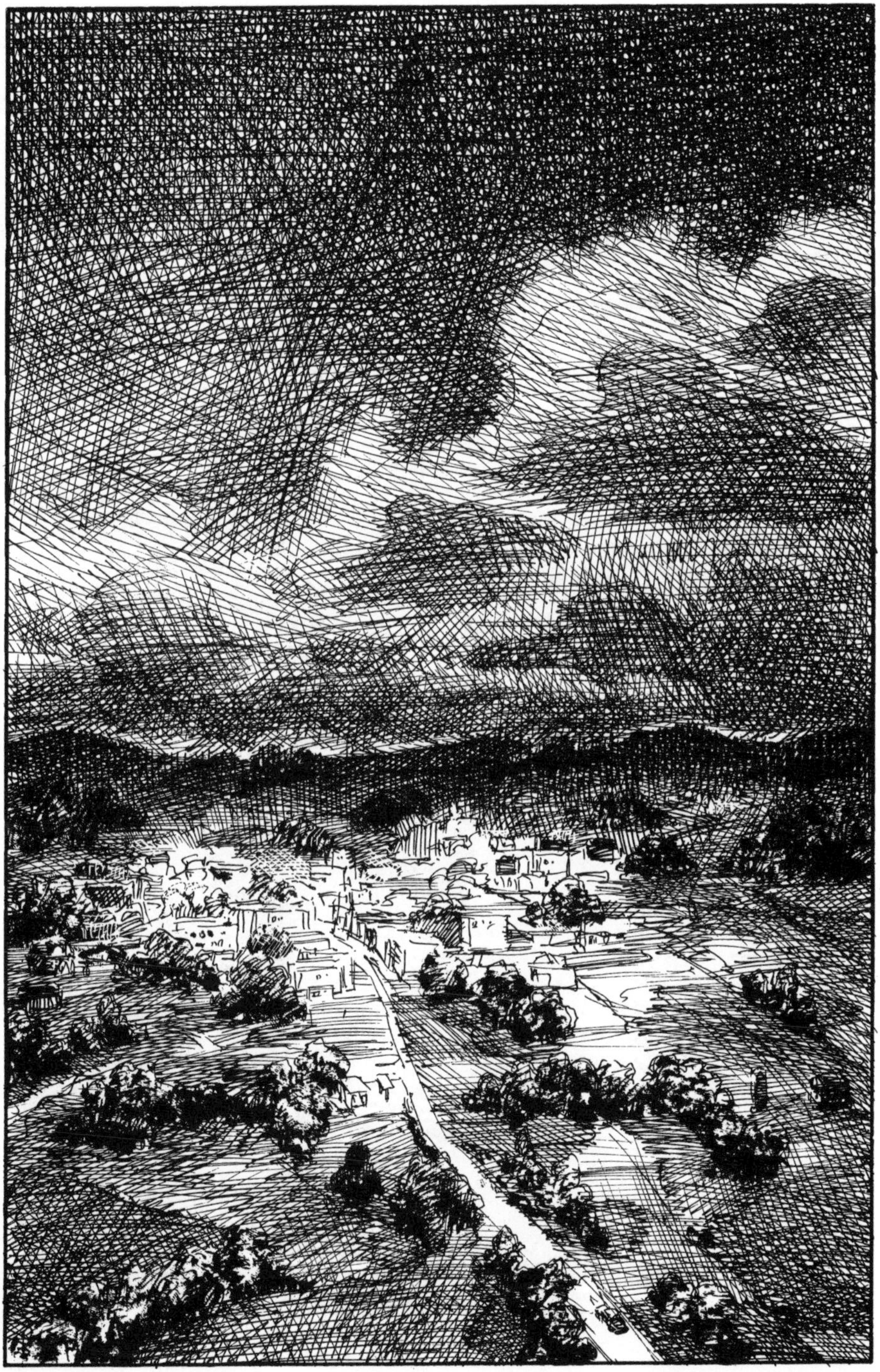

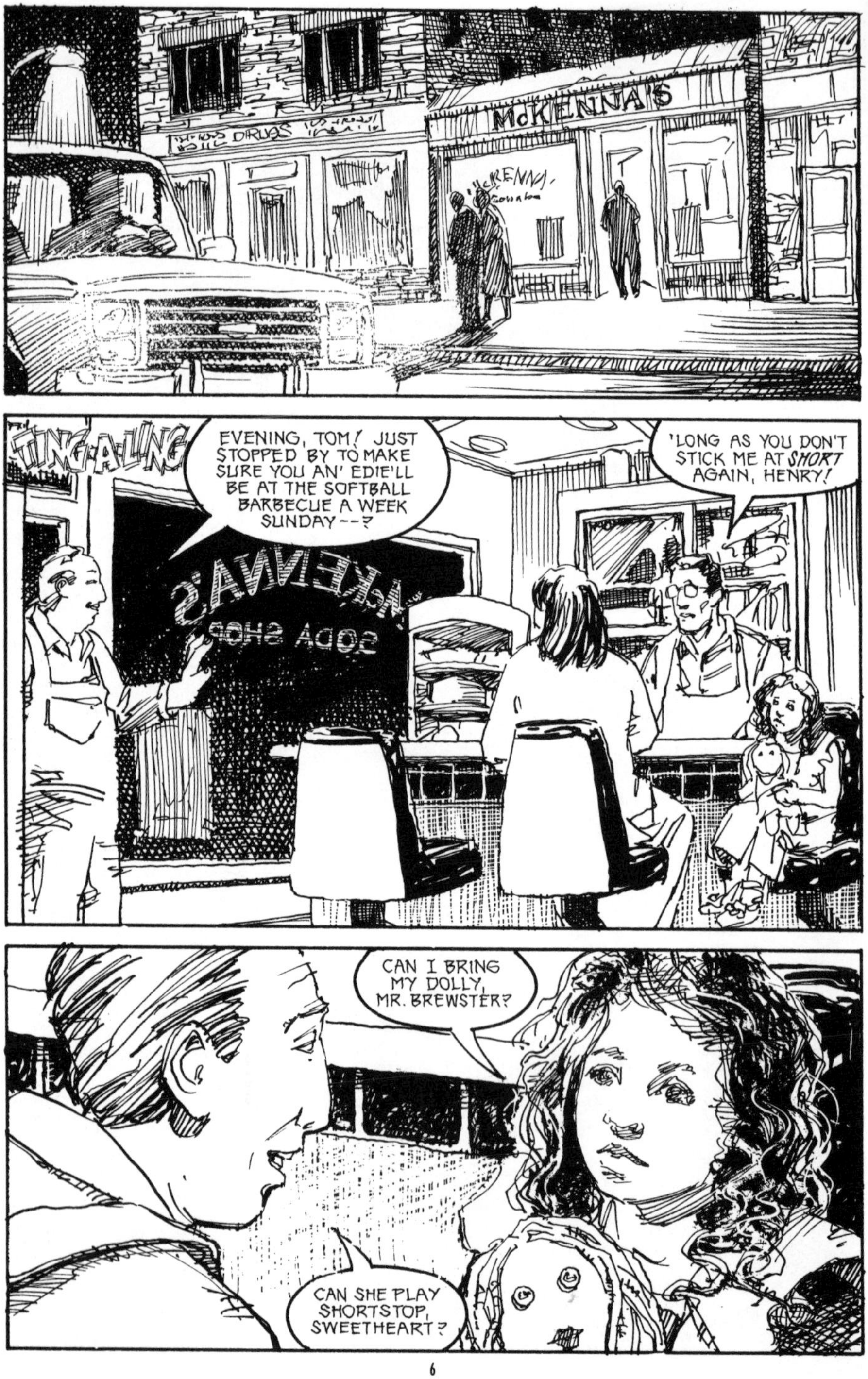
DRUGS
McKENNA'S
TING-A-LING
EVENING, TOM! JUST STOPPED BY TO MAKE SURE YOU AN' EDIE'LL BE AT THE SOFTBALL BARBECUE A WEEK SUNDAY--?
'LONG AS YOU DON'T STICK ME AT SHORT AGAIN, HENRY!
CAN I BRING MY DOLLY, MR. BREWSTER?
CAN SHE PLAY SHORTSTOP, SWEETHEART?

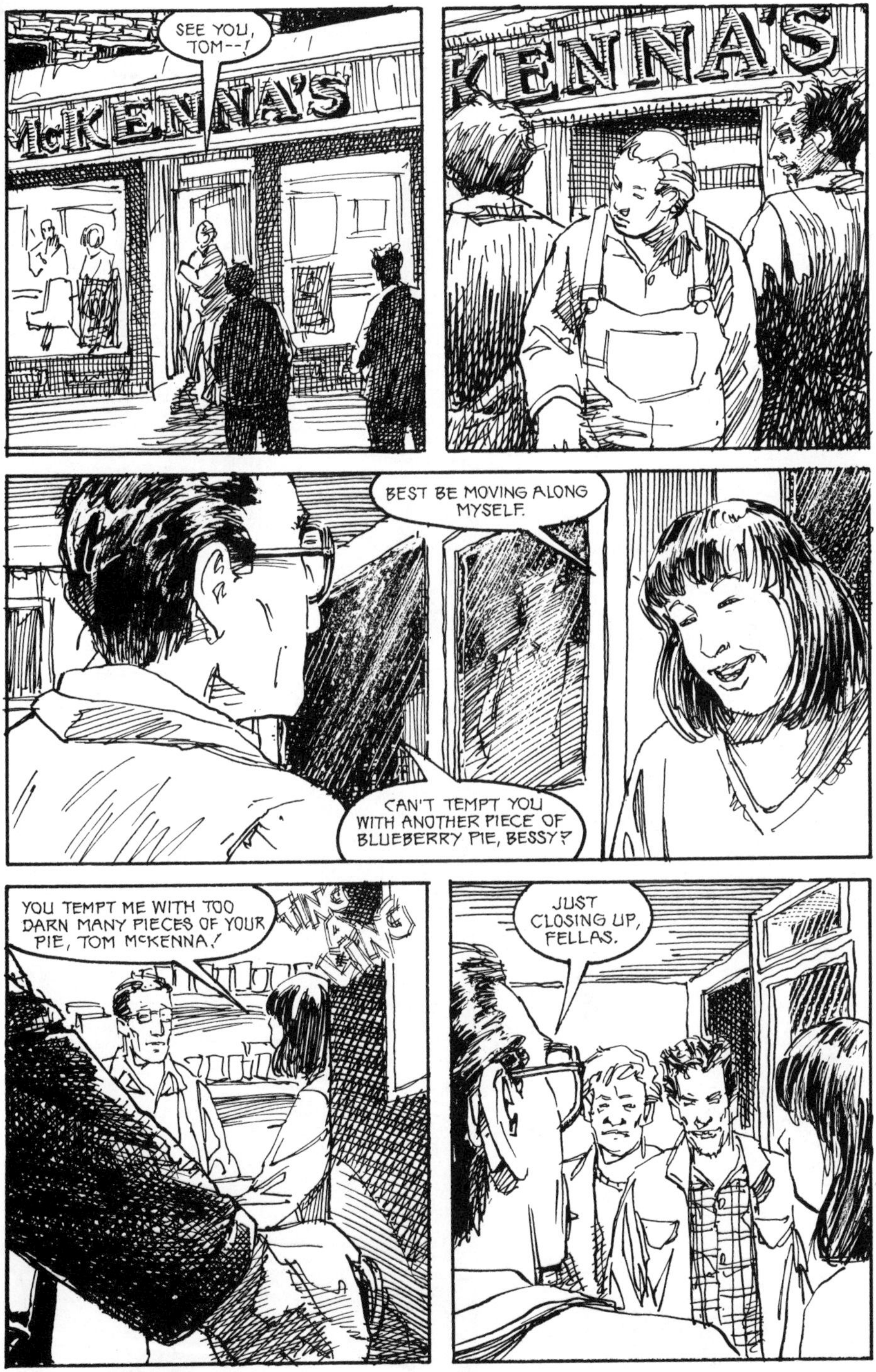

McKENNA'S
SEE YOU, TOM--!
KENNA'S
BEST BE MOVING ALONG MYSELF.
CAN'T TEMPT YOU WITH ANOTHER PIECE OF BLUEBERRY PIE, BESSY?
YOU TEMPT ME WITH TOO DARN MANY PIECES OF YOUR PIE, TOM McKENNA!
JUST CLOSING UP, FELLAS.

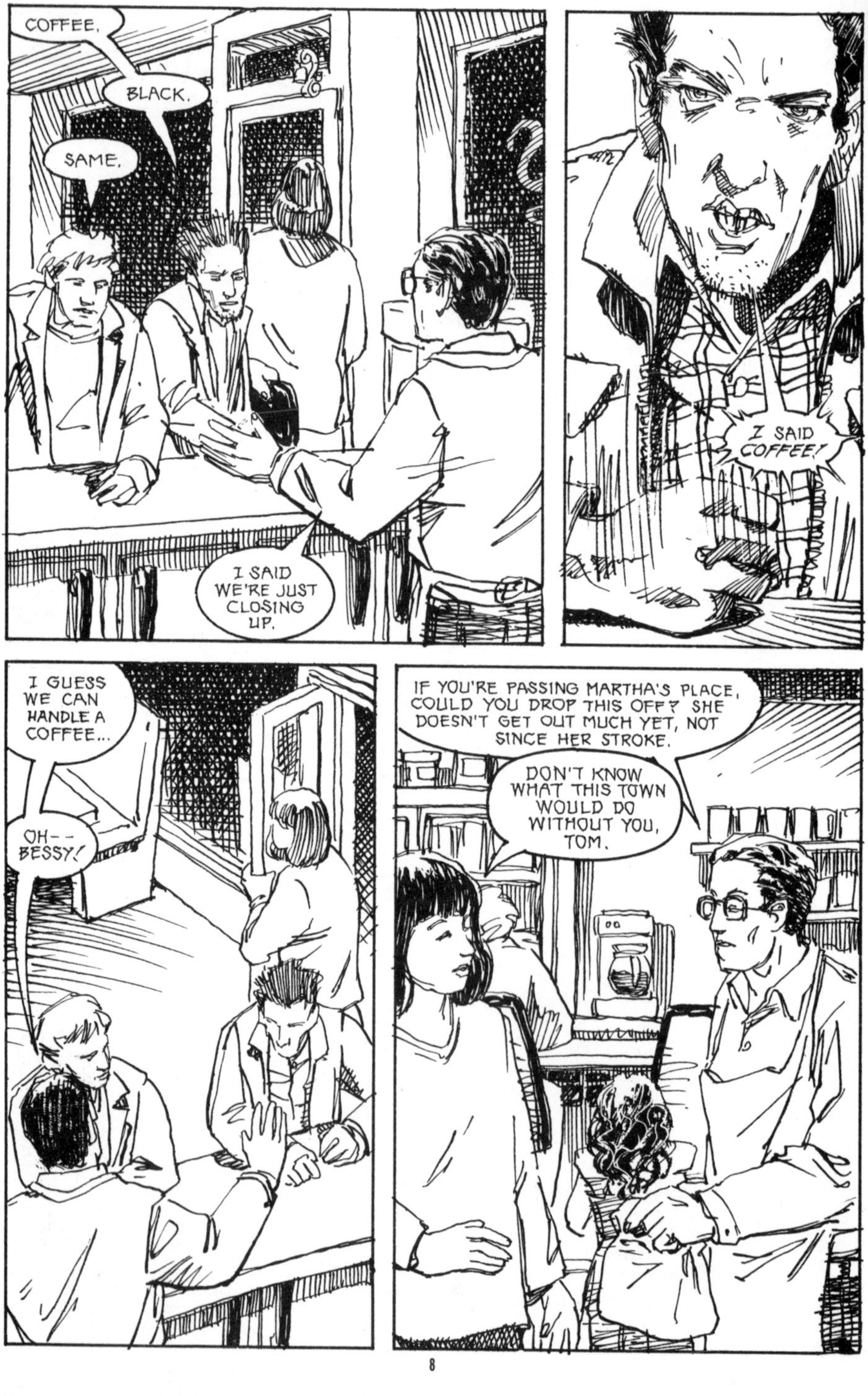
COFFEE,
BLACK.
SAME.
I SAID WE'RE JUST CLOSING UP.
I SAID COFFEE!
I GUESS WE CAN HANDLE A COFFEE...
OH-- BESSY!
IF YOU'RE PASSING MARTHA'S PLACE, COULD YOU DROP THIS OFF? SHE DOESN'T GET OUT MUCH YET, NOT SINCE HER STROKE.
DON'T KNOW WHAT THIS TOWN WOULD DO WITHOUT YOU, TOM.

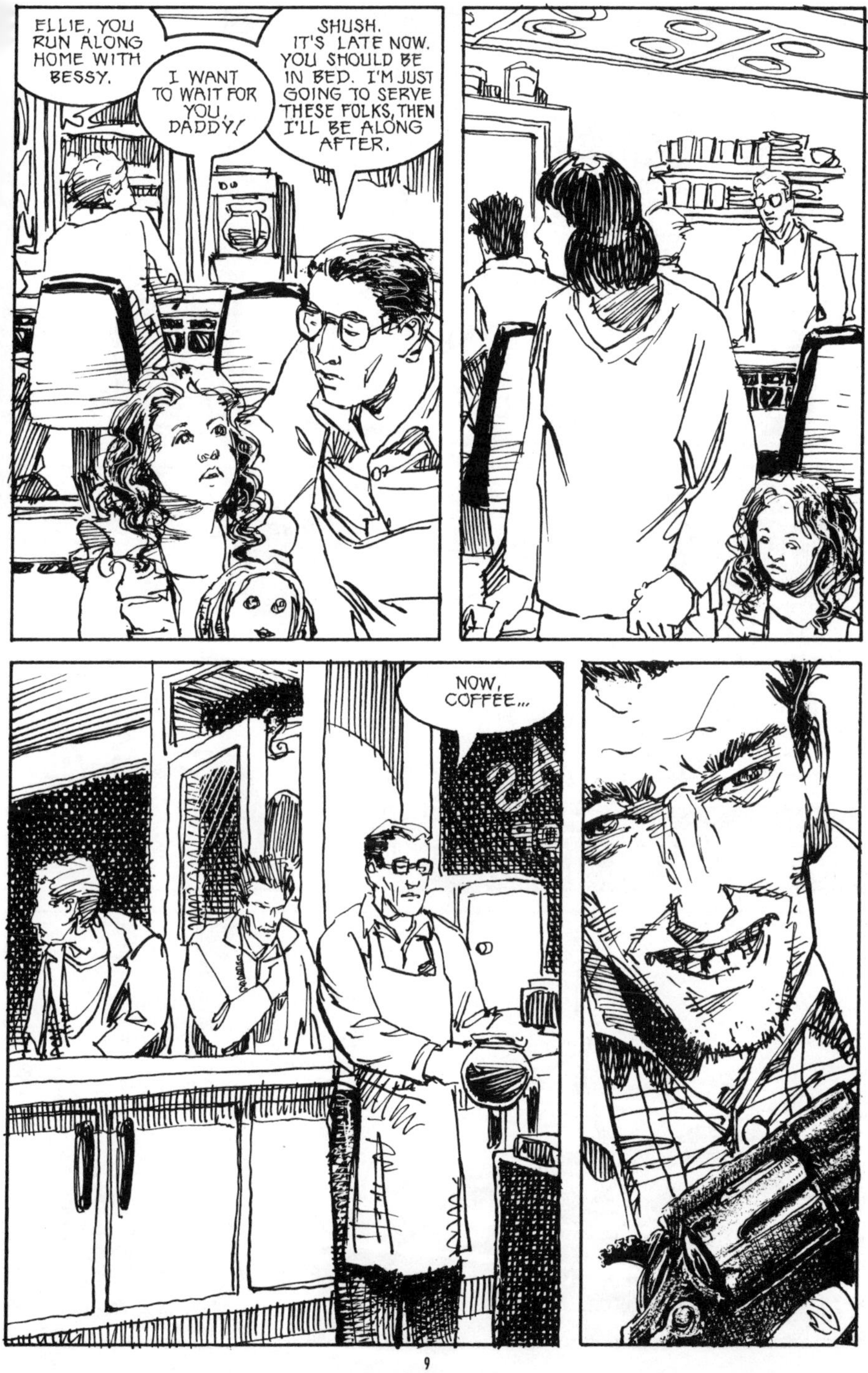
ELLIE, YOU RUN ALONG HOME WITH BESSY.
I WANT TO WAIT FOR YOU, DADDY!
SHUSH. IT'S LATE NOW. YOU SHOULD BE IN BED. I'M JUST GOING TO SERVE THESE FOLKS, THEN I'LL BE ALONG AFTER.
NOW, COFFEE...

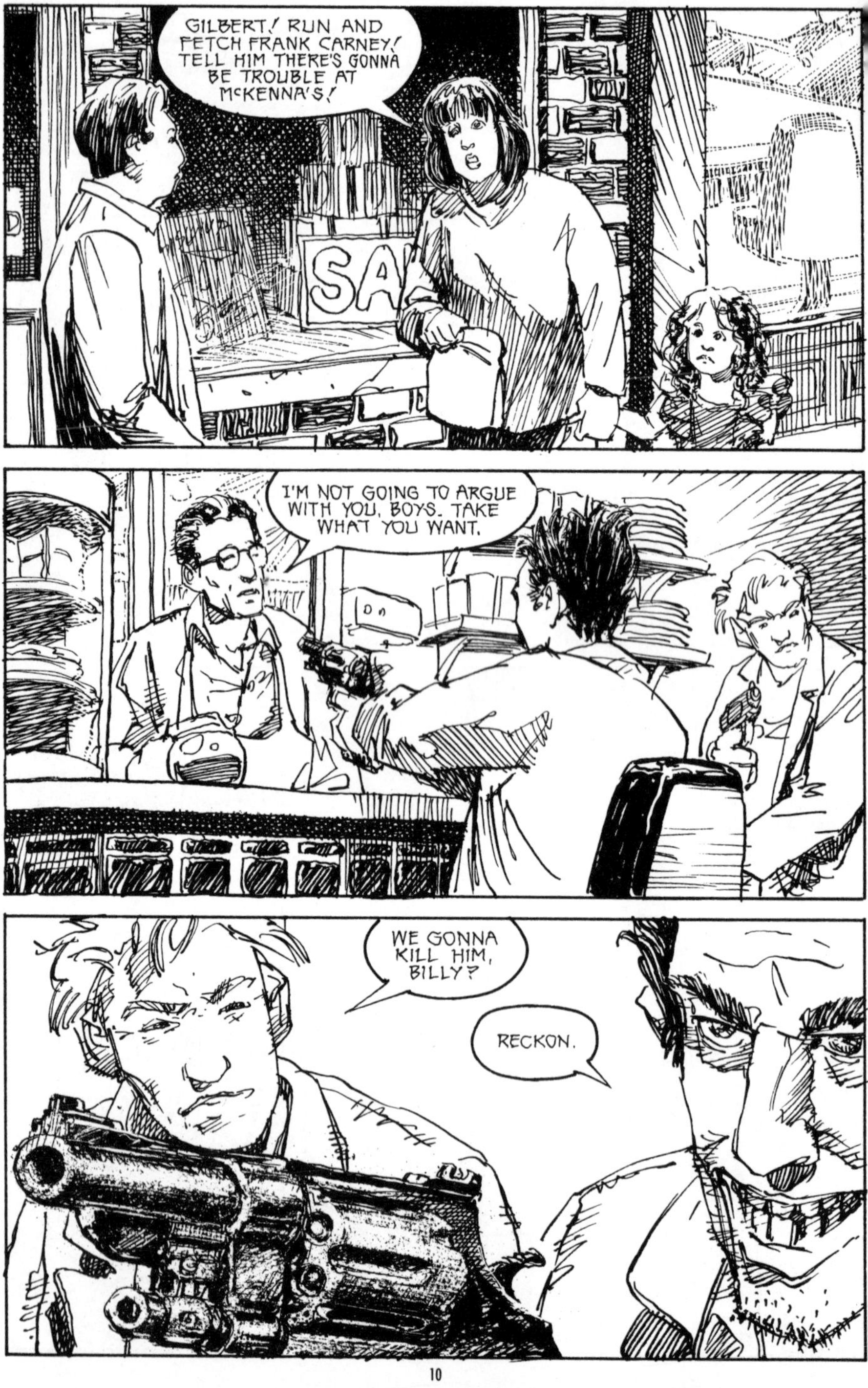
GILBERT! RUN AND FETCH FRANK CARNEY! TELL HIM THERE'S GONNA BE TROUBLE AT McKENNA'S!
I'M NOT GOING TO ARGUE WITH YOU, BOYS. TAKE WHAT YOU WANT.
WE GONNA KILL HIM, BILLY?
RECKON.

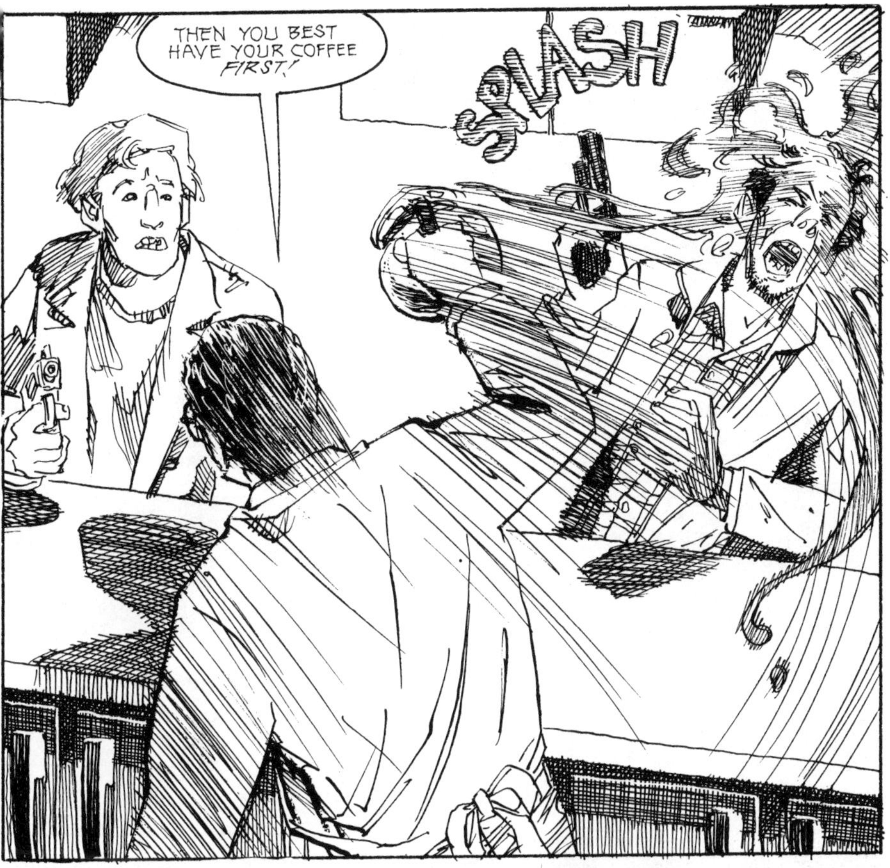
THEN YOU BEST HAVE YOUR COFFEE FIRST!
SPLASH

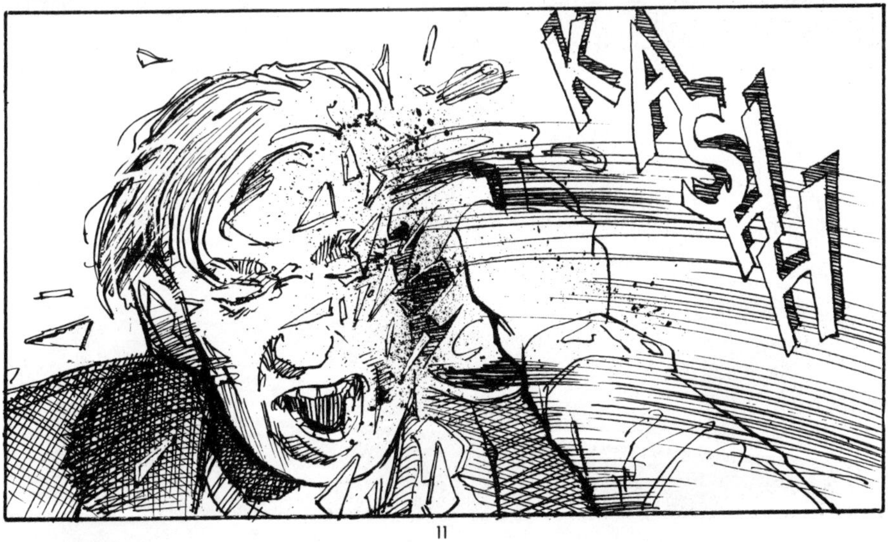
KASSH

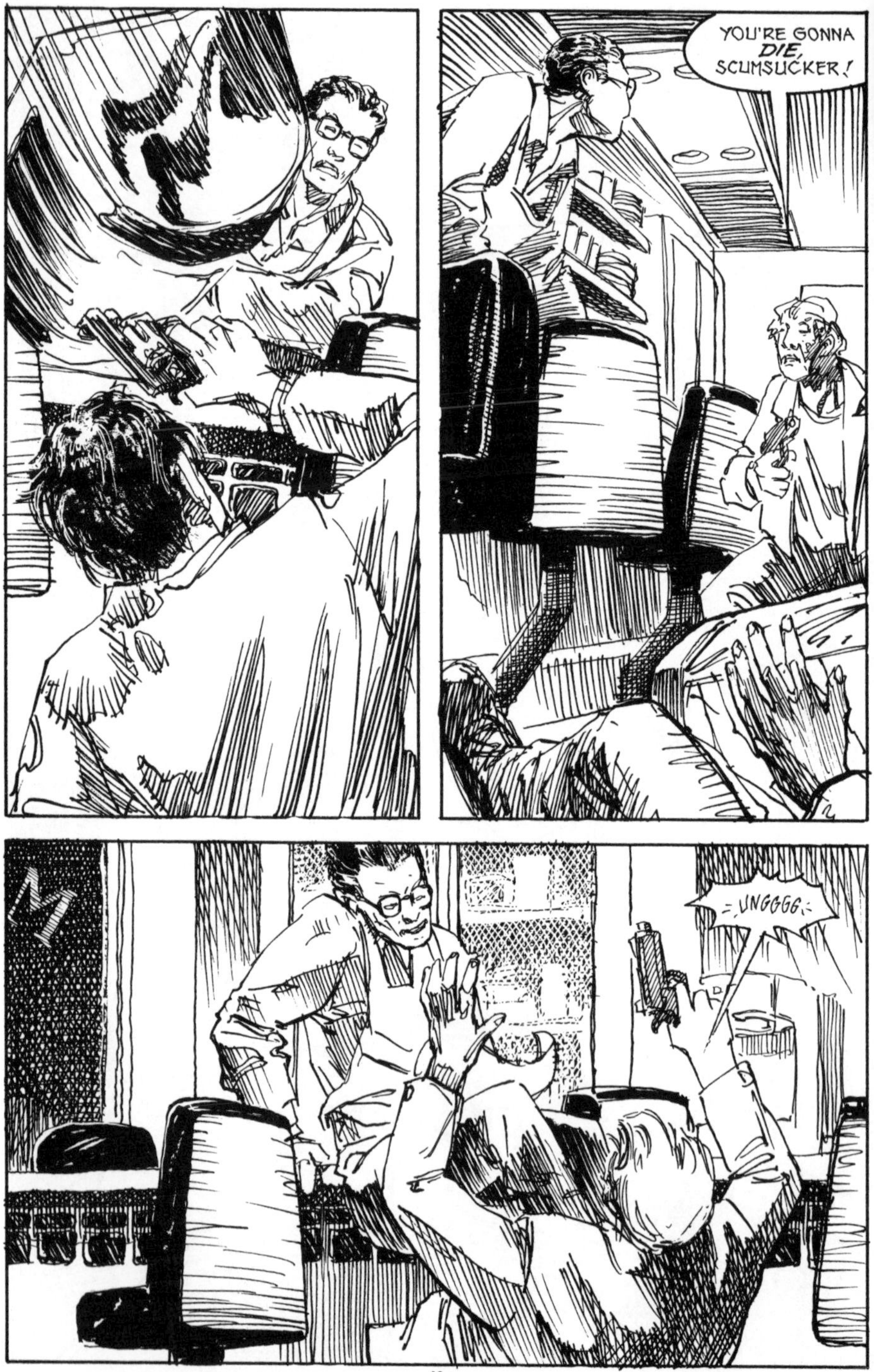
YOU'RE GONNA *DIE*, SCUMSUCKER!
UNGGGG

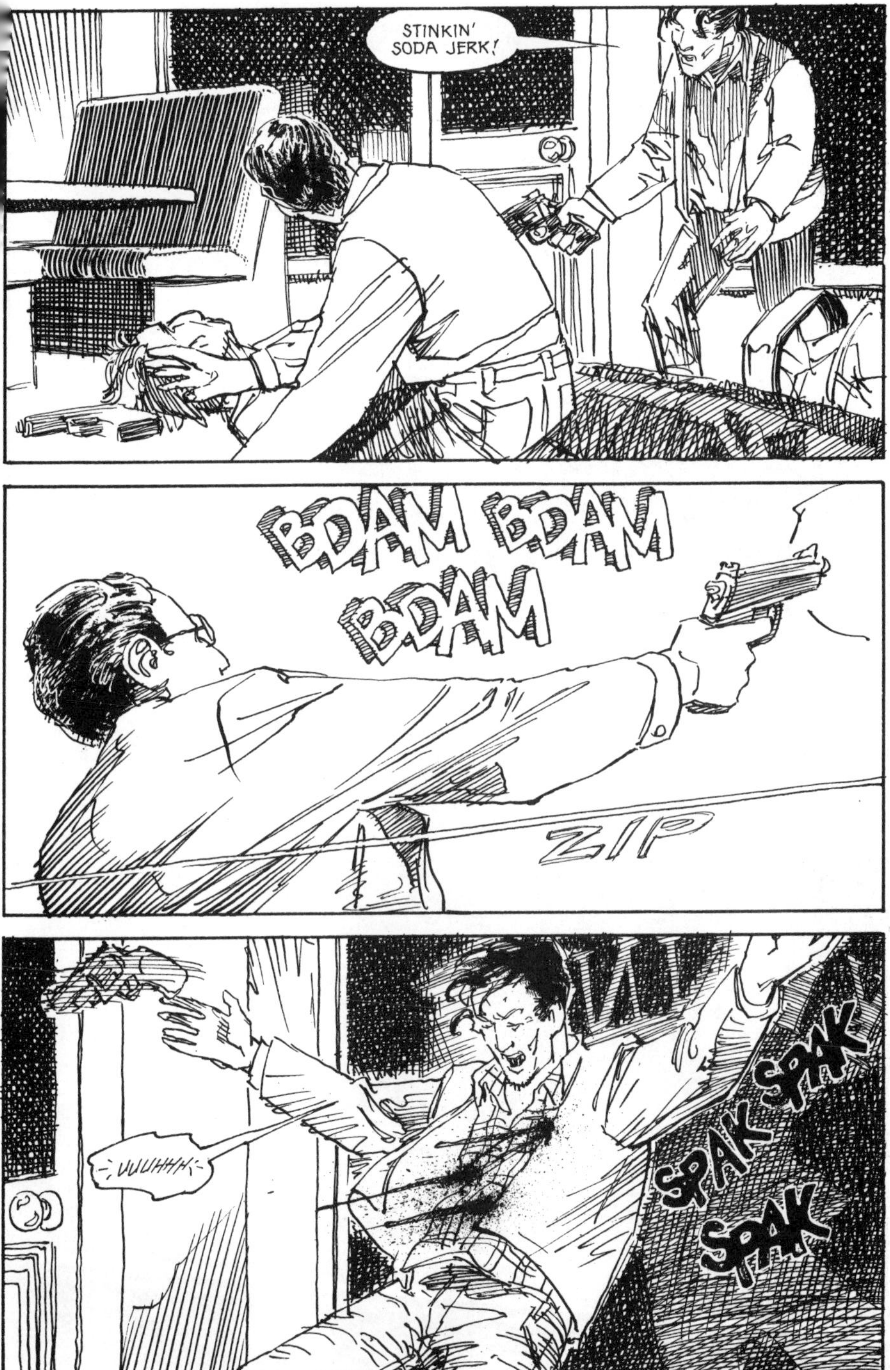
STINKIN' SODA JERK!
BDAM BDAM
BDAM
ZIP
UUUHHH
SPAK SPAK
SPAK
SPAK

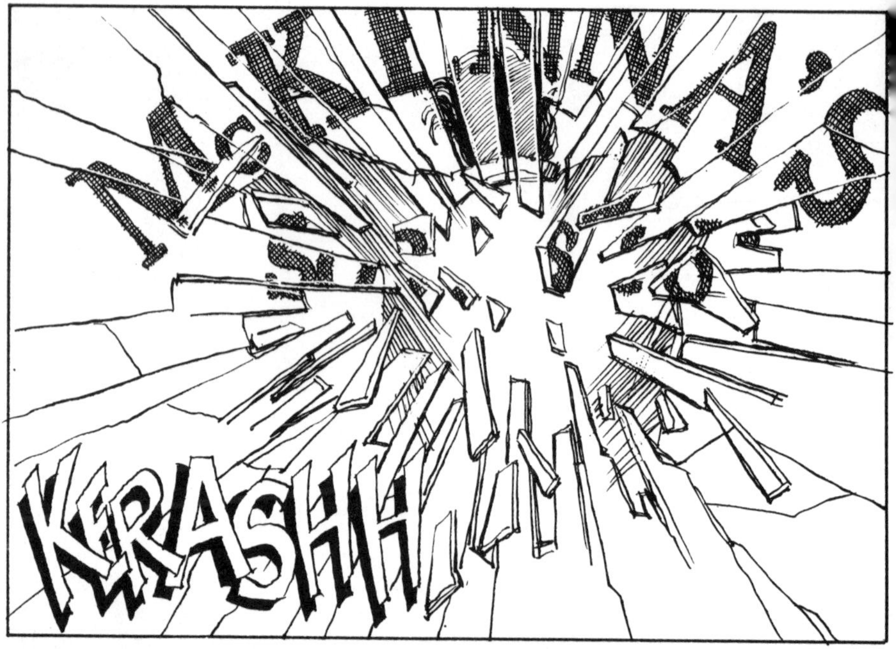
KERASHH

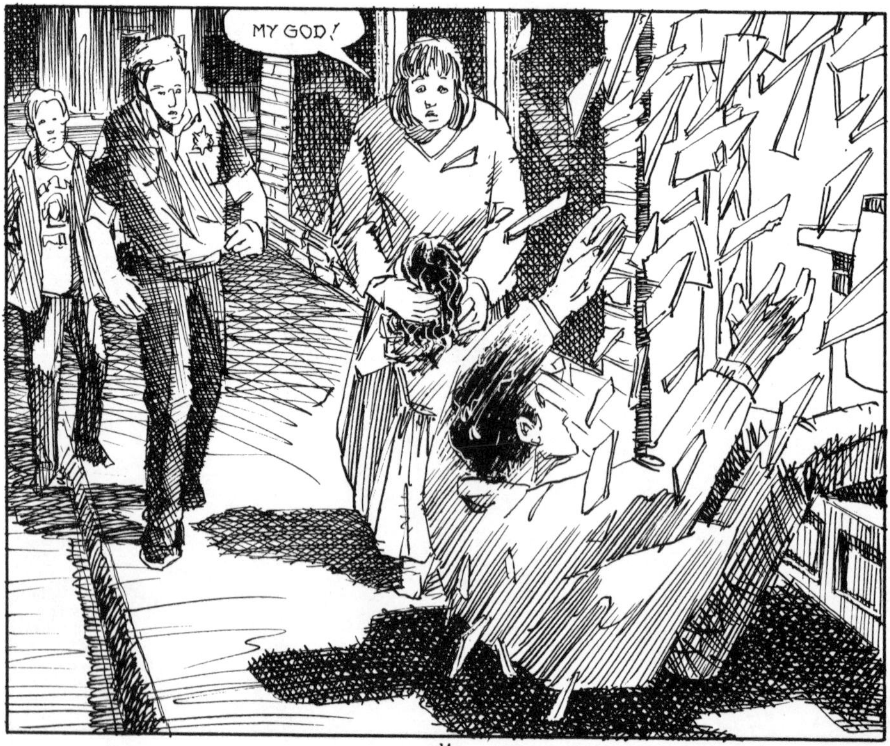
MY GOD!

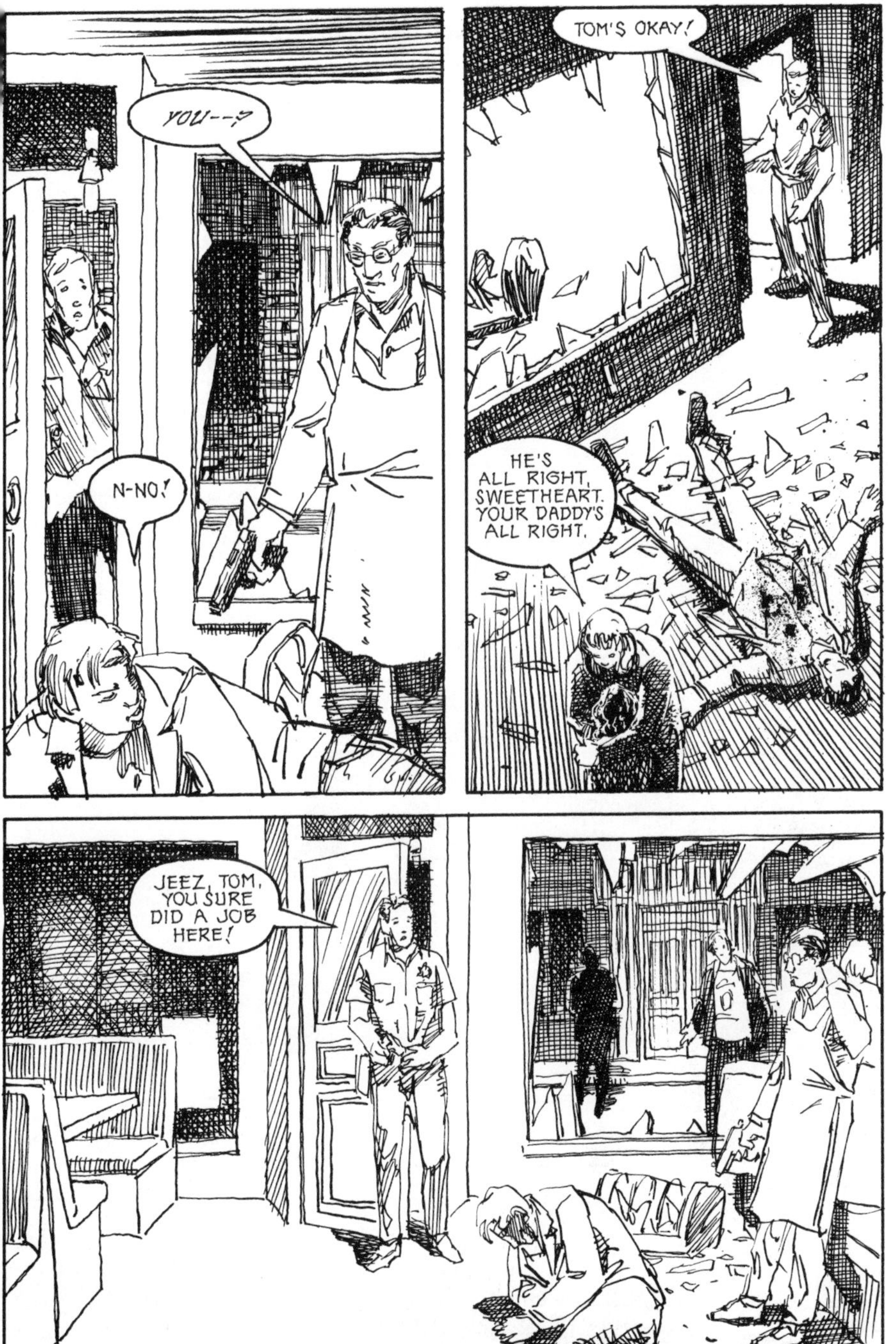
YOU--?
N-NO!
TOM'S OKAY!
HE'S ALL RIGHT, SWEETHEART. YOUR DADDY'S ALL RIGHT.
JEEZ, TOM, YOU SURE DID A JOB HERE!

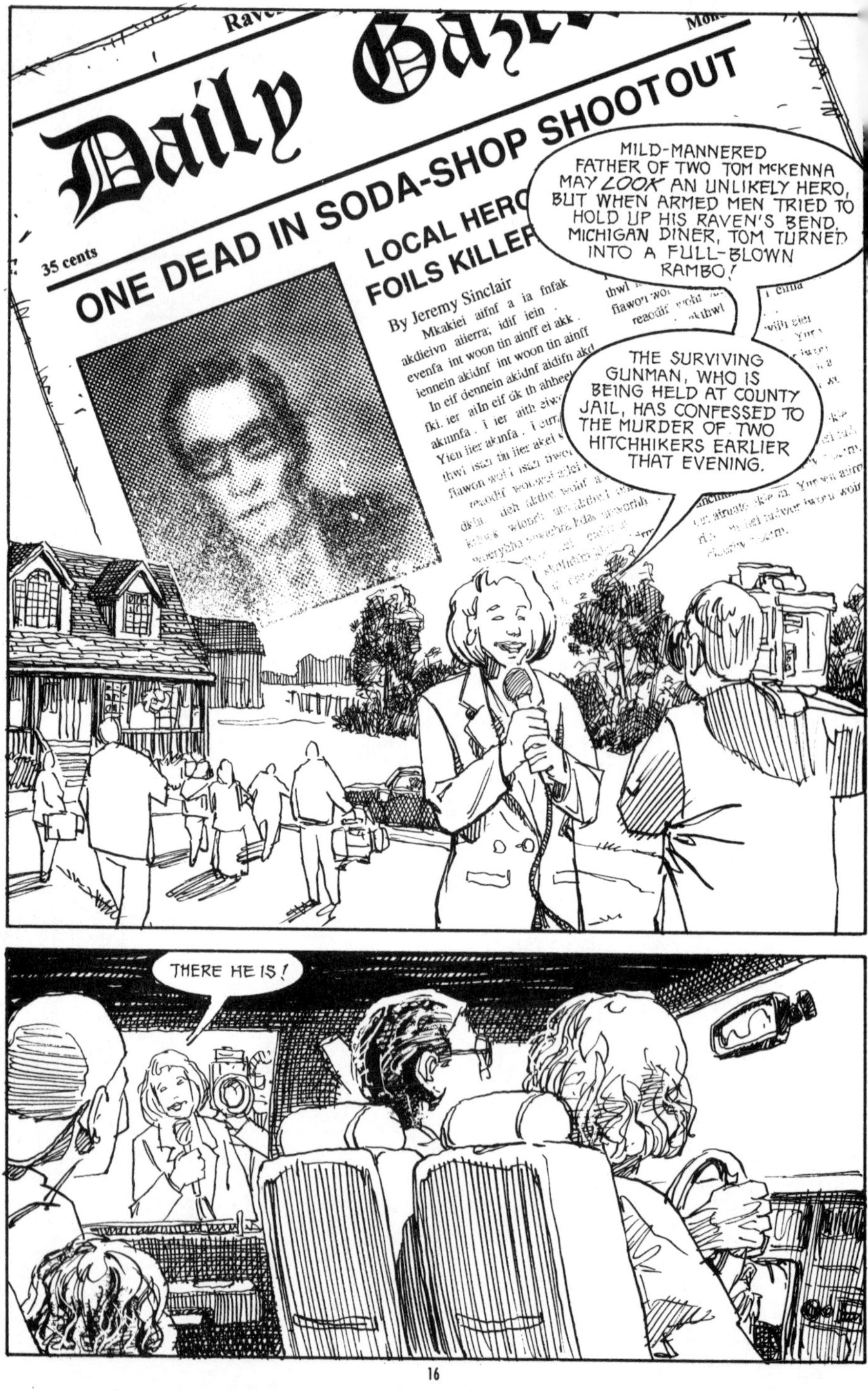
Daily Gazette
35 cents
ONE DEAD IN SODA-SHOP SHOOTOUT
LOCAL HERO FOILS KILLER
By Jeremy Sinclair
MILD-MANNERED FATHER OF TWO TOM McKENNA MAY LOOK AN UNLIKELY HERO, BUT WHEN ARMED MEN TRIED TO HOLD UP HIS RAVEN'S BEND, MICHIGAN DINER, TOM TURNED INTO A FULL-BLOWN RAMBO!
THE SURVIVING GUNMAN, WHO IS BEING HELD AT COUNTY JAIL, HAS CONFESSED TO THE MURDER OF TWO HITCHHIKERS EARLIER THAT EVENING.
THERE HE IS!

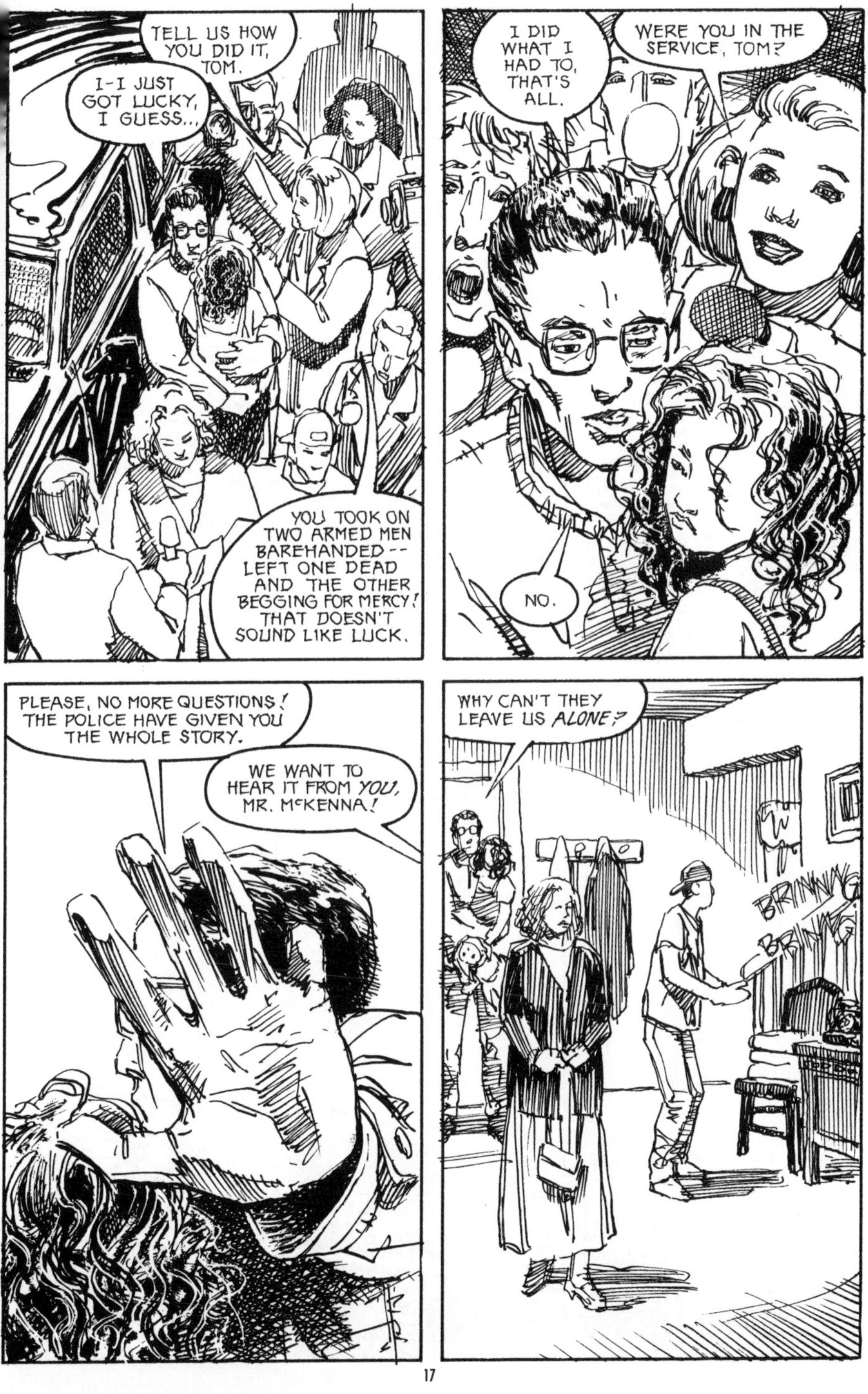
TELL US HOW YOU DID IT, TOM.
I-I JUST GOT LUCKY, I GUESS...
YOU TOOK ON TWO ARMED MEN BAREHANDED-- LEFT ONE DEAD AND THE OTHER BEGGING FOR MERCY! THAT DOESN'T SOUND LIKE LUCK.
WERE YOU IN THE SERVICE, TOM?
I DID WHAT I HAD TO, THAT'S ALL.
NO.
PLEASE, NO MORE QUESTIONS! THE POLICE HAVE GIVEN YOU THE WHOLE STORY.
WE WANT TO HEAR IT FROM *YOU*, MR. McKENNA!
WHY CAN'T THEY LEAVE US *ALONE*?
BRINNG
BRINNG

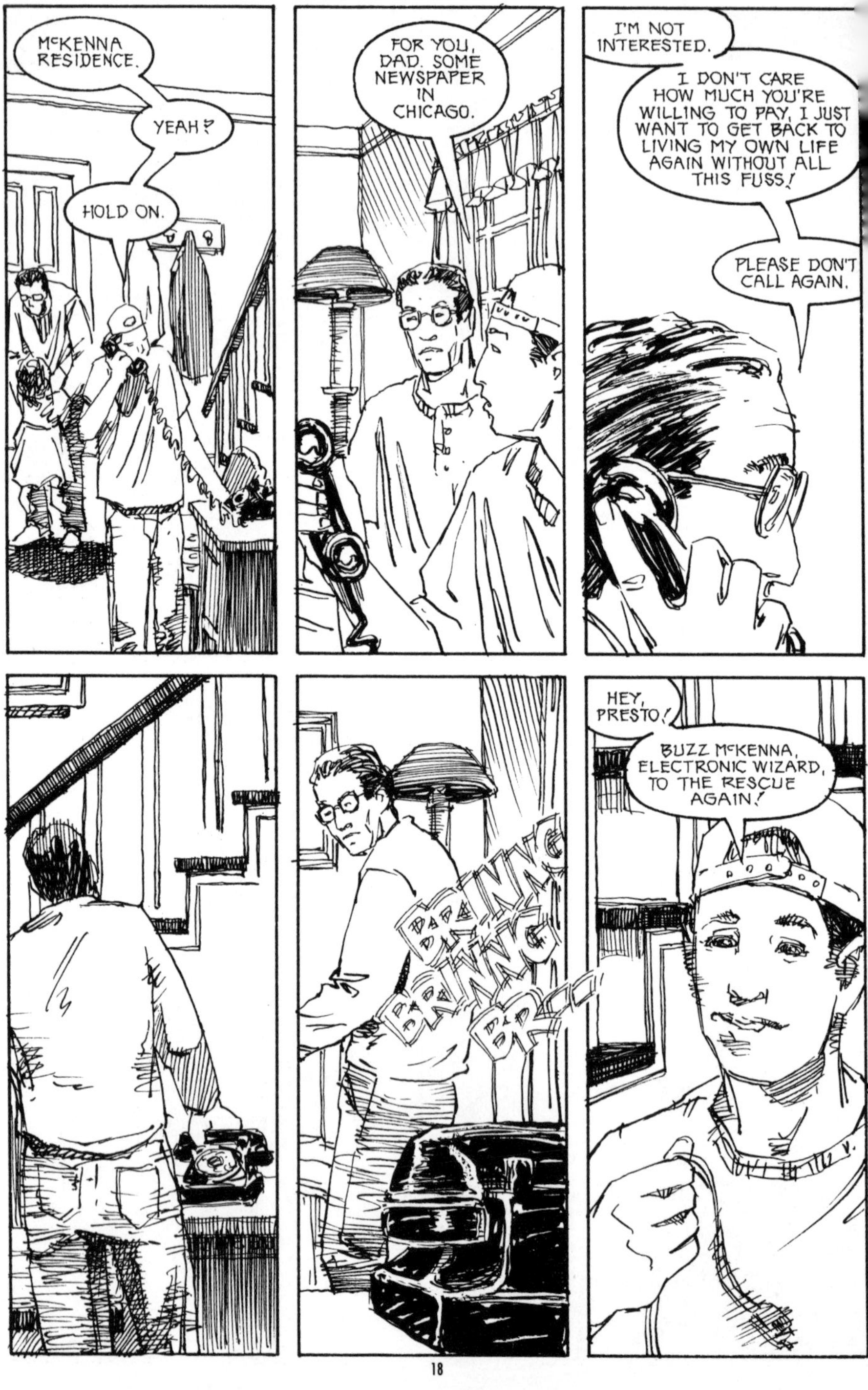
McKENNA RESIDENCE.
YEAH?
HOLD ON.
FOR YOU, DAD. SOME NEWSPAPER IN CHICAGO.
I'M NOT INTERESTED.
I DON'T CARE HOW MUCH YOU'RE WILLING TO PAY, I JUST WANT TO GET BACK TO LIVING MY OWN LIFE AGAIN WITHOUT ALL THIS FUSS!
PLEASE DON'T CALL AGAIN.
HEY, PRESTO!
BUZZ McKENNA, ELECTRONIC WIZARD, TO THE RESCUE AGAIN!

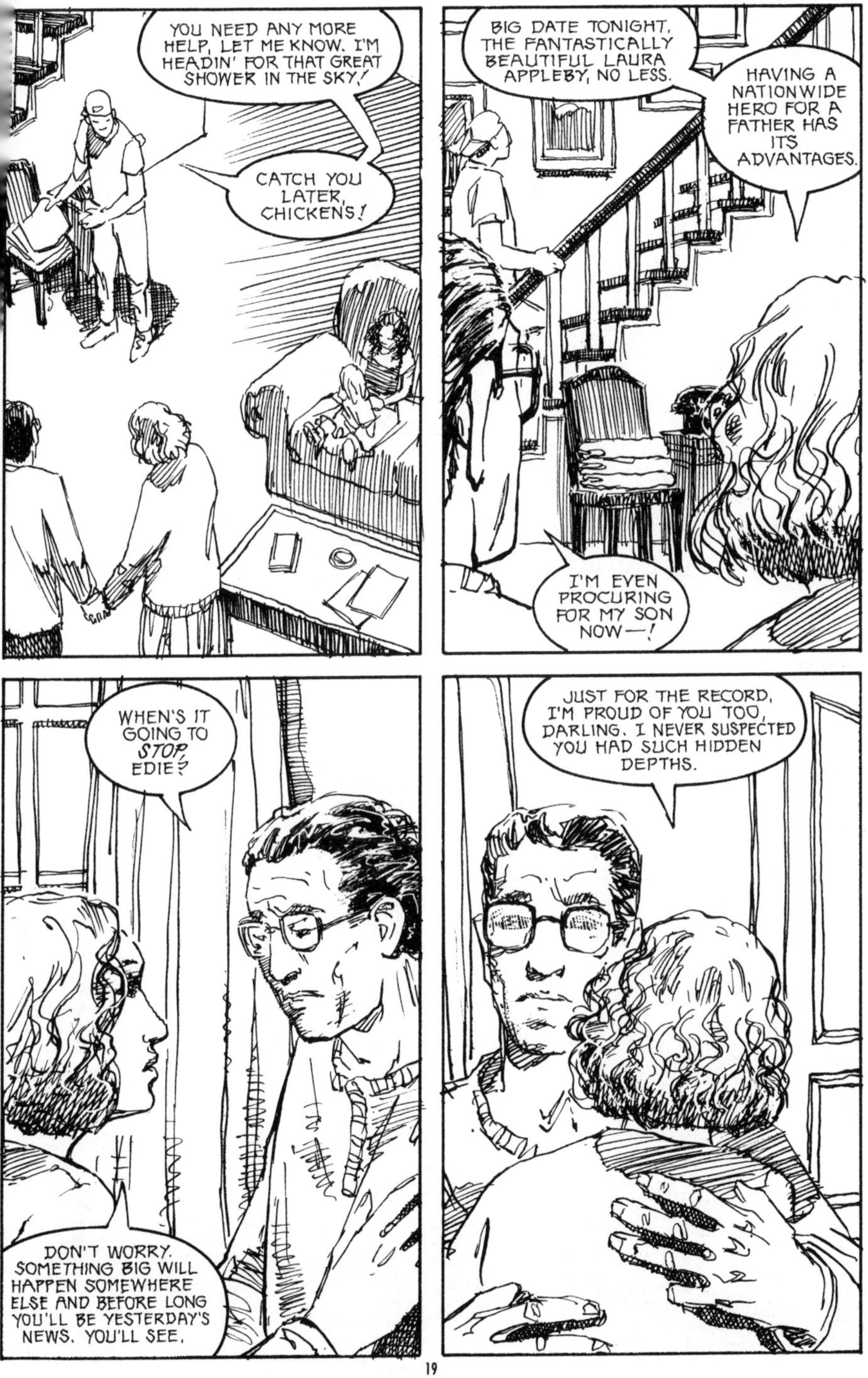
YOU NEED ANY MORE HELP, LET ME KNOW. I'M HEADIN' FOR THAT GREAT SHOWER IN THE SKY!
CATCH YOU LATER, CHICKENS!
BIG DATE TONIGHT, THE FANTASTICALLY BEAUTIFUL LAURA APPLEBY, NO LESS.
HAVING A NATIONWIDE HERO FOR A FATHER HAS ITS ADVANTAGES.
I'M EVEN PROCURING FOR MY SON NOW—!
WHEN'S IT GOING TO STOP, EDIE?
DON'T WORRY. SOMETHING BIG WILL HAPPEN SOMEWHERE ELSE AND BEFORE LONG YOU'LL BE YESTERDAY'S NEWS. YOU'LL SEE.
JUST FOR THE RECORD, I'M PROUD OF YOU TOO, DARLING. I NEVER SUSPECTED YOU HAD SUCH HIDDEN DEPTHS.

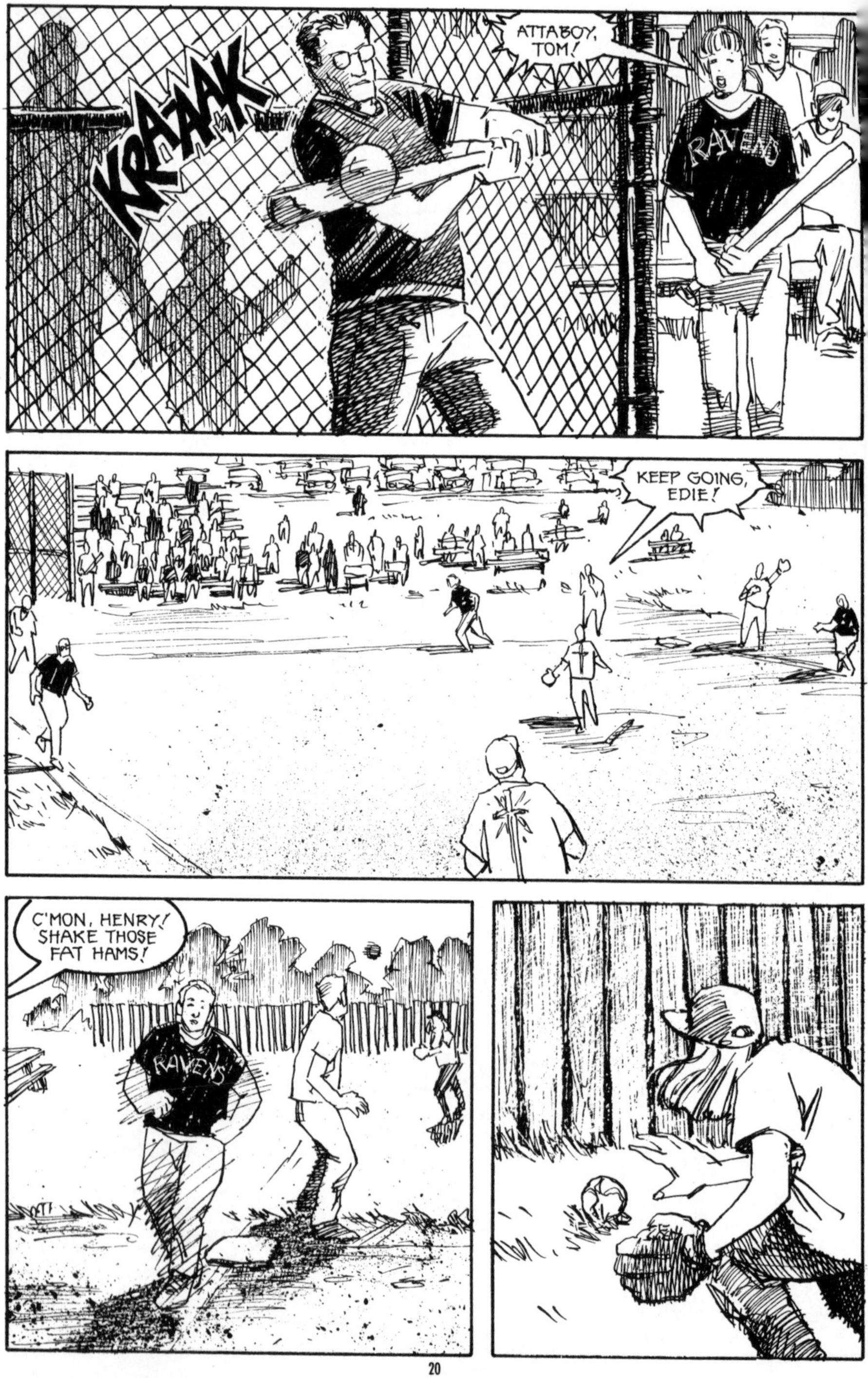
ATTABOY, TOM!
KRAAAK
RAVENS
KEEP GOING, EDIE!
C'MON, HENRY! SHAKE THOSE FAT HAMS!
RAVENS

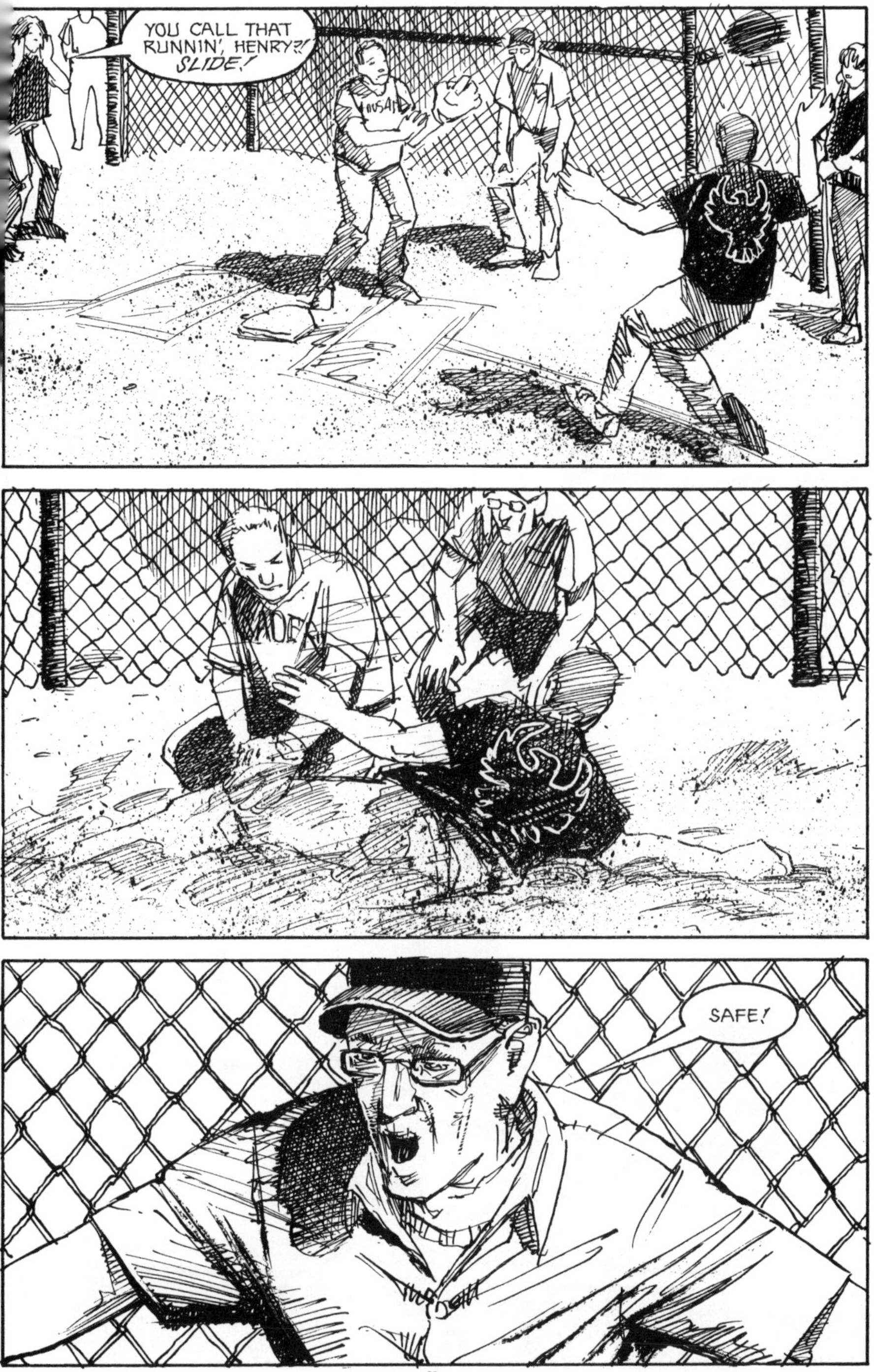
YOU CALL THAT RUNNIN', HENRY?!
SLIDE!
SAFE!

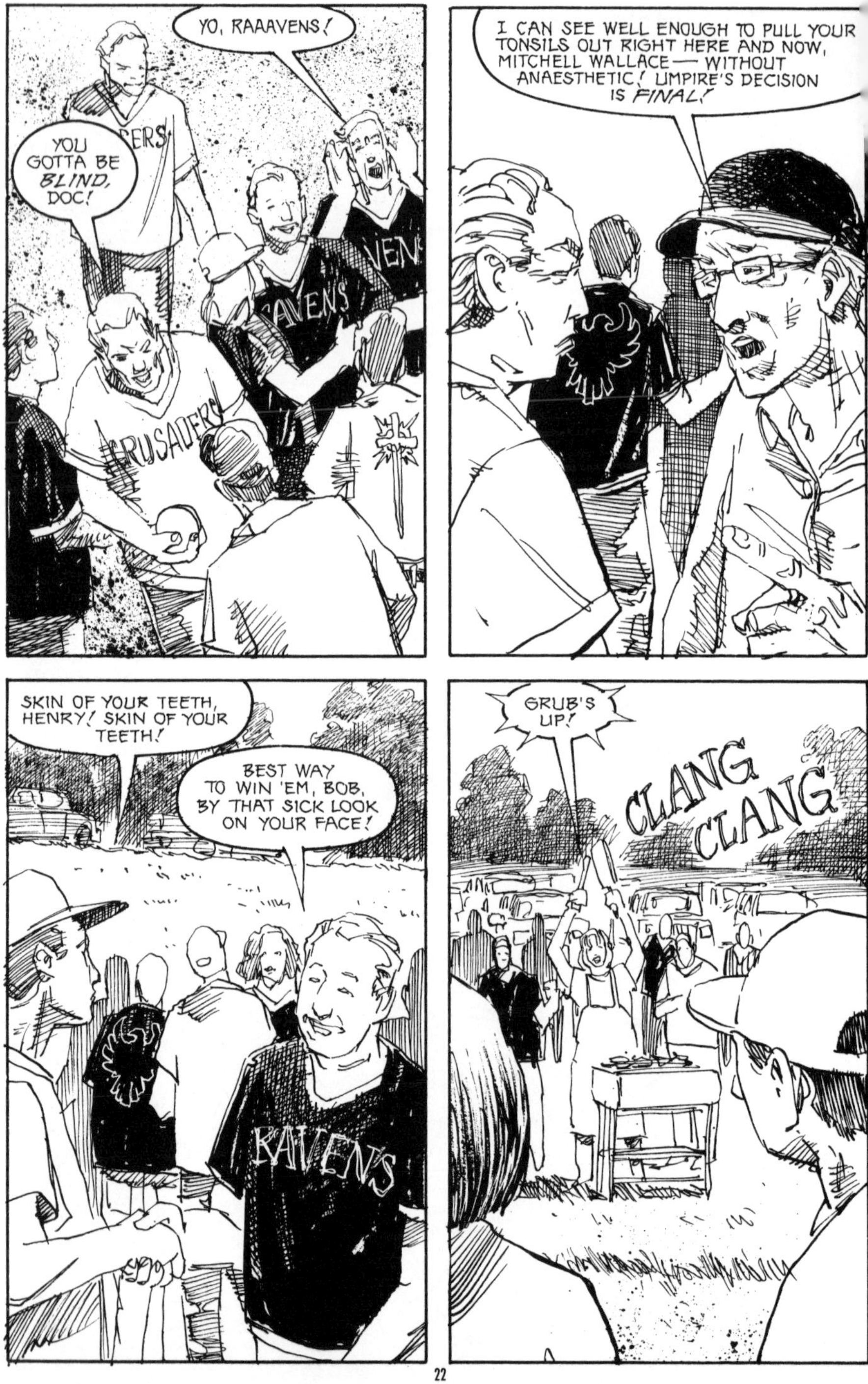
YO, RAAAVENS!
YOU GOTTA BE BLIND, DOC!
I CAN SEE WELL ENOUGH TO PULL YOUR TONSILS OUT RIGHT HERE AND NOW, MITCHELL WALLACE— WITHOUT ANAESTHETIC! UMPIRE'S DECISION IS FINAL!
SKIN OF YOUR TEETH, HENRY! SKIN OF YOUR TEETH!
BEST WAY TO WIN 'EM, BOB, BY THAT SICK LOOK ON YOUR FACE!
GRUB'S UP!
CLANG CLANG

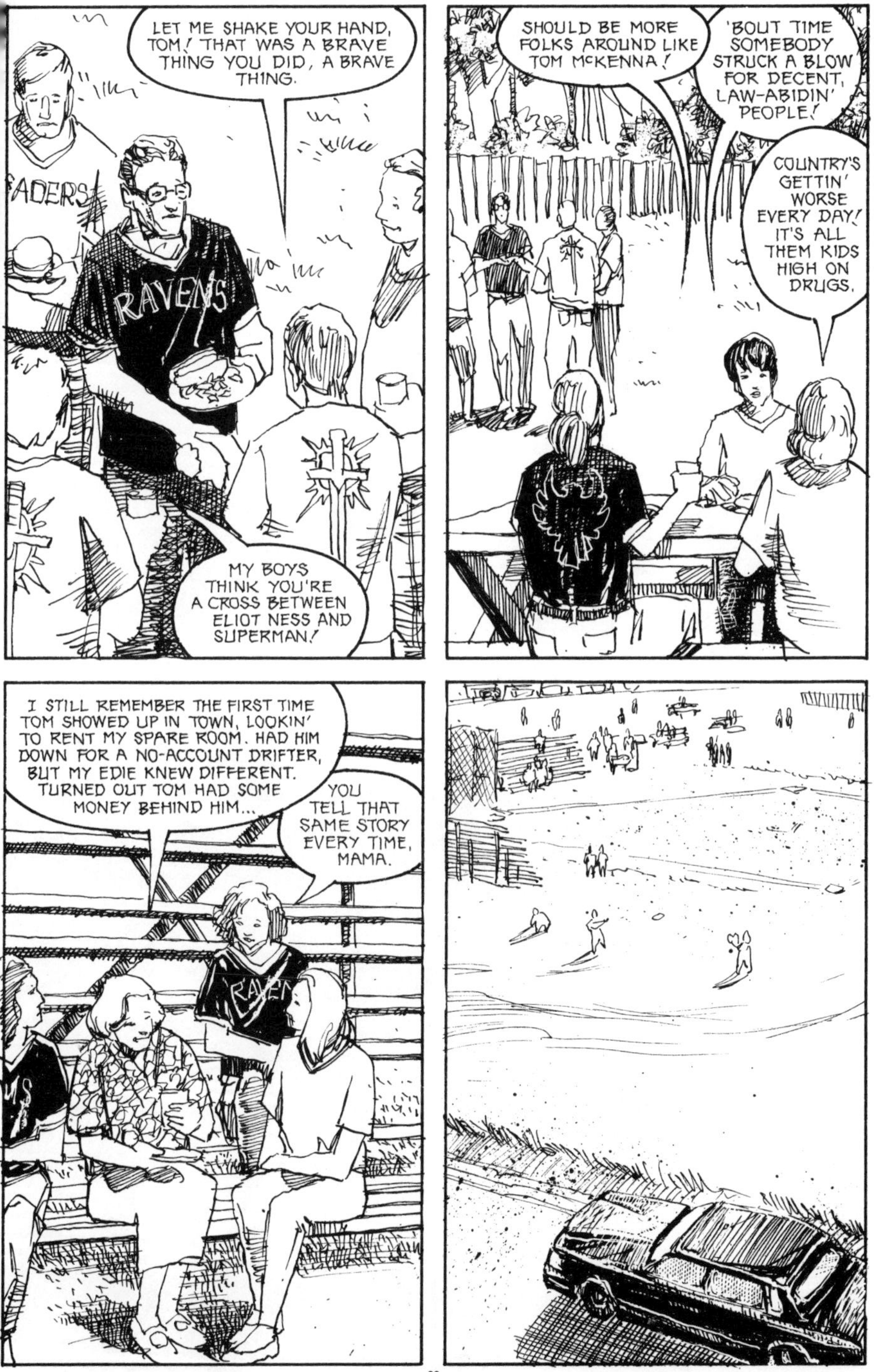
LET ME SHAKE YOUR HAND, TOM! THAT WAS A BRAVE THING YOU DID, A BRAVE THING.
RAVENS
MY BOYS THINK YOU'RE A CROSS BETWEEN ELIOT NESS AND SUPERMAN!
SHOULD BE MORE FOLKS AROUND LIKE TOM McKENNA!
'BOUT TIME SOMEBODY STRUCK A BLOW FOR DECENT, LAW-ABIDIN' PEOPLE!
COUNTRY'S GETTIN' WORSE EVERY DAY! IT'S ALL THEM KIDS HIGH ON DRUGS.
I STILL REMEMBER THE FIRST TIME TOM SHOWED UP IN TOWN, LOOKIN' TO RENT MY SPARE ROOM. HAD HIM DOWN FOR A NO-ACCOUNT DRIFTER, BUT MY EDIE KNEW DIFFERENT. TURNED OUT TOM HAD SOME MONEY BEHIND HIM...
YOU TELL THAT SAME STORY EVERY TIME, MAMA.

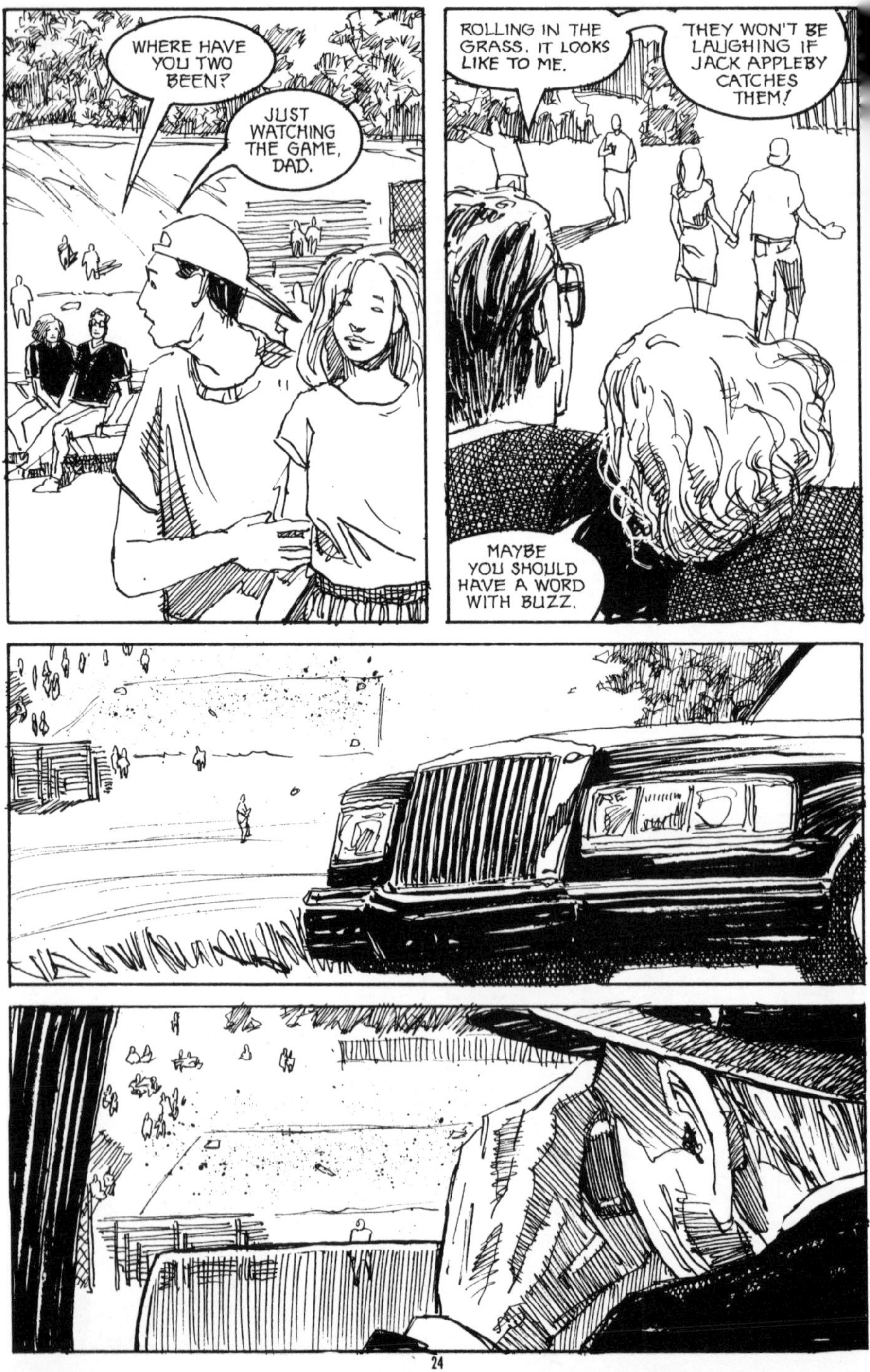
WHERE HAVE YOU TWO BEEN?
JUST WATCHING THE GAME, DAD.
ROLLING IN THE GRASS, IT LOOKS LIKE TO ME.
THEY WON'T BE LAUGHING IF JACK APPLEBY CATCHES THEM!
MAYBE YOU SHOULD HAVE A WORD WITH BUZZ.

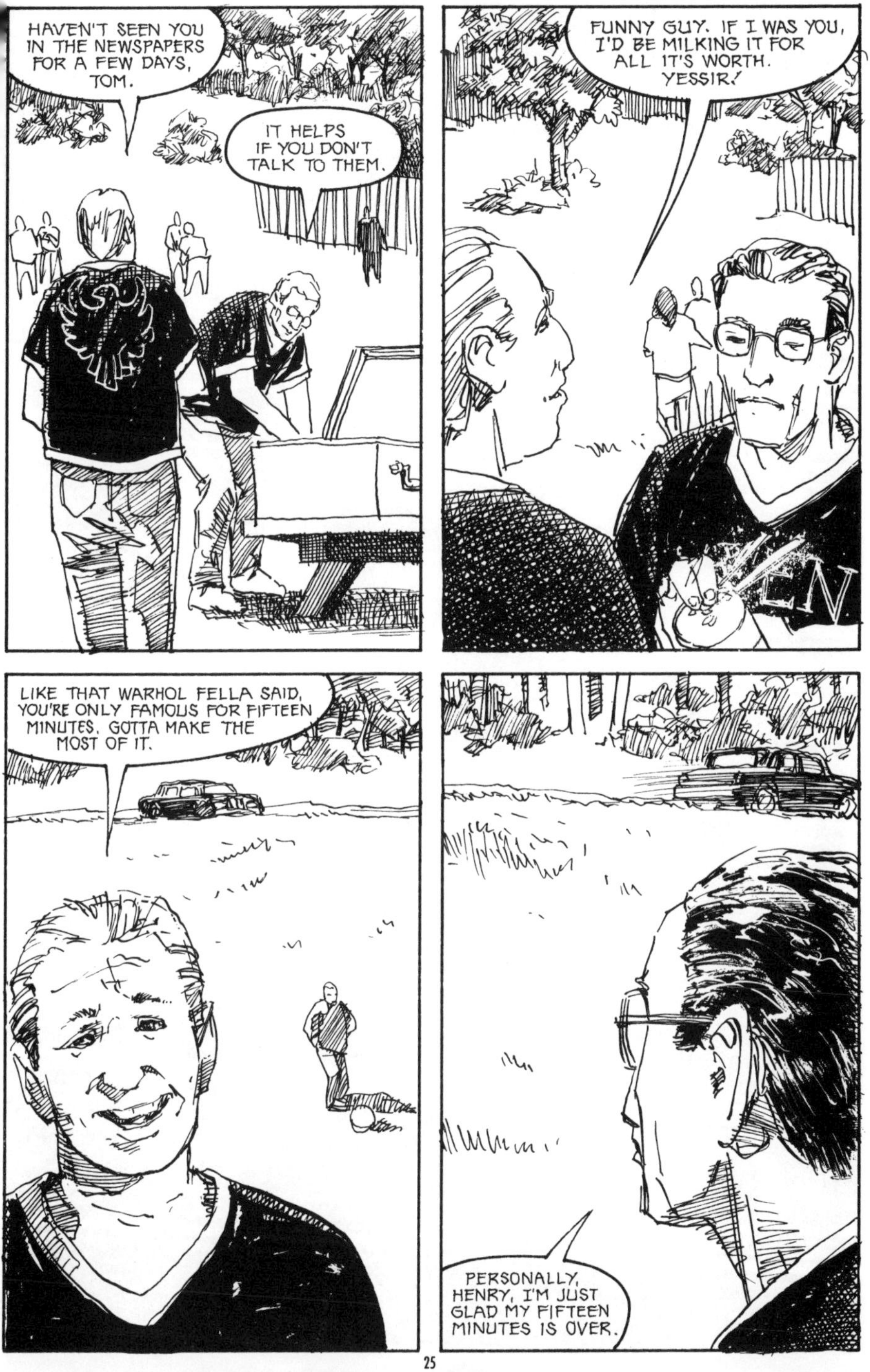
HAVEN'T SEEN YOU IN THE NEWSPAPERS FOR A FEW DAYS, TOM.
IT HELPS IF YOU DON'T TALK TO THEM.
FUNNY GUY. IF I WAS YOU, I'D BE MILKING IT FOR ALL IT'S WORTH. YESSIR!
LIKE THAT WARHOL FELLA SAID, YOU'RE ONLY FAMOUS FOR FIFTEEN MINUTES. GOTTA MAKE THE MOST OF IT.
PERSONALLY, HENRY, I'M JUST GLAD MY FIFTEEN MINUTES IS OVER.

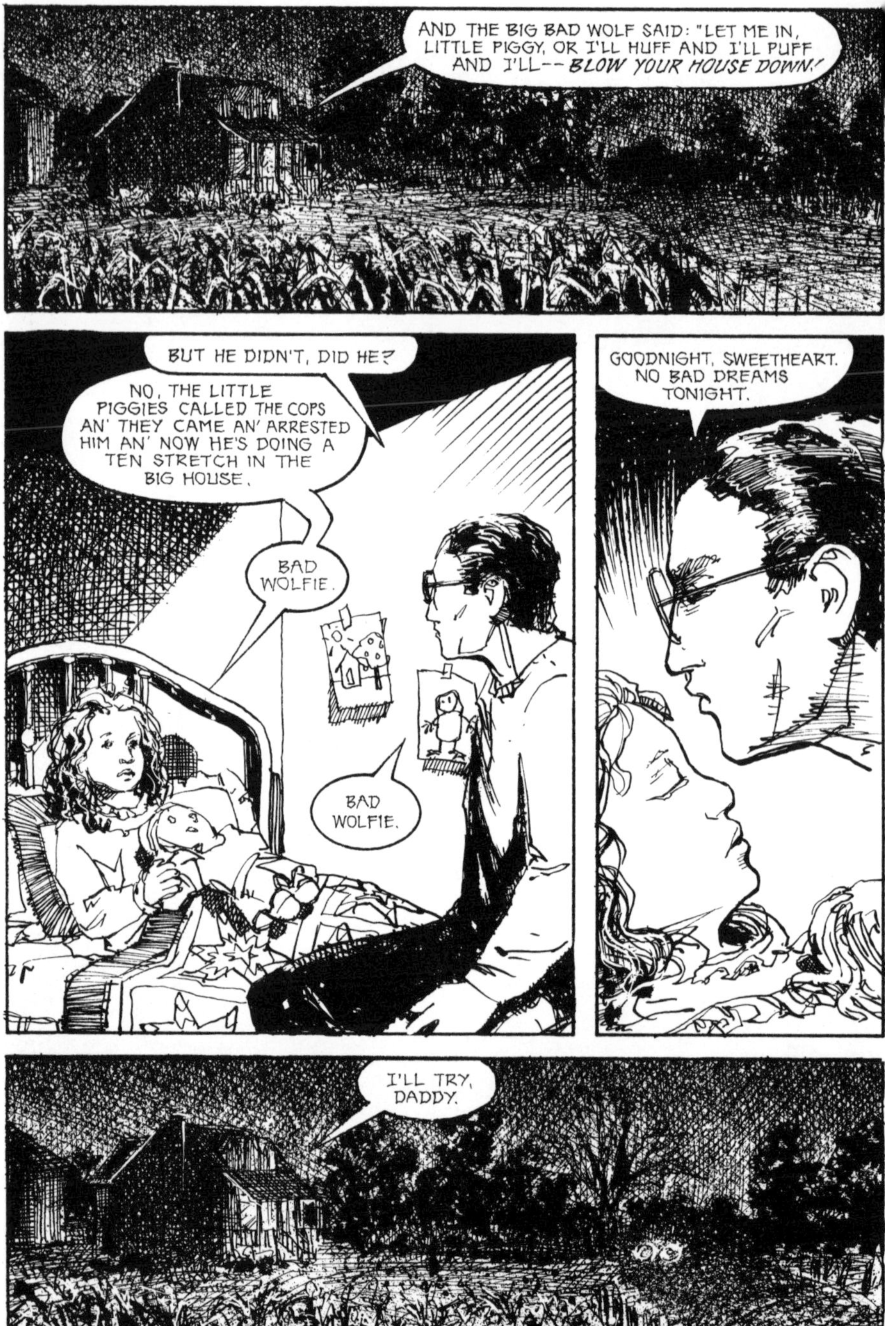
AND THE BIG BAD WOLF SAID: "LET ME IN, LITTLE PIGGY, OR I'LL HUFF AND I'LL PUFF AND I'LL-- BLOW YOUR HOUSE DOWN!"
BUT HE DIDN'T, DID HE?
NO, THE LITTLE PIGGIES CALLED THE COPS AN' THEY CAME AN' ARRESTED HIM AN' NOW HE'S DOING A TEN STRETCH IN THE BIG HOUSE.
BAD WOLFIE.
BAD WOLFIE.
GOODNIGHT, SWEETHEART. NO BAD DREAMS TONIGHT.
I'LL TRY, DADDY.

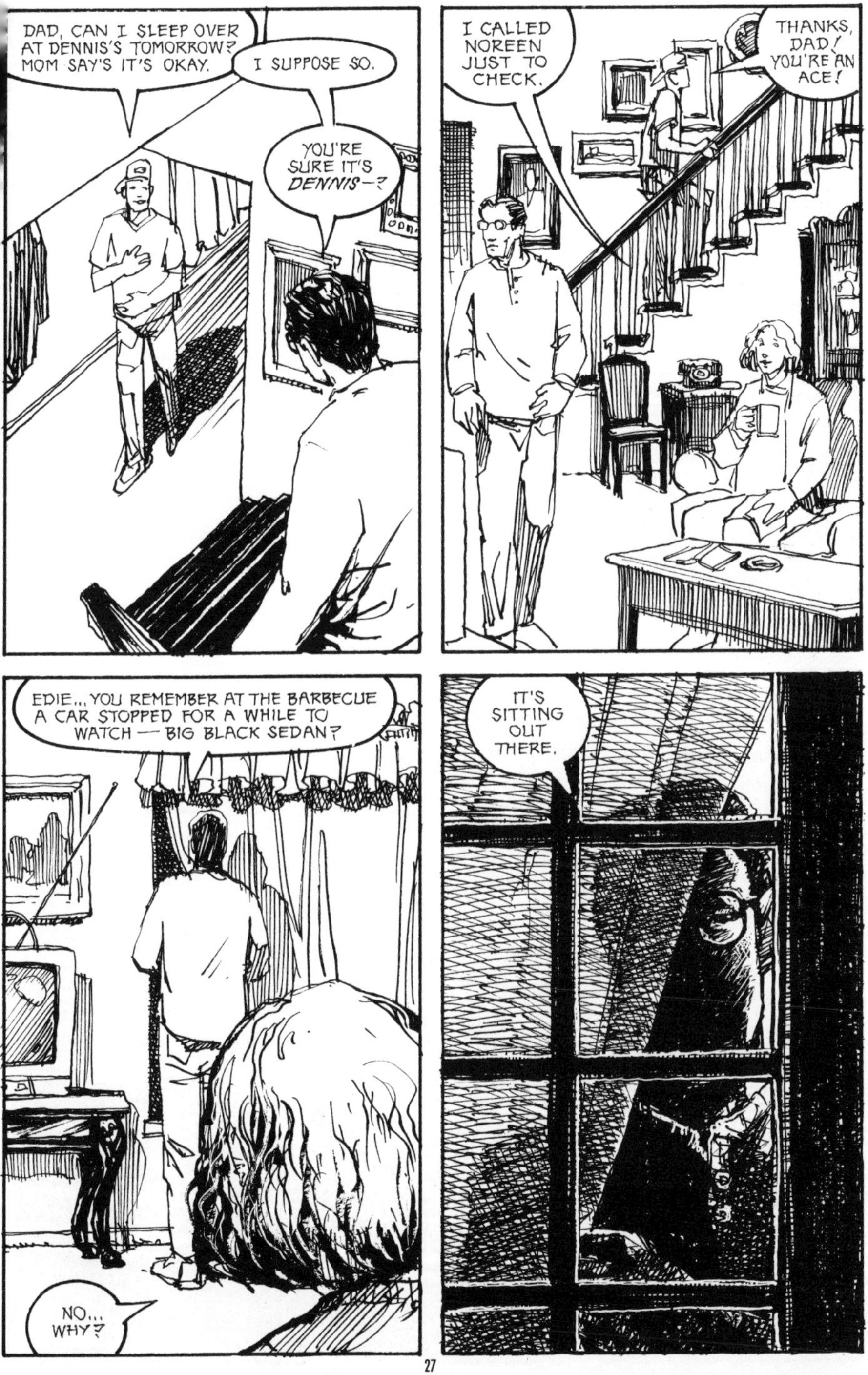
DAD, CAN I SLEEP OVER AT DENNIS'S TOMORROW? MOM SAY'S IT'S OKAY.
I SUPPOSE SO.
YOU'RE SURE IT'S DENNIS—?
I CALLED NOREEN JUST TO CHECK.
THANKS, DAD! YOU'RE AN ACE!
EDIE... YOU REMEMBER AT THE BARBECUE A CAR STOPPED FOR A WHILE TO WATCH — BIG BLACK SEDAN?
NO... WHY?
IT'S SITTING OUT THERE.

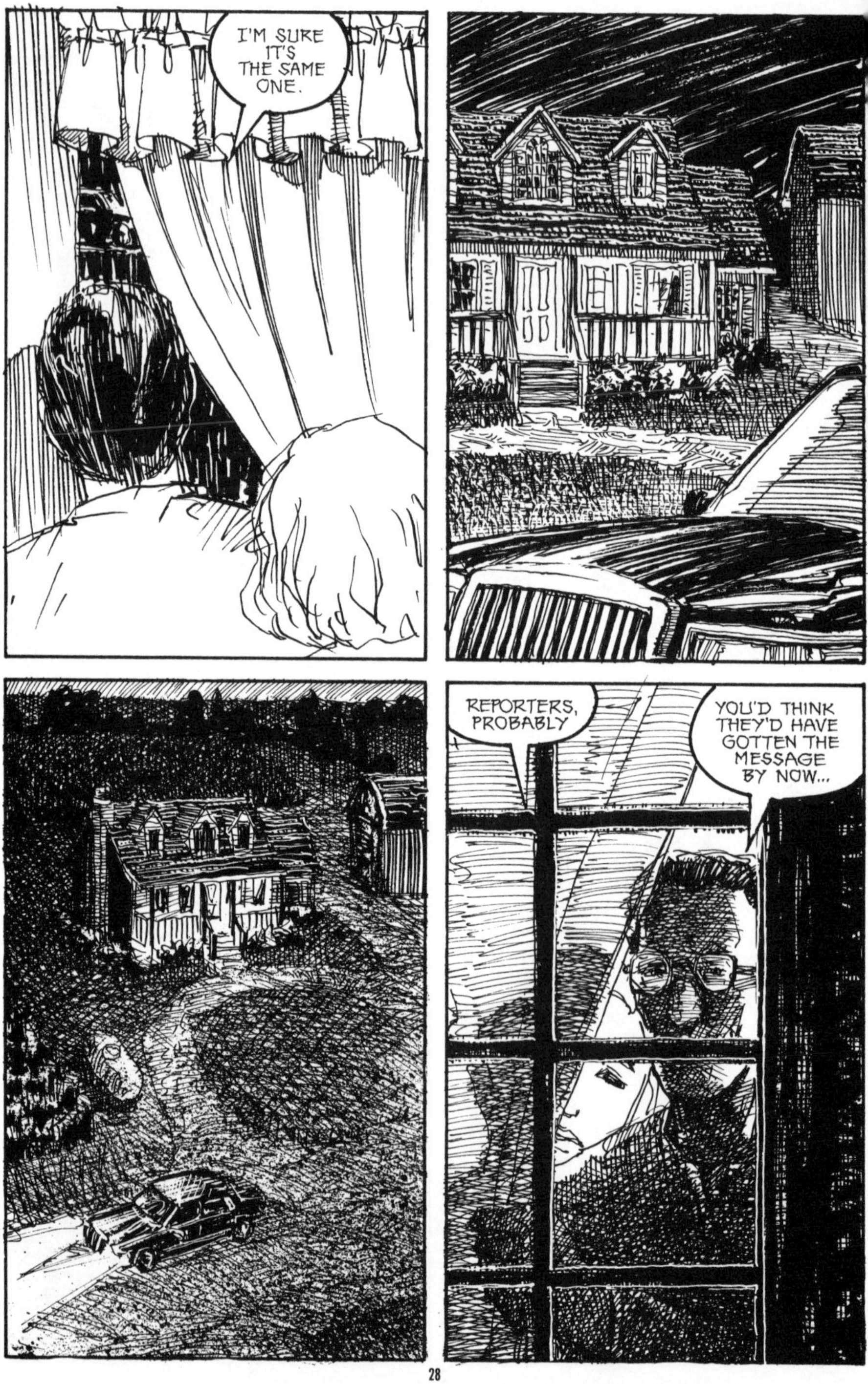
I'M SURE IT'S THE SAME ONE.
REPORTERS, PROBABLY
YOU'D THINK THEY'D HAVE GOTTEN THE MESSAGE BY NOW...

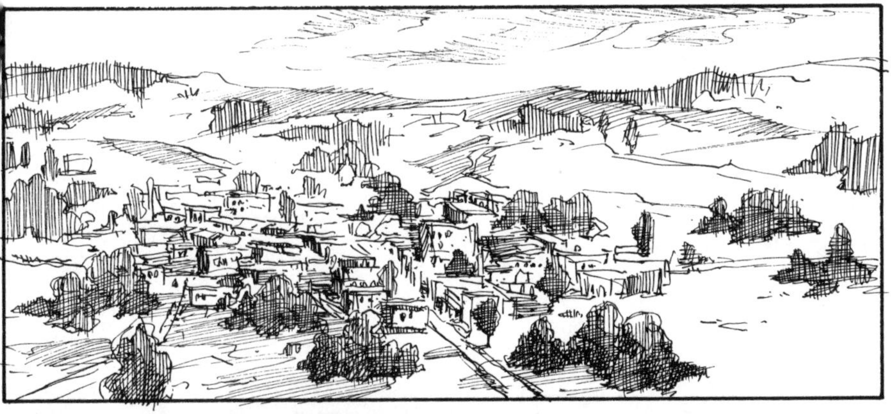

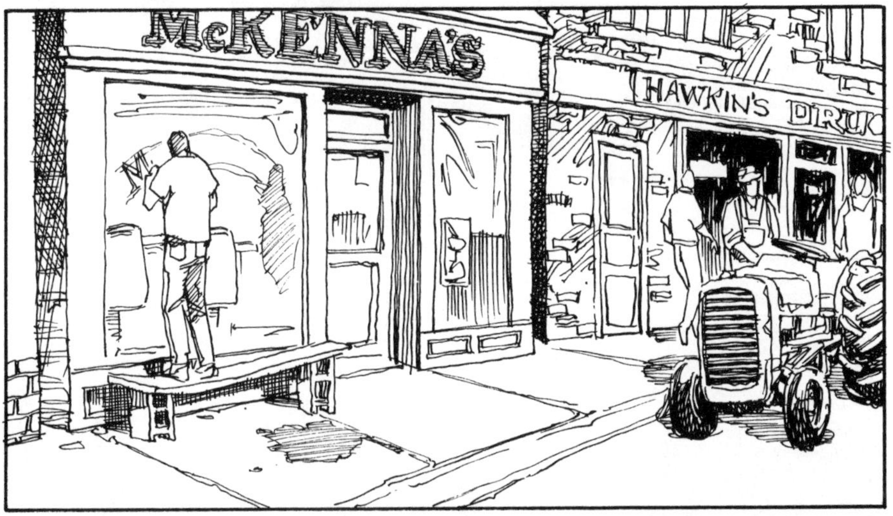
McKENNA'S
HAWKIN'S

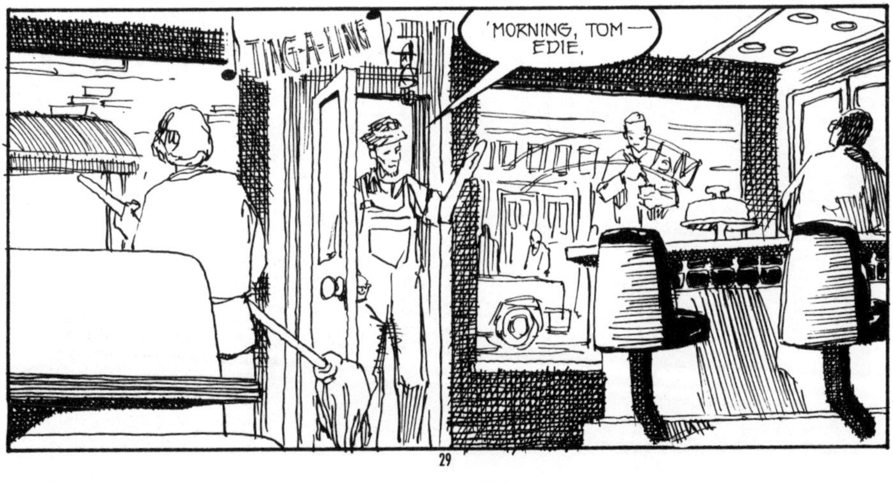
TING-A-LING
'MORNING, TOM — EDIE.

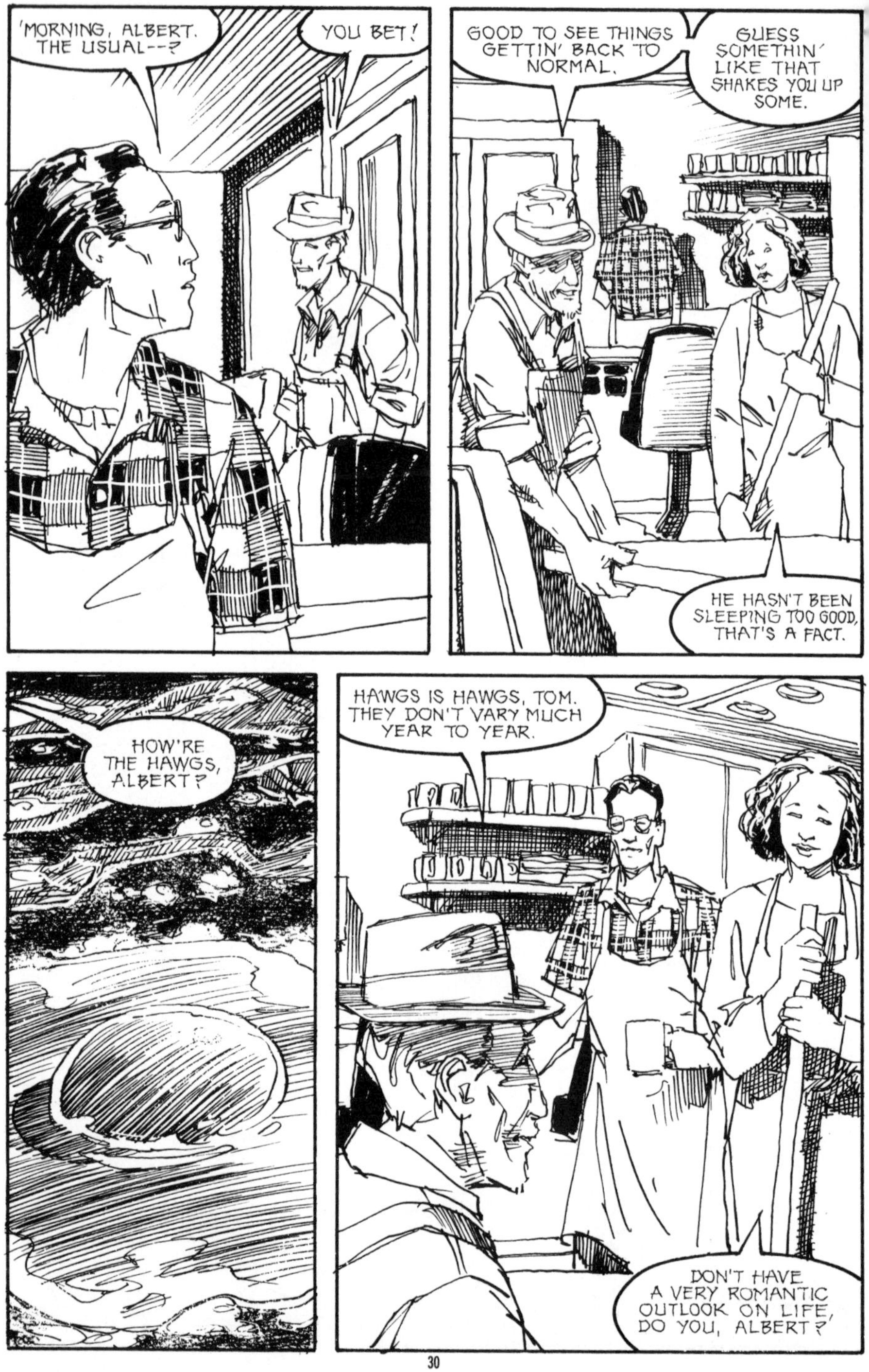
'MORNING, ALBERT. THE USUAL--?
YOU BET!
GOOD TO SEE THINGS GETTIN' BACK TO NORMAL.
GUESS SOMETHIN' LIKE THAT SHAKES YOU UP SOME.
HE HASN'T BEEN SLEEPING TOO GOOD, THAT'S A FACT.
HOW'RE THE HAWGS, ALBERT?
HAWGS IS HAWGS, TOM. THEY DON'T VARY MUCH YEAR TO YEAR.
DON'T HAVE A VERY ROMANTIC OUTLOOK ON LIFE, DO YOU, ALBERT?

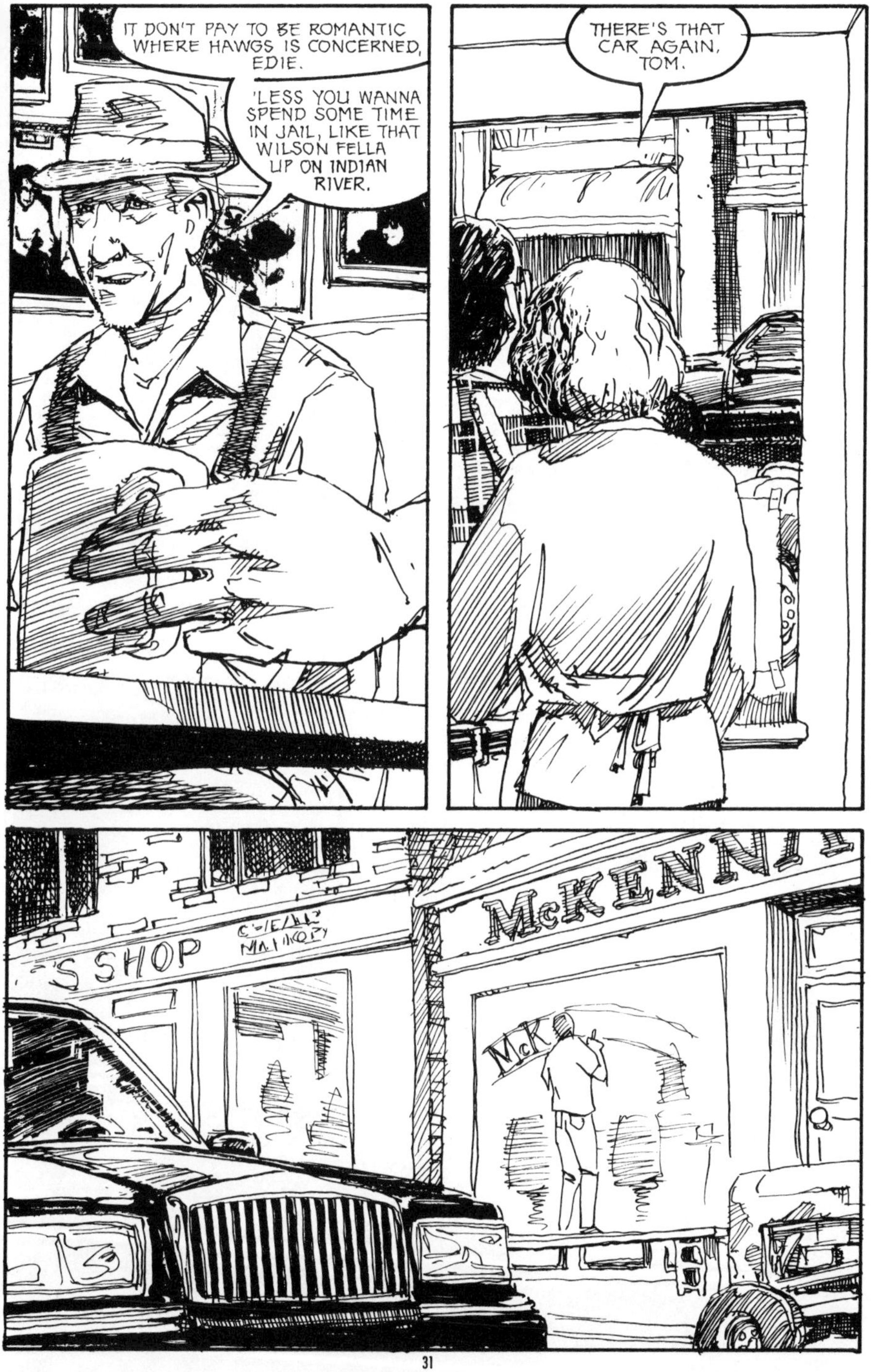
IT DON'T PAY TO BE ROMANTIC WHERE HAWGS IS CONCERNED, EDIE.
'LESS YOU WANNA SPEND SOME TIME IN JAIL, LIKE THAT WILSON FELLA UP ON INDIAN RIVER.
THERE'S THAT CAR AGAIN, TOM.

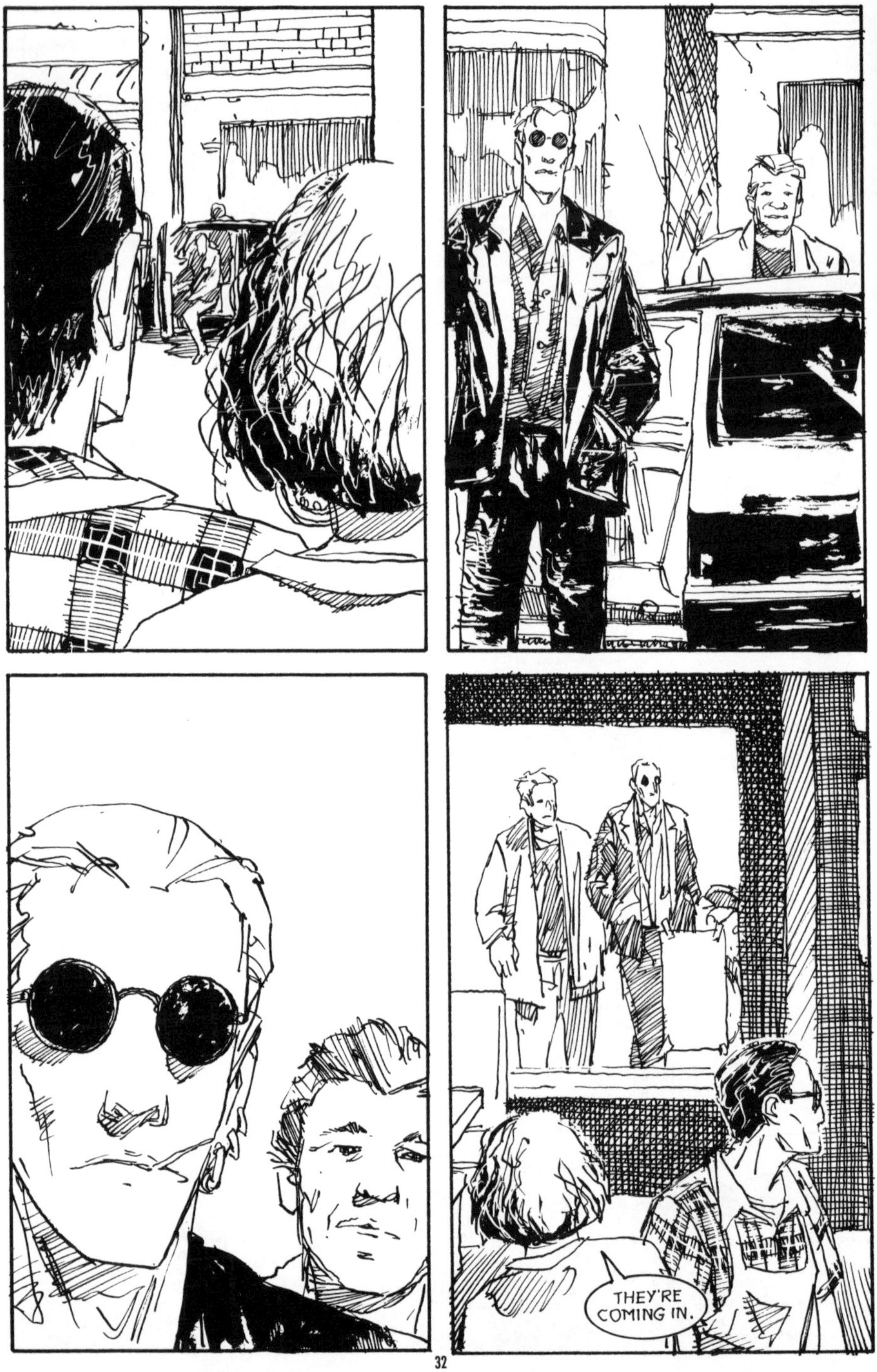
THEY'RE COMING IN.

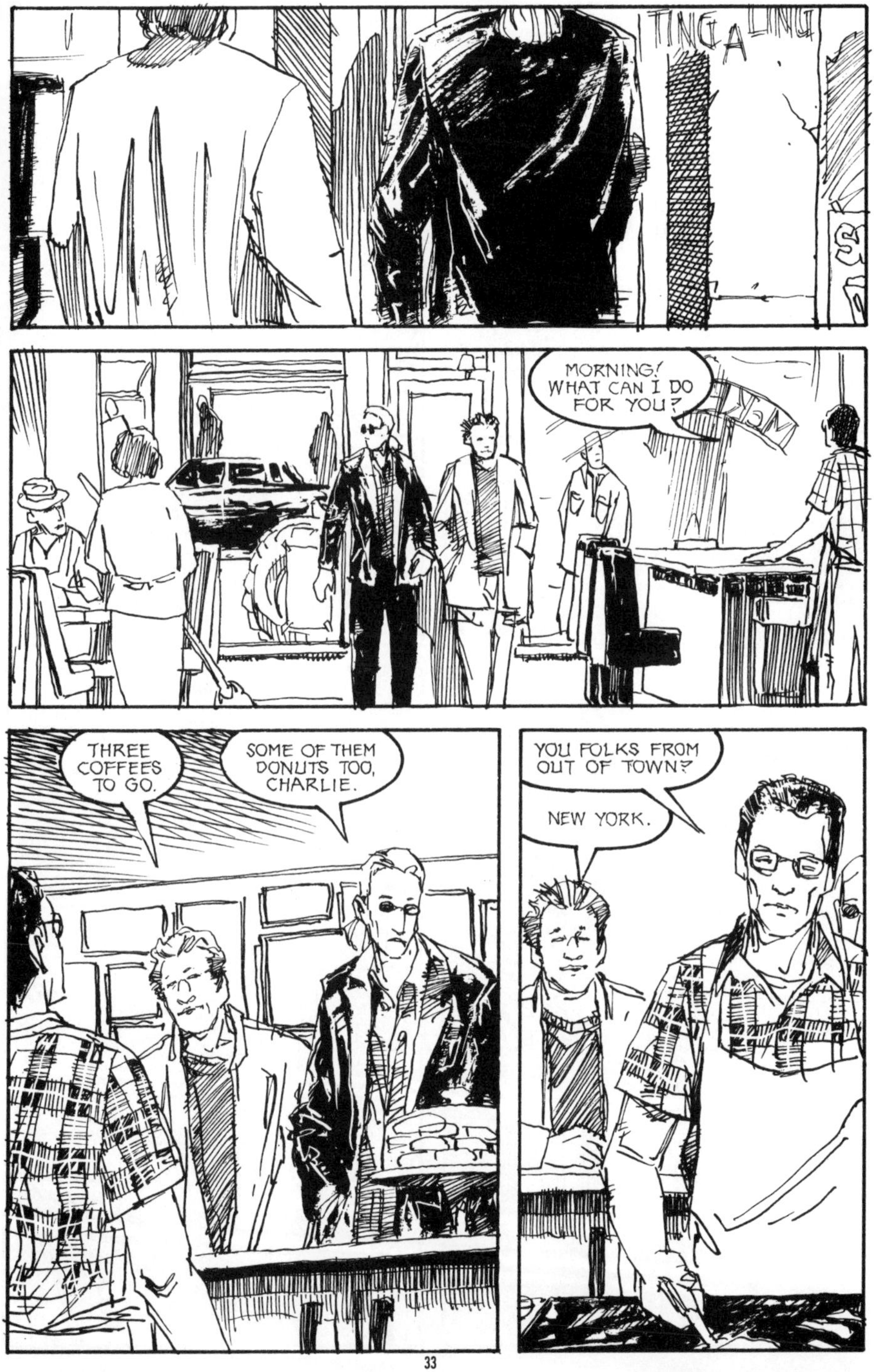
TINGALING
MORNING! WHAT CAN I DO FOR YOU?
THREE COFFEES TO GO.
SOME OF THEM DONUTS TOO, CHARLIE.
YOU FOLKS FROM OUT OF TOWN?
NEW YORK.

SAY, AIN'T I SEEN YOU SOMEPLACE BEFORE--?

WAIT A MINUTE-- THAT'S RIGHT! ON THE TV NEWS! YOU'RE THAT HERO GUY-- MCKENNA.

YEAH, THAT'S IT! SEE THAT, TONY? IT'S MCKENNA-- THAT SODA JERK WHO BLASTED THEM NO-GOODS. *TOM*, AIN'T IT?

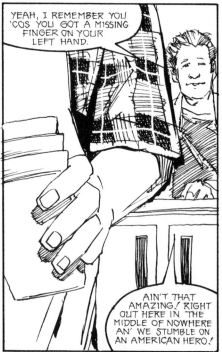

YEAH, I REMEMBER YOU 'COS YOU GOT A MISSING FINGER ON YOUR LEFT HAND.

AIN'T THAT AMAZING! RIGHT OUT HERE IN THE MIDDLE OF NOWHERE AN' WE STUMBLE ON AN AMERICAN HERO!

THIS IS WHERE IT HAPPENED, HUH? HEY, TELL YOU WHAT, WE'LL JUST HAVE THEM COFFEES RIGHT HERE!

LOOK, I'M GONNA GO OUT AN' GET OUR FRIEND, OKAY? HE WOULDN'T WANNA PASS THROUGH WITHOUT MEETIN' *THE* TOM MCKENNA--!

34

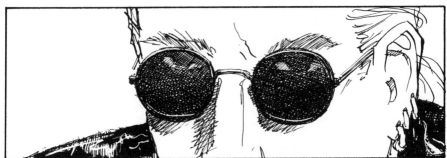

STING SLING

THAT'S HIM, MR. TORRINO!

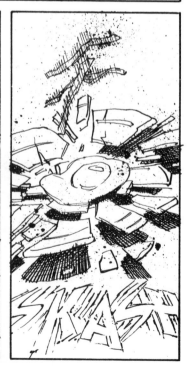

SMASH

36

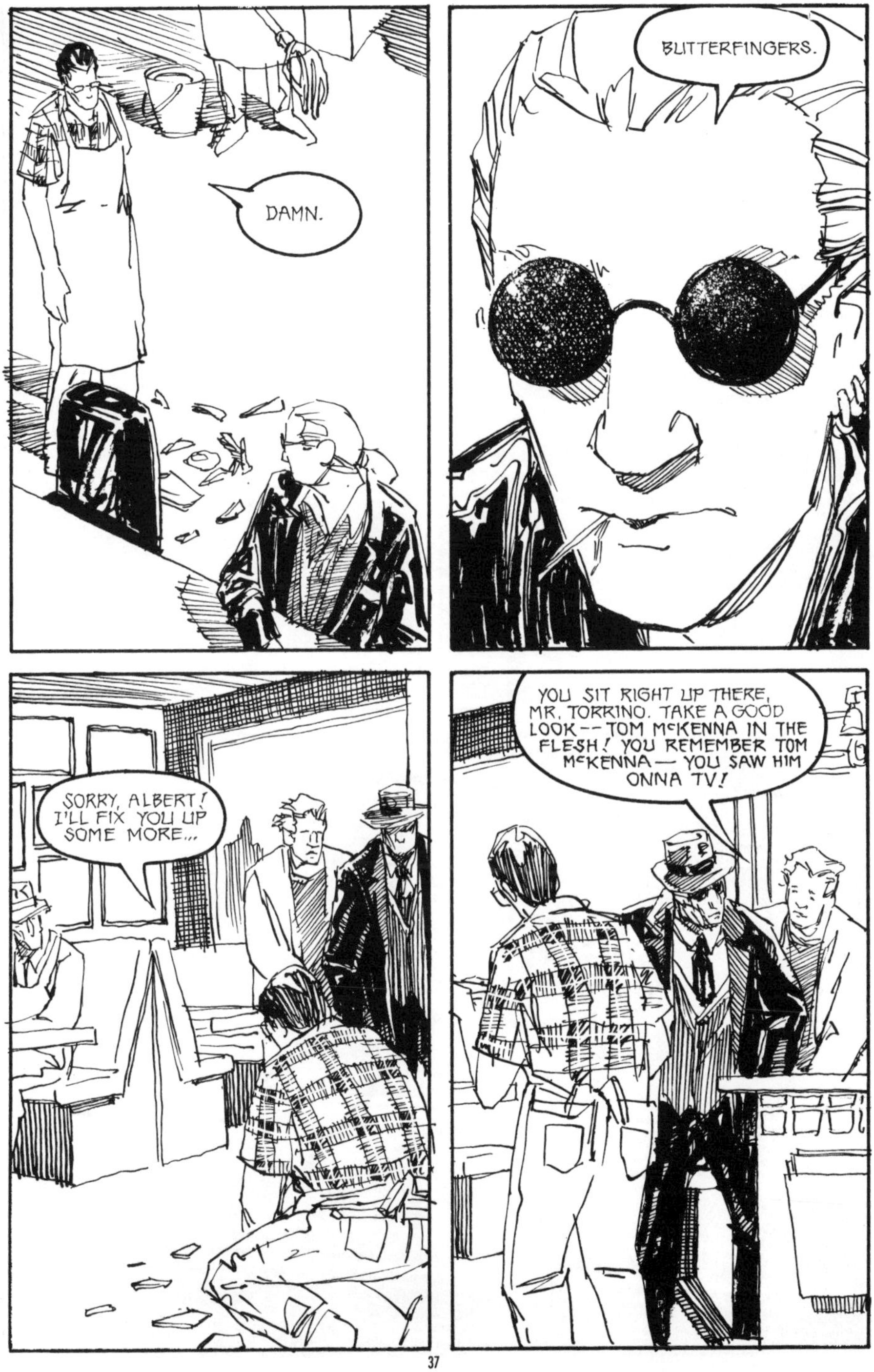
DAMN.
BUTTERFINGERS.
SORRY, ALBERT! I'LL FIX YOU UP SOME MORE...
YOU SIT RIGHT UP THERE, MR. TORRINO. TAKE A GOOD LOOK-- TOM McKENNA IN THE FLESH! YOU REMEMBER TOM McKENNA— YOU SAW HIM ONNA TV!

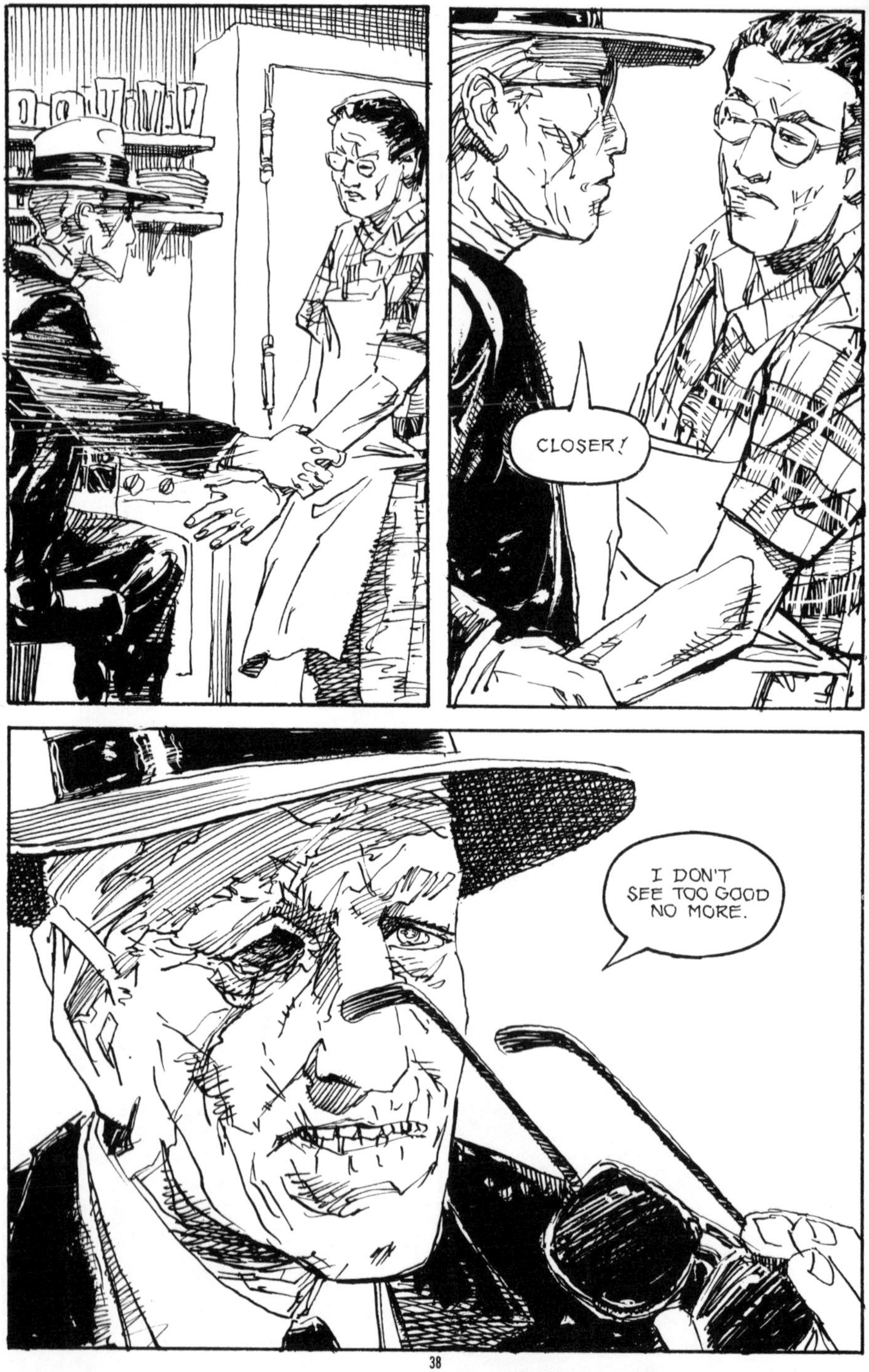
CLOSER!
I DON'T SEE TOO GOOD NO MORE.

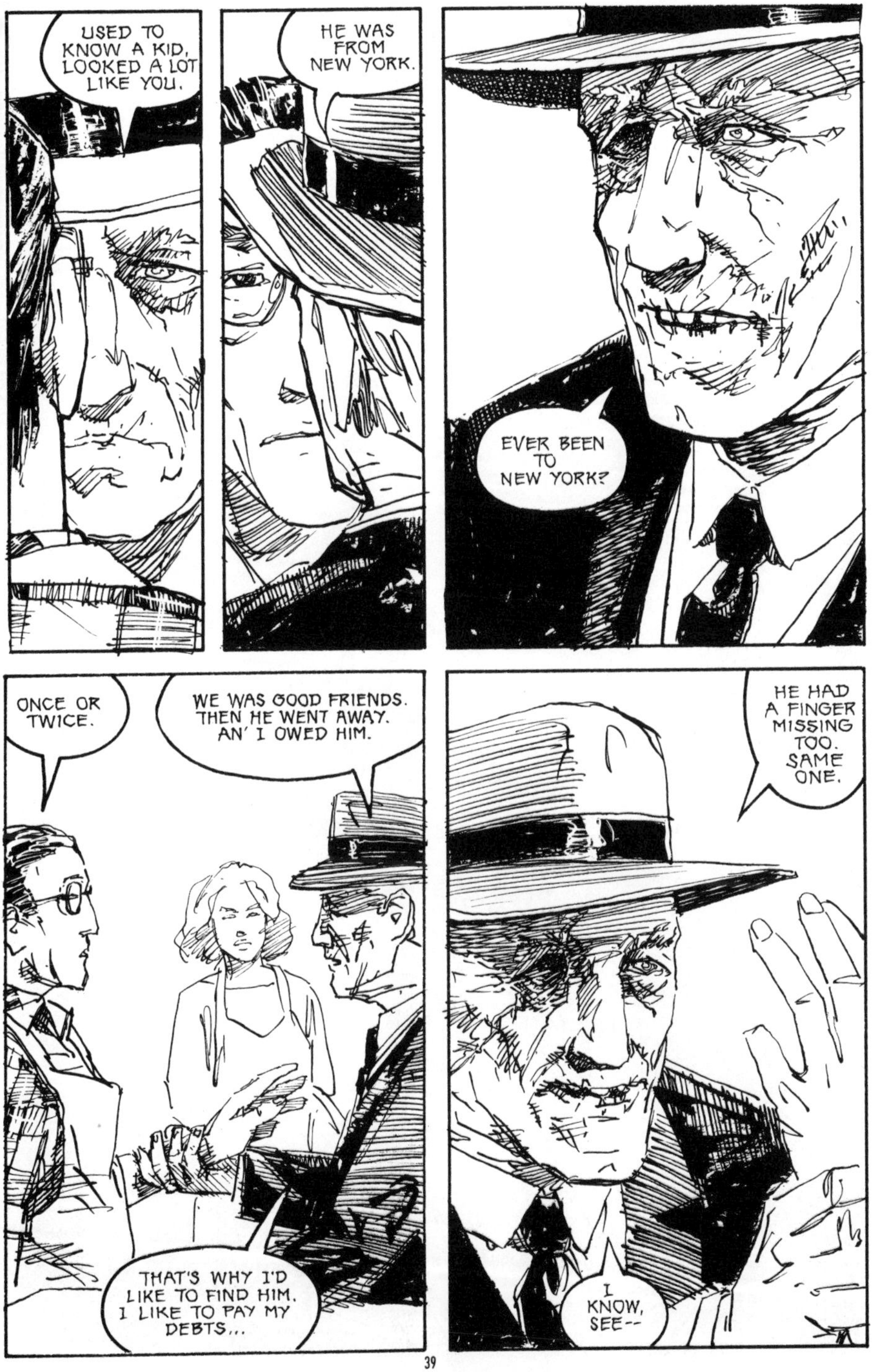
USED TO KNOW A KID, LOOKED A LOT LIKE YOU.
HE WAS FROM NEW YORK.
EVER BEEN TO NEW YORK?
ONCE OR TWICE.
WE WAS GOOD FRIENDS. THEN HE WENT AWAY. AN' I OWED HIM.
THAT'S WHY I'D LIKE TO FIND HIM. I LIKE TO PAY MY DEBTS...
HE HAD A FINGER MISSING TOO. SAME ONE.
I KNOW, SEE--

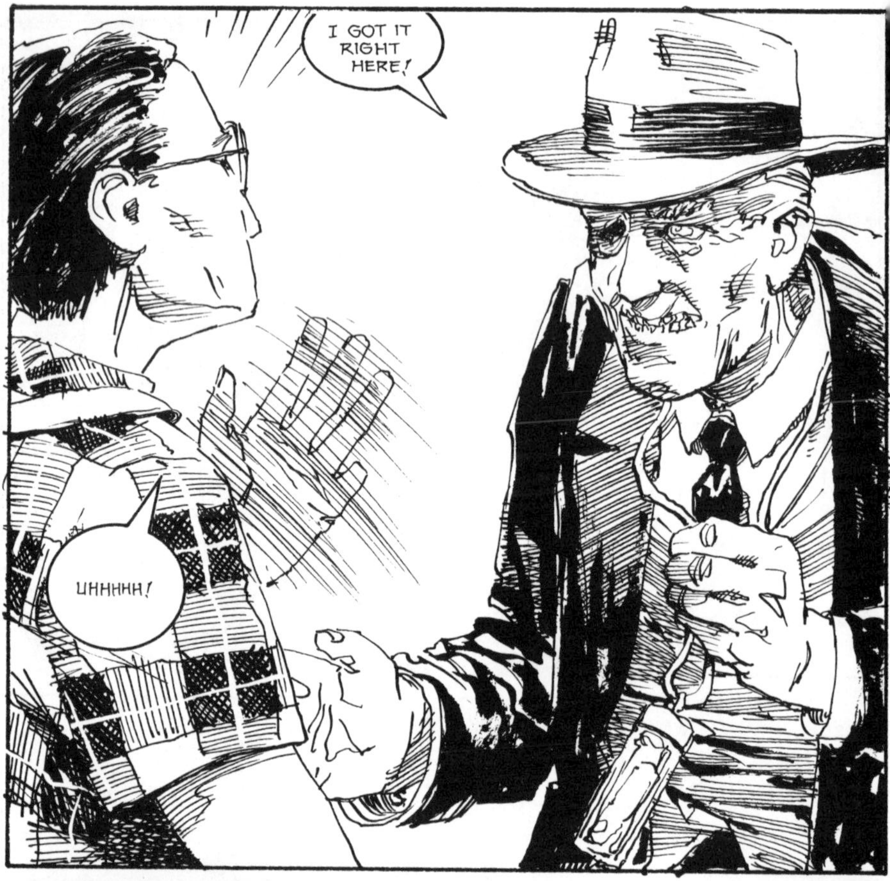
I GOT IT RIGHT HERE!
UHHHHH!

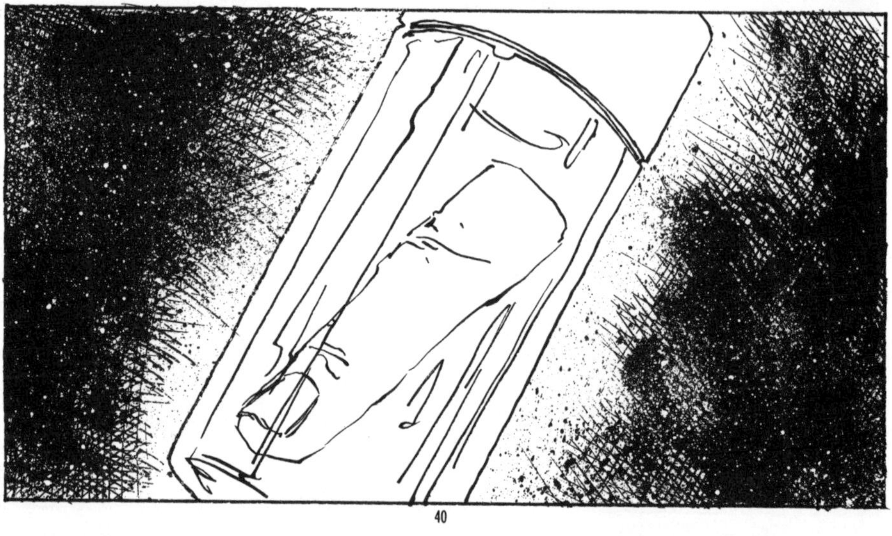

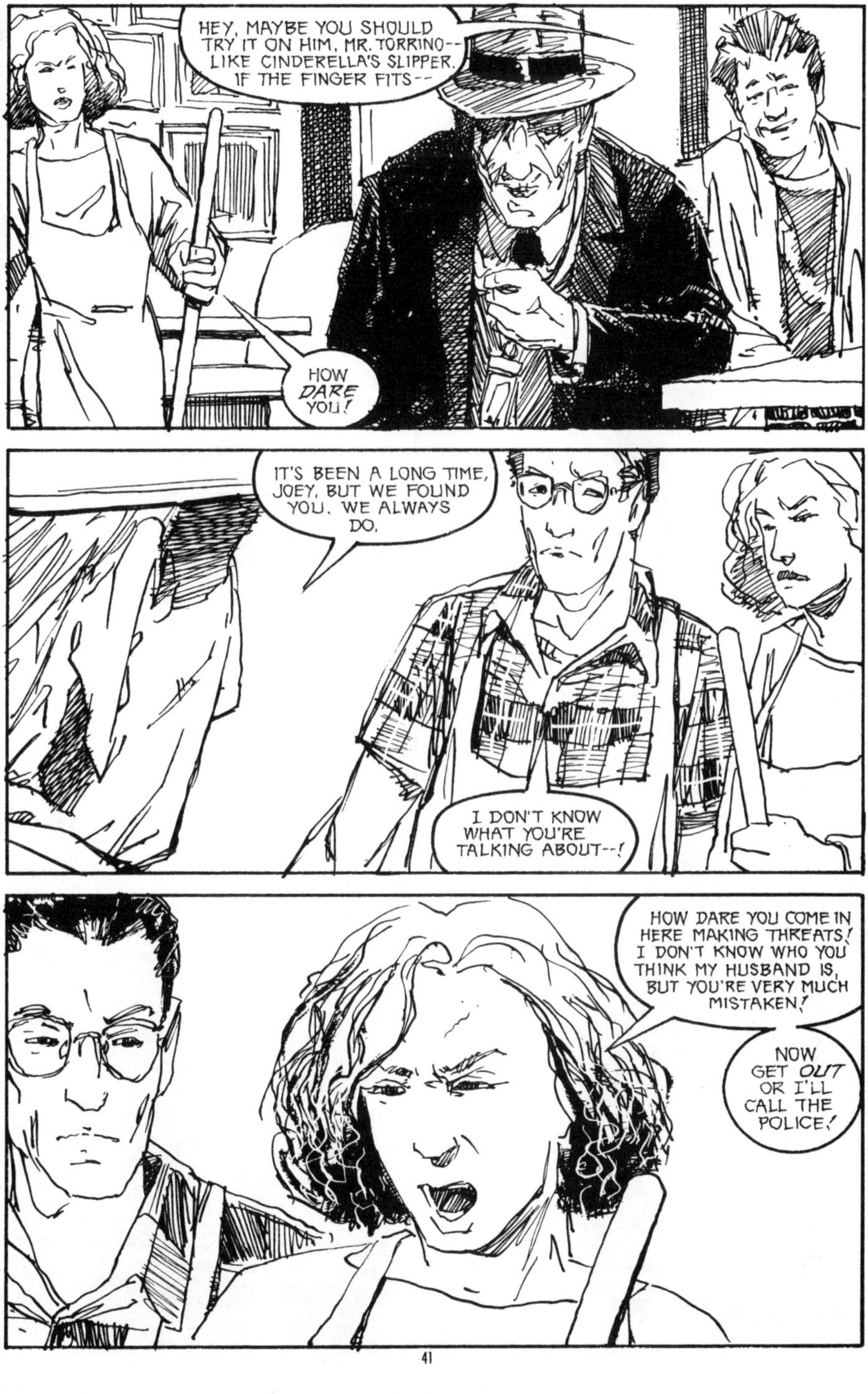
HEY, MAYBE YOU SHOULD TRY IT ON HIM, MR. TORRINO-- LIKE CINDERELLA'S SLIPPER. IF THE FINGER FITS--
HOW DARE YOU!
IT'S BEEN A LONG TIME, JOEY, BUT WE FOUND YOU. WE ALWAYS DO.
I DON'T KNOW WHAT YOU'RE TALKING ABOUT--!
HOW DARE YOU COME IN HERE MAKING THREATS! I DON'T KNOW WHO YOU THINK MY HUSBAND IS, BUT YOU'RE VERY MUCH MISTAKEN!
NOW GET OUT OR I'LL CALL THE POLICE!

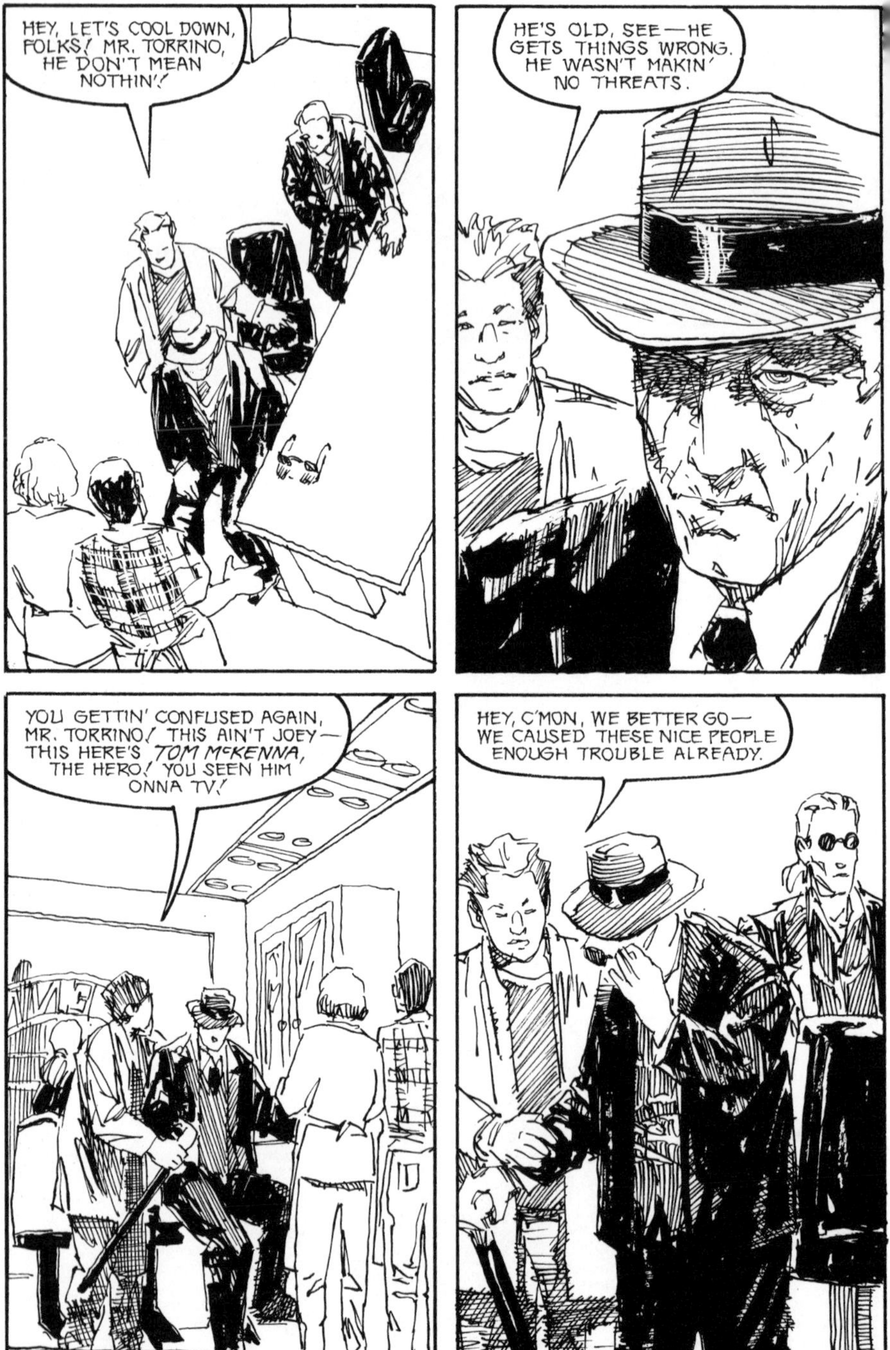
HEY, LET'S COOL DOWN, FOLKS! MR. TORRINO, HE DON'T MEAN NOTHIN'!
HE'S OLD, SEE—HE GETS THINGS WRONG. HE WASN'T MAKIN' NO THREATS.
YOU GETTIN' CONFUSED AGAIN, MR. TORRINO! THIS AIN'T JOEY— THIS HERE'S *TOM McKENNA*, THE HERO! YOU SEEN HIM ONNA TV!
HEY, C'MON, WE BETTER GO— WE CAUSED THESE NICE PEOPLE ENOUGH TROUBLE ALREADY.

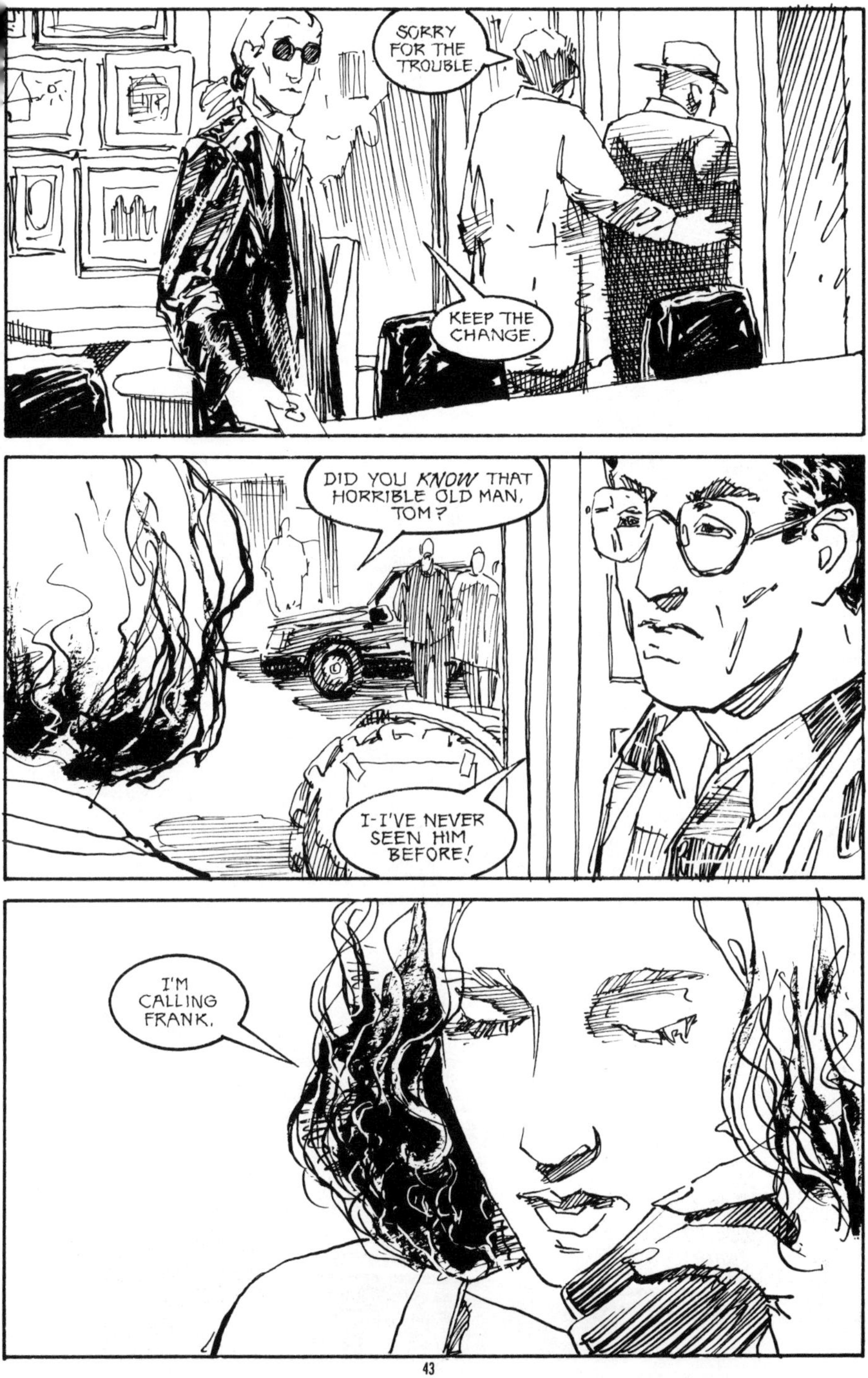
SORRY FOR THE TROUBLE.
KEEP THE CHANGE.
DID YOU *KNOW* THAT HORRIBLE OLD MAN, TOM?
I-I'VE NEVER SEEN HIM BEFORE!
I'M CALLING FRANK.

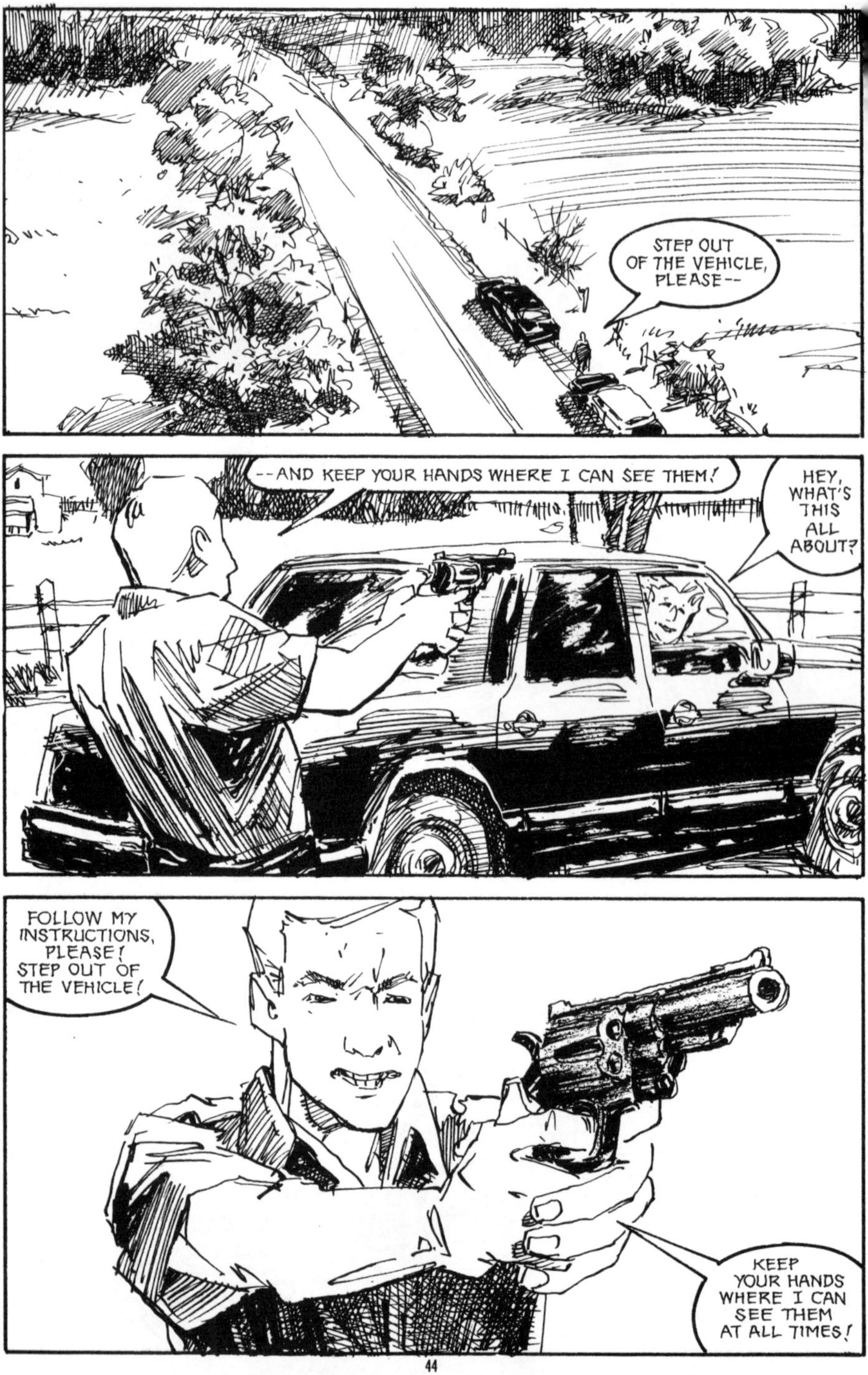
STEP OUT OF THE VEHICLE, PLEASE--
--AND KEEP YOUR HANDS WHERE I CAN SEE THEM!
HEY, WHAT'S THIS ALL ABOUT?
FOLLOW MY INSTRUCTIONS, PLEASE! STEP OUT OF THE VEHICLE!
KEEP YOUR HANDS WHERE I CAN SEE THEM AT ALL TIMES!

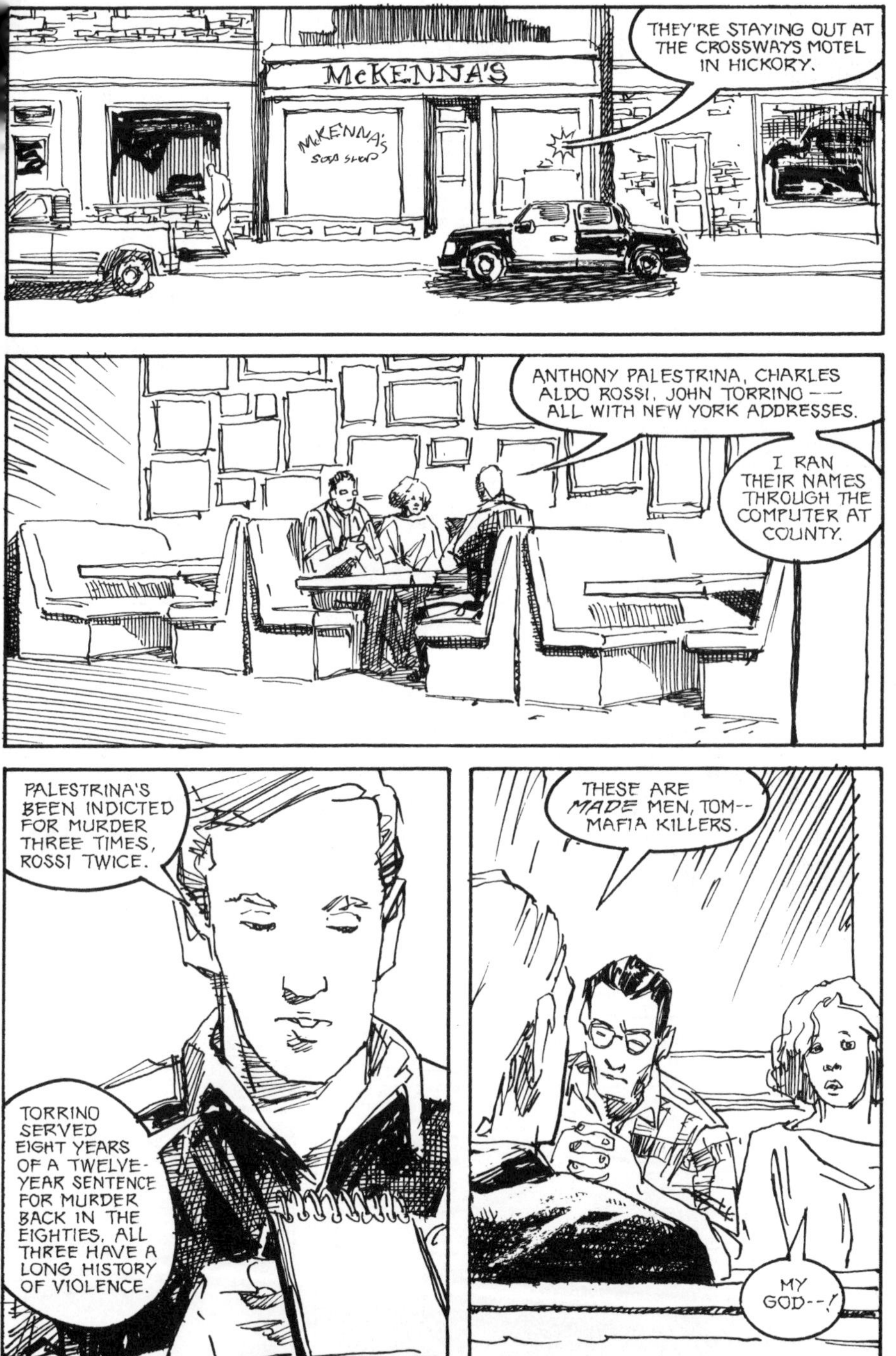
McKENNA'S
McKENNA'S SODA SHOP
THEY'RE STAYING OUT AT THE CROSSWAYS MOTEL IN HICKORY.
ANTHONY PALESTRINA, CHARLES ALDO ROSSI, JOHN TORRINO -- ALL WITH NEW YORK ADDRESSES.
I RAN THEIR NAMES THROUGH THE COMPUTER AT COUNTY.
PALESTRINA'S BEEN INDICTED FOR MURDER THREE TIMES, ROSSI TWICE.
TORRINO SERVED EIGHT YEARS OF A TWELVE-YEAR SENTENCE FOR MURDER BACK IN THE EIGHTIES. ALL THREE HAVE A LONG HISTORY OF VIOLENCE.
THESE ARE MADE MEN, TOM-- MAFIA KILLERS.
MY GOD--!

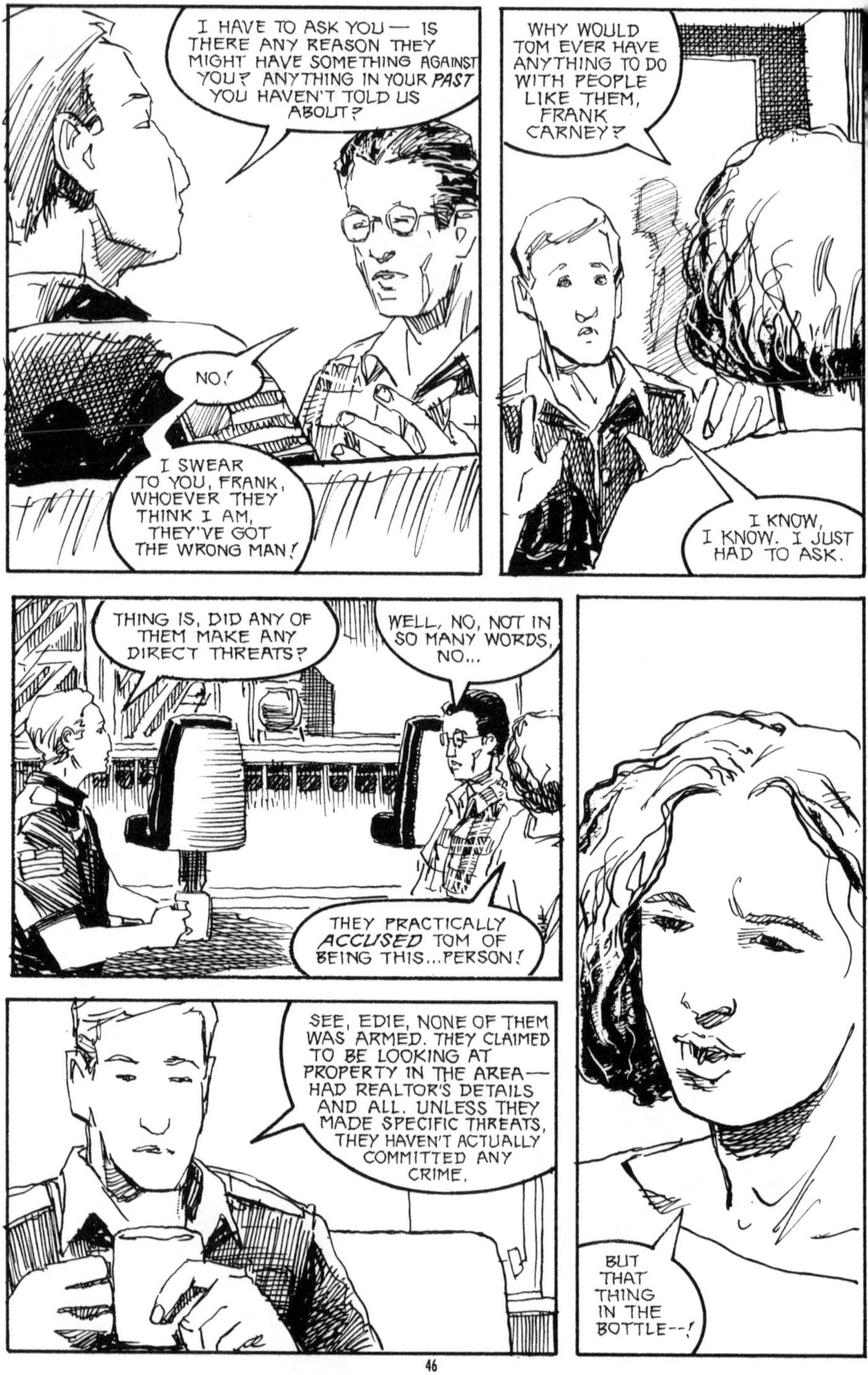
I HAVE TO ASK YOU— IS THERE ANY REASON THEY MIGHT HAVE SOMETHING AGAINST YOU? ANYTHING IN YOUR PAST YOU HAVEN'T TOLD US ABOUT?
NO!
I SWEAR TO YOU, FRANK, WHOEVER THEY THINK I AM, THEY'VE GOT THE WRONG MAN!
WHY WOULD TOM EVER HAVE ANYTHING TO DO WITH PEOPLE LIKE THEM, FRANK CARNEY?
I KNOW, I KNOW. I JUST HAD TO ASK.
THING IS, DID ANY OF THEM MAKE ANY DIRECT THREATS?
WELL, NO, NOT IN SO MANY WORDS, NO...
THEY PRACTICALLY ACCUSED TOM OF BEING THIS...PERSON!
SEE, EDIE, NONE OF THEM WAS ARMED. THEY CLAIMED TO BE LOOKING AT PROPERTY IN THE AREA— HAD REALTOR'S DETAILS AND ALL. UNLESS THEY MADE SPECIFIC THREATS, THEY HAVEN'T ACTUALLY COMMITTED ANY CRIME.
BUT THAT THING IN THE BOTTLE--!

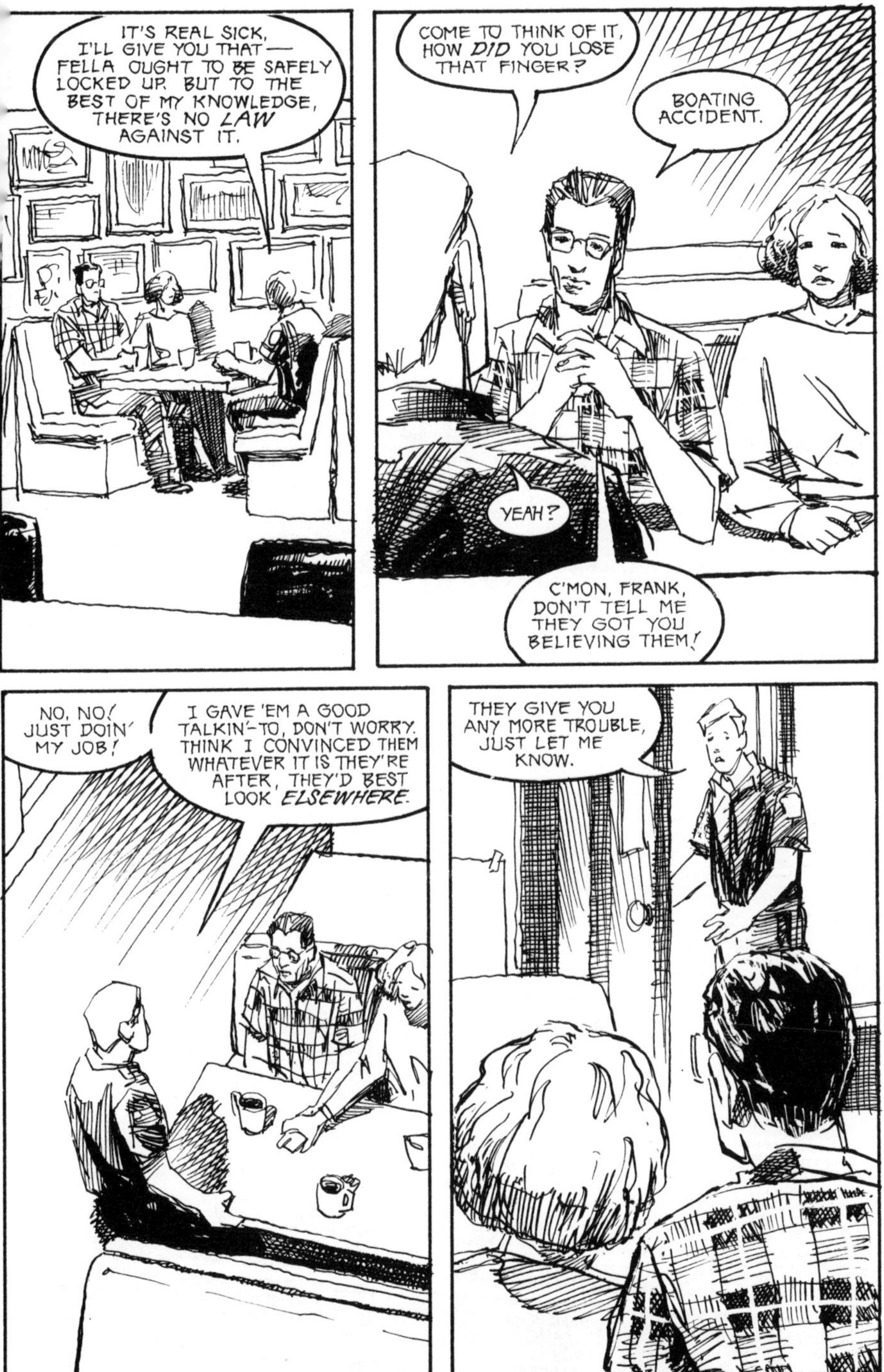
IT'S REAL SICK, I'LL GIVE YOU THAT— FELLA OUGHT TO BE SAFELY LOCKED UP. BUT TO THE BEST OF MY KNOWLEDGE, THERE'S NO LAW AGAINST IT.
COME TO THINK OF IT, HOW DID YOU LOSE THAT FINGER?
BOATING ACCIDENT.
YEAH?
C'MON, FRANK, DON'T TELL ME THEY GOT YOU BELIEVING THEM!
NO, NO! JUST DOIN' MY JOB!
I GAVE 'EM A GOOD TALKIN'-TO, DON'T WORRY. THINK I CONVINCED THEM WHATEVER IT IS THEY'RE AFTER, THEY'D BEST LOOK ELSEWHERE.
THEY GIVE YOU ANY MORE TROUBLE, JUST LET ME KNOW.

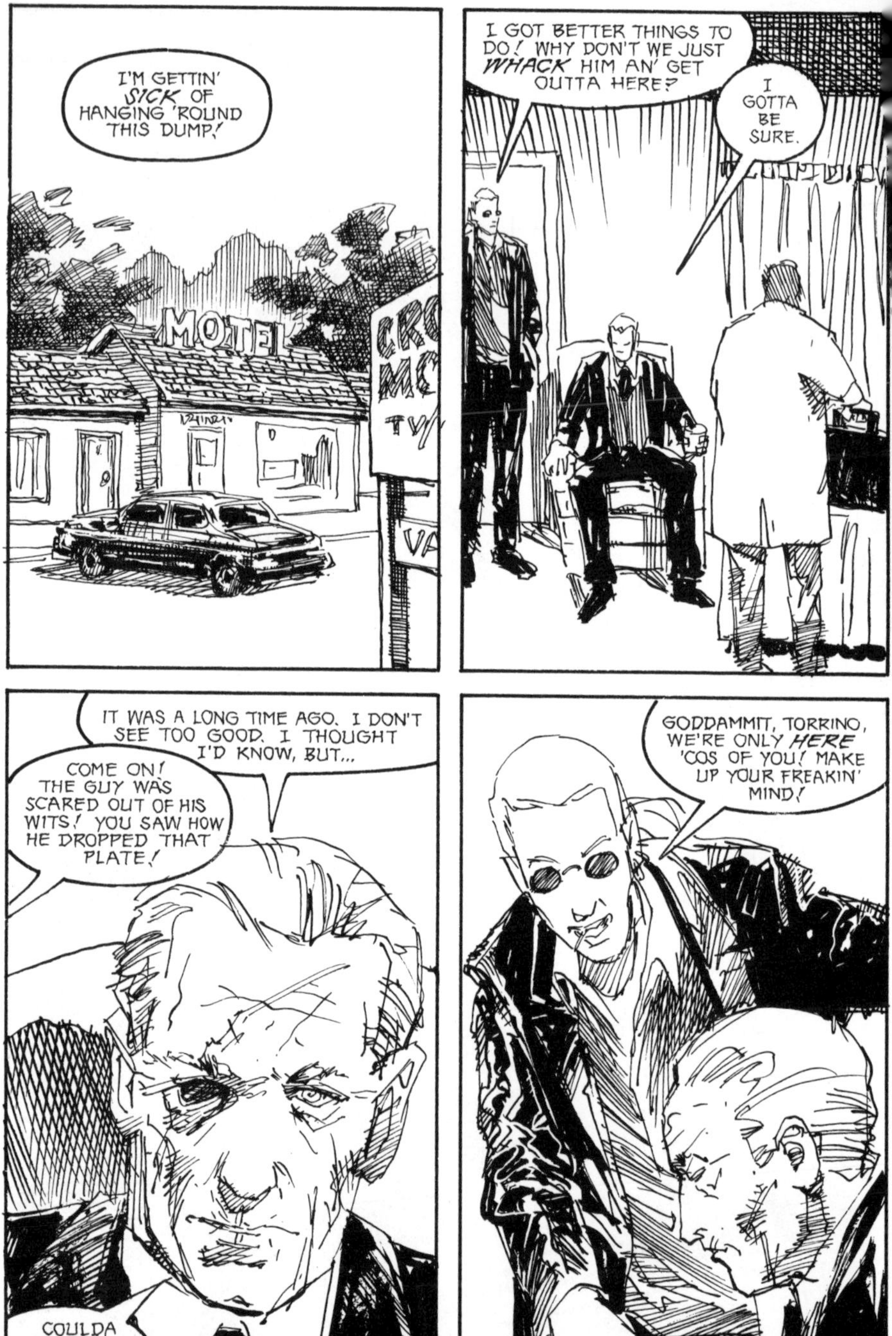
I'M GETTIN' SICK OF HANGING 'ROUND THIS DUMP!
MOTEL
I GOT BETTER THINGS TO DO! WHY DON'T WE JUST WHACK HIM AN' GET OUTTA HERE?
I GOTTA BE SURE.
IT WAS A LONG TIME AGO. I DON'T SEE TOO GOOD. I THOUGHT I'D KNOW, BUT...
COME ON! THE GUY WAS SCARED OUT OF HIS WITS! YOU SAW HOW HE DROPPED THAT PLATE!
COULDA BEEN AN ACCIDENT.
GODDAMMIT, TORRINO, WE'RE ONLY HERE 'COS OF YOU! MAKE UP YOUR FREAKIN' MIND!

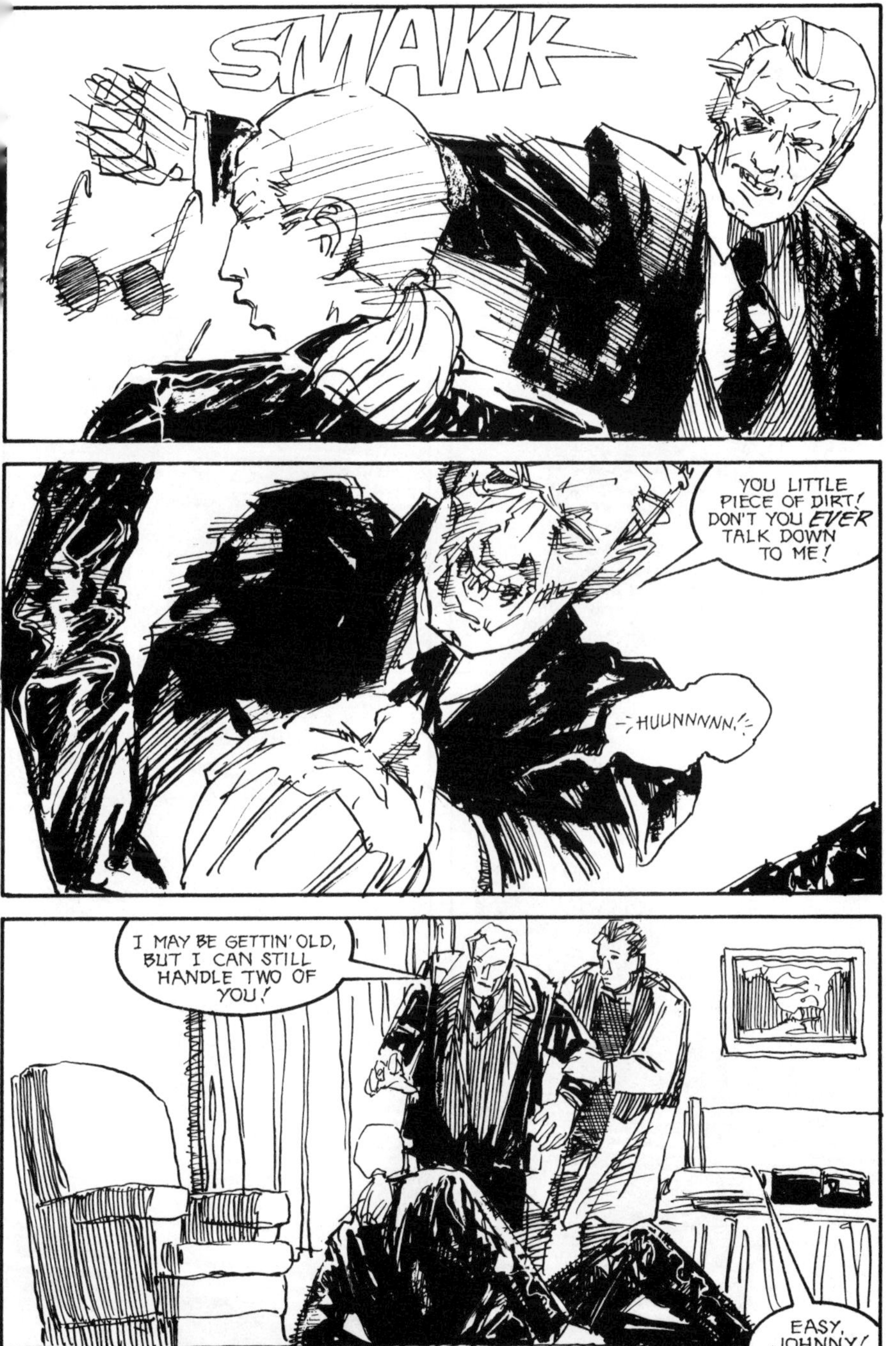
SMAKK
YOU LITTLE PIECE OF DIRT! DON'T YOU EVER TALK DOWN TO ME!
HUUNNNNN!
I MAY BE GETTIN' OLD, BUT I CAN STILL HANDLE TWO OF YOU!
EASY, JOHNNY! EASY!

LITTLE SHIT! MOUTH OFF TO ME AGAIN AN' I'LL *KILL* YOU!

C'MON, JOHNNY-- TONY DIDN'T MEAN NOTHIN', OKAY?

ANYWAY, HE'S GOT A POINT. IF THIS GEEK AIN'T JOEY, WHY DON'T WE JUST SCRAM, HUH?

NO! IT'S HIM! I JUST GOT TO BE SURE, THAT'S ALL....!

THEN WE'RE GONNA HAVE TO FLUSH HIM OUT.

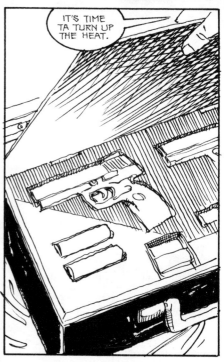

IT'S TIME TA TURN UP THE HEAT.

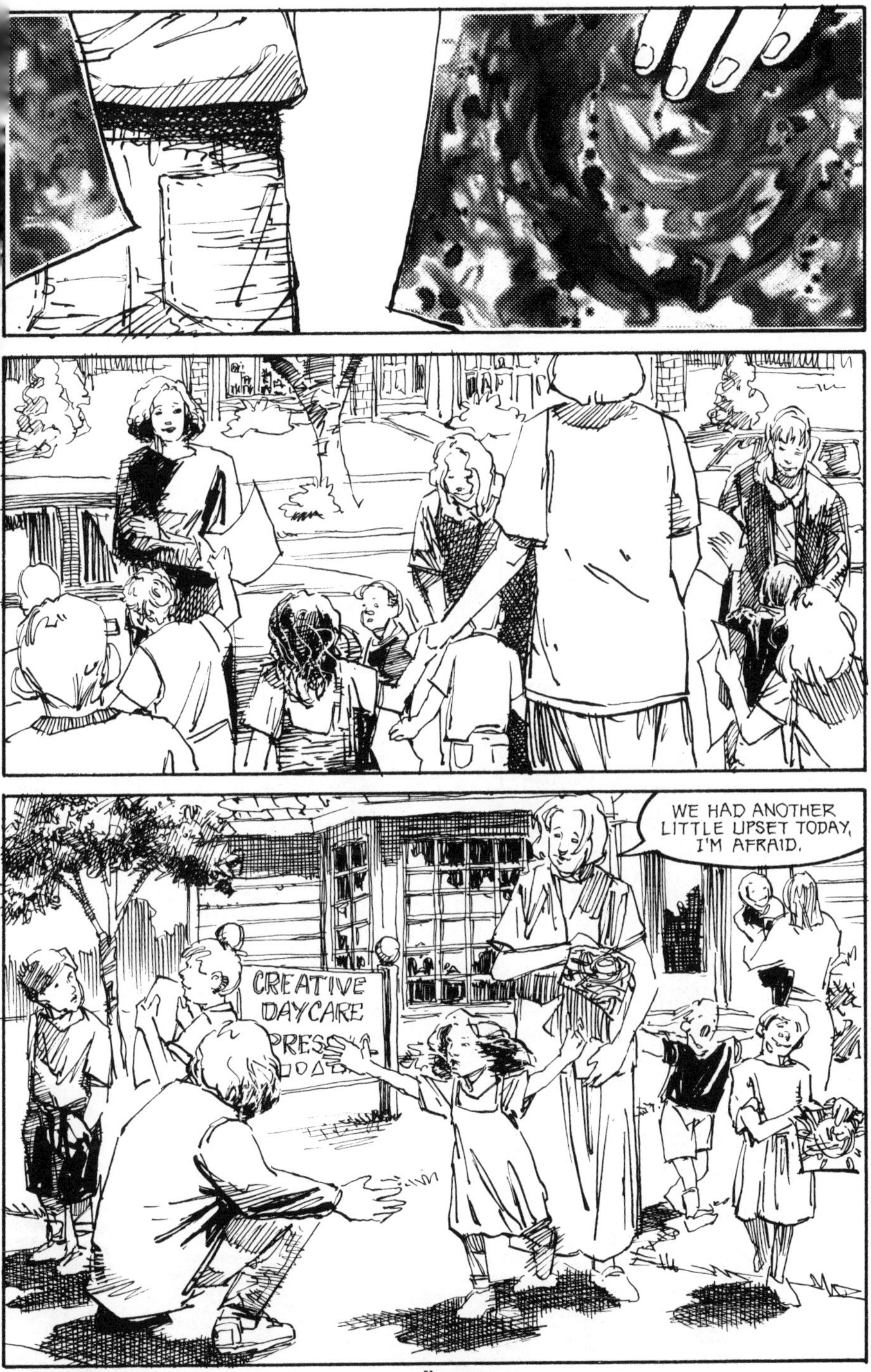
CREATIVE
DAYCARE
WE HAD ANOTHER LITTLE UPSET TODAY, I'M AFRAID.

POOR LITTLE MITE, THE SHOOTIN' MUST HAVE SHOOK HER UP PRETTY BAD.

BUT SHE'LL GET OVER IT, JUST TAKES TIME.

WE'RE TRYING TO MAKE LIFE AS NORMAL AS POSSIBLE FOR HER. AT LEAST THE REPORTERS HAVE STOPPED BOTHERING US.

TROUBLE IS, HOW DO YOU REASSURE A CHILD THE WORLD'S A SAFE PLACE WHEN YOU KNOW FULL WELL IT'S NOT?

WE'RE DROPPING BY THE MALL. ANYTHING I CAN PICK UP FOR YOU, PRU?

NO THANKS. GOT TO GO MYSELF.

TELL TOM *ROY'S* GONNA RING HIM TONIGHT ABOUT THAT HUNTIN' TRIP.

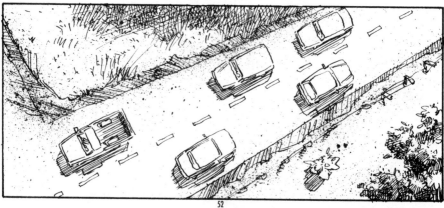

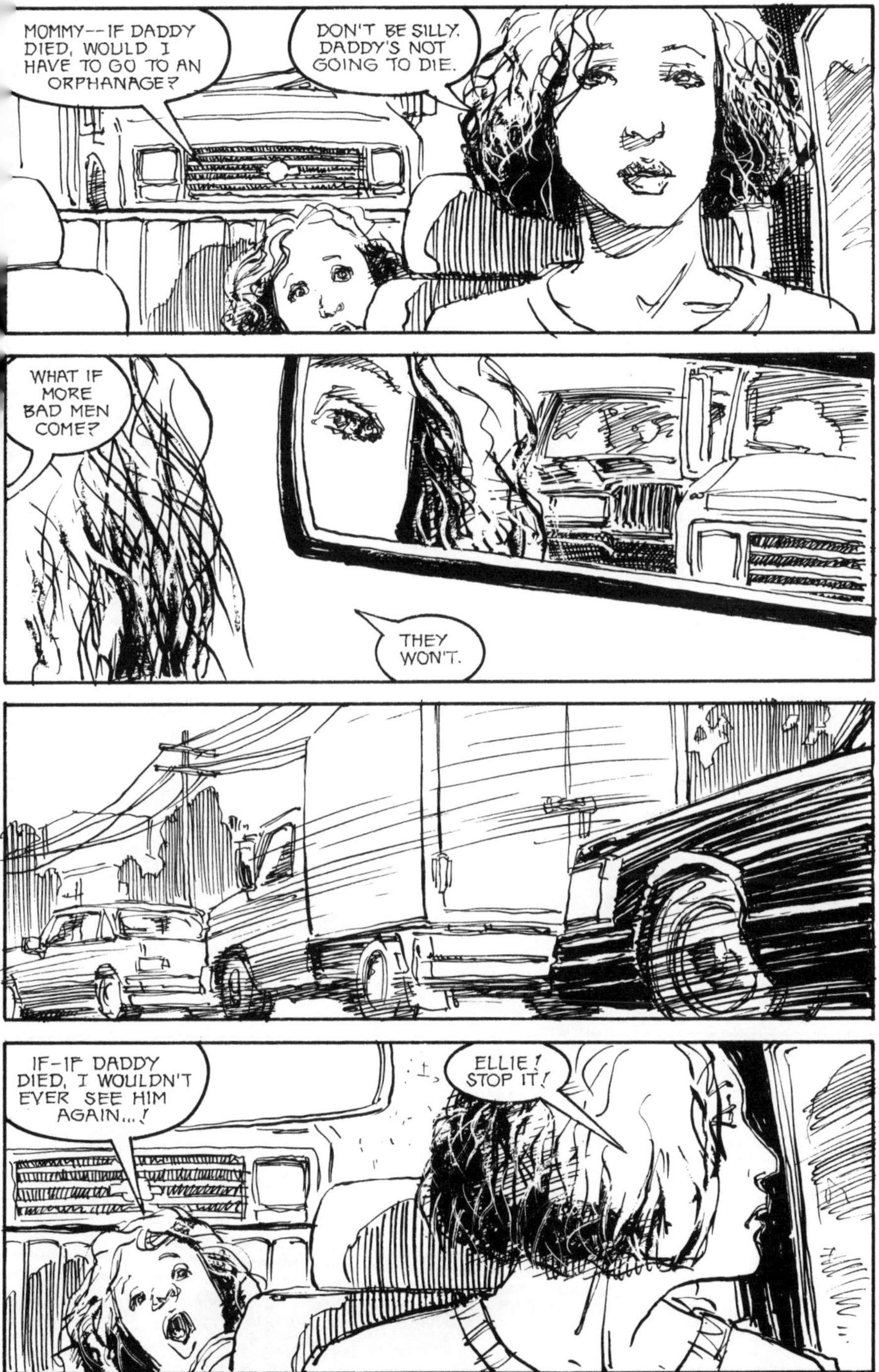
MOMMY--IF DADDY DIED, WOULD I HAVE TO GO TO AN ORPHANAGE?
DON'T BE SILLY. DADDY'S NOT GOING TO DIE.
WHAT IF MORE BAD MEN COME?
THEY WON'T.
IF-IF DADDY DIED, I WOULDN'T EVER SEE HIM AGAIN...!
ELLIE! STOP IT!

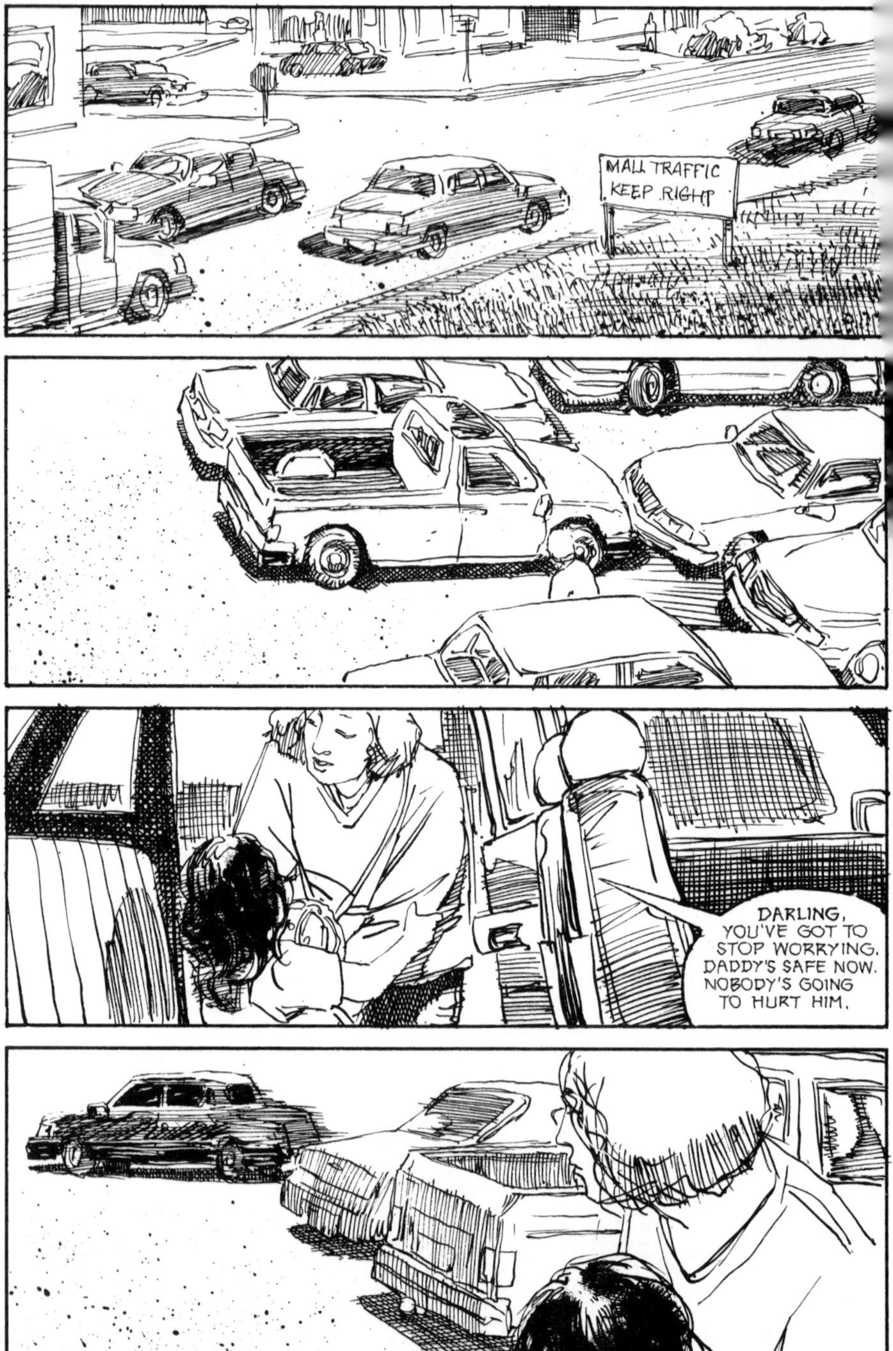
MALL TRAFFIC
KEEP RIGHT
DARLING, YOU'VE GOT TO STOP WORRYING. DADDY'S SAFE NOW. NOBODY'S GOING TO HURT HIM.

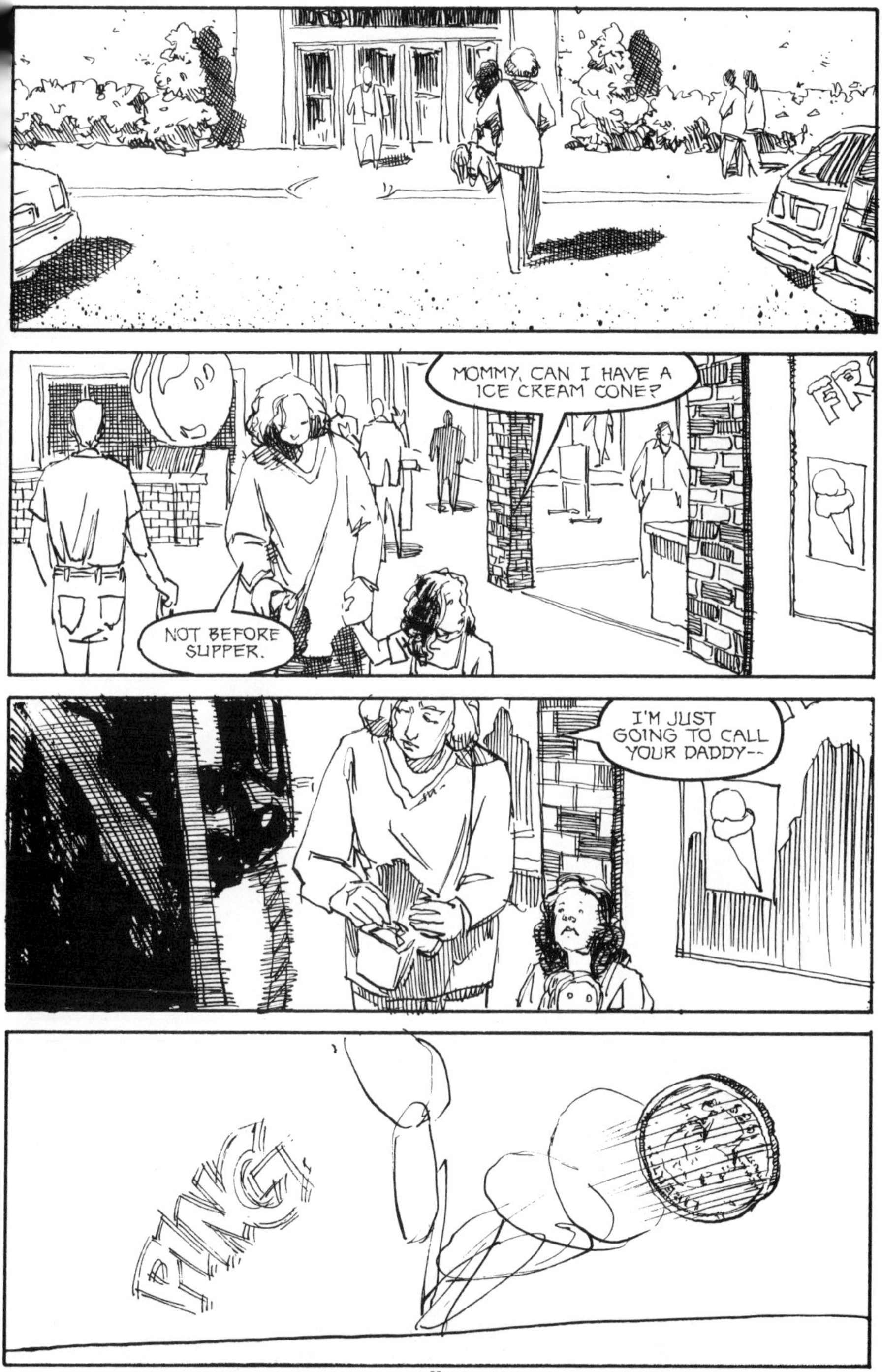
MOMMY, CAN I HAVE A ICE CREAM CONE?
NOT BEFORE SUPPER.
I'M JUST GOING TO CALL YOUR DADDY--
PING!

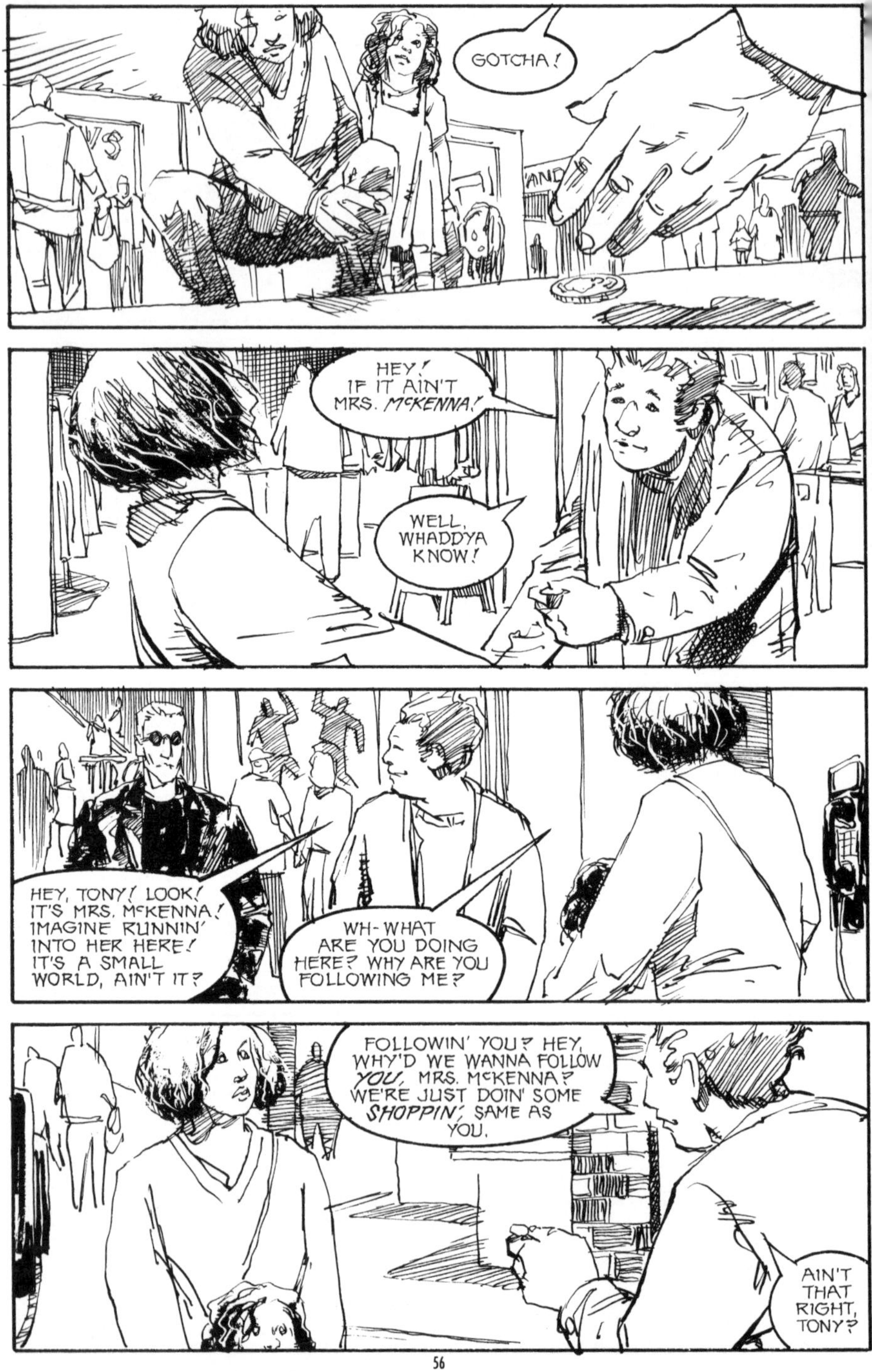
GOTCHA!
HEY! IF IT AIN'T MRS. McKENNA!
WELL, WHADDYA KNOW!
HEY, TONY! LOOK! IT'S MRS. McKENNA! IMAGINE RUNNIN' INTO HER HERE! IT'S A SMALL WORLD, AIN'T IT?
WH-WHAT ARE YOU DOING HERE? WHY ARE YOU FOLLOWING ME?
FOLLOWIN' YOU? HEY, WHY'D WE WANNA FOLLOW YOU, MRS. McKENNA? WE'RE JUST DOIN' SOME SHOPPIN', SAME AS YOU.
AIN'T THAT RIGHT, TONY?

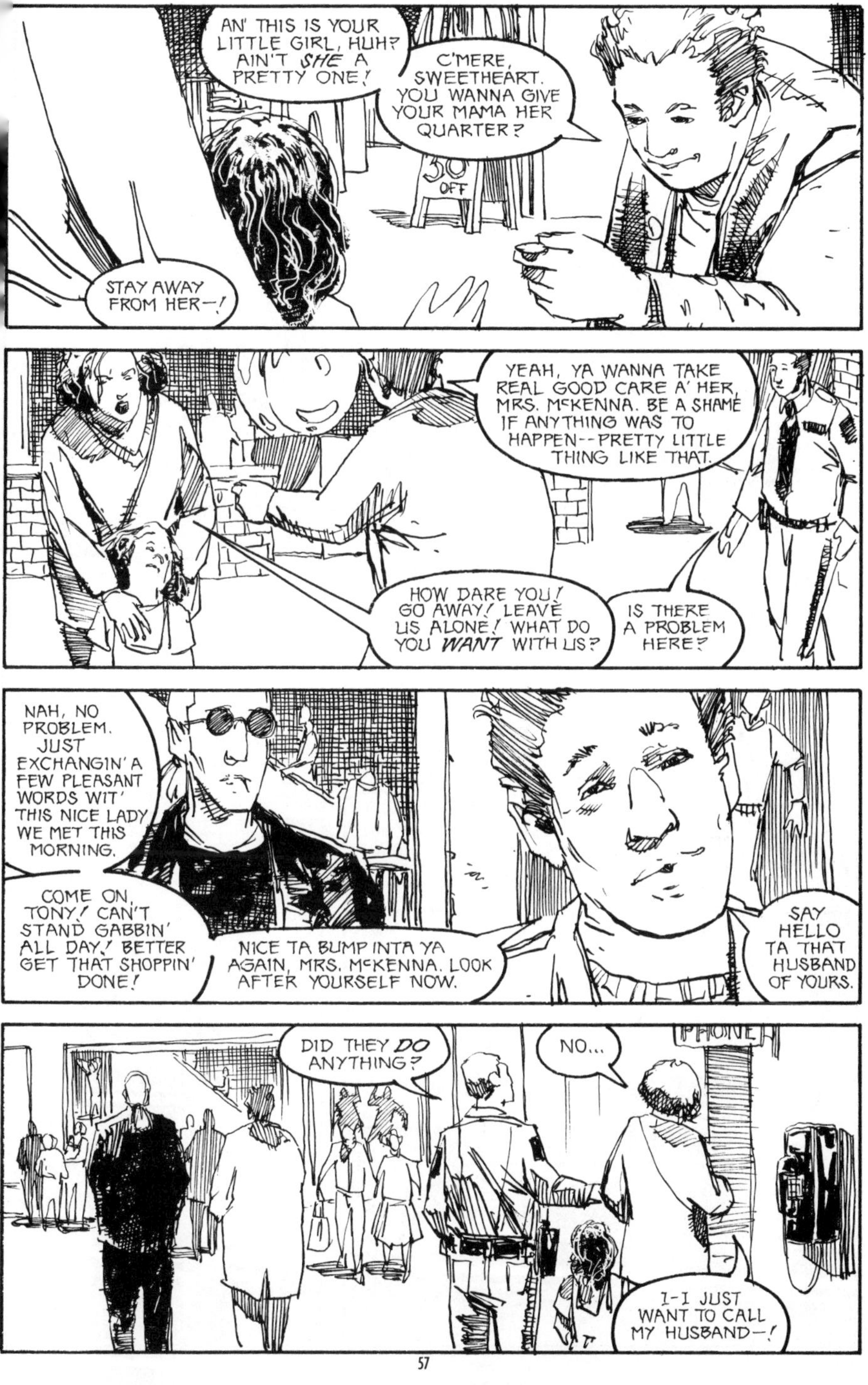
AN' THIS IS YOUR LITTLE GIRL, HUH? AIN'T *SHE* A PRETTY ONE!
C'MERE, SWEETHEART. YOU WANNA GIVE YOUR MAMA HER QUARTER?
30 OFF
STAY AWAY FROM HER—!
YEAH, YA WANNA TAKE REAL GOOD CARE A' HER, MRS. McKENNA. BE A SHAME IF ANYTHING WAS TO HAPPEN--PRETTY LITTLE THING LIKE THAT.
HOW DARE YOU! GO AWAY! LEAVE US ALONE! WHAT DO YOU *WANT* WITH US?
IS THERE A PROBLEM HERE?
NAH, NO PROBLEM. JUST EXCHANGIN' A FEW PLEASANT WORDS WIT' THIS NICE LADY WE MET THIS MORNING.
COME ON, TONY! CAN'T STAND GABBIN' ALL DAY! BETTER GET THAT SHOPPIN' DONE!
NICE TA BUMP INTA YA AGAIN, MRS. McKENNA. LOOK AFTER YOURSELF NOW.
SAY HELLO TA THAT HUSBAND OF YOURS.
PHONE
DID THEY *DO* ANYTHING?
NO...
I-I JUST WANT TO CALL MY HUSBAND—!

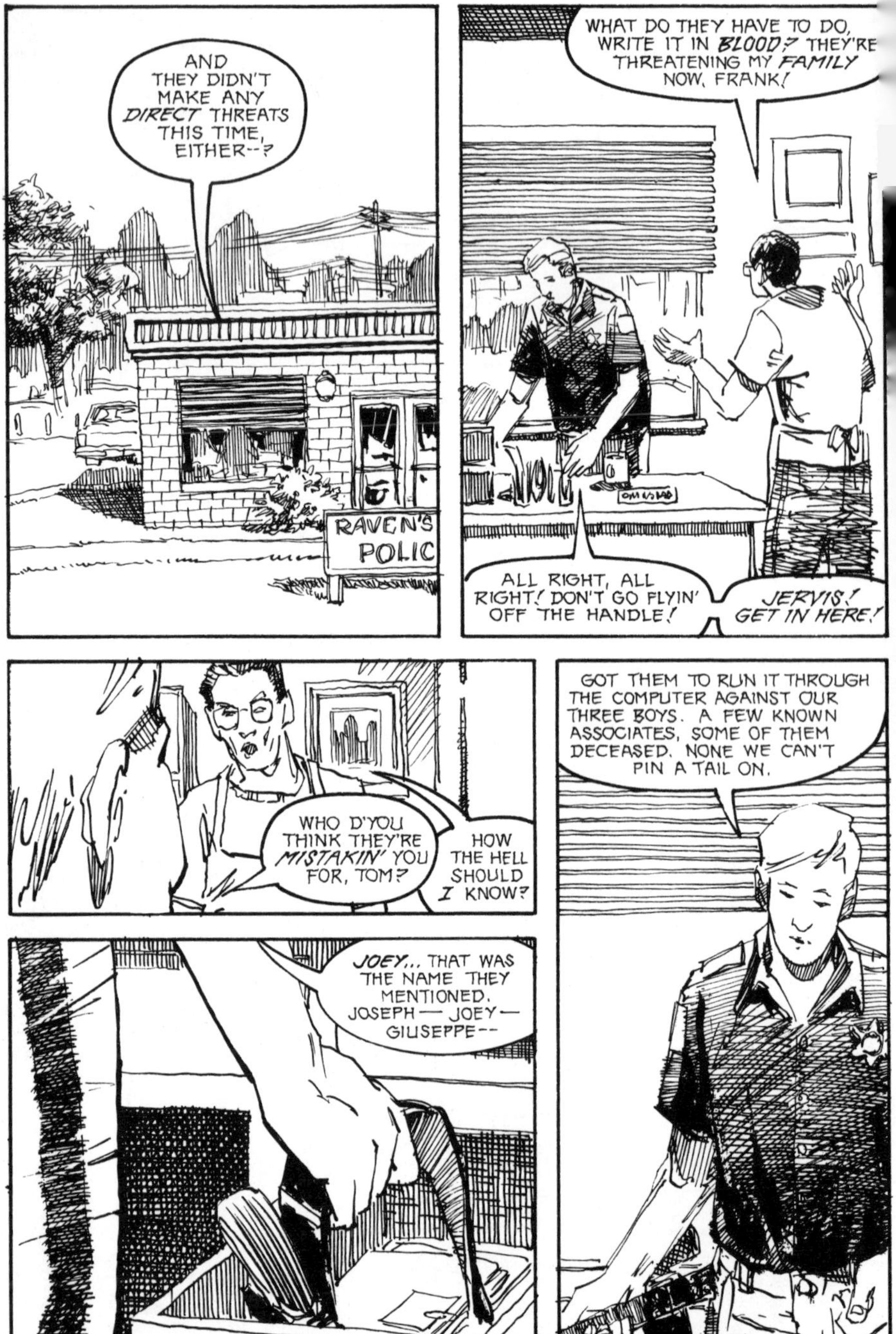
AND THEY DIDN'T MAKE ANY DIRECT THREATS THIS TIME, EITHER--?
RAVEN'S POLIC
WHAT DO THEY HAVE TO DO, WRITE IT IN BLOOD? THEY'RE THREATENING MY FAMILY NOW, FRANK!
ALL RIGHT, ALL RIGHT! DON'T GO FLYIN' OFF THE HANDLE!
JERVIS! GET IN HERE!
WHO D'YOU THINK THEY'RE MISTAKIN' YOU FOR, TOM?
HOW THE HELL SHOULD I KNOW?
GOT THEM TO RUN IT THROUGH THE COMPUTER AGAINST OUR THREE BOYS. A FEW KNOWN ASSOCIATES, SOME OF THEM DECEASED. NONE WE CAN'T PIN A TAIL ON.
JOEY... THAT WAS THE NAME THEY MENTIONED. JOSEPH — JOEY — GIUSEPPE--

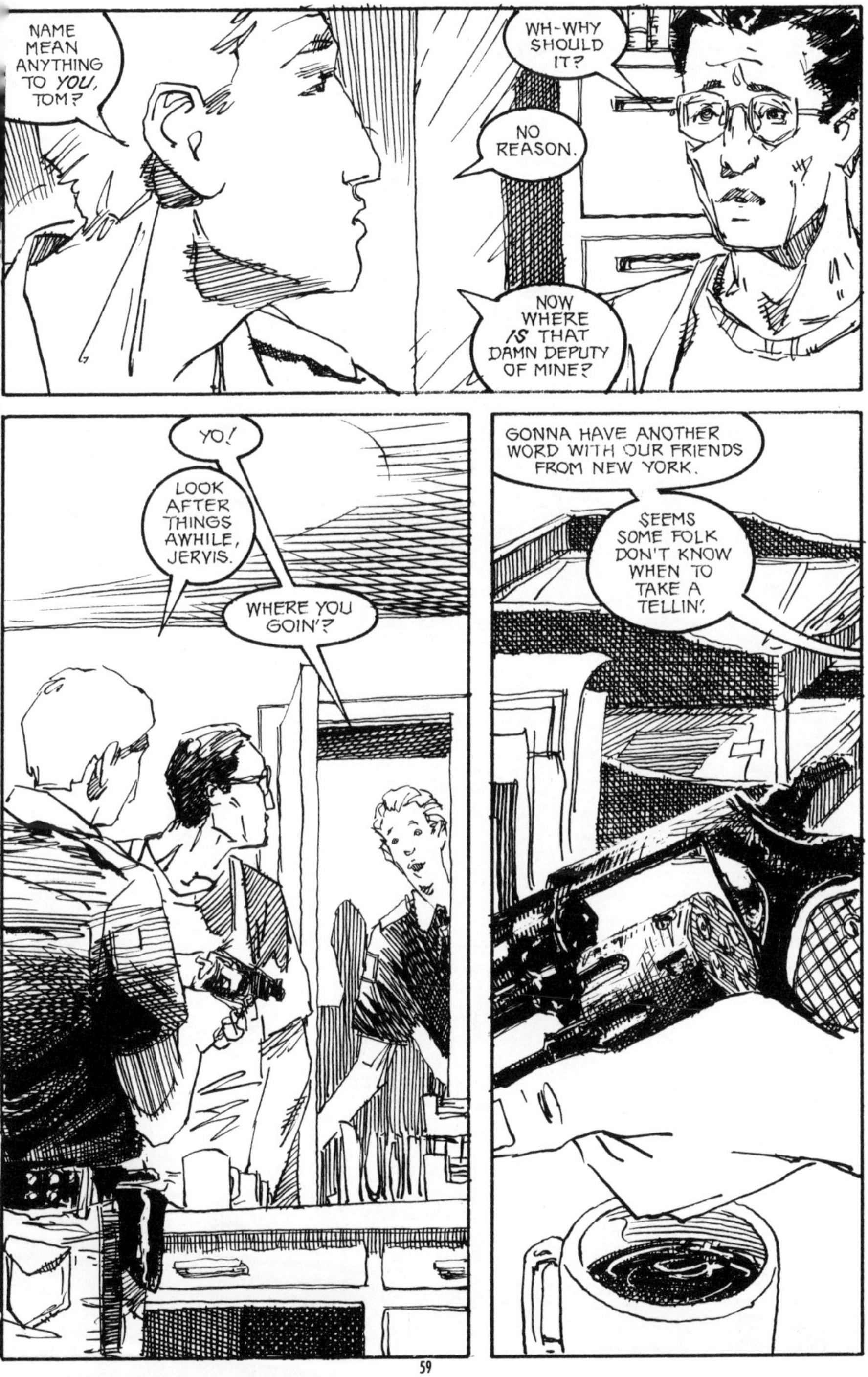
NAME MEAN ANYTHING TO *YOU*, TOM?
WH-WHY SHOULD IT?
NO REASON.
NOW WHERE *IS* THAT DAMN DEPUTY OF MINE?
YO!
LOOK AFTER THINGS AWHILE, JERVIS.
WHERE YOU GOIN'?
GONNA HAVE ANOTHER WORD WITH OUR FRIENDS FROM NEW YORK.
SEEMS SOME FOLK DON'T KNOW WHEN TO TAKE A TELLIN'.

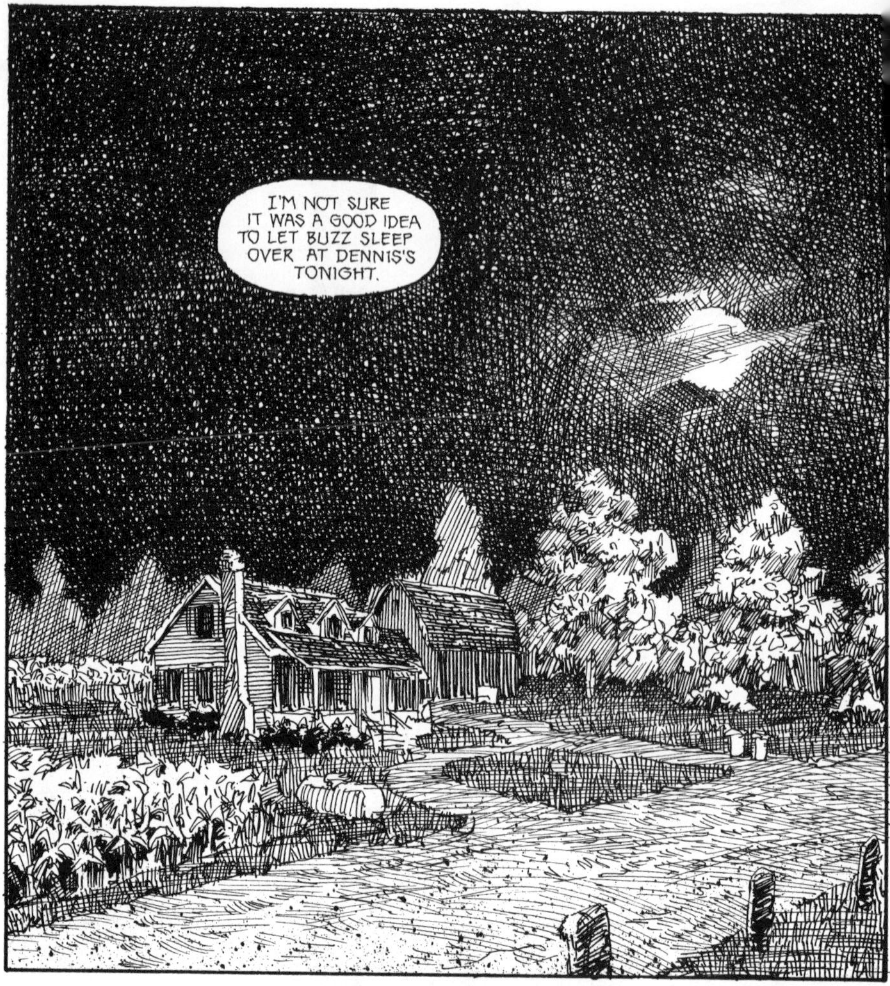
I'M NOT SURE IT WAS A GOOD IDEA TO LET BUZZ SLEEP OVER AT DENNIS'S TONIGHT.

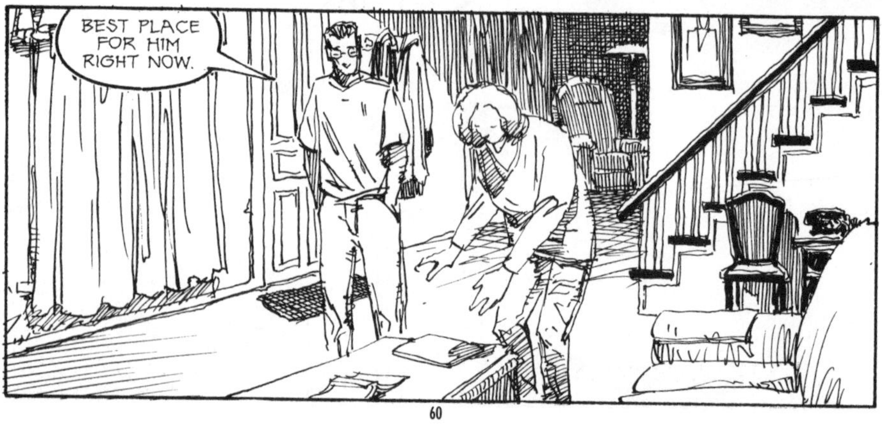
BEST PLACE FOR HIM RIGHT NOW.

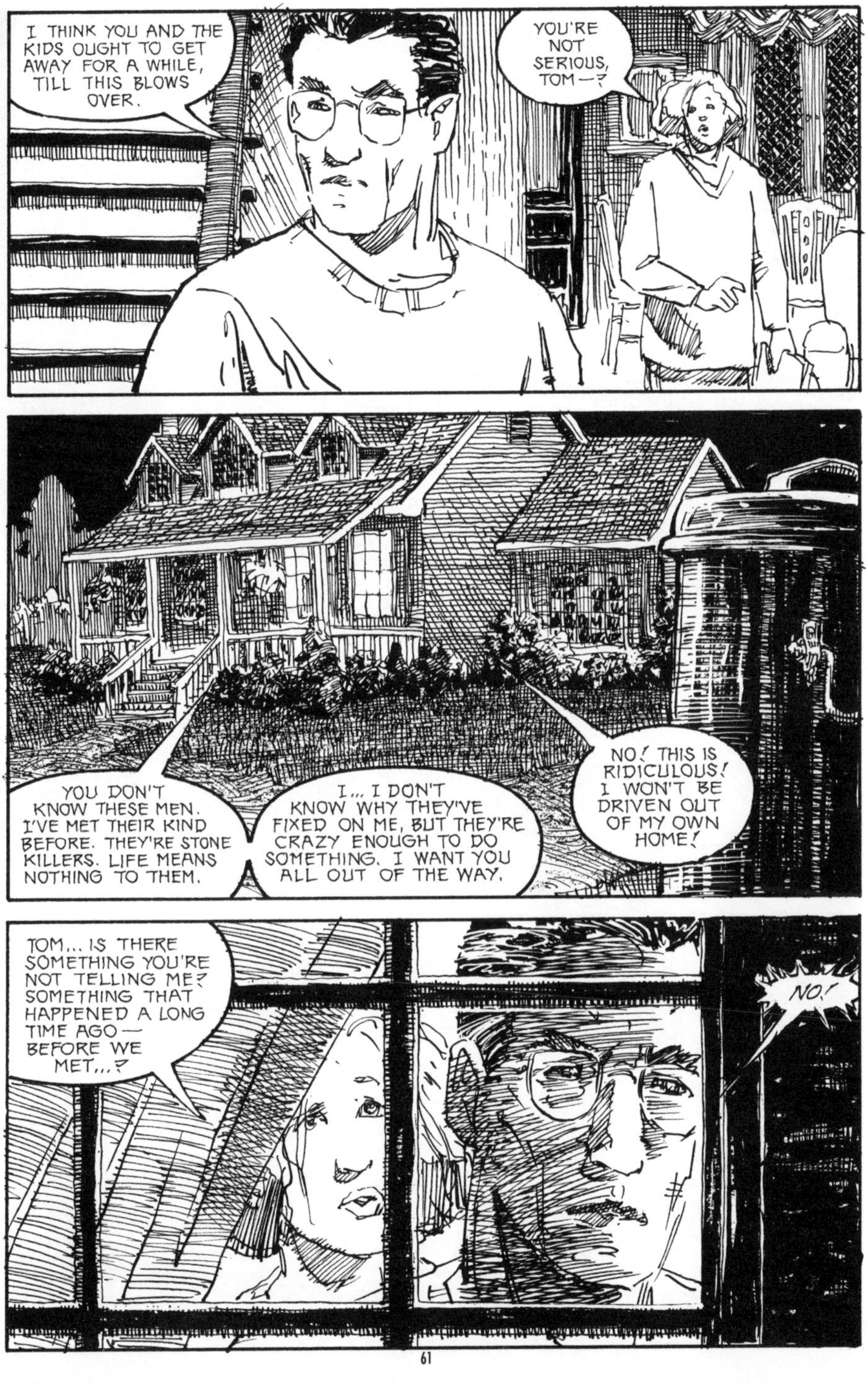
I THINK YOU AND THE KIDS OUGHT TO GET AWAY FOR A WHILE, TILL THIS BLOWS OVER.
YOU'RE NOT SERIOUS, TOM—?
YOU DON'T KNOW THESE MEN. I'VE MET THEIR KIND BEFORE. THEY'RE STONE KILLERS. LIFE MEANS NOTHING TO THEM.
I... I DON'T KNOW WHY THEY'VE FIXED ON ME, BUT THEY'RE CRAZY ENOUGH TO DO SOMETHING. I WANT YOU ALL OUT OF THE WAY.
NO! THIS IS RIDICULOUS! I WON'T BE DRIVEN OUT OF MY OWN HOME!
TOM... IS THERE SOMETHING YOU'RE NOT TELLING ME? SOMETHING THAT HAPPENED A LONG TIME AGO— BEFORE WE MET...?
NO!

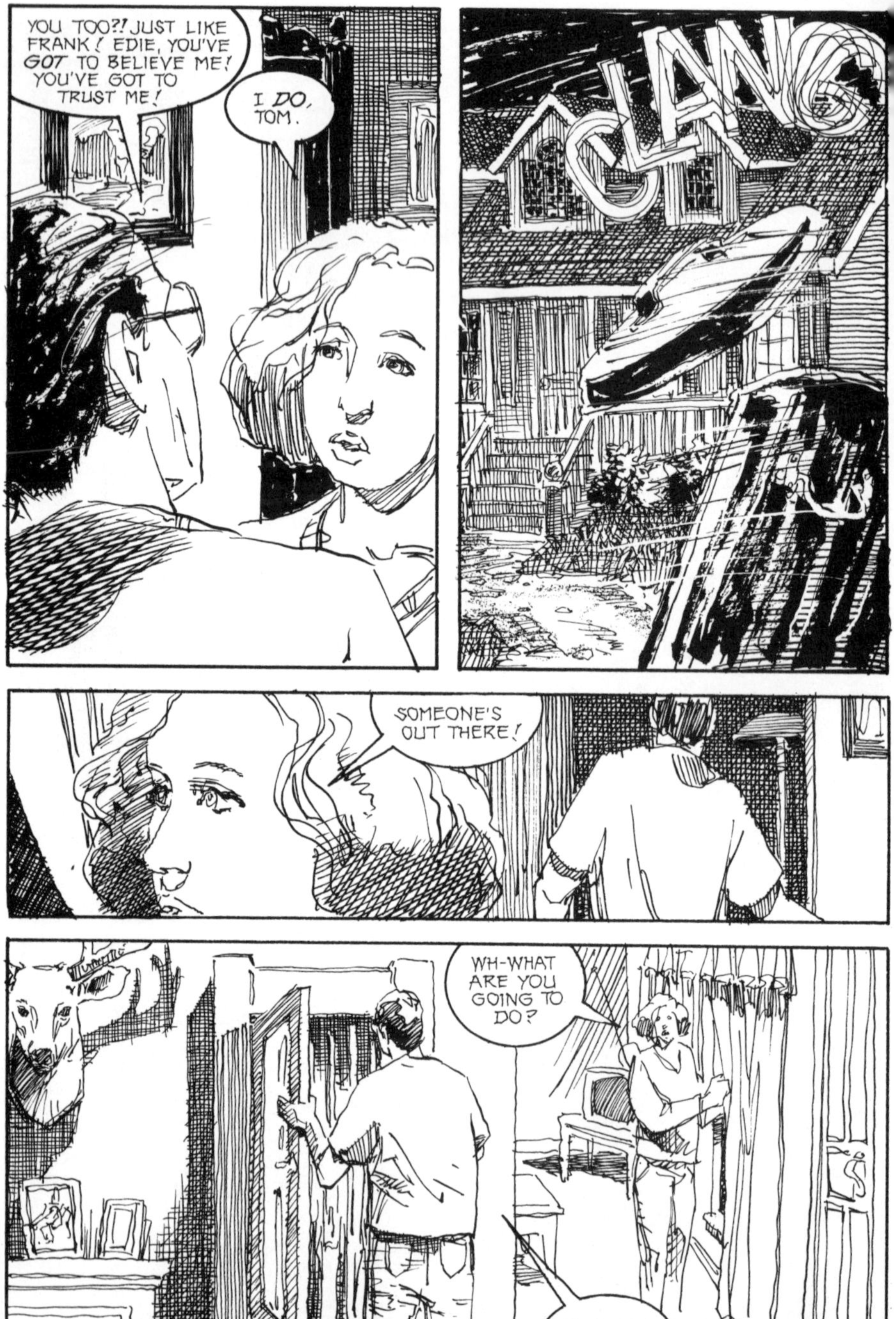

YOU TOO?! JUST LIKE FRANK! EDIE, YOU'VE *GOT* TO BELIEVE ME! YOU'VE GOT TO TRUST ME!
I *DO*, TOM.
CLANG
SOMEONE'S OUT THERE!
WH-WHAT ARE YOU GOING TO DO?
I'VE HAD *ENOUGH*, DAMMIT!

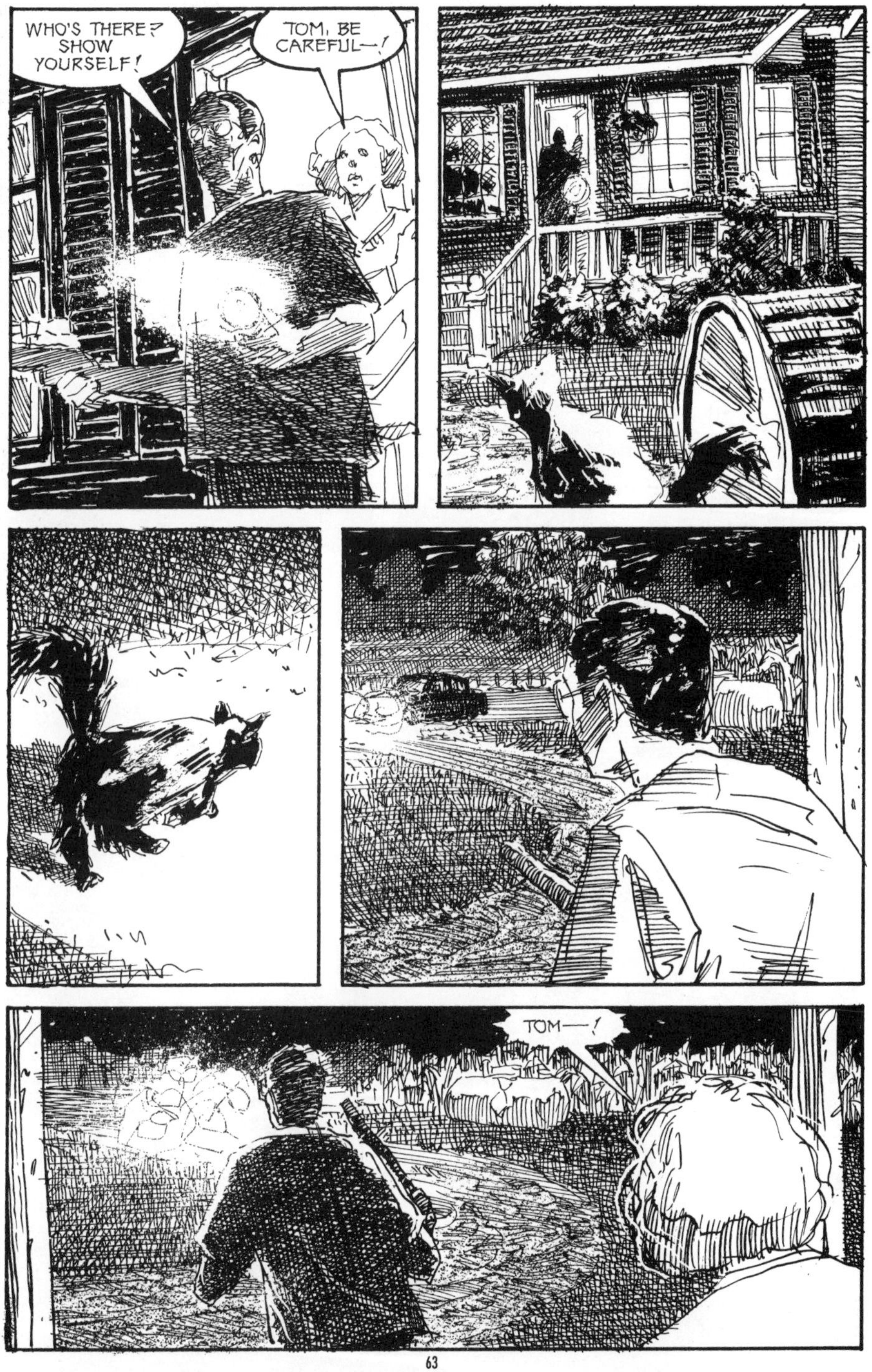
WHO'S THERE? SHOW YOURSELF!
TOM, BE CAREFUL—!
TOM—!

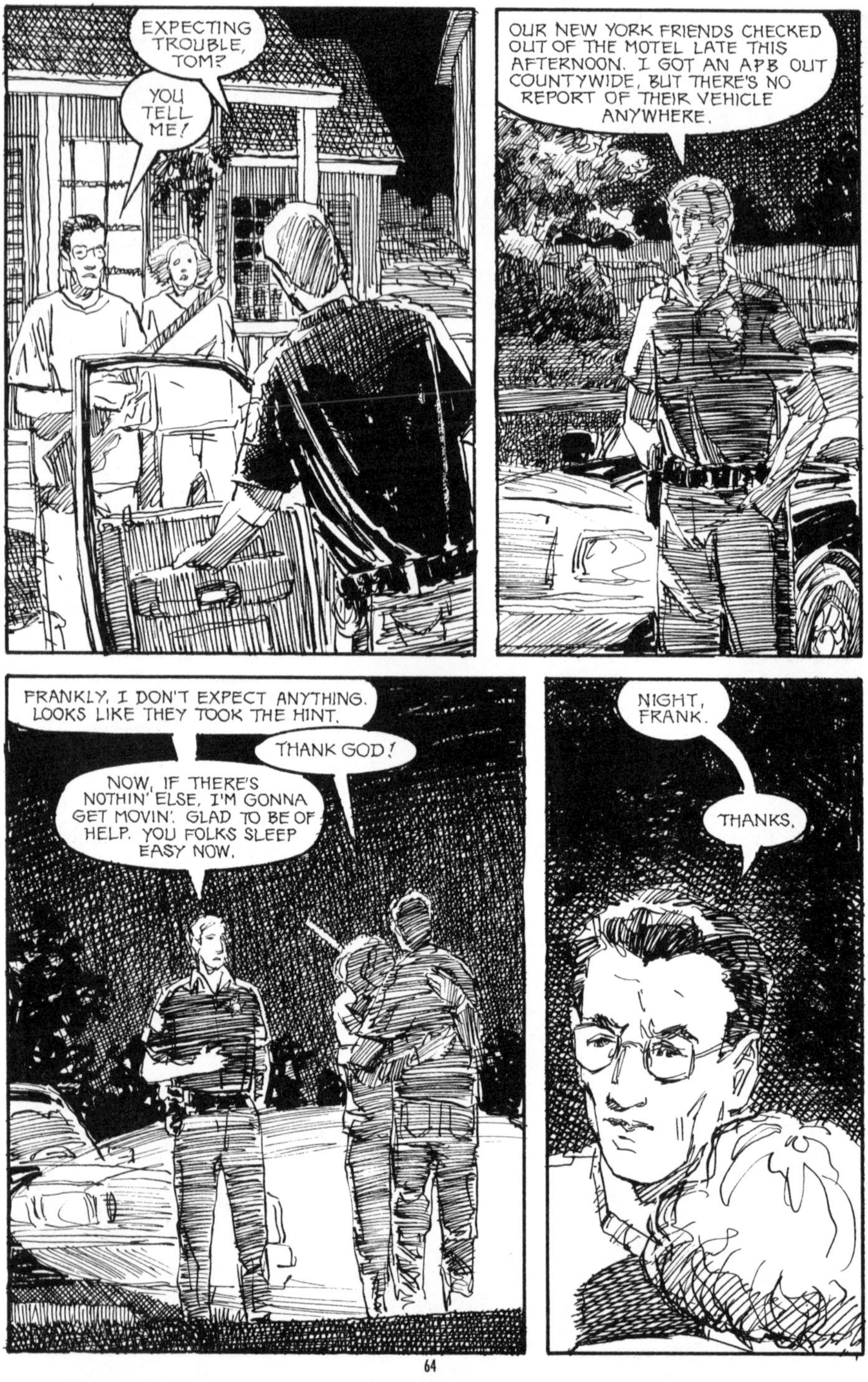
EXPECTING TROUBLE, TOM?
YOU TELL ME!
OUR NEW YORK FRIENDS CHECKED OUT OF THE MOTEL LATE THIS AFTERNOON. I GOT AN APB OUT COUNTYWIDE, BUT THERE'S NO REPORT OF THEIR VEHICLE ANYWHERE.
FRANKLY, I DON'T EXPECT ANYTHING. LOOKS LIKE THEY TOOK THE HINT.
THANK GOD!
NOW, IF THERE'S NOTHIN' ELSE, I'M GONNA GET MOVIN'. GLAD TO BE OF HELP. YOU FOLKS SLEEP EASY NOW.
NIGHT, FRANK.
THANKS.

MAYBE WE OUGHT TO GET AWAY FOR A WHILE ANYWAY, TOM—ALL OF US. WE COULD ALL DO WITH A BREAK.

WE'VE ALWAYS PROMISED TO TAKE THEM TO DISNEYLAND. HOW ABOUT IT? IT'S JUST WHAT ELLIE NEEDS TO HELP HER FORGET THIS WHOLE HORRIBLE BUSINESS.

MMM, YES...

BRINNGGG

TOM McKENNA.

THAT'LL BE ROY. PRU SAID HE'D CALL.

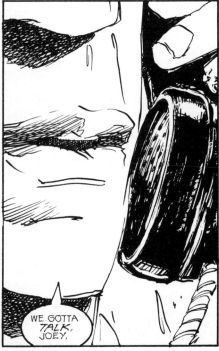

WE GOTTA *TALK,* JOEY.

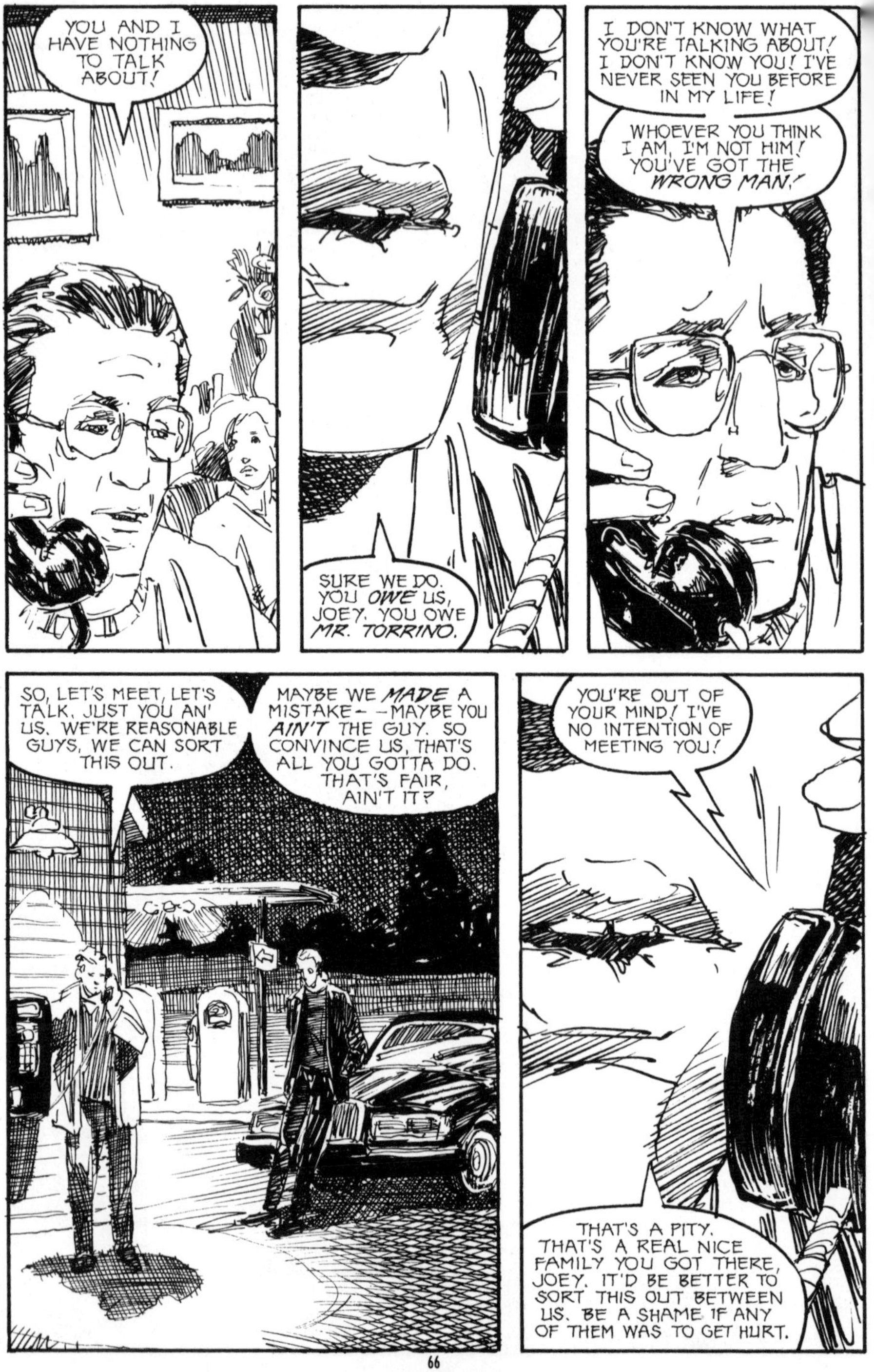
YOU AND I HAVE NOTHING TO TALK ABOUT!
SURE WE DO. YOU OWE US, JOEY. YOU OWE MR. TORRINO.
I DON'T KNOW WHAT YOU'RE TALKING ABOUT! I DON'T KNOW YOU! I'VE NEVER SEEN YOU BEFORE IN MY LIFE!
WHOEVER YOU THINK I AM, I'M NOT HIM! YOU'VE GOT THE WRONG MAN!
SO, LET'S MEET, LET'S TALK. JUST YOU AN' US. WE'RE REASONABLE GUYS, WE CAN SORT THIS OUT.
MAYBE WE MADE A MISTAKE-- --MAYBE YOU AIN'T THE GUY. SO CONVINCE US, THAT'S ALL YOU GOTTA DO. THAT'S FAIR, AIN'T IT?
YOU'RE OUT OF YOUR MIND! I'VE NO INTENTION OF MEETING YOU!
THAT'S A PITY. THAT'S A REAL NICE FAMILY YOU GOT THERE, JOEY. IT'D BE BETTER TO SORT THIS OUT BETWEEN US. BE A SHAME IF ANY OF THEM WAS TO GET HURT.

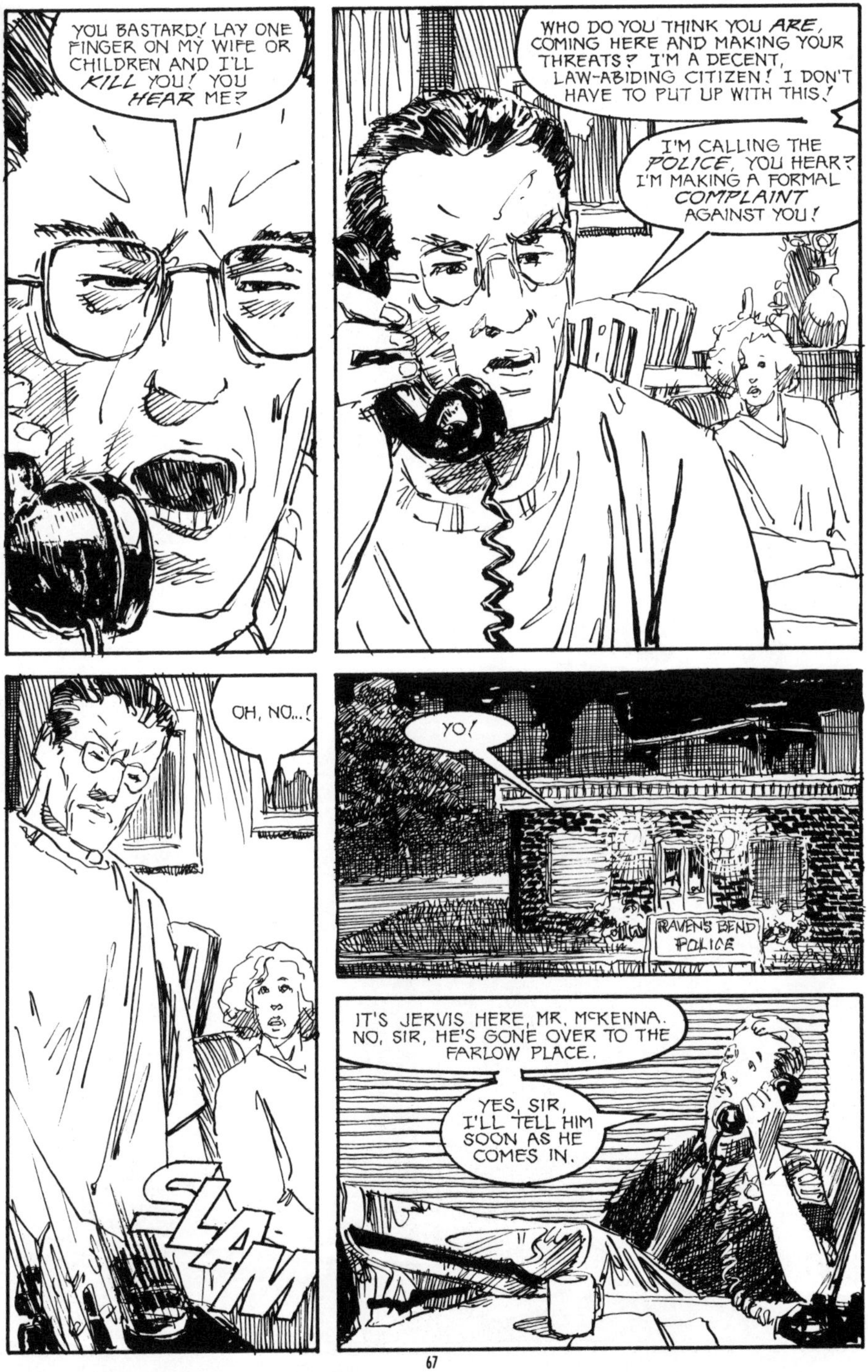
YOU BASTARD! LAY ONE FINGER ON MY WIFE OR CHILDREN AND I'LL KILL YOU! YOU HEAR ME?
WHO DO YOU THINK YOU ARE, COMING HERE AND MAKING YOUR THREATS? I'M A DECENT, LAW-ABIDING CITIZEN! I DON'T HAVE TO PUT UP WITH THIS!
I'M CALLING THE POLICE, YOU HEAR? I'M MAKING A FORMAL COMPLAINT AGAINST YOU!
OH, NO...!
SLAM
YO!
RAVEN'S BEND POLICE
IT'S JERVIS HERE, MR. McKENNA. NO, SIR, HE'S GONE OVER TO THE FARLOW PLACE.
YES, SIR, I'LL TELL HIM SOON AS HE COMES IN.

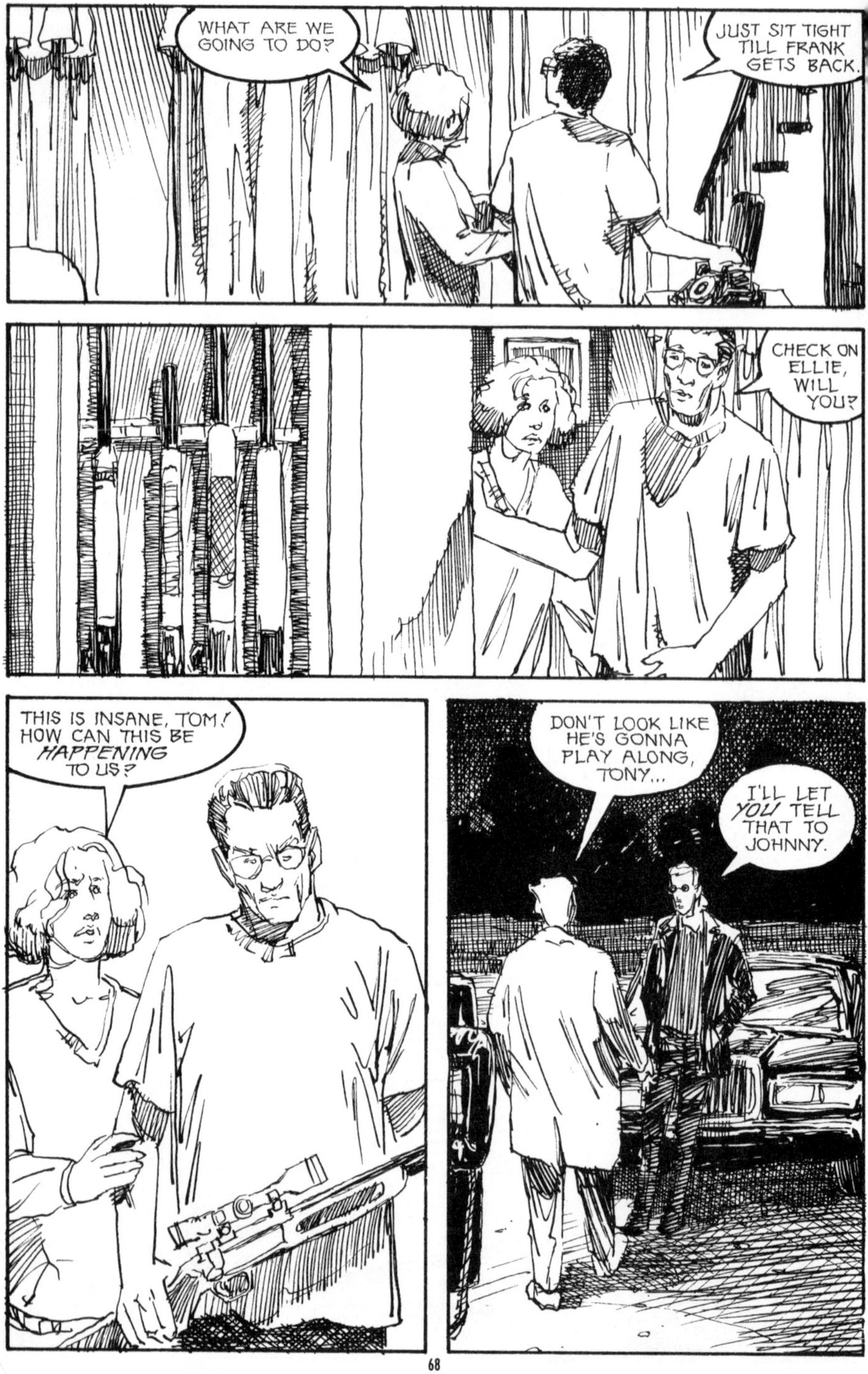
WHAT ARE WE GOING TO DO?
JUST SIT TIGHT TILL FRANK GETS BACK.
CHECK ON ELLIE, WILL YOU?
THIS IS INSANE, TOM! HOW CAN THIS BE *HAPPENING* TO US?
DON'T LOOK LIKE HE'S GONNA PLAY ALONG, TONY...
I'LL LET *YOU* TELL THAT TO JOHNNY.

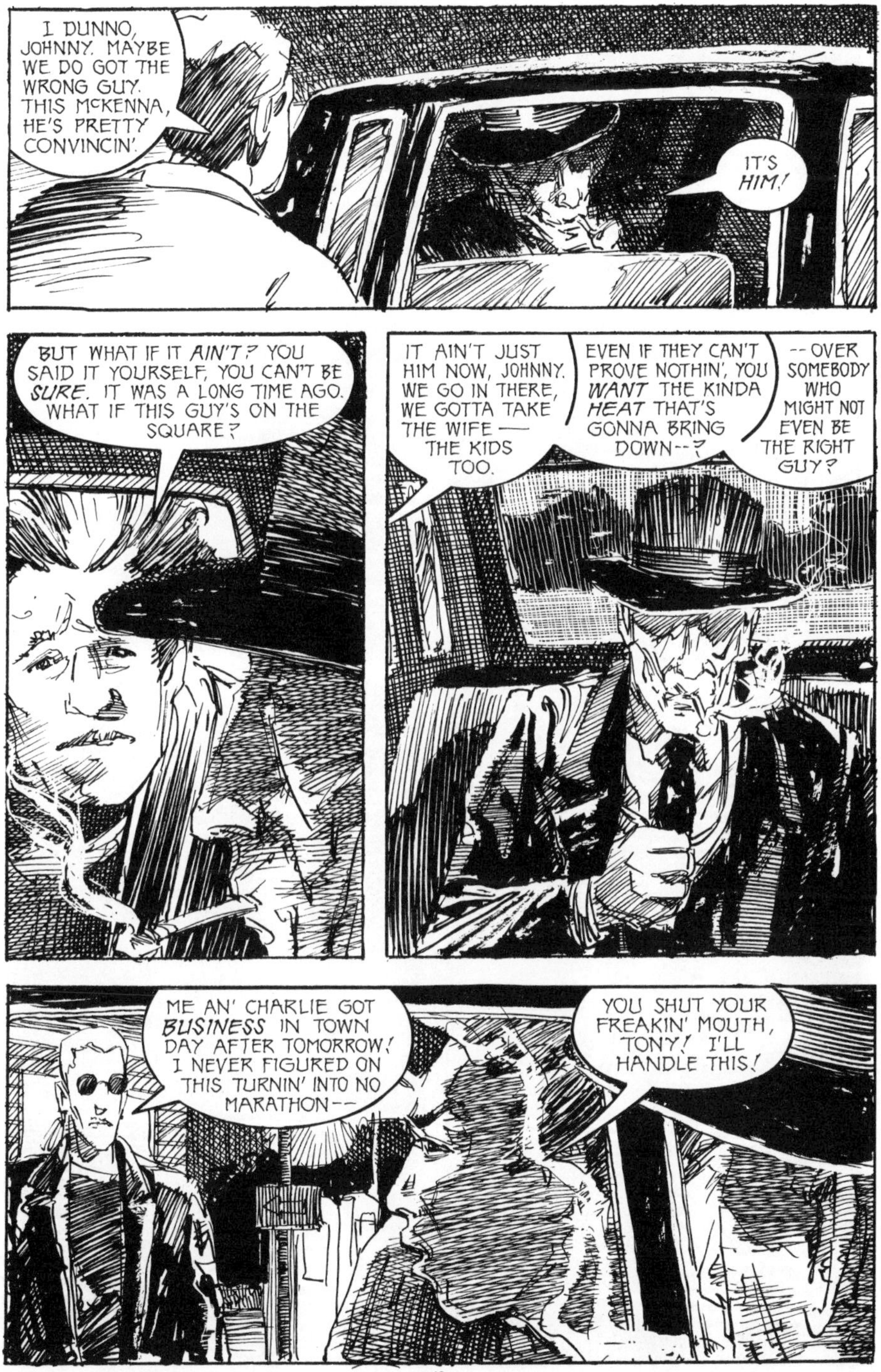
I DUNNO, JOHNNY. MAYBE WE DO GOT THE WRONG GUY. THIS McKENNA, HE'S PRETTY CONVINCIN'.
IT'S HIM!
BUT WHAT IF IT AIN'T? YOU SAID IT YOURSELF, YOU CAN'T BE SURE. IT WAS A LONG TIME AGO. WHAT IF THIS GUY'S ON THE SQUARE?
IT AIN'T JUST HIM NOW, JOHNNY. WE GO IN THERE, WE GOTTA TAKE THE WIFE — THE KIDS TOO.
EVEN IF THEY CAN'T PROVE NOTHIN', YOU WANT THE KINDA HEAT THAT'S GONNA BRING DOWN--?
--OVER SOMEBODY WHO MIGHT NOT EVEN BE THE RIGHT GUY?
ME AN' CHARLIE GOT BUSINESS IN TOWN DAY AFTER TOMORROW! I NEVER FIGURED ON THIS TURNIN' INTO NO MARATHON--
YOU SHUT YOUR FREAKIN' MOUTH, TONY! I'LL HANDLE THIS!

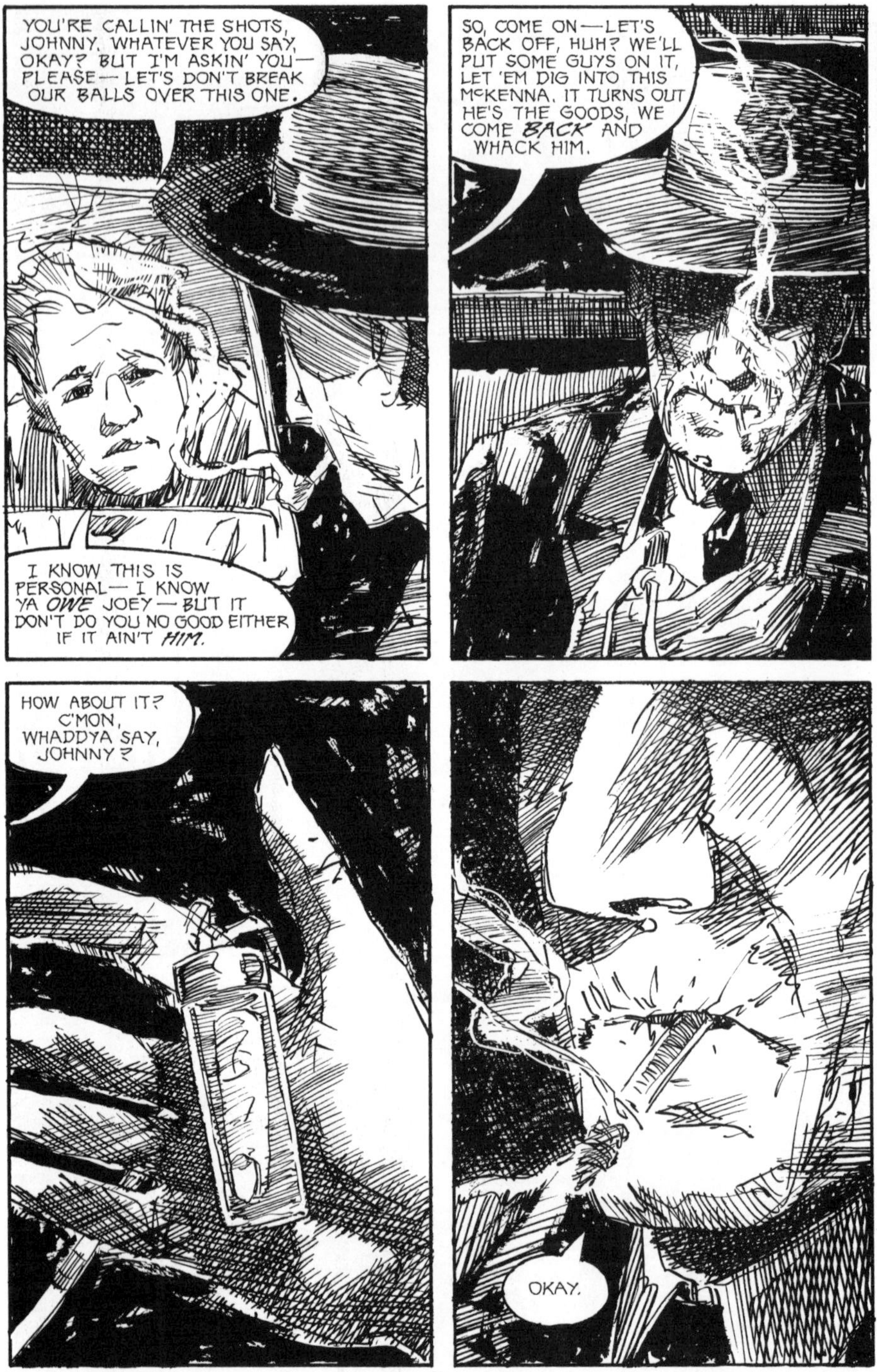
YOU'RE CALLIN' THE SHOTS, JOHNNY. WHATEVER YOU SAY, OKAY? BUT I'M ASKIN' YOU— PLEASE— LET'S DON'T BREAK OUR BALLS OVER THIS ONE.
I KNOW THIS IS PERSONAL— I KNOW YA OWE JOEY— BUT IT DON'T DO YOU NO GOOD EITHER IF IT AIN'T HIM.
SO, COME ON—LET'S BACK OFF, HUH? WE'LL PUT SOME GUYS ON IT, LET 'EM DIG INTO THIS McKENNA. IT TURNS OUT HE'S THE GOODS, WE COME BACK AND WHACK HIM.
HOW ABOUT IT? C'MON, WHADDYA SAY, JOHNNY?
OKAY.

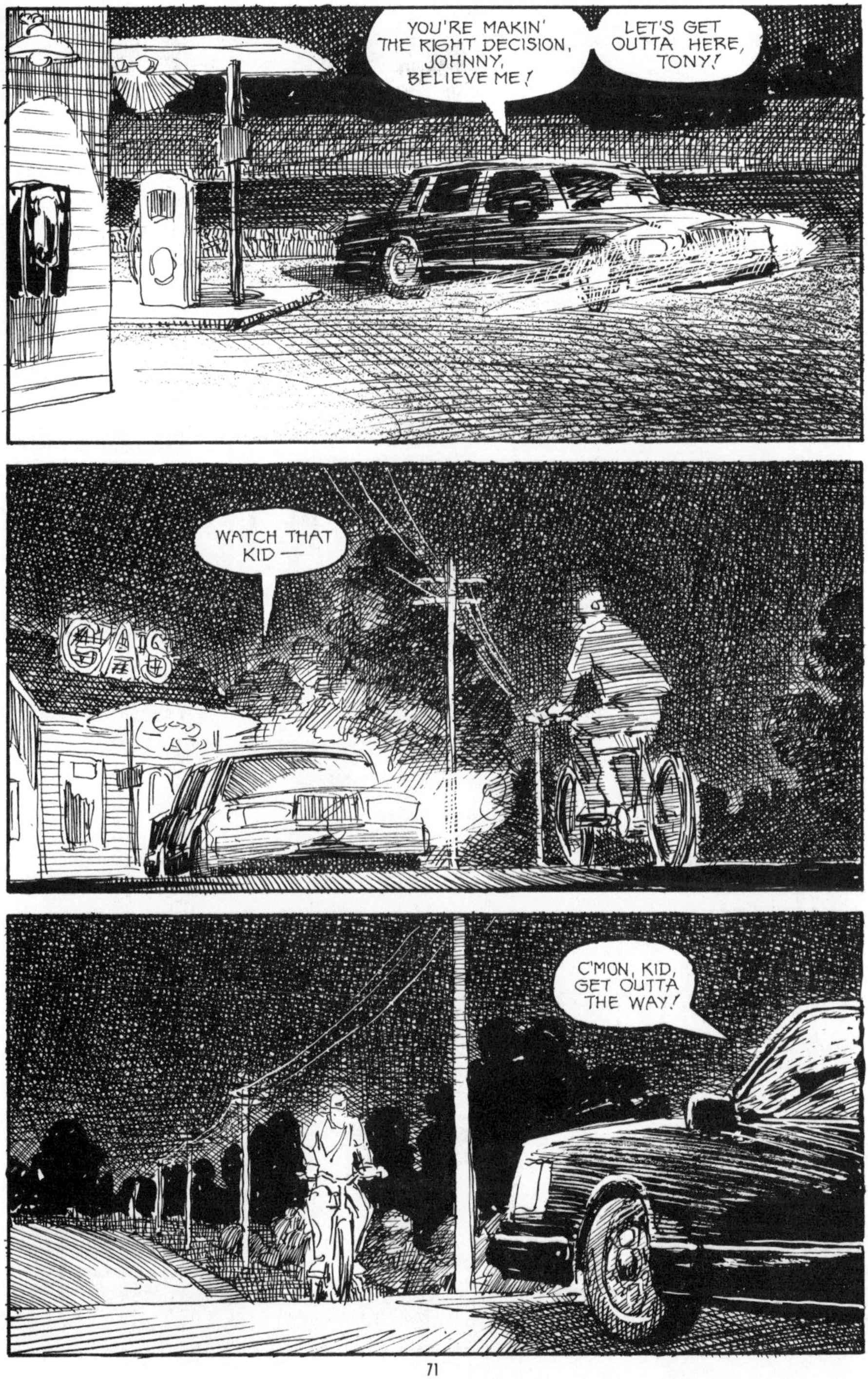
YOU'RE MAKIN' THE RIGHT DECISION, JOHNNY, BELIEVE ME!
LET'S GET OUTTA HERE, TONY!
WATCH THAT KID —
GAS
C'MON, KID, GET OUTTA THE WAY!

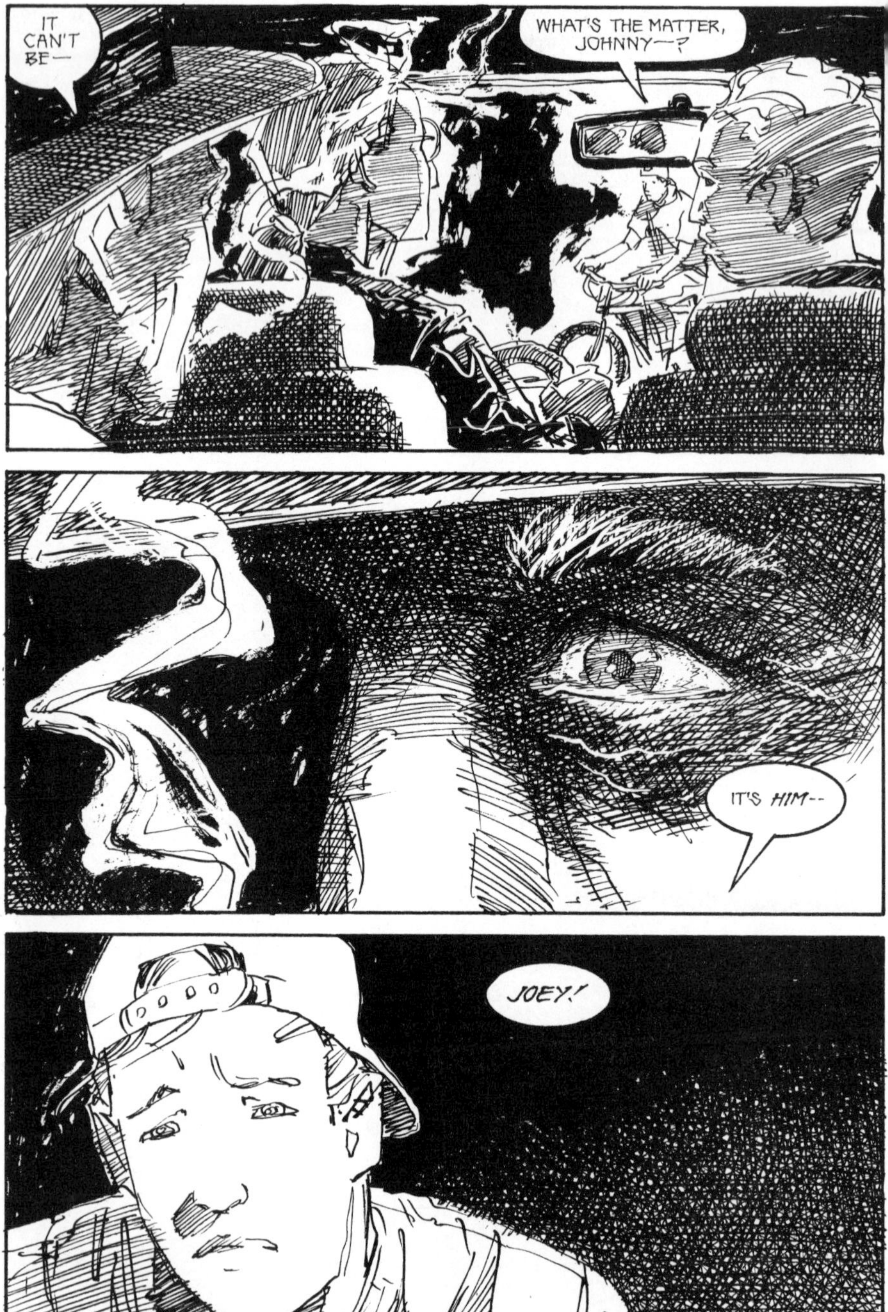
IT CAN'T BE—
WHAT'S THE MATTER, JOHNNY—?
IT'S *HIM*--
JOEY!

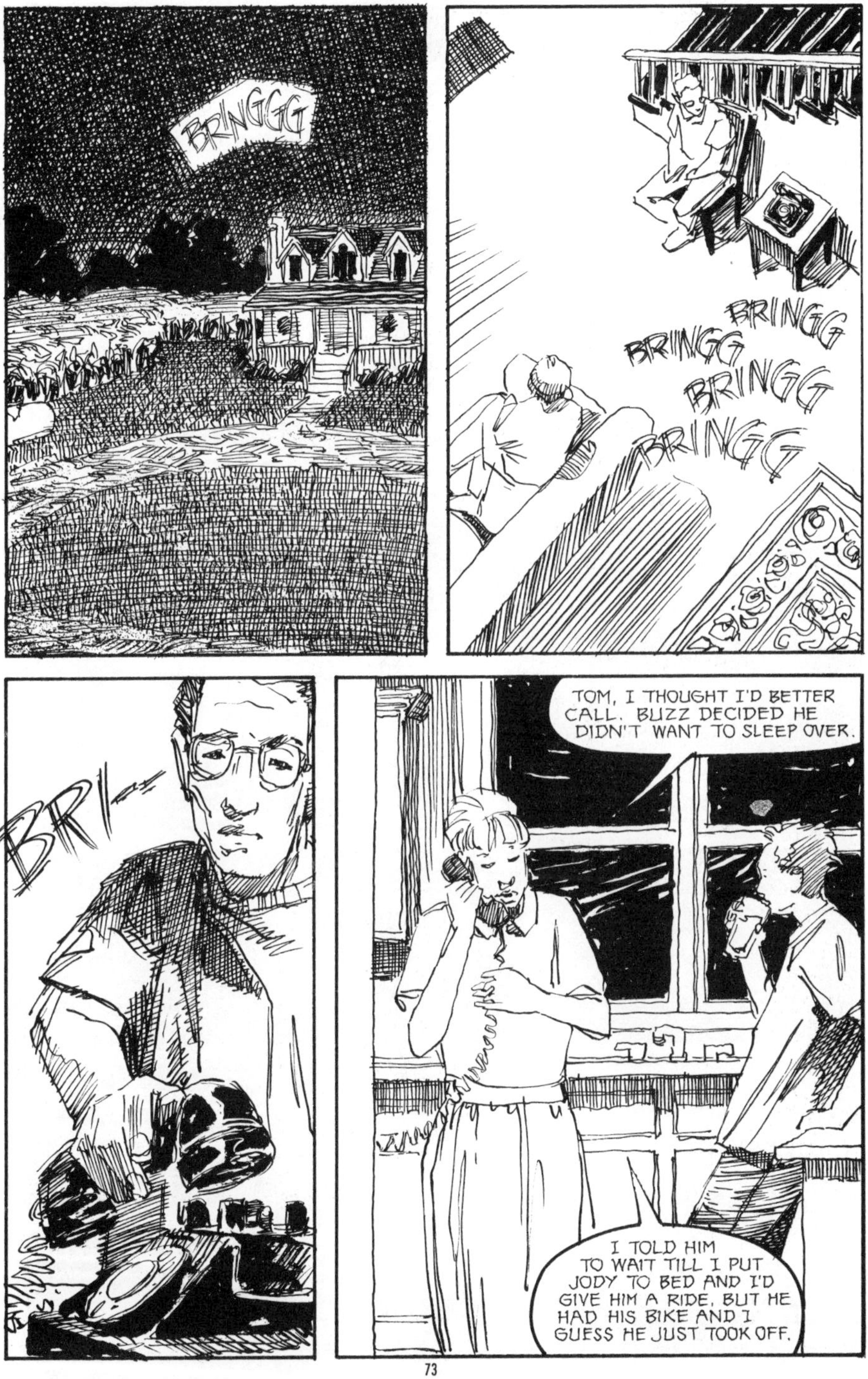
BRINGG
BRINGG
BRINGG
BRINGG
BRINGG
BRI--
TOM, I THOUGHT I'D BETTER CALL. BUZZ DECIDED HE DIDN'T WANT TO SLEEP OVER.
I TOLD HIM TO WAIT TILL I PUT JODY TO BED AND I'D GIVE HIM A RIDE, BUT HE HAD HIS BIKE AND I GUESS HE JUST TOOK OFF.

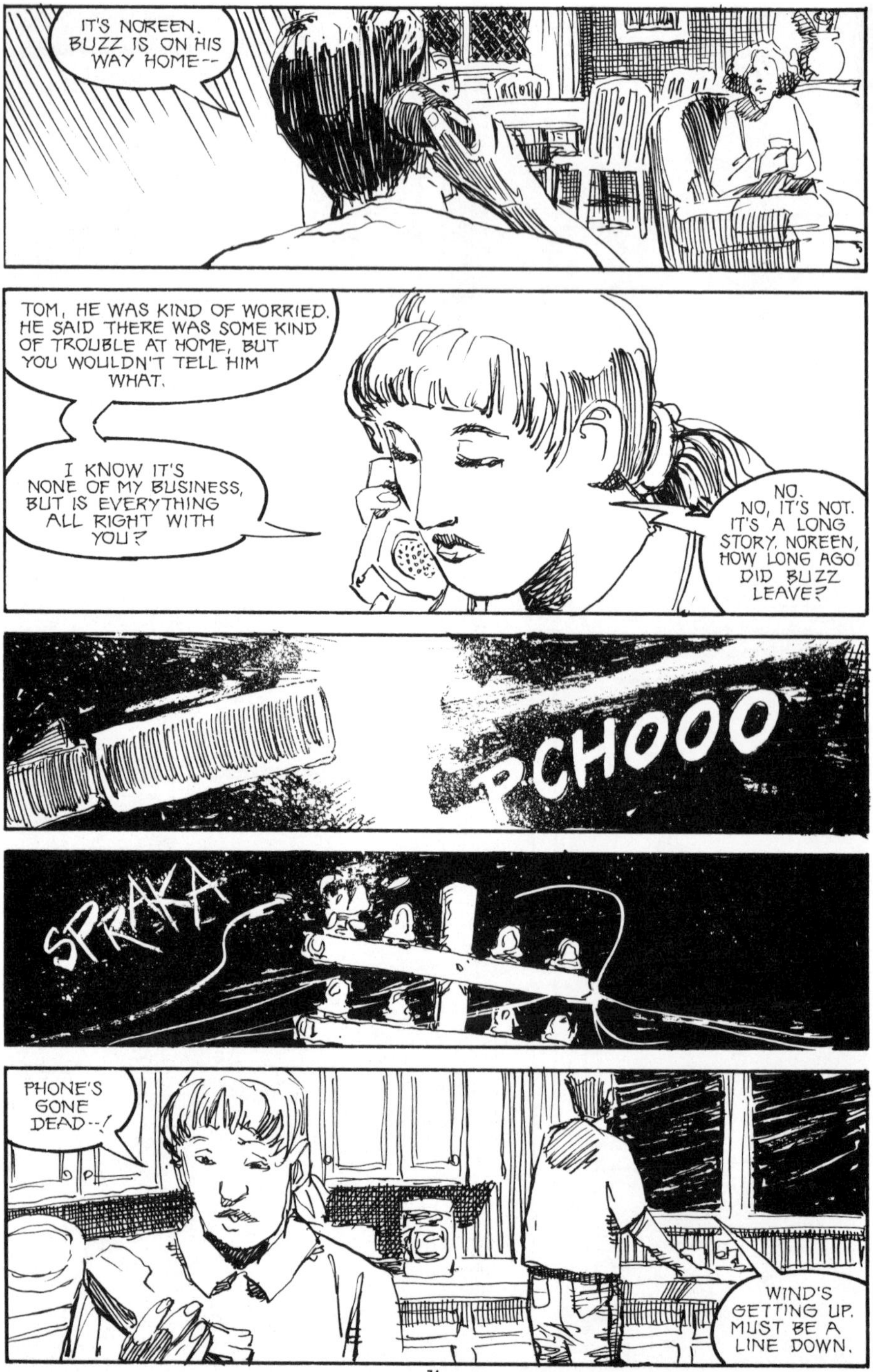
IT'S NOREEN. BUZZ IS ON HIS WAY HOME--
TOM, HE WAS KIND OF WORRIED. HE SAID THERE WAS SOME KIND OF TROUBLE AT HOME, BUT YOU WOULDN'T TELL HIM WHAT.
I KNOW IT'S NONE OF MY BUSINESS, BUT IS EVERYTHING ALL RIGHT WITH YOU?
NO. NO, IT'S NOT. IT'S A LONG STORY, NOREEN. HOW LONG AGO DID BUZZ LEAVE?
PCHOOO
SPRAKA
PHONE'S GONE DEAD--!
WIND'S GETTING UP. MUST BE A LINE DOWN.

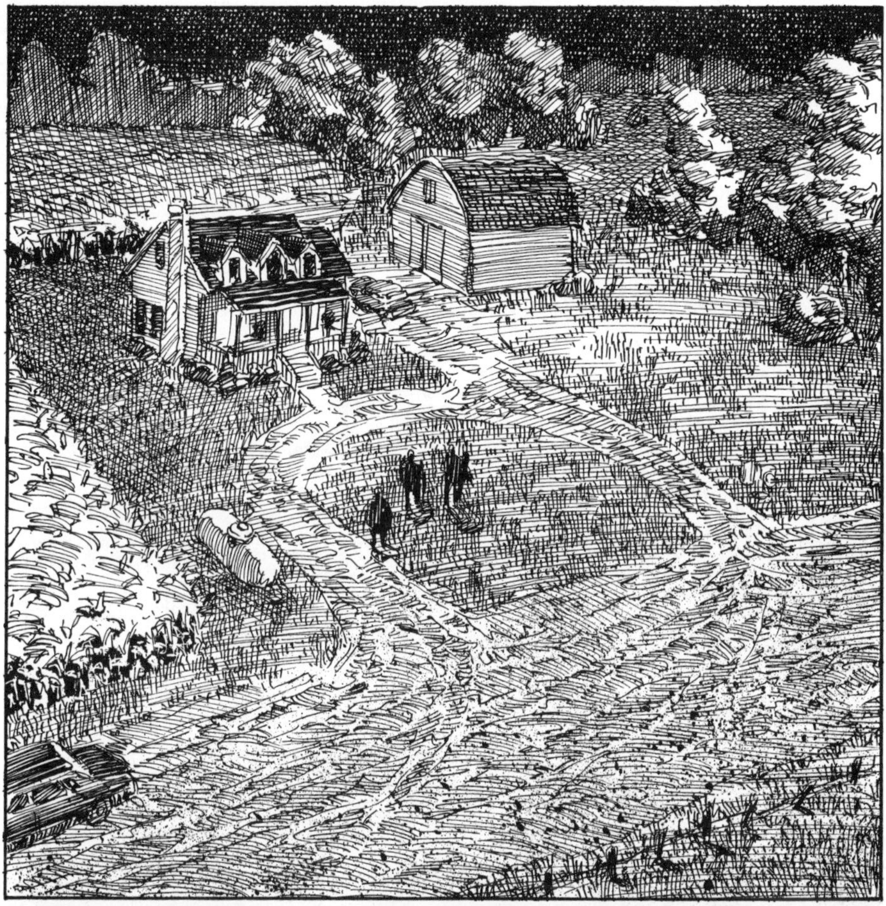

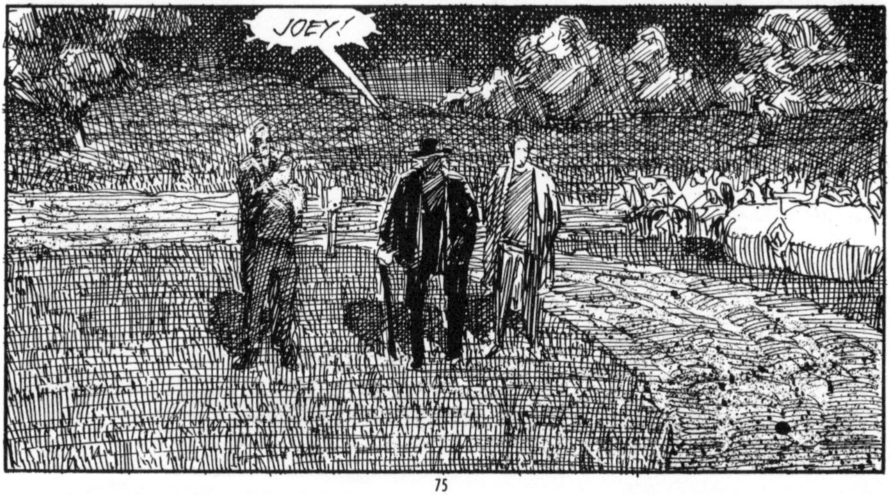
JOEY!

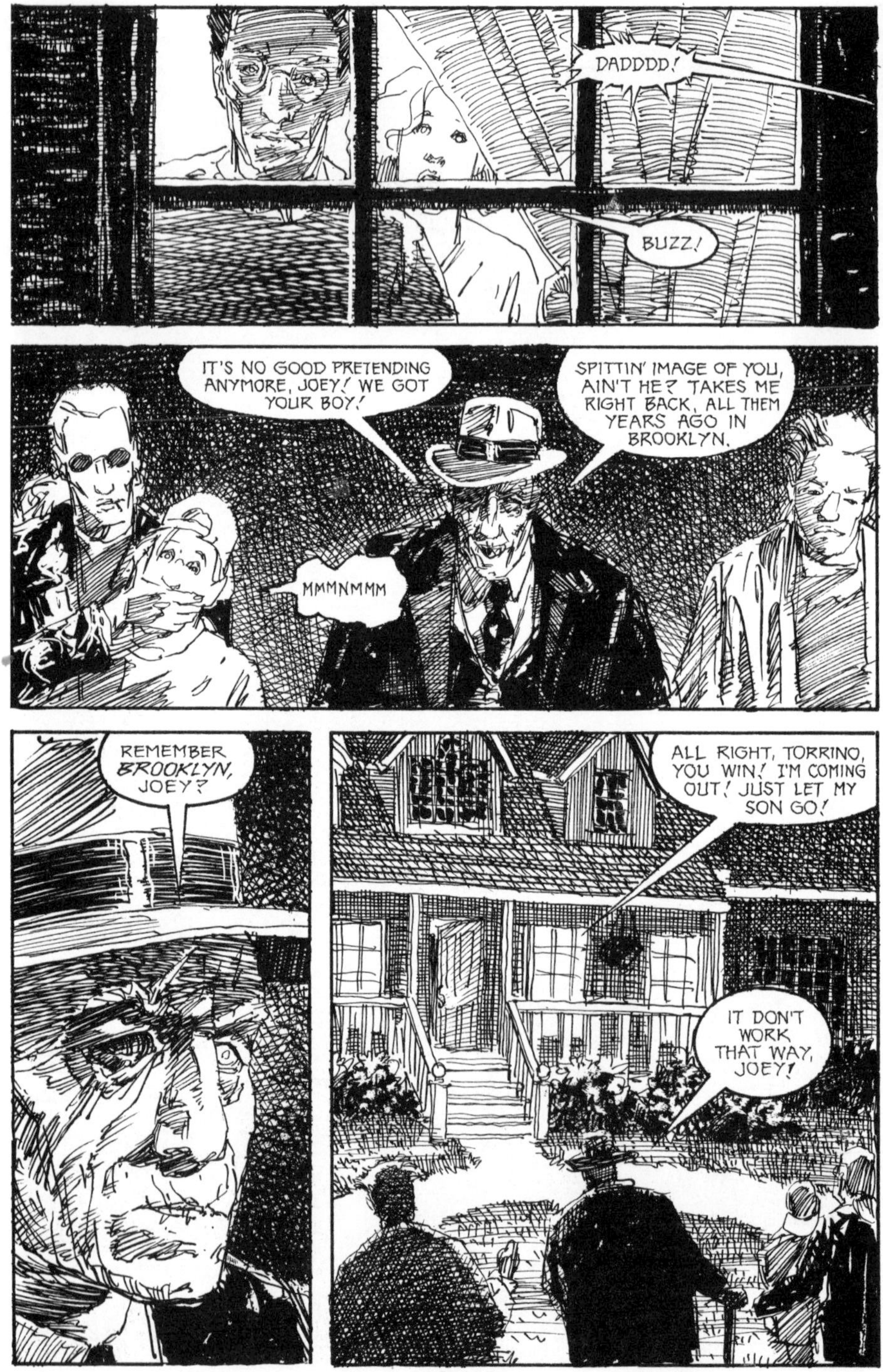
DADDDD!
BUZZ!
IT'S NO GOOD PRETENDING ANYMORE, JOEY! WE GOT YOUR BOY!
SPITTIN' IMAGE OF YOU, AIN'T HE? TAKES ME RIGHT BACK, ALL THEM YEARS AGO IN BROOKLYN.
MMMNMMM
REMEMBER *BROOKLYN*, JOEY?
ALL RIGHT, TORRINO, YOU WIN! I'M COMING OUT! JUST LET MY SON GO!
IT DON'T WORK THAT WAY, JOEY!

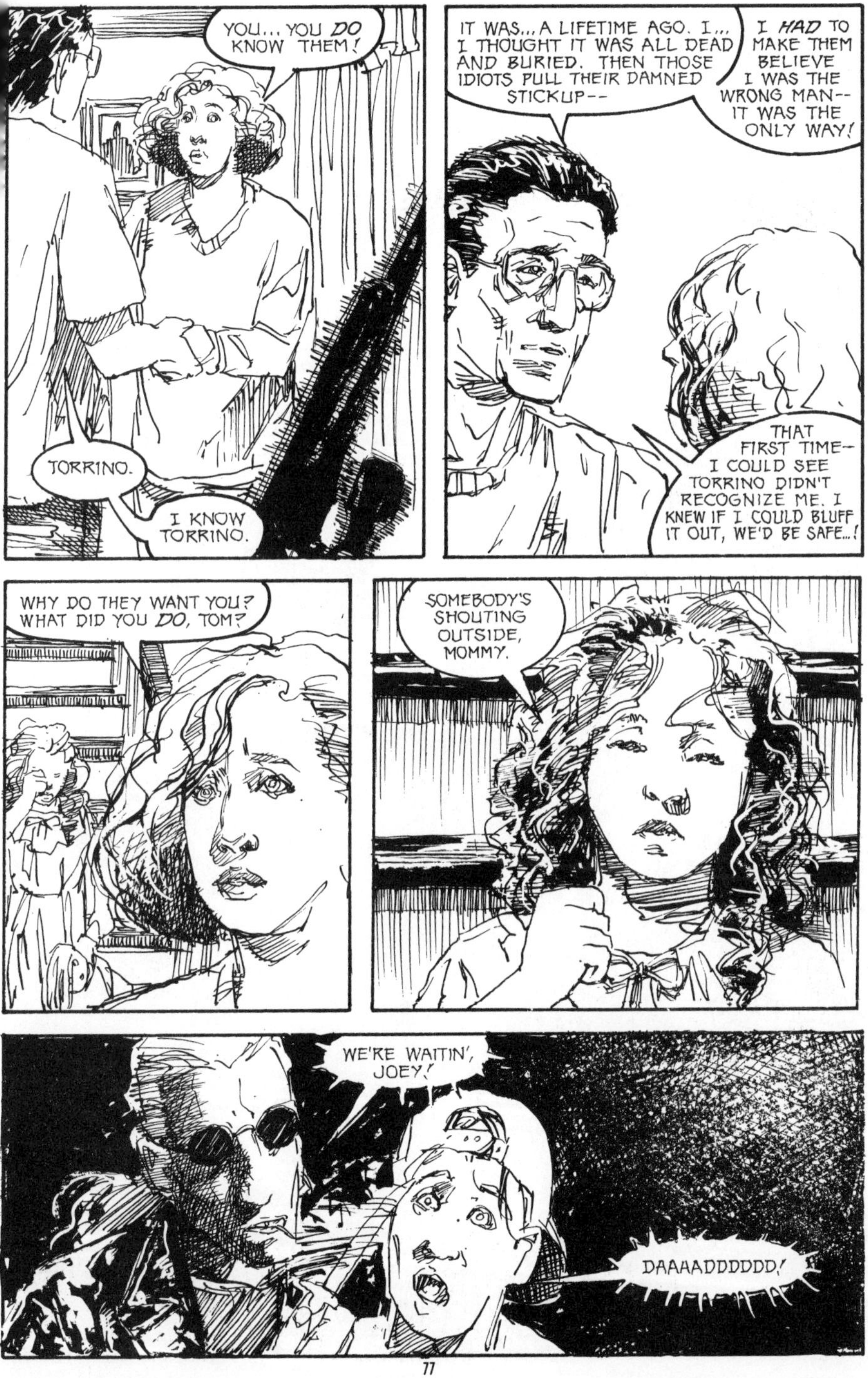
YOU... YOU *DO* KNOW THEM!
TORRINO.
I KNOW TORRINO.
IT WAS... A LIFETIME AGO. I... I THOUGHT IT WAS ALL DEAD AND BURIED. THEN THOSE IDIOTS PULL THEIR DAMNED STICKUP--
I *HAD* TO MAKE THEM BELIEVE I WAS THE WRONG MAN-- IT WAS THE ONLY WAY!
THAT FIRST TIME-- I COULD SEE TORRINO DIDN'T RECOGNIZE ME. I KNEW IF I COULD BLUFF IT OUT, WE'D BE SAFE...!
WHY DO THEY WANT YOU? WHAT DID YOU *DO*, TOM?
SOMEBODY'S SHOUTING OUTSIDE, MOMMY.
WE'RE WAITIN', JOEY!
DAAAADDDDDD!

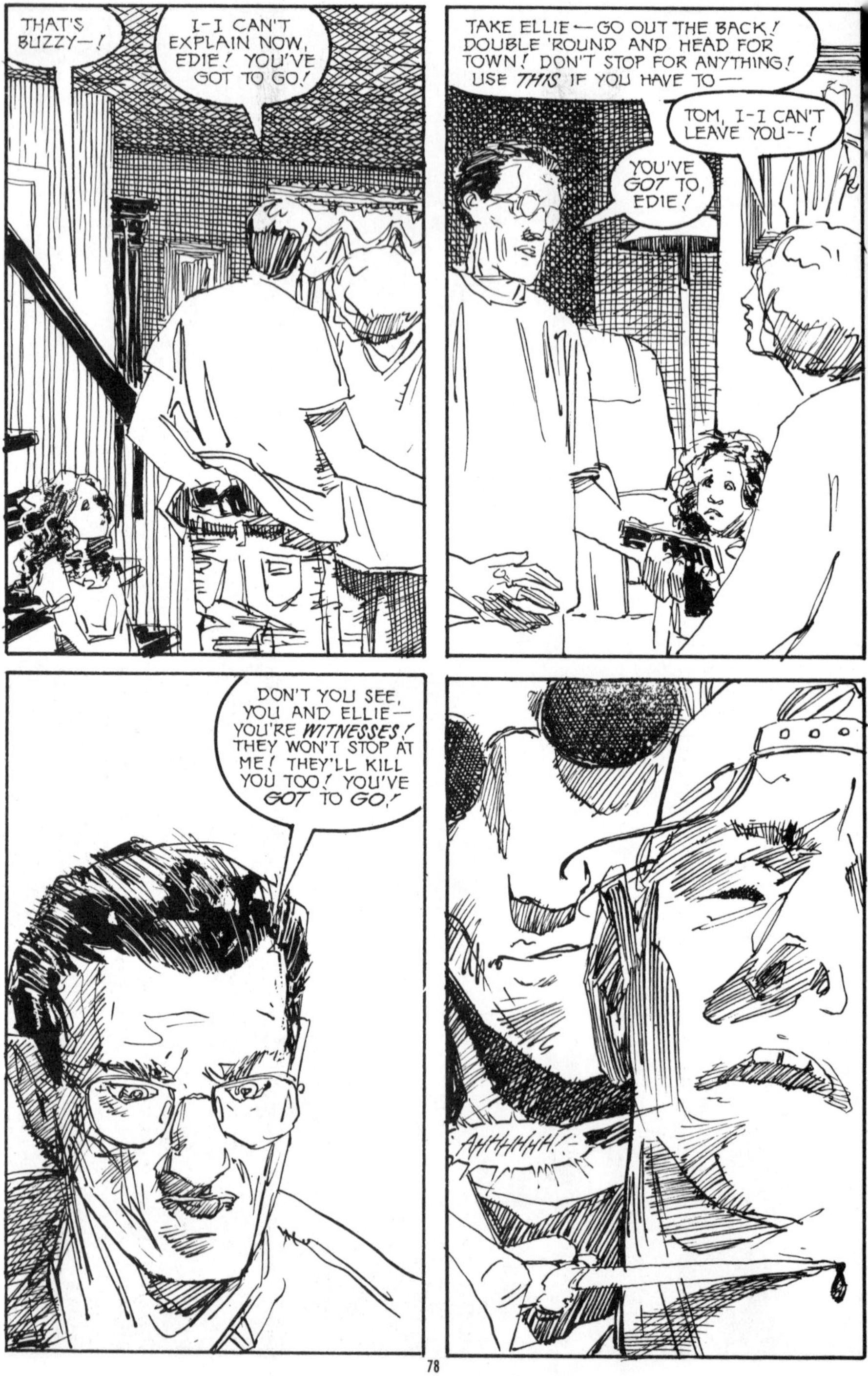
THAT'S BUZZY--!
I-I CAN'T EXPLAIN NOW, EDIE! YOU'VE GOT TO GO!
TAKE ELLIE--GO OUT THE BACK! DOUBLE 'ROUND AND HEAD FOR TOWN! DON'T STOP FOR ANYTHING! USE THIS IF YOU HAVE TO--
TOM, I-I CAN'T LEAVE YOU--!
YOU'VE GOT TO, EDIE!
DON'T YOU SEE, YOU AND ELLIE--YOU'RE WITNESSES! THEY WON'T STOP AT ME! THEY'LL KILL YOU TOO! YOU'VE GOT TO GO!
AHHHHHH!--

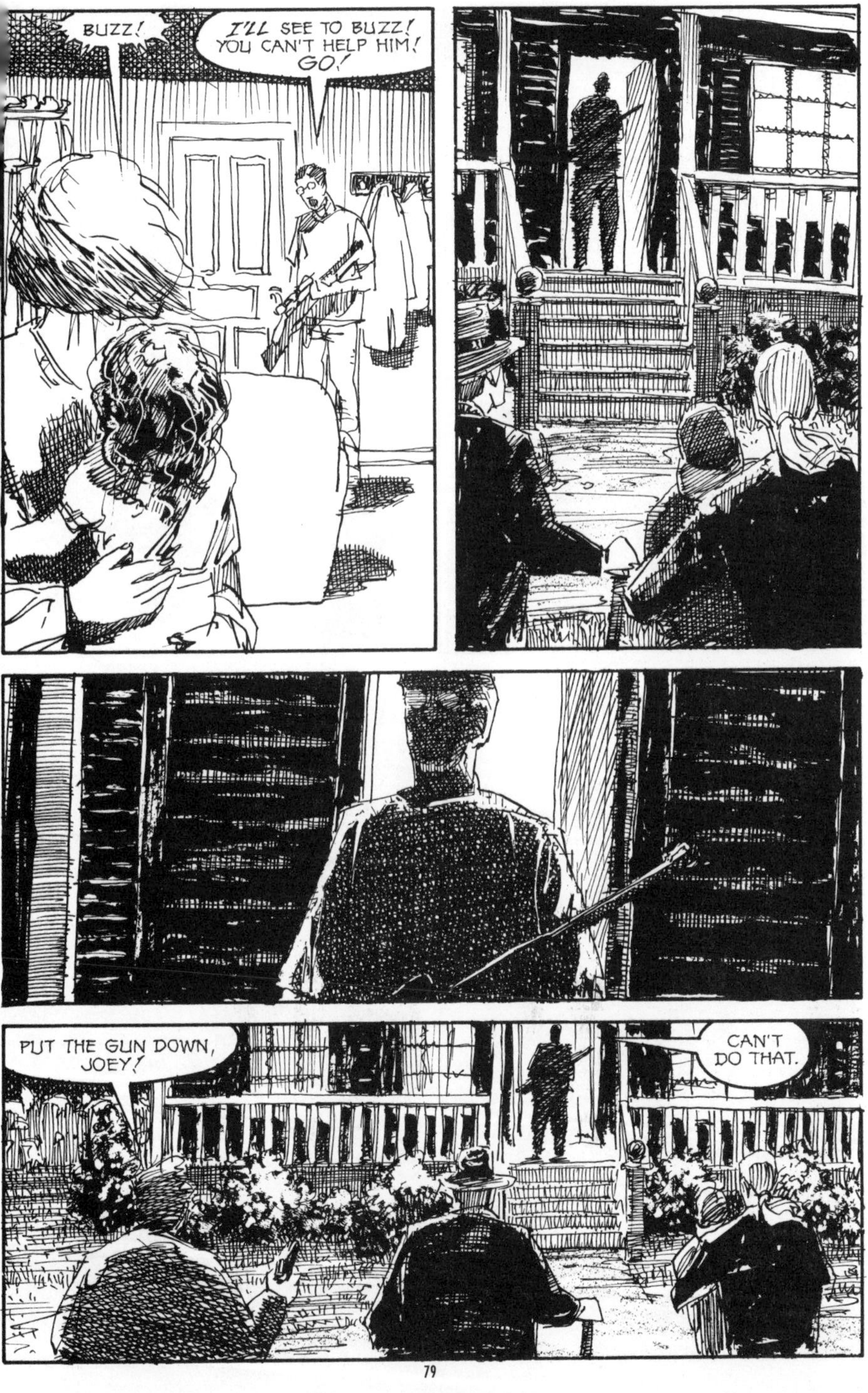
BUZZ!
I'LL SEE TO BUZZ! YOU CAN'T HELP HIM! GO!
PUT THE GUN DOWN, JOEY!
CAN'T DO THAT.

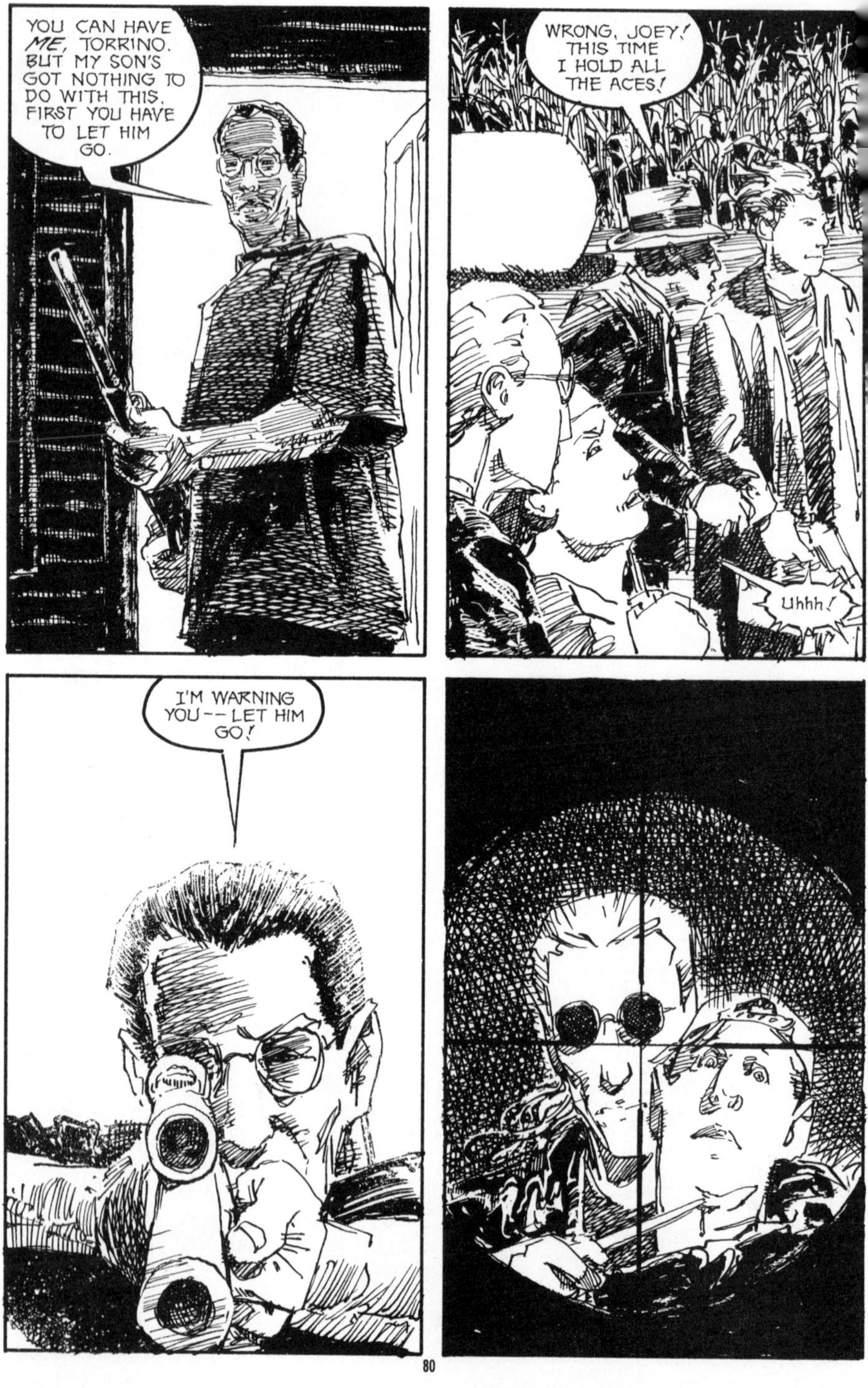
YOU CAN HAVE ME, TORRINO. BUT MY SON'S GOT NOTHING TO DO WITH THIS. FIRST YOU HAVE TO LET HIM GO.
WRONG, JOEY! THIS TIME I HOLD ALL THE ACES!
Uhhh!
I'M WARNING YOU--LET HIM GO!

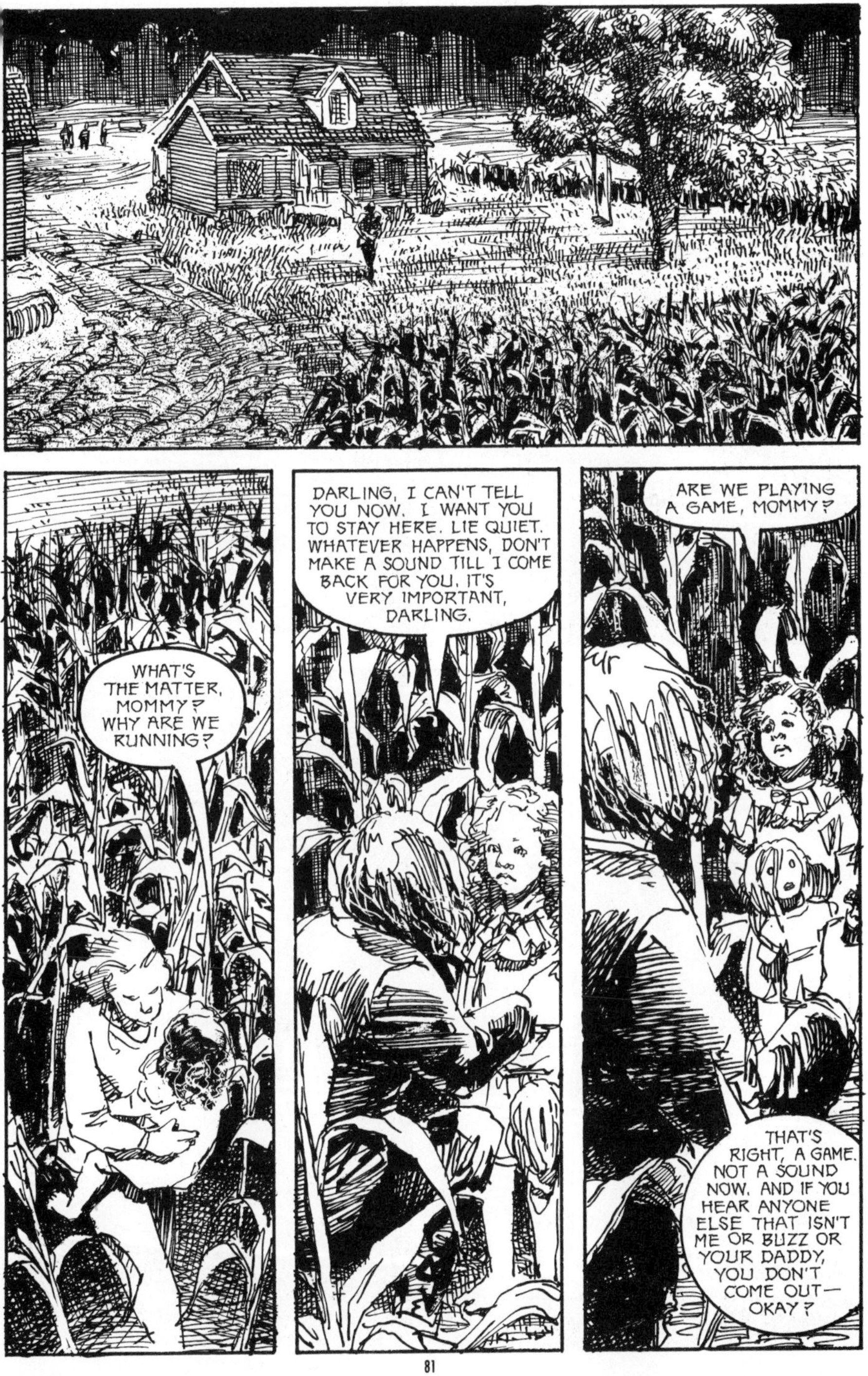
WHAT'S THE MATTER, MOMMY? WHY ARE WE RUNNING?
DARLING, I CAN'T TELL YOU NOW. I WANT YOU TO STAY HERE. LIE QUIET. WHATEVER HAPPENS, DON'T MAKE A SOUND TILL I COME BACK FOR YOU. IT'S VERY IMPORTANT, DARLING.
ARE WE PLAYING A GAME, MOMMY?
THAT'S RIGHT, A GAME. NOT A SOUND NOW. AND IF YOU HEAR ANYONE ELSE THAT ISN'T ME OR BUZZ OR YOUR DADDY, YOU DON'T COME OUT— OKAY?

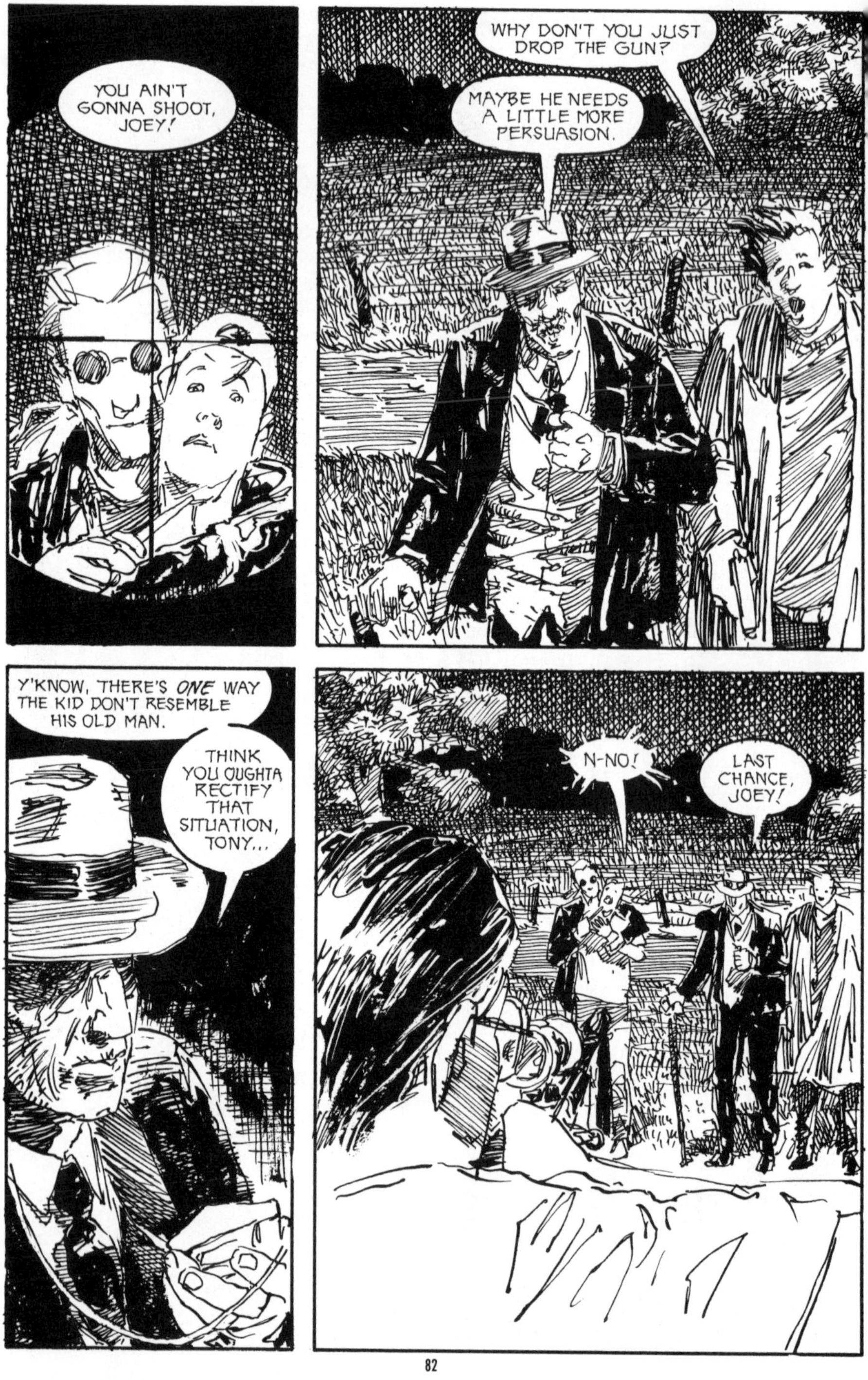
YOU AIN'T GONNA SHOOT, JOEY!
WHY DON'T YOU JUST DROP THE GUN?
MAYBE HE NEEDS A LITTLE MORE PERSUASION.
Y'KNOW, THERE'S ONE WAY THE KID DON'T RESEMBLE HIS OLD MAN.
THINK YOU OUGHTA RECTIFY THAT SITUATION, TONY...
N-NO!
LAST CHANCE, JOEY!

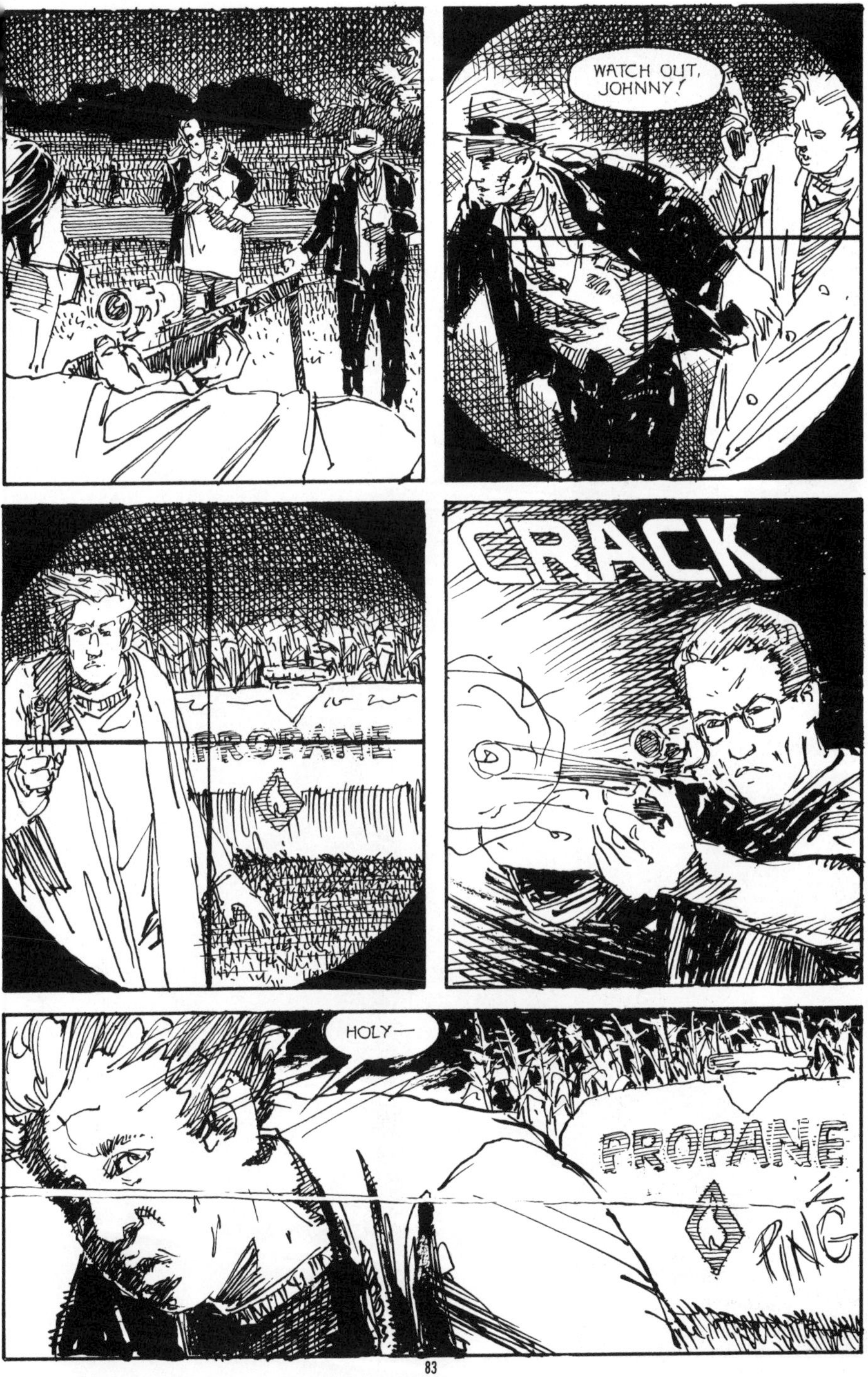
WATCH OUT, JOHNNY!
PROPANE
CRACK
HOLY—
PROPANE
PING

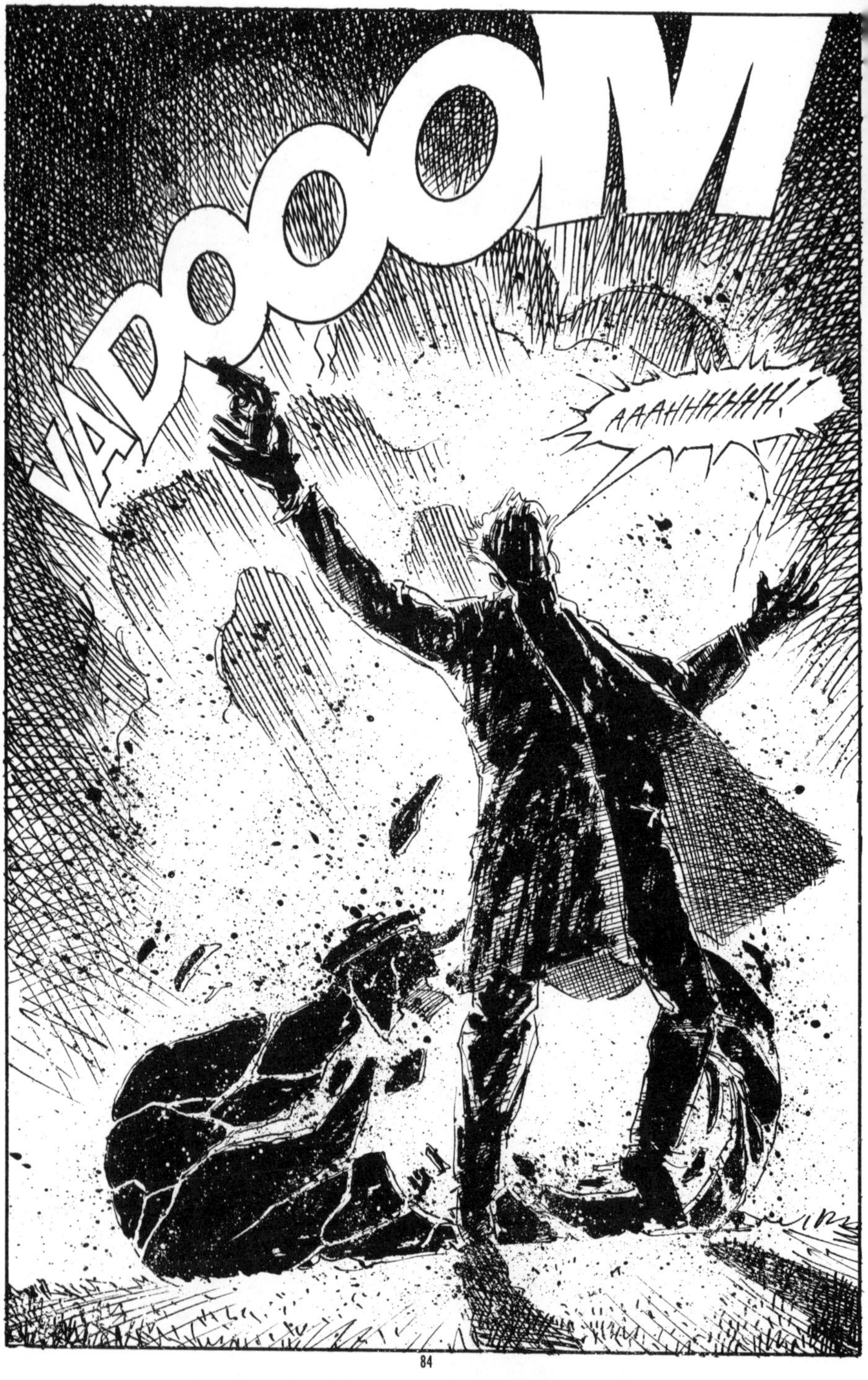
VADOOOOM!
AAAHHHHHH!

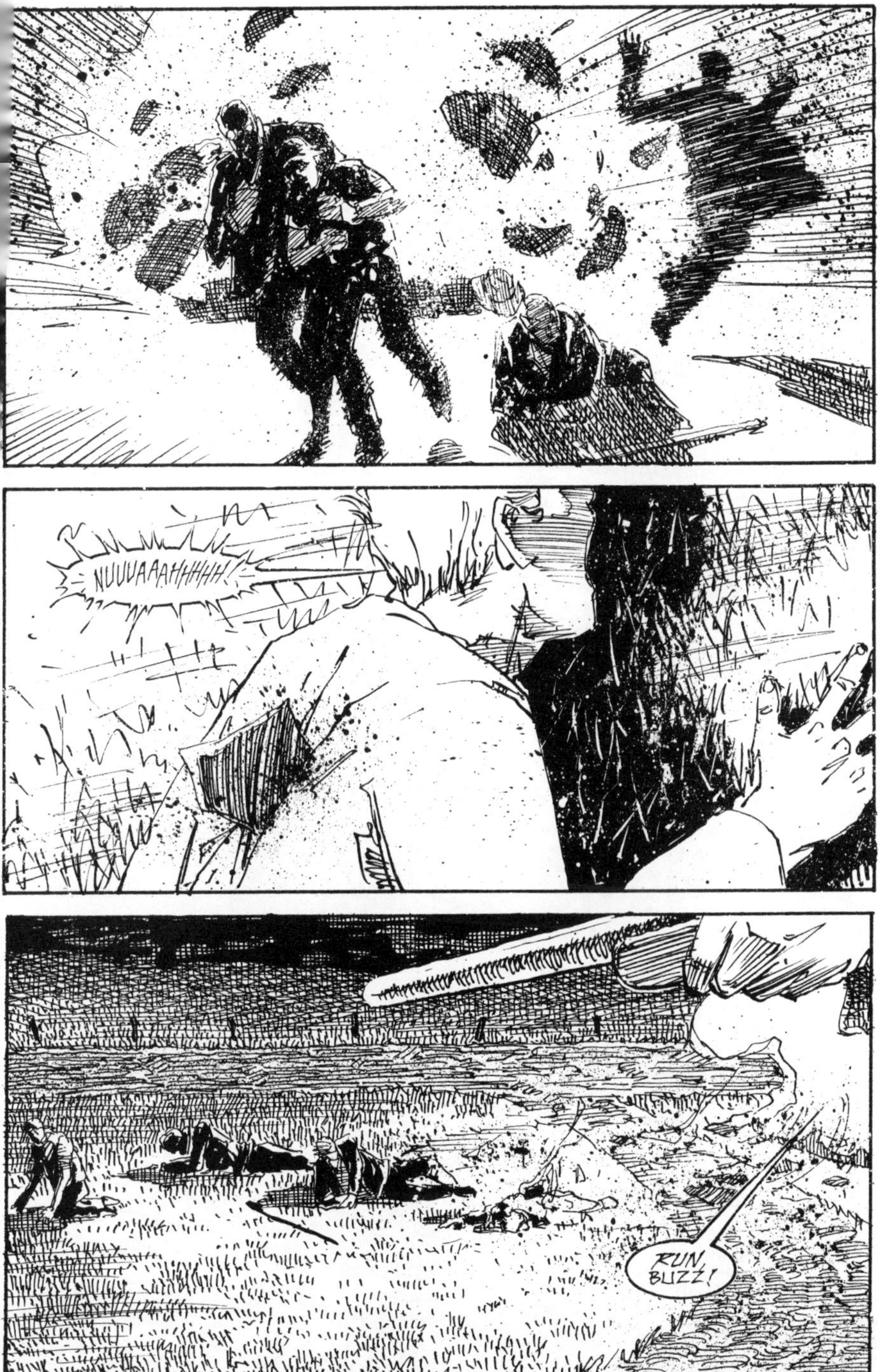
NUUUAAAHHHHH!
RUN, BUZZ!

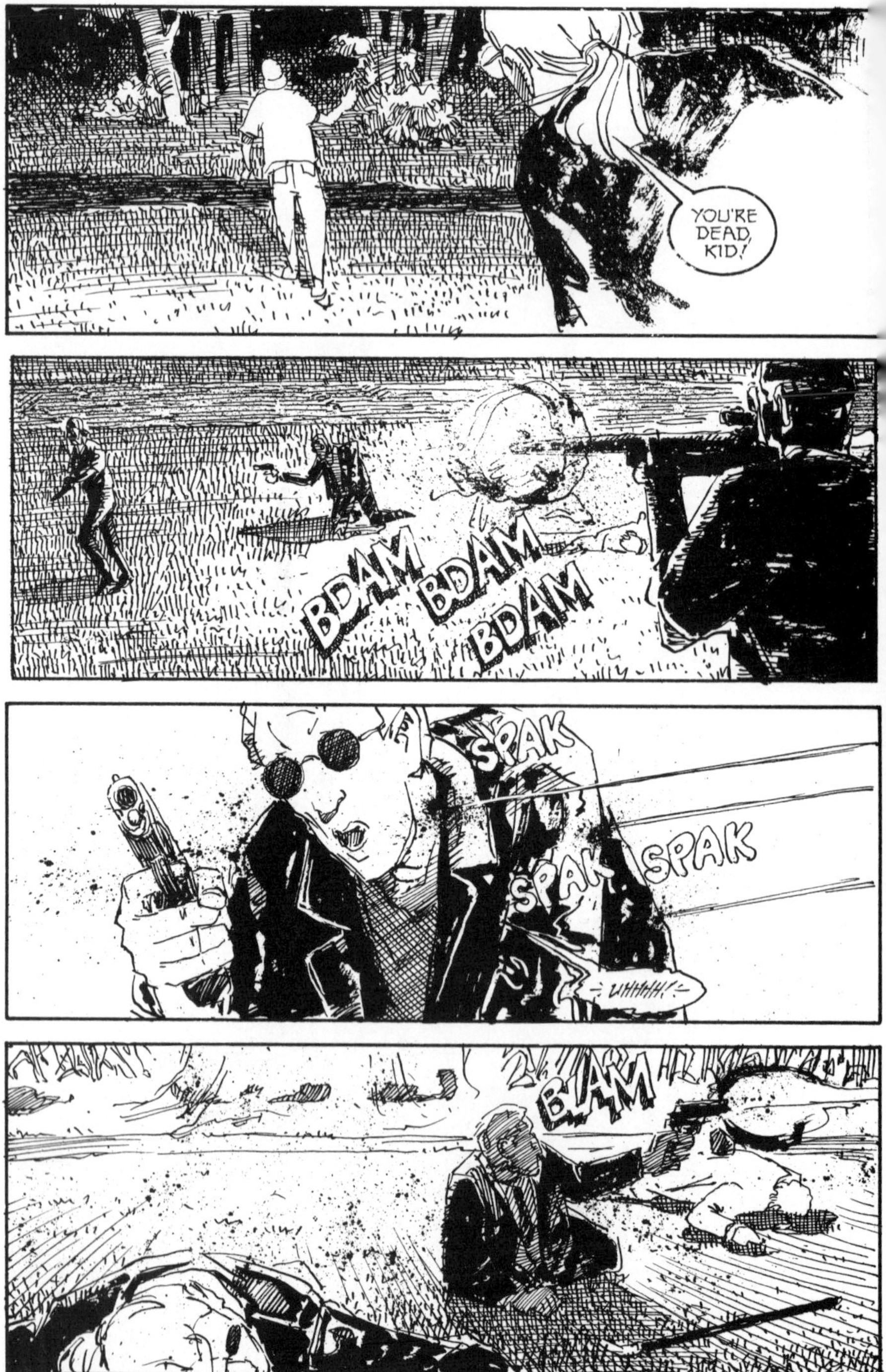
YOU'RE DEAD, KID!
BDAM
BDAM
BDAM
BDAM
SPAK
SPAK
SPAK
UHHHH!
BLAM

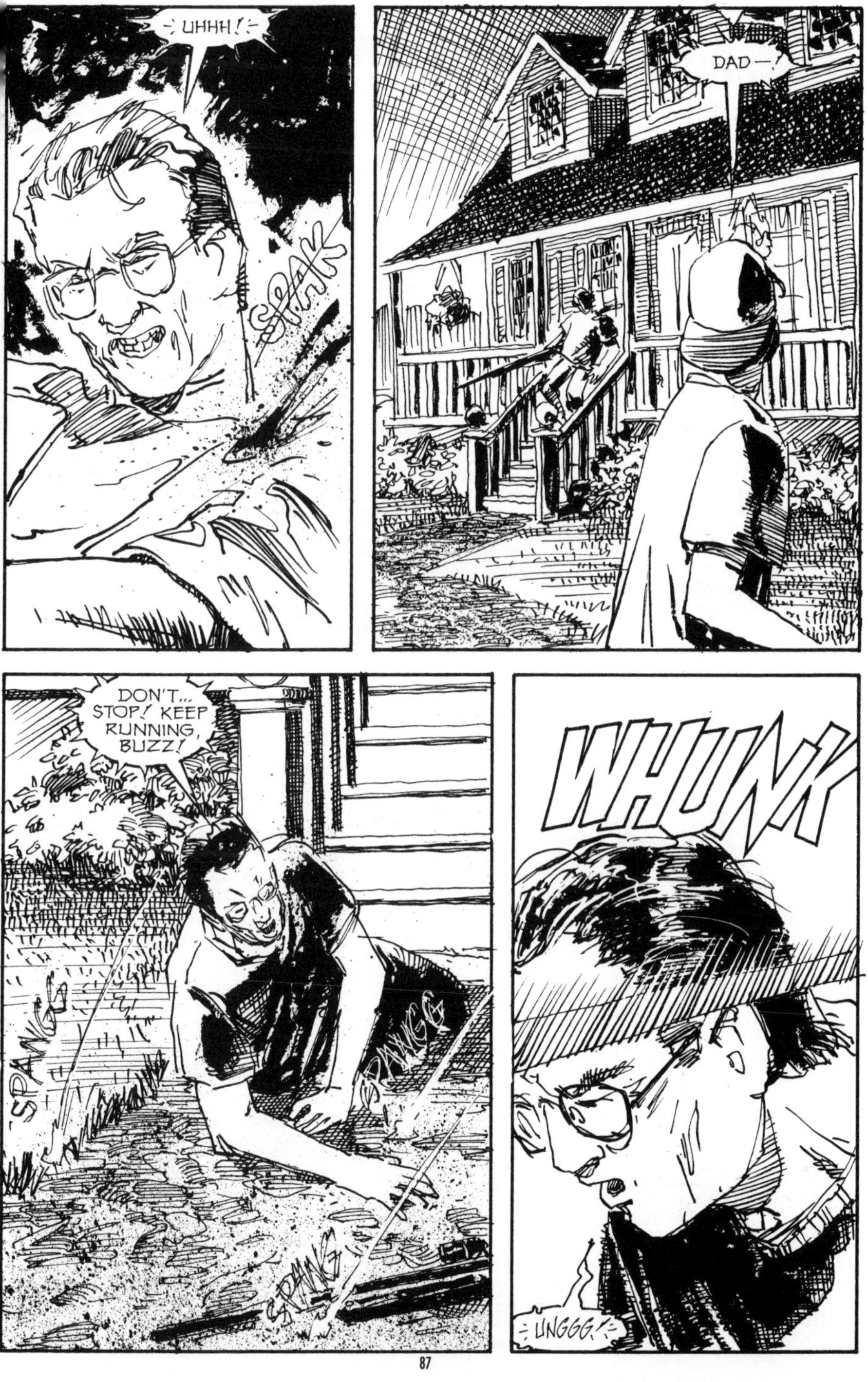
UHHH!
SPAK
DAD—!
DON'T... STOP! KEEP RUNNING, BUZZ!
SPANG
SPANG
SPANG
WHUNK
UNGGG!

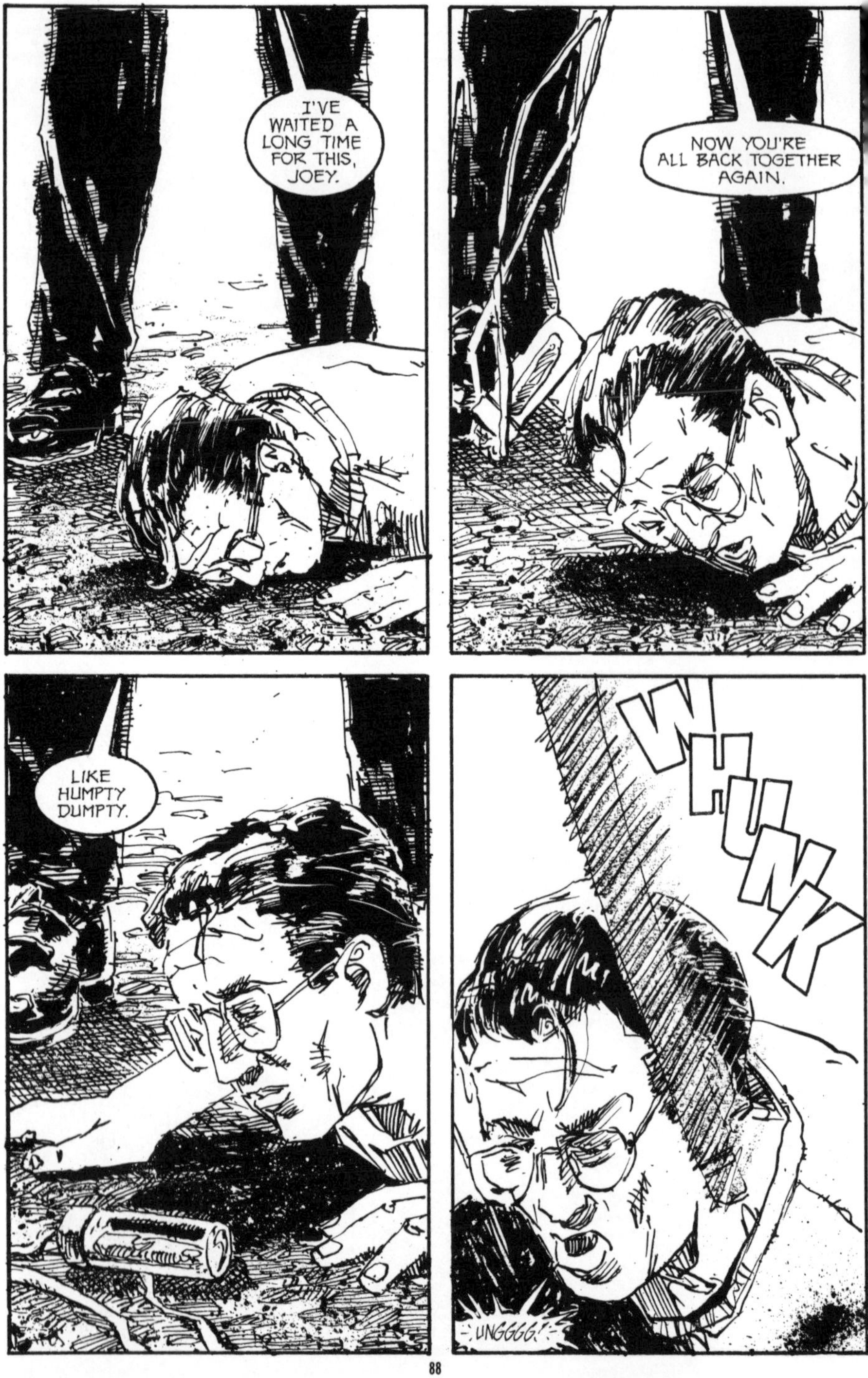
I'VE WAITED A LONG TIME FOR THIS, JOEY.
NOW YOU'RE ALL BACK TOGETHER AGAIN.
LIKE HUMPTY DUMPTY.
WHUNK
UNGGGG!

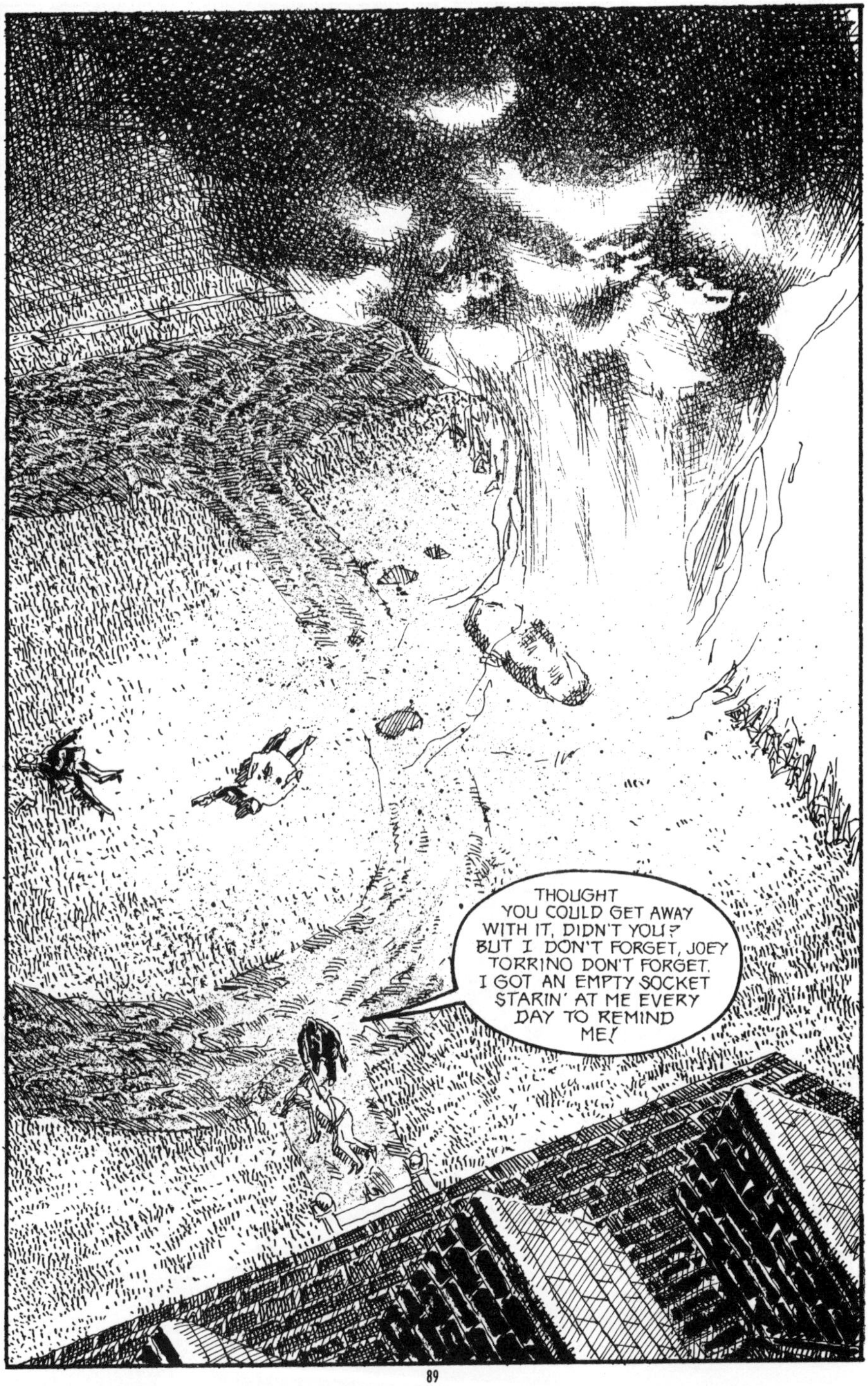
THOUGHT YOU COULD GET AWAY WITH IT, DIDN'T YOU? BUT I DON'T FORGET, JOEY TORRINO DON'T FORGET. I GOT AN EMPTY SOCKET STARIN' AT ME EVERY DAY TO REMIND ME!

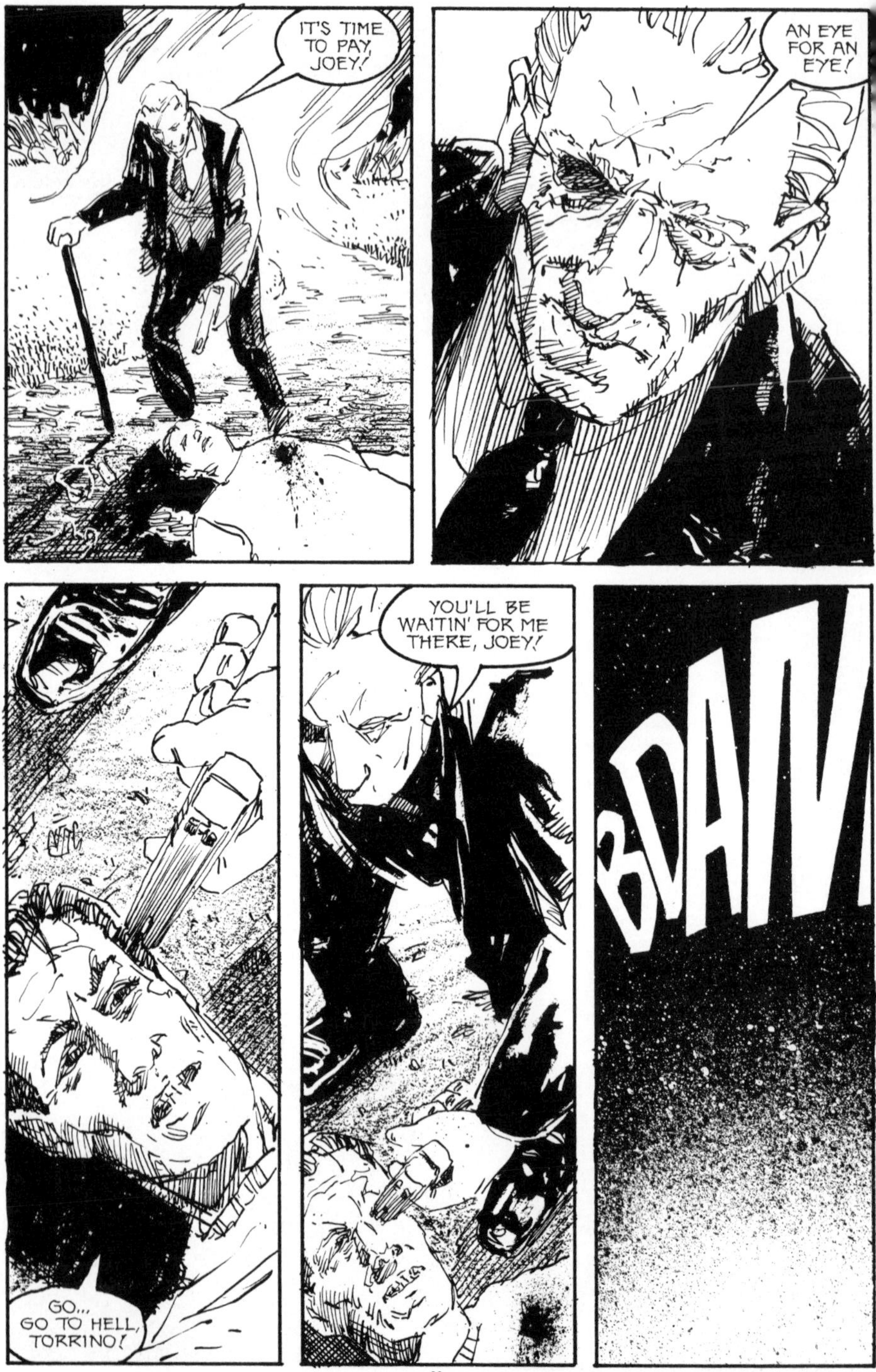
IT'S TIME TO PAY, JOEY!
AN EYE FOR AN EYE!
GO... GO TO HELL, TORRINO!
YOU'LL BE WAITIN' FOR ME THERE, JOEY!
BLAM

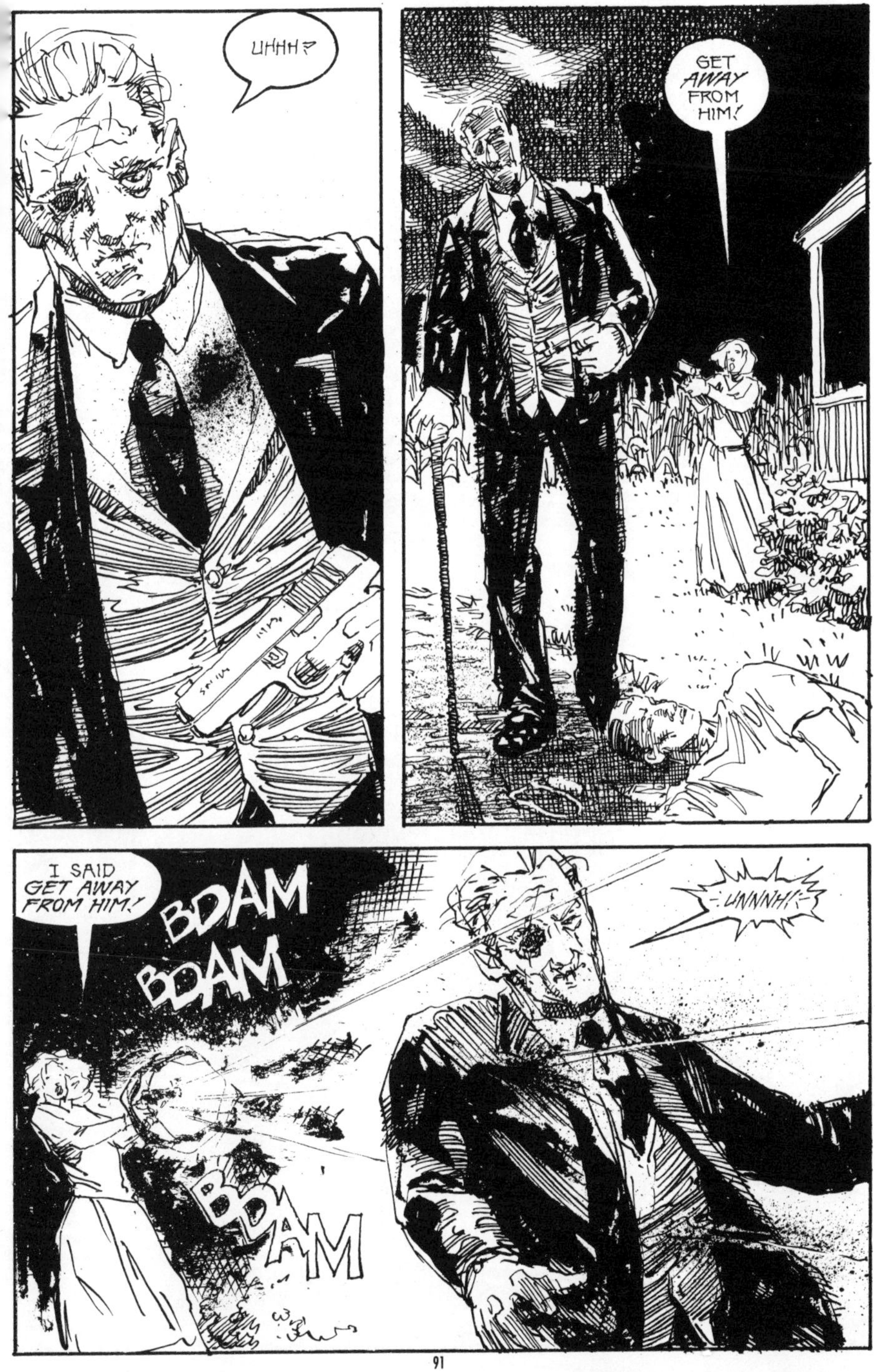
UHHH?
GET AWAY FROM HIM!
I SAID GET AWAY FROM HIM!
BDAM
BDAM
UNNNH!
BDAM

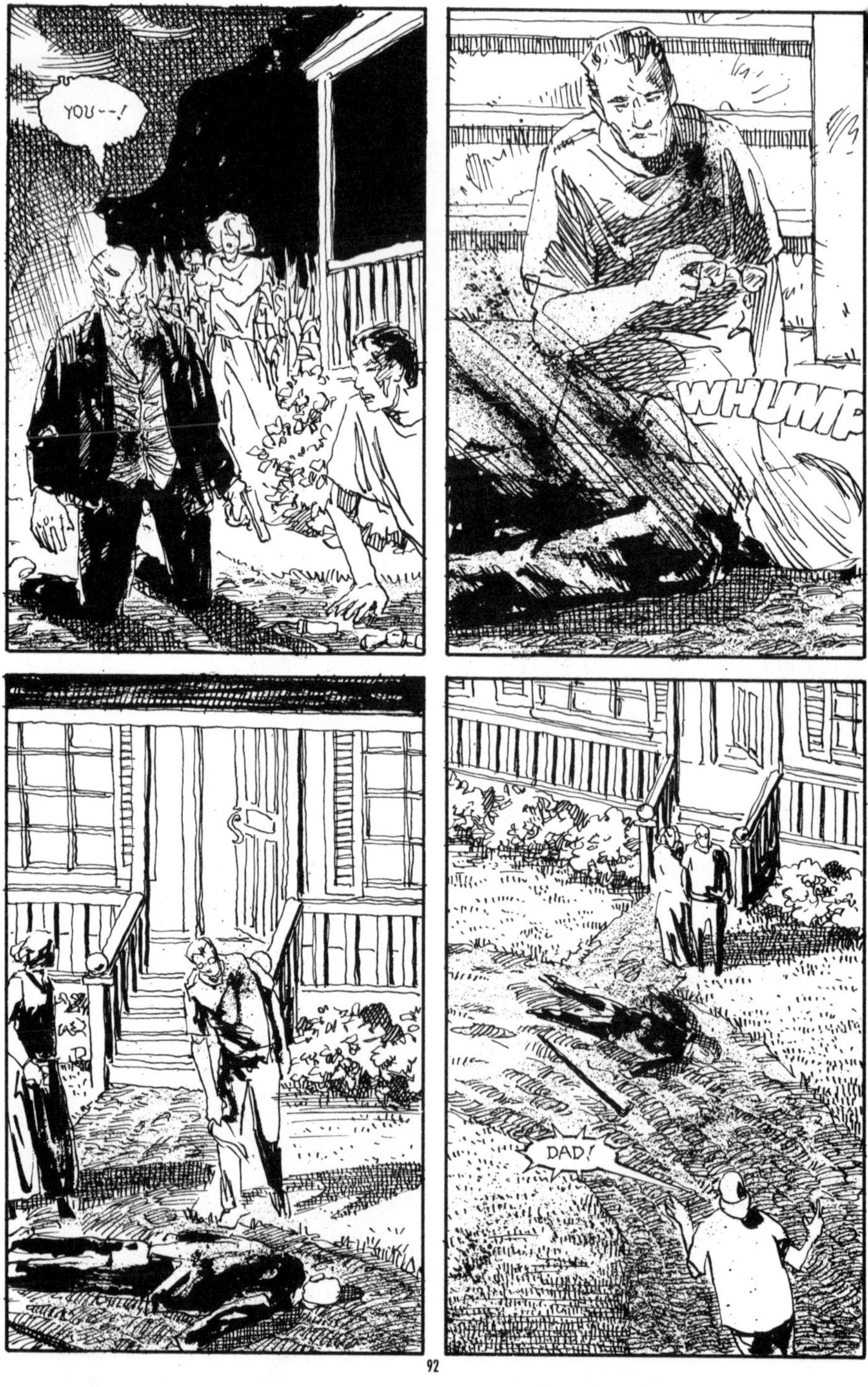
YOU--!
WHUMP
DAD!

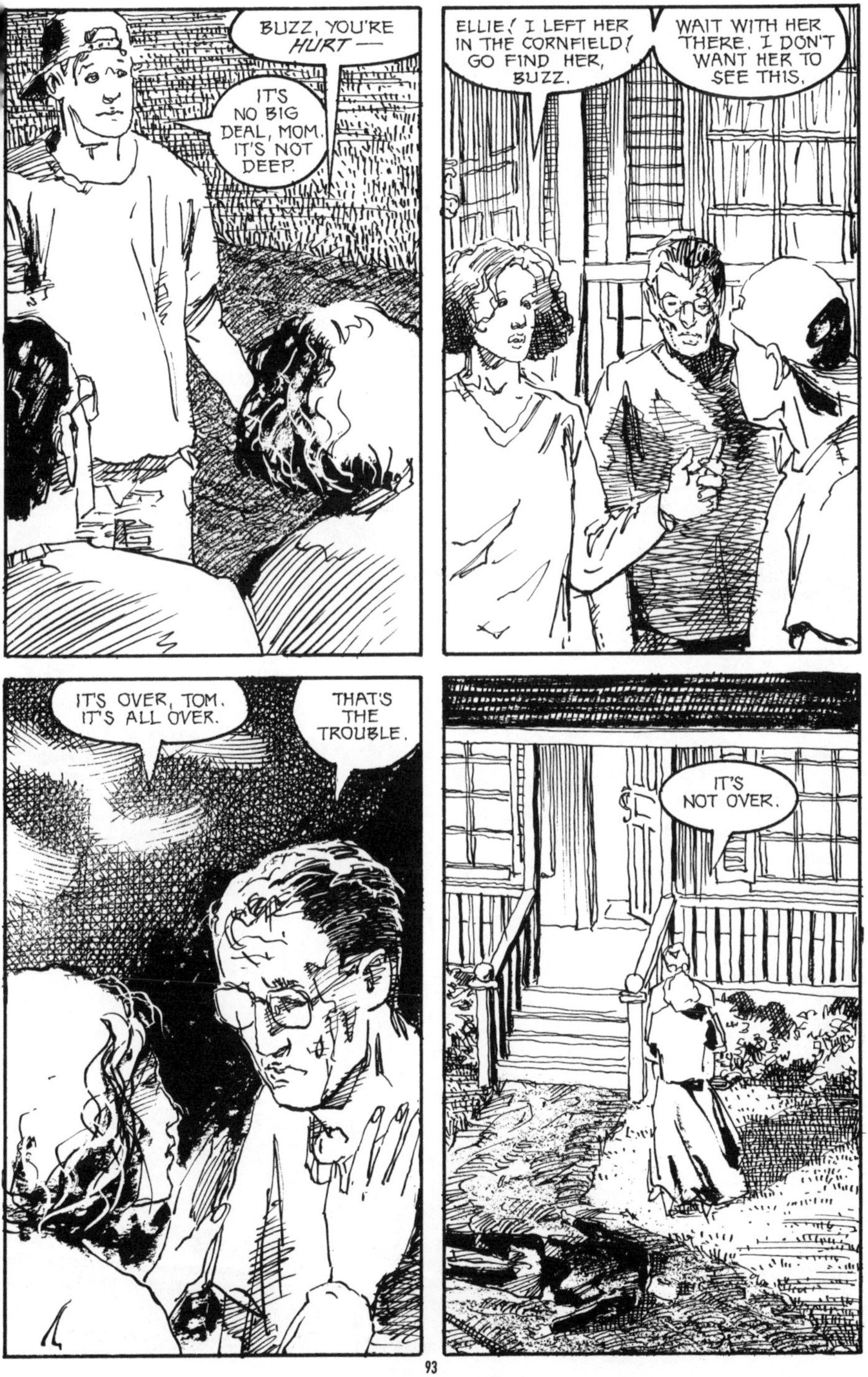
BUZZ, YOU'RE *HURT*—
IT'S NO BIG DEAL, MOM. IT'S NOT DEEP.
ELLIE! I LEFT HER IN THE CORNFIELD! GO FIND HER, BUZZ.
WAIT WITH HER THERE. I DON'T WANT HER TO SEE THIS.
IT'S OVER, TOM. IT'S ALL OVER.
THAT'S THE TROUBLE.
IT'S NOT OVER.

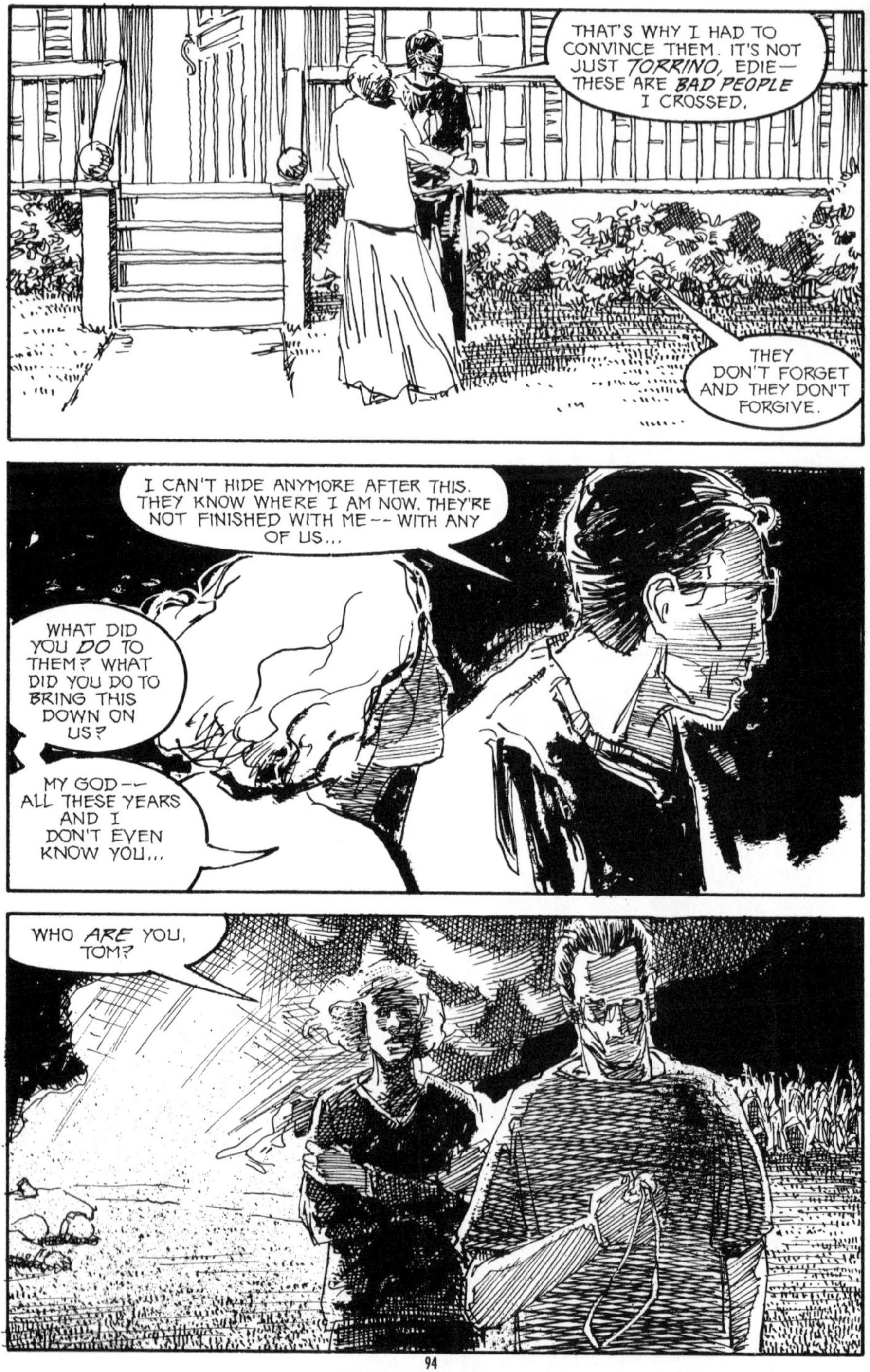
THAT'S WHY I HAD TO CONVINCE THEM. IT'S NOT JUST TORRINO, EDIE-- THESE ARE BAD PEOPLE I CROSSED.
THEY DON'T FORGET AND THEY DON'T FORGIVE.
I CAN'T HIDE ANYMORE AFTER THIS. THEY KNOW WHERE I AM NOW. THEY'RE NOT FINISHED WITH ME-- WITH ANY OF US...
WHAT DID YOU DO TO THEM? WHAT DID YOU DO TO BRING THIS DOWN ON US?
MY GOD-- ALL THESE YEARS AND I DON'T EVEN KNOW YOU...
WHO ARE YOU, TOM?

CHAPTER 2

THE BROOKLYN MURDERS

"Through the jungle

very softly flits

a shadow and a sigh -

He is Fear,

O Little Hunter,

he is Fear!"

-KIPLING

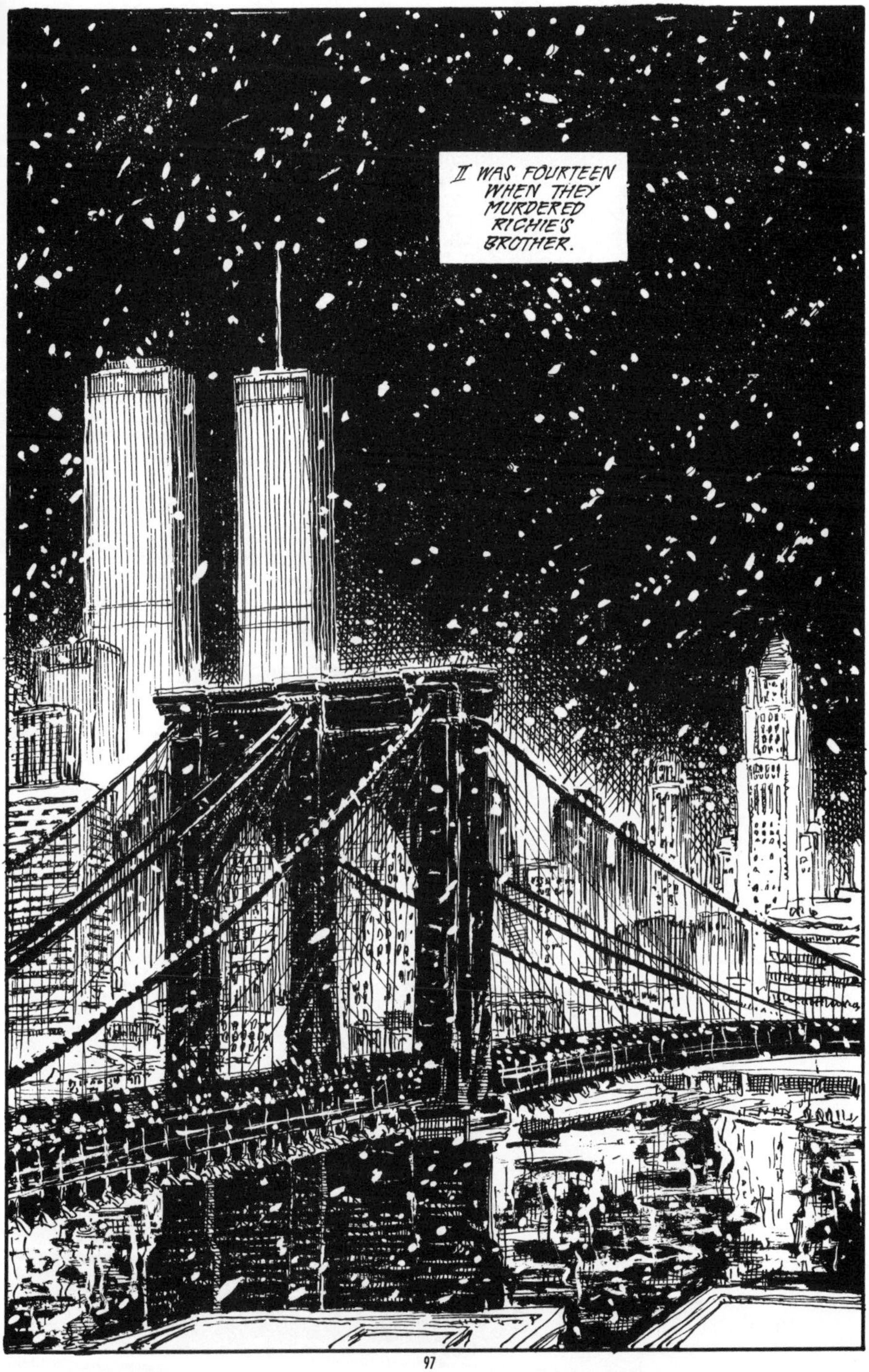
I WAS FOURTEEN WHEN THEY MURDERED RICHIE'S BROTHER.

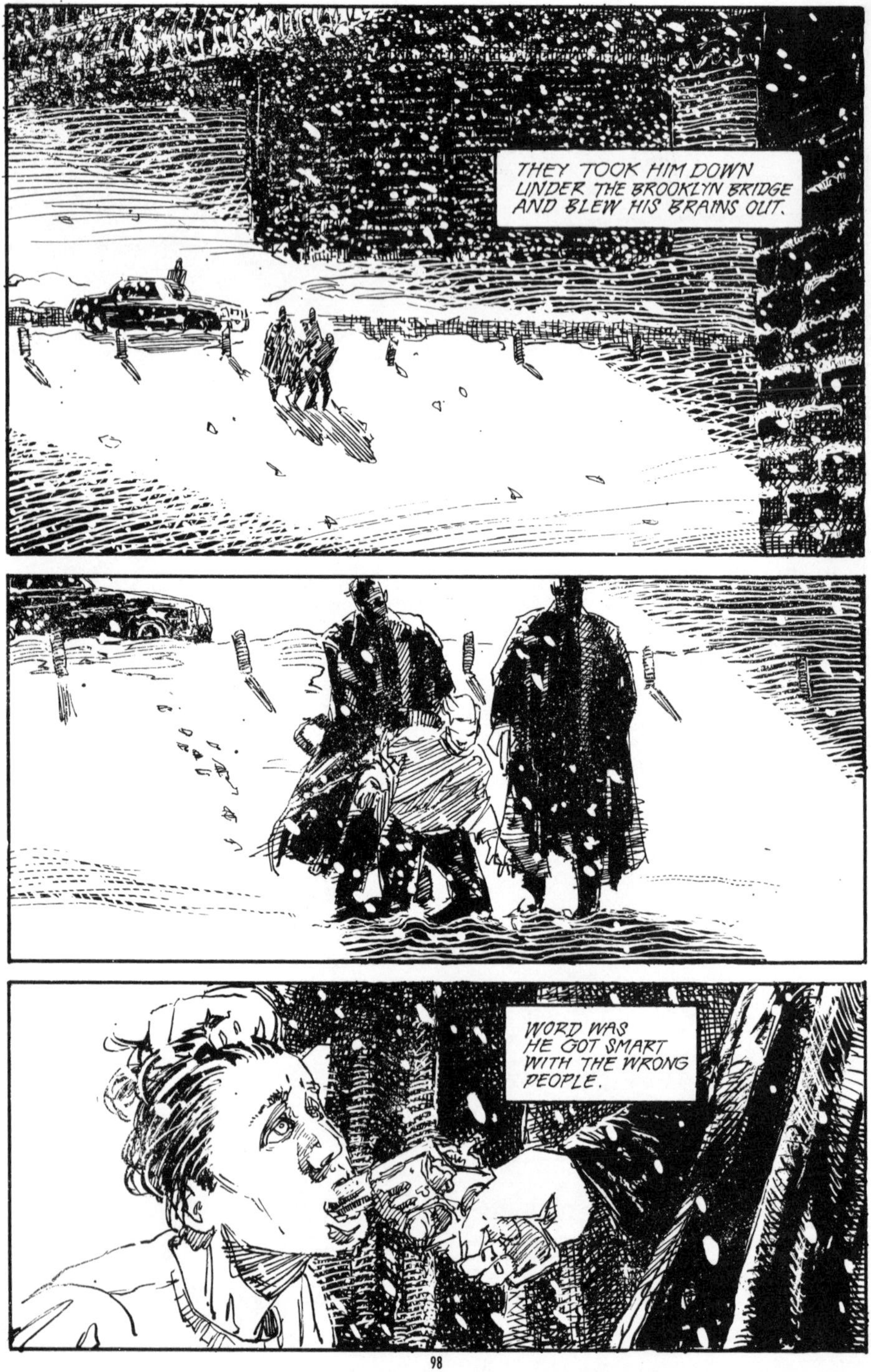
THEY TOOK HIM DOWN UNDER THE BROOKLYN BRIDGE AND BLEW HIS BRAINS OUT.
WORD WAS HE GOT SMART WITH THE WRONG PEOPLE.

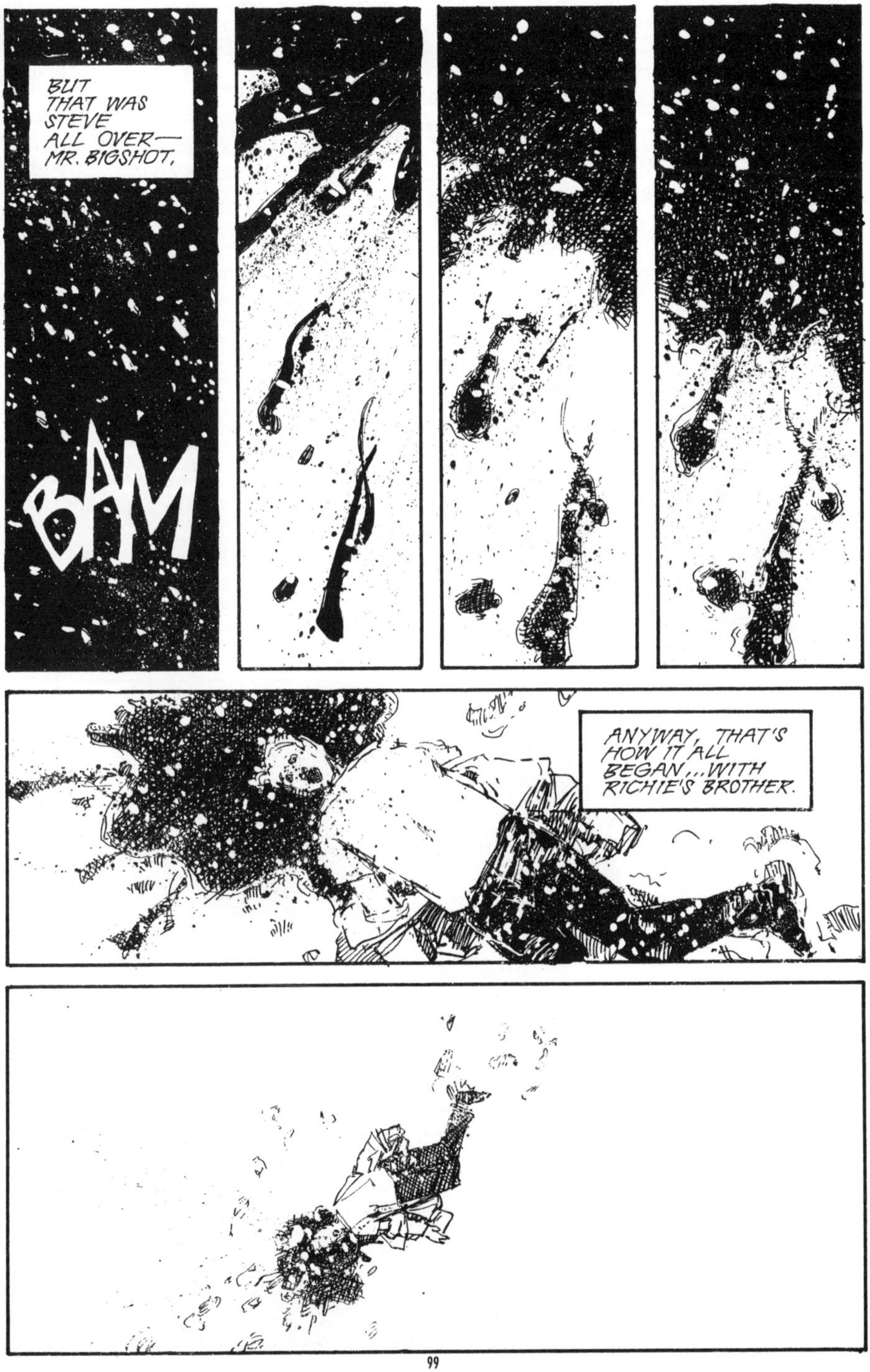
BUT THAT WAS STEVE ALL OVER— MR. BIGSHOT.
BAM
ANYWAY, THAT'S HOW IT ALL BEGAN...WITH RICHIE'S BROTHER.

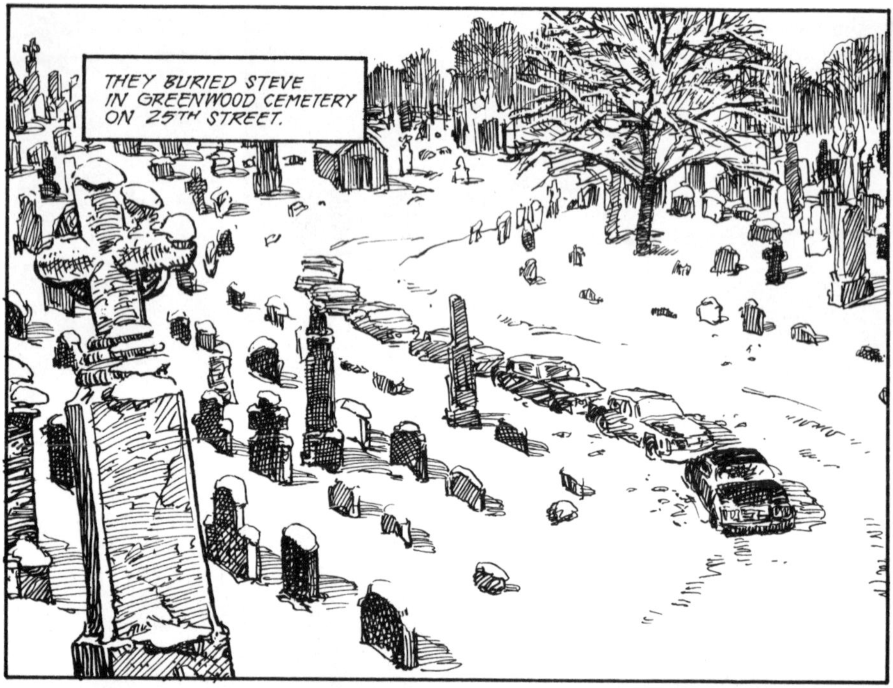
THEY BURIED STEVE IN GREENWOOD CEMETERY ON 25TH STREET.

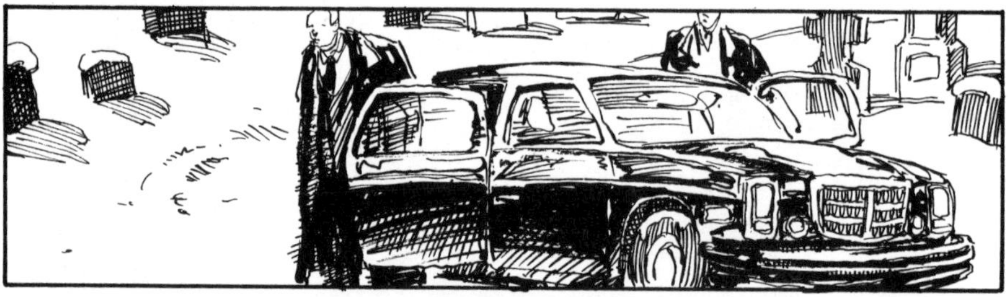

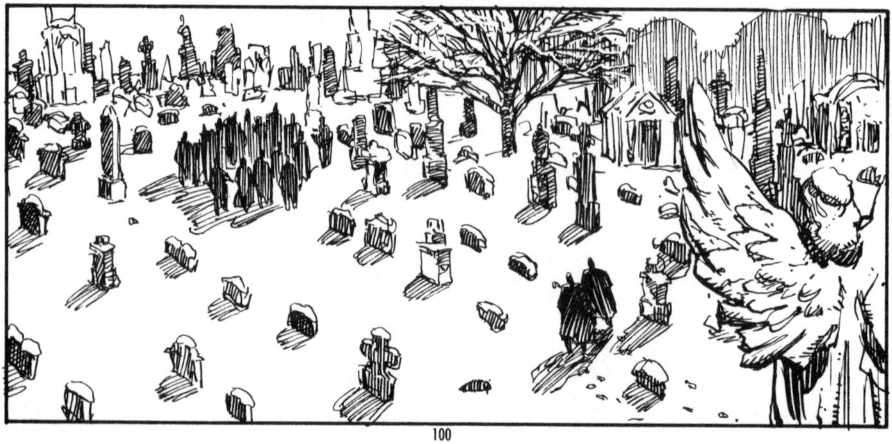

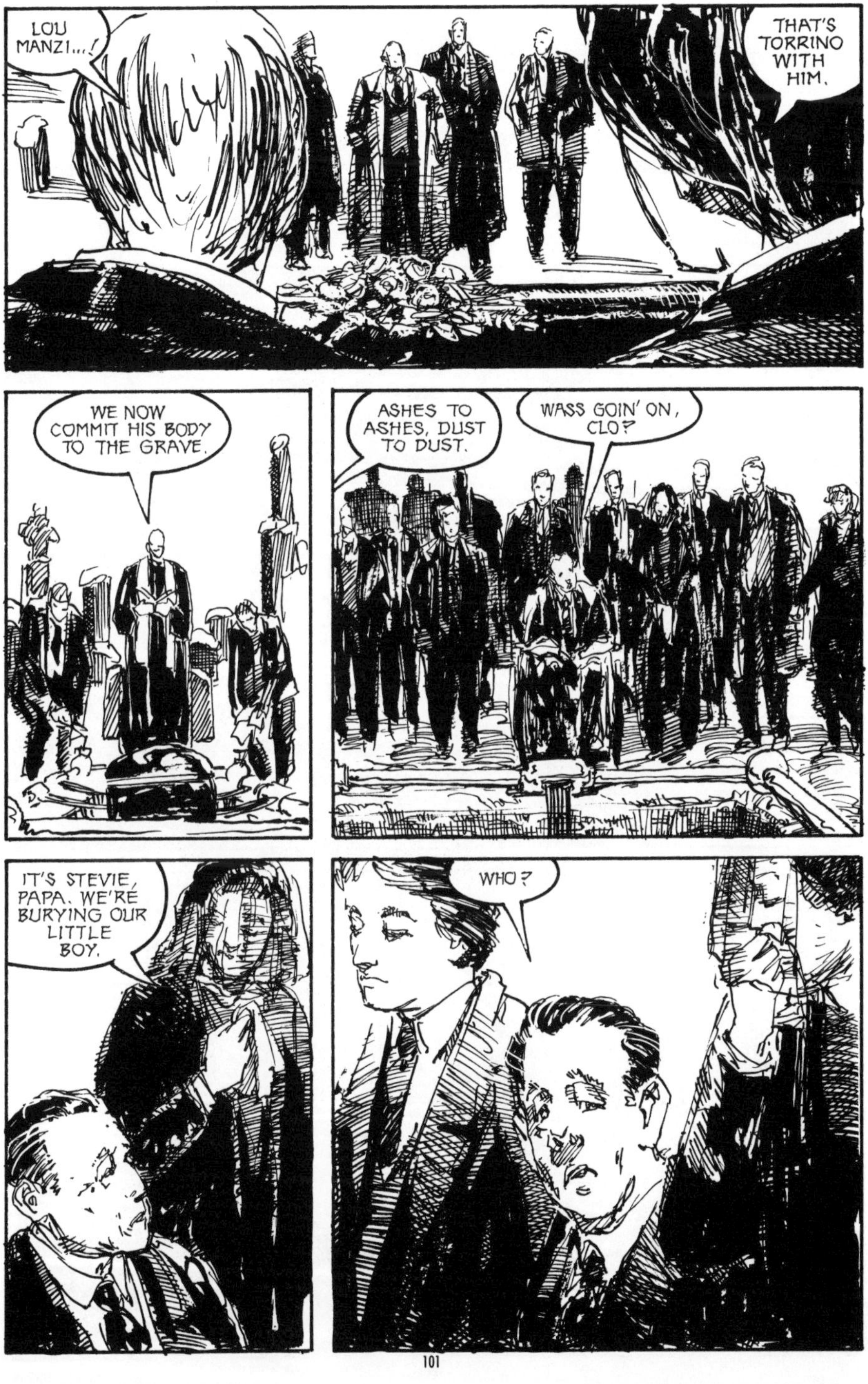
LOU MANZI...!
THAT'S TORRINO WITH HIM.
WE NOW COMMIT HIS BODY TO THE GRAVE.
ASHES TO ASHES, DUST TO DUST.
WASS GOIN' ON, CLO?
IT'S STEVIE, PAPA. WE'RE BURYING OUR LITTLE BOY.
WHO?

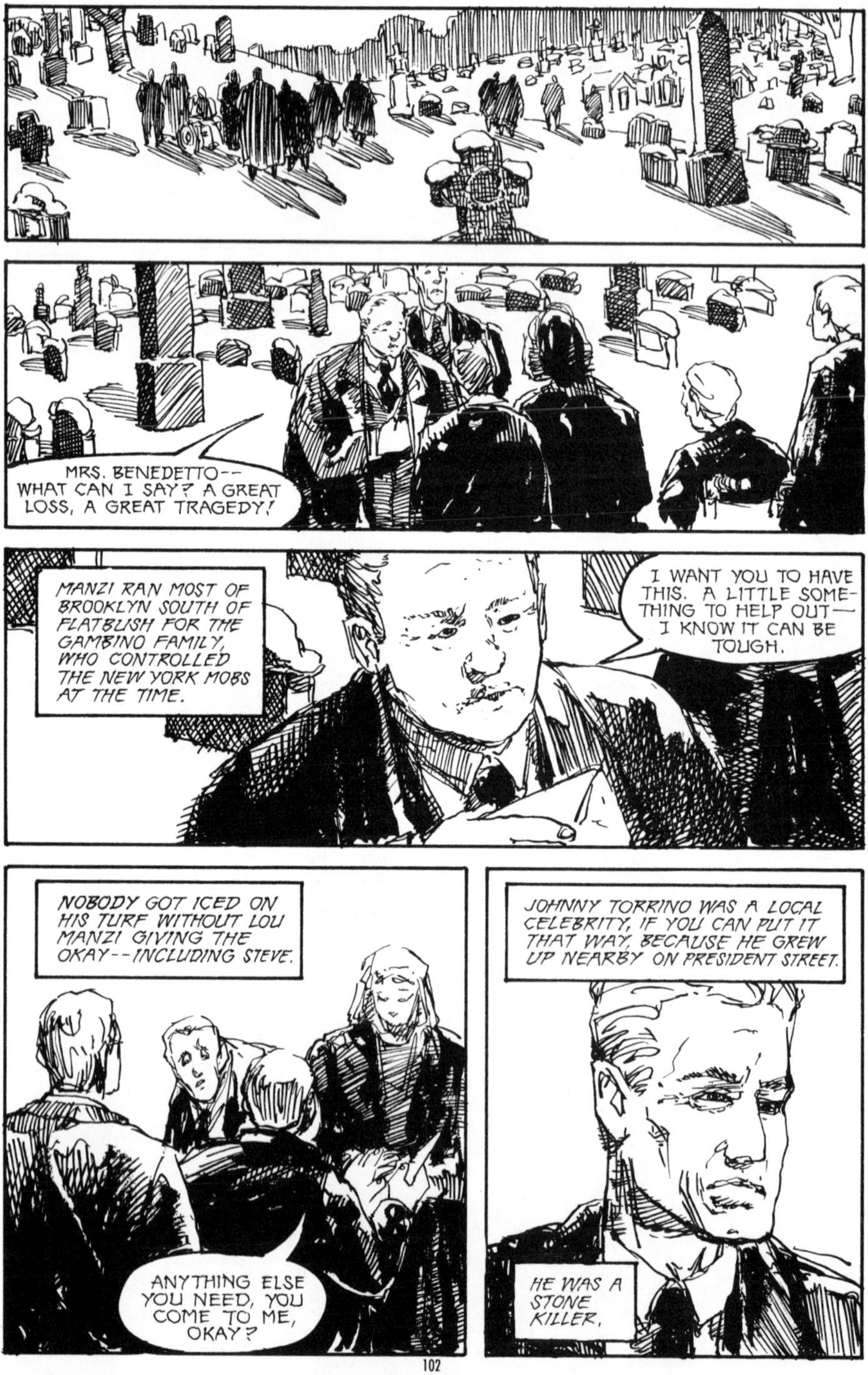
MRS. BENEDETTO-- WHAT CAN I SAY? A GREAT LOSS, A GREAT TRAGEDY!
MANZI RAN MOST OF BROOKLYN SOUTH OF FLATBUSH FOR THE GAMBINO FAMILY, WHO CONTROLLED THE NEW YORK MOBS AT THE TIME.
I WANT YOU TO HAVE THIS. A LITTLE SOMETHING TO HELP OUT— I KNOW IT CAN BE TOUGH.
NOBODY GOT ICED ON HIS TURF WITHOUT LOU MANZI GIVING THE OKAY--INCLUDING STEVE.
ANYTHING ELSE YOU NEED, YOU COME TO ME, OKAY?
JOHNNY TORRINO WAS A LOCAL CELEBRITY, IF YOU CAN PUT IT THAT WAY, BECAUSE HE GREW UP NEARBY ON PRESIDENT STREET.
HE WAS A STONE KILLER.

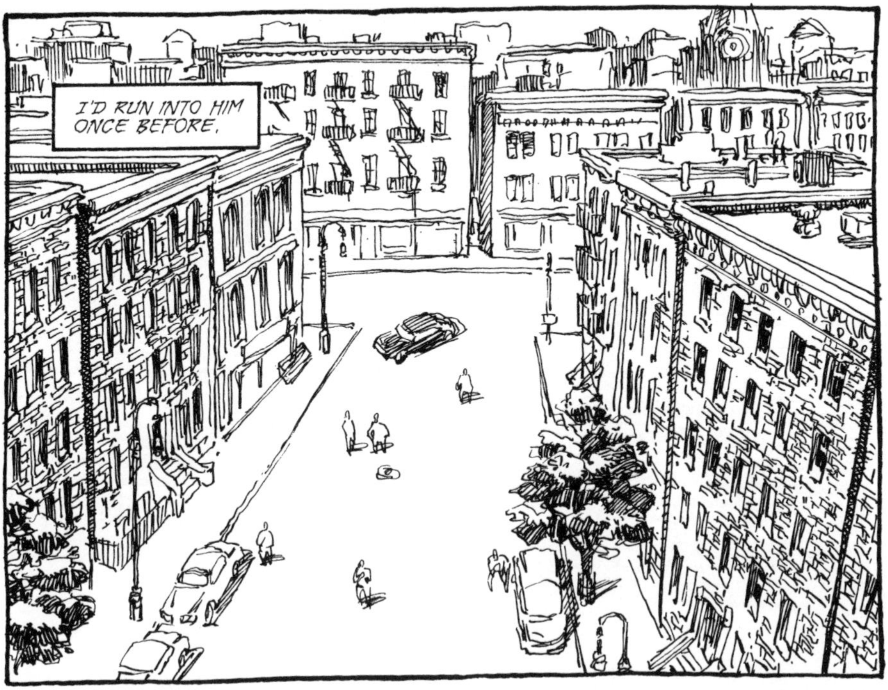
I'D RUN INTO HIM ONCE BEFORE.

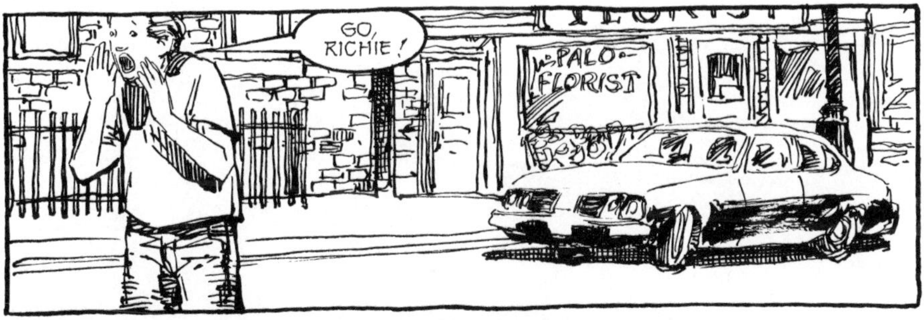
GO, RICHIE!
PALO FLORIST

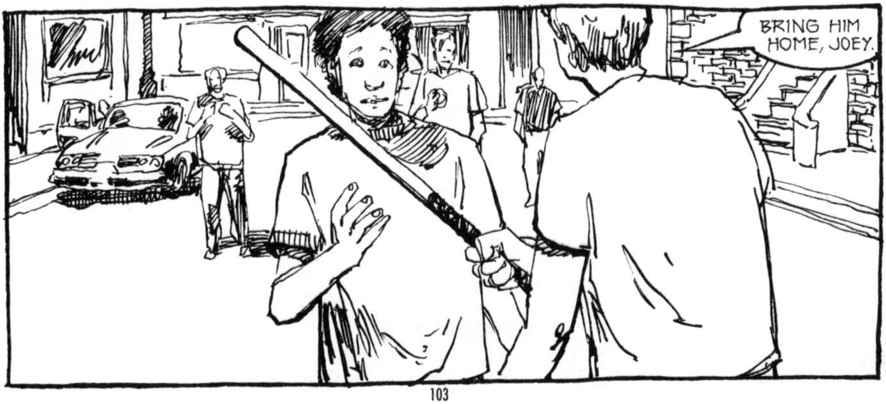
BRING HIM HOME, JOEY.

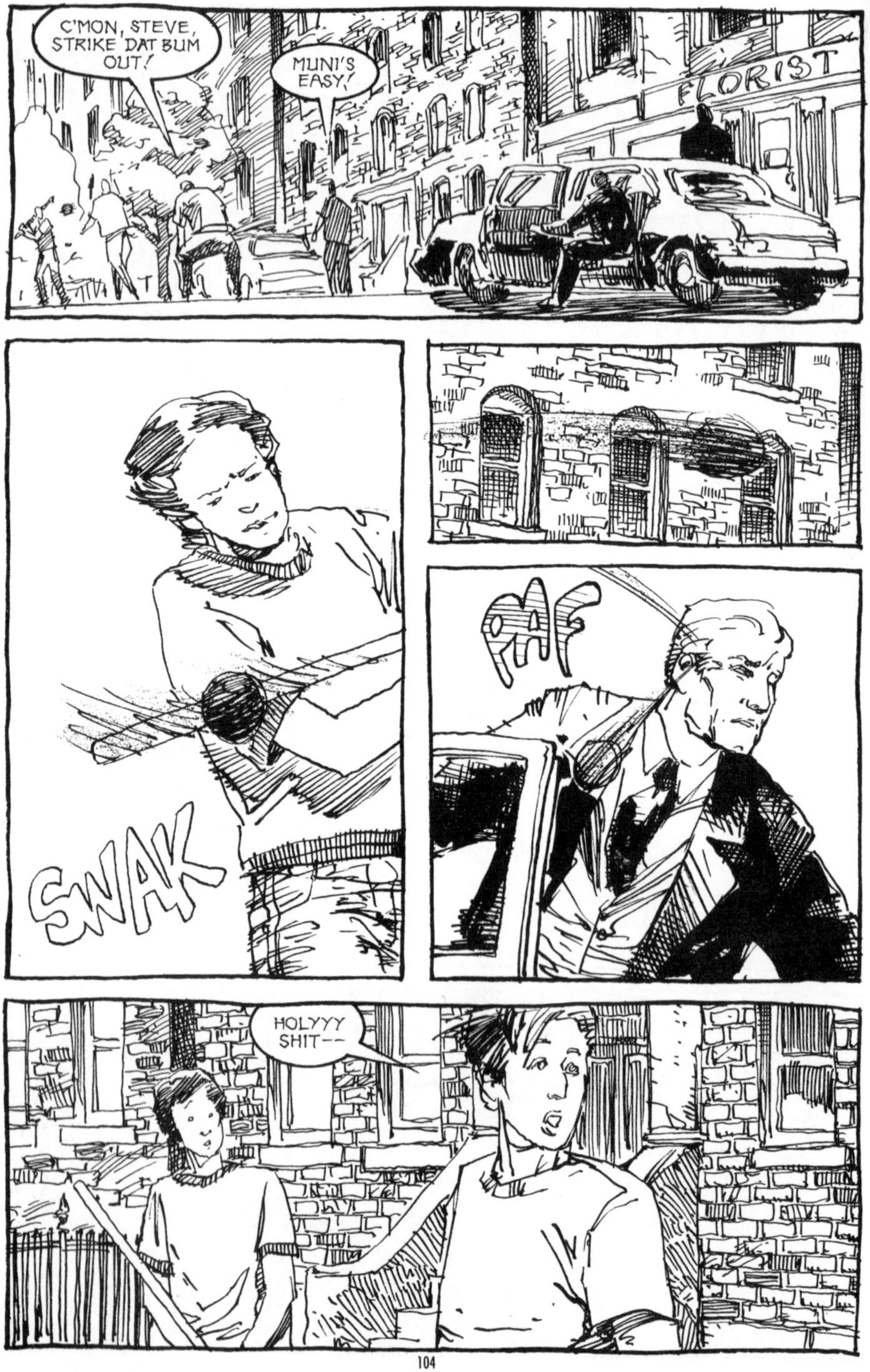
C'MON, STEVE, STRIKE DAT BUM OUT!
MUNI'S EASY!
FLORIST
SWAK
PAF
HOLYYY SHIT--

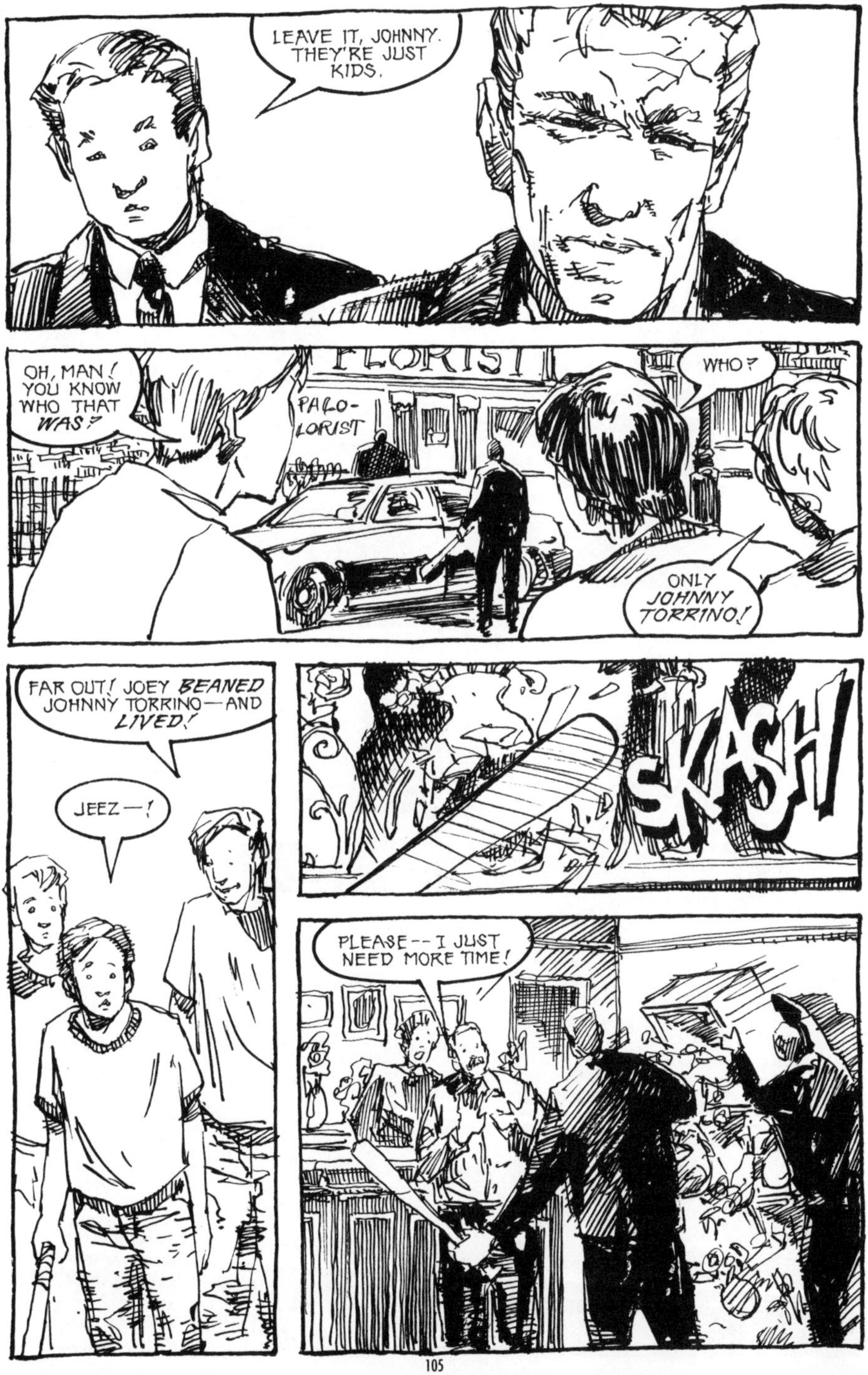
LEAVE IT, JOHNNY. THEY'RE JUST KIDS.
FLORIST
OH, MAN! YOU KNOW WHO THAT WAS?
PALO-LORIST
WHO?
ONLY JOHNNY TORRINO!
FAR OUT! JOEY BEANED JOHNNY TORRINO—AND LIVED!
JEEZ—!
SKASH
PLEASE--I JUST NEED MORE TIME!

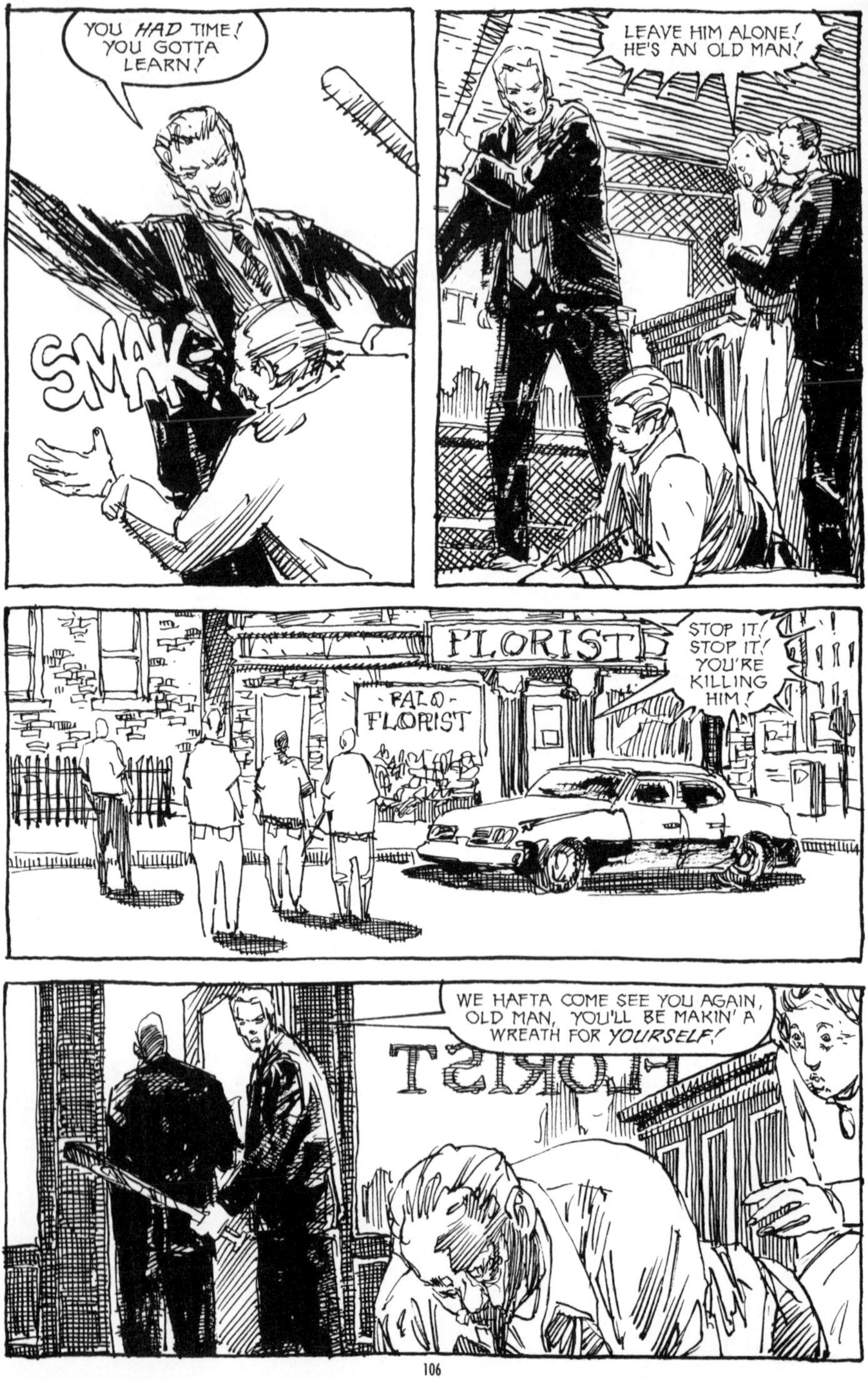
YOU *HAD* TIME! YOU GOTTA LEARN!
SMAK
LEAVE HIM ALONE! HE'S AN OLD MAN!
FLORIST
PALO FLORIST
STOP IT! STOP IT! YOU'RE KILLING HIM!
WE HAFTA COME SEE YOU AGAIN, OLD MAN, YOU'LL BE MAKIN' A WREATH FOR *YOURSELF*!

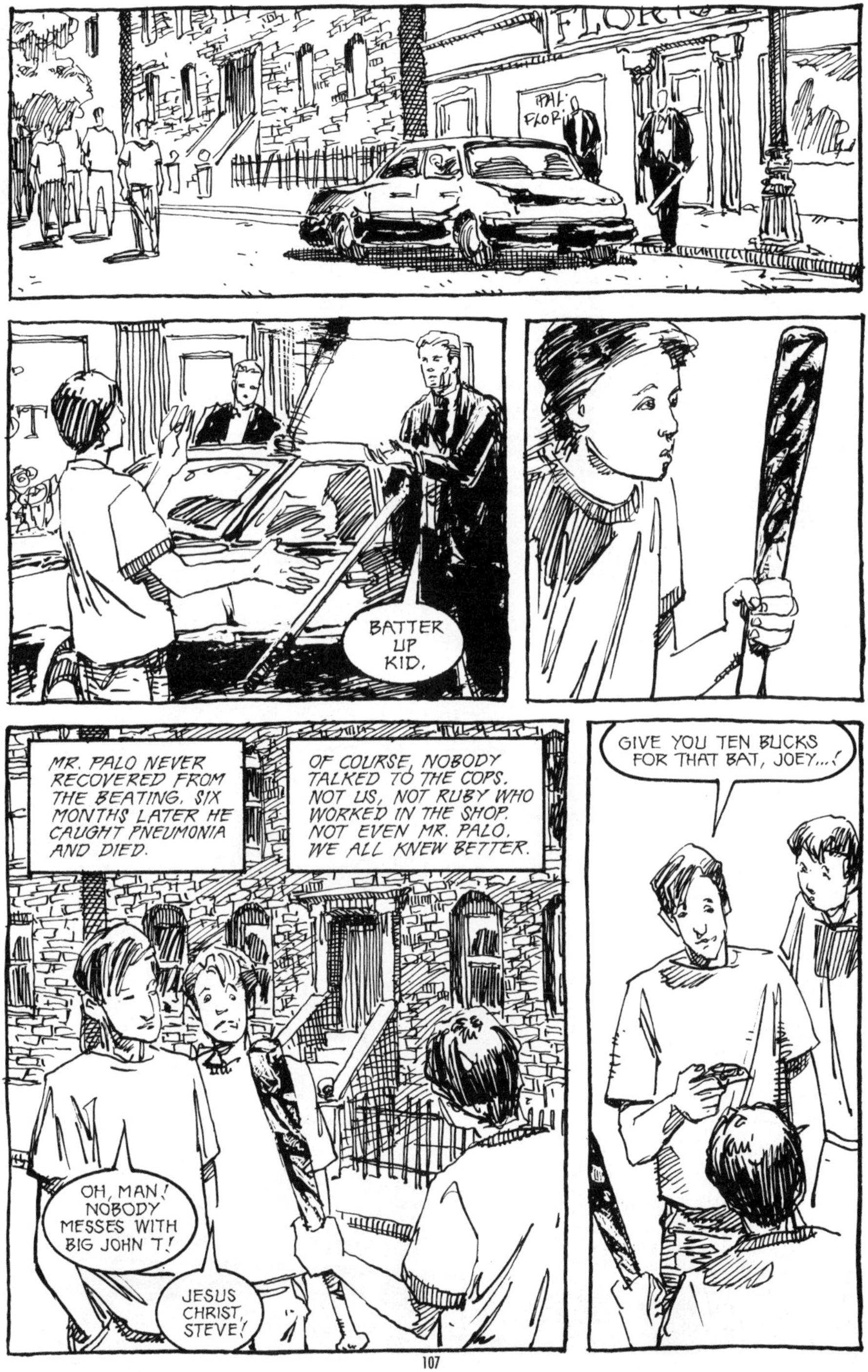

BATTER UP KID.
MR. PALO NEVER RECOVERED FROM THE BEATING. SIX MONTHS LATER HE CAUGHT PNEUMONIA AND DIED.
OF COURSE, NOBODY TALKED TO THE COPS. NOT US, NOT RUBY WHO WORKED IN THE SHOP. NOT EVEN MR. PALO. WE ALL KNEW BETTER.
OH, MAN! NOBODY MESSES WITH BIG JOHN T!
JESUS CHRIST, STEVE!
GIVE YOU TEN BUCKS FOR THAT BAT, JOEY...!

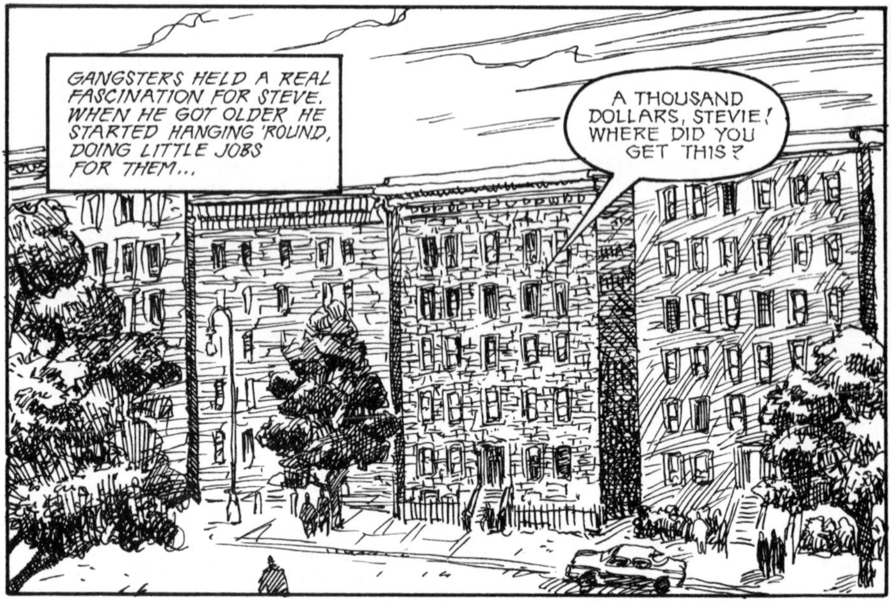
GANGSTERS HELD A REAL FASCINATION FOR STEVE. WHEN HE GOT OLDER HE STARTED HANGING 'ROUND, DOING LITTLE JOBS FOR THEM...
A THOUSAND DOLLARS, STEVIE! WHERE DID YOU GET THIS?

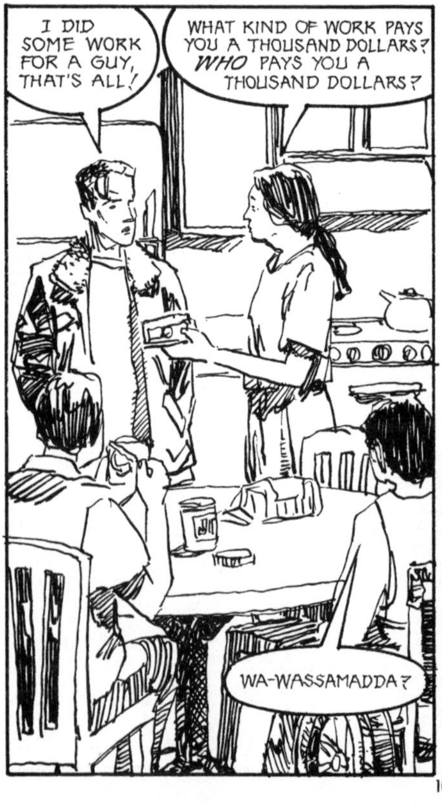
I DID SOME WORK FOR A GUY, THAT'S ALL!
WHAT KIND OF WORK PAYS YOU A THOUSAND DOLLARS? *WHO* PAYS YOU A THOUSAND DOLLARS?
WA-WASSAMADDA?

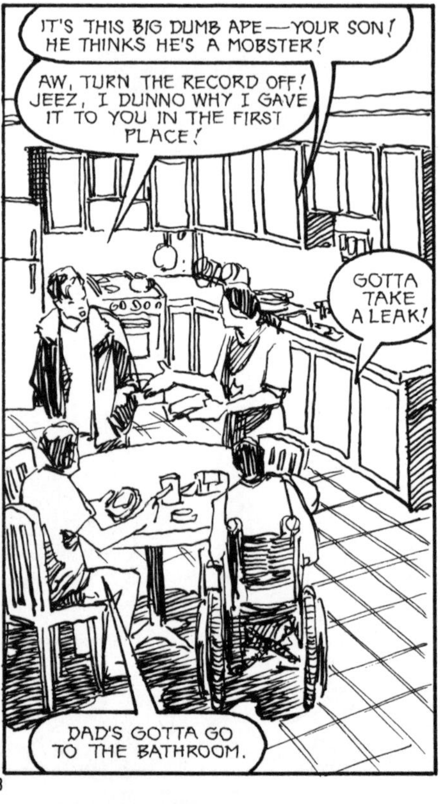
IT'S THIS BIG DUMB APE—YOUR SON! HE THINKS HE'S A MOBSTER!
AW, TURN THE RECORD OFF! JEEZ, I DUNNO WHY I GAVE IT TO YOU IN THE FIRST PLACE!
GOTTA TAKE A LEAK!
DAD'S GOTTA GO TO THE BATHROOM.

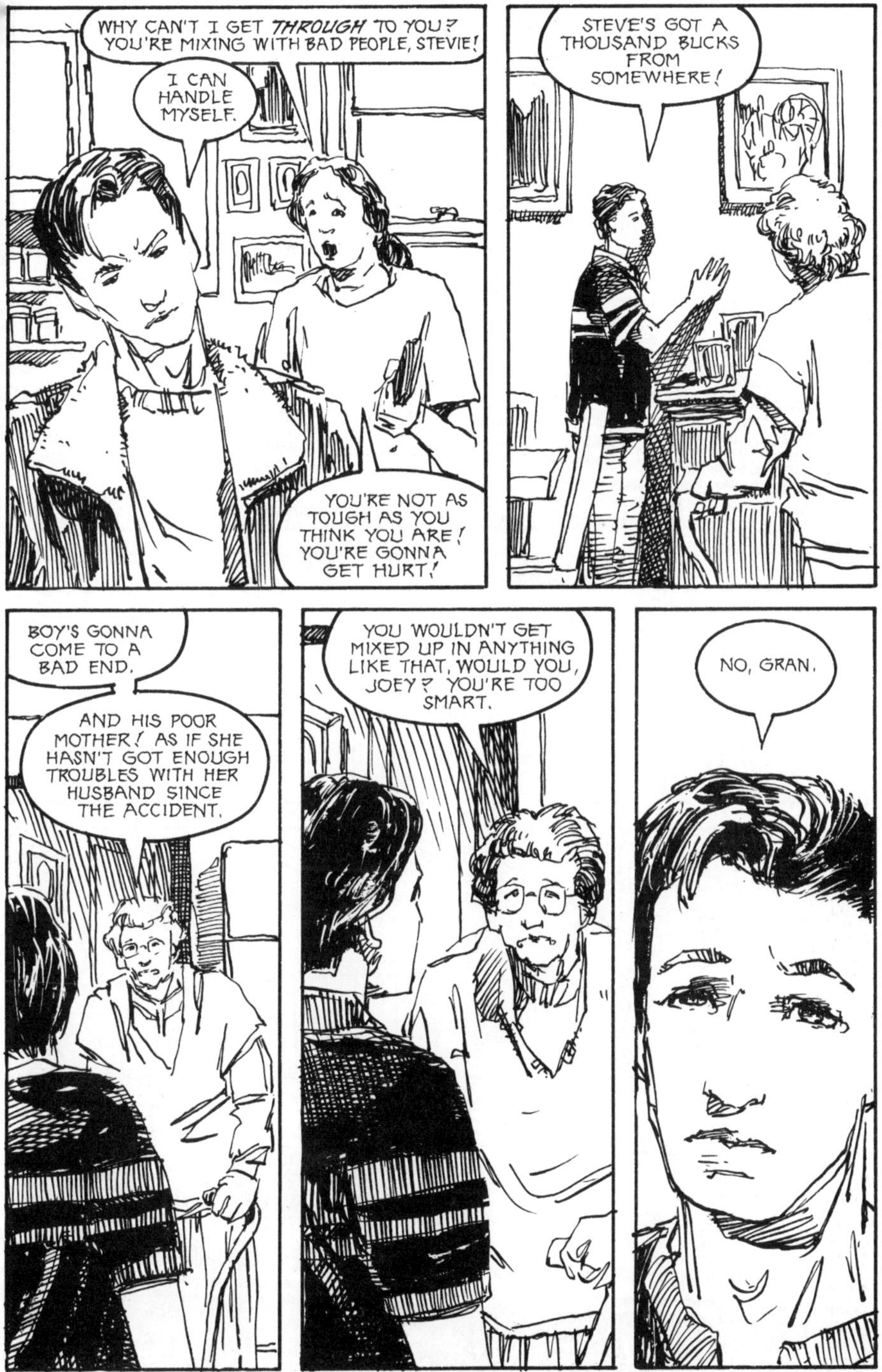
WHY CAN'T I GET THROUGH TO YOU? YOU'RE MIXING WITH BAD PEOPLE, STEVIE!
I CAN HANDLE MYSELF.
YOU'RE NOT AS TOUGH AS YOU THINK YOU ARE! YOU'RE GONNA GET HURT!
STEVE'S GOT A THOUSAND BUCKS FROM SOMEWHERE!
BOY'S GONNA COME TO A BAD END.
AND HIS POOR MOTHER! AS IF SHE HASN'T GOT ENOUGH TROUBLES WITH HER HUSBAND SINCE THE ACCIDENT.
YOU WOULDN'T GET MIXED UP IN ANYTHING LIKE THAT, WOULD YOU, JOEY? YOU'RE TOO SMART.
NO, GRAN.

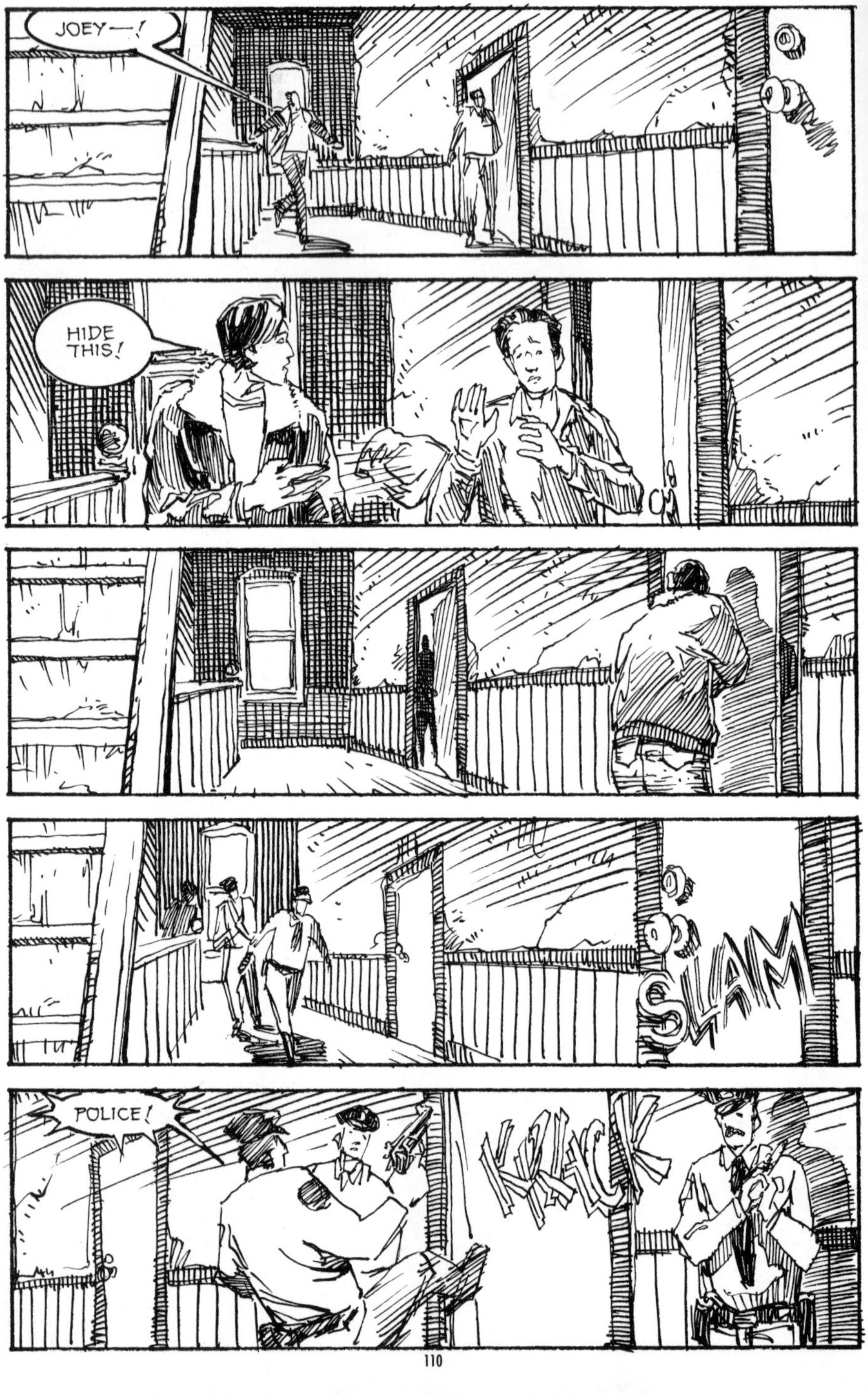
JOEY—!
HIDE THIS!
SLAM
POLICE!
KRACK

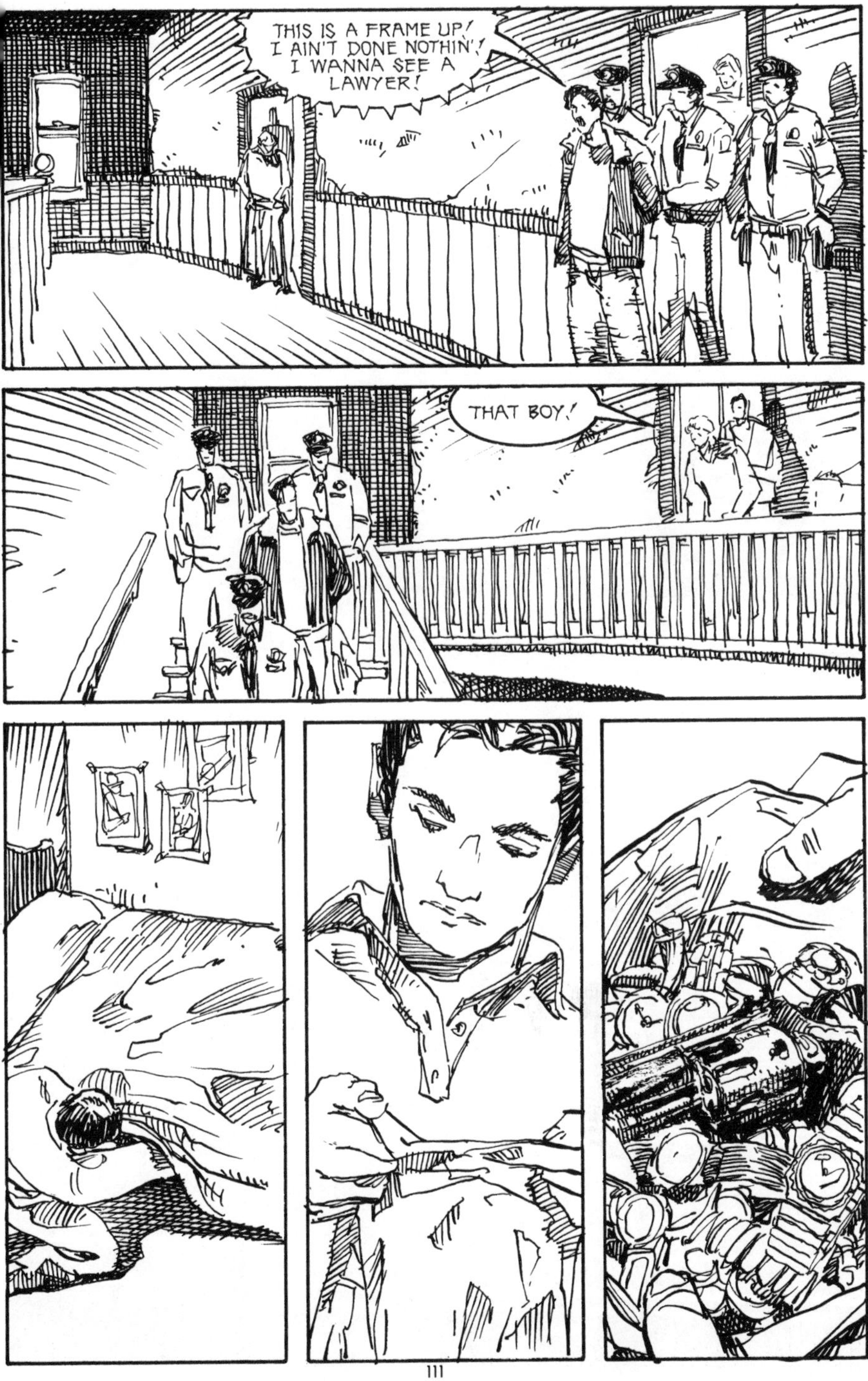
THIS IS A FRAME UP! I AIN'T DONE NOTHIN'! I WANNA SEE A LAWYER!
THAT BOY!

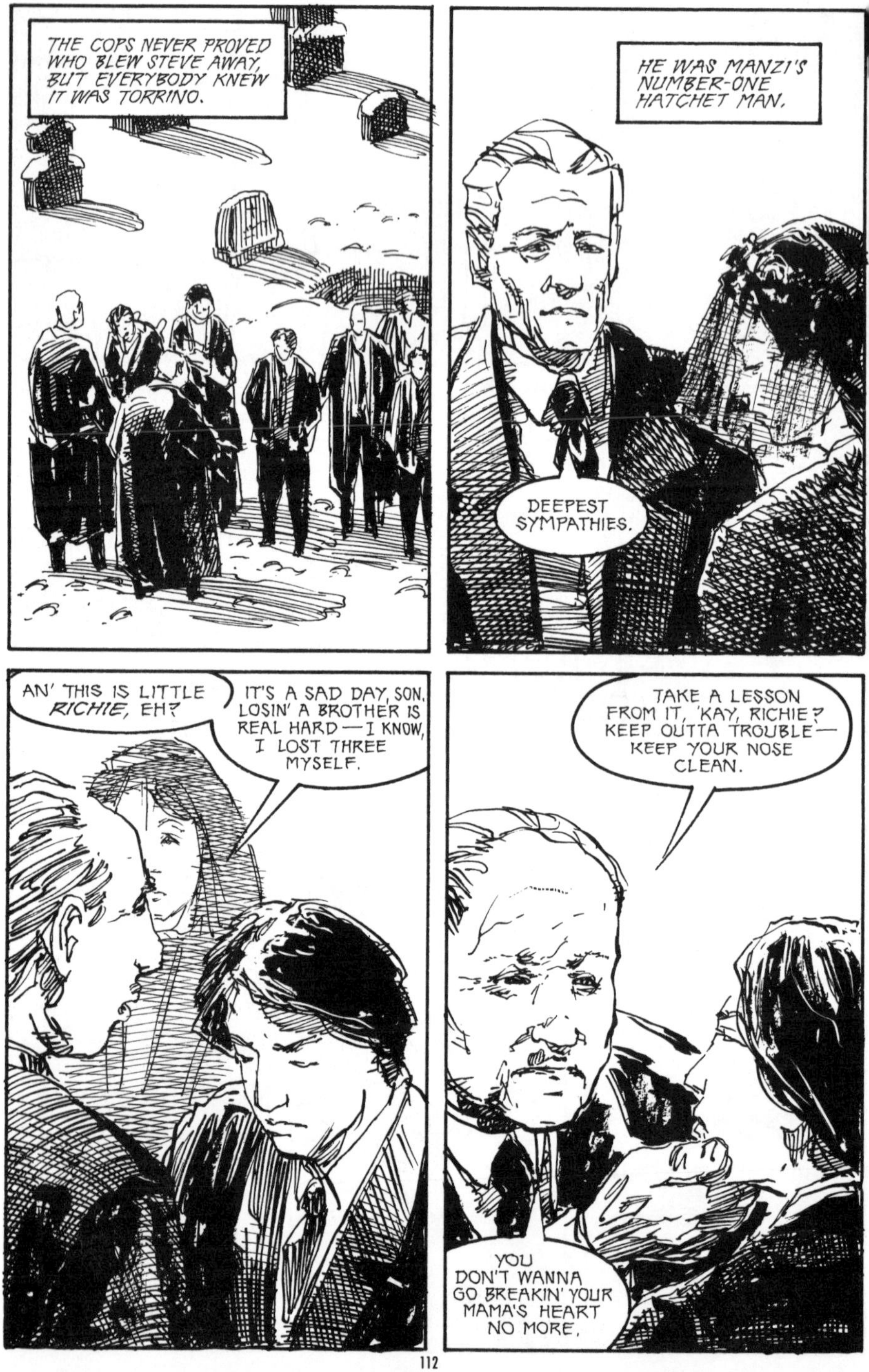
THE COPS NEVER PROVED WHO BLEW STEVE AWAY, BUT EVERYBODY KNEW IT WAS TORRINO.
HE WAS MANZI'S NUMBER-ONE HATCHET MAN.
DEEPEST SYMPATHIES.
AN' THIS IS LITTLE *RICHIE,* EH?
IT'S A SAD DAY, SON. LOSIN' A BROTHER IS REAL HARD — I KNOW, I LOST THREE MYSELF.
TAKE A LESSON FROM IT, 'KAY, RICHIE? KEEP OUTTA TROUBLE — KEEP YOUR NOSE CLEAN.
YOU DON'T WANNA GO BREAKIN' YOUR MAMA'S HEART NO MORE.

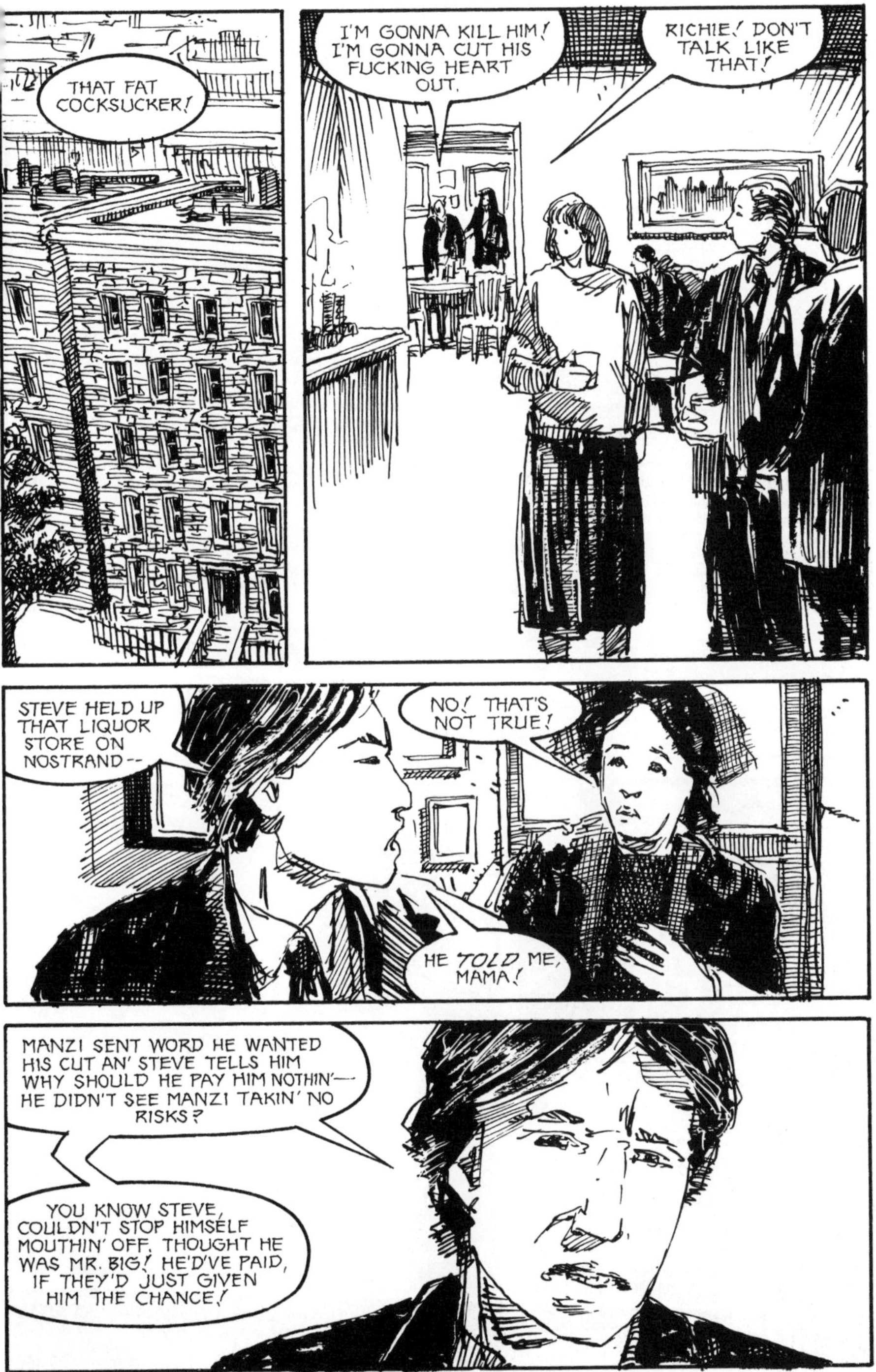
THAT FAT COCKSUCKER!
I'M GONNA KILL HIM! I'M GONNA CUT HIS FUCKING HEART OUT.
RICHIE! DON'T TALK LIKE THAT!
STEVE HELD UP THAT LIQUOR STORE ON NOSTRAND--
NO! THAT'S NOT TRUE!
HE *TOLD* ME, MAMA!
MANZI SENT WORD HE WANTED HIS CUT AN' STEVE TELLS HIM WHY SHOULD HE PAY HIM NOTHIN'— HE DIDN'T SEE MANZI TAKIN' NO RISKS?
YOU KNOW STEVE, COULDN'T STOP HIMSELF MOUTHIN' OFF. THOUGHT HE WAS MR. BIG! HE'D'VE PAID, IF THEY'D JUST GIVEN HIM THE CHANCE!

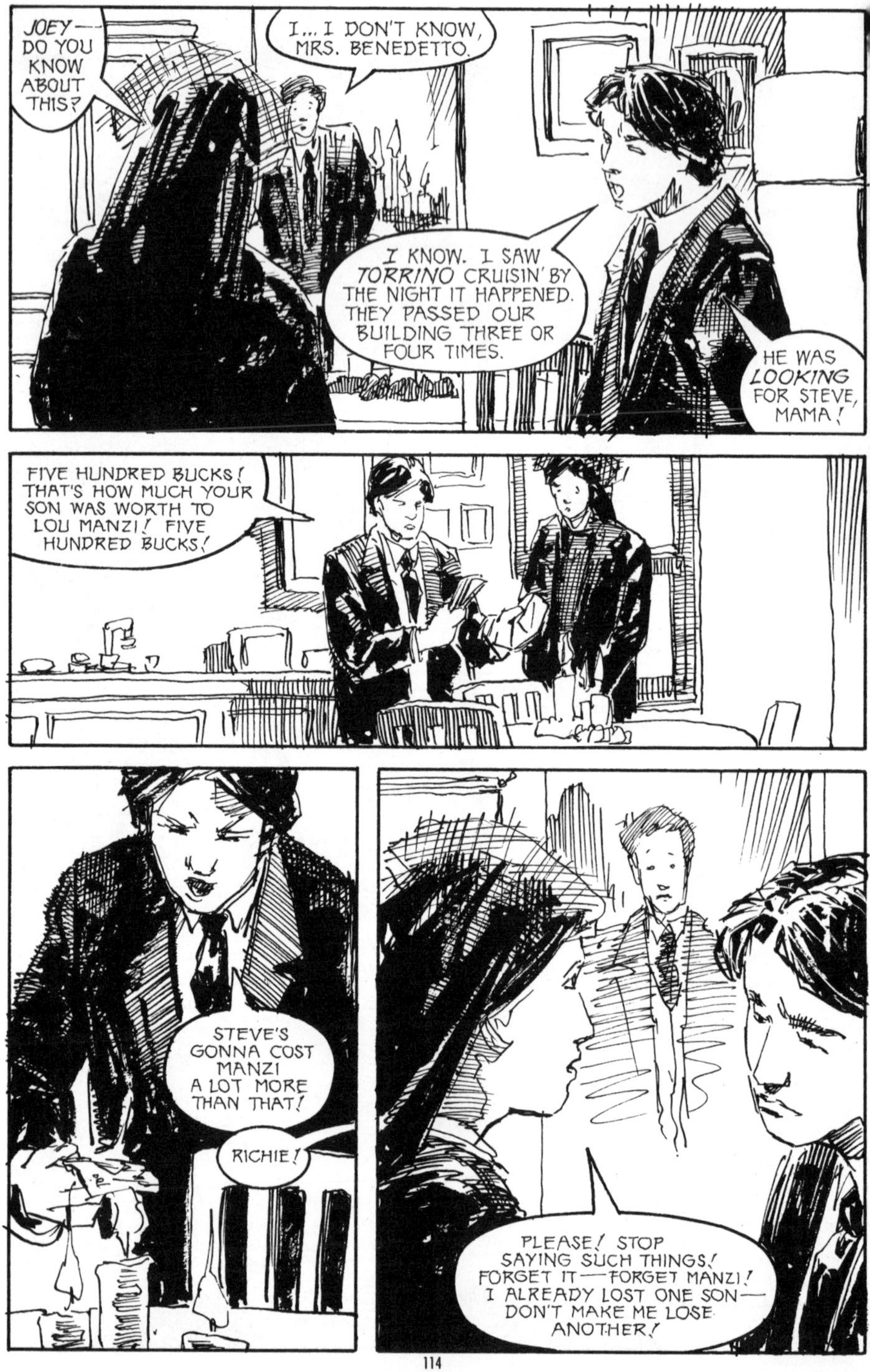
JOEY— DO YOU KNOW ABOUT THIS?
I... I DON'T KNOW, MRS. BENEDETTO.
I KNOW. I SAW TORRINO CRUISIN' BY THE NIGHT IT HAPPENED. THEY PASSED OUR BUILDING THREE OR FOUR TIMES.
HE WAS LOOKING FOR STEVE, MAMA!
FIVE HUNDRED BUCKS! THAT'S HOW MUCH YOUR SON WAS WORTH TO LOU MANZI! FIVE HUNDRED BUCKS!
STEVE'S GONNA COST MANZI A LOT MORE THAN THAT!
RICHIE!
PLEASE! STOP SAYING SUCH THINGS! FORGET IT—FORGET MANZI! I ALREADY LOST ONE SON— DON'T MAKE ME LOSE ANOTHER!

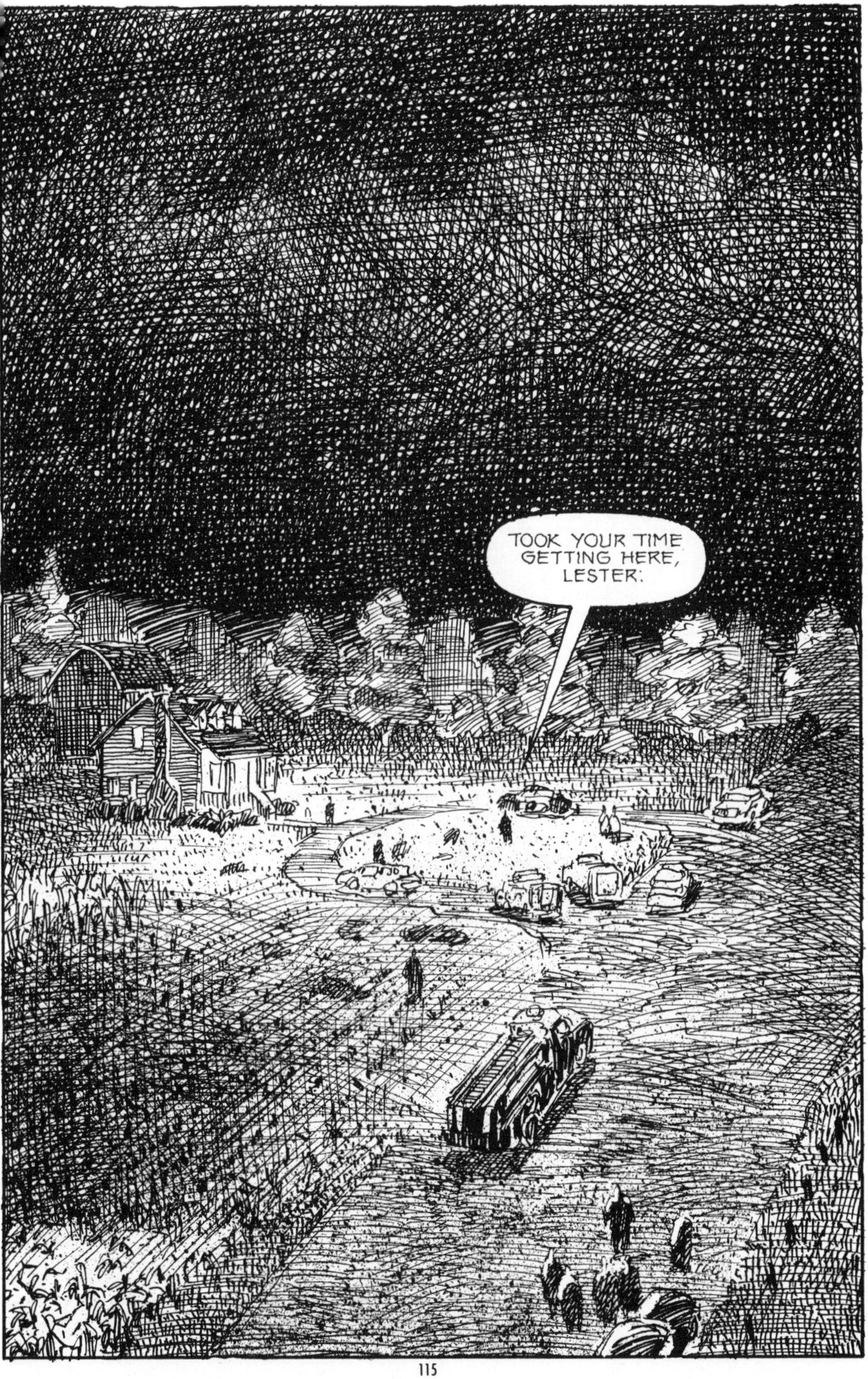
TOOK YOUR TIME GETTING HERE, LESTER.

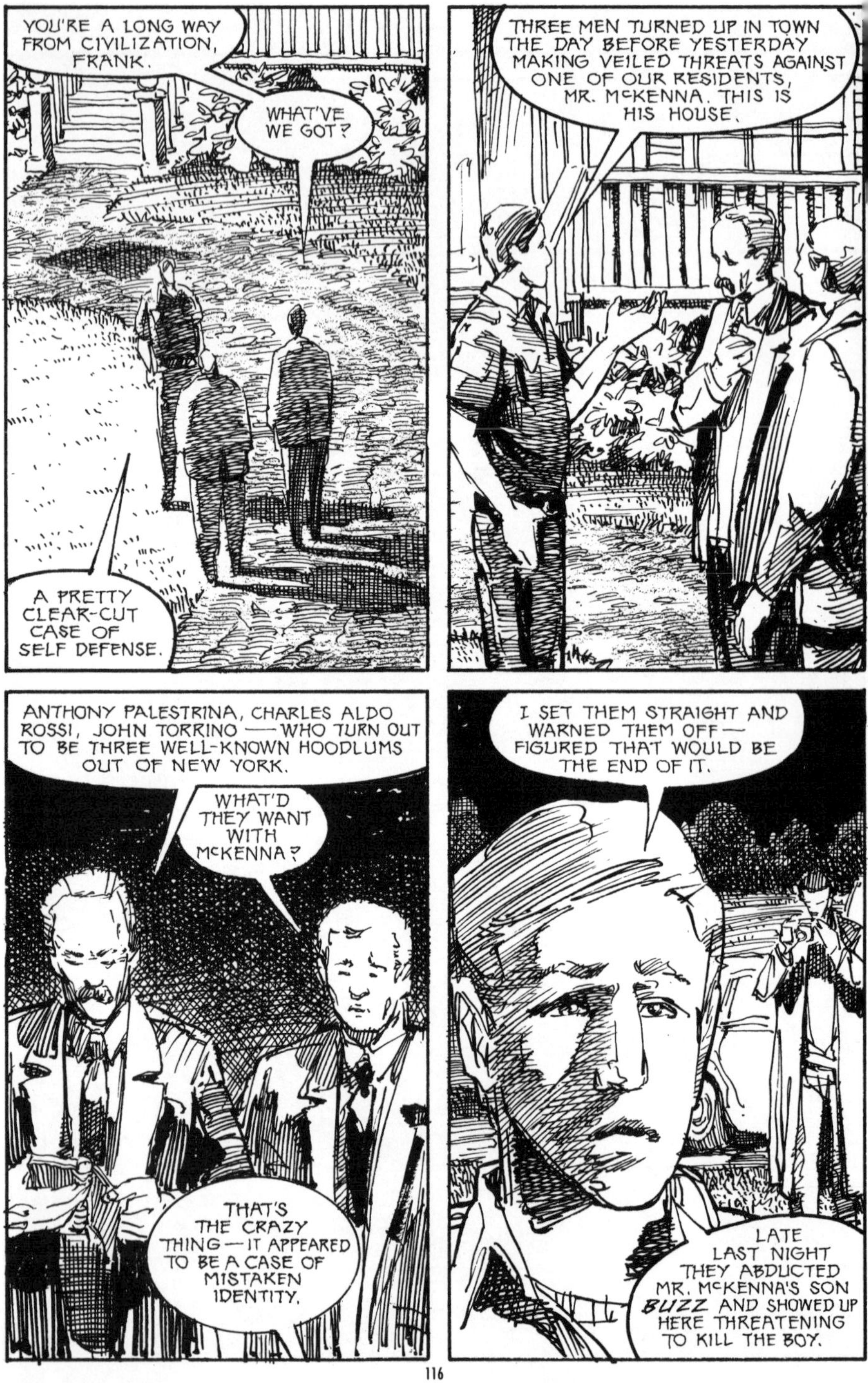
YOU'RE A LONG WAY FROM CIVILIZATION, FRANK.
WHAT'VE WE GOT?
A PRETTY CLEAR-CUT CASE OF SELF DEFENSE.
THREE MEN TURNED UP IN TOWN THE DAY BEFORE YESTERDAY MAKING VEILED THREATS AGAINST ONE OF OUR RESIDENTS, MR. McKENNA. THIS IS HIS HOUSE.
ANTHONY PALESTRINA, CHARLES ALDO ROSSI, JOHN TORRINO — WHO TURN OUT TO BE THREE WELL-KNOWN HOODLUMS OUT OF NEW YORK.
WHAT'D THEY WANT WITH McKENNA?
THAT'S THE CRAZY THING — IT APPEARED TO BE A CASE OF MISTAKEN IDENTITY.
I SET THEM STRAIGHT AND WARNED THEM OFF — FIGURED THAT WOULD BE THE END OF IT.
LATE LAST NIGHT THEY ABDUCTED MR. McKENNA'S SON BUZZ AND SHOWED UP HERE THREATENING TO KILL THE BOY.

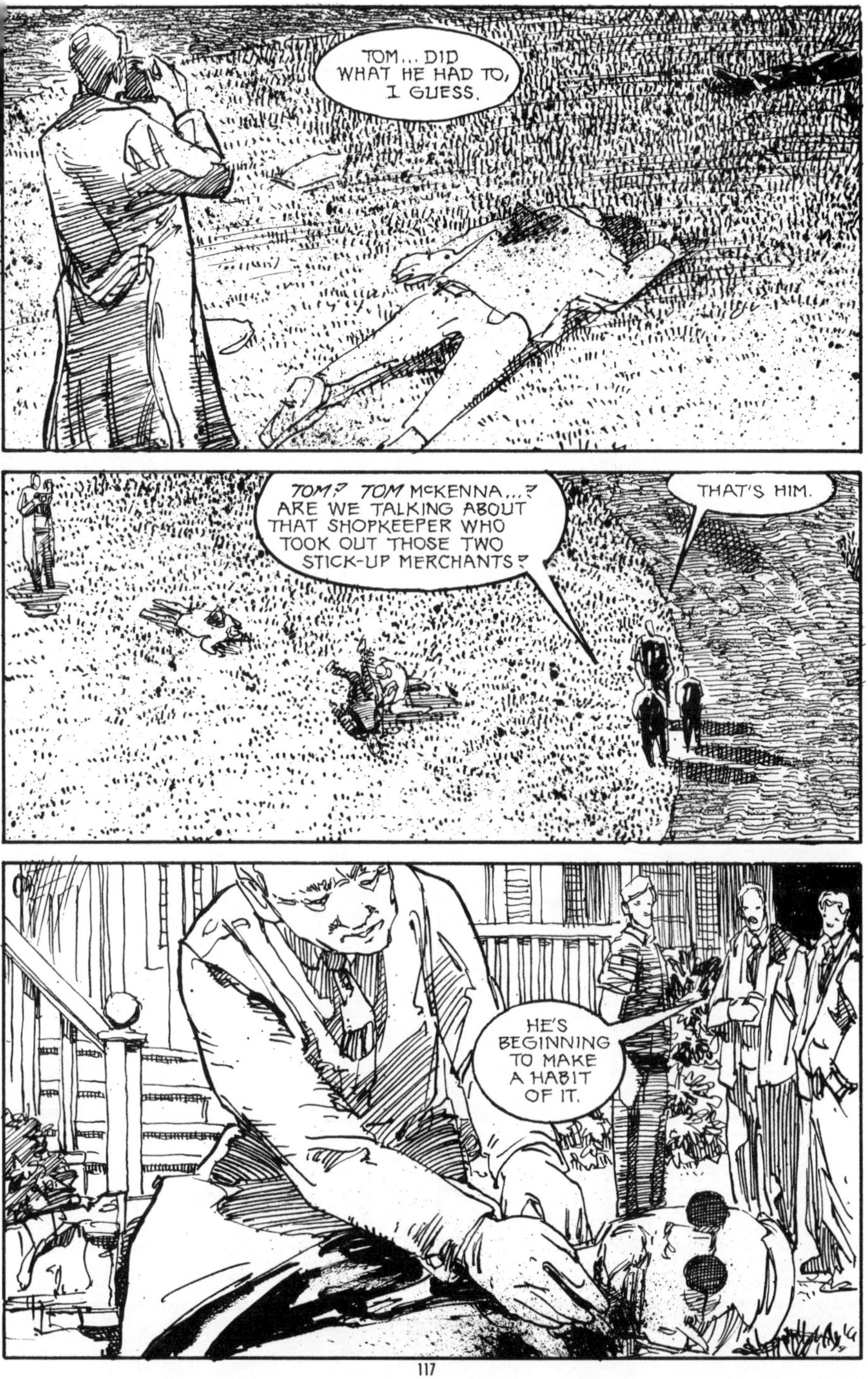
TOM... DID WHAT HE HAD TO, I GUESS.
TOM? TOM McKENNA...? ARE WE TALKING ABOUT THAT SHOPKEEPER WHO TOOK OUT THOSE TWO STICK-UP MERCHANTS?
THAT'S HIM.
HE'S BEGINNING TO MAKE A HABIT OF IT.

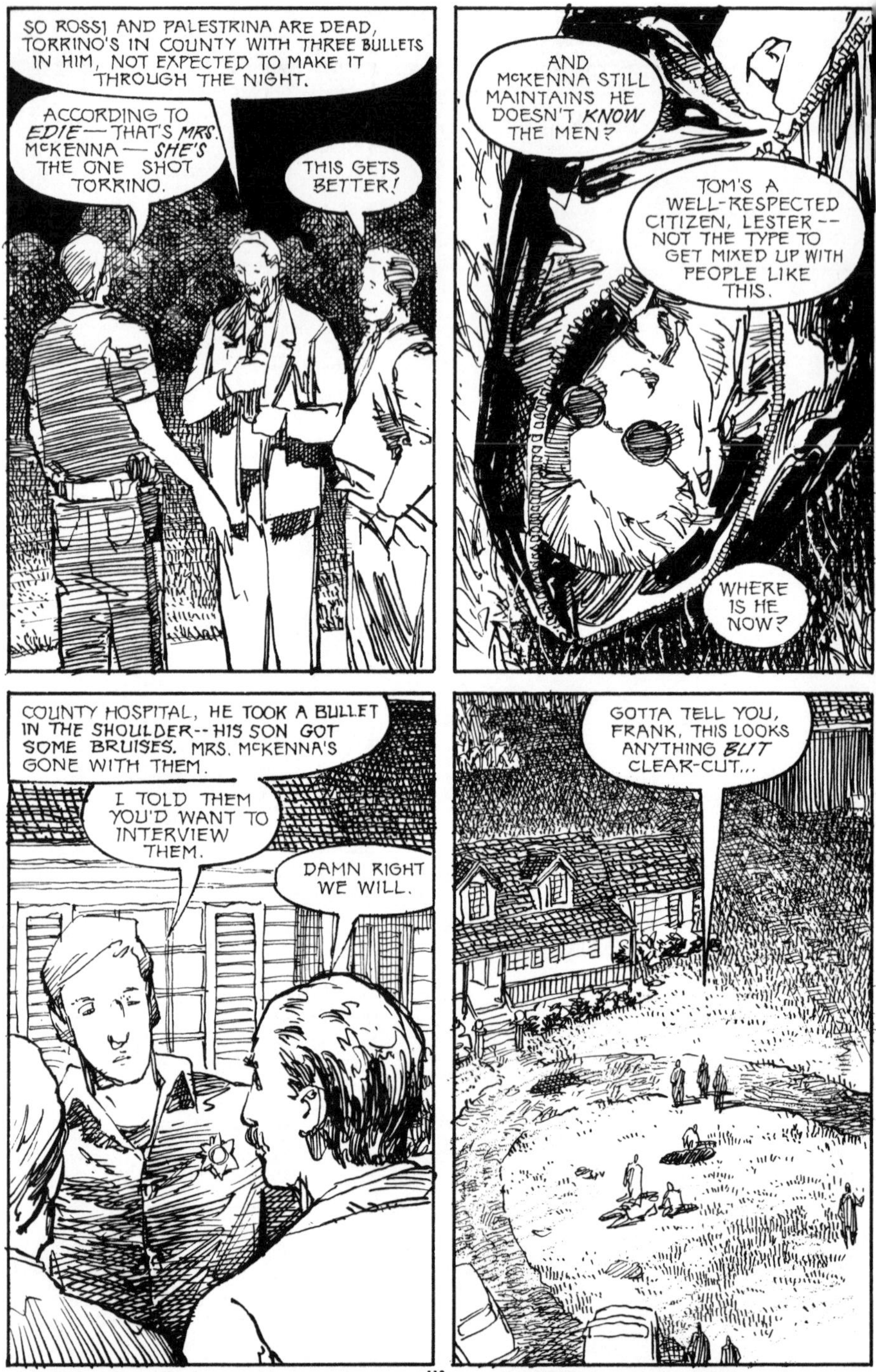
SO ROSSI AND PALESTRINA ARE DEAD, TORRINO'S IN COUNTY WITH THREE BULLETS IN HIM, NOT EXPECTED TO MAKE IT THROUGH THE NIGHT.
ACCORDING TO EDIE — THAT'S MRS. McKENNA — SHE'S THE ONE SHOT TORRINO.
THIS GETS BETTER!
AND McKENNA STILL MAINTAINS HE DOESN'T KNOW THE MEN?
TOM'S A WELL-RESPECTED CITIZEN, LESTER -- NOT THE TYPE TO GET MIXED UP WITH PEOPLE LIKE THIS.
WHERE IS HE NOW?
COUNTY HOSPITAL, HE TOOK A BULLET IN THE SHOULDER -- HIS SON GOT SOME BRUISES. MRS. McKENNA'S GONE WITH THEM.
I TOLD THEM YOU'D WANT TO INTERVIEW THEM.
DAMN RIGHT WE WILL.
GOTTA TELL YOU, FRANK, THIS LOOKS ANYTHING BUT CLEAR-CUT...

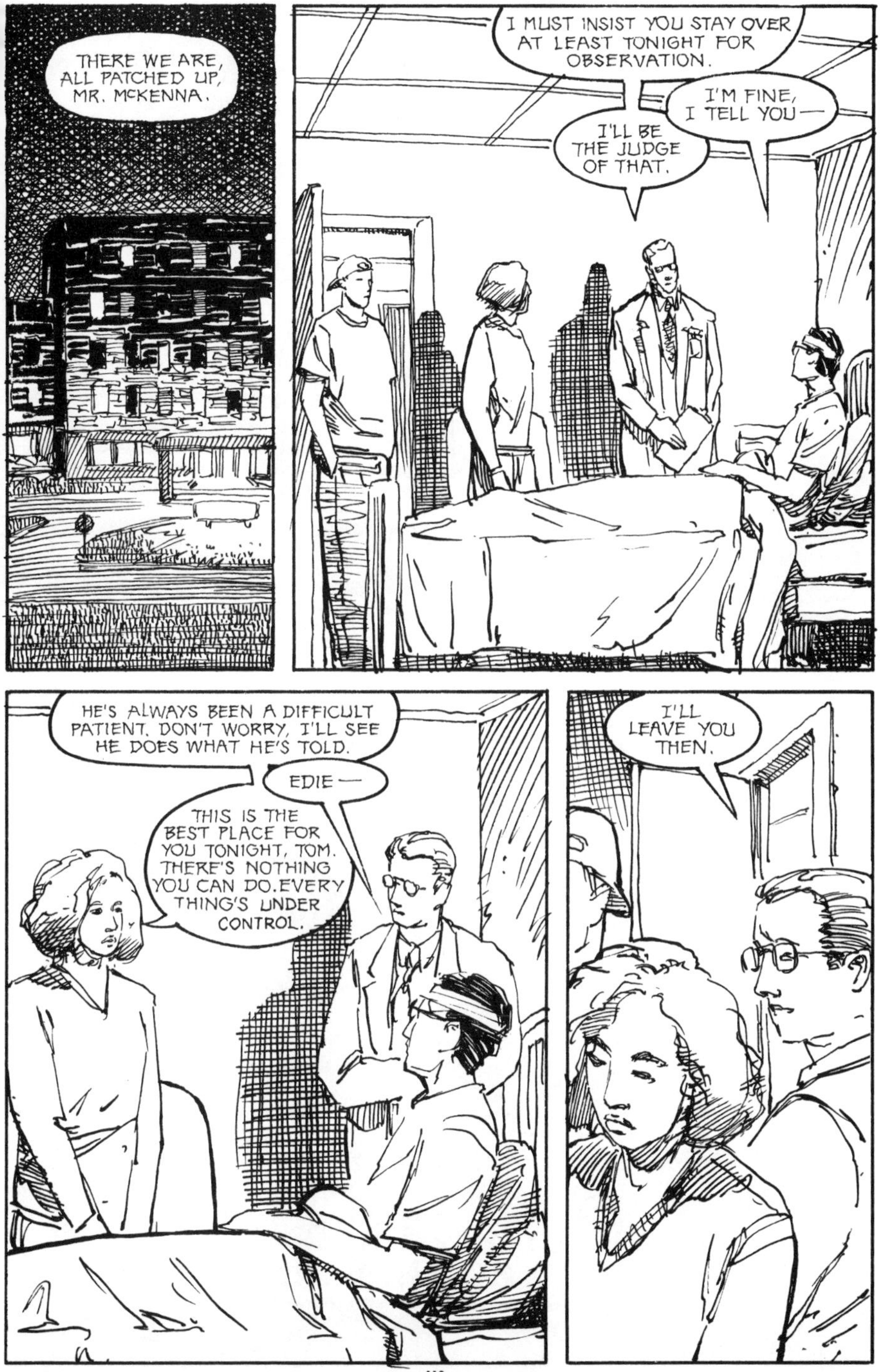
THERE WE ARE, ALL PATCHED UP, MR. MCKENNA.
I MUST INSIST YOU STAY OVER AT LEAST TONIGHT FOR OBSERVATION.
I'M FINE, I TELL YOU—
I'LL BE THE JUDGE OF THAT.
HE'S ALWAYS BEEN A DIFFICULT PATIENT. DON'T WORRY, I'LL SEE HE DOES WHAT HE'S TOLD.
EDIE—
THIS IS THE BEST PLACE FOR YOU TONIGHT, TOM. THERE'S NOTHING YOU CAN DO. EVERY THING'S UNDER CONTROL.
I'LL LEAVE YOU THEN.

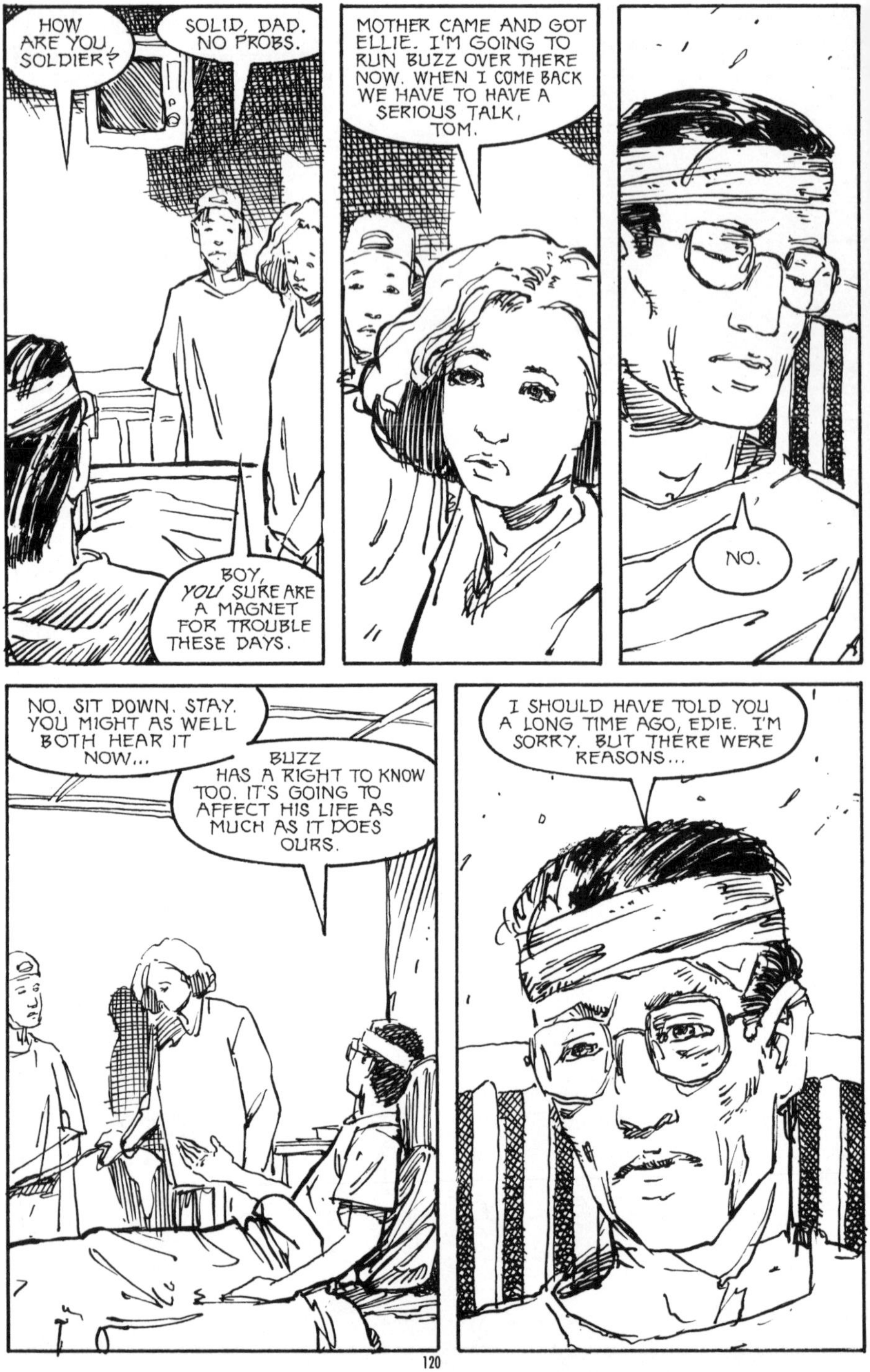
HOW ARE YOU, SOLDIER?
SOLID, DAD. NO PROBS.
BOY, *YOU* SURE ARE A MAGNET FOR TROUBLE THESE DAYS.
MOTHER CAME AND GOT ELLIE. I'M GOING TO RUN BUZZ OVER THERE NOW. WHEN I COME BACK WE HAVE TO HAVE A SERIOUS TALK, TOM.
NO.
NO, SIT DOWN. STAY. YOU MIGHT AS WELL BOTH HEAR IT NOW...
BUZZ HAS A RIGHT TO KNOW TOO. IT'S GOING TO AFFECT HIS LIFE AS MUCH AS IT DOES OURS.
I SHOULD HAVE TOLD YOU A LONG TIME AGO, EDIE. I'M SORRY. BUT THERE WERE REASONS...

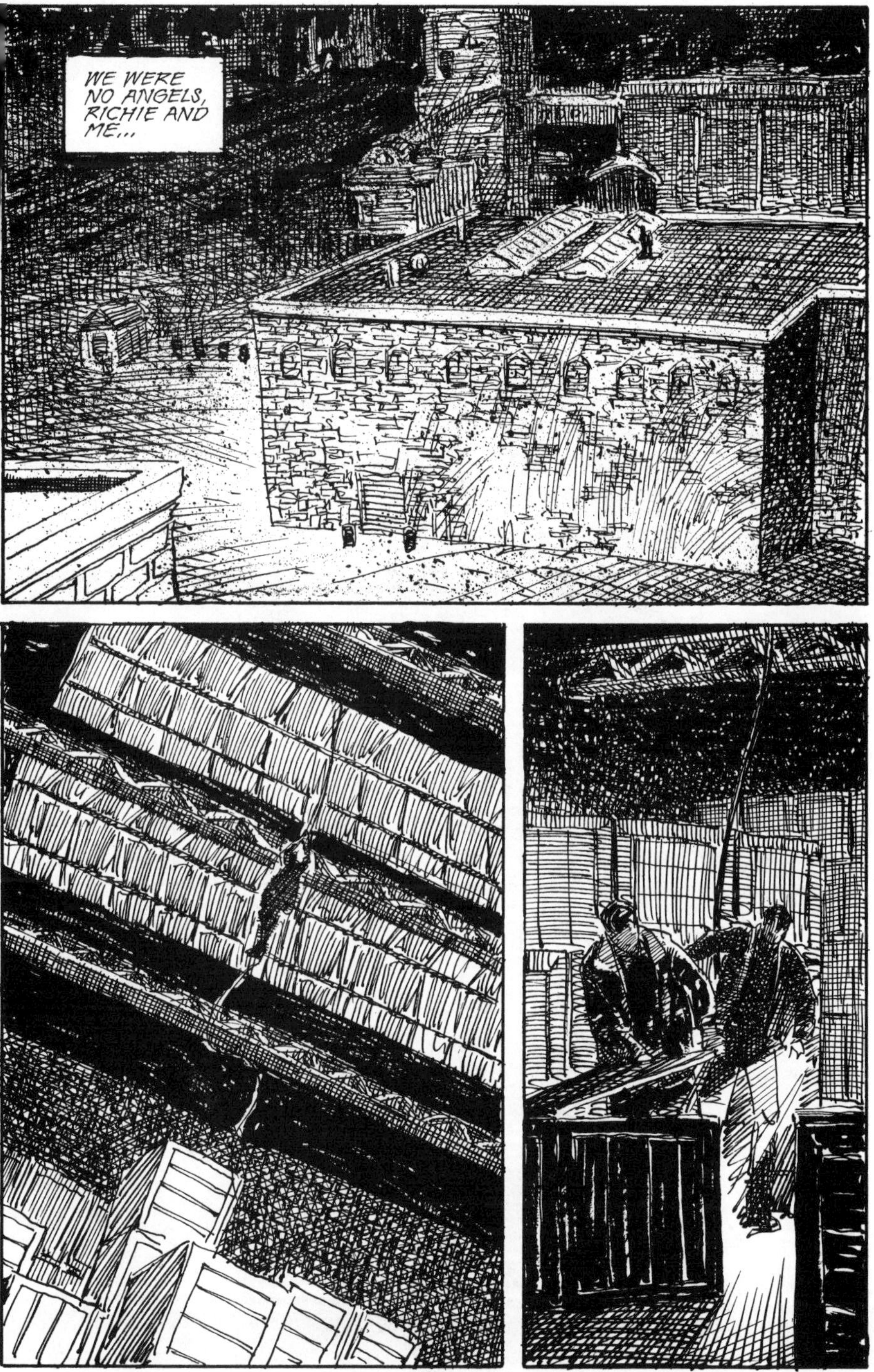
WE WERE NO ANGELS, RICHIE AND ME...

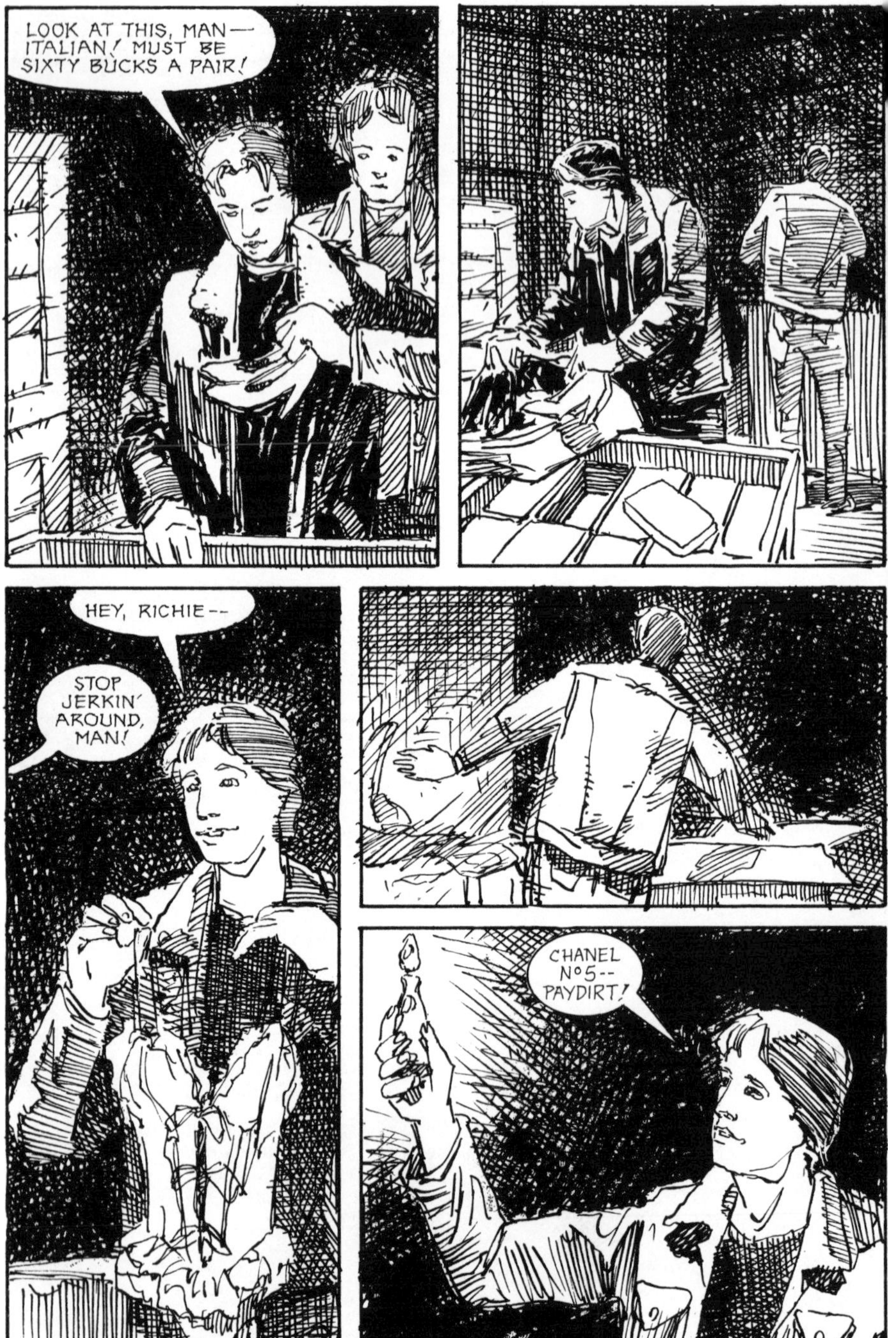
LOOK AT THIS, MAN— ITALIAN! MUST BE SIXTY BUCKS A PAIR!
HEY, RICHIE--
STOP JERKIN' AROUND, MAN!
CHANEL Nº5-- PAYDIRT!

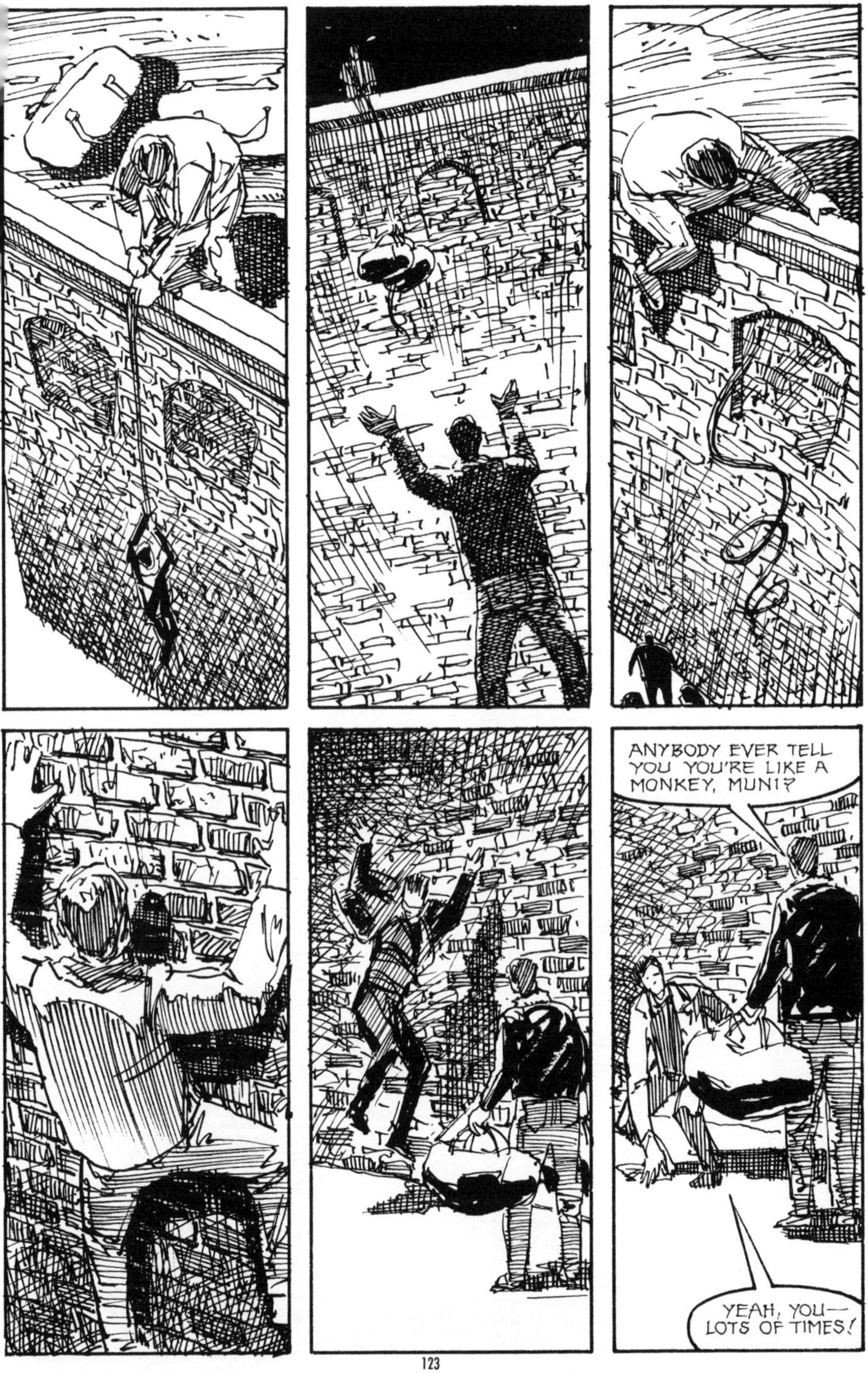
ANYBODY EVER TELL YOU YOU'RE LIKE A MONKEY, MUNI?
YEAH, YOU— LOTS OF TIMES!

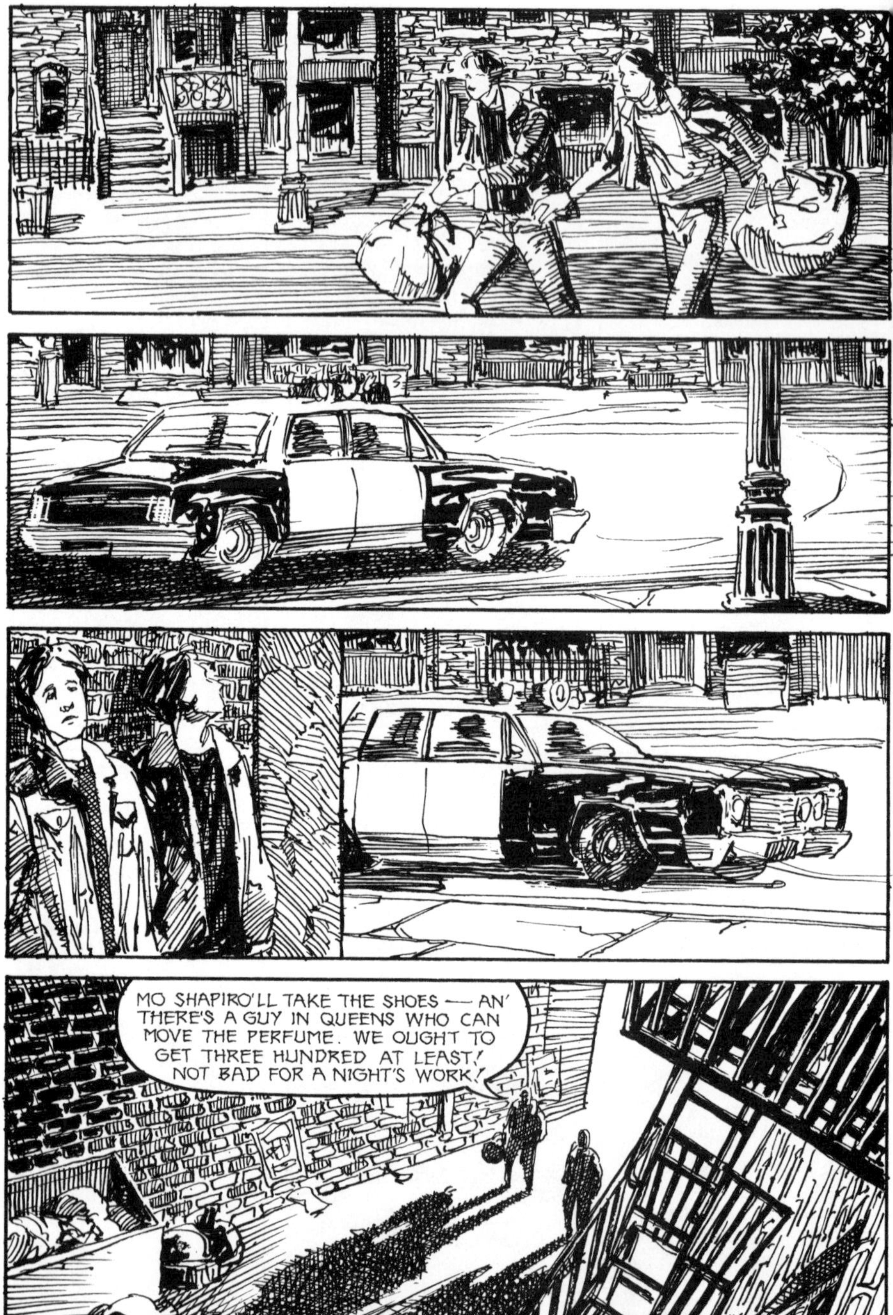
MO SHAPIRO'LL TAKE THE SHOES — AN' THERE'S A GUY IN QUEENS WHO CAN MOVE THE PERFUME. WE OUGHT TO GET THREE HUNDRED AT LEAST! NOT BAD FOR A NIGHT'S WORK!

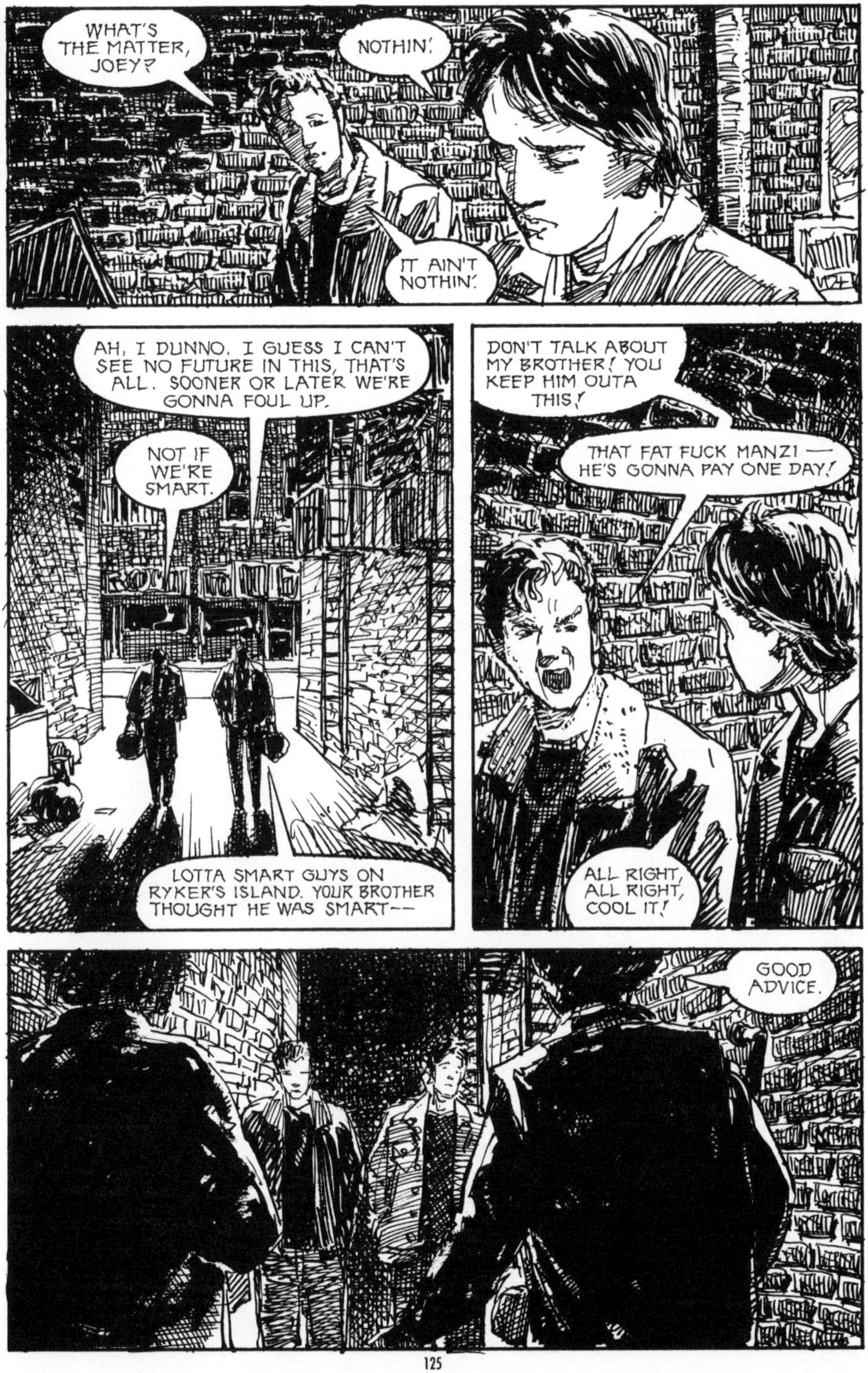
WHAT'S THE MATTER, JOEY?
NOTHIN'.
IT AIN'T NOTHIN'.
AH, I DUNNO. I GUESS I CAN'T SEE NO FUTURE IN THIS, THAT'S ALL. SOONER OR LATER WE'RE GONNA FOUL UP.
NOT IF WE'RE SMART.
LOTTA SMART GUYS ON RYKER'S ISLAND. YOUR BROTHER THOUGHT HE WAS SMART--
DON'T TALK ABOUT MY BROTHER! YOU KEEP HIM OUTA THIS!
THAT FAT FUCK MANZI — HE'S GONNA PAY ONE DAY!
ALL RIGHT, ALL RIGHT, COOL IT!
GOOD ADVICE.

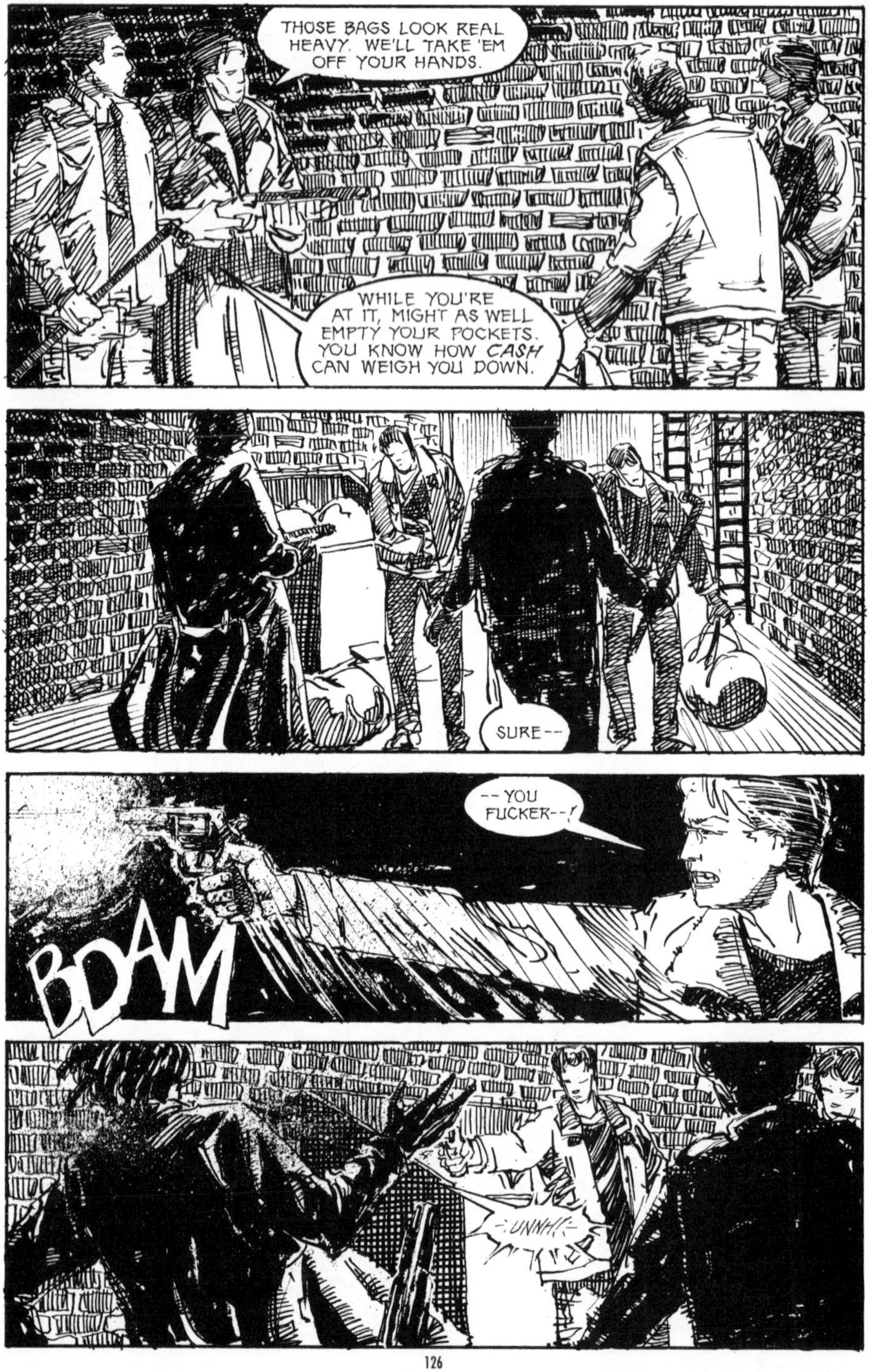
THOSE BAGS LOOK REAL HEAVY. WE'LL TAKE 'EM OFF YOUR HANDS.
WHILE YOU'RE AT IT, MIGHT AS WELL EMPTY YOUR POCKETS. YOU KNOW HOW CASH CAN WEIGH YOU DOWN.
SURE--
--YOU FUCKER--!
BDAM
UNNH!

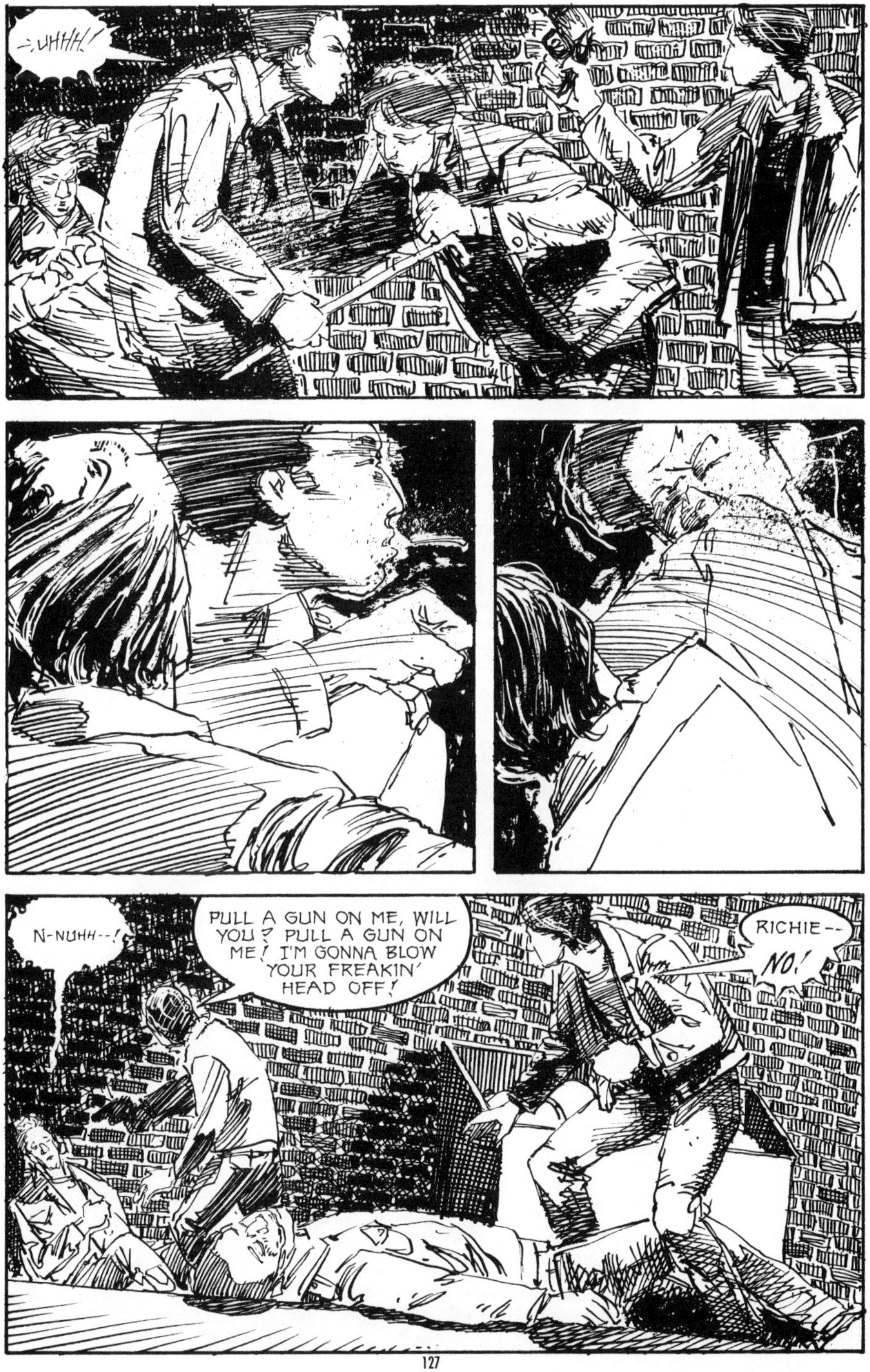
-;UHHH!
N-NUHH--!
PULL A GUN ON ME, WILL YOU? PULL A GUN ON ME! I'M GONNA BLOW YOUR FREAKIN' HEAD OFF!
RICHIE-- NO!

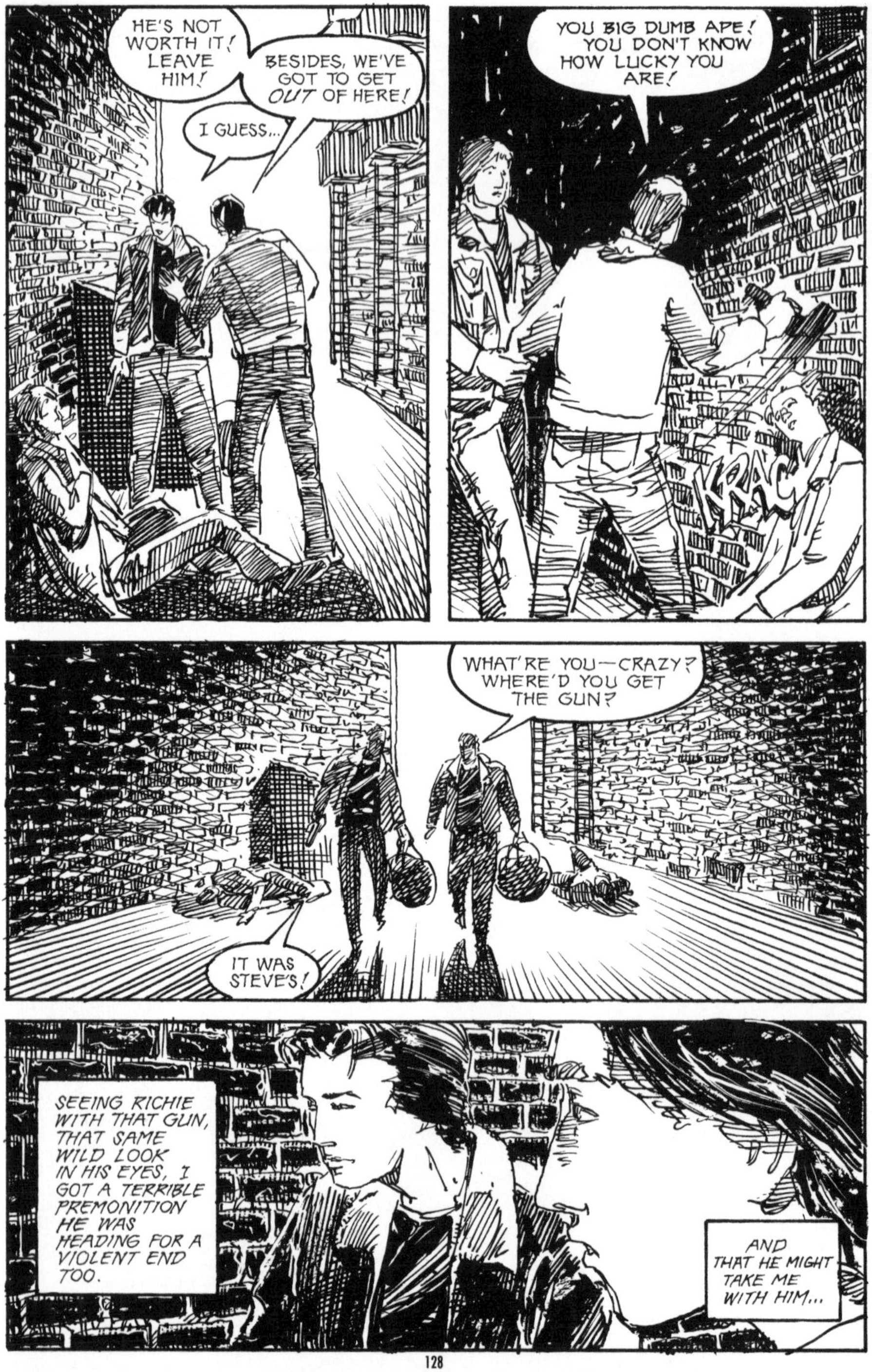
HE'S NOT WORTH IT! LEAVE HIM!
BESIDES, WE'VE GOT TO GET OUT OF HERE!
I GUESS...
YOU BIG DUMB APE! YOU DON'T KNOW HOW LUCKY YOU ARE!
KRAC
WHAT'RE YOU—CRAZY? WHERE'D YOU GET THE GUN?
IT WAS STEVE'S!
SEEING RICHIE WITH THAT GUN, THAT SAME WILD LOOK IN HIS EYES, I GOT A TERRIBLE PREMONITION HE WAS HEADING FOR A VIOLENT END TOO.
AND THAT HE MIGHT TAKE ME WITH HIM...

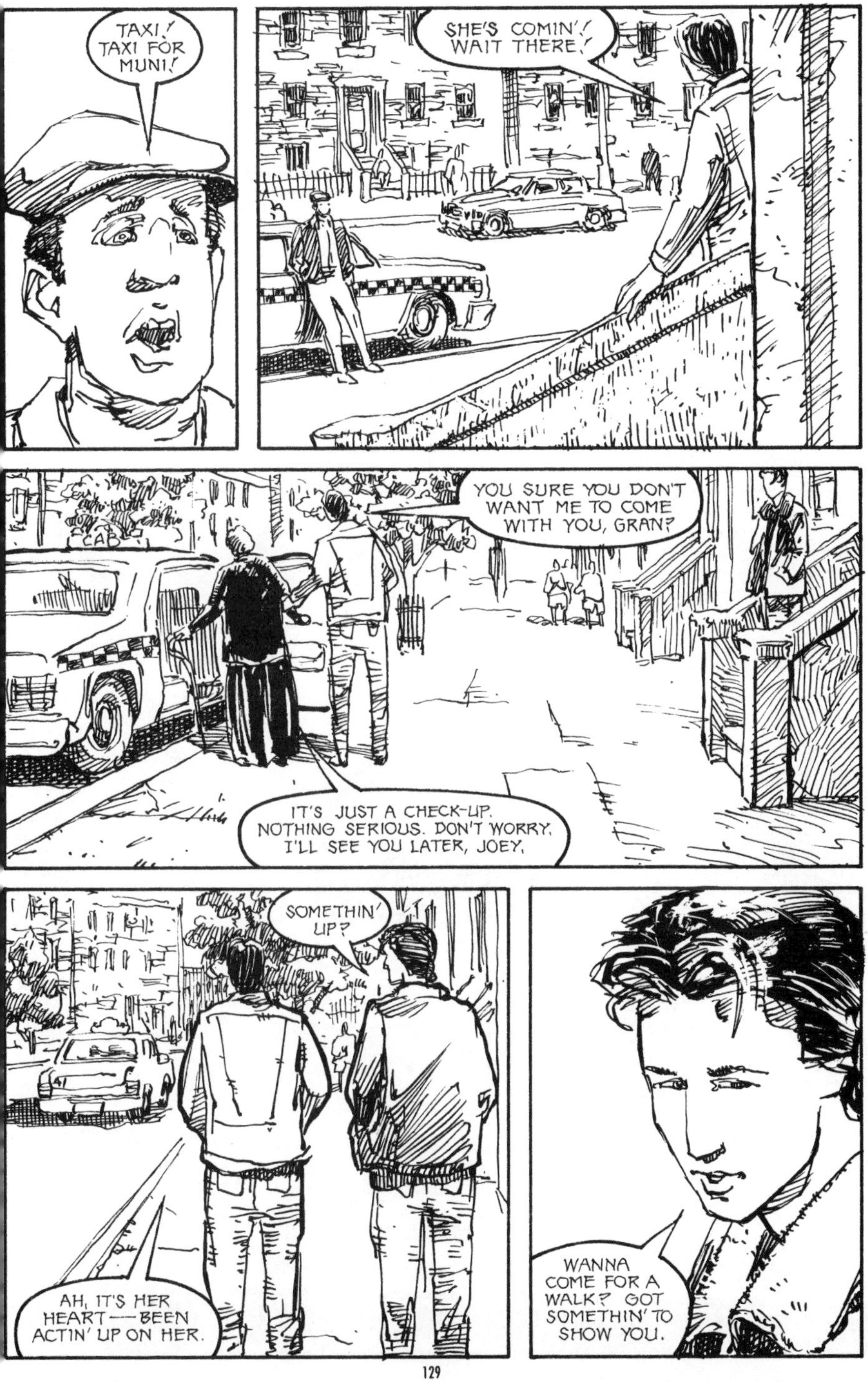
TAXI! TAXI FOR MUNI!
SHE'S COMIN'! WAIT THERE!
YOU SURE YOU DON'T WANT ME TO COME WITH YOU, GRAN?
IT'S JUST A CHECK-UP. NOTHING SERIOUS. DON'T WORRY. I'LL SEE YOU LATER, JOEY.
SOMETHIN' UP?
AH, IT'S HER HEART——BEEN ACTIN' UP ON HER.
WANNA COME FOR A WALK? GOT SOMETHIN' TO SHOW YOU.

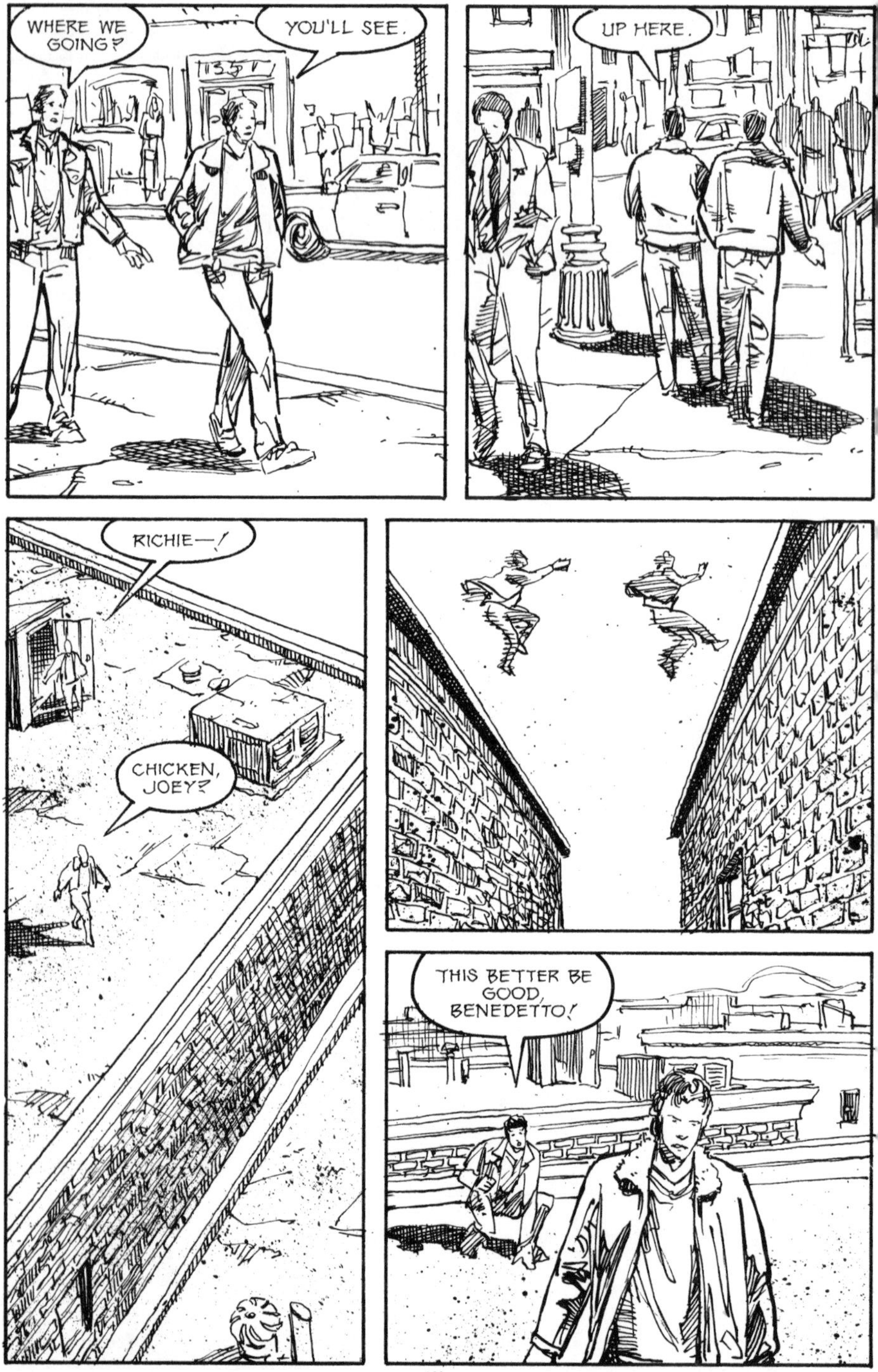
WHERE WE GOING?
YOU'LL SEE.
UP HERE.
RICHIE—!
CHICKEN, JOEY?
THIS BETTER BE GOOD, BENEDETTO!

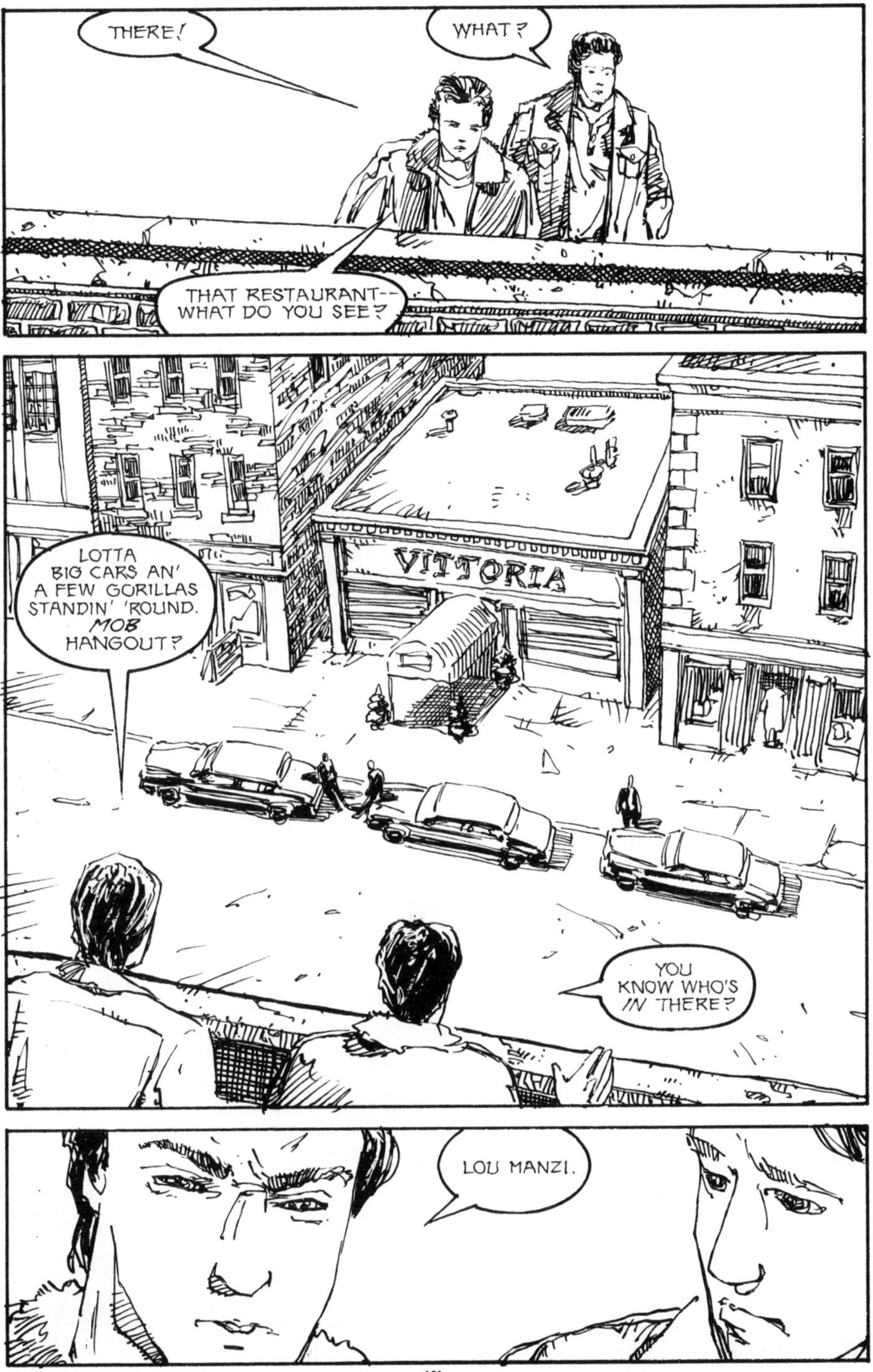
THERE!
WHAT?
THAT RESTAURANT-- WHAT DO YOU SEE?
VITTORIA
LOTTA BIG CARS AN' A FEW GORILLAS STANDIN' 'ROUND. MOB HANGOUT?
YOU KNOW WHO'S IN THERE?
LOU MANZI.

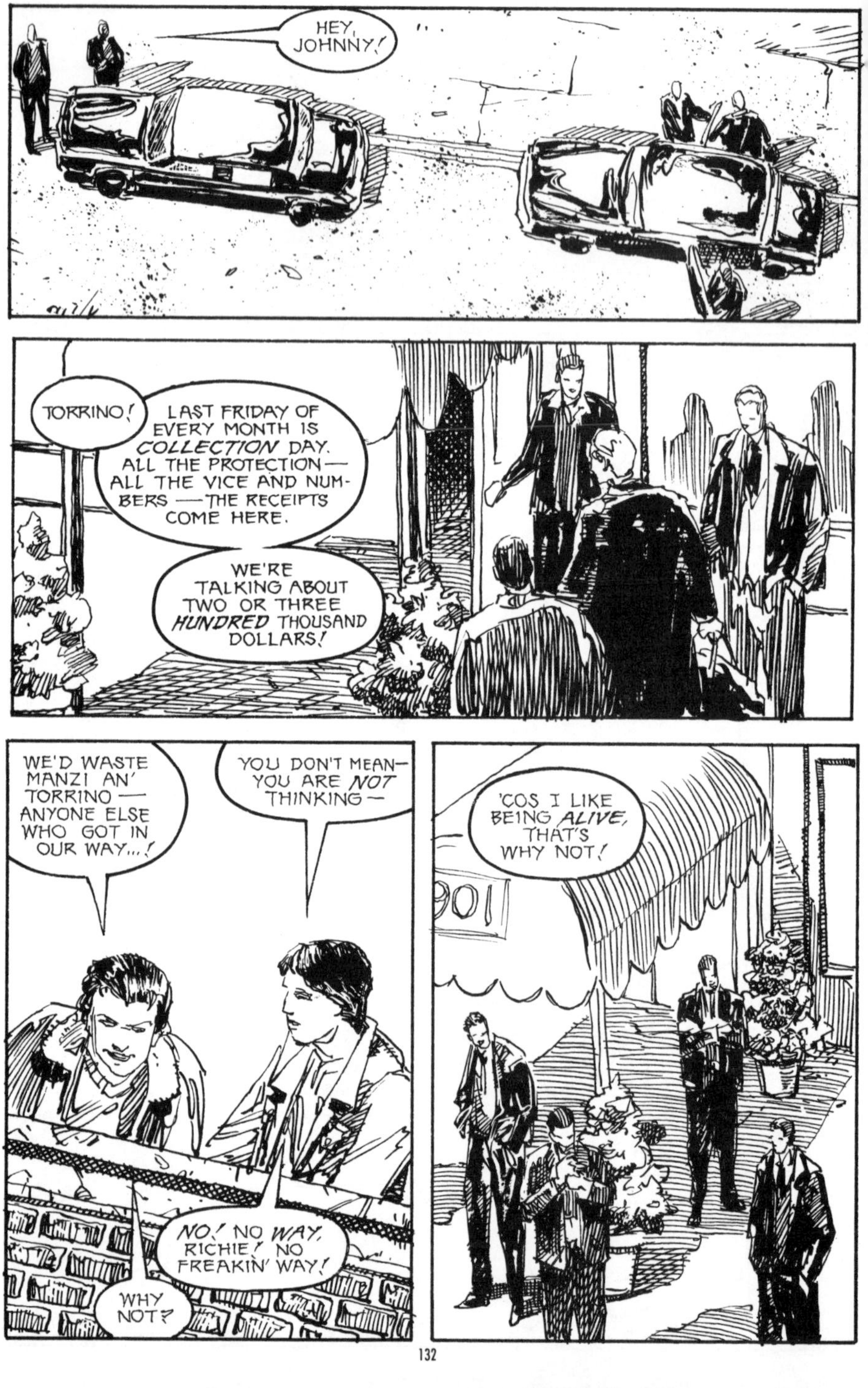
HEY, JOHNNY!
TORRINO!
LAST FRIDAY OF EVERY MONTH IS *COLLECTION* DAY. ALL THE PROTECTION— ALL THE VICE AND NUMBERS —THE RECEIPTS COME HERE.
WE'RE TALKING ABOUT TWO OR THREE *HUNDRED* THOUSAND DOLLARS!
WE'D WASTE MANZI AN' TORRINO — ANYONE ELSE WHO GOT IN OUR WAY...!
YOU DON'T MEAN— YOU ARE *NOT* THINKING—
NO! NO *WAY,* RICHIE! NO FREAKIN' WAY!
WHY NOT?
'COS I LIKE BEING *ALIVE,* THAT'S WHY NOT!
901

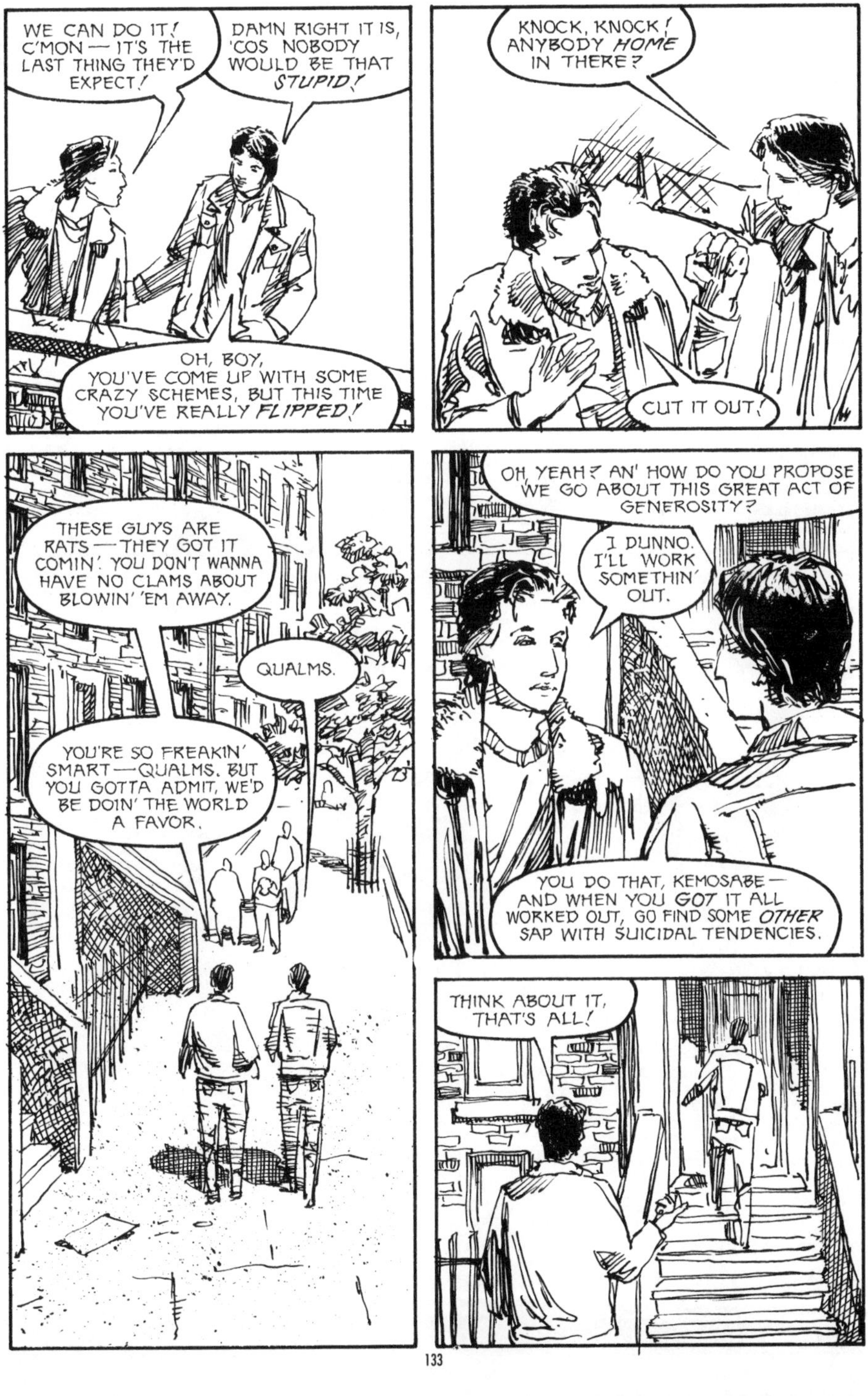
WE CAN DO IT! C'MON — IT'S THE LAST THING THEY'D EXPECT!
DAMN RIGHT IT IS, 'COS NOBODY WOULD BE THAT STUPID!
OH, BOY, YOU'VE COME UP WITH SOME CRAZY SCHEMES, BUT THIS TIME YOU'VE REALLY FLIPPED!
KNOCK, KNOCK! ANYBODY HOME IN THERE?
CUT IT OUT!
THESE GUYS ARE RATS — THEY GOT IT COMIN'. YOU DON'T WANNA HAVE NO CLAMS ABOUT BLOWIN' 'EM AWAY.
QUALMS.
YOU'RE SO FREAKIN' SMART — QUALMS. BUT YOU GOTTA ADMIT, WE'D BE DOIN' THE WORLD A FAVOR.
OH, YEAH? AN' HOW DO YOU PROPOSE WE GO ABOUT THIS GREAT ACT OF GENEROSITY?
I DUNNO. I'LL WORK SOMETHIN' OUT.
YOU DO THAT, KEMOSABE — AND WHEN YOU GOT IT ALL WORKED OUT, GO FIND SOME OTHER SAP WITH SUICIDAL TENDENCIES.
THINK ABOUT IT, THAT'S ALL!

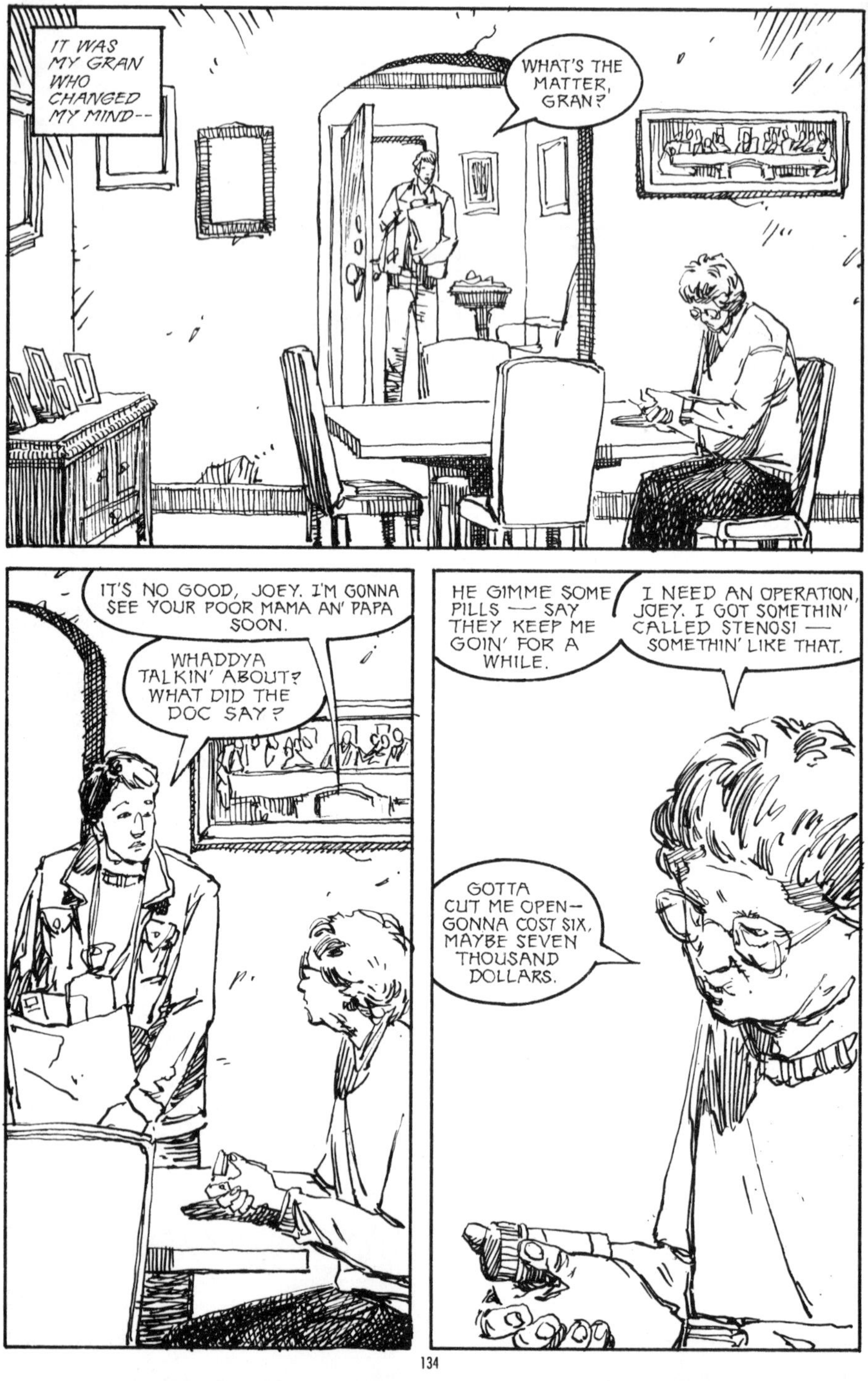
IT WAS MY GRAN WHO CHANGED MY MIND--
WHAT'S THE MATTER, GRAN?
IT'S NO GOOD, JOEY. I'M GONNA SEE YOUR POOR MAMA AN' PAPA SOON.
WHADDYA TALKIN' ABOUT? WHAT DID THE DOC SAY?
HE GIMME SOME PILLS — SAY THEY KEEP ME GOIN' FOR A WHILE.
I NEED AN OPERATION, JOEY. I GOT SOMETHIN' CALLED STENOSI — SOMETHIN' LIKE THAT.
GOTTA CUT ME OPEN-- GONNA COST SIX, MAYBE SEVEN THOUSAND DOLLARS.

DOCTOR SAYS I WAIT TILL I GET ANOTHER ATTACK, IT'S GONNA BE TOO LATE. WHAT CAN I DO? I GOT NO HEALTH INSURANCE.

DON'T WORRY, GRAN, *I'LL* GET THE MONEY.

SIX THOUSAND DOLLARS? WHERE YOU GONNA GET THAT? AND THAT'S NO THE END OF IT. WITH HOSPITAL, WHAT'S IT GONNA BE — TEN — TWENTY, I DUNNO...

I SAID I'D *GET* IT, GRAN.

AH, JOEY, YOU A GOOD BOY. FORGET IT. DON'T WORRY. I'LL BE FINE.

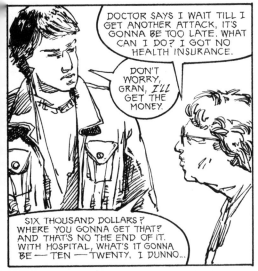

HEY, RICHIE--!

YO!

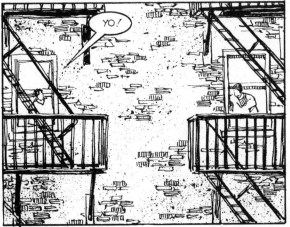

LET'S *TALK*, KEMOSABE.

135

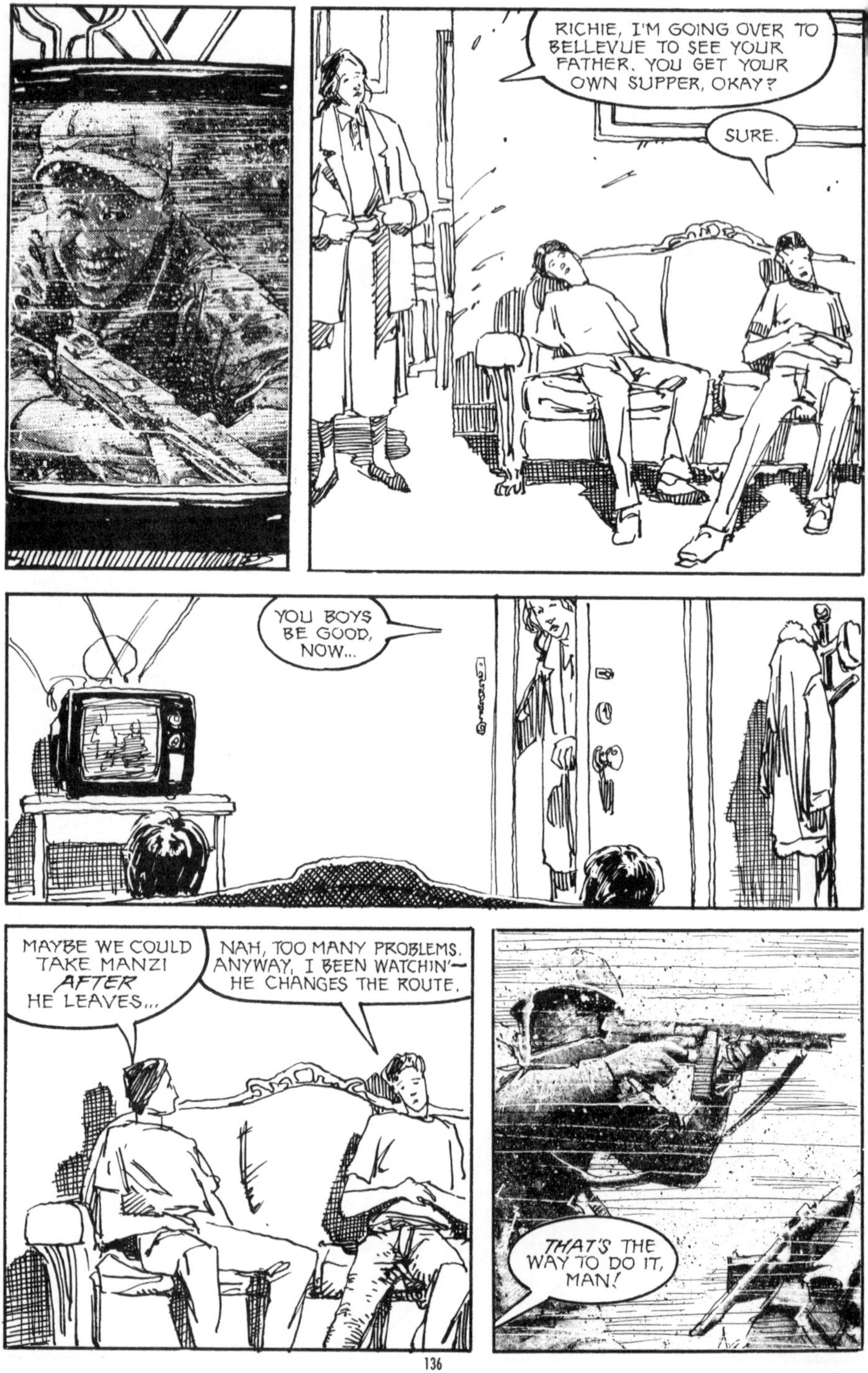
RICHIE, I'M GOING OVER TO BELLEVUE TO SEE YOUR FATHER. YOU GET YOUR OWN SUPPER, OKAY?
SURE.
YOU BOYS BE GOOD, NOW...
MAYBE WE COULD TAKE MANZI *AFTER* HE LEAVES...
NAH, TOO MANY PROBLEMS. ANYWAY, I BEEN WATCHIN'— HE CHANGES THE ROUTE.
THAT'S THE WAY TO DO IT, MAN!

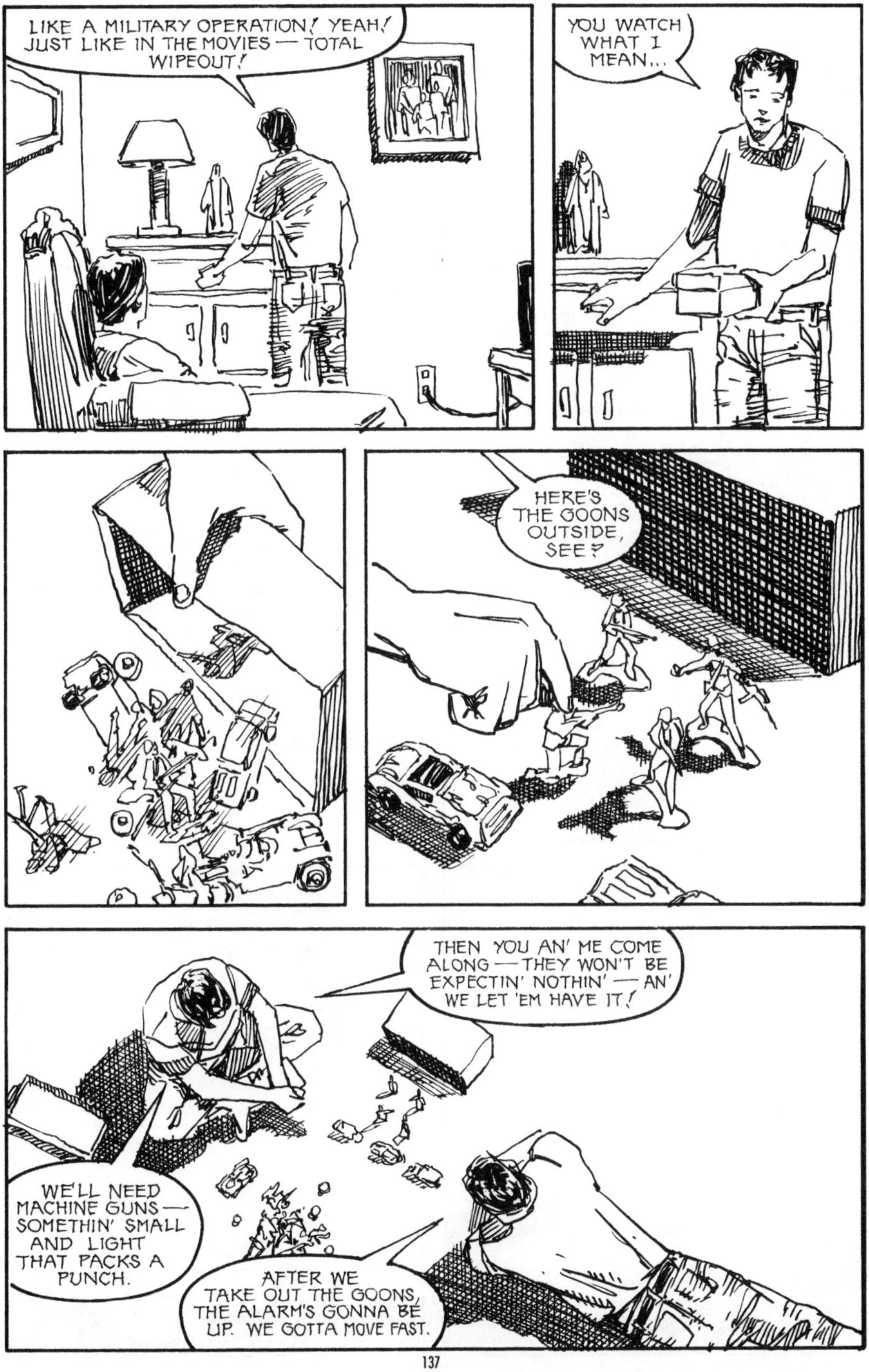
LIKE A MILITARY OPERATION! YEAH! JUST LIKE IN THE MOVIES — TOTAL WIPEOUT!
YOU WATCH WHAT I MEAN...
HERE'S THE GOONS OUTSIDE, SEE?
THEN YOU AN' ME COME ALONG — THEY WON'T BE EXPECTIN' NOTHIN' — AN' WE LET 'EM HAVE IT!
WE'LL NEED MACHINE GUNS — SOMETHIN' SMALL AND LIGHT THAT PACKS A PUNCH.
AFTER WE TAKE OUT THE GOONS, THE ALARM'S GONNA BE UP. WE GOTTA MOVE FAST.

WE NEED SOMETHIN' BIG — LIKE A BAZOOKA!

THAT'D BLOW THE *MONEY* UP TOO, MEATHEAD!

TEAR GAS — THAT'S BETTER. EASIER TO GET HOLD OF, TOO!

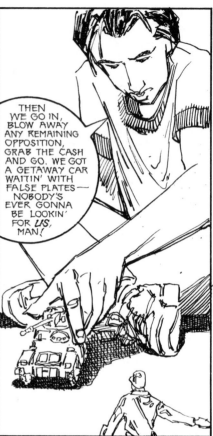

THEN WE GO IN, BLOW AWAY ANY REMAINING OPPOSITION, GRAB THE CASH AND GO. WE GOT A GETAWAY CAR WAITIN' WITH FALSE PLATES — NOBODY'S EVER GONNA BE LOOKIN' FOR *US,* MAN!

SO, ALL WE NEED IS MACHINE GUNS, TEAR GAS AND A HOT CAR.

DREAM ON!

DON'T WORRY, I'LL WORK ON IT.

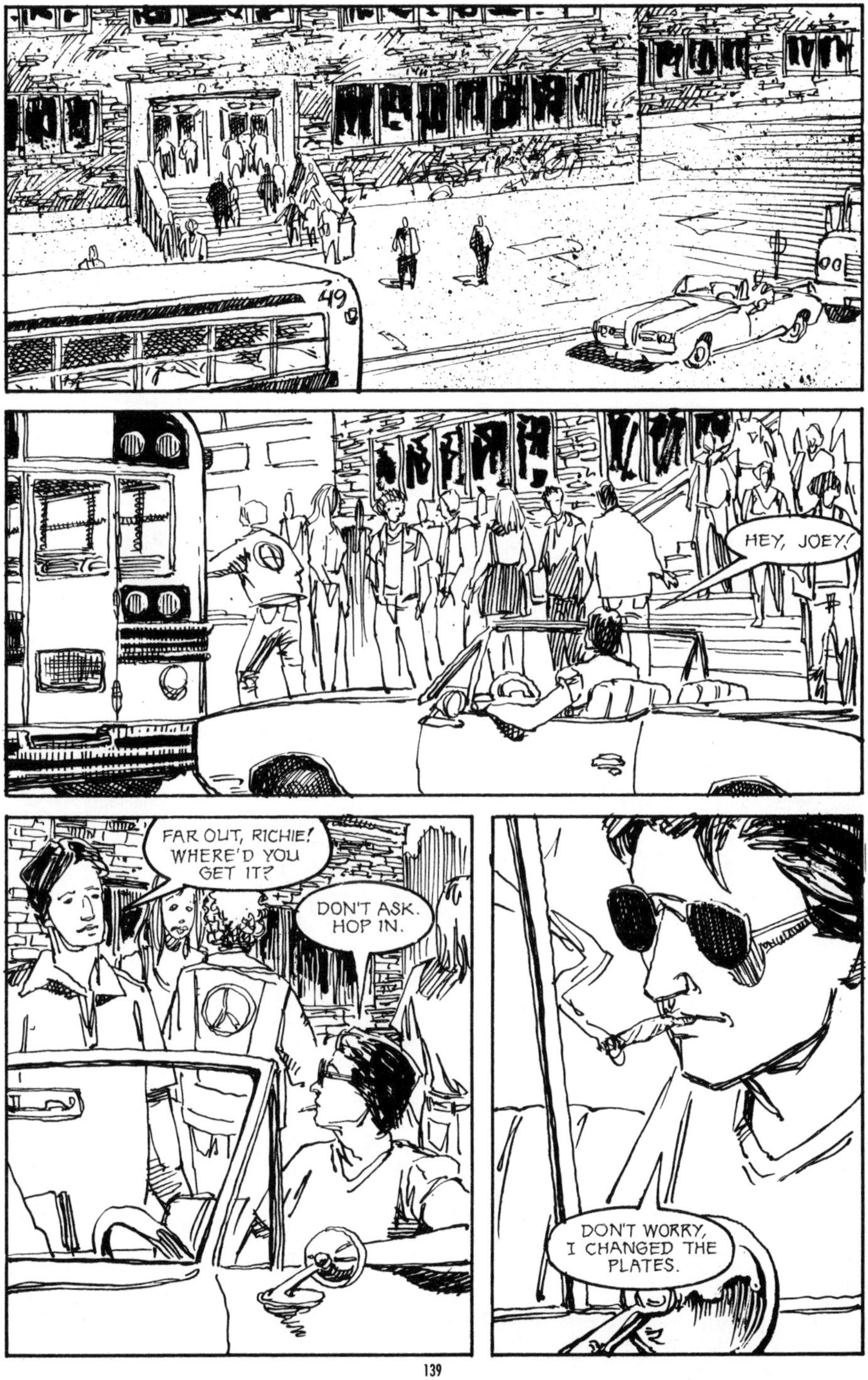
HEY, JOEY!
FAR OUT, RICHIE! WHERE'D YOU GET IT?
DON'T ASK. HOP IN.
DON'T WORRY, I CHANGED THE PLATES.

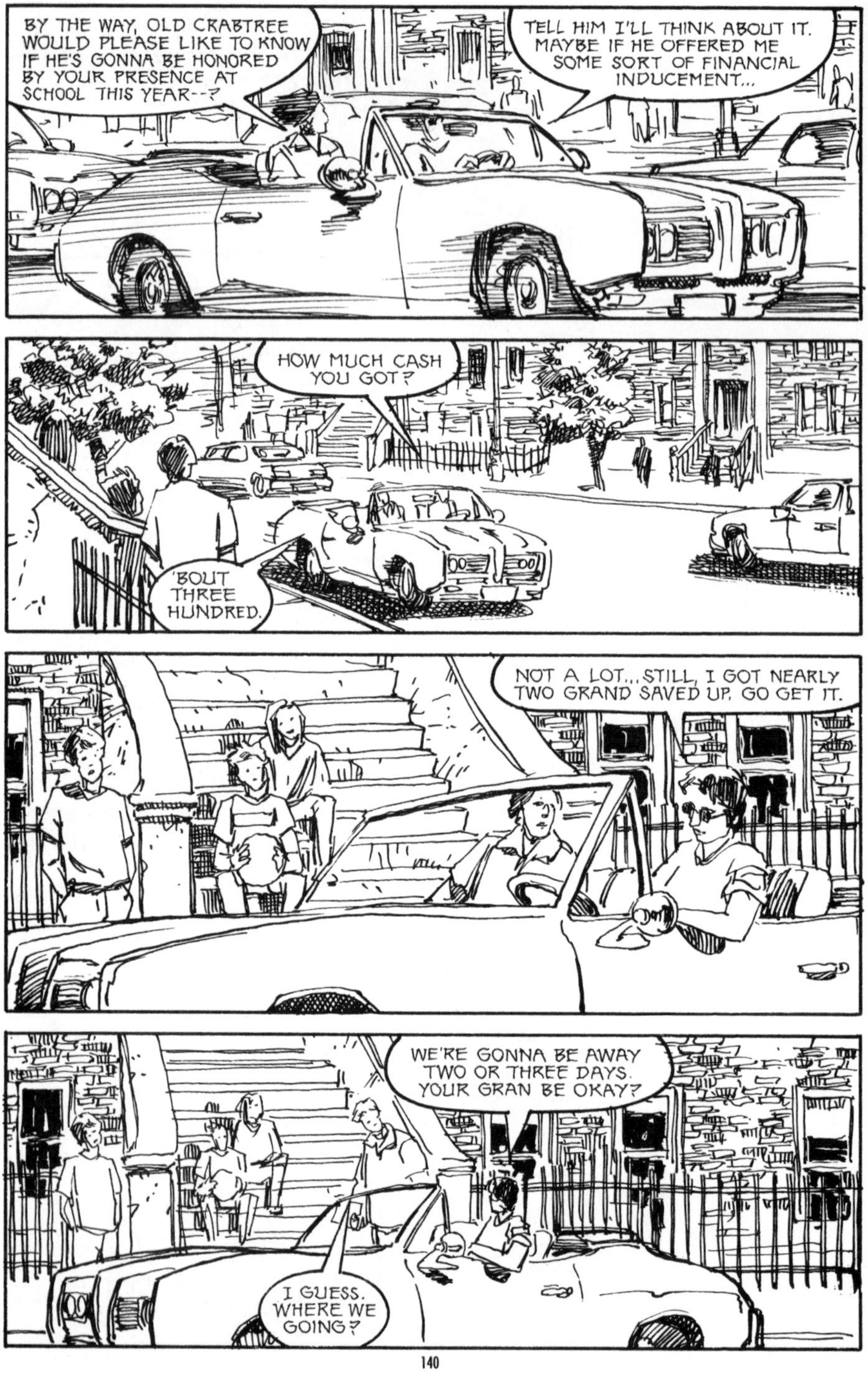
BY THE WAY, OLD CRABTREE WOULD PLEASE LIKE TO KNOW IF HE'S GONNA BE HONORED BY YOUR PRESENCE AT SCHOOL THIS YEAR--?
TELL HIM I'LL THINK ABOUT IT. MAYBE IF HE OFFERED ME SOME SORT OF FINANCIAL INDUCEMENT...
HOW MUCH CASH YOU GOT?
'BOUT THREE HUNDRED.
NOT A LOT... STILL, I GOT NEARLY TWO GRAND SAVED UP. GO GET IT.
WE'RE GONNA BE AWAY TWO OR THREE DAYS. YOUR GRAN BE OKAY?
I GUESS. WHERE WE GOING?

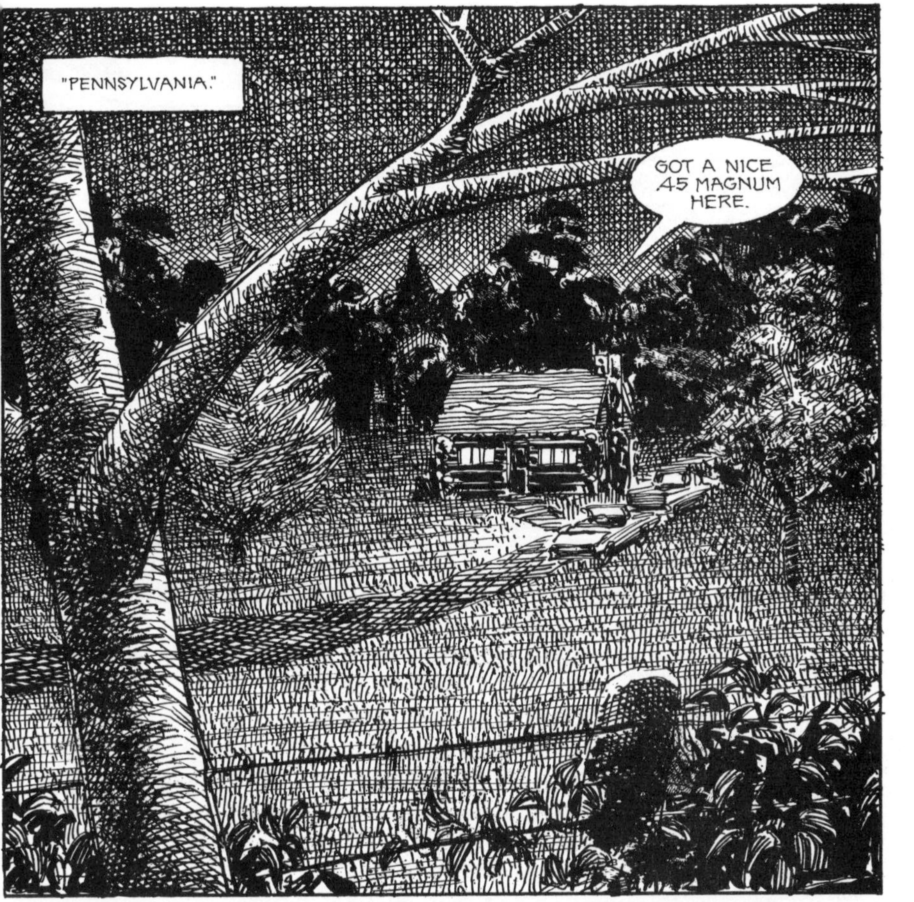
"PENNSYLVANIA."
GOT A NICE .45 MAGNUM HERE.

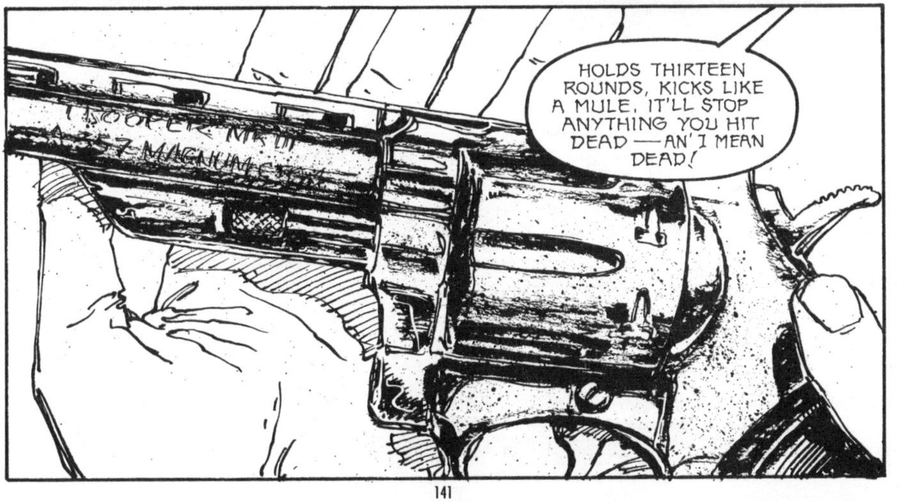
HOLDS THIRTEEN ROUNDS, KICKS LIKE A MULE, IT'LL STOP ANYTHING YOU HIT DEAD — AN' I MEAN DEAD!

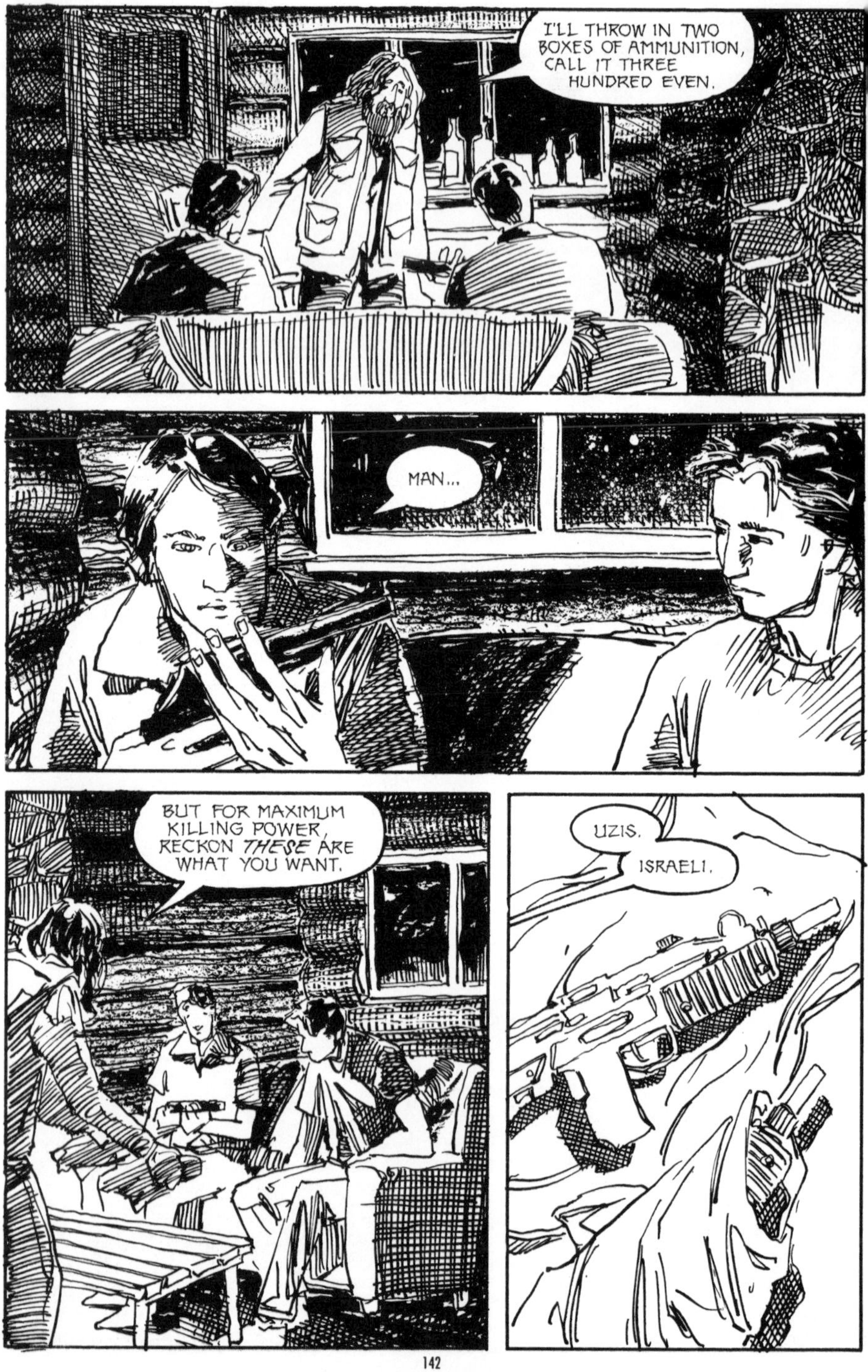
I'LL THROW IN TWO BOXES OF AMMUNITION, CALL IT THREE HUNDRED EVEN.
MAN...
BUT FOR MAXIMUM KILLING POWER, RECKON *THESE* ARE WHAT YOU WANT.
UZIS.
ISRAELI.

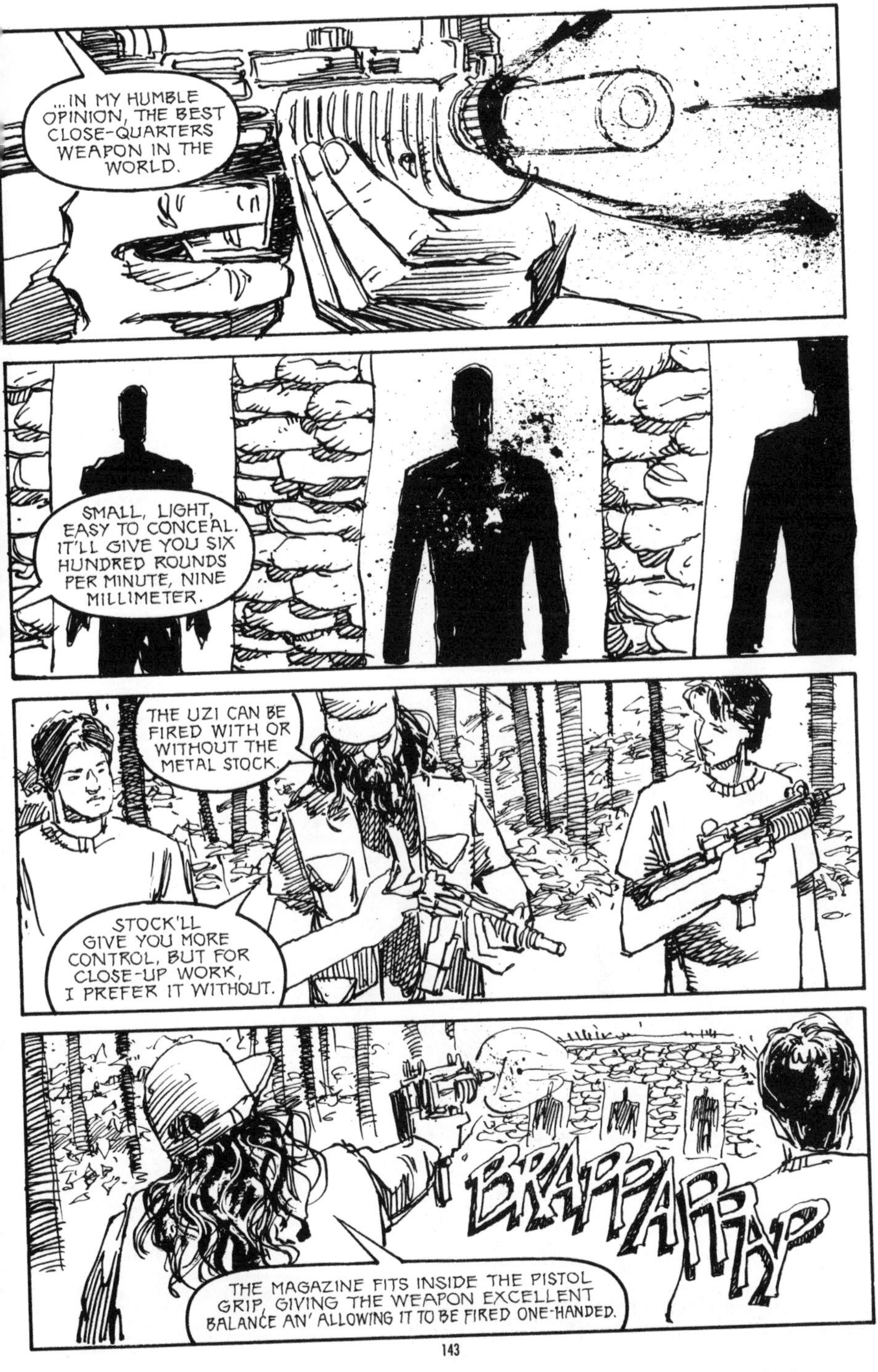
...IN MY HUMBLE OPINION, THE BEST CLOSE-QUARTERS WEAPON IN THE WORLD.
SMALL, LIGHT, EASY TO CONCEAL. IT'LL GIVE YOU SIX HUNDRED ROUNDS PER MINUTE, NINE MILLIMETER.
THE UZI CAN BE FIRED WITH OR WITHOUT THE METAL STOCK.
STOCK'LL GIVE YOU MORE CONTROL, BUT FOR CLOSE-UP WORK, I PREFER IT WITHOUT.
BRAPPAPPAP
THE MAGAZINE FITS INSIDE THE PISTOL GRIP, GIVING THE WEAPON EXCELLENT BALANCE AN' ALLOWING IT TO BE FIRED ONE-HANDED.

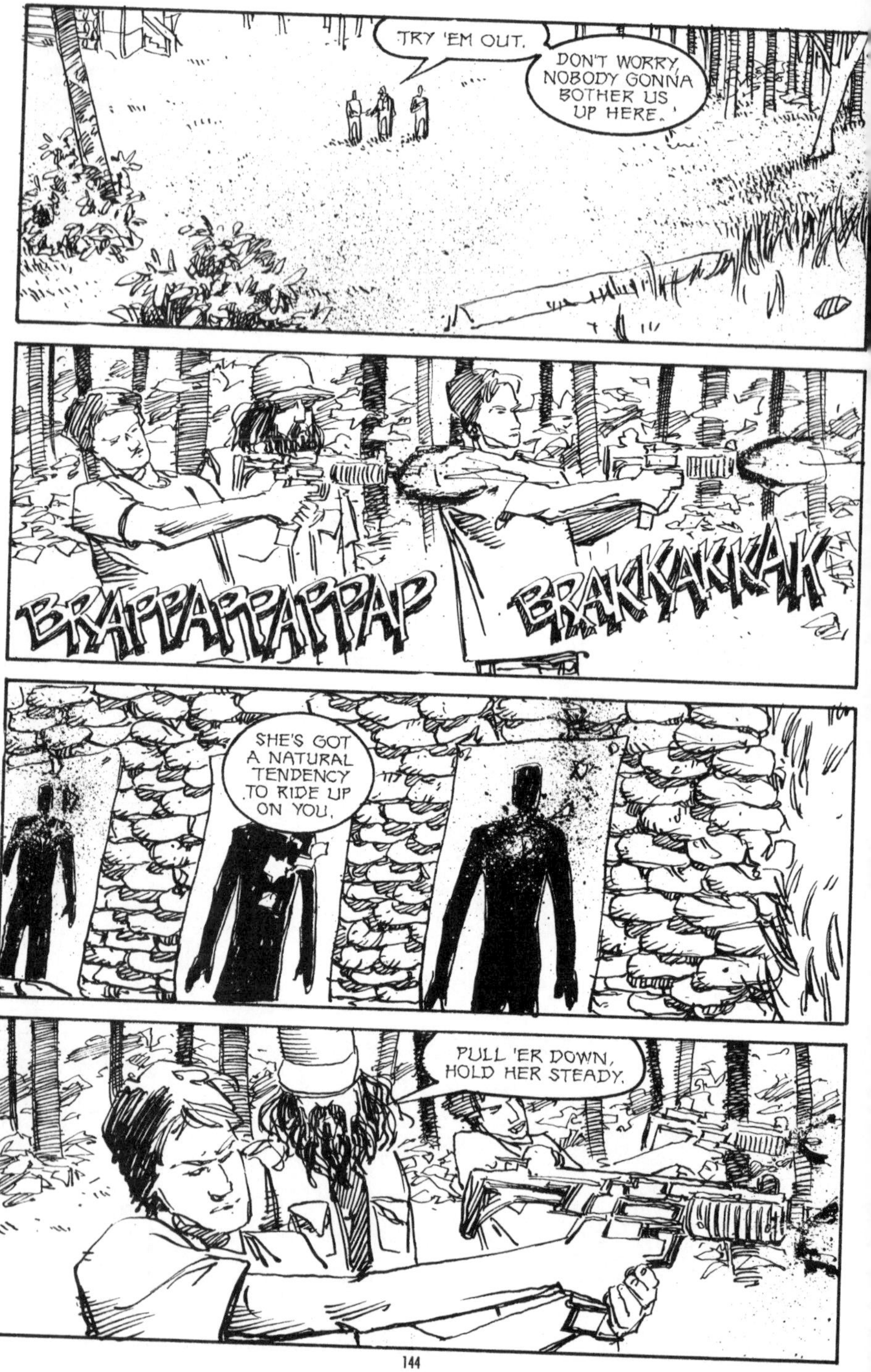
TRY 'EM OUT.
DON'T WORRY, NOBODY GONNA BOTHER US UP HERE.
BRAPPAPPAPPAP
BRAKKAKKAK
SHE'S GOT A NATURAL TENDENCY TO RIDE UP ON YOU.
PULL 'ER DOWN, HOLD HER STEADY.

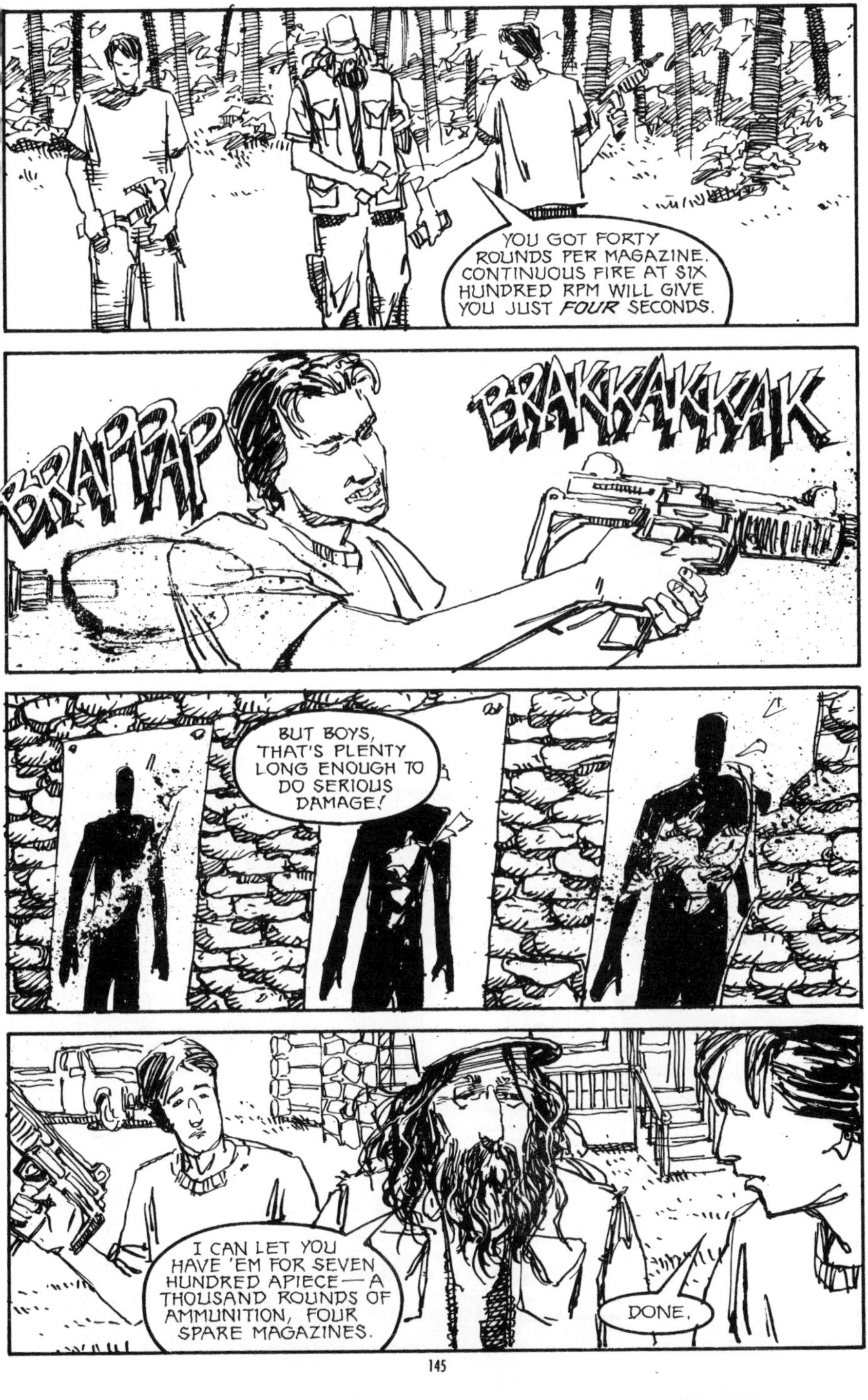
YOU GOT FORTY ROUNDS PER MAGAZINE. CONTINUOUS FIRE AT SIX HUNDRED RPM WILL GIVE YOU JUST *FOUR* SECONDS.
BRAPPAP
BRAKKAKKAK
BUT BOYS, THAT'S PLENTY LONG ENOUGH TO DO SERIOUS DAMAGE!
I CAN LET YOU HAVE 'EM FOR SEVEN HUNDRED APIECE — A THOUSAND ROUNDS OF AMMUNITION, FOUR SPARE MAGAZINES.
DONE.

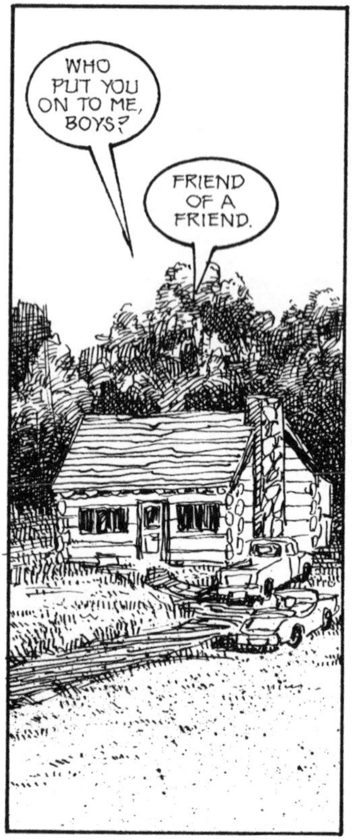
WHO PUT YOU ON TO ME, BOYS?
FRIEND OF A FRIEND.

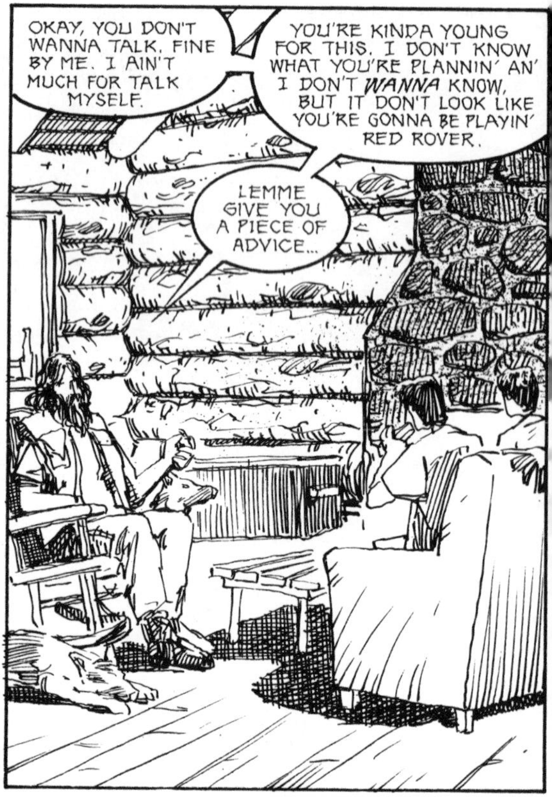
OKAY, YOU DON'T WANNA TALK. FINE BY ME. I AIN'T MUCH FOR TALK MYSELF.
YOU'RE KINDA YOUNG FOR THIS. I DON'T KNOW WHAT YOU'RE PLANNIN' AN' I DON'T WANNA KNOW, BUT IT DON'T LOOK LIKE YOU'RE GONNA BE PLAYIN' RED ROVER.
LEMME GIVE YOU A PIECE OF ADVICE...

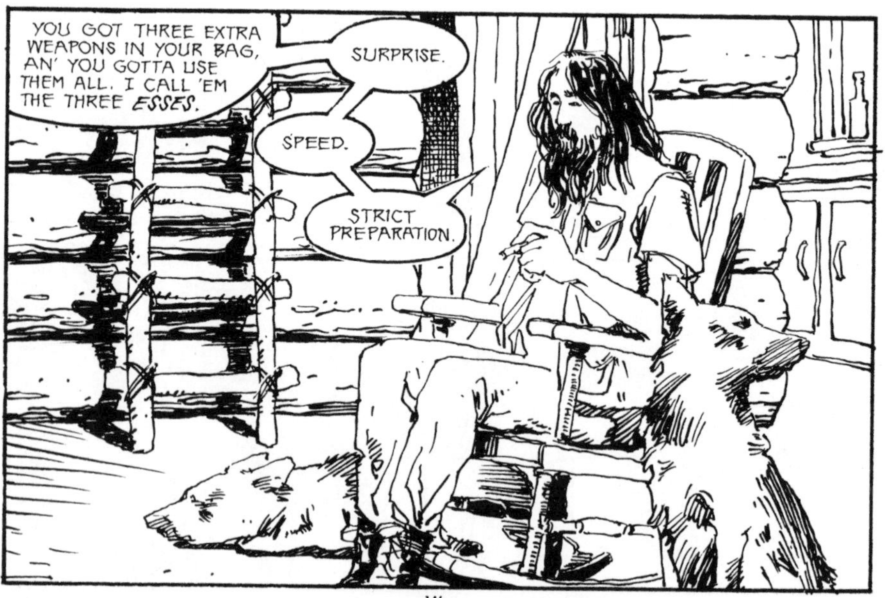
YOU GOT THREE EXTRA WEAPONS IN YOUR BAG, AN' YOU GOTTA USE THEM ALL. I CALL 'EM THE THREE ESSES.
SURPRISE.
SPEED.
STRICT PREPARATION.

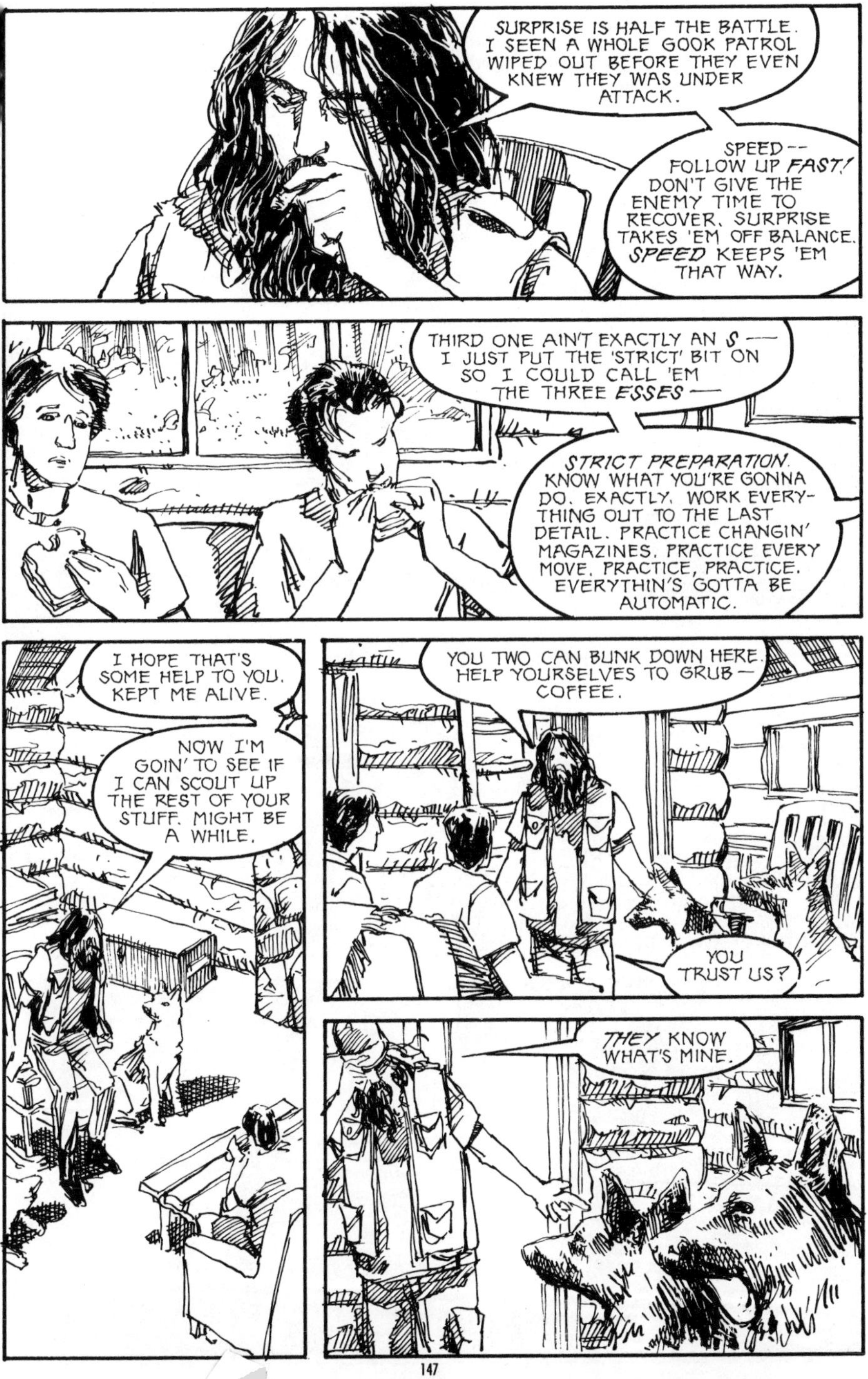
SURPRISE IS HALF THE BATTLE. I SEEN A WHOLE GOOK PATROL WIPED OUT BEFORE THEY EVEN KNEW THEY WAS UNDER ATTACK.
SPEED-- FOLLOW UP FAST! DON'T GIVE THE ENEMY TIME TO RECOVER. SURPRISE TAKES 'EM OFF BALANCE. SPEED KEEPS 'EM THAT WAY.
THIRD ONE AIN'T EXACTLY AN S -- I JUST PUT THE 'STRICT' BIT ON SO I COULD CALL 'EM THE THREE ESSES --
STRICT PREPARATION. KNOW WHAT YOU'RE GONNA DO. EXACTLY. WORK EVERYTHING OUT TO THE LAST DETAIL. PRACTICE CHANGIN' MAGAZINES. PRACTICE EVERY MOVE. PRACTICE, PRACTICE. EVERYTHIN'S GOTTA BE AUTOMATIC.
I HOPE THAT'S SOME HELP TO YOU. KEPT ME ALIVE.
NOW I'M GOIN' TO SEE IF I CAN SCOUT UP THE REST OF YOUR STUFF. MIGHT BE A WHILE.
YOU TWO CAN BUNK DOWN HERE. HELP YOURSELVES TO GRUB -- COFFEE.
YOU TRUST US?
THEY KNOW WHAT'S MINE.

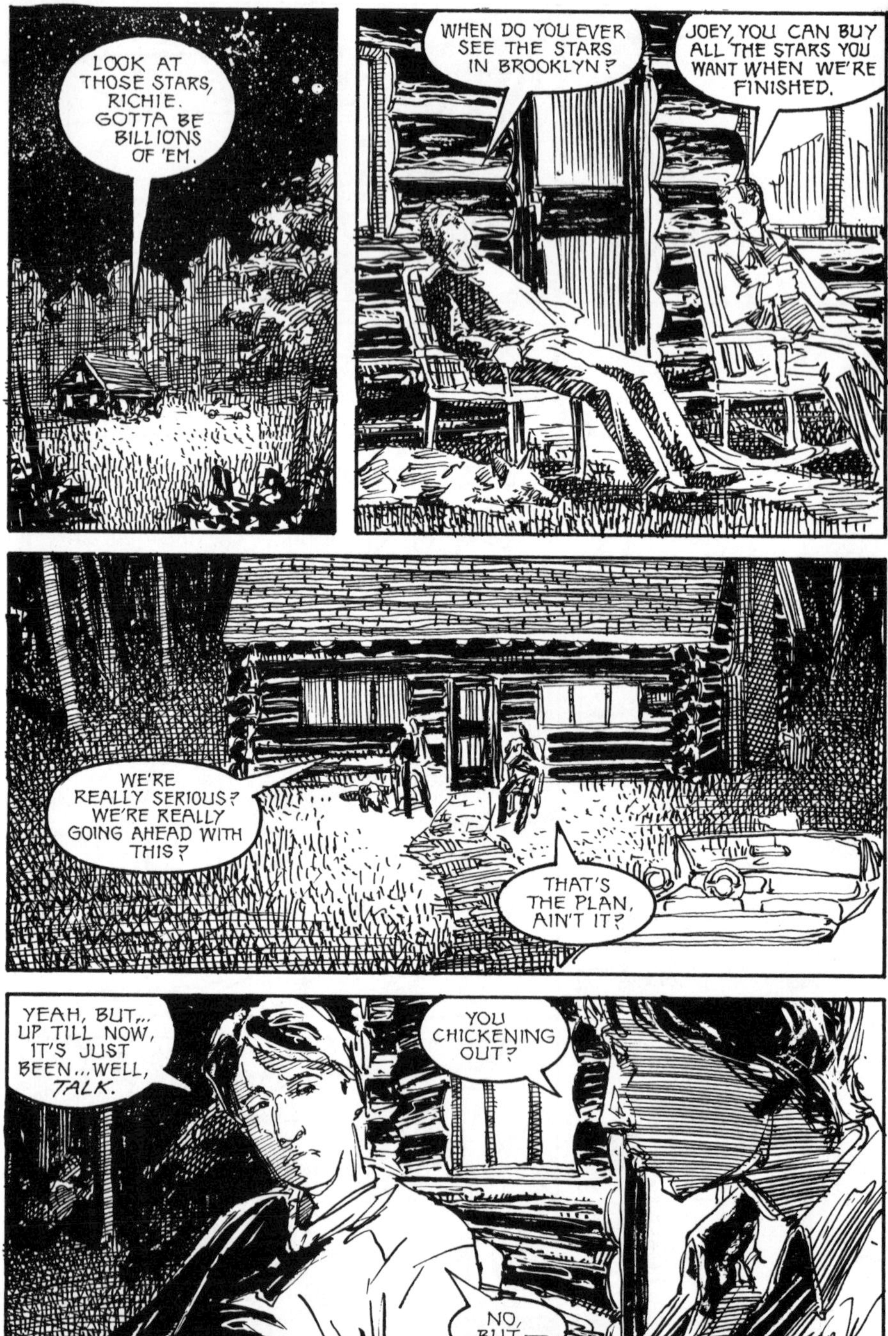
LOOK AT THOSE STARS, RICHIE. GOTTA BE BILLIONS OF 'EM.
WHEN DO YOU EVER SEE THE STARS IN BROOKLYN?
JOEY, YOU CAN BUY ALL THE STARS YOU WANT WHEN WE'RE FINISHED.
WE'RE REALLY SERIOUS? WE'RE REALLY GOING AHEAD WITH THIS?
THAT'S THE PLAN, AIN'T IT?
YEAH, BUT... UP TILL NOW, IT'S JUST BEEN... WELL, *TALK*.
YOU CHICKENING OUT?
NO, BUT—

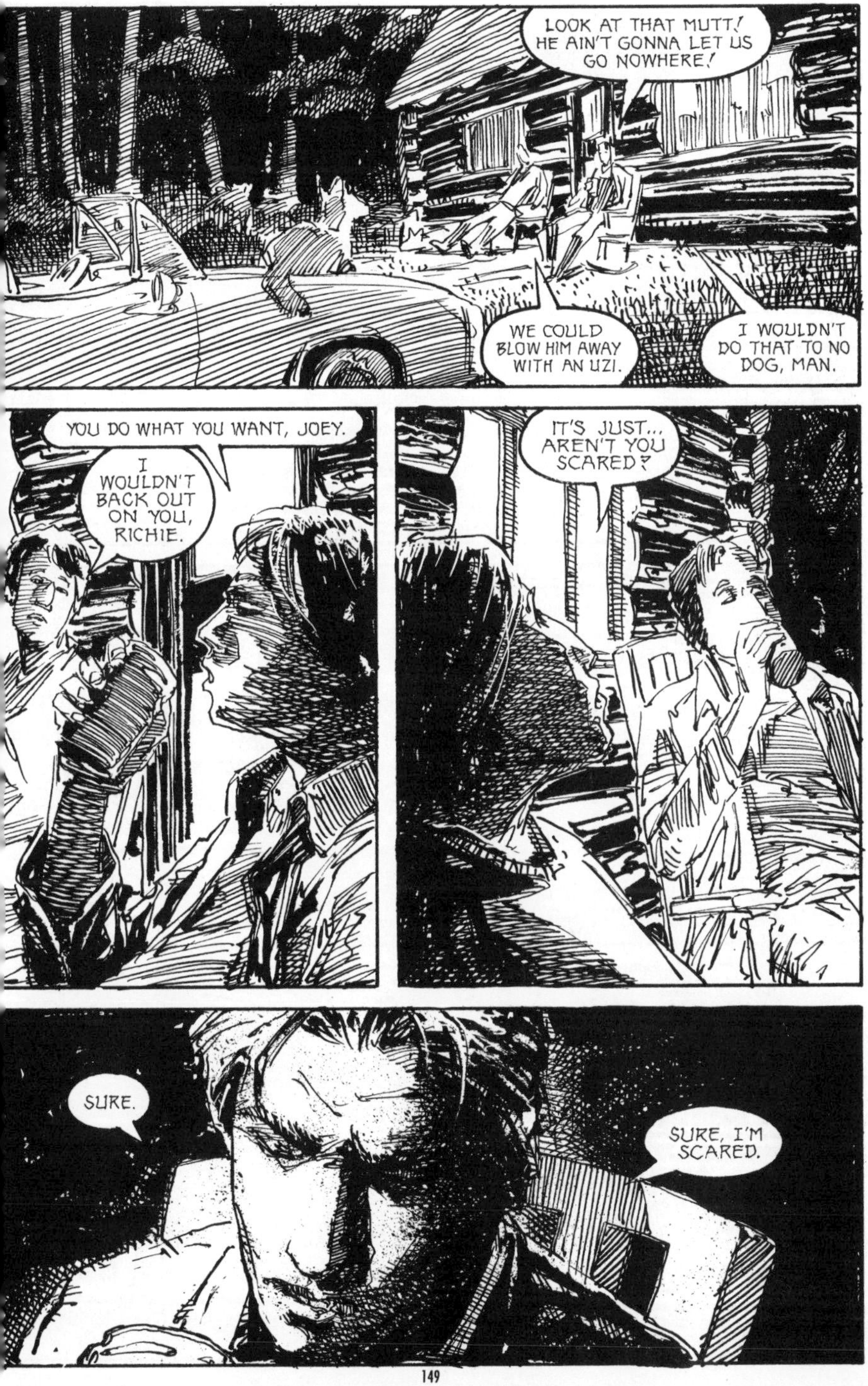

LOOK AT THAT MUTT! HE AIN'T GONNA LET US GO NOWHERE!
WE COULD BLOW HIM AWAY WITH AN UZI.
I WOULDN'T DO THAT TO NO DOG, MAN.
YOU DO WHAT YOU WANT, JOEY.
I WOULDN'T BACK OUT ON YOU, RICHIE.
IT'S JUST... AREN'T YOU SCARED?
SURE.
SURE, I'M SCARED.

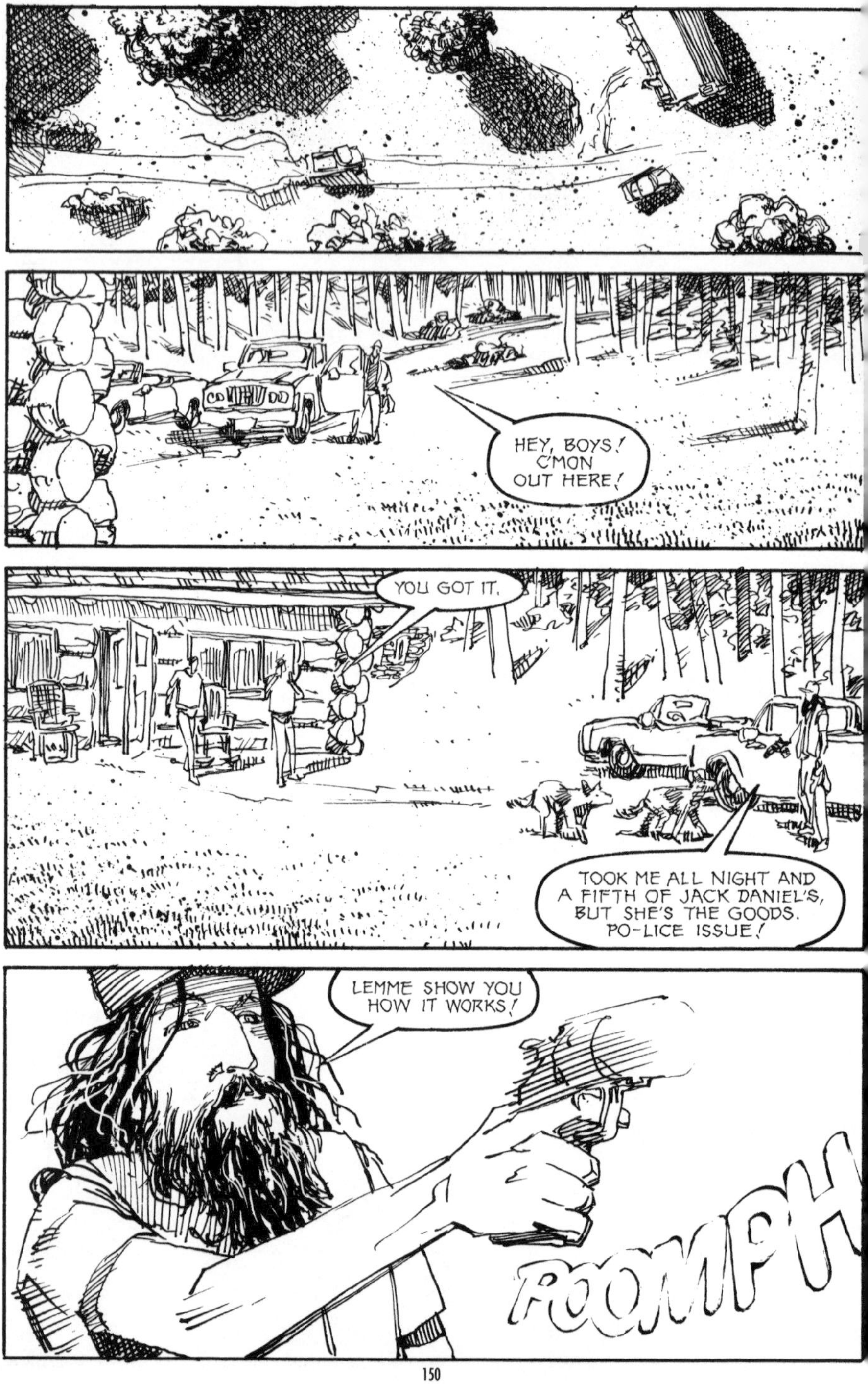
HEY, BOYS! C'MON OUT HERE!
YOU GOT IT.
TOOK ME ALL NIGHT AND A FIFTH OF JACK DANIEL'S, BUT SHE'S THE GOODS. PO-LICE ISSUE!
LEMME SHOW YOU HOW IT WORKS!
POOMPH

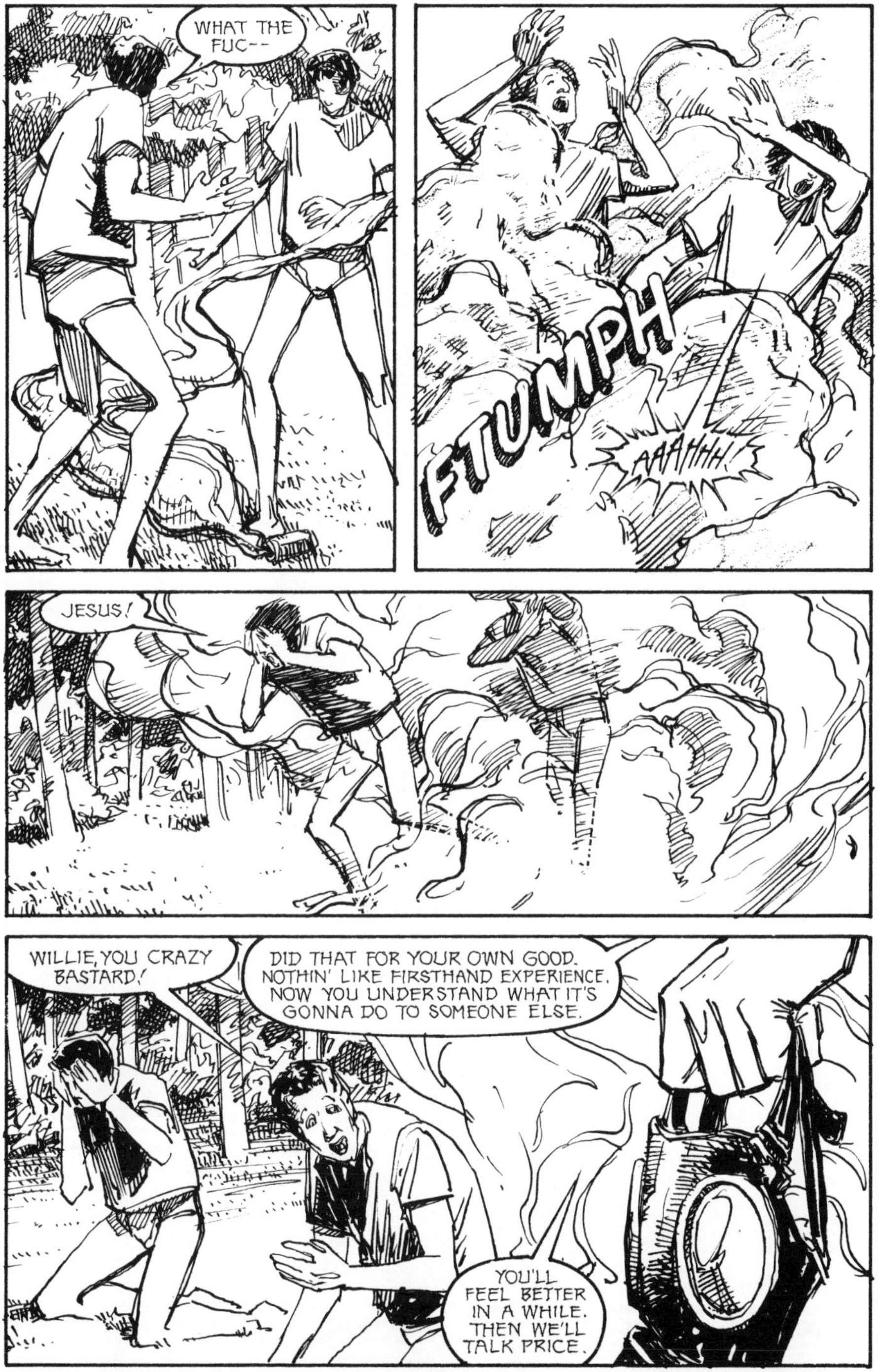
WHAT THE FUC--
FTUMPH
AAAHHH!
JESUS!
WILLIE, YOU CRAZY BASTARD!
DID THAT FOR YOUR OWN GOOD. NOTHIN' LIKE FIRSTHAND EXPERIENCE. NOW YOU UNDERSTAND WHAT IT'S GONNA DO TO SOMEONE ELSE.
YOU'LL FEEL BETTER IN A WHILE. THEN WE'LL TALK PRICE.

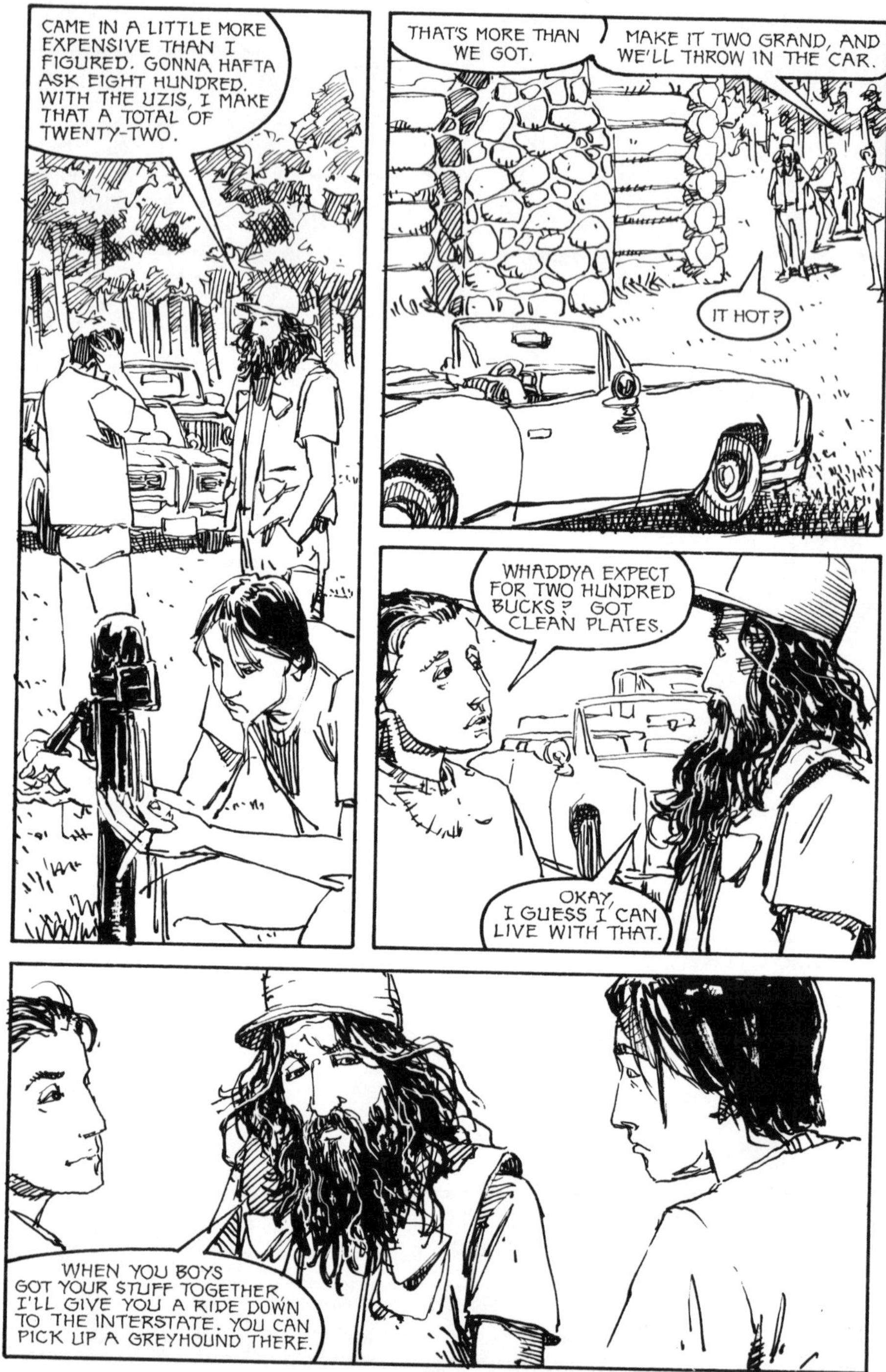
CAME IN A LITTLE MORE EXPENSIVE THAN I FIGURED. GONNA HAFTA ASK EIGHT HUNDRED. WITH THE UZIS, I MAKE THAT A TOTAL OF TWENTY-TWO.
THAT'S MORE THAN WE GOT.
MAKE IT TWO GRAND, AND WE'LL THROW IN THE CAR.
IT HOT?
WHADDYA EXPECT FOR TWO HUNDRED BUCKS? GOT CLEAN PLATES.
OKAY, I GUESS I CAN LIVE WITH THAT.
WHEN YOU BOYS GOT YOUR STUFF TOGETHER, I'LL GIVE YOU A RIDE DOWN TO THE INTERSTATE. YOU CAN PICK UP A GREYHOUND THERE.

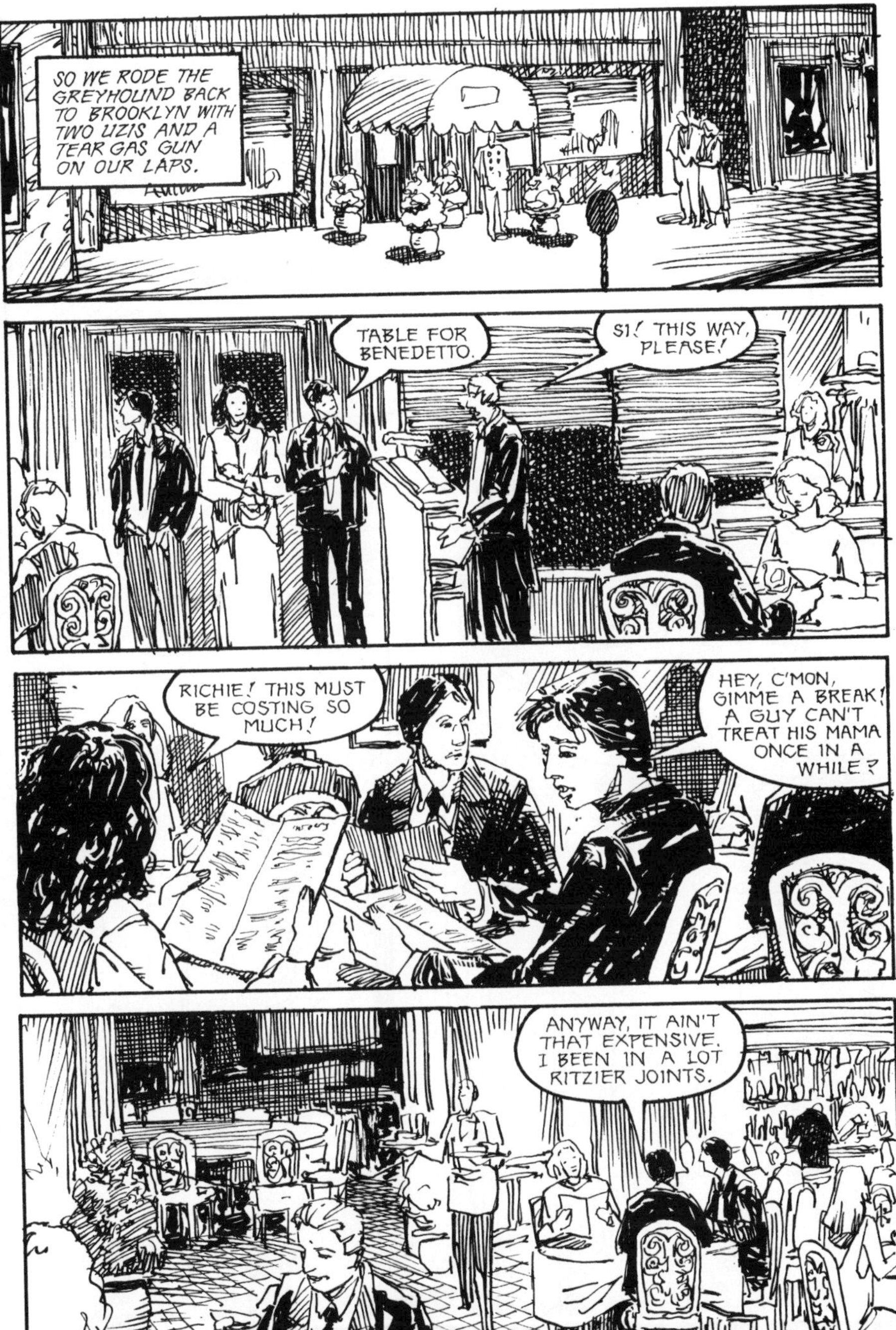
SO WE RODE THE GREYHOUND BACK TO BROOKLYN WITH TWO UZIS AND A TEAR GAS GUN ON OUR LAPS.
TABLE FOR BENEDETTO.
SI! THIS WAY, PLEASE!
RICHIE! THIS MUST BE COSTING SO MUCH!
HEY, C'MON, GIMME A BREAK! A GUY CAN'T TREAT HIS MAMA ONCE IN A WHILE?
ANYWAY, IT AIN'T THAT EXPENSIVE. I BEEN IN A LOT RITZIER JOINTS.

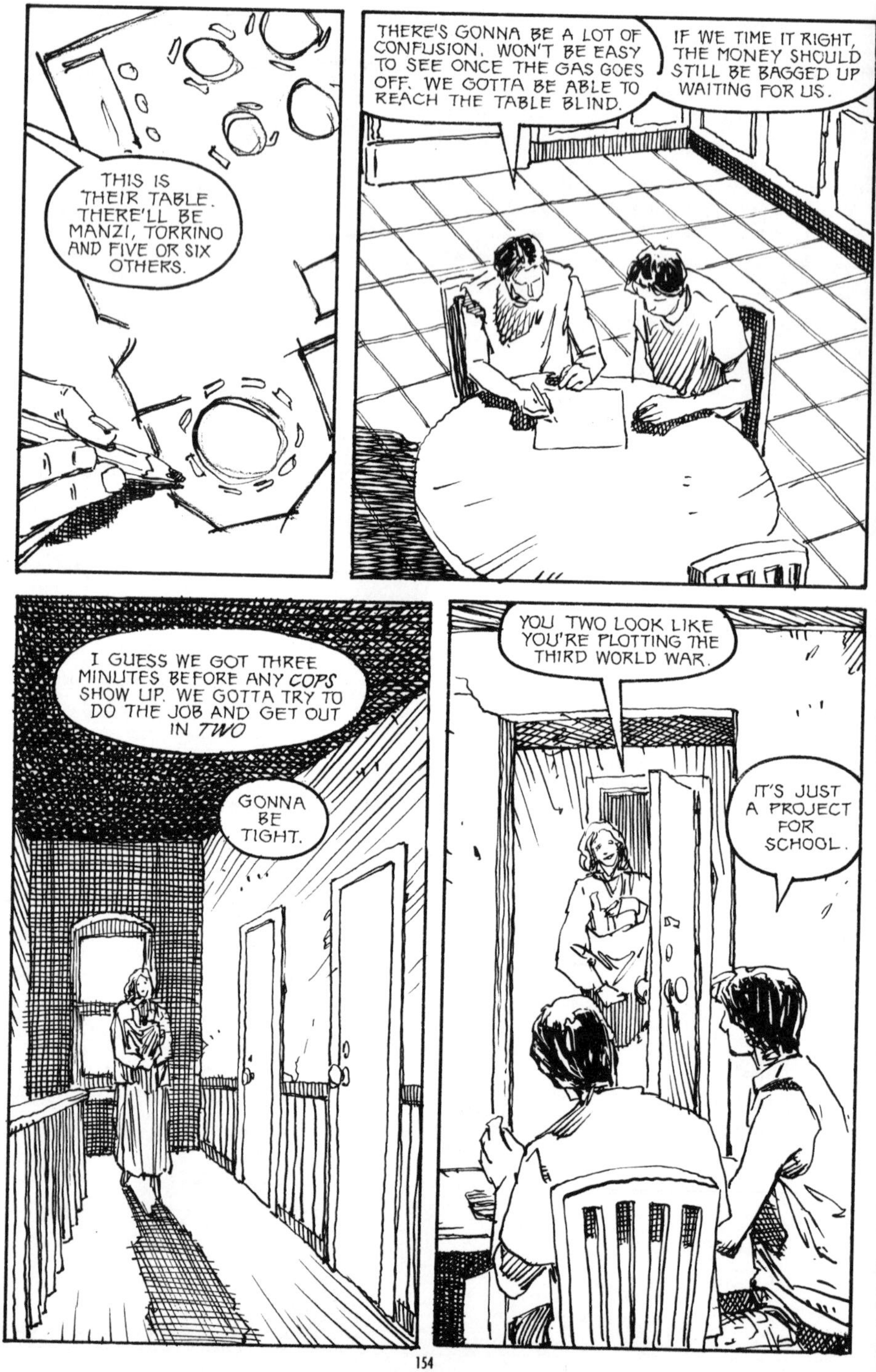
THIS IS THEIR TABLE. THERE'LL BE MANZI, TORRINO AND FIVE OR SIX OTHERS.
THERE'S GONNA BE A LOT OF CONFUSION. WON'T BE EASY TO SEE ONCE THE GAS GOES OFF. WE GOTTA BE ABLE TO REACH THE TABLE BLIND.
IF WE TIME IT RIGHT, THE MONEY SHOULD STILL BE BAGGED UP WAITING FOR US.
I GUESS WE GOT THREE MINUTES BEFORE ANY COPS SHOW UP. WE GOTTA TRY TO DO THE JOB AND GET OUT IN TWO
GONNA BE TIGHT.
YOU TWO LOOK LIKE YOU'RE PLOTTING THE THIRD WORLD WAR.
IT'S JUST A PROJECT FOR SCHOOL.

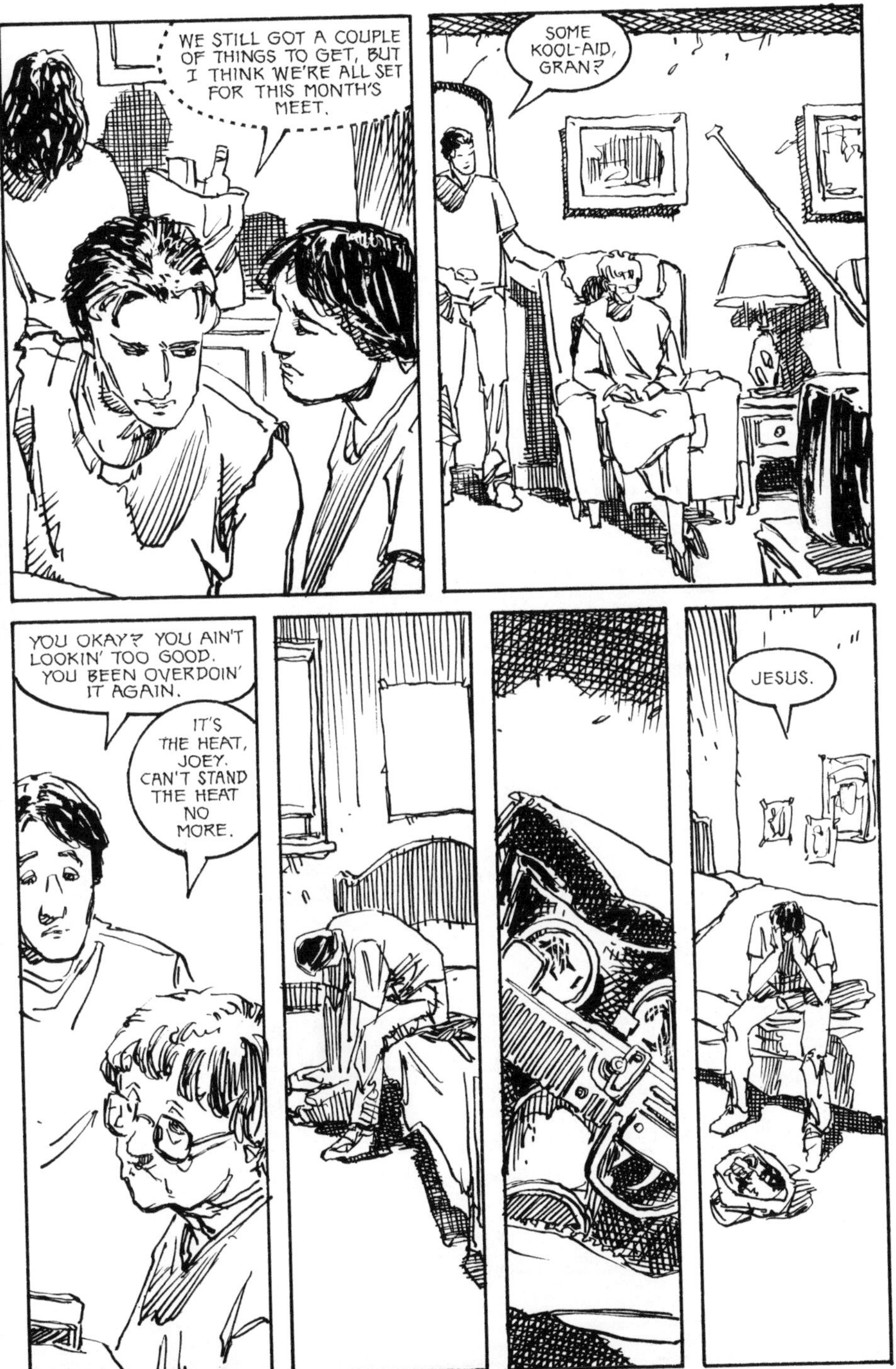
WE STILL GOT A COUPLE OF THINGS TO GET, BUT I THINK WE'RE ALL SET FOR THIS MONTH'S MEET.
SOME KOOL-AID, GRAN?
YOU OKAY? YOU AIN'T LOOKIN' TOO GOOD. YOU BEEN OVERDOIN' IT AGAIN.
IT'S THE HEAT, JOEY. CAN'T STAND THE HEAT NO MORE.
JESUS.

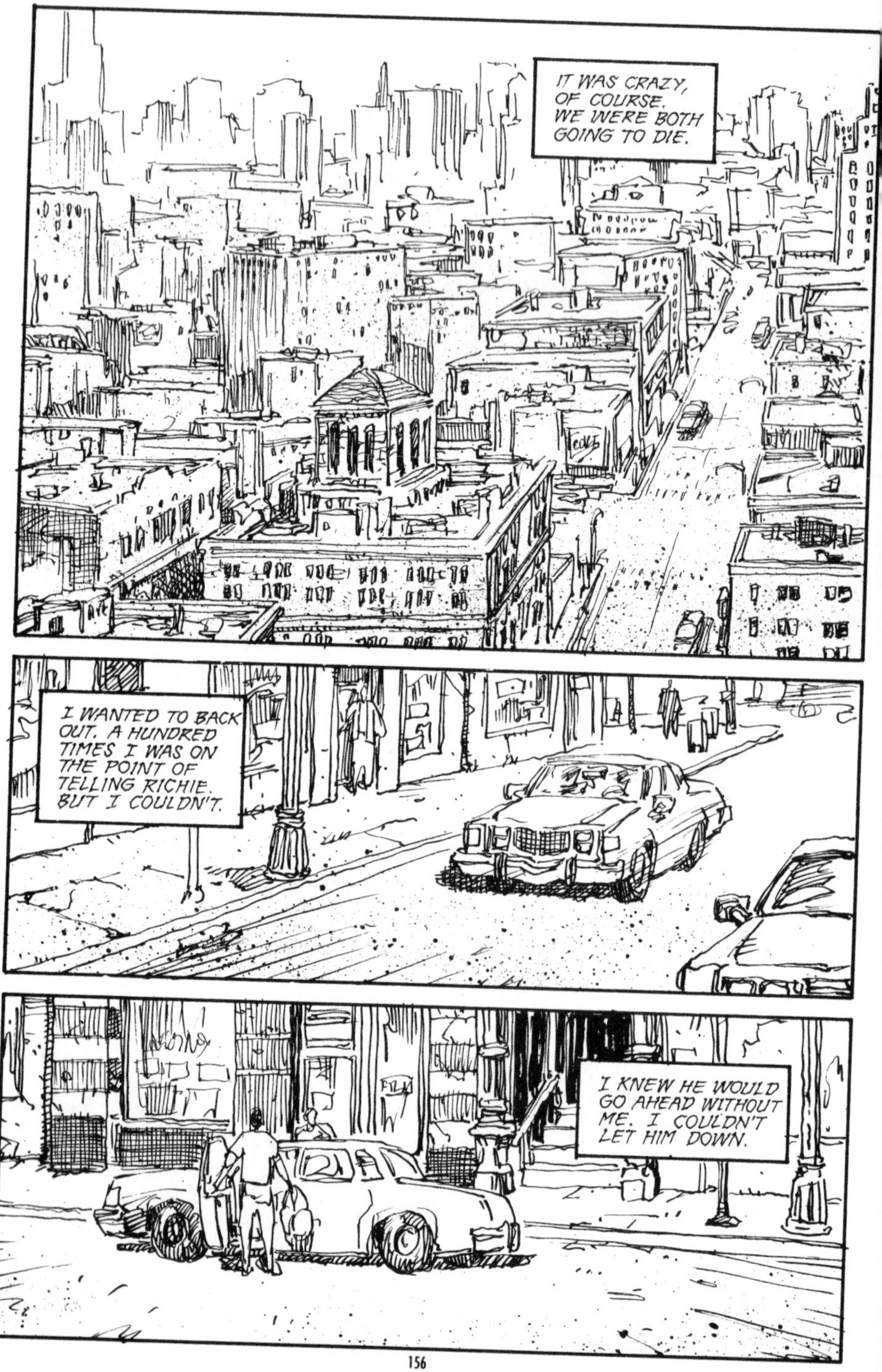
IT WAS CRAZY, OF COURSE. WE WERE BOTH GOING TO DIE.
I WANTED TO BACK OUT. A HUNDRED TIMES I WAS ON THE POINT OF TELLING RICHIE. BUT I COULDN'T.
I KNEW HE WOULD GO AHEAD WITHOUT ME. I COULDN'T LET HIM DOWN.

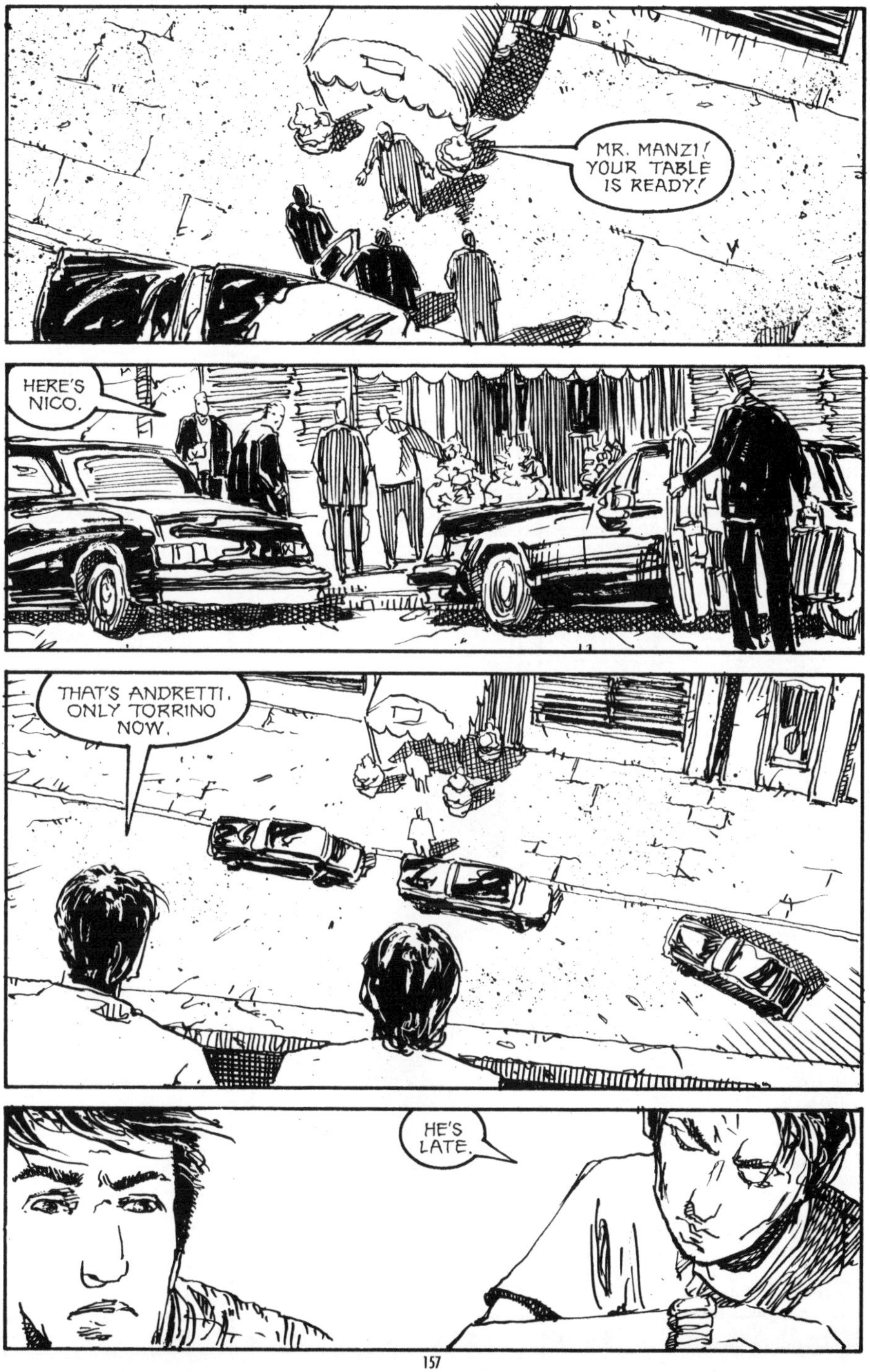
MR. MANZI! YOUR TABLE IS READY!
HERE'S NICO.
THAT'S ANDRETTI. ONLY TORRINO NOW.
HE'S LATE.

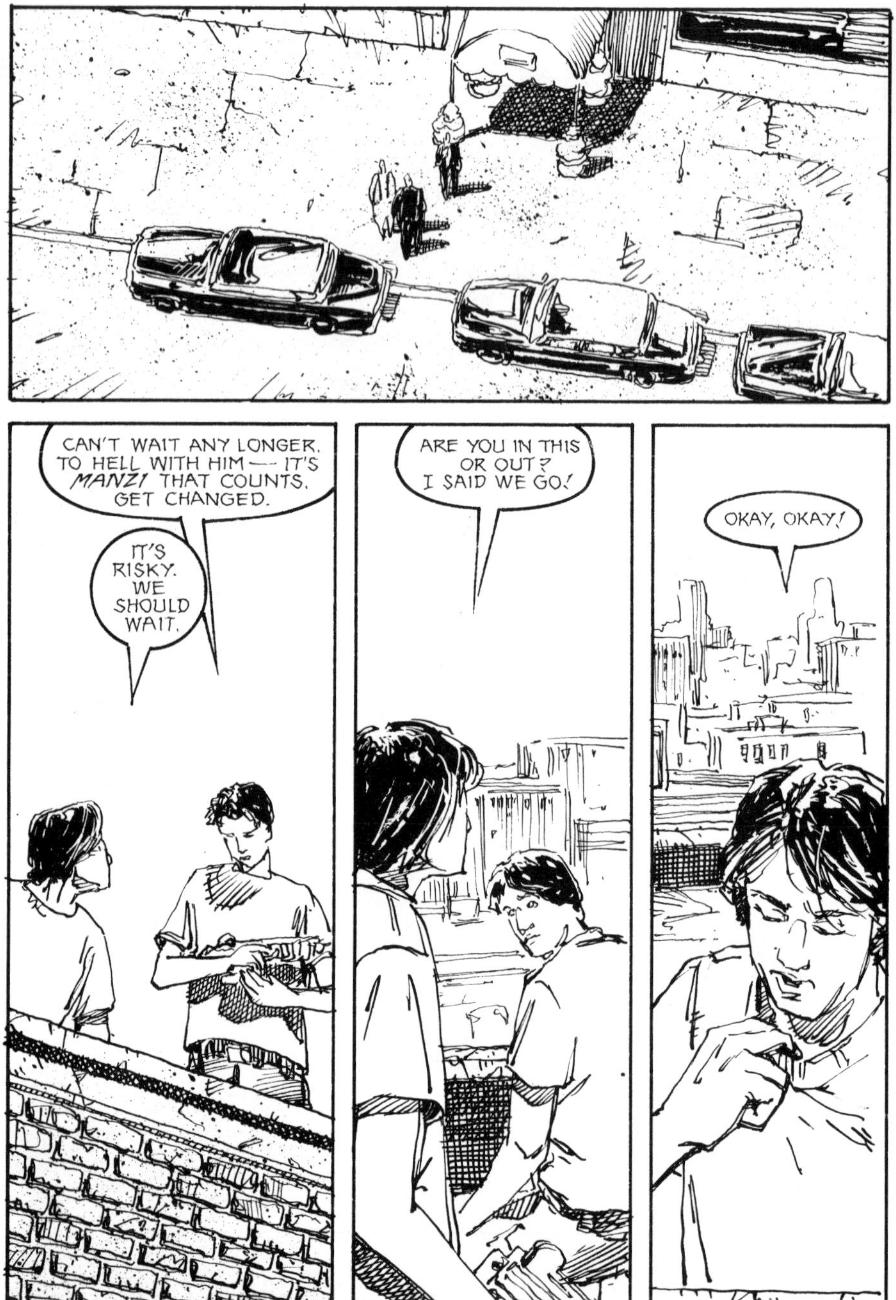
CAN'T WAIT ANY LONGER. TO HELL WITH HIM — IT'S MANZI THAT COUNTS. GET CHANGED.
IT'S RISKY. WE SHOULD WAIT.
ARE YOU IN THIS OR OUT? I SAID WE GO!
OKAY, OKAY!

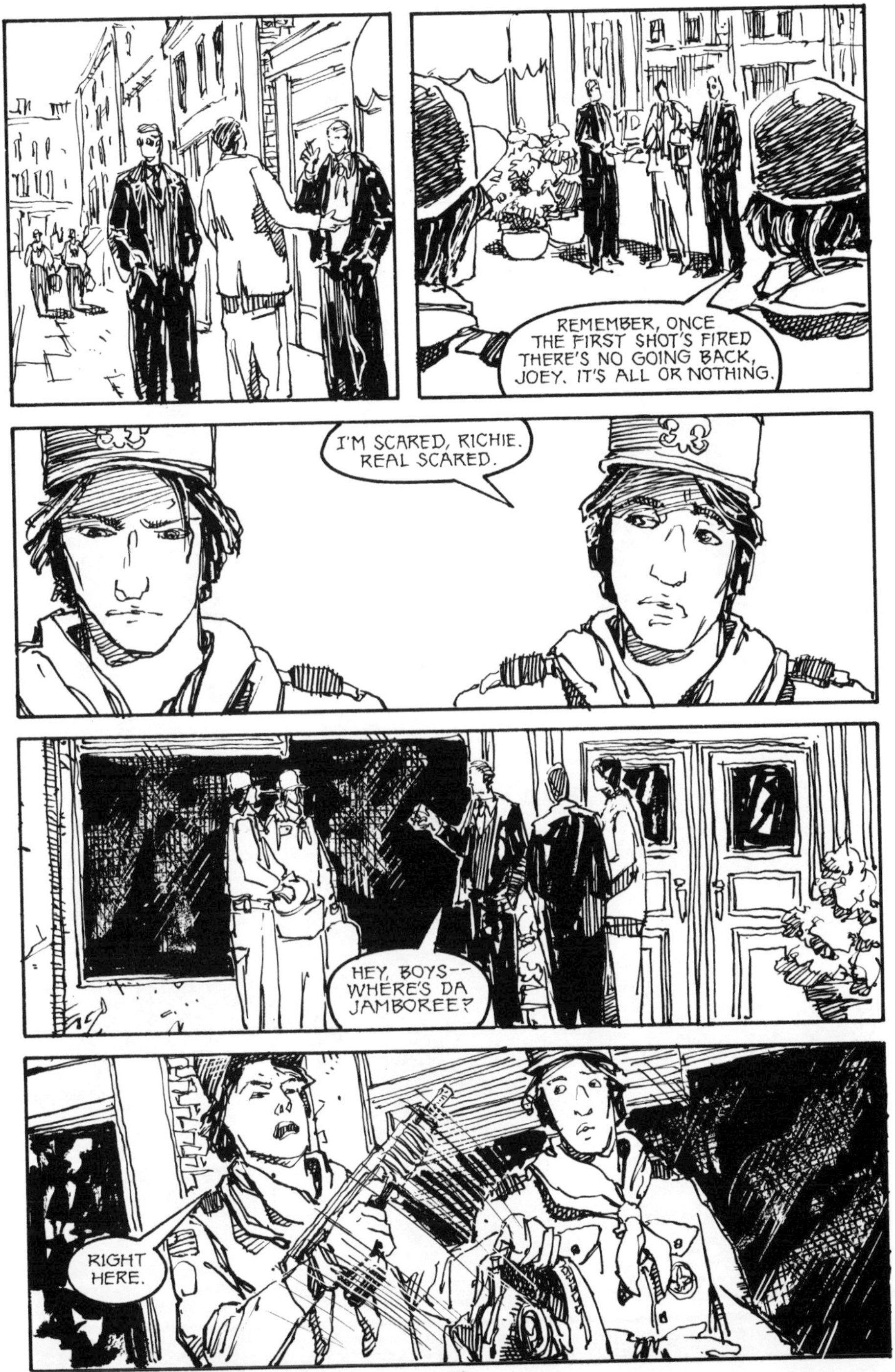
REMEMBER, ONCE THE FIRST SHOT'S FIRED THERE'S NO GOING BACK, JOEY. IT'S ALL OR NOTHING.
I'M SCARED, RICHIE. REAL SCARED.
HEY, BOYS-- WHERE'S DA JAMBOREE?
RIGHT HERE.

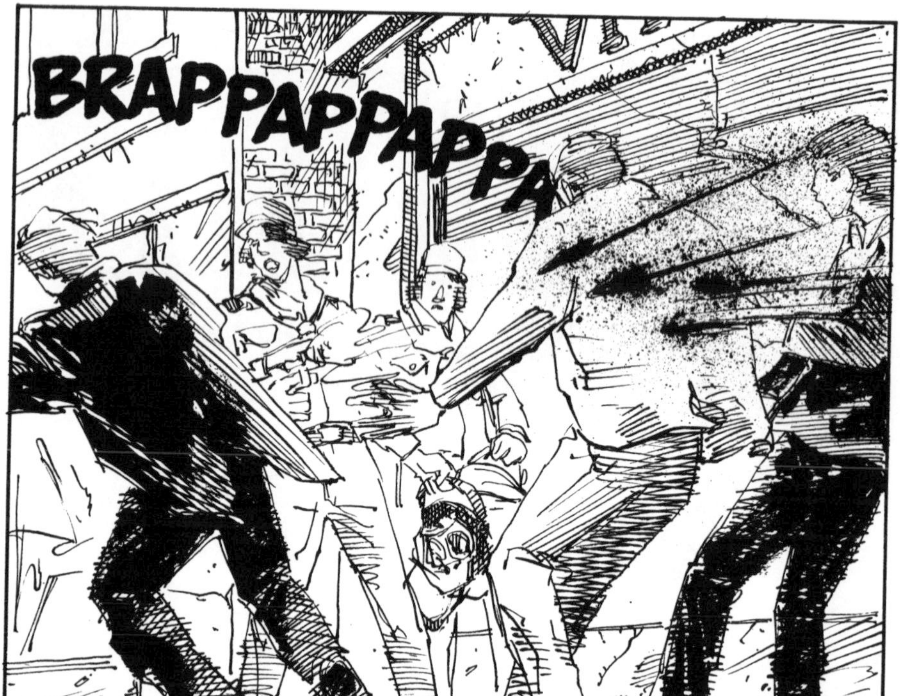
BRAPPAPPAPPA

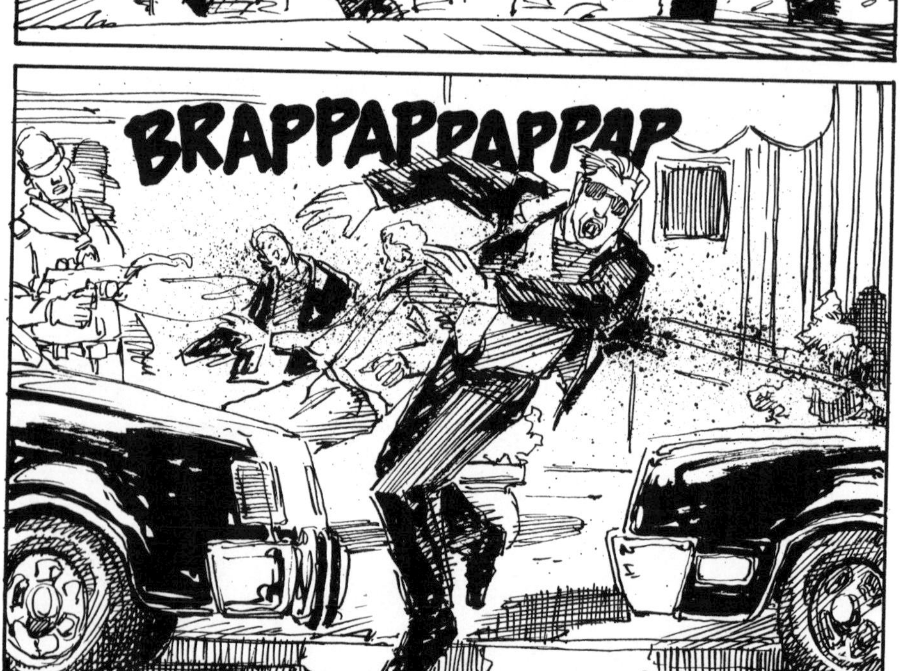
BRAPPAPPAPPAP

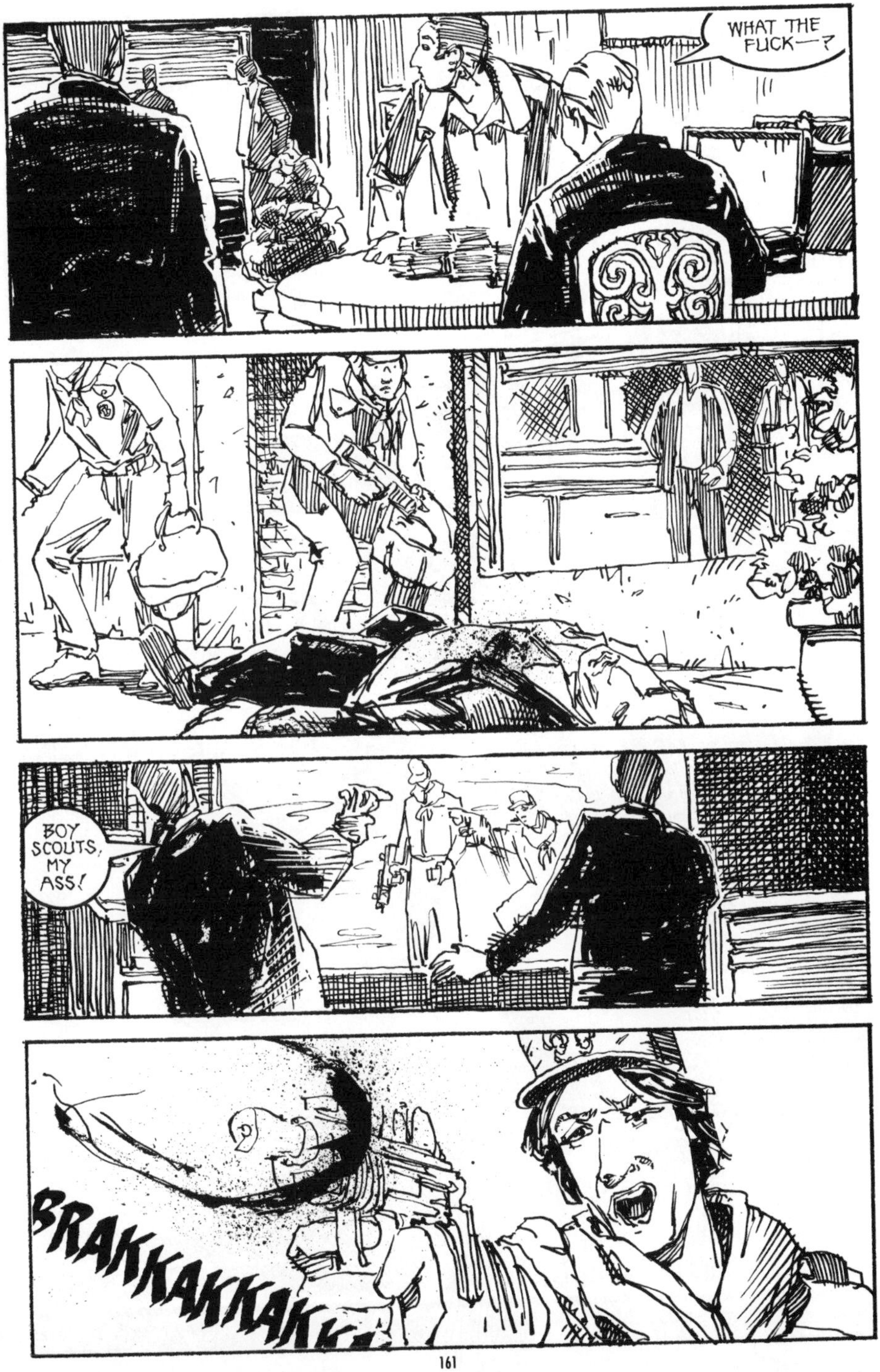
WHAT THE FUCK—?
BOY SCOUTS, MY ASS!
BRAKKAKKAKK

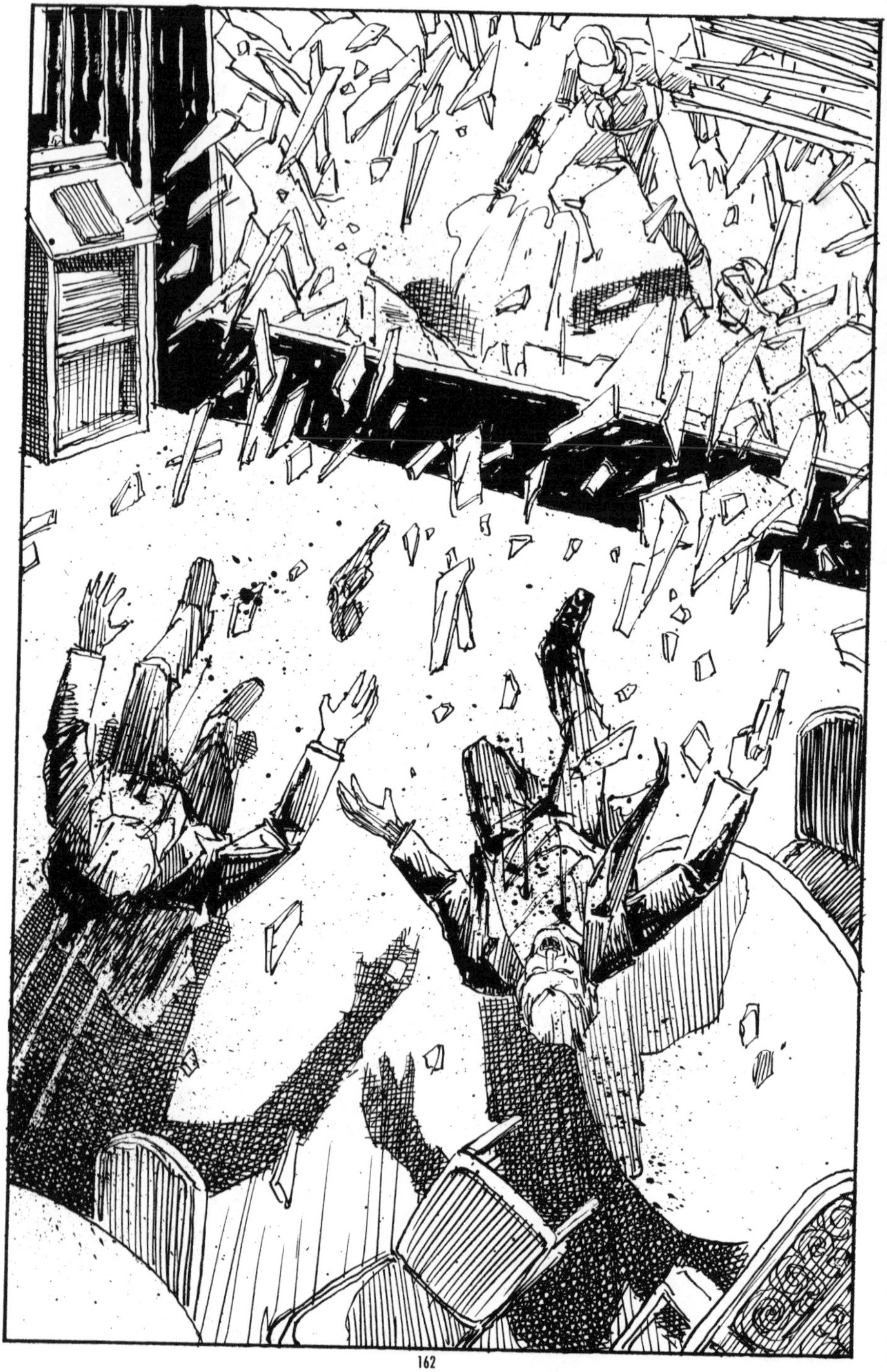

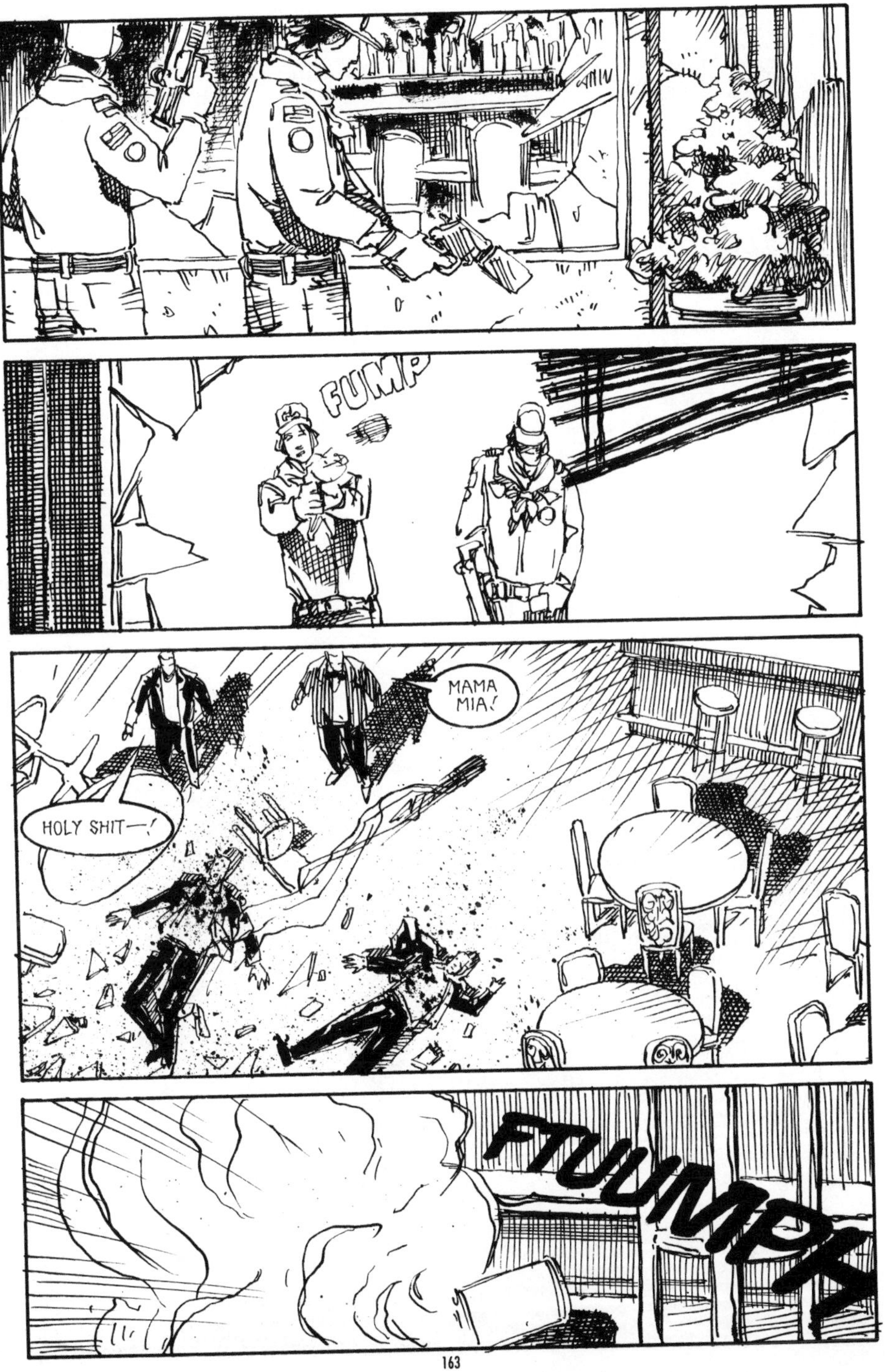
FUMP
MAMA MIA!
HOLY SHIT—!
FTUUMPK

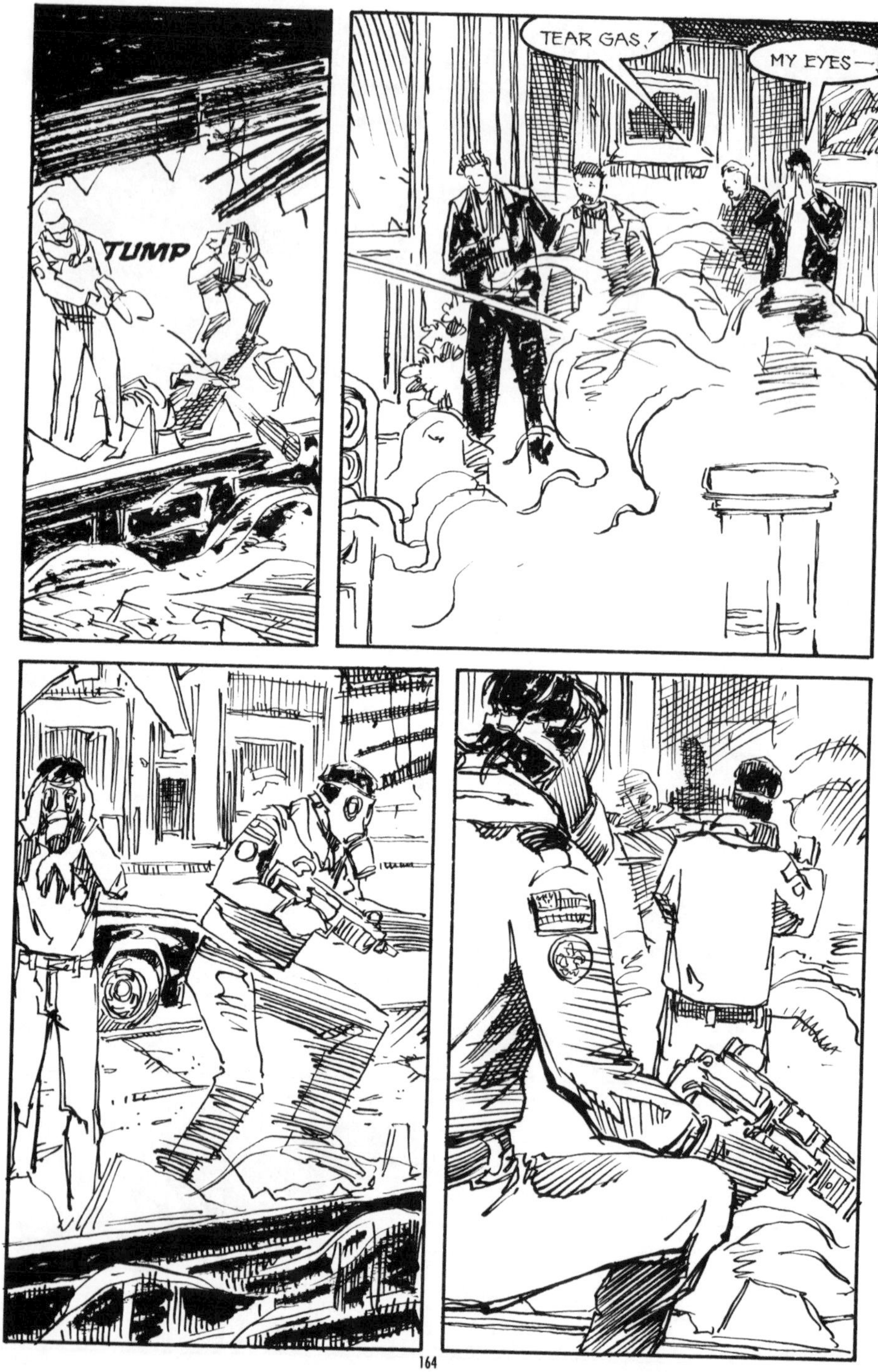
TUMP
TEAR GAS!
MY EYES—!

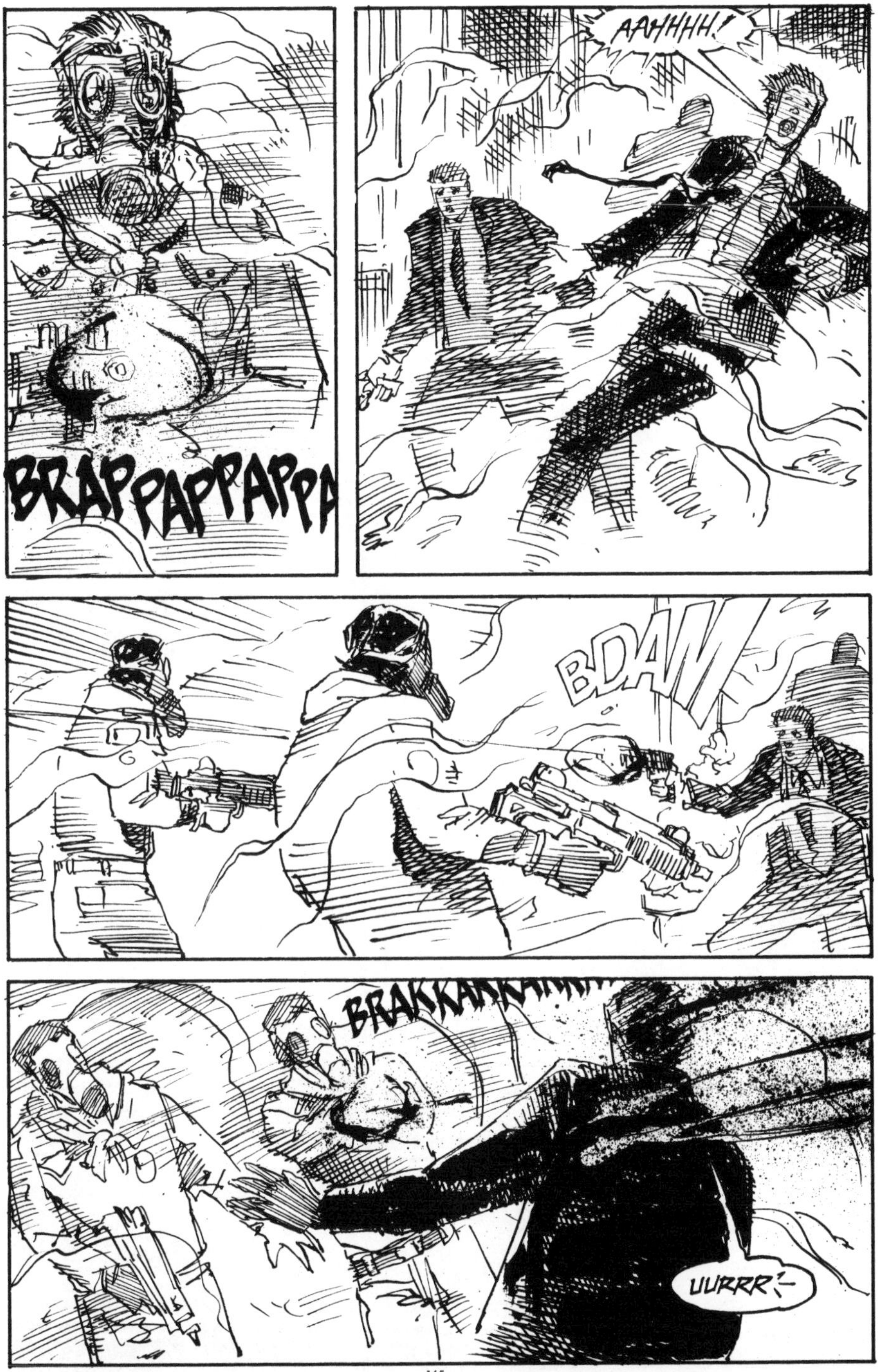
BRAPPAPPAPPA
AAHHHH!
BDAM
BRAKKAKKAKKKK
UURRR

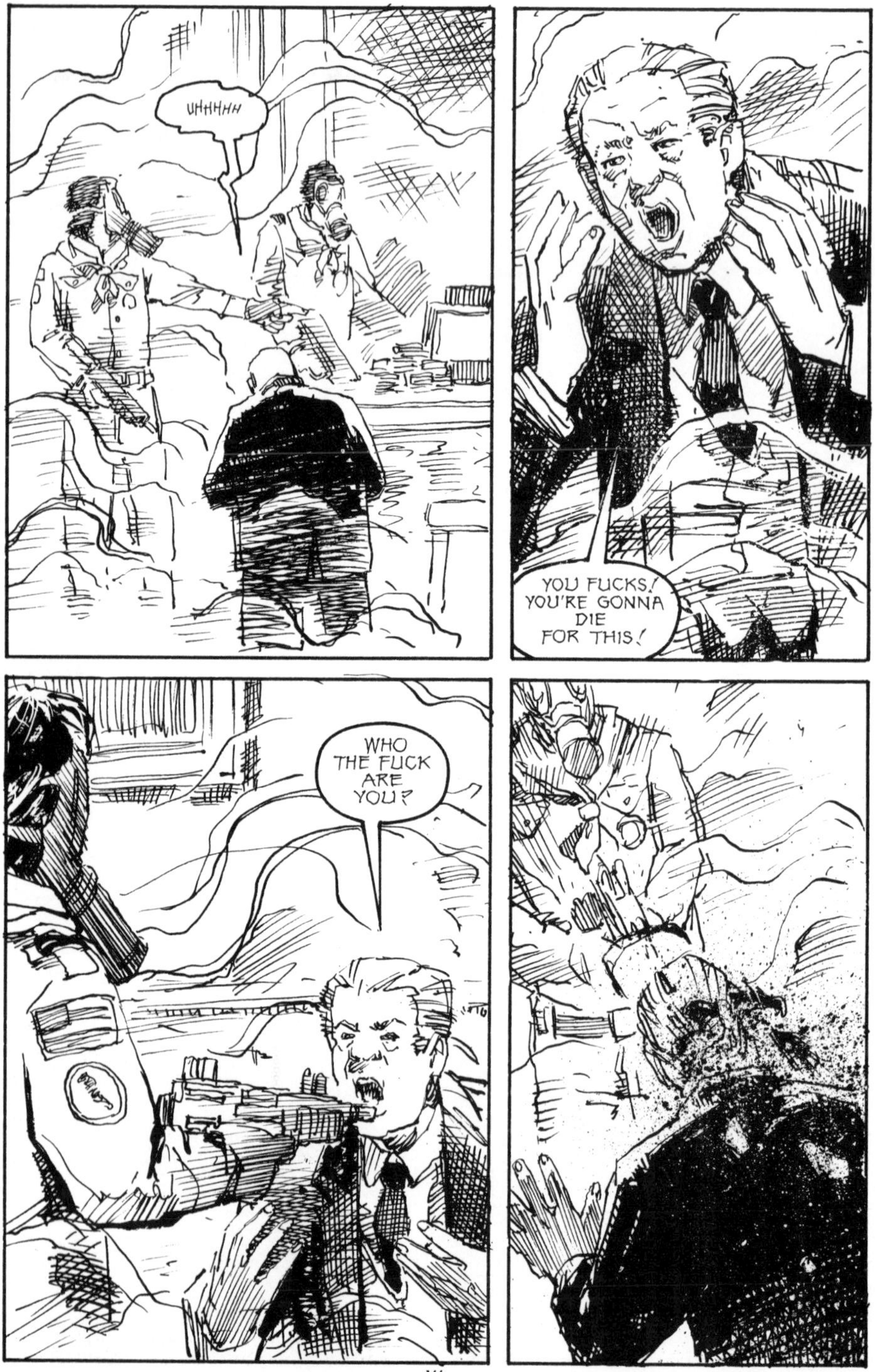
UHHHHH
YOU FUCKS! YOU'RE GONNA DIE FOR THIS!
WHO THE FUCK ARE YOU?

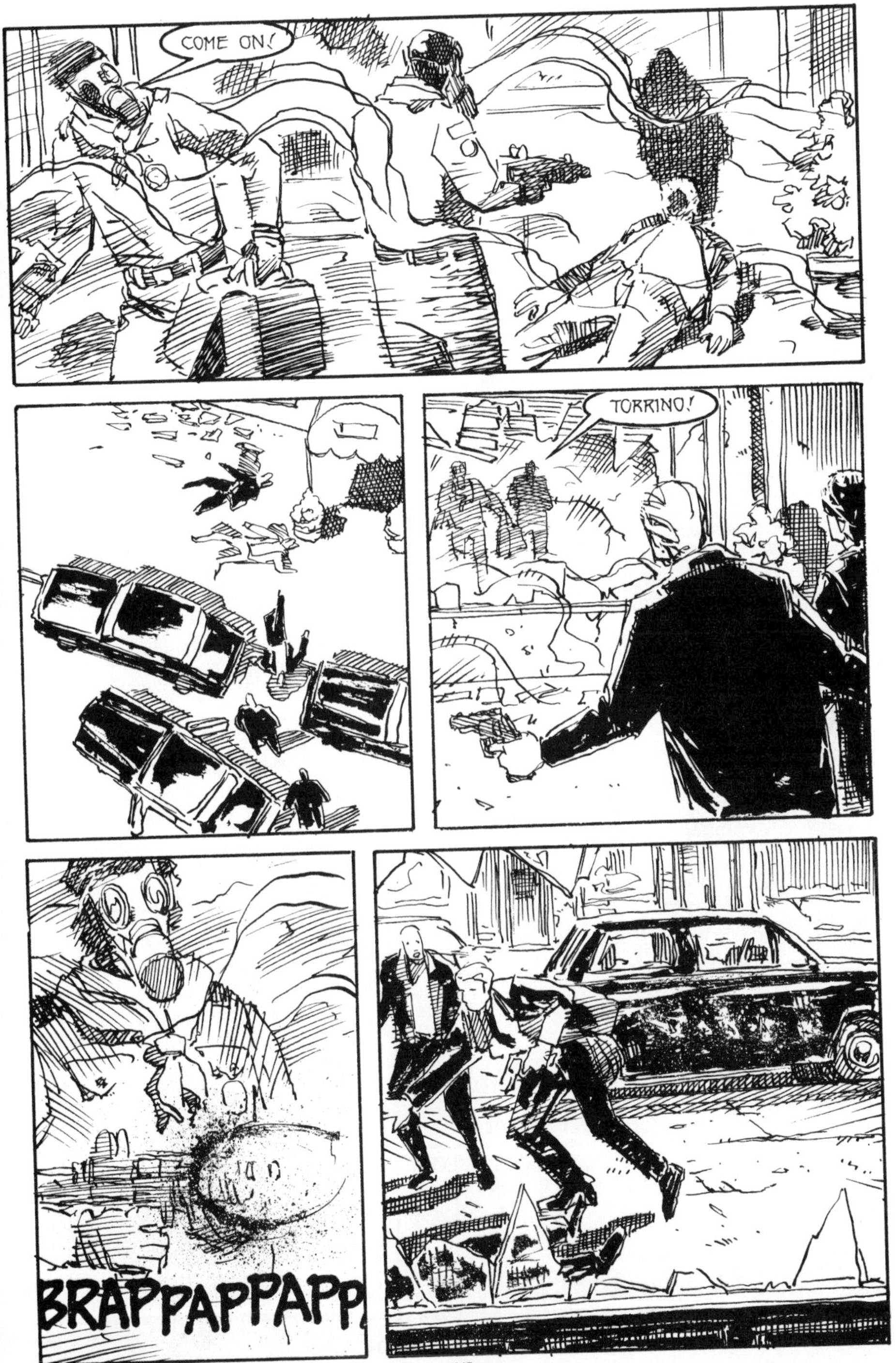
COME ON!
TORRINO!
BRAPPAPPAPP

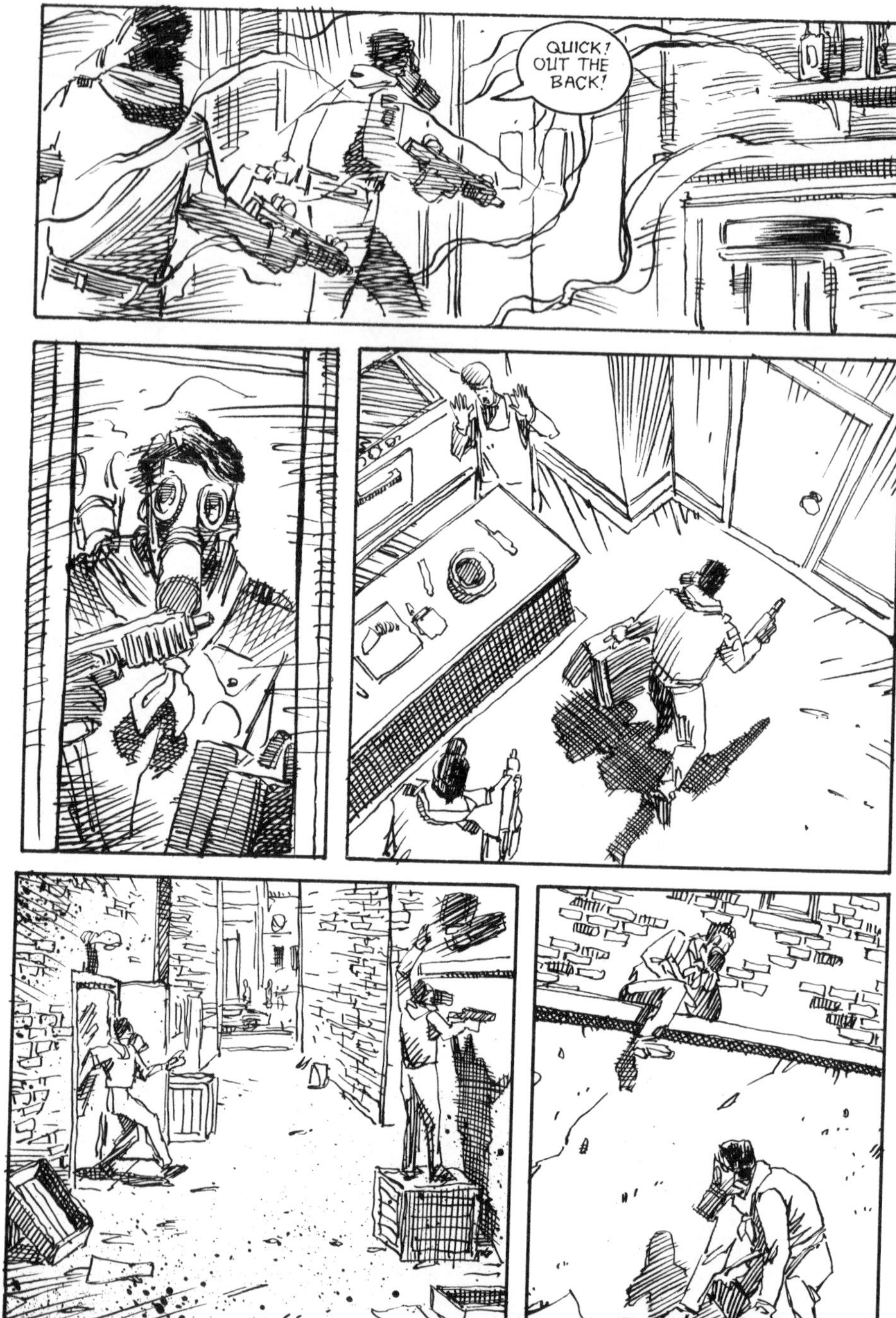
QUICK! OUT THE BACK!

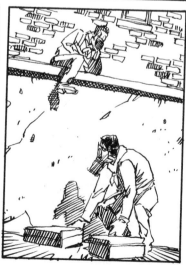

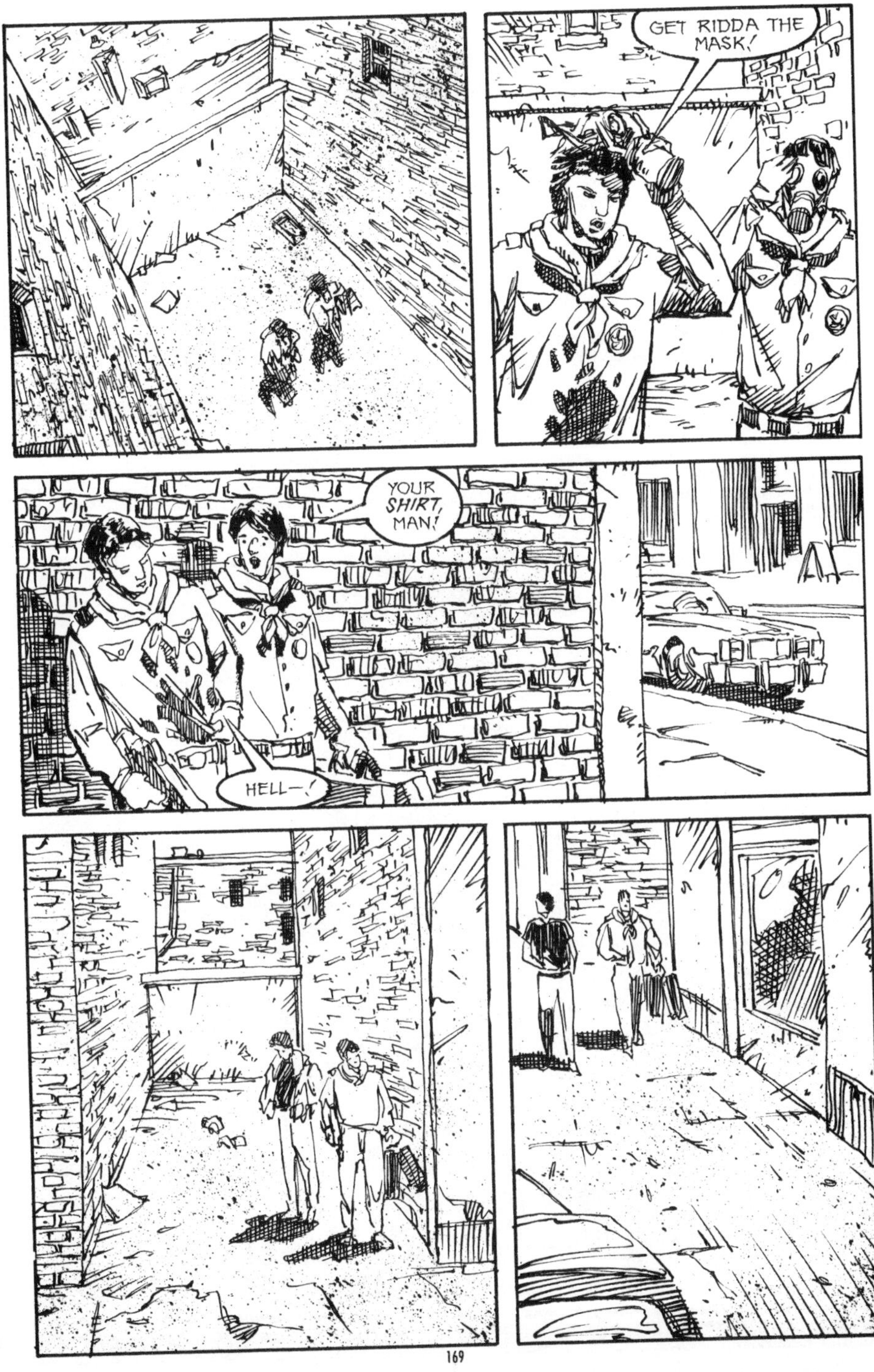
GET RIDDA THE MASK!
YOUR SHIRT, MAN!
HELL—!

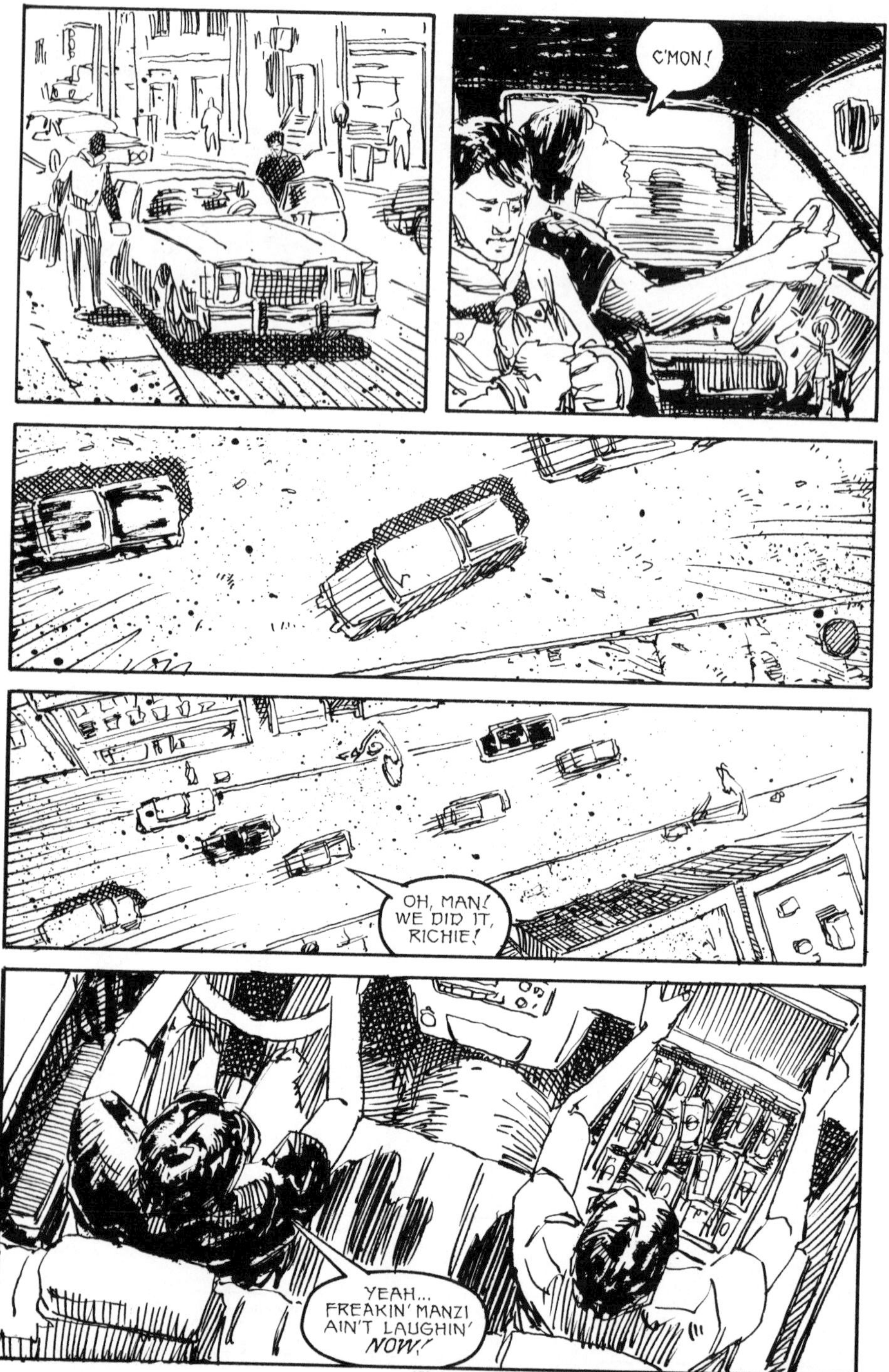
C'MON!
OH, MAN! WE DID IT, RICHIE!
YEAH... FREAKIN' MANZI AIN'T LAUGHIN' NOW!

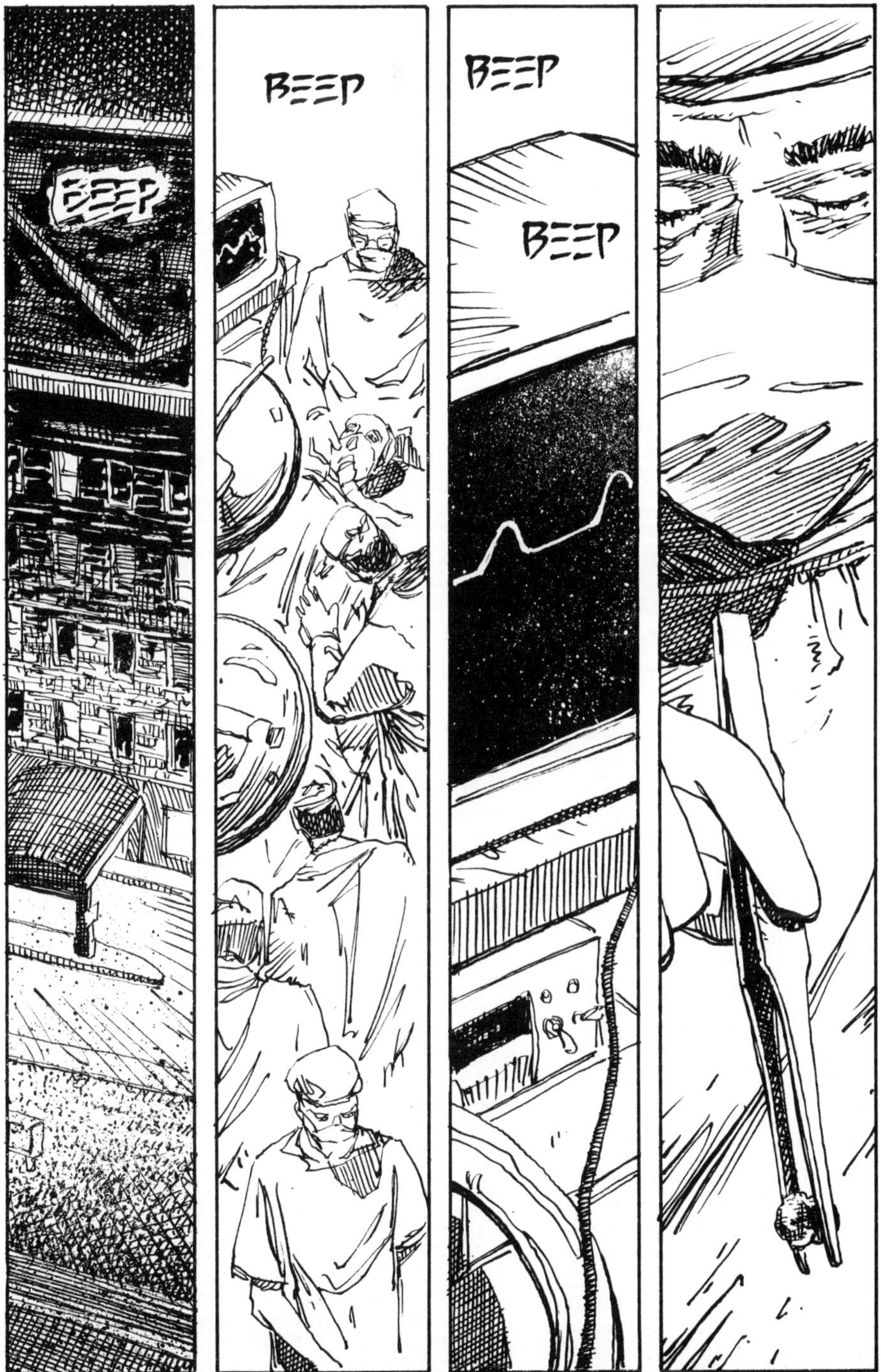
BEEP
BEEP
BEEP
BEEP

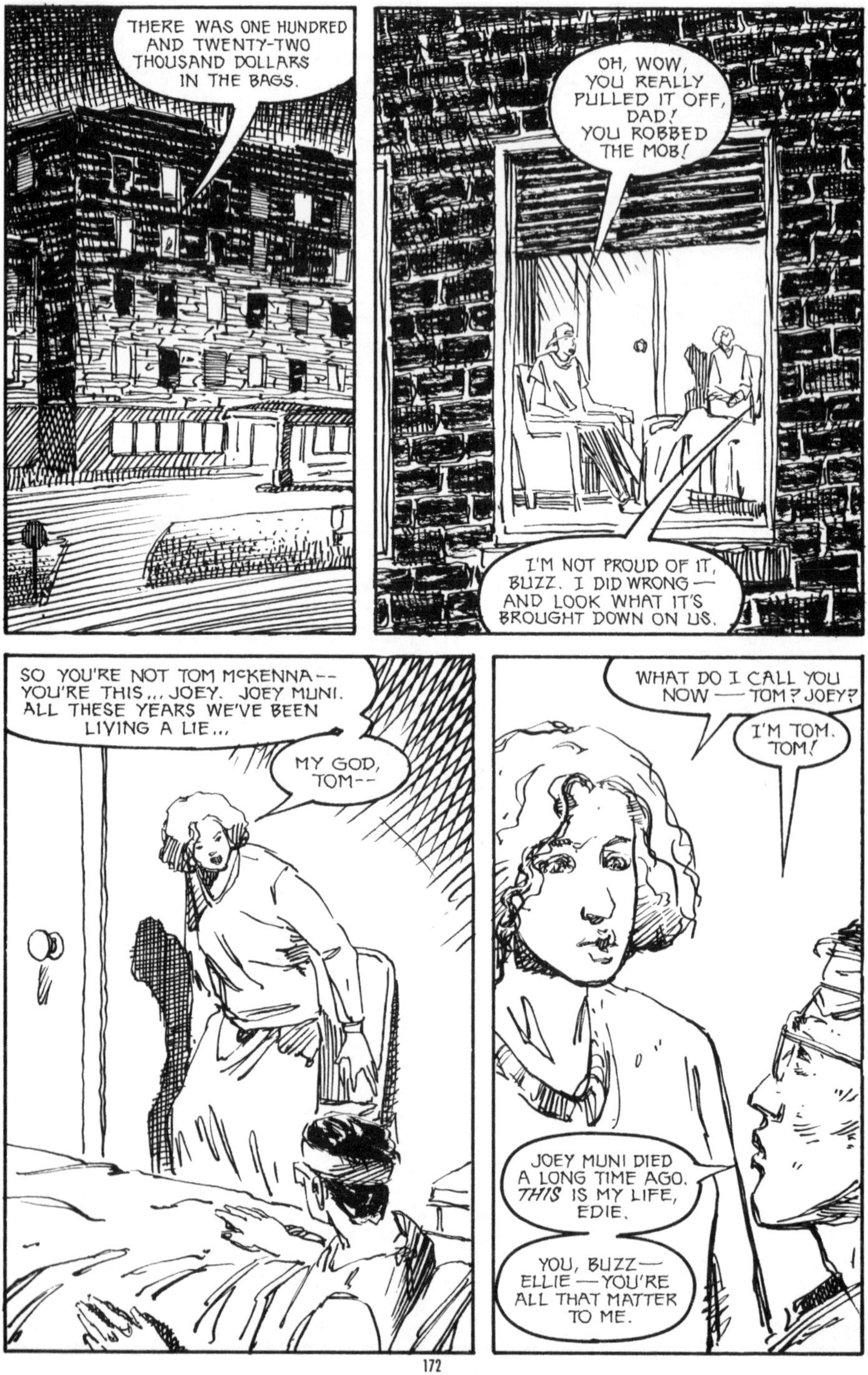
THERE WAS ONE HUNDRED AND TWENTY-TWO THOUSAND DOLLARS IN THE BAGS.
OH, WOW, YOU REALLY PULLED IT OFF, DAD! YOU ROBBED THE MOB!
I'M NOT PROUD OF IT, BUZZ. I DID WRONG— AND LOOK WHAT IT'S BROUGHT DOWN ON US.
SO YOU'RE NOT TOM McKENNA-- YOU'RE THIS... JOEY. JOEY MUNI. ALL THESE YEARS WE'VE BEEN LIVING A LIE...
MY GOD, TOM--
WHAT DO I CALL YOU NOW — TOM? JOEY?
I'M TOM. TOM!
JOEY MUNI DIED A LONG TIME AGO. *THIS* IS MY LIFE, EDIE.
YOU, BUZZ— ELLIE — YOU'RE ALL THAT MATTER TO ME.

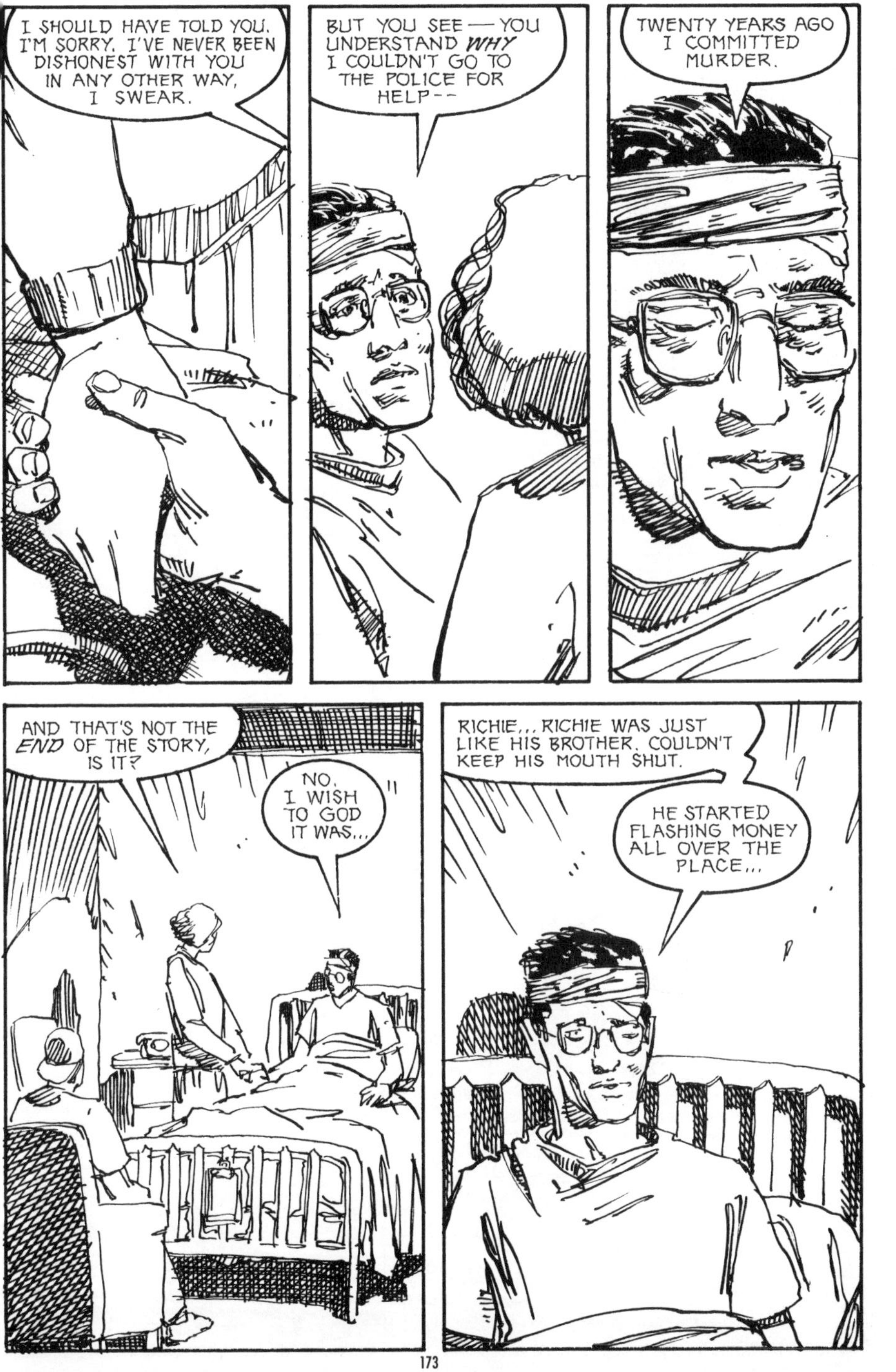
I SHOULD HAVE TOLD YOU. I'M SORRY. I'VE NEVER BEEN DISHONEST WITH YOU IN ANY OTHER WAY, I SWEAR.
BUT YOU SEE—YOU UNDERSTAND WHY I COULDN'T GO TO THE POLICE FOR HELP--
TWENTY YEARS AGO I COMMITTED MURDER.
AND THAT'S NOT THE END OF THE STORY, IS IT?
NO. I WISH TO GOD IT WAS...
RICHIE... RICHIE WAS JUST LIKE HIS BROTHER. COULDN'T KEEP HIS MOUTH SHUT.
HE STARTED FLASHING MONEY ALL OVER THE PLACE...

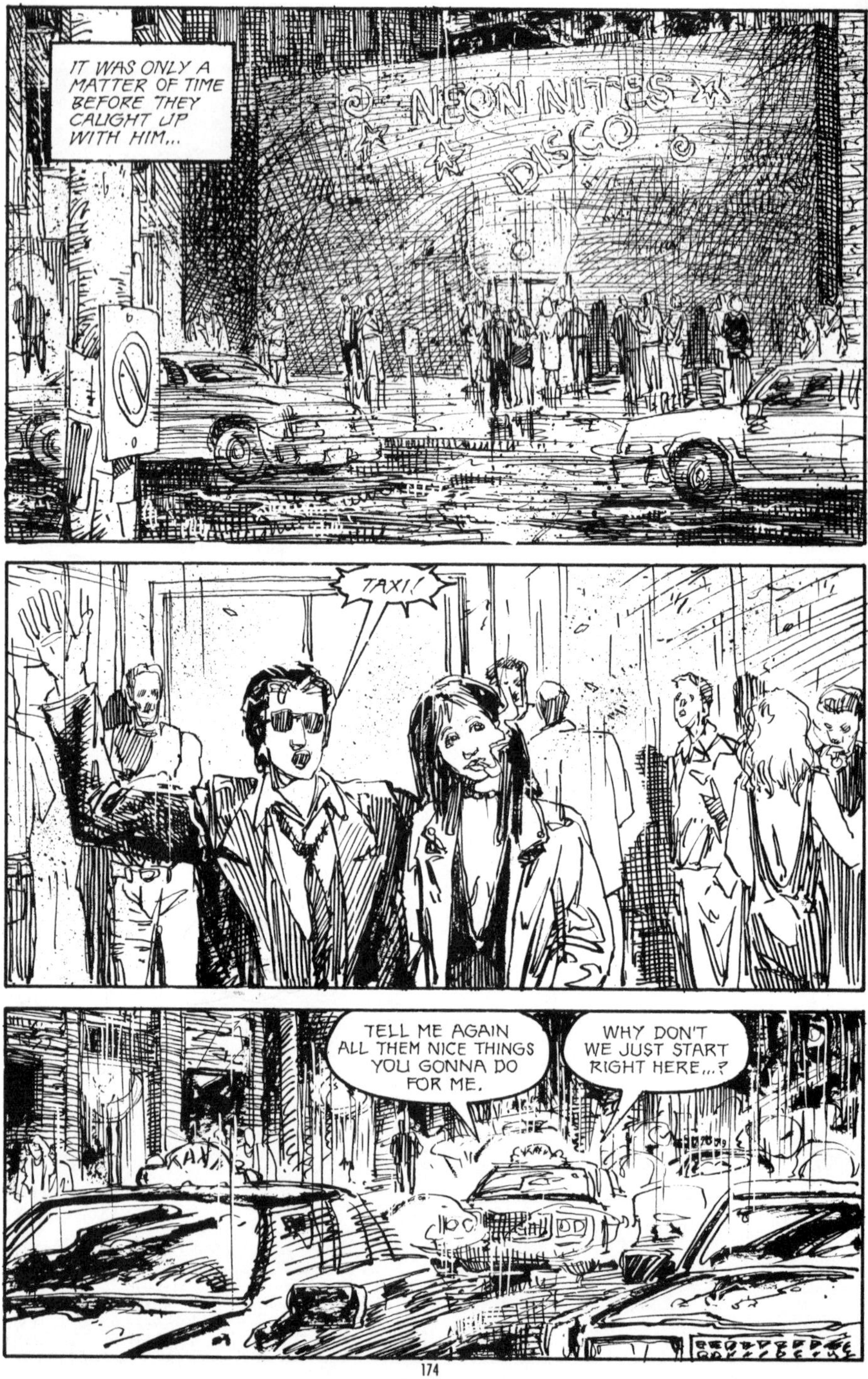
IT WAS ONLY A MATTER OF TIME BEFORE THEY CAUGHT UP WITH HIM...
NEON NITES DISCO
TAXI!
TELL ME AGAIN ALL THEM NICE THINGS YOU GONNA DO FOR ME.
WHY DON'T WE JUST START RIGHT HERE...?

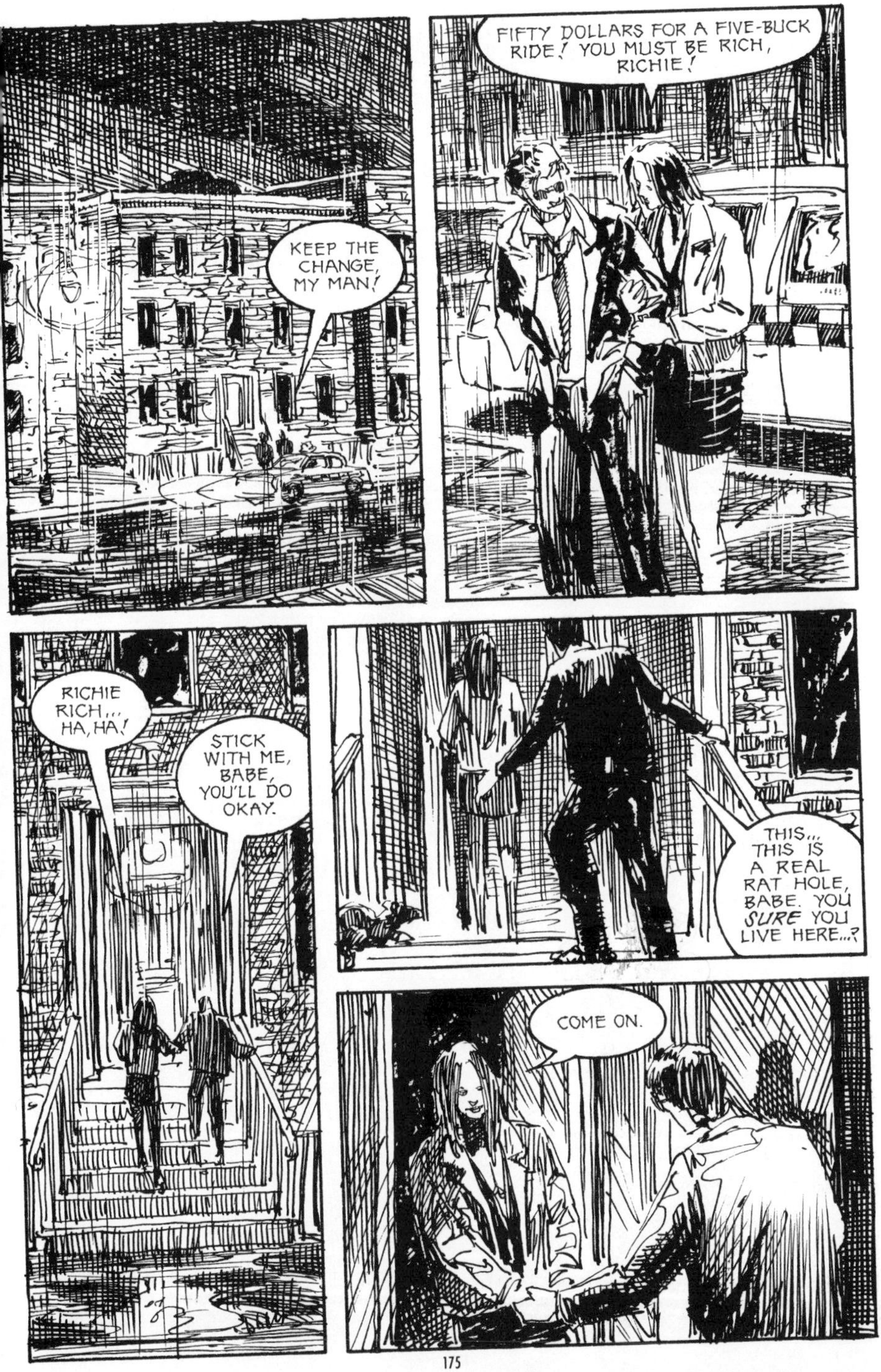
KEEP THE CHANGE, MY MAN!
FIFTY DOLLARS FOR A FIVE-BUCK RIDE! YOU MUST BE RICH, RICHIE!
RICHIE RICH... HA, HA!
STICK WITH ME, BABE, YOU'LL DO OKAY.
THIS... THIS IS A REAL RAT HOLE, BABE. YOU *SURE* YOU LIVE HERE...?
COME ON.

SLAM

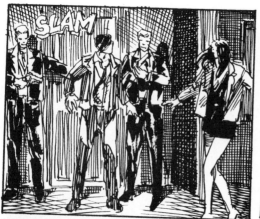

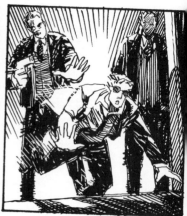

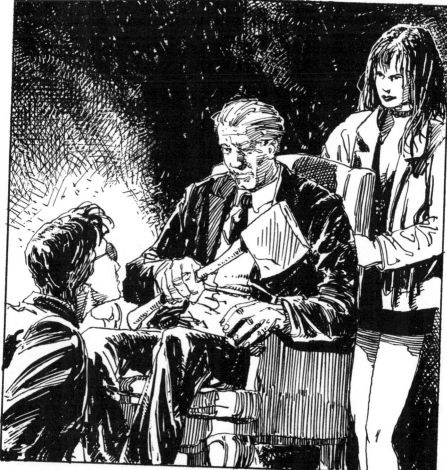

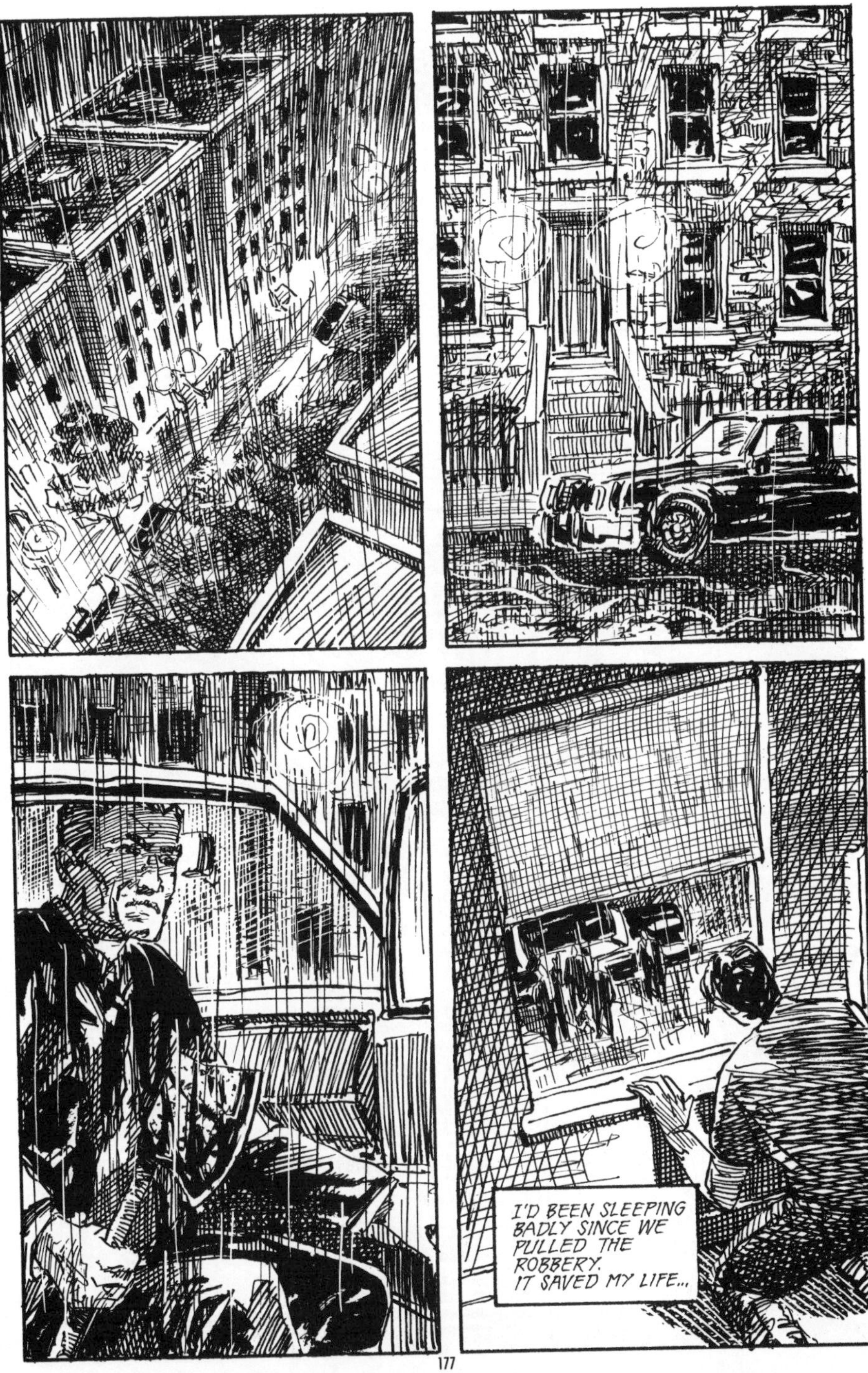
I'D BEEN SLEEPING BADLY SINCE WE PULLED THE ROBBERY. IT SAVED MY LIFE...

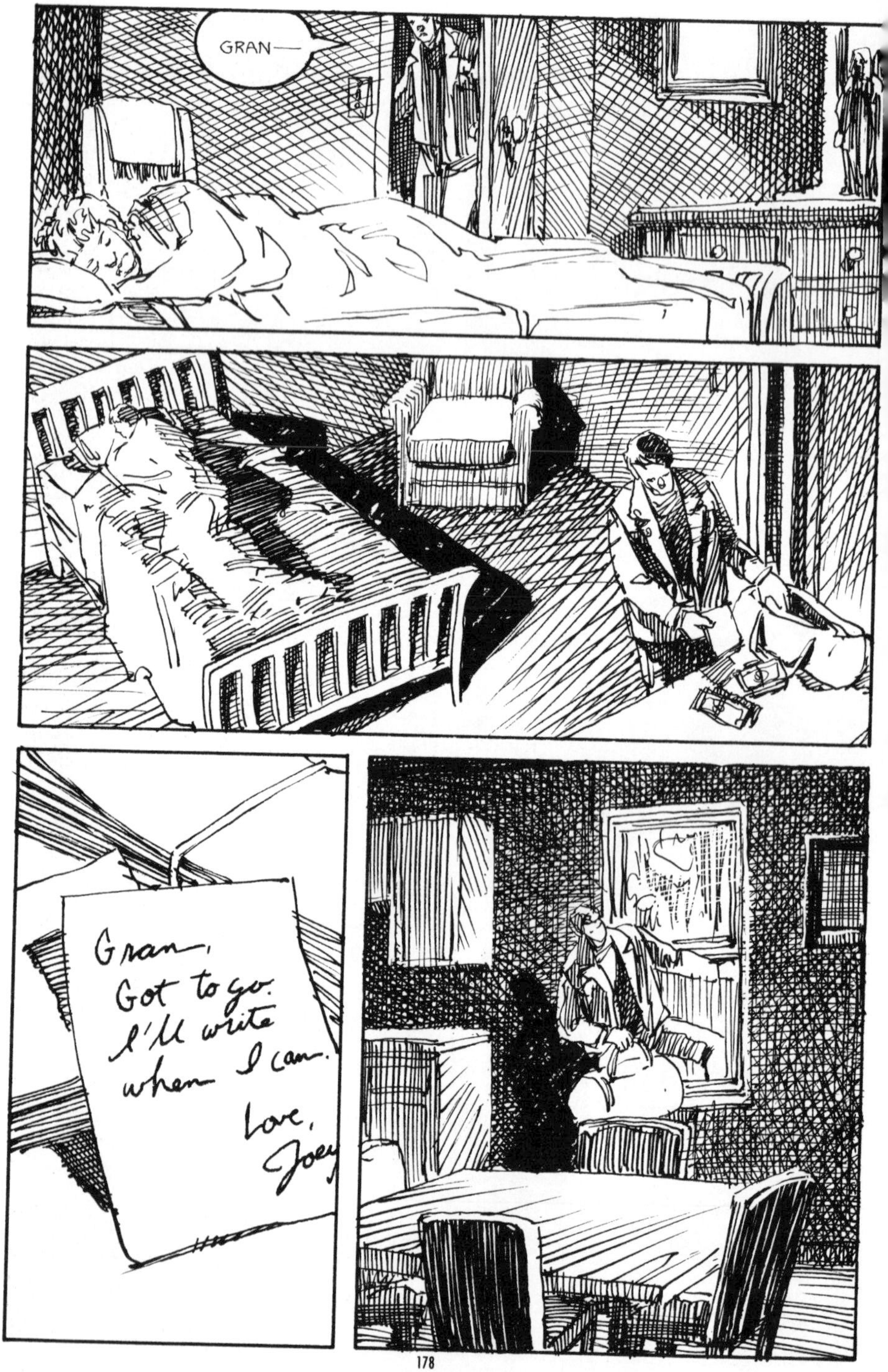
GRAN—
Gran,
Got to go.
I'll write
when I can.
Love,
Joey

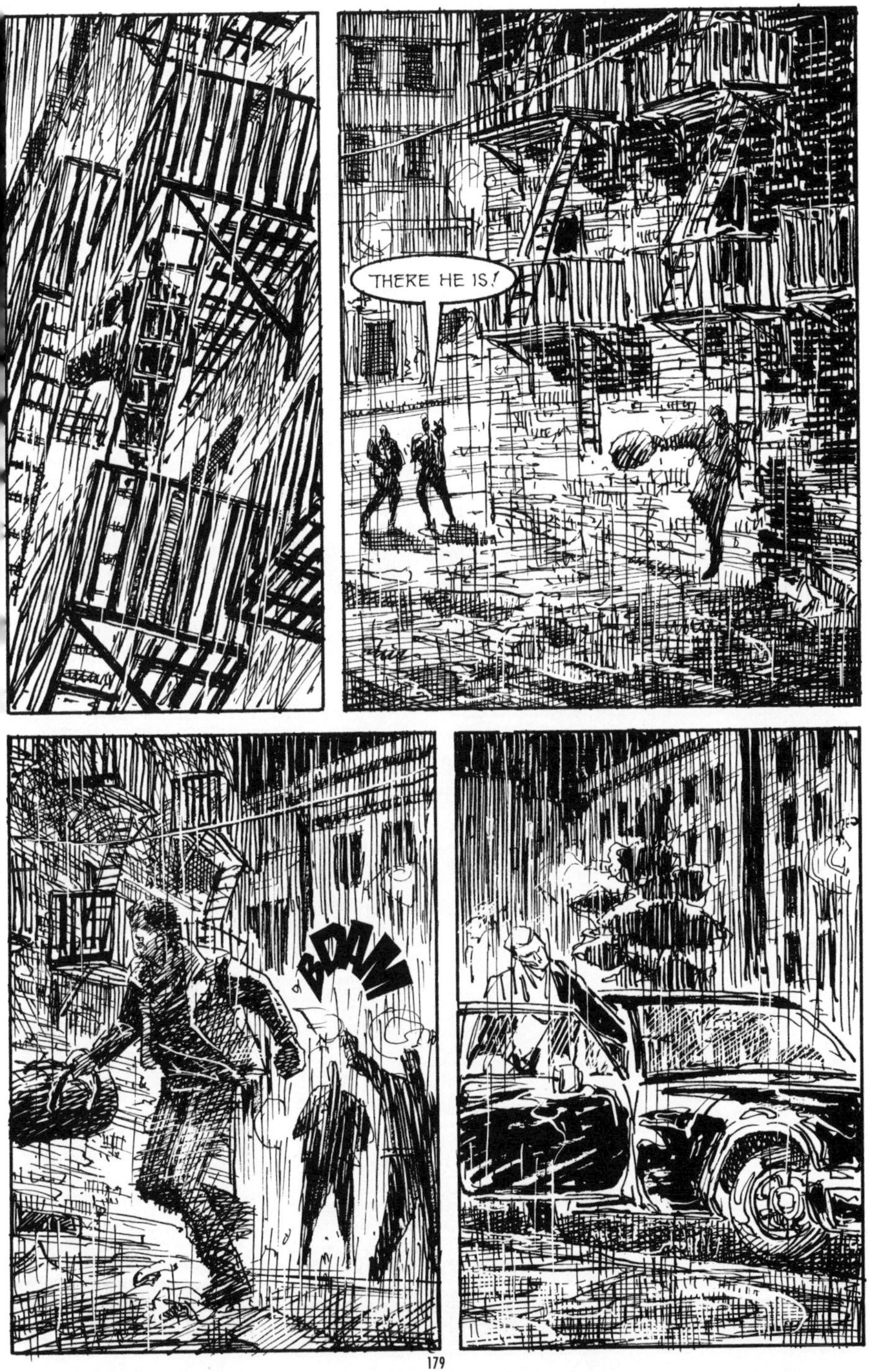
THERE HE IS!
BDAM

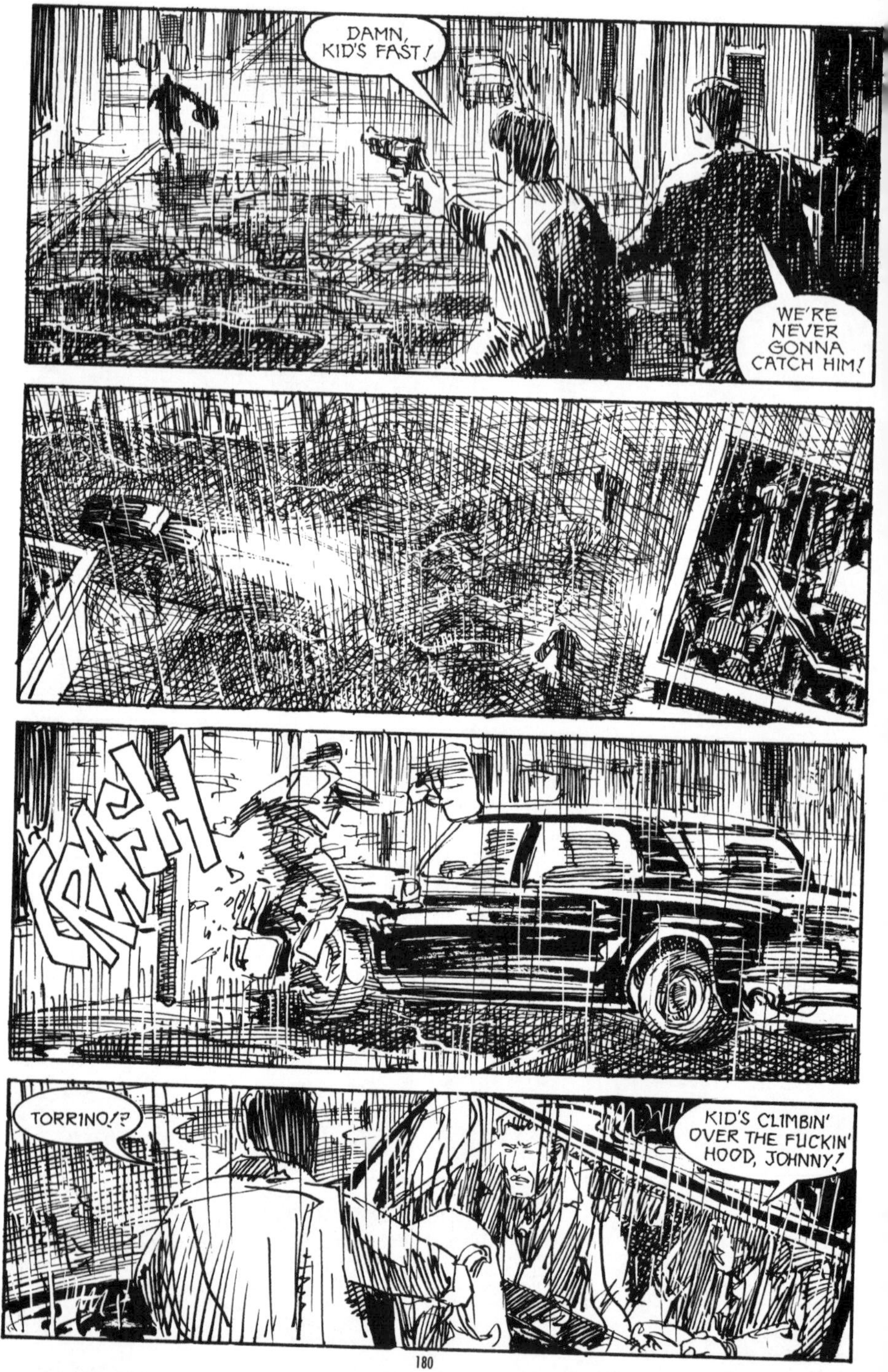
DAMN, KID'S FAST!
WE'RE NEVER GONNA CATCH HIM!
KRASH
TORRINO!?
KID'S CLIMBIN' OVER THE FUCKIN' HOOD, JOHNNY!

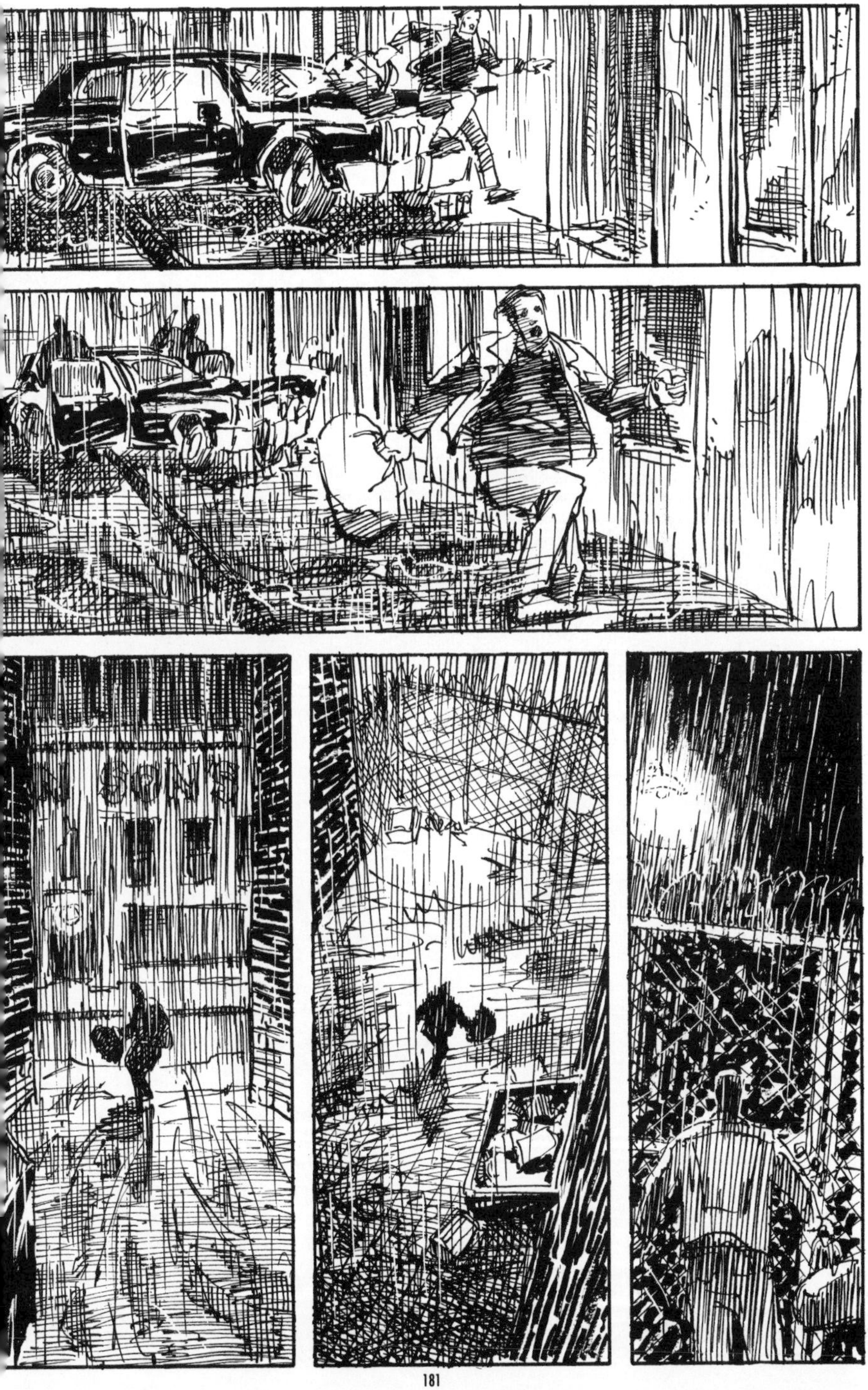

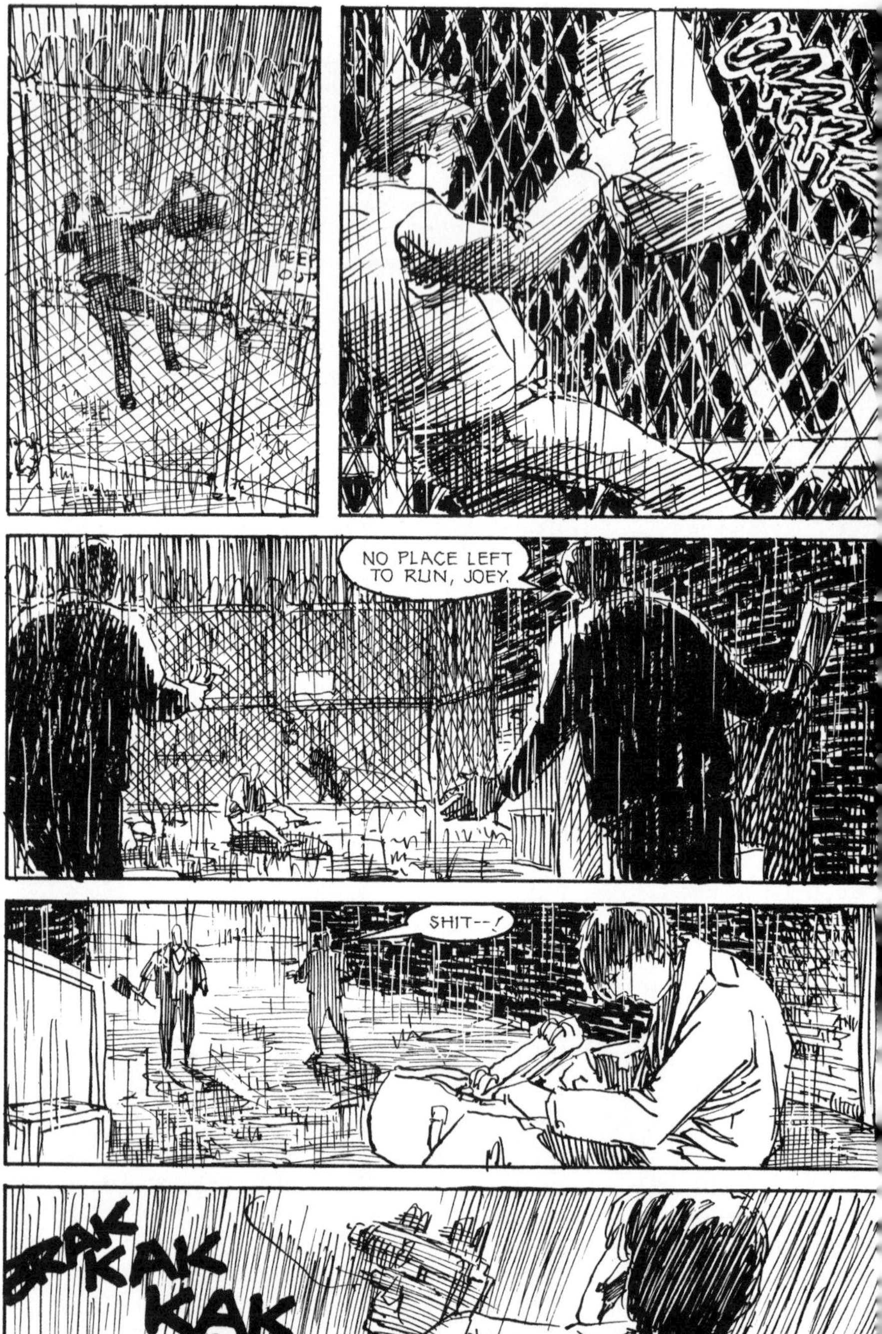
KEEP OUT
NO PLACE LEFT TO RUN, JOEY.
SHIT--!
BRAK KAK KAK KAK

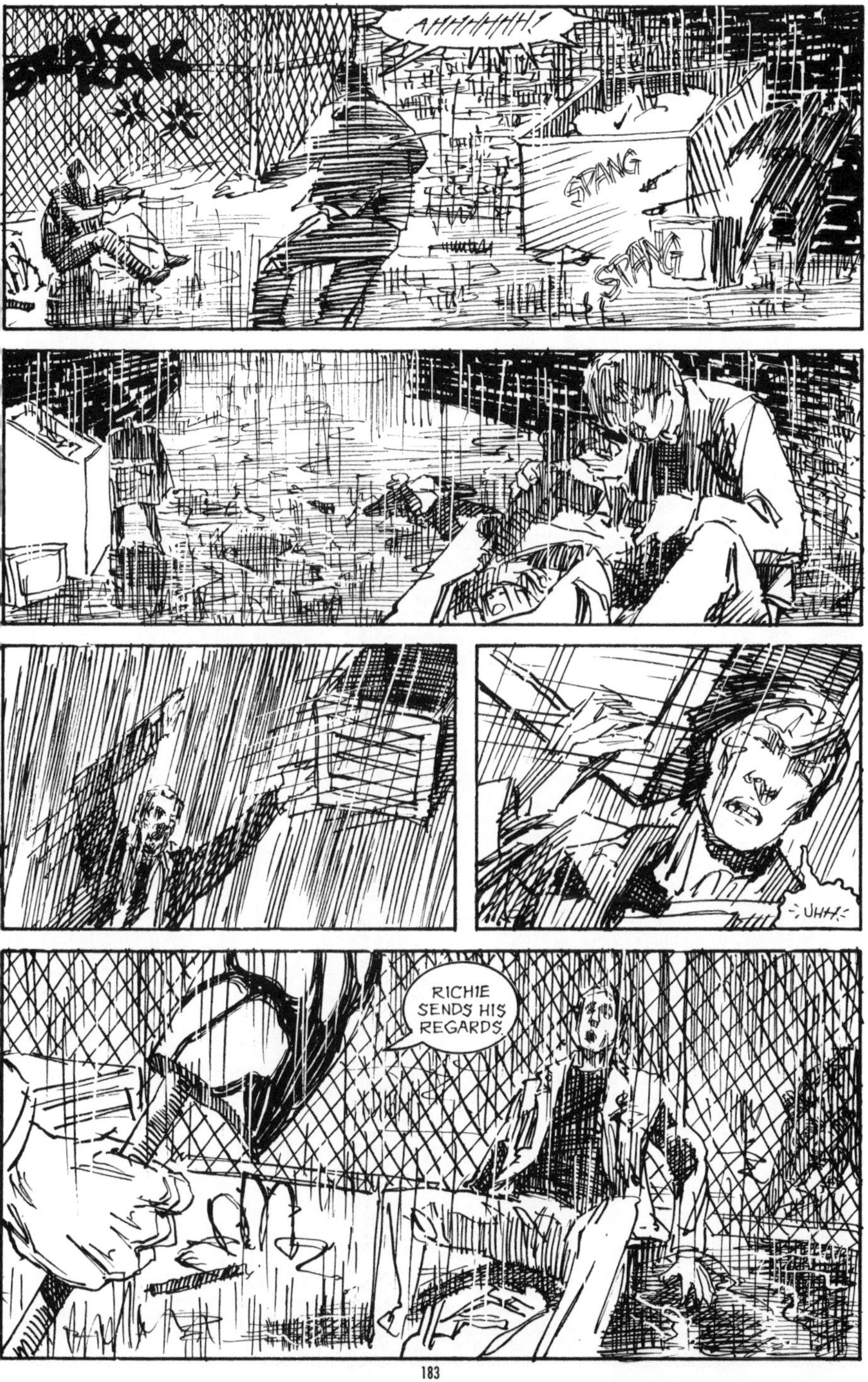
AHHHHHHH!
SPANG
SPANG
UHH
RICHIE SENDS HIS REGARDS.

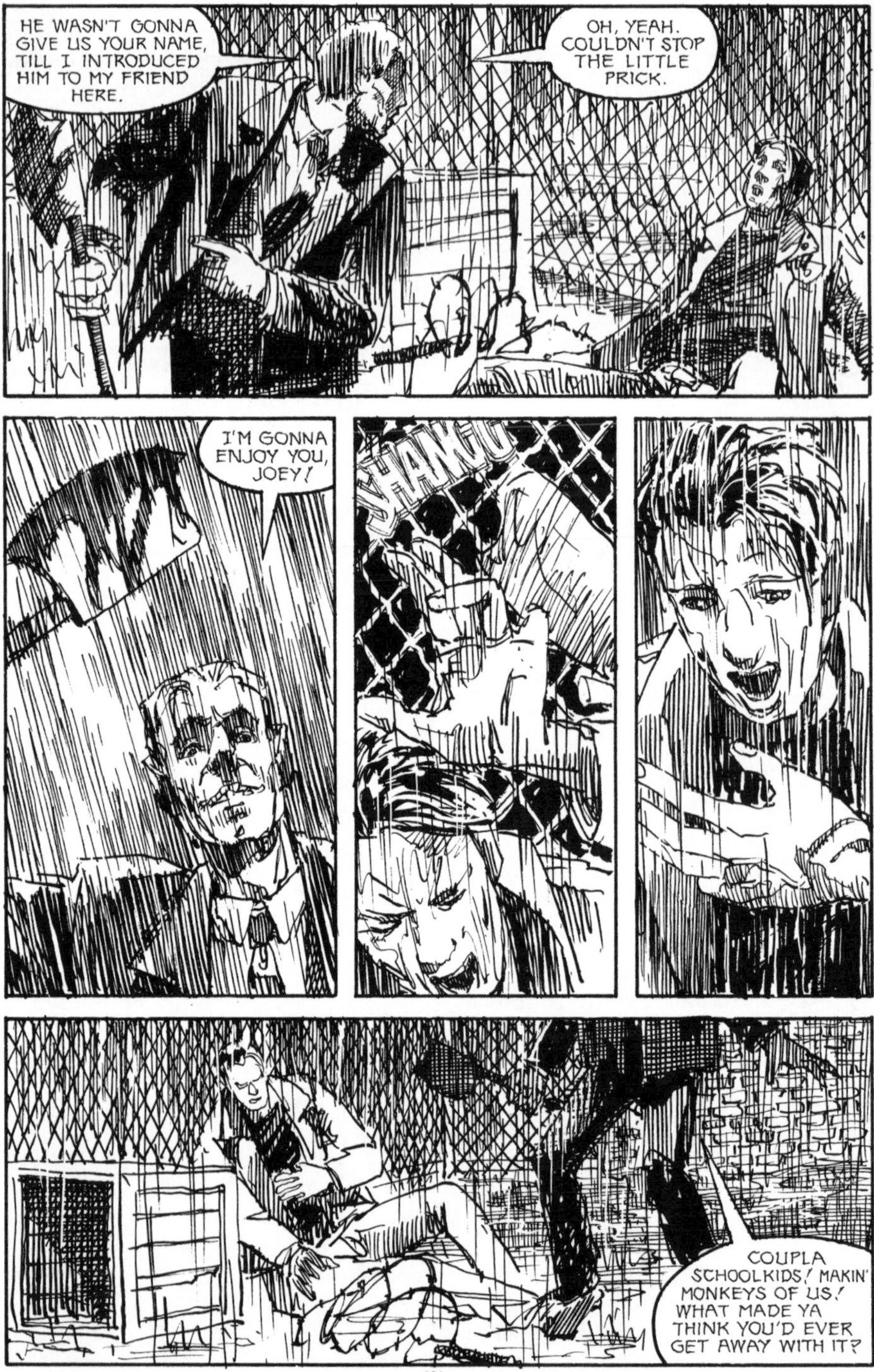
HE WASN'T GONNA GIVE US YOUR NAME, TILL I INTRODUCED HIM TO MY FRIEND HERE.
OH, YEAH. COULDN'T STOP THE LITTLE PRICK.
I'M GONNA ENJOY YOU, JOEY!
COUPLA SCHOOLKIDS! MAKIN' MONKEYS OF US! WHAT MADE YA THINK YOU'D EVER GET AWAY WITH IT?

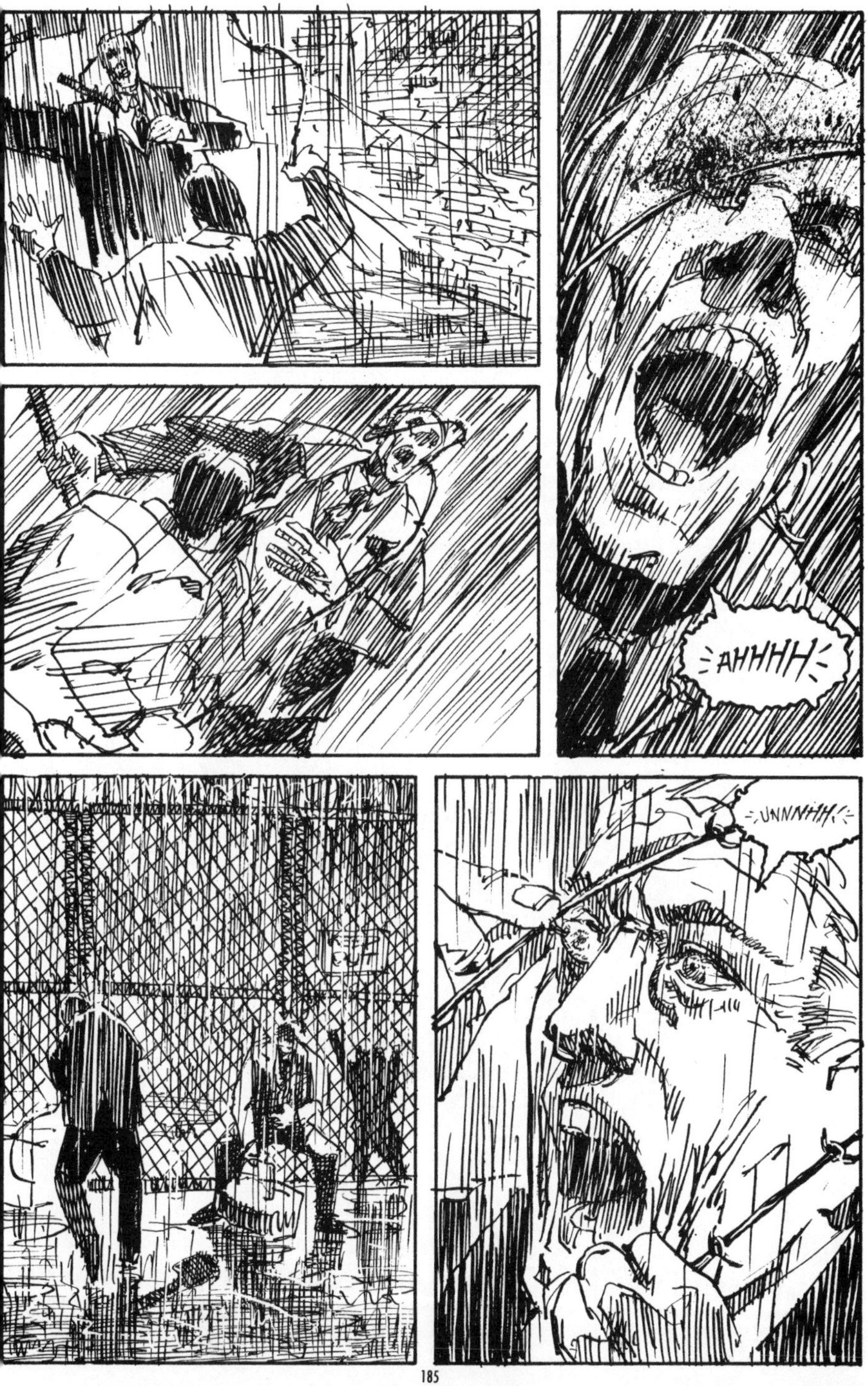
AHHHH
UNNNHH

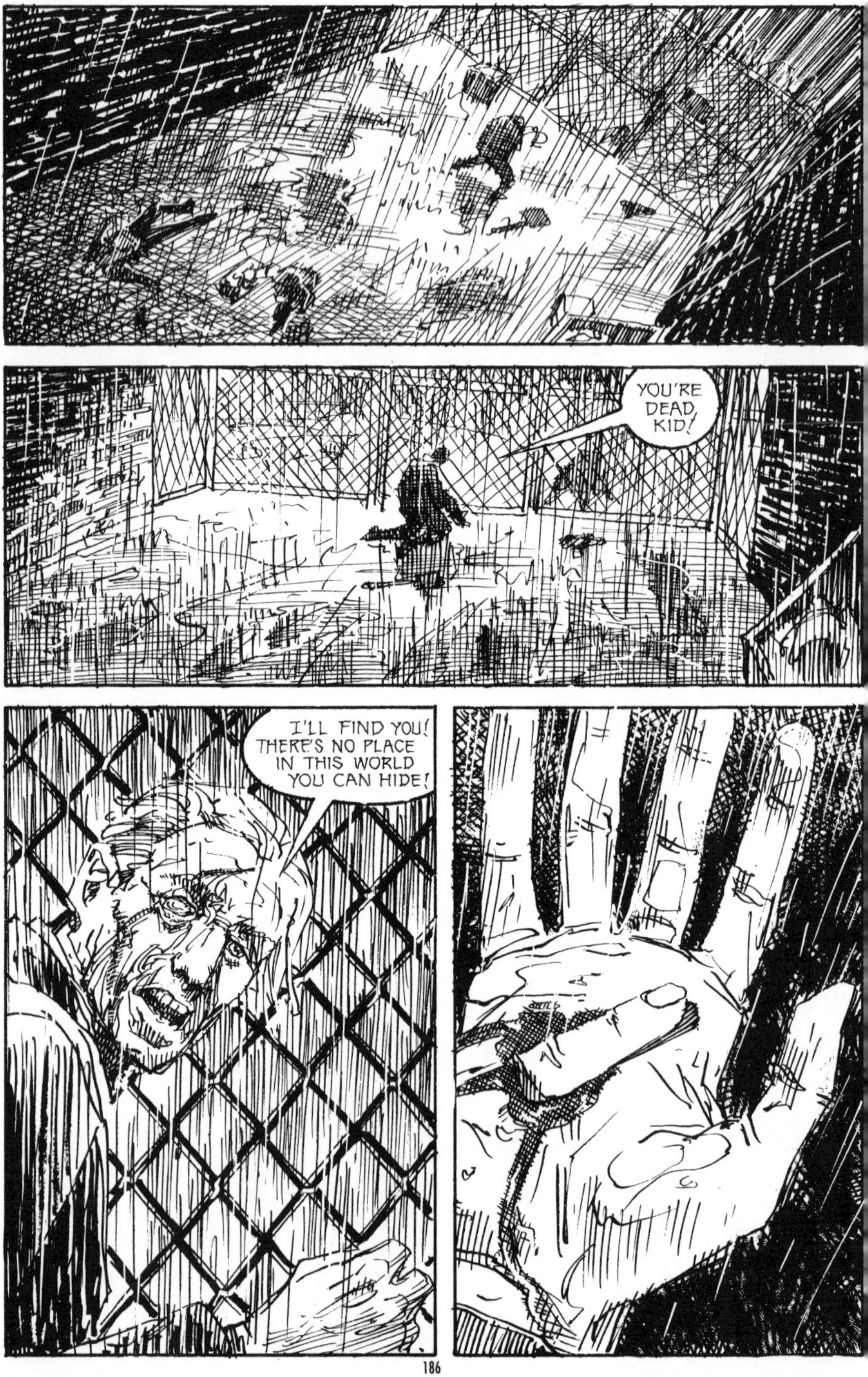
YOU'RE DEAD, KID!
I'LL FIND YOU! THERE'S NO PLACE IN THIS WORLD YOU CAN HIDE!

I NEVER SAW MY GRAN AGAIN. I COULDN'T GO BACK, COULDN'T WRITE. IT WAS TOO DANGEROUS.

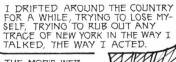

I DRIFTED AROUND THE COUNTRY FOR A WHILE, TRYING TO LOSE MY-SELF, TRYING TO RUB OUT ANY TRACE OF NEW YORK IN THE WAY I TALKED, THE WAY I ACTED.

THE MOB'S WEB SPREADS EVERYWHERE, AND THEY DON'T FORGET. IF I WAS TO HAVE ANY CHANCE OF STAYING ALIVE, I HAD TO DIS-APPEAR COMPLETELY-- COMPLETELY AND FOREVER.

EVENTUALLY I TURNED UP HERE... AND MET YOU.

BUT YOU WERE TOM MCKENNA — YOU HAD A DRIVER'S LICENSE, A SOCIAL SECURITY NUMBER--

THERE WAS A REAL TOM MCKENNA. HE DIED. IT'S NOT SO DIFFICULT WHEN YOU KNOW HOW...

AND TORRINO DID FIND YOU. WHAT AN EVIL, EVIL MAN!

WHATEVER YOU DID, DAD, THEY HAD IT COMING!

DO YOU FORGIVE ME, EDIE?

OF COURSE I DO, TOM. IT'S ALL BEEN A... A BIT OF A SHOCK, THAT'S ALL.

YOU'RE STILL THE MAN I MARRIED — THE MAN I LOVE.

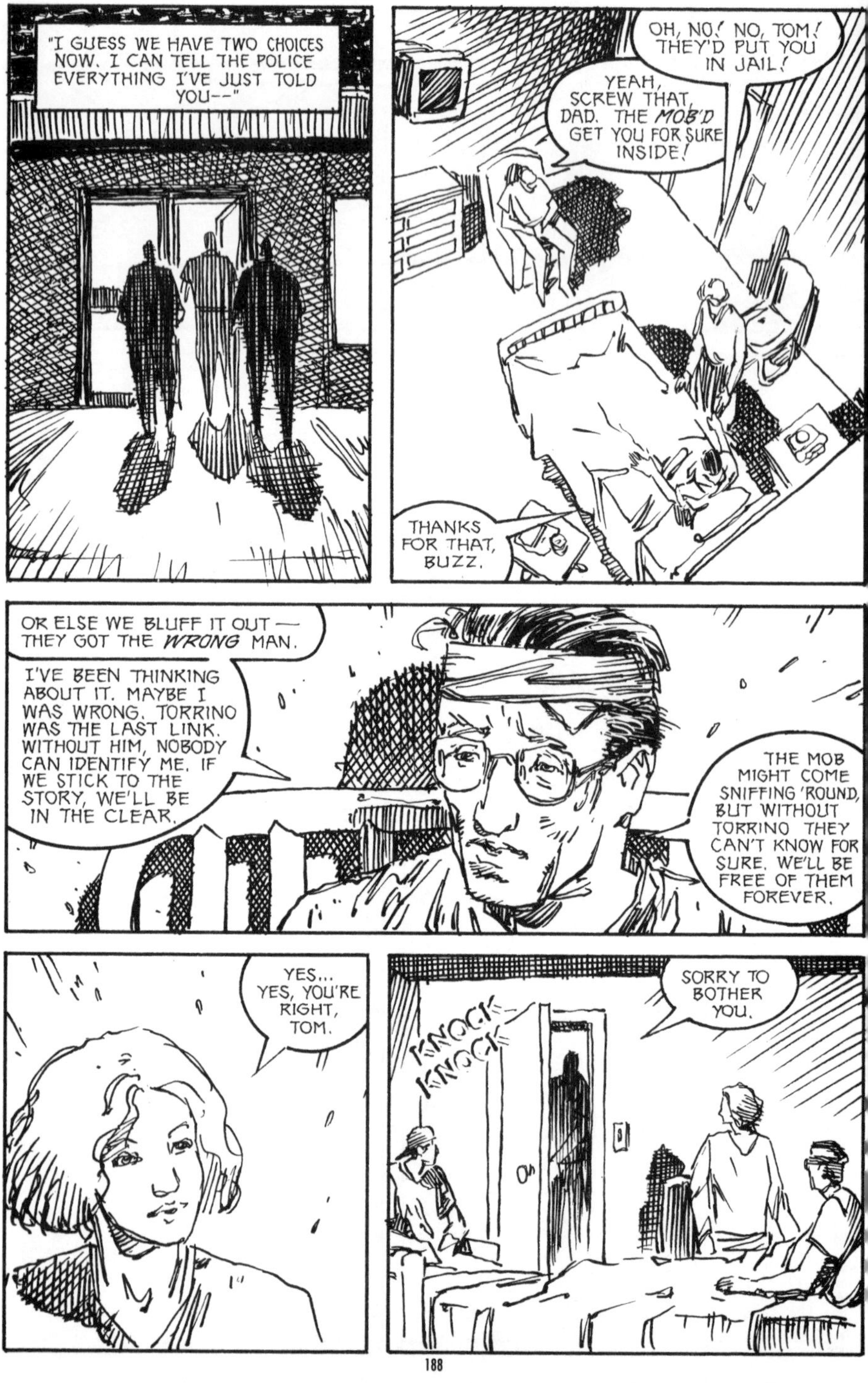
"I GUESS WE HAVE TWO CHOICES NOW. I CAN TELL THE POLICE EVERYTHING I'VE JUST TOLD YOU--"
OH, NO! NO, TOM! THEY'D PUT YOU IN JAIL!
YEAH, SCREW THAT, DAD. THE MOB'D GET YOU FOR SURE INSIDE!
THANKS FOR THAT, BUZZ.
OR ELSE WE BLUFF IT OUT— THEY GOT THE WRONG MAN.
I'VE BEEN THINKING ABOUT IT. MAYBE I WAS WRONG. TORRINO WAS THE LAST LINK. WITHOUT HIM, NOBODY CAN IDENTIFY ME. IF WE STICK TO THE STORY, WE'LL BE IN THE CLEAR.
THE MOB MIGHT COME SNIFFING 'ROUND, BUT WITHOUT TORRINO THEY CAN'T KNOW FOR SURE. WE'LL BE FREE OF THEM FOREVER.
YES... YES, YOU'RE RIGHT, TOM.
SORRY TO BOTHER YOU.
KNOCK KNOCK

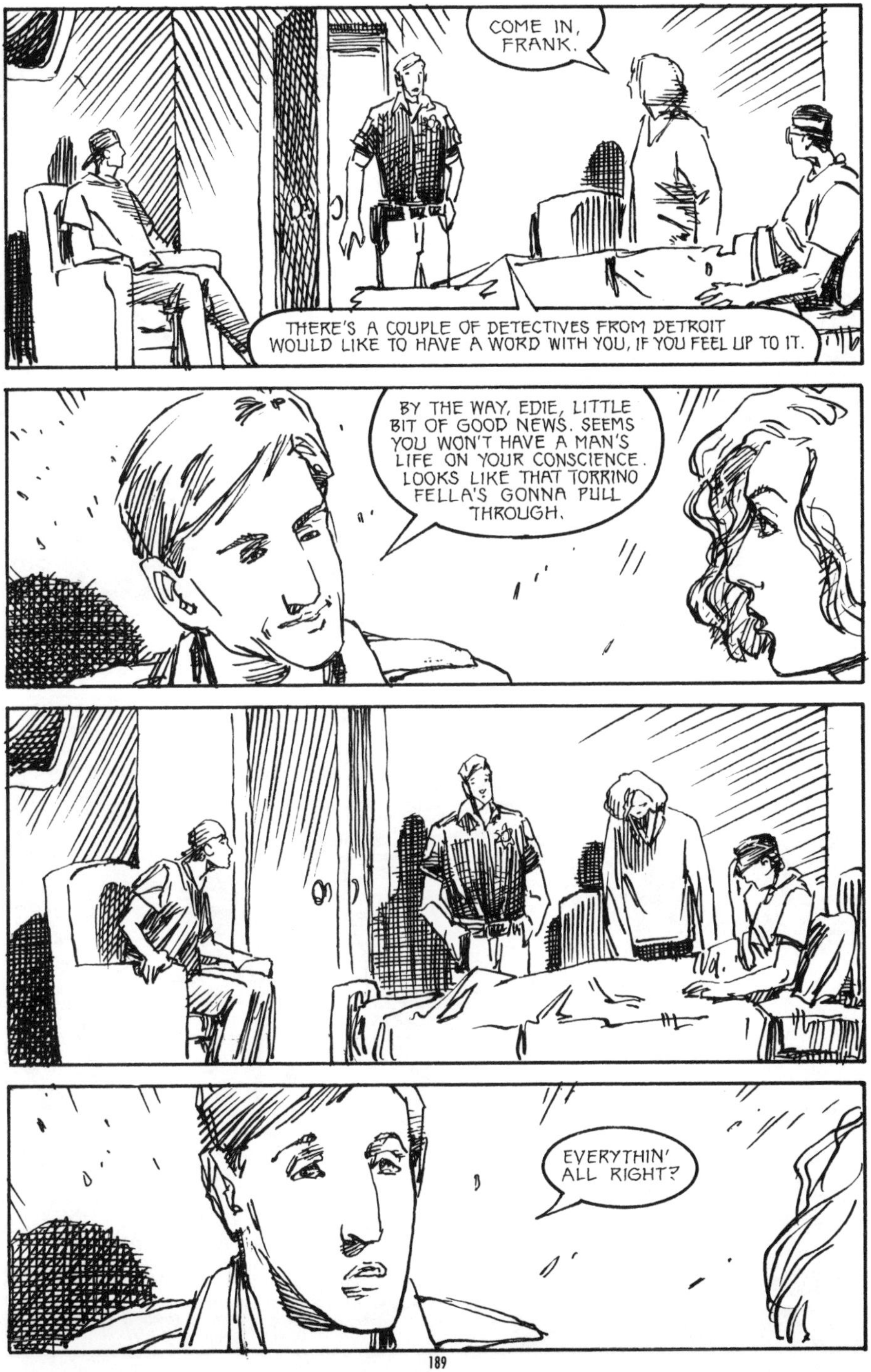
COME IN, FRANK.
THERE'S A COUPLE OF DETECTIVES FROM DETROIT WOULD LIKE TO HAVE A WORD WITH YOU, IF YOU FEEL UP TO IT.
BY THE WAY, EDIE, LITTLE BIT OF GOOD NEWS. SEEMS YOU WON'T HAVE A MAN'S LIFE ON YOUR CONSCIENCE. LOOKS LIKE THAT TORRINO FELLA'S GONNA PULL THROUGH.
EVERYTHIN' ALL RIGHT?

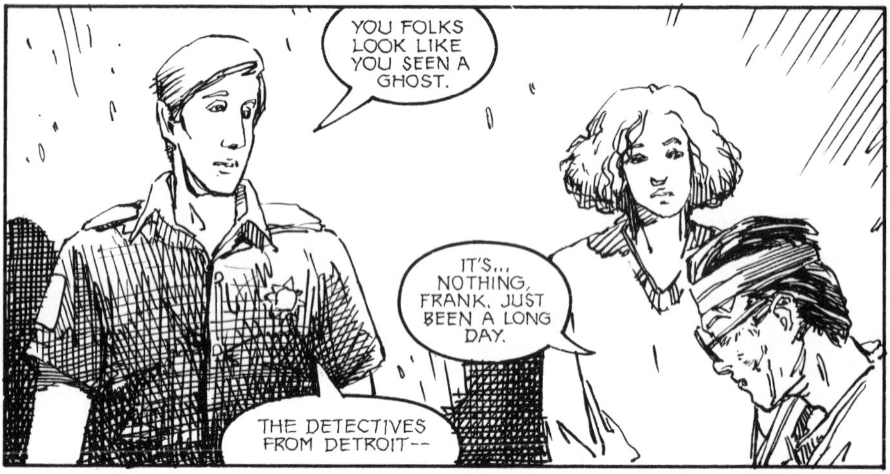
YOU FOLKS LOOK LIKE YOU SEEN A GHOST.
THE DETECTIVES FROM DETROIT--
IT'S... NOTHING, FRANK. JUST BEEN A LONG DAY.

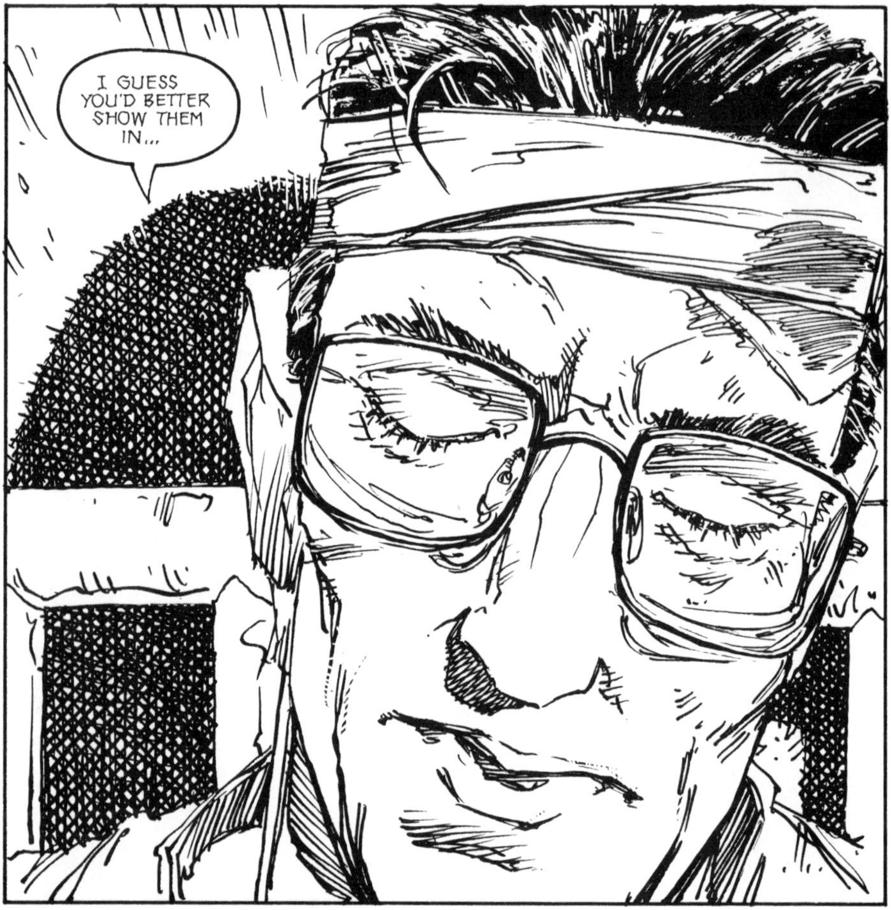
I GUESS YOU'D BETTER SHOW THEM IN...

CHAPTER 3
WITH EVIL INTENT

"They have sown the wind,

and they shall reap the whirlwind."

-HOSEA 8:7

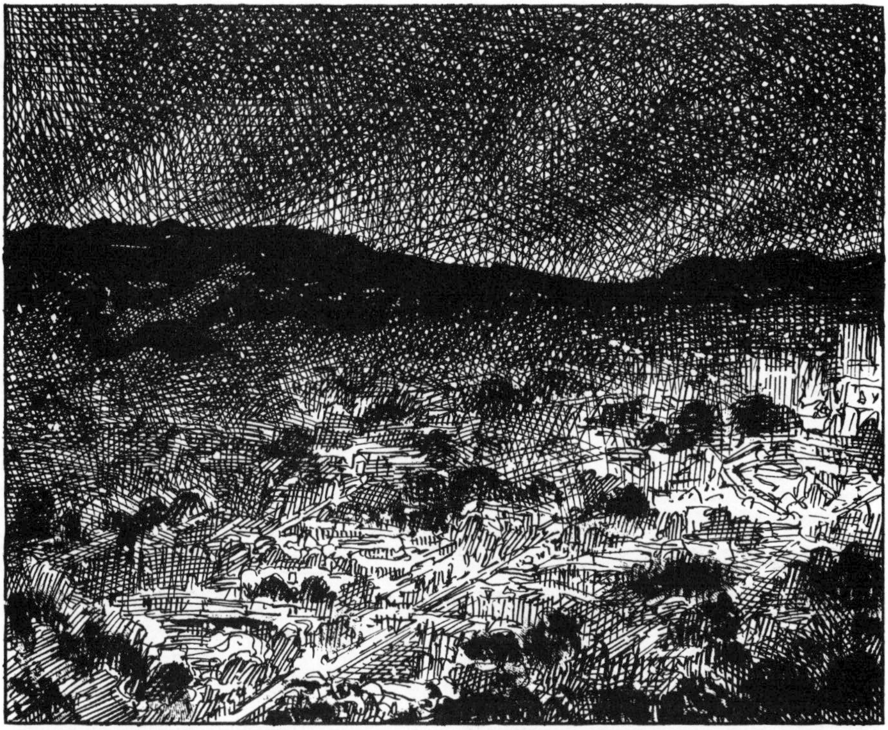

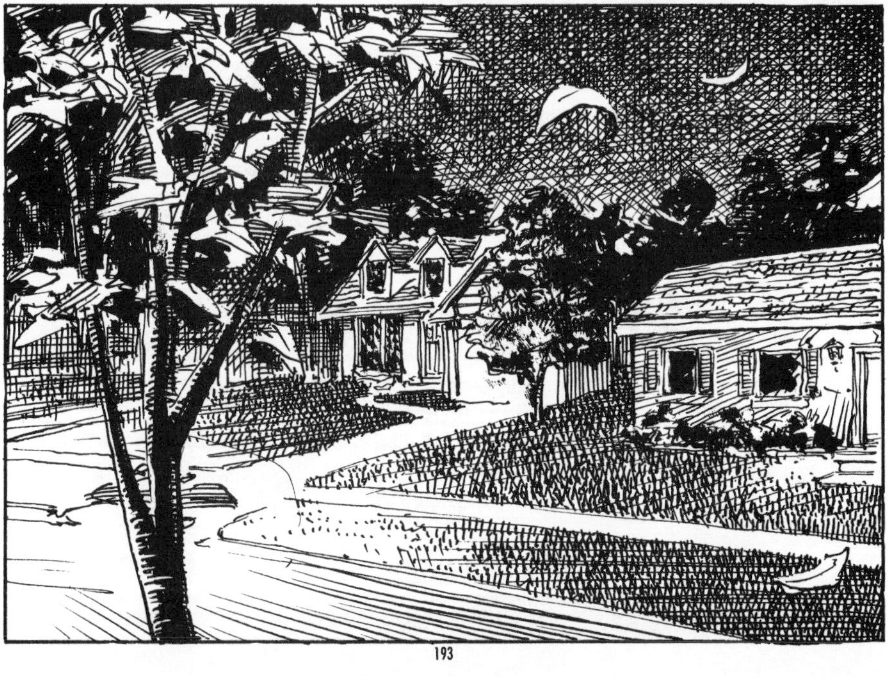

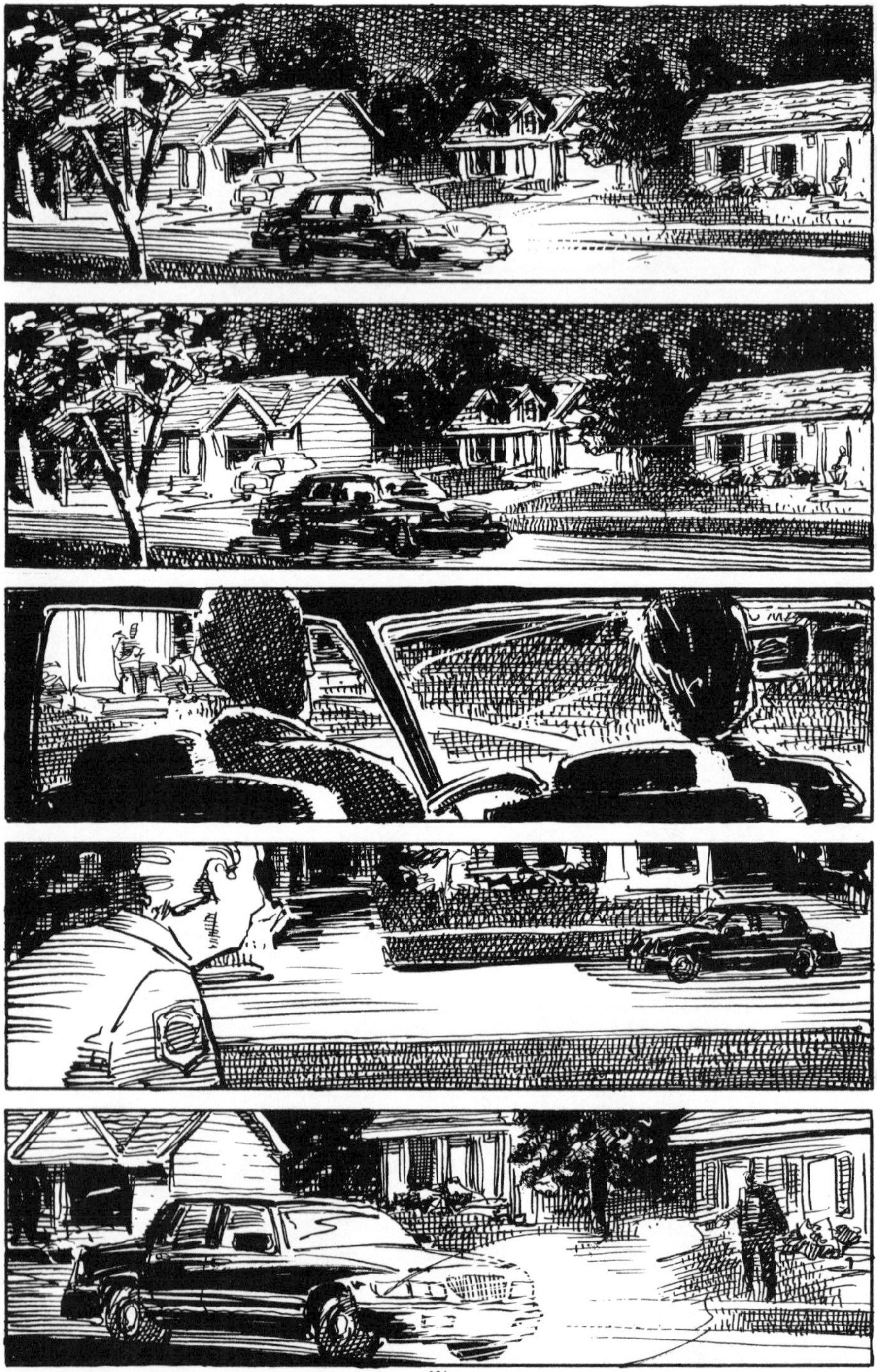

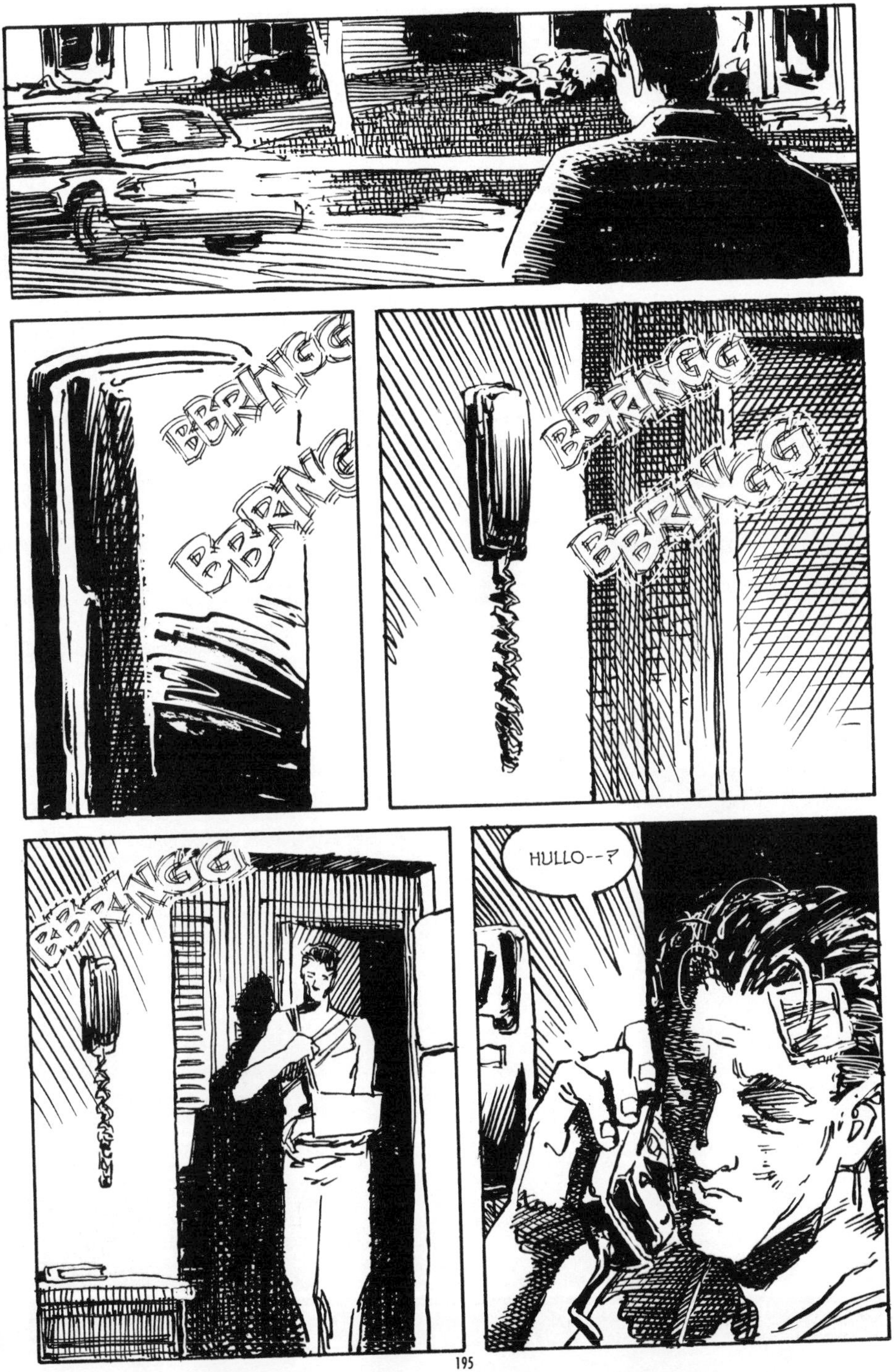
BBRINGG
BBRINGG
BBRINGG
BBRINGG
BBRINGG
HULLO--?

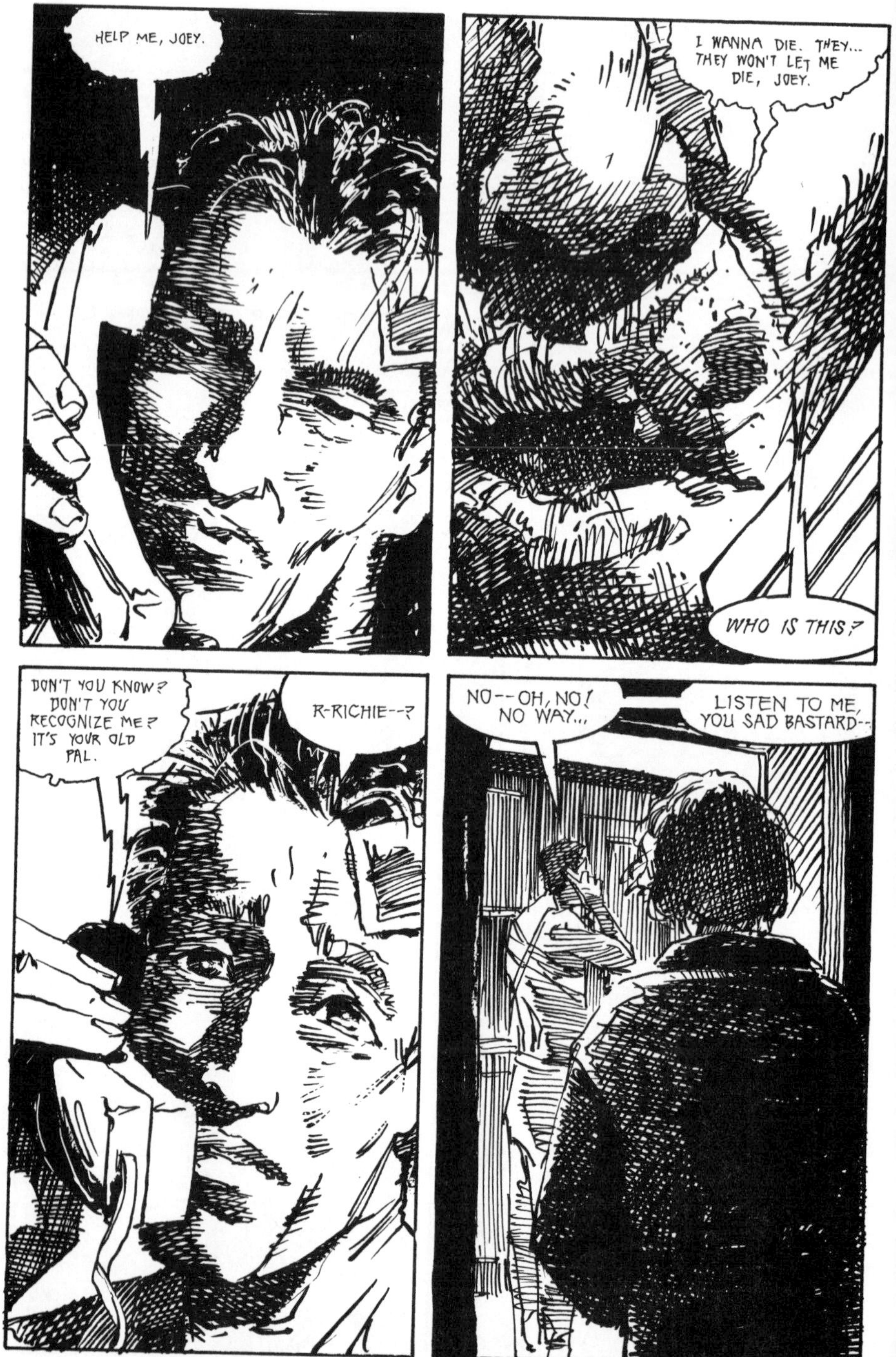
HELP ME, JOEY.
I WANNA DIE. THEY... THEY WON'T LET ME DIE, JOEY.
WHO IS THIS?
DON'T YOU KNOW? DON'T YOU RECOGNIZE ME? IT'S YOUR OLD PAL.
R-RICHIE--?
NO--OH, NO! NO WAY...
LISTEN TO ME, YOU SAD BASTARD--

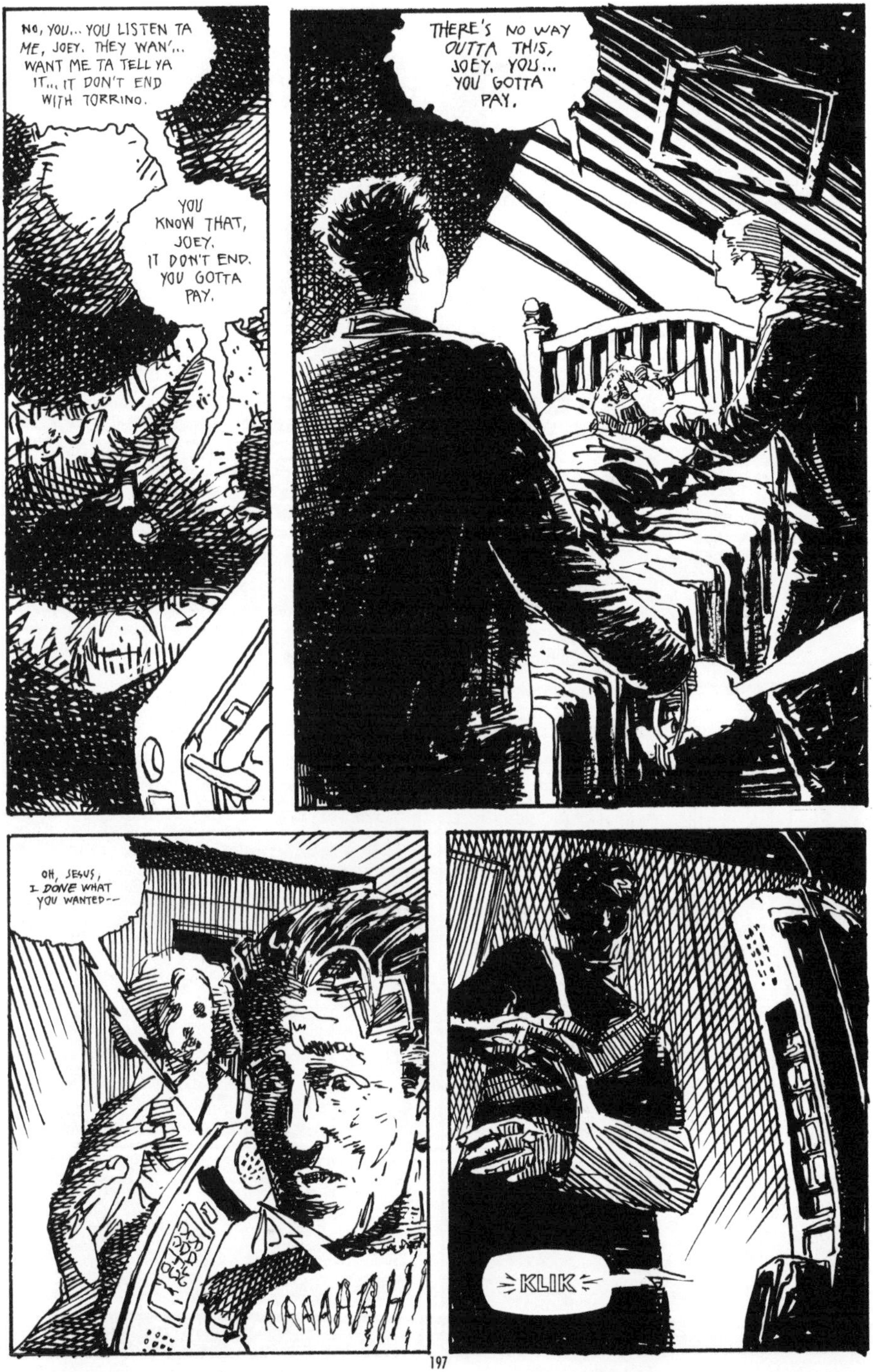
NO, YOU... YOU LISTEN TA ME, JOEY. THEY WAN'... WANT ME TA TELL YA IT... IT DON'T END WITH TORRINO.
YOU KNOW THAT, JOEY. IT DON'T END. YOU GOTTA PAY.
THERE'S NO WAY OUTTA THIS, JOEY. YOU... YOU GOTTA PAY.
OH, JESUS, I DONE WHAT YOU WANTED--
ARRAAAAH!
KLIK

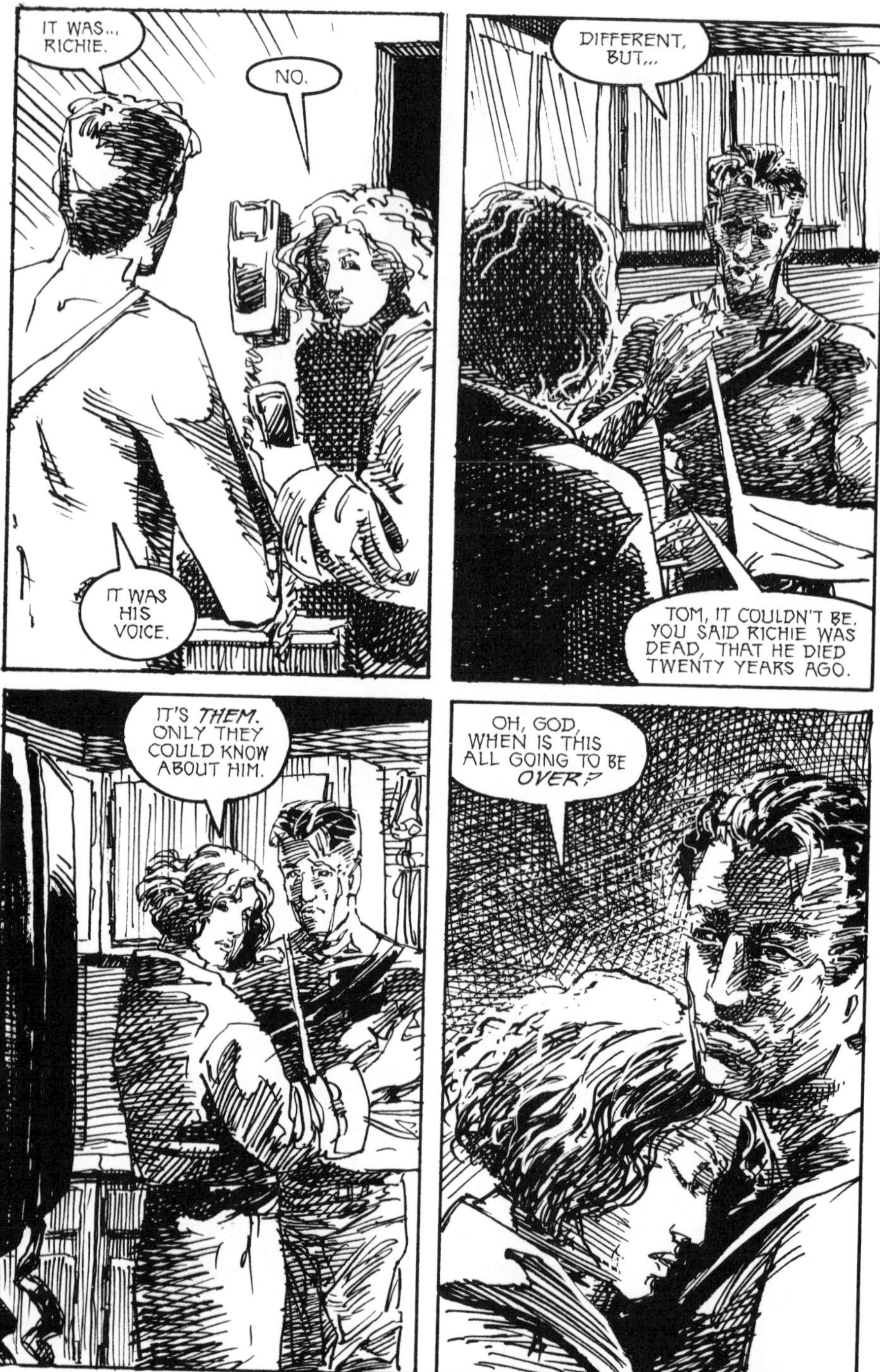
IT WAS... RICHIE.
NO.
IT WAS HIS VOICE.
DIFFERENT, BUT...
TOM, IT COULDN'T BE. YOU SAID RICHIE WAS DEAD, THAT HE DIED TWENTY YEARS AGO.
IT'S *THEM*. ONLY THEY COULD KNOW ABOUT HIM.
OH, GOD, WHEN IS THIS ALL GOING TO BE *OVER?*

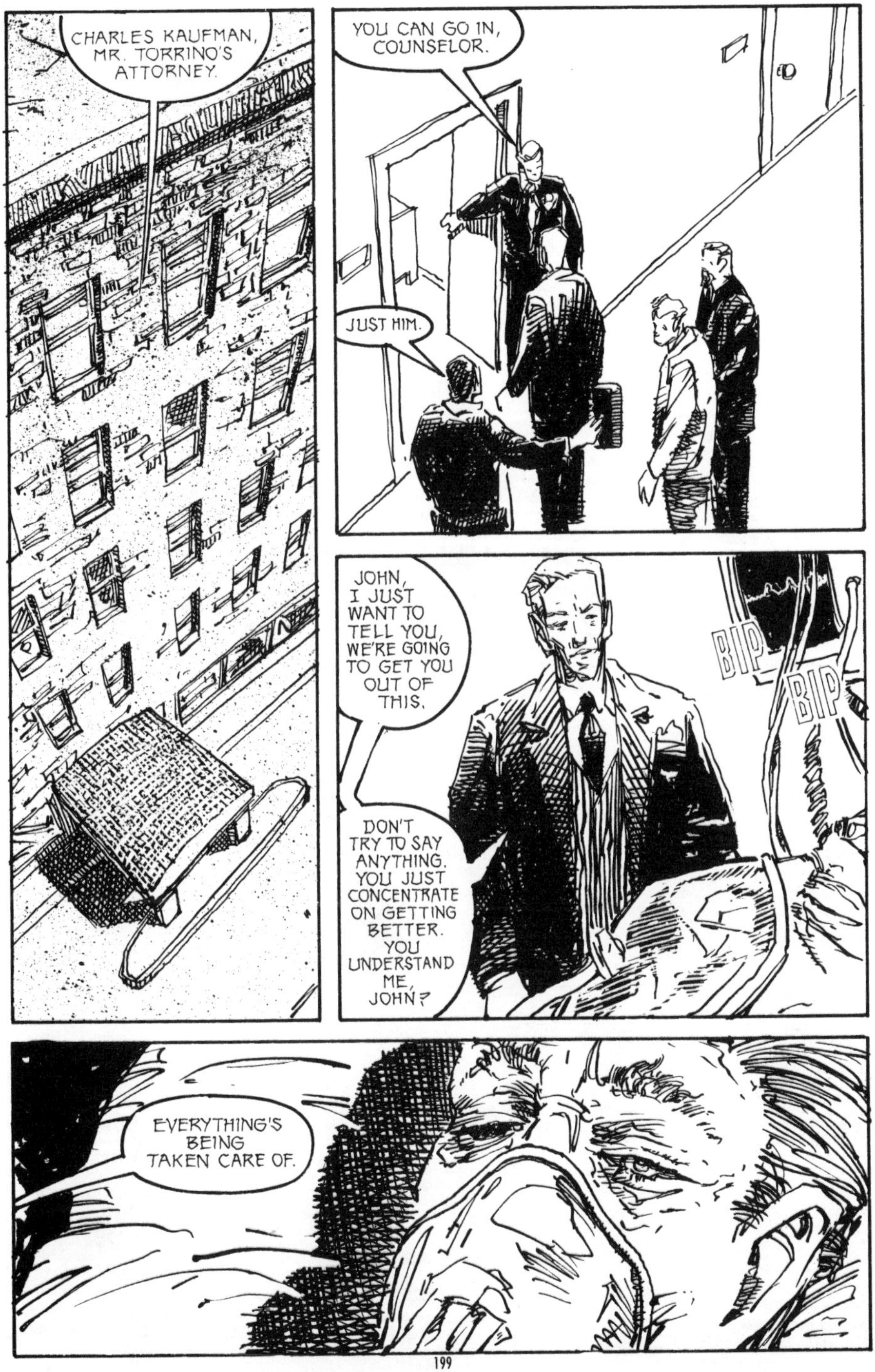

CHARLES KAUFMAN, MR. TORRINO'S ATTORNEY.
YOU CAN GO IN, COUNSELOR.
JUST HIM.
JOHN, I JUST WANT TO TELL YOU, WE'RE GOING TO GET YOU OUT OF THIS.
BIP
BIP
DON'T TRY TO SAY ANYTHING. YOU JUST CONCENTRATE ON GETTING BETTER. YOU UNDERSTAND ME, JOHN?
EVERYTHING'S BEING TAKEN CARE OF.

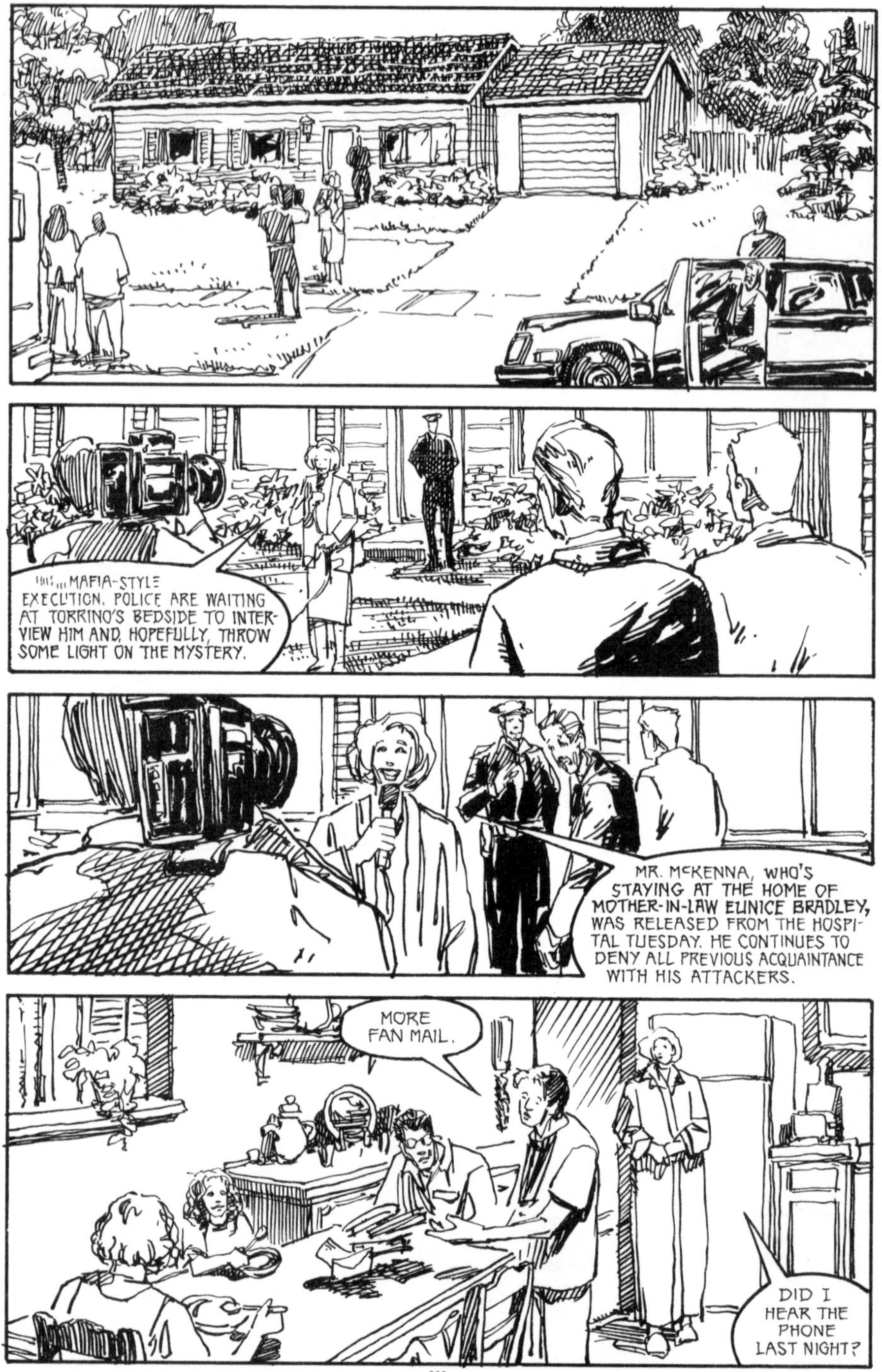
...MAFIA-STYLE EXECUTION. POLICE ARE WAITING AT TORRINO'S BEDSIDE TO INTERVIEW HIM AND, HOPEFULLY, THROW SOME LIGHT ON THE MYSTERY.
MR. McKENNA, WHO'S STAYING AT THE HOME OF MOTHER-IN-LAW EUNICE BRADLEY, WAS RELEASED FROM THE HOSPITAL TUESDAY. HE CONTINUES TO DENY ALL PREVIOUS ACQUAINTANCE WITH HIS ATTACKERS.
MORE FAN MAIL.
DID I HEAR THE PHONE LAST NIGHT?

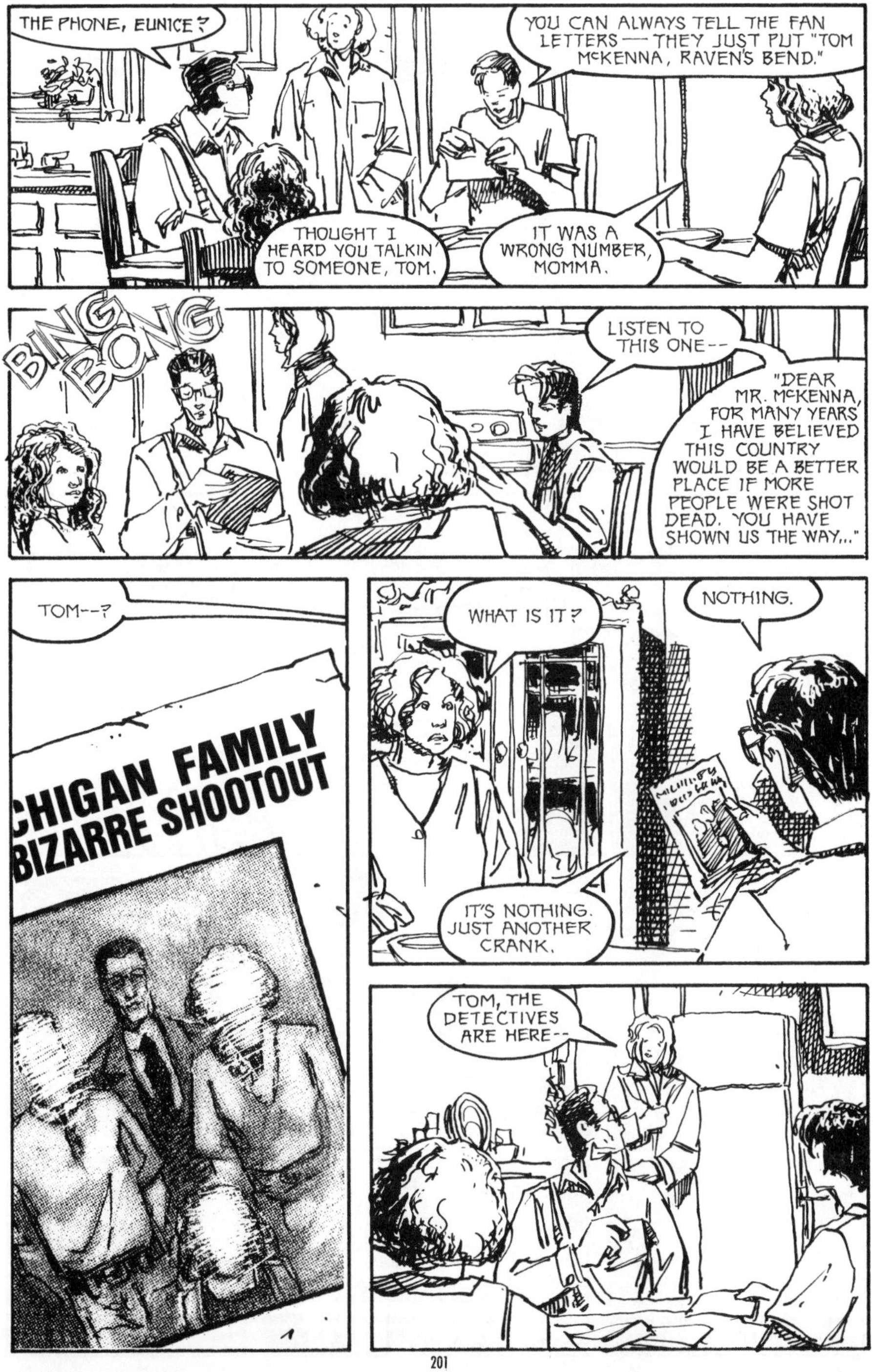
THE PHONE, EUNICE?
YOU CAN ALWAYS TELL THE FAN LETTERS — THEY JUST PUT "TOM McKENNA, RAVEN'S BEND."
THOUGHT I HEARD YOU TALKIN' TO SOMEONE, TOM.
IT WAS A WRONG NUMBER, MOMMA.
BING BONG
LISTEN TO THIS ONE--
"DEAR MR. McKENNA, FOR MANY YEARS I HAVE BELIEVED THIS COUNTRY WOULD BE A BETTER PLACE IF MORE PEOPLE WERE SHOT DEAD. YOU HAVE SHOWN US THE WAY..."
TOM--?
CHIGAN FAMILY
BIZARRE SHOOTOUT
WHAT IS IT?
NOTHING.
IT'S NOTHING. JUST ANOTHER CRANK.
TOM, THE DETECTIVES ARE HERE--

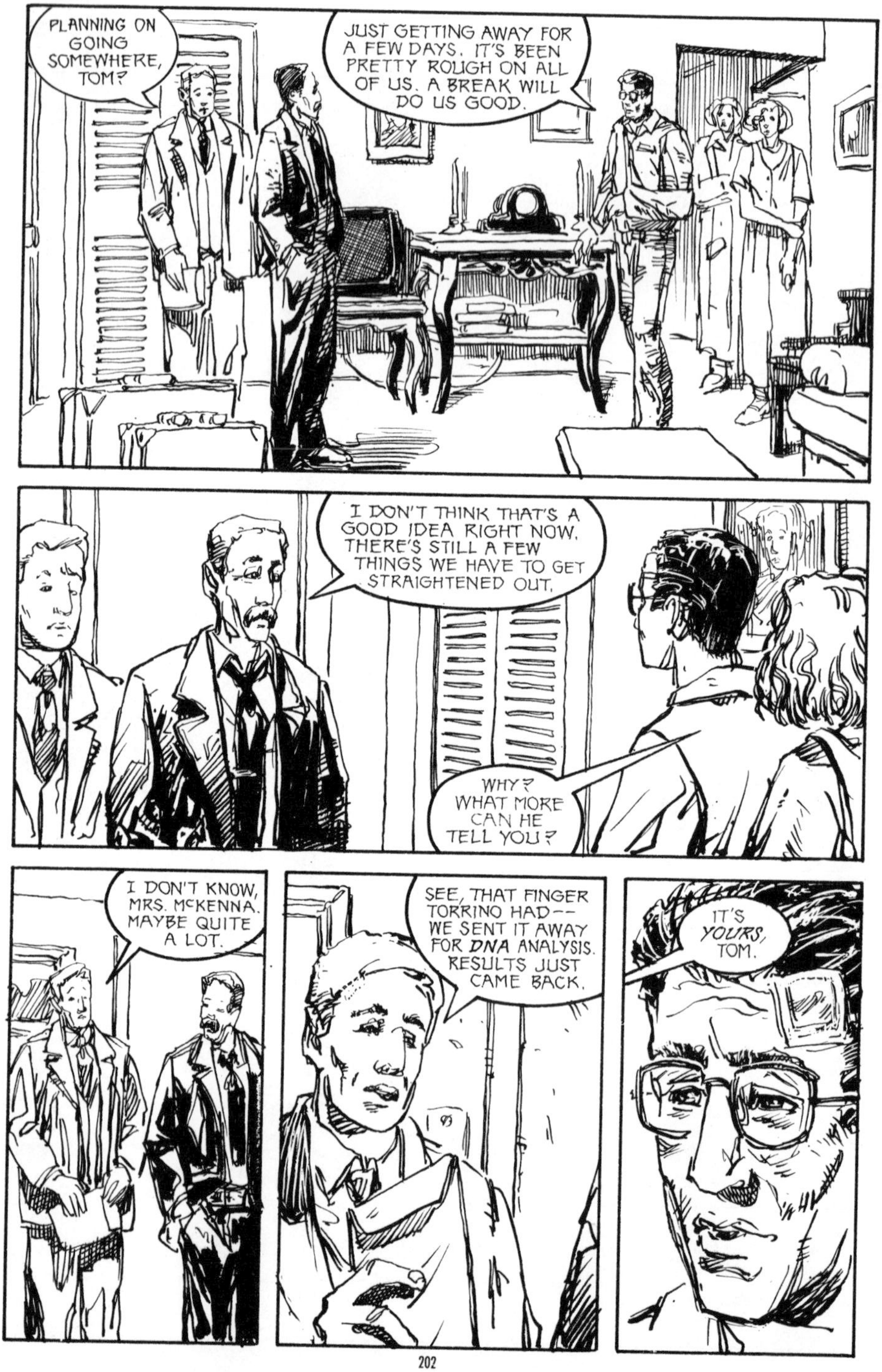
PLANNING ON GOING SOMEWHERE, TOM?
JUST GETTING AWAY FOR A FEW DAYS. IT'S BEEN PRETTY ROUGH ON ALL OF US. A BREAK WILL DO US GOOD.
I DON'T THINK THAT'S A GOOD IDEA RIGHT NOW. THERE'S STILL A FEW THINGS WE HAVE TO GET STRAIGHTENED OUT.
WHY? WHAT MORE CAN HE TELL YOU?
I DON'T KNOW, MRS. McKENNA. MAYBE QUITE A LOT.
SEE, THAT FINGER TORRINO HAD-- WE SENT IT AWAY FOR *DNA* ANALYSIS. RESULTS JUST CAME BACK.
IT'S *YOURS,* TOM.

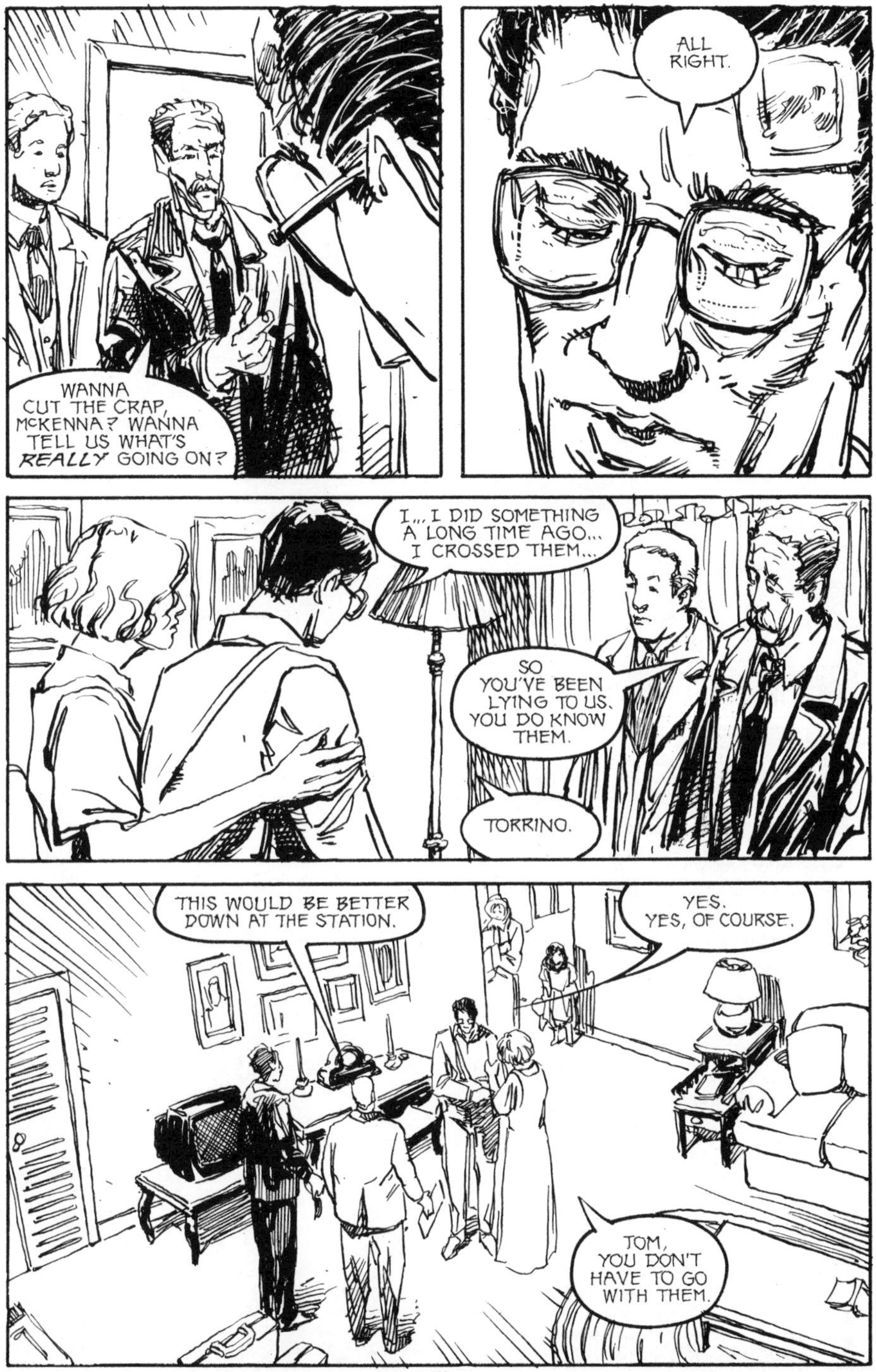
WANNA CUT THE CRAP, McKENNA? WANNA TELL US WHAT'S REALLY GOING ON?
ALL RIGHT.
I... I DID SOMETHING A LONG TIME AGO... I CROSSED THEM...
SO YOU'VE BEEN LYING TO US. YOU DO KNOW THEM.
TORRINO.
THIS WOULD BE BETTER DOWN AT THE STATION.
YES. YES, OF COURSE.
TOM, YOU DON'T HAVE TO GO WITH THEM.

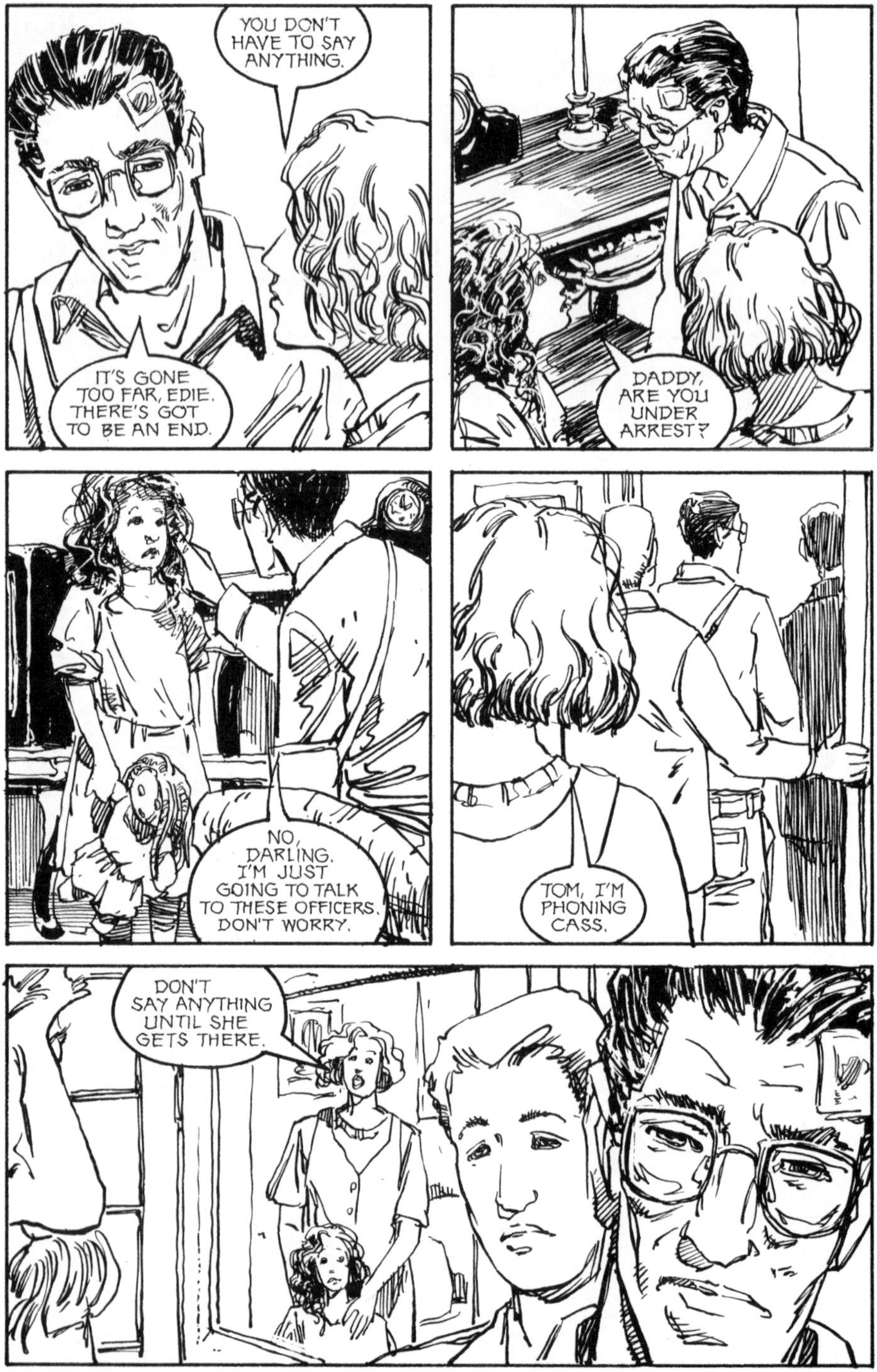

YOU DON'T HAVE TO SAY ANYTHING.
IT'S GONE TOO FAR, EDIE. THERE'S GOT TO BE AN END.
DADDY, ARE YOU UNDER ARREST?
NO, DARLING. I'M JUST GOING TO TALK TO THESE OFFICERS. DON'T WORRY.
TOM, I'M PHONING CASS.
DON'T SAY ANYTHING UNTIL SHE GETS THERE.

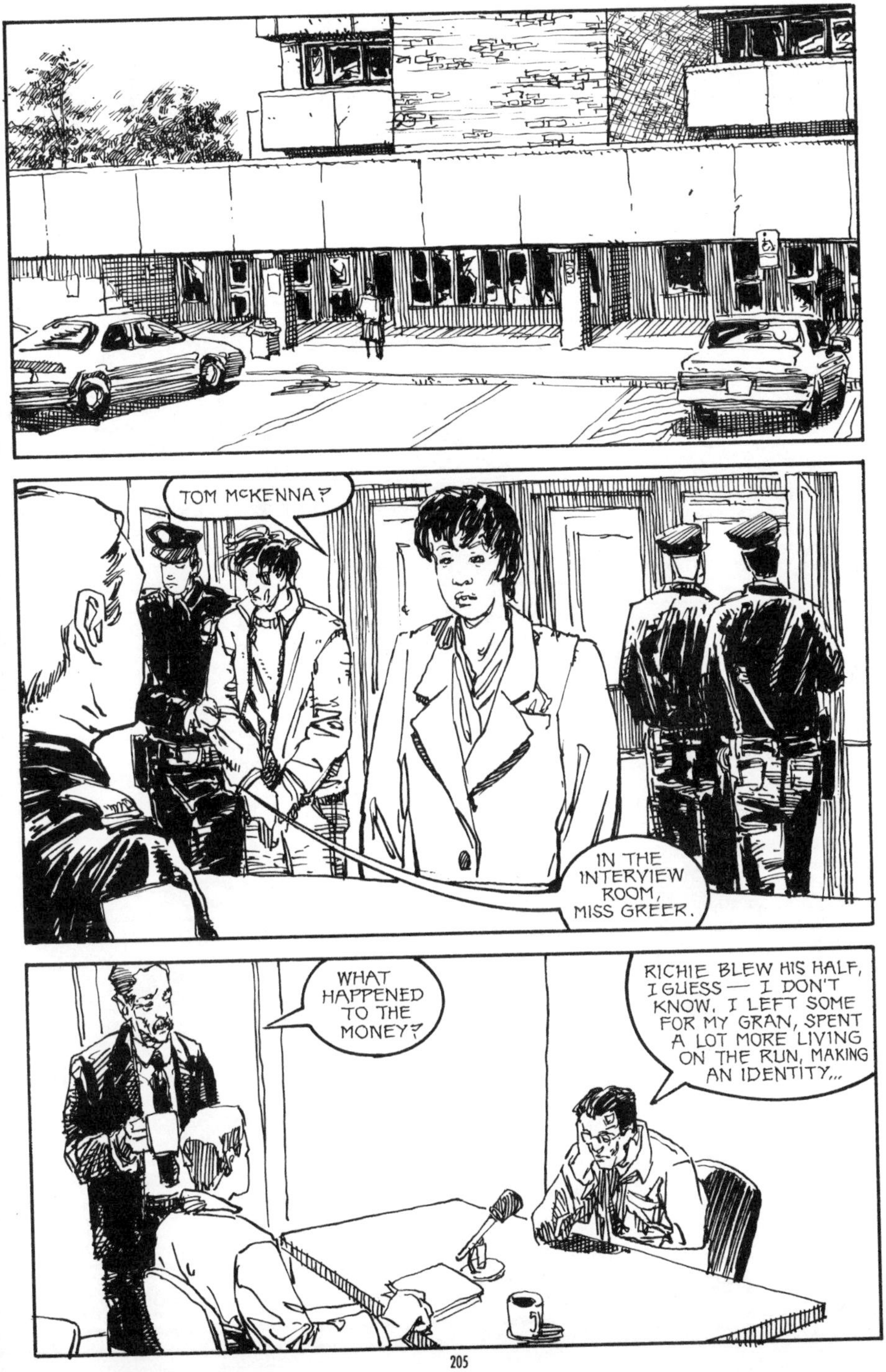
TOM McKENNA?
IN THE INTERVIEW ROOM, MISS GREER.
WHAT HAPPENED TO THE MONEY?
RICHIE BLEW HIS HALF, I GUESS — I DON'T KNOW. I LEFT SOME FOR MY GRAN, SPENT A LOT MORE LIVING ON THE RUN, MAKING AN IDENTITY...

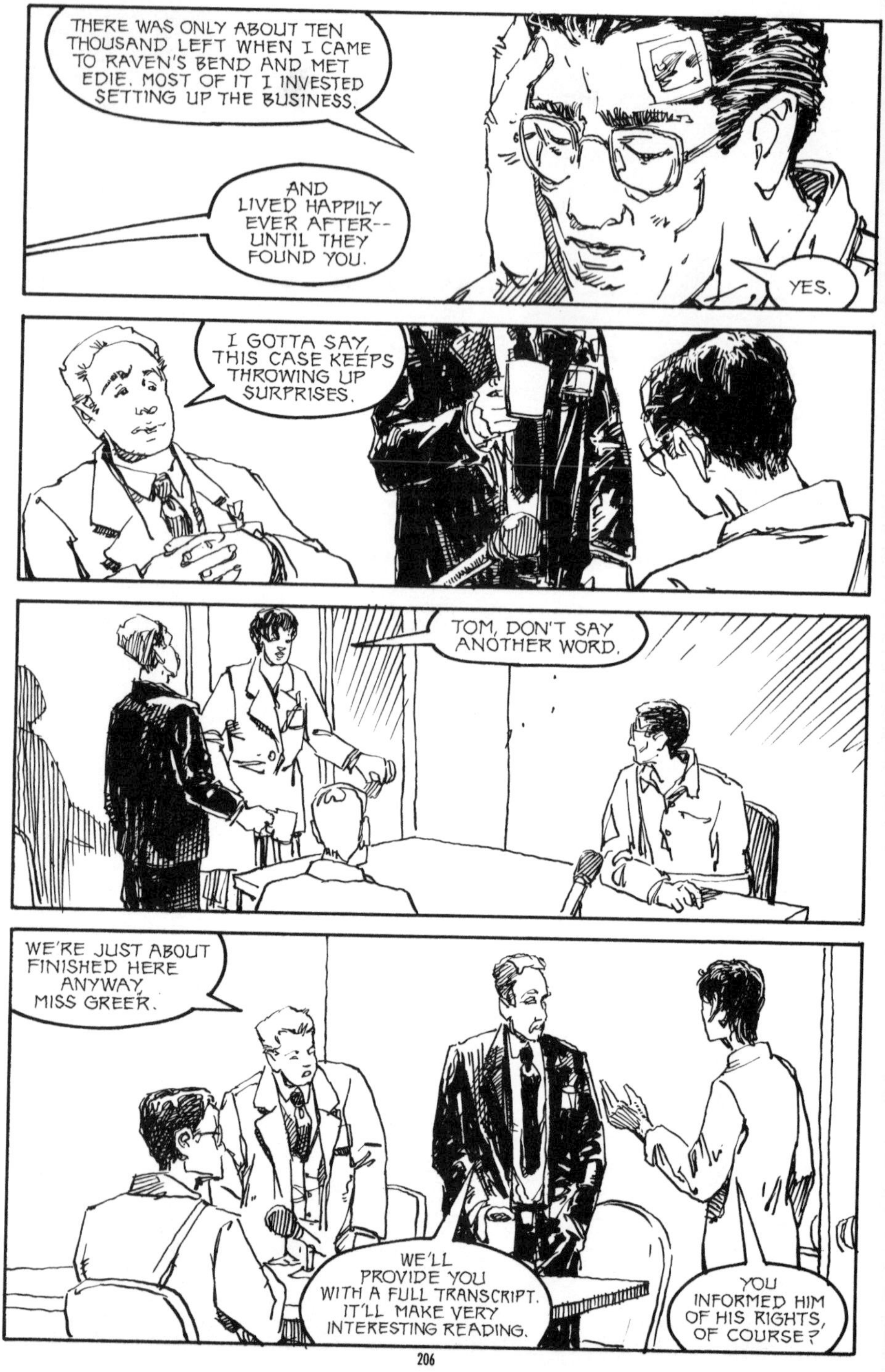
THERE WAS ONLY ABOUT TEN THOUSAND LEFT WHEN I CAME TO RAVEN'S BEND AND MET EDIE. MOST OF IT I INVESTED SETTING UP THE BUSINESS.
AND LIVED HAPPILY EVER AFTER-- UNTIL THEY FOUND YOU.
YES.
I GOTTA SAY, THIS CASE KEEPS THROWING UP SURPRISES.
TOM, DON'T SAY ANOTHER WORD.
WE'RE JUST ABOUT FINISHED HERE ANYWAY, MISS GREER.
WE'LL PROVIDE YOU WITH A FULL TRANSCRIPT. IT'LL MAKE VERY INTERESTING READING.
YOU INFORMED HIM OF HIS RIGHTS, OF COURSE?

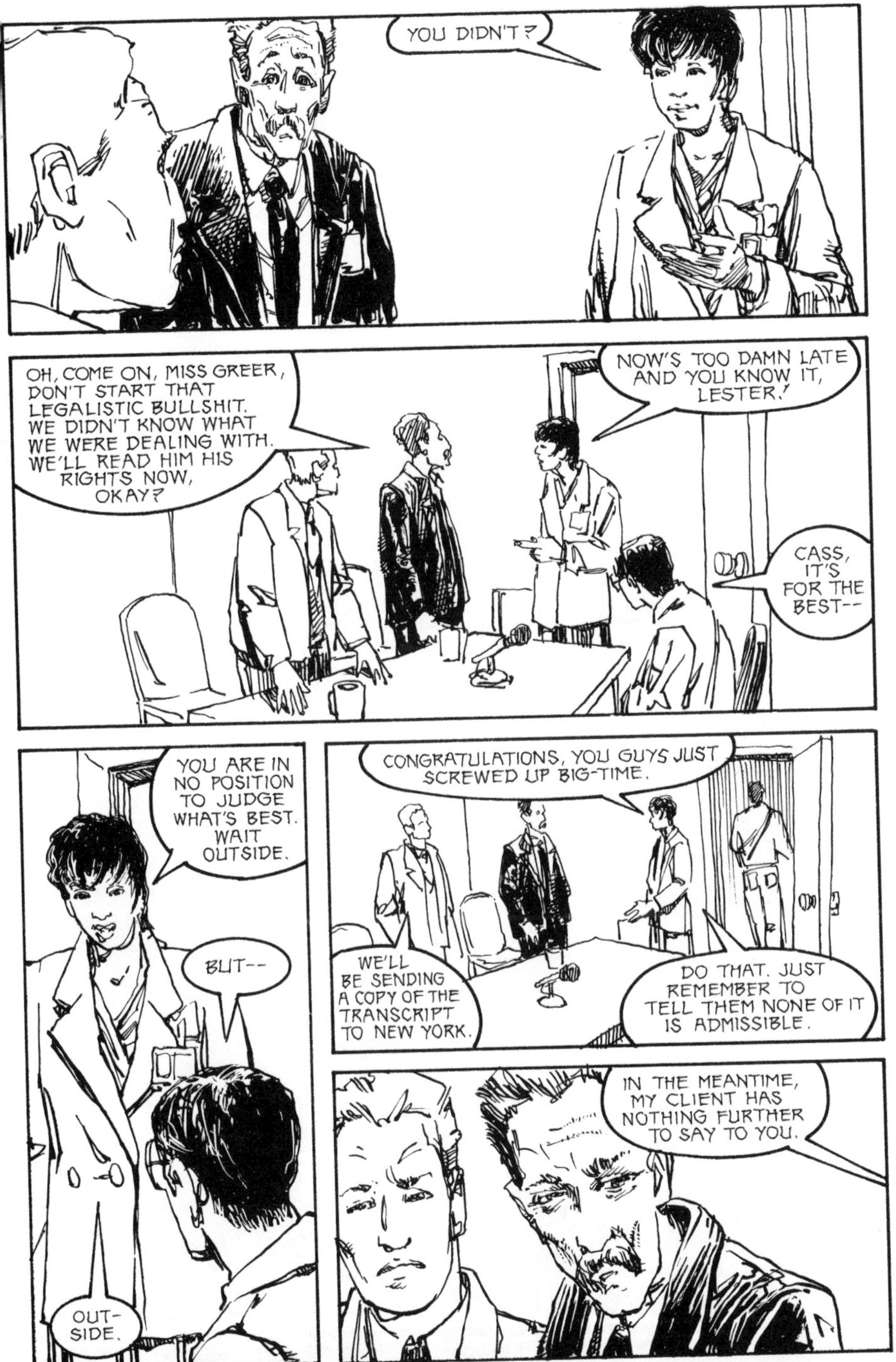
YOU DIDN'T?
OH, COME ON, MISS GREER, DON'T START THAT LEGALISTIC BULLSHIT. WE DIDN'T KNOW WHAT WE WERE DEALING WITH. WE'LL READ HIM HIS RIGHTS NOW, OKAY?
NOW'S TOO DAMN LATE AND YOU KNOW IT, LESTER!
CASS, IT'S FOR THE BEST--
YOU ARE IN NO POSITION TO JUDGE WHAT'S BEST. WAIT OUTSIDE.
BUT--
OUT-SIDE.
CONGRATULATIONS, YOU GUYS JUST SCREWED UP BIG-TIME.
WE'LL BE SENDING A COPY OF THE TRANSCRIPT TO NEW YORK.
DO THAT. JUST REMEMBER TO TELL THEM NONE OF IT IS ADMISSIBLE.
IN THE MEANTIME, MY CLIENT HAS NOTHING FURTHER TO SAY TO YOU.

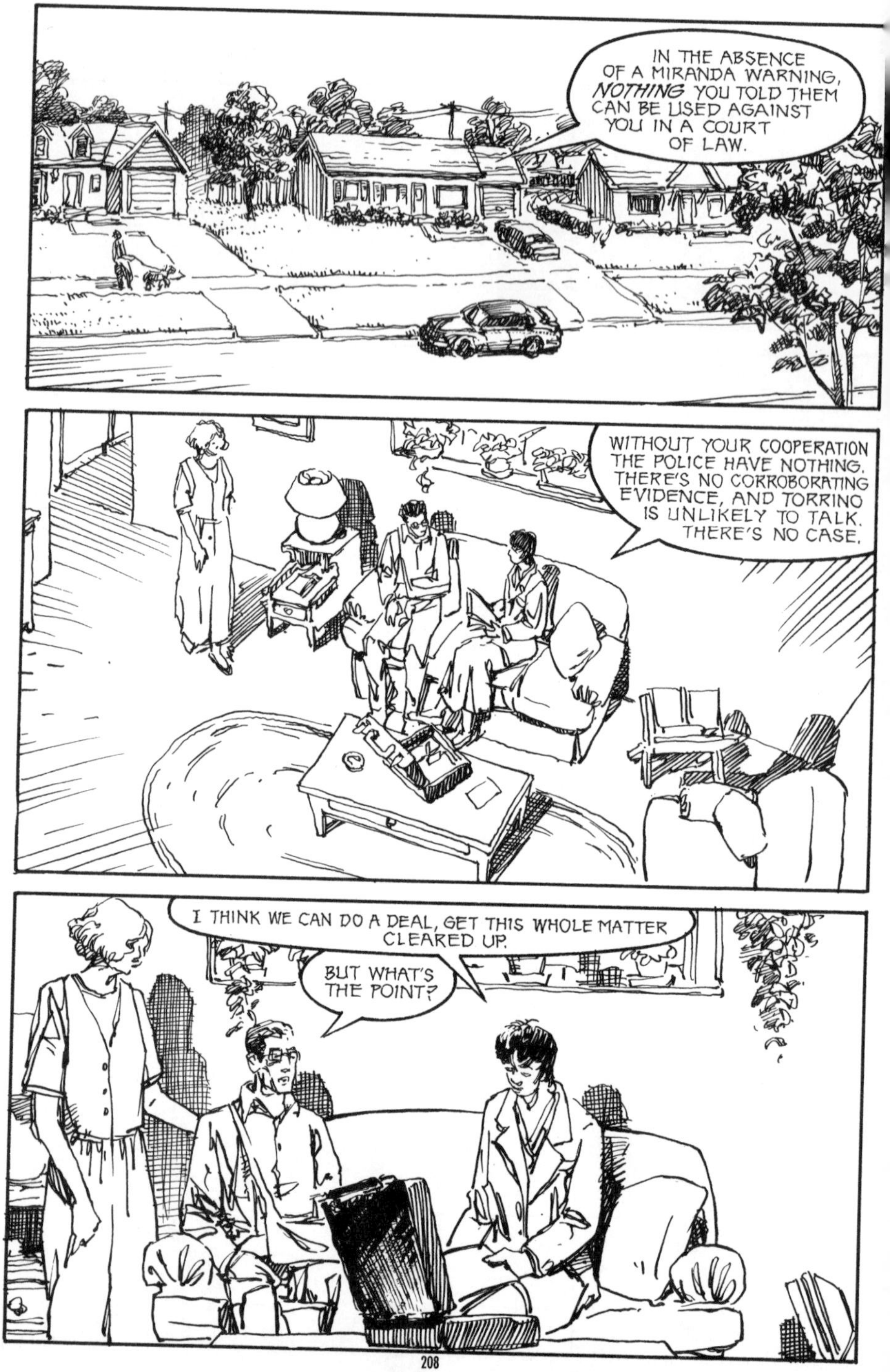
IN THE ABSENCE OF A MIRANDA WARNING, *NOTHING* YOU TOLD THEM CAN BE USED AGAINST YOU IN A COURT OF LAW.
WITHOUT YOUR COOPERATION THE POLICE HAVE NOTHING. THERE'S NO CORROBORATING EVIDENCE, AND TORRINO IS UNLIKELY TO TALK. THERE'S NO CASE.
I THINK WE CAN DO A DEAL, GET THIS WHOLE MATTER CLEARED UP.
BUT WHAT'S THE POINT?

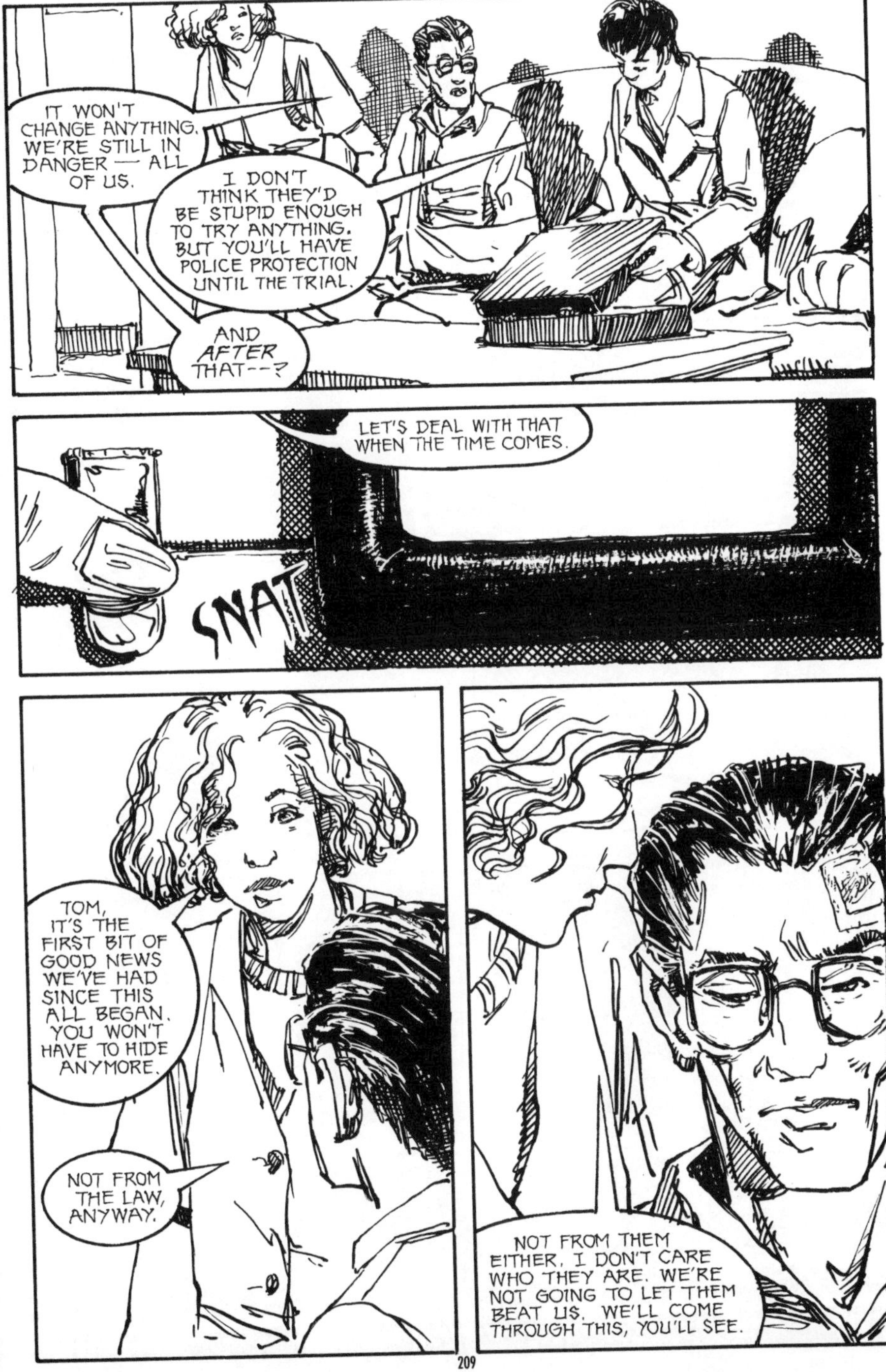
IT WON'T CHANGE ANYTHING. WE'RE STILL IN DANGER — ALL OF US.
I DON'T THINK THEY'D BE STUPID ENOUGH TO TRY ANYTHING. BUT YOU'LL HAVE POLICE PROTECTION UNTIL THE TRIAL.
AND *AFTER* THAT--?
LET'S DEAL WITH THAT WHEN THE TIME COMES.
SNAT
TOM, IT'S THE FIRST BIT OF GOOD NEWS WE'VE HAD SINCE THIS ALL BEGAN. YOU WON'T HAVE TO HIDE ANYMORE.
NOT FROM THE LAW, ANYWAY.
NOT FROM THEM EITHER. I DON'T CARE WHO THEY ARE. WE'RE NOT GOING TO LET THEM BEAT US. WE'LL COME THROUGH THIS, YOU'LL SEE.

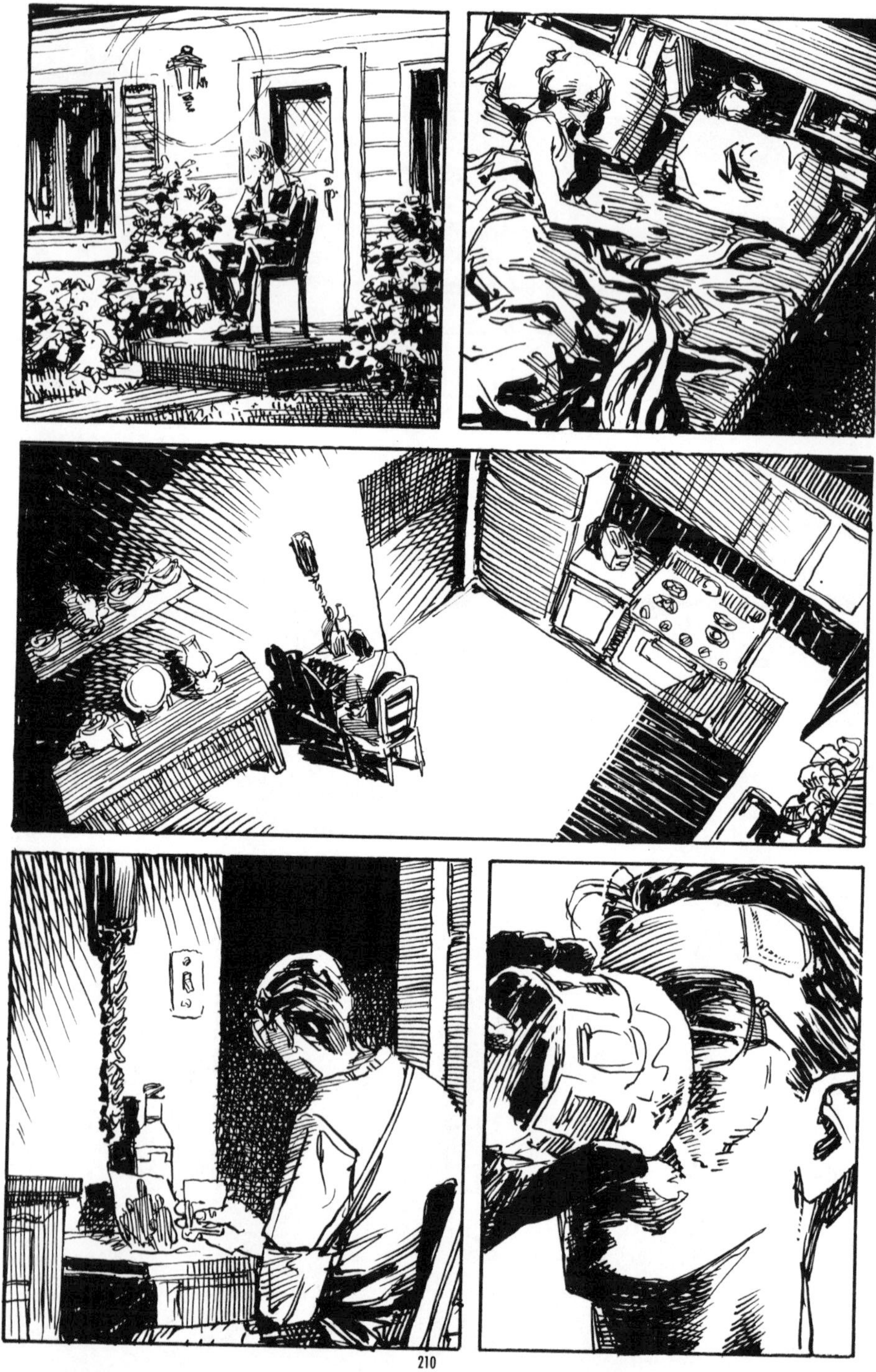

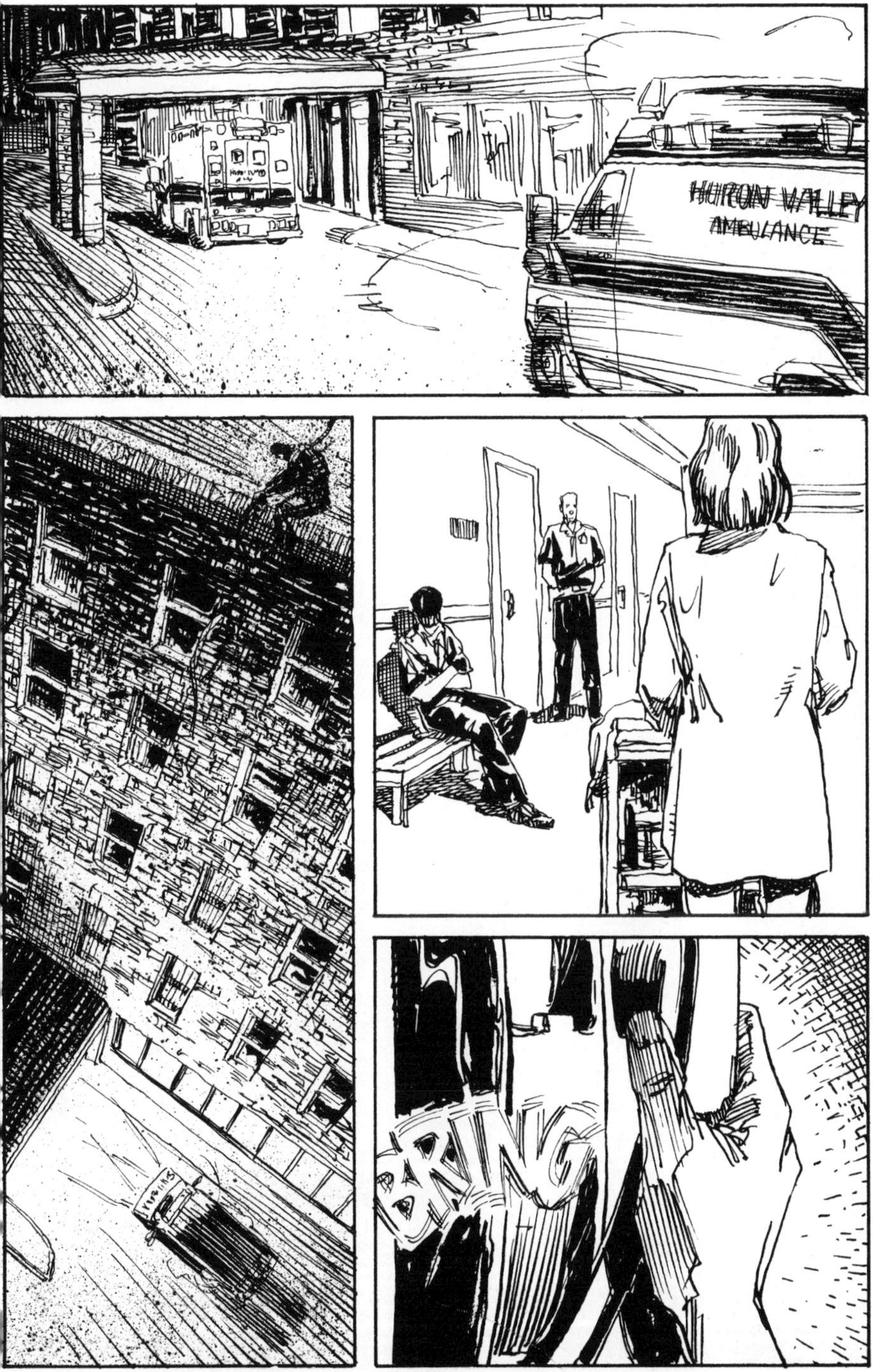
HURON VALLEY
AMBULANCE
BRRING

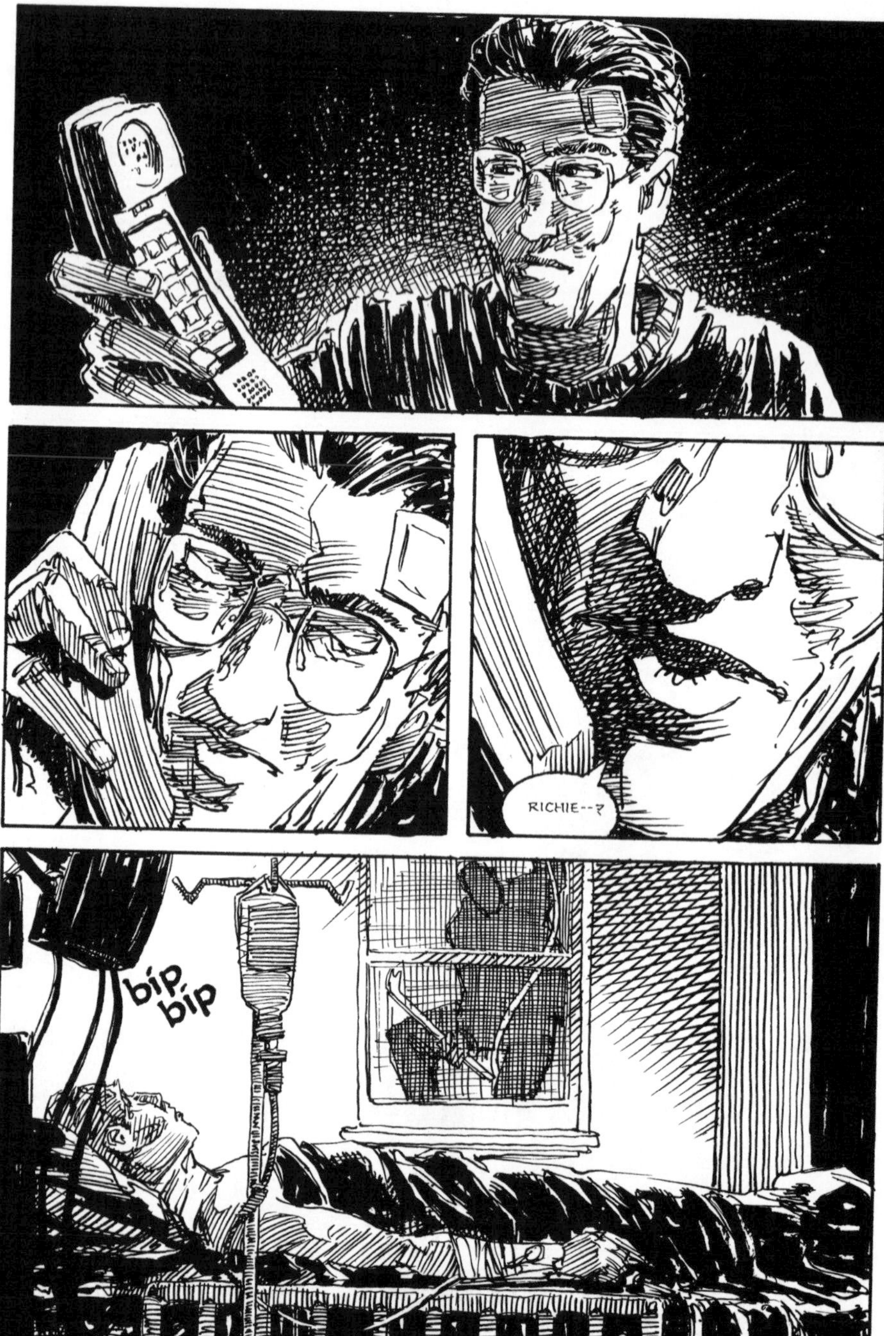
RICHIE--?
bip, bip

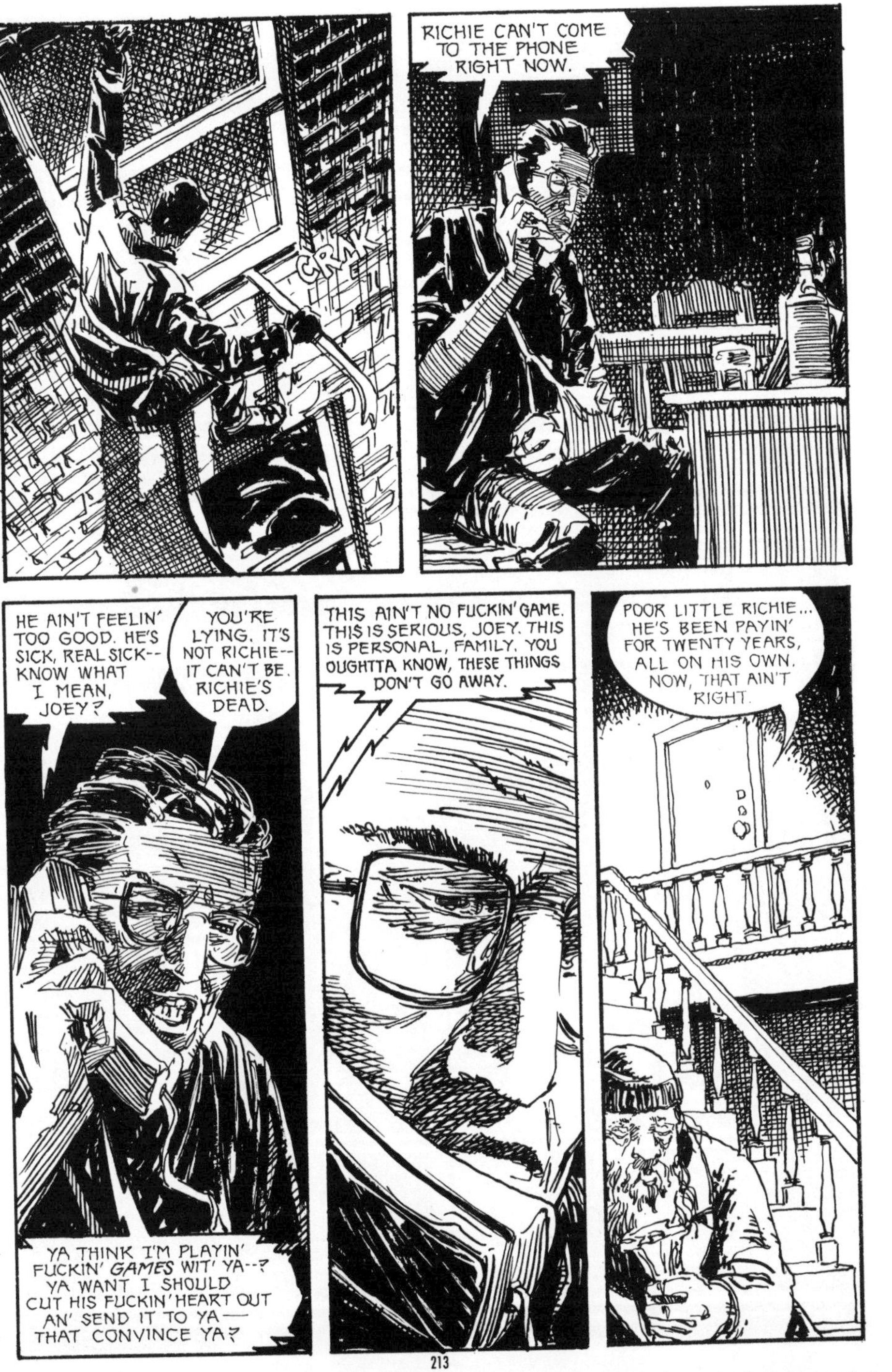
CRAK
RICHIE CAN'T COME TO THE PHONE RIGHT NOW.
HE AIN'T FEELIN' TOO GOOD. HE'S SICK, REAL SICK-- KNOW WHAT I MEAN, JOEY?
YOU'RE LYING. IT'S NOT RICHIE-- IT CAN'T BE. RICHIE'S DEAD.
YA THINK I'M PLAYIN' FUCKIN' GAMES WIT' YA--? YA WANT I SHOULD CUT HIS FUCKIN' HEART OUT AN' SEND IT TO YA— THAT CONVINCE YA?
THIS AIN'T NO FUCKIN' GAME. THIS IS SERIOUS, JOEY. THIS IS PERSONAL, FAMILY. YOU OUGHTTA KNOW, THESE THINGS DON'T GO AWAY.
POOR LITTLE RICHIE... HE'S BEEN PAYIN' FOR TWENTY YEARS, ALL ON HIS OWN. NOW, THAT AIN'T RIGHT.

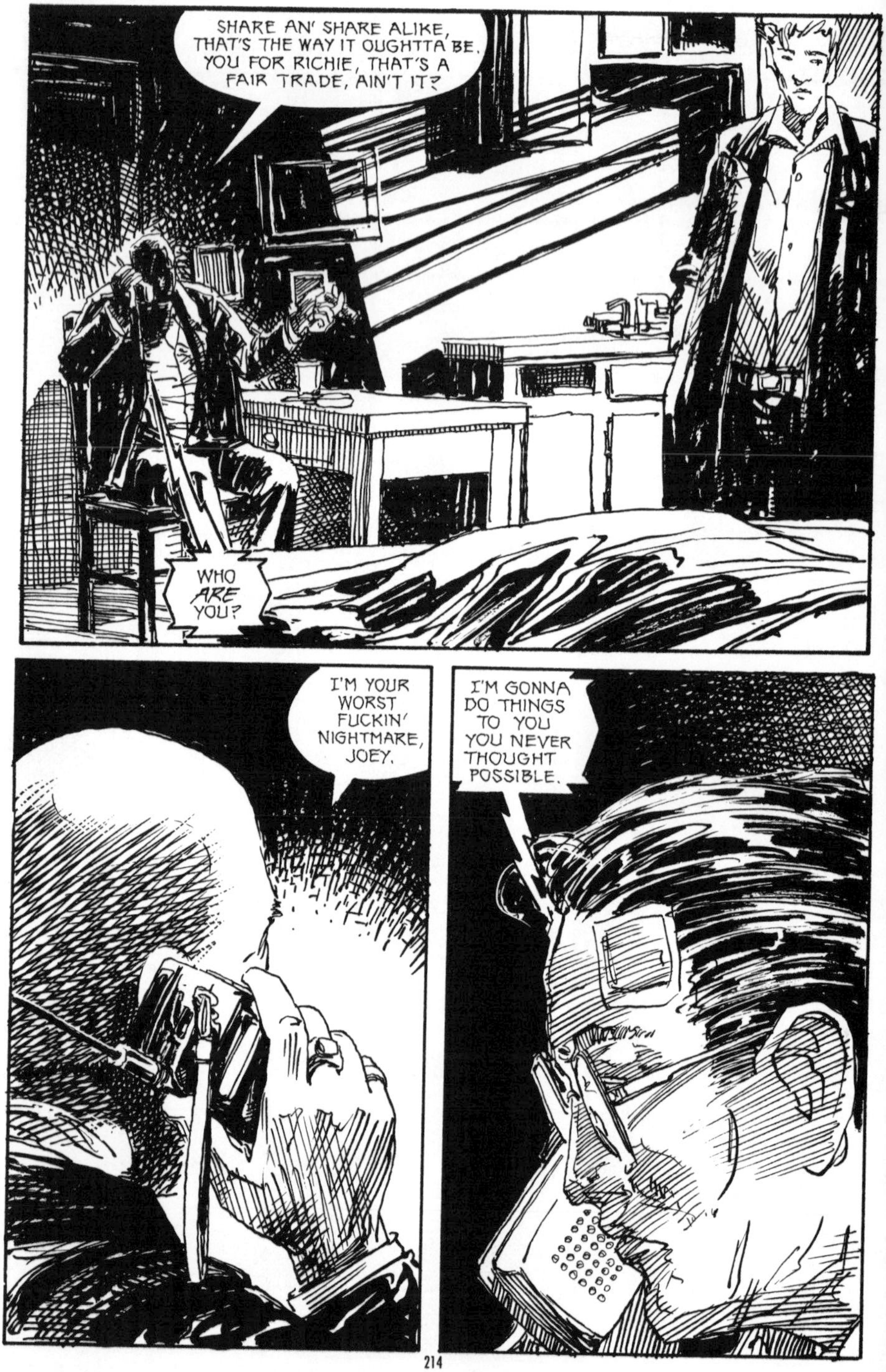
SHARE AN' SHARE ALIKE, THAT'S THE WAY IT OUGHTTA BE. YOU FOR RICHIE, THAT'S A FAIR TRADE, AIN'T IT?
WHO *ARE* YOU?
I'M YOUR WORST FUCKIN' NIGHTMARE, JOEY.
I'M GONNA DO THINGS TO YOU YOU NEVER THOUGHT POSSIBLE.

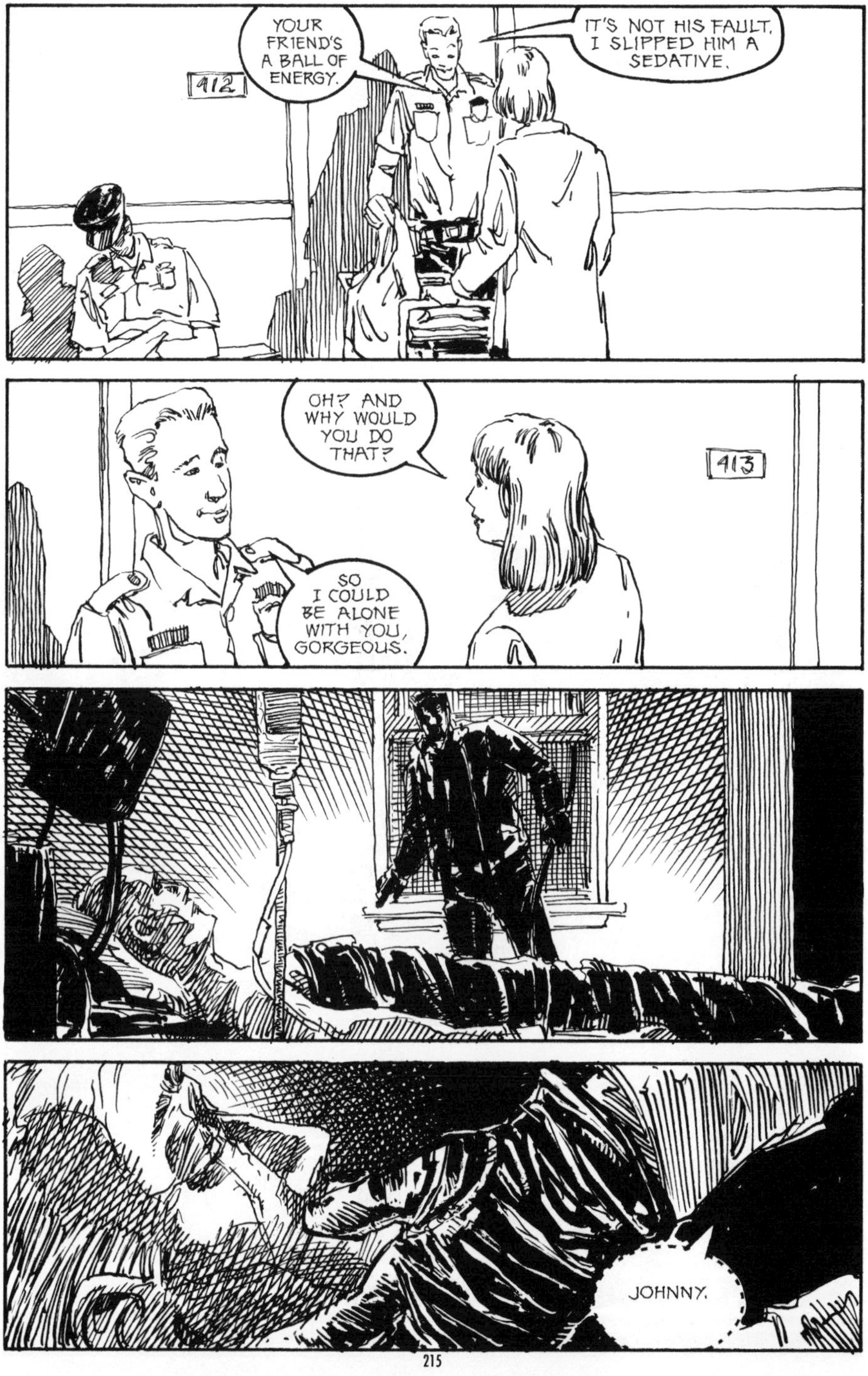
412
YOUR FRIEND'S A BALL OF ENERGY.
IT'S NOT HIS FAULT. I SLIPPED HIM A SEDATIVE.
OH? AND WHY WOULD YOU DO THAT?
413
SO I COULD BE ALONE WITH YOU, GORGEOUS.
JOHNNY.

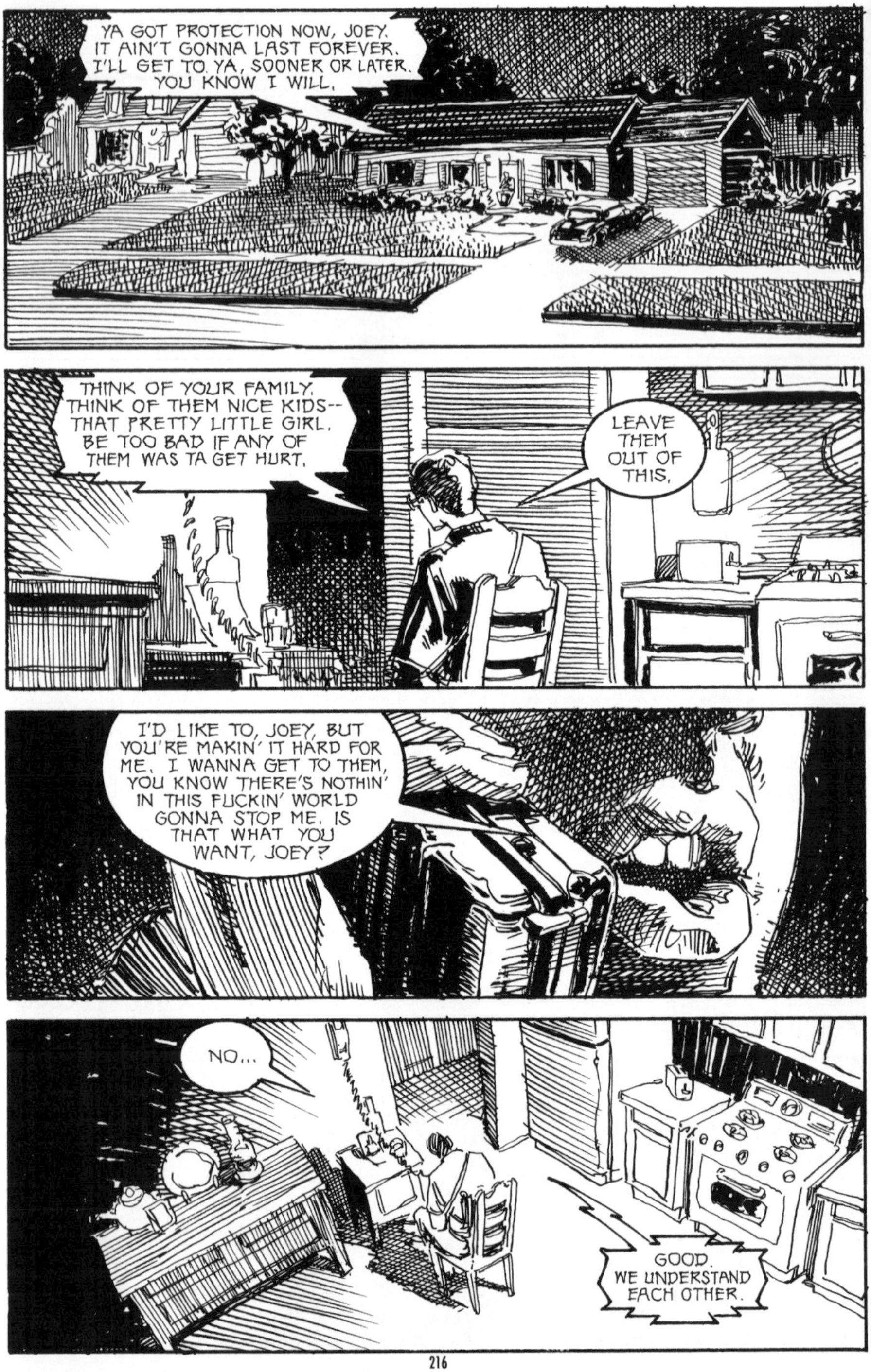
YA GOT PROTECTION NOW, JOEY. IT AIN'T GONNA LAST FOREVER. I'LL GET TO YA, SOONER OR LATER. YOU KNOW I WILL.
THINK OF YOUR FAMILY. THINK OF THEM NICE KIDS-- THAT PRETTY LITTLE GIRL. BE TOO BAD IF ANY OF THEM WAS TA GET HURT.
LEAVE THEM OUT OF THIS.
I'D LIKE TO, JOEY, BUT YOU'RE MAKIN' IT HARD FOR ME. I WANNA GET TO THEM, YOU KNOW THERE'S NOTHIN' IN THIS FUCKIN' WORLD GONNA STOP ME. IS THAT WHAT YOU WANT, JOEY?
NO...
GOOD. WE UNDERSTAND EACH OTHER.

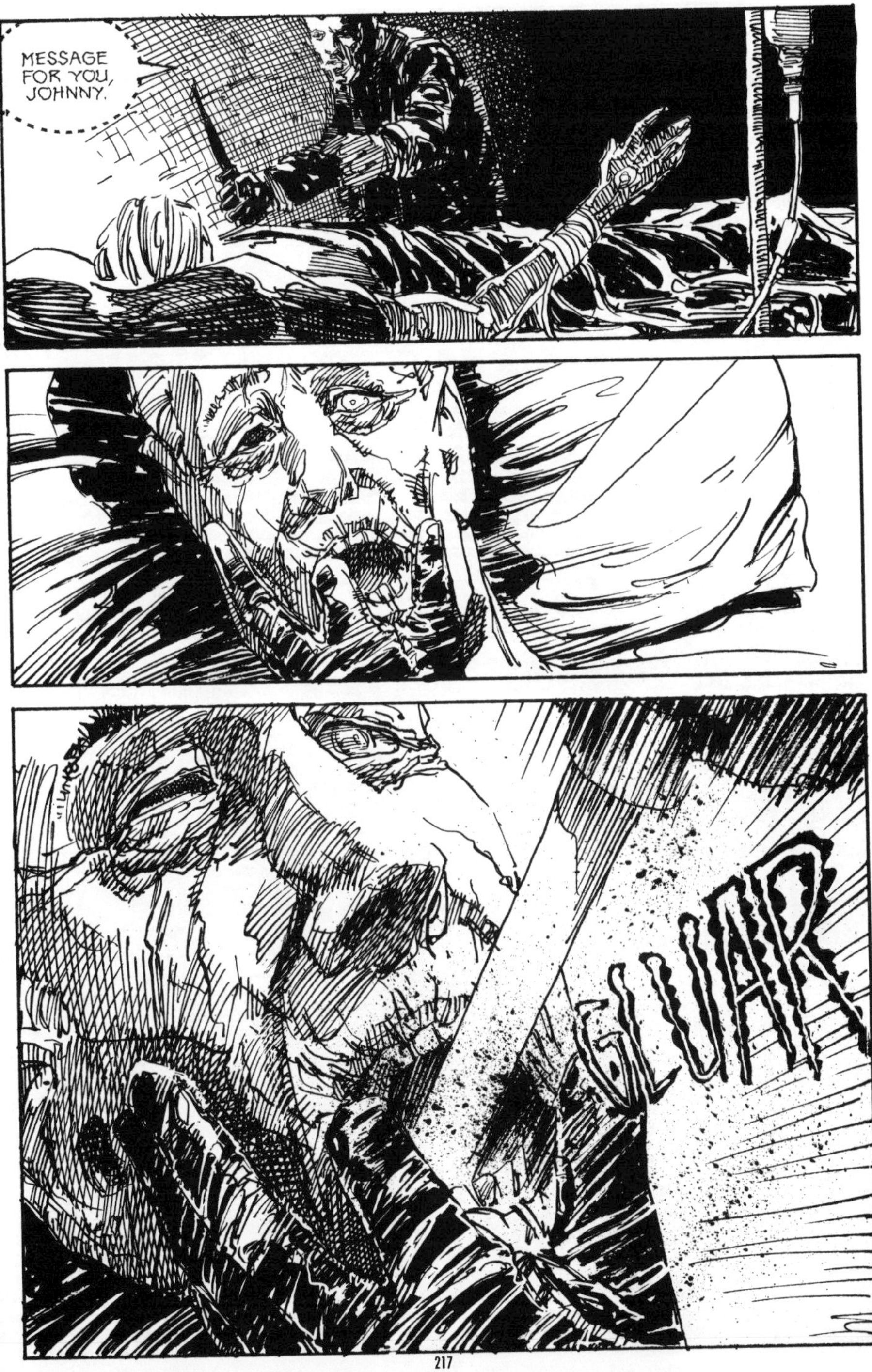
MESSAGE FOR YOU, JOHNNY.
GLUAR

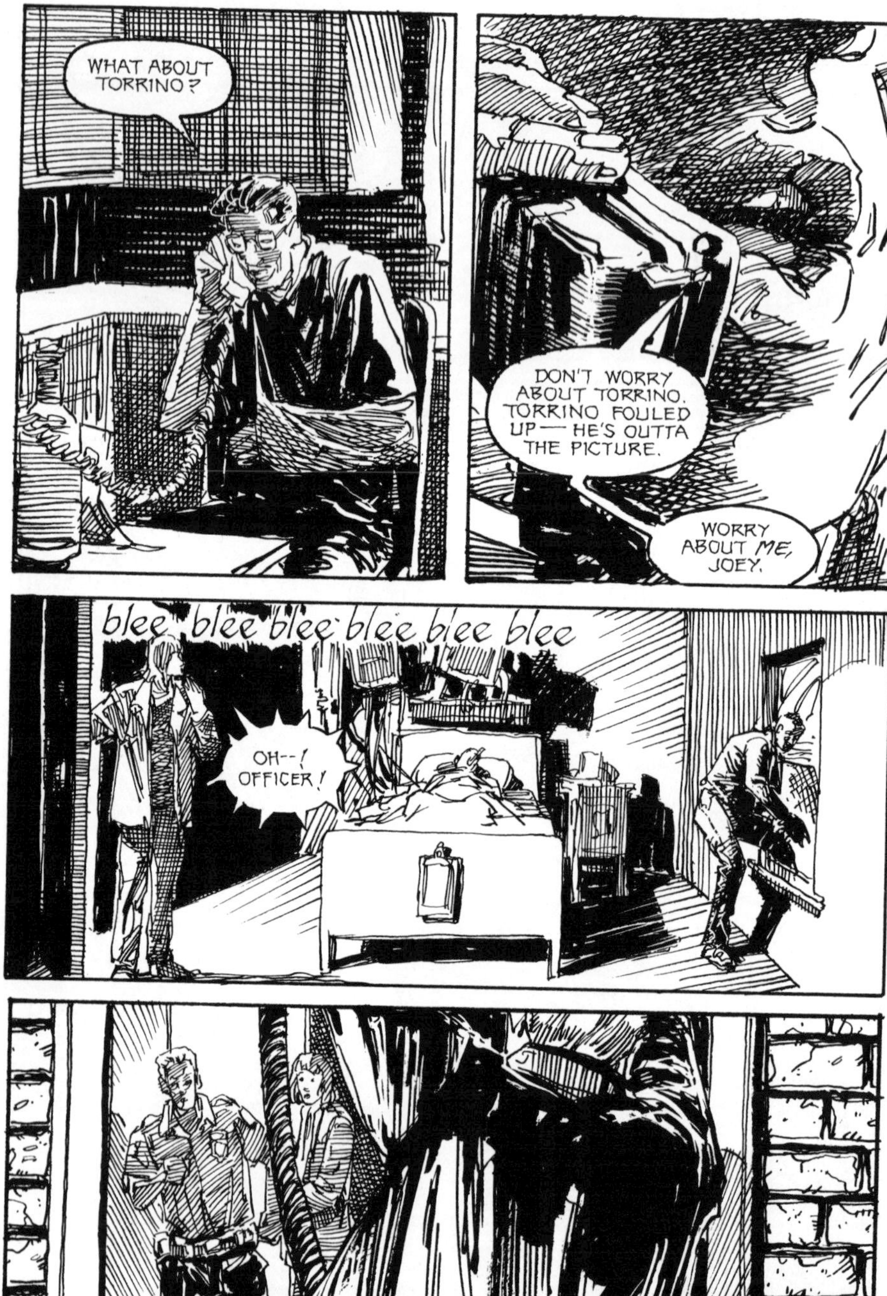
WHAT ABOUT TORRINO?
DON'T WORRY ABOUT TORRINO. TORRINO FOULED UP— HE'S OUTTA THE PICTURE.
WORRY ABOUT *ME*, JOEY.
blee blee blee blee blee blee
OH--! OFFICER!

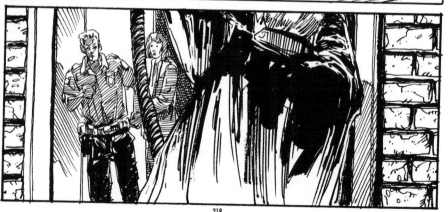

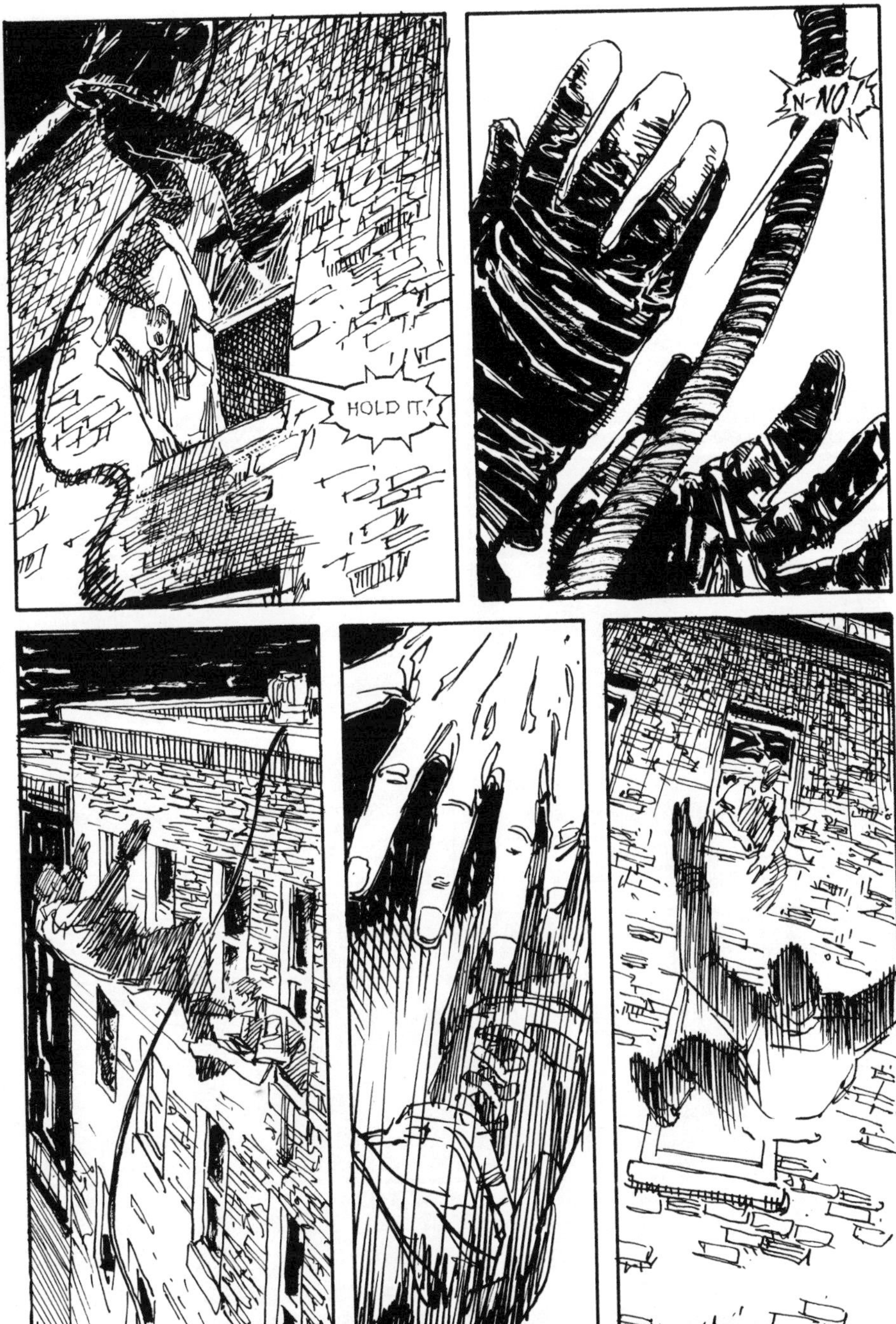
HOLD IT!
N-NO!

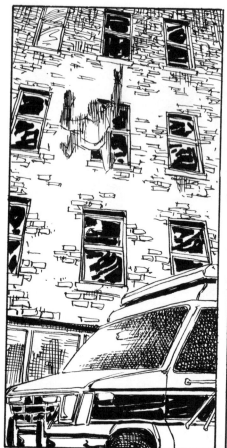

THRUNG

blee blee blee ble

OH MY GOD.

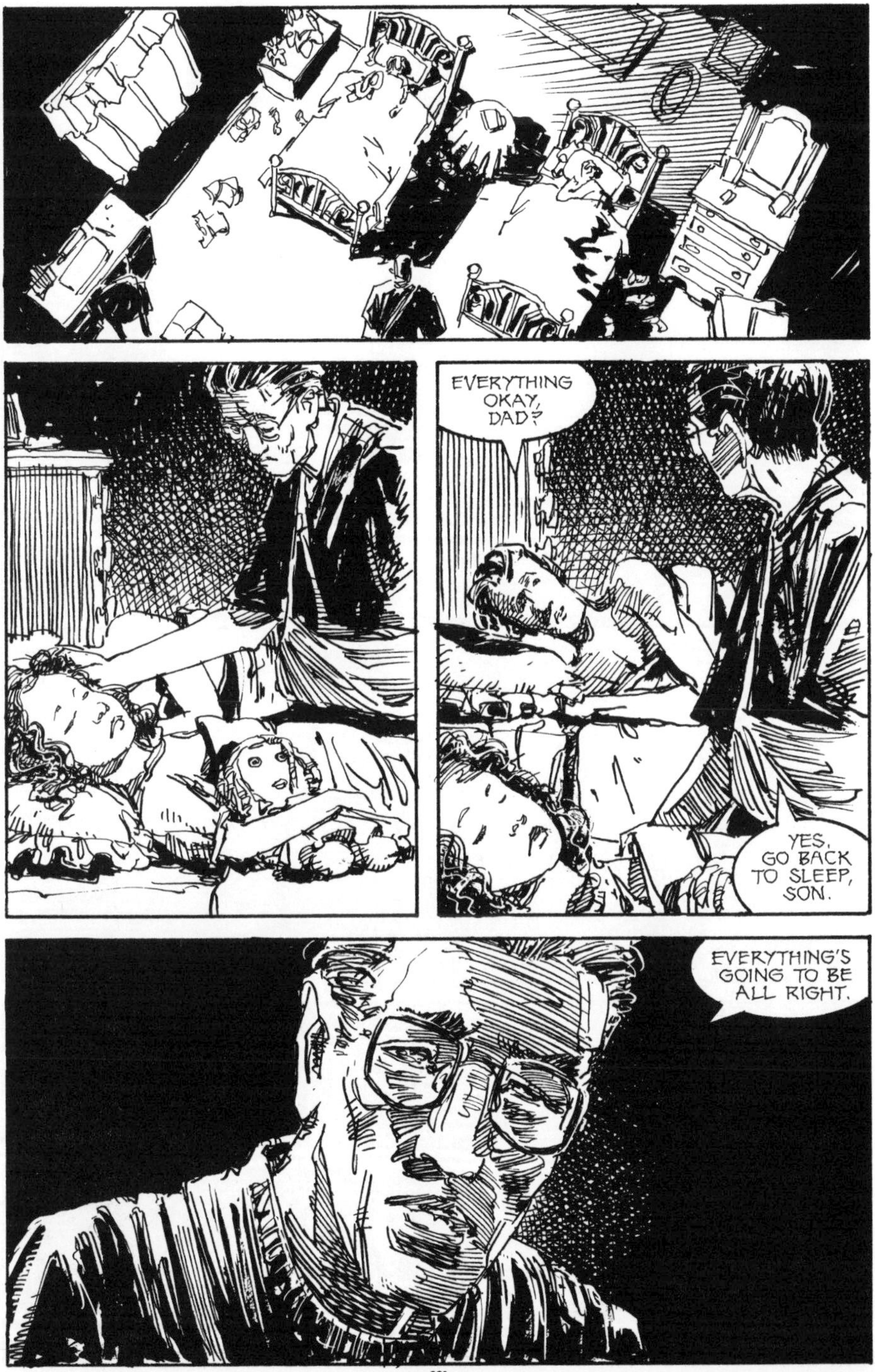
EVERYTHING OKAY, DAD?
YES, GO BACK TO SLEEP, SON.
EVERYTHING'S GOING TO BE ALL RIGHT.

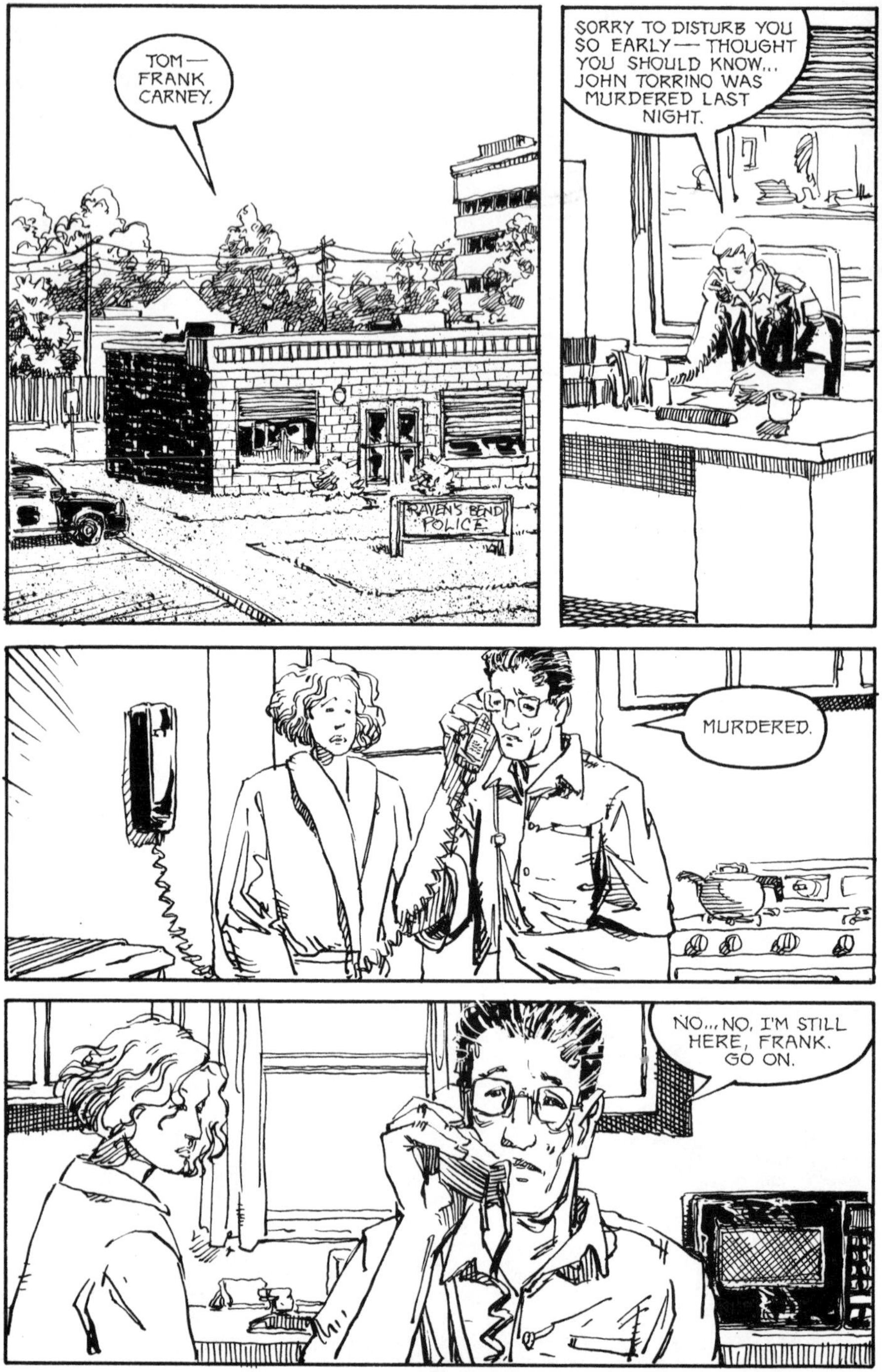
TOM— FRANK CARNEY.
RAVEN'S BEND POLICE
SORRY TO DISTURB YOU SO EARLY— THOUGHT YOU SHOULD KNOW... JOHN TORRINO WAS MURDERED LAST NIGHT.
MURDERED.
NO...NO, I'M STILL HERE, FRANK. GO ON.

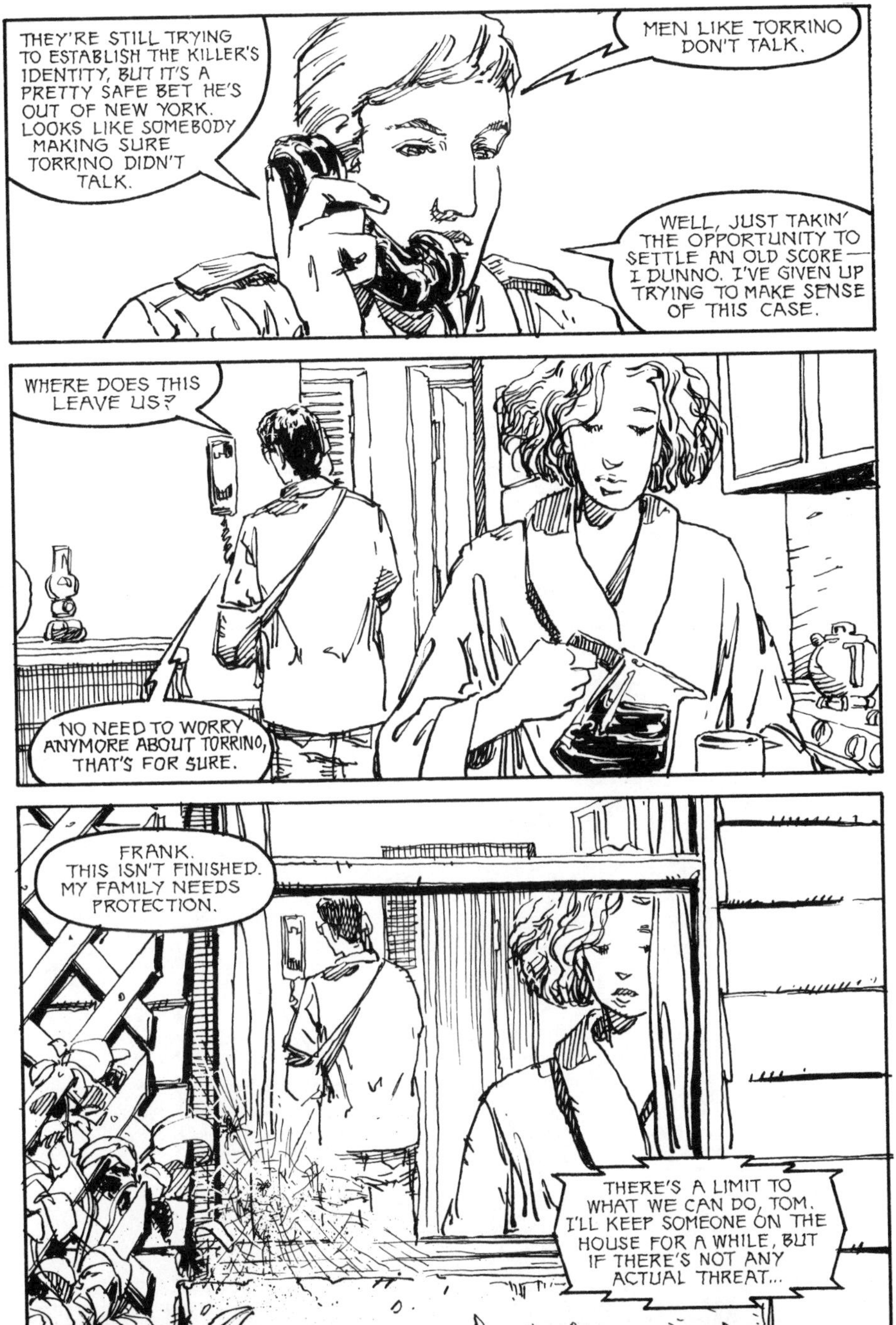
THEY'RE STILL TRYING TO ESTABLISH THE KILLER'S IDENTITY, BUT IT'S A PRETTY SAFE BET HE'S OUT OF NEW YORK. LOOKS LIKE SOMEBODY MAKING SURE TORRINO DIDN'T TALK.
MEN LIKE TORRINO DON'T TALK.
WELL, JUST TAKIN' THE OPPORTUNITY TO SETTLE AN OLD SCORE— I DUNNO. I'VE GIVEN UP TRYING TO MAKE SENSE OF THIS CASE.
WHERE DOES THIS LEAVE US?
NO NEED TO WORRY ANYMORE ABOUT TORRINO, THAT'S FOR SURE.
FRANK. THIS ISN'T FINISHED. MY FAMILY NEEDS PROTECTION.
THERE'S A LIMIT TO WHAT WE CAN DO, TOM. I'LL KEEP SOMEONE ON THE HOUSE FOR A WHILE, BUT IF THERE'S NOT ANY ACTUAL THREAT...

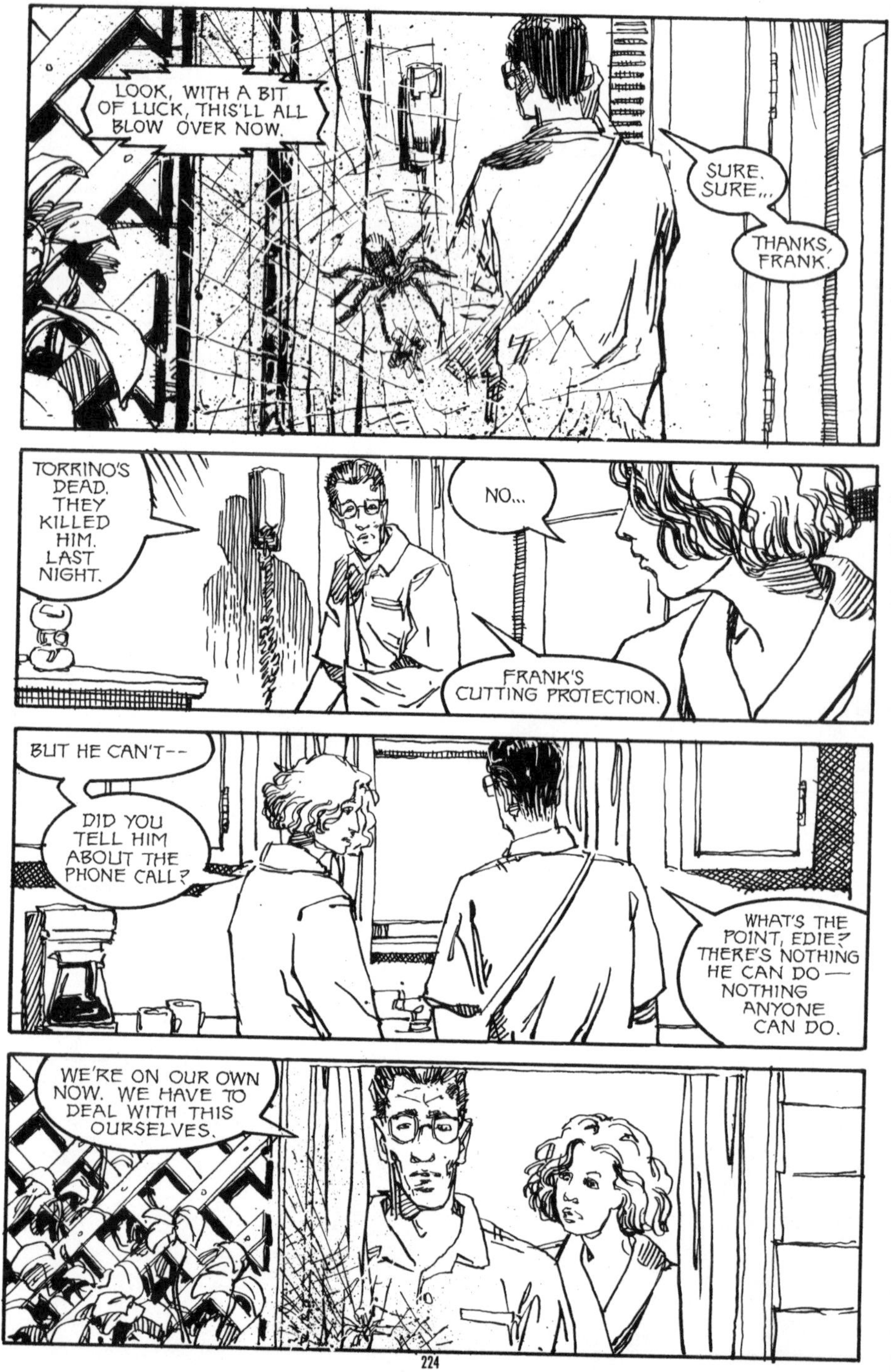
LOOK, WITH A BIT OF LUCK, THIS'LL ALL BLOW OVER NOW.
SURE. SURE...
THANKS, FRANK.
TORRINO'S DEAD. THEY KILLED HIM. LAST NIGHT.
NO...
FRANK'S CUTTING PROTECTION.
BUT HE CAN'T--
DID YOU TELL HIM ABOUT THE PHONE CALL?
WHAT'S THE POINT, EDIE? THERE'S NOTHING HE CAN DO — NOTHING ANYONE CAN DO.
WE'RE ON OUR OWN NOW. WE HAVE TO DEAL WITH THIS OURSELVES.

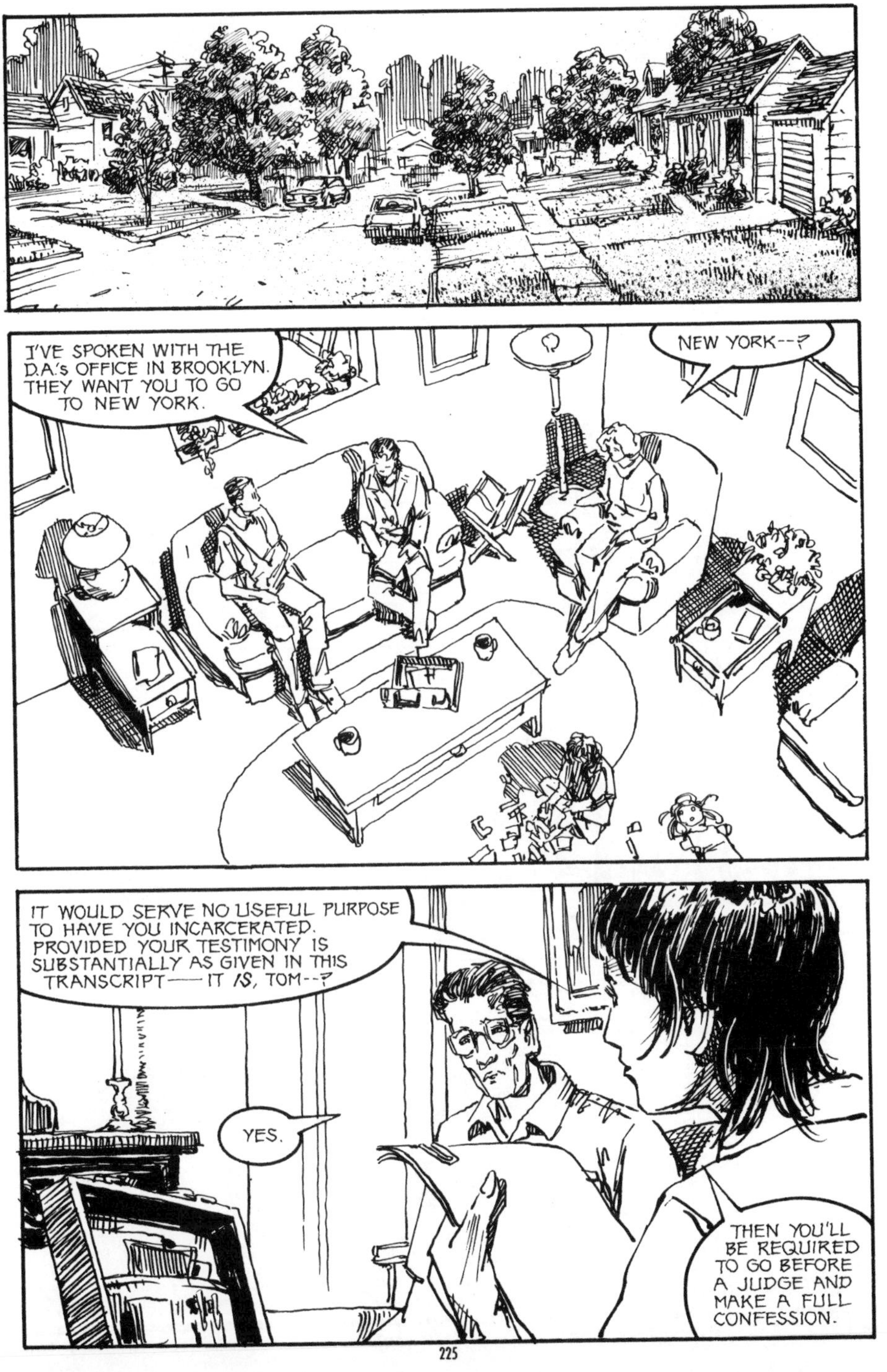
I'VE SPOKEN WITH THE D.A.'s OFFICE IN BROOKLYN. THEY WANT YOU TO GO TO NEW YORK.
NEW YORK--?
IT WOULD SERVE NO USEFUL PURPOSE TO HAVE YOU INCARCERATED. PROVIDED YOUR TESTIMONY IS SUBSTANTIALLY AS GIVEN IN THIS TRANSCRIPT—— IT *IS*, TOM--?
YES.
THEN YOU'LL BE REQUIRED TO GO BEFORE A JUDGE AND MAKE A FULL CONFESSION.

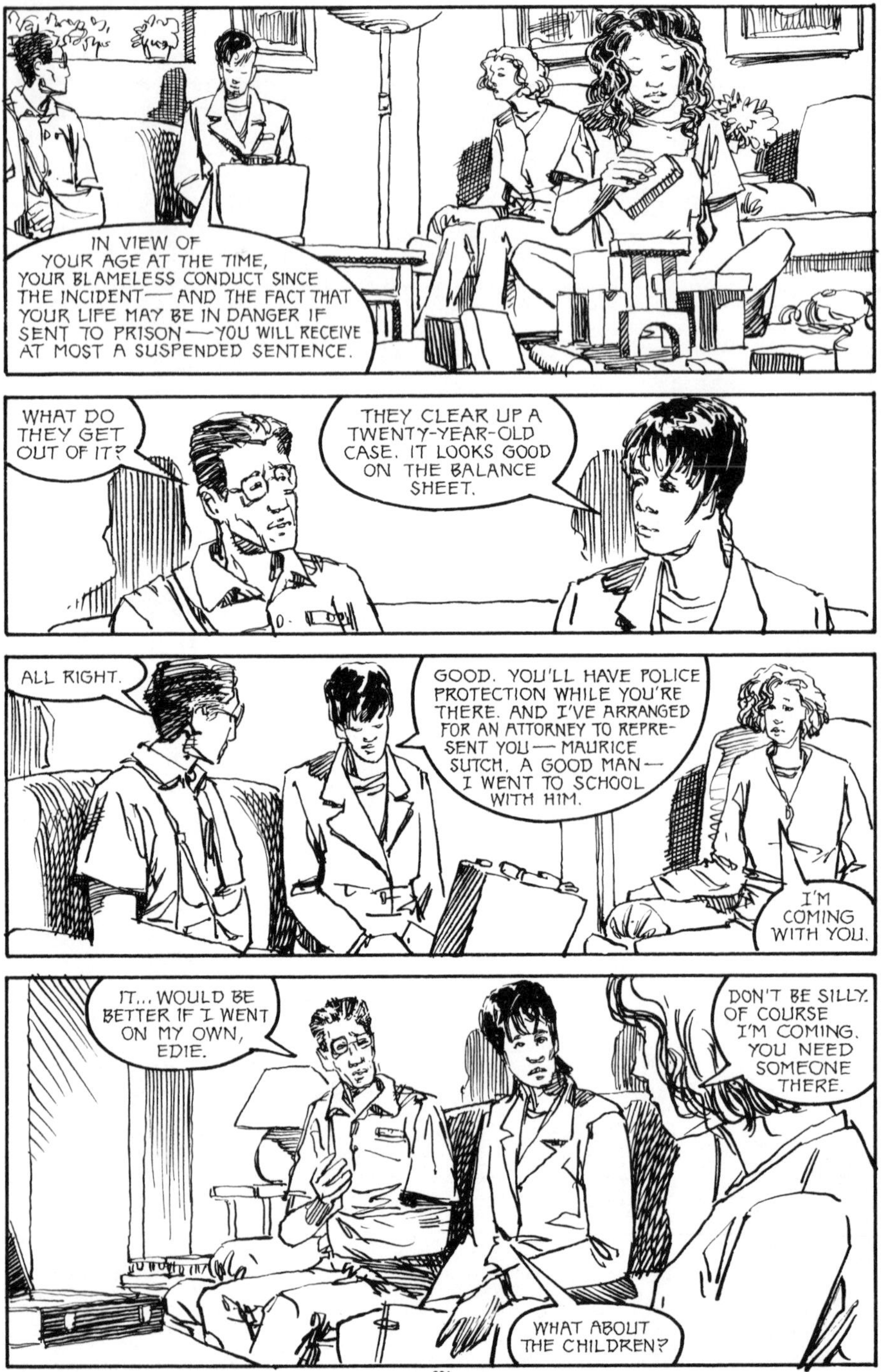
IN VIEW OF YOUR AGE AT THE TIME, YOUR BLAMELESS CONDUCT SINCE THE INCIDENT— AND THE FACT THAT YOUR LIFE MAY BE IN DANGER IF SENT TO PRISON —YOU WILL RECEIVE AT MOST A SUSPENDED SENTENCE.
WHAT DO THEY GET OUT OF IT?
THEY CLEAR UP A TWENTY-YEAR-OLD CASE. IT LOOKS GOOD ON THE BALANCE SHEET.
ALL RIGHT.
GOOD. YOU'LL HAVE POLICE PROTECTION WHILE YOU'RE THERE. AND I'VE ARRANGED FOR AN ATTORNEY TO REPRESENT YOU— MAURICE SUTCH. A GOOD MAN— I WENT TO SCHOOL WITH HIM.
I'M COMING WITH YOU.
IT... WOULD BE BETTER IF I WENT ON MY OWN, EDIE.
DON'T BE SILLY. OF COURSE I'M COMING. YOU NEED SOMEONE THERE.
WHAT ABOUT THE CHILDREN?

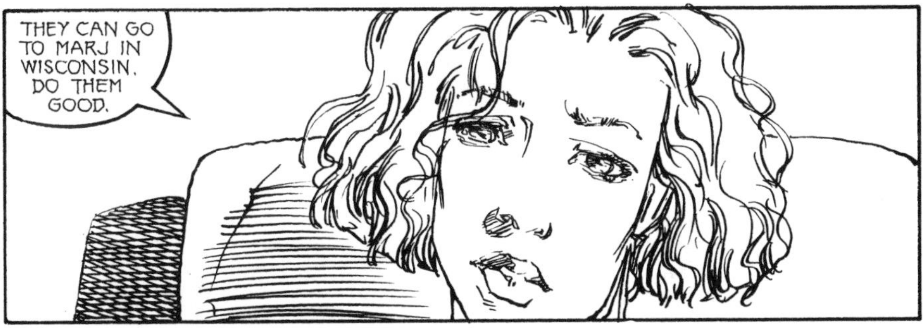
THEY CAN GO TO MARJ IN WISCONSIN. DO THEM GOOD.

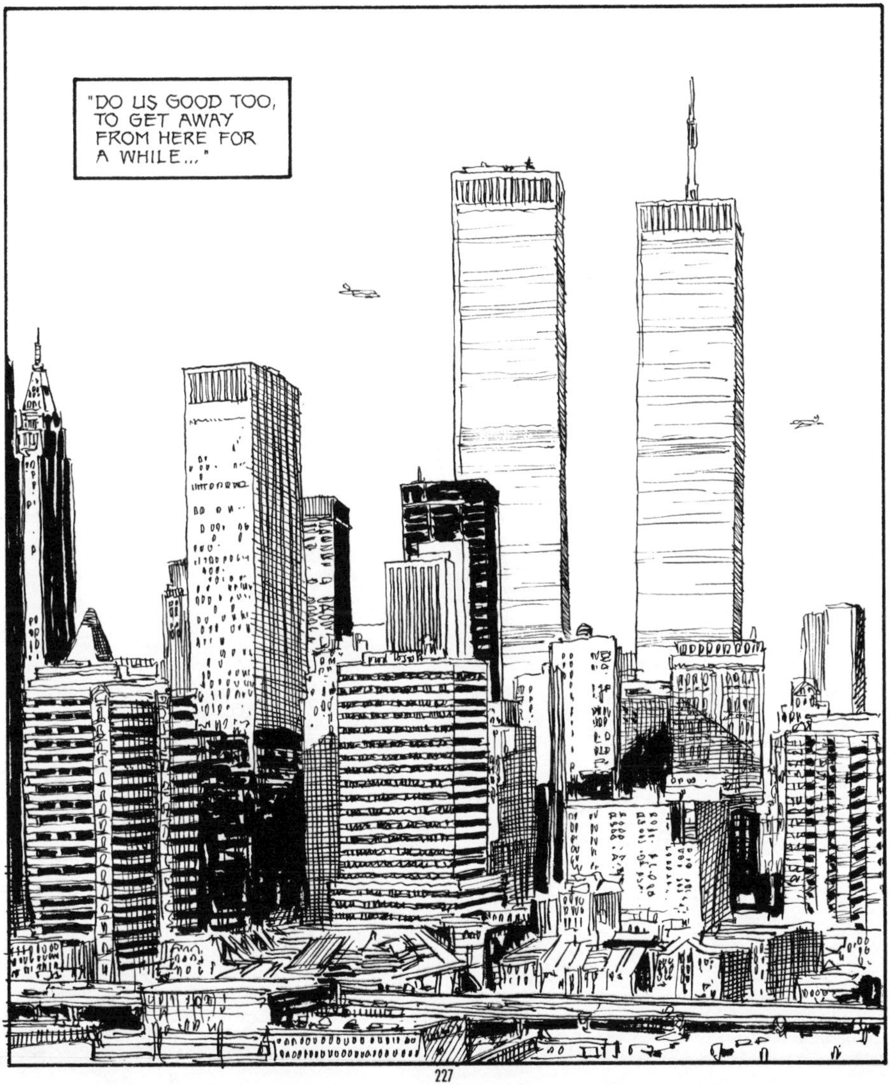
"DO US GOOD TOO, TO GET AWAY FROM HERE FOR A WHILE..."

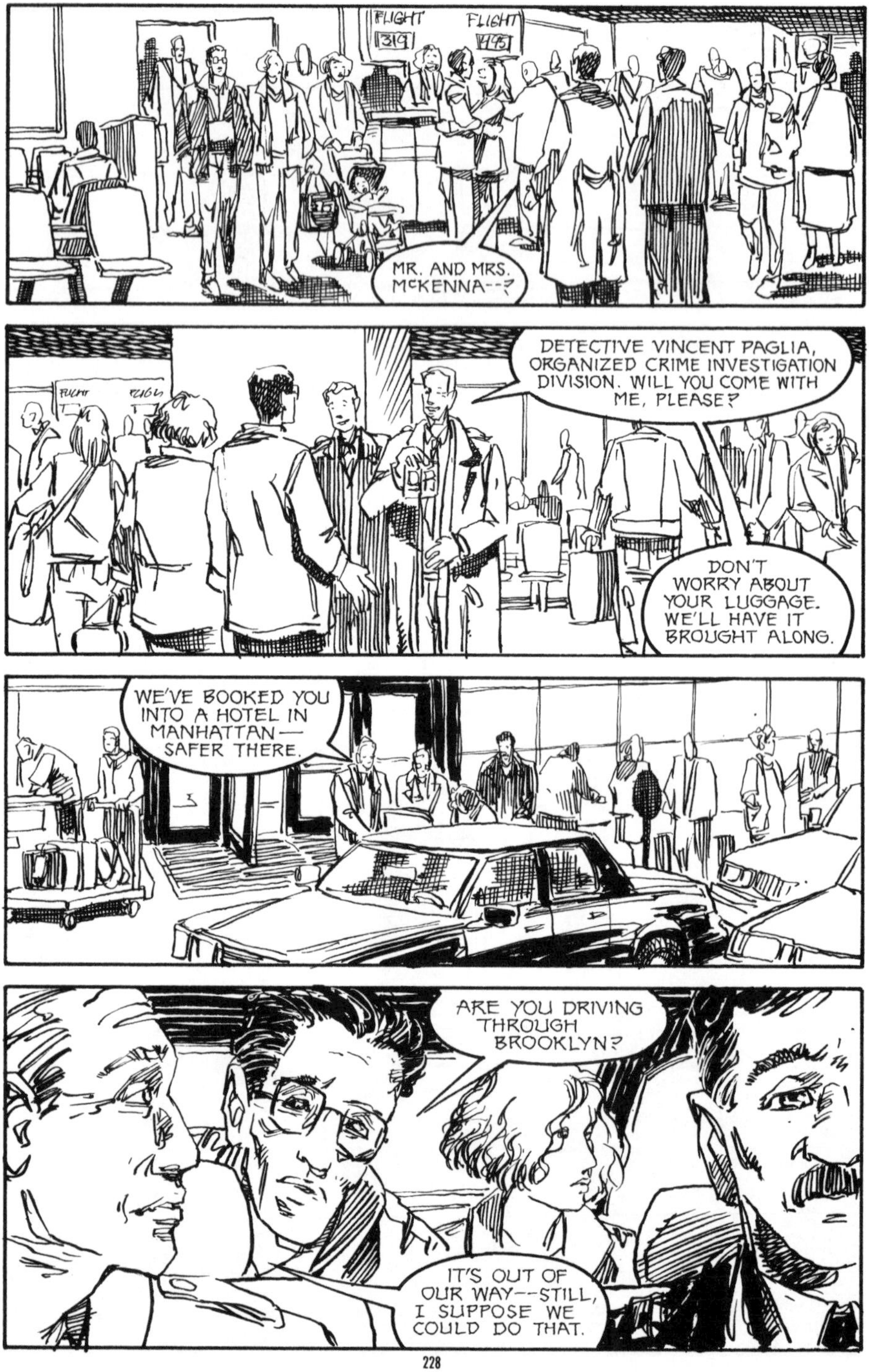
FLIGHT 319
FLIGHT 495
MR. AND MRS. McKENNA--?
DETECTIVE VINCENT PAGLIA, ORGANIZED CRIME INVESTIGATION DIVISION. WILL YOU COME WITH ME, PLEASE?
DON'T WORRY ABOUT YOUR LUGGAGE. WE'LL HAVE IT BROUGHT ALONG.
WE'VE BOOKED YOU INTO A HOTEL IN MANHATTAN— SAFER THERE.
ARE YOU DRIVING THROUGH BROOKLYN?
IT'S OUT OF OUR WAY--STILL, I SUPPOSE WE COULD DO THAT.

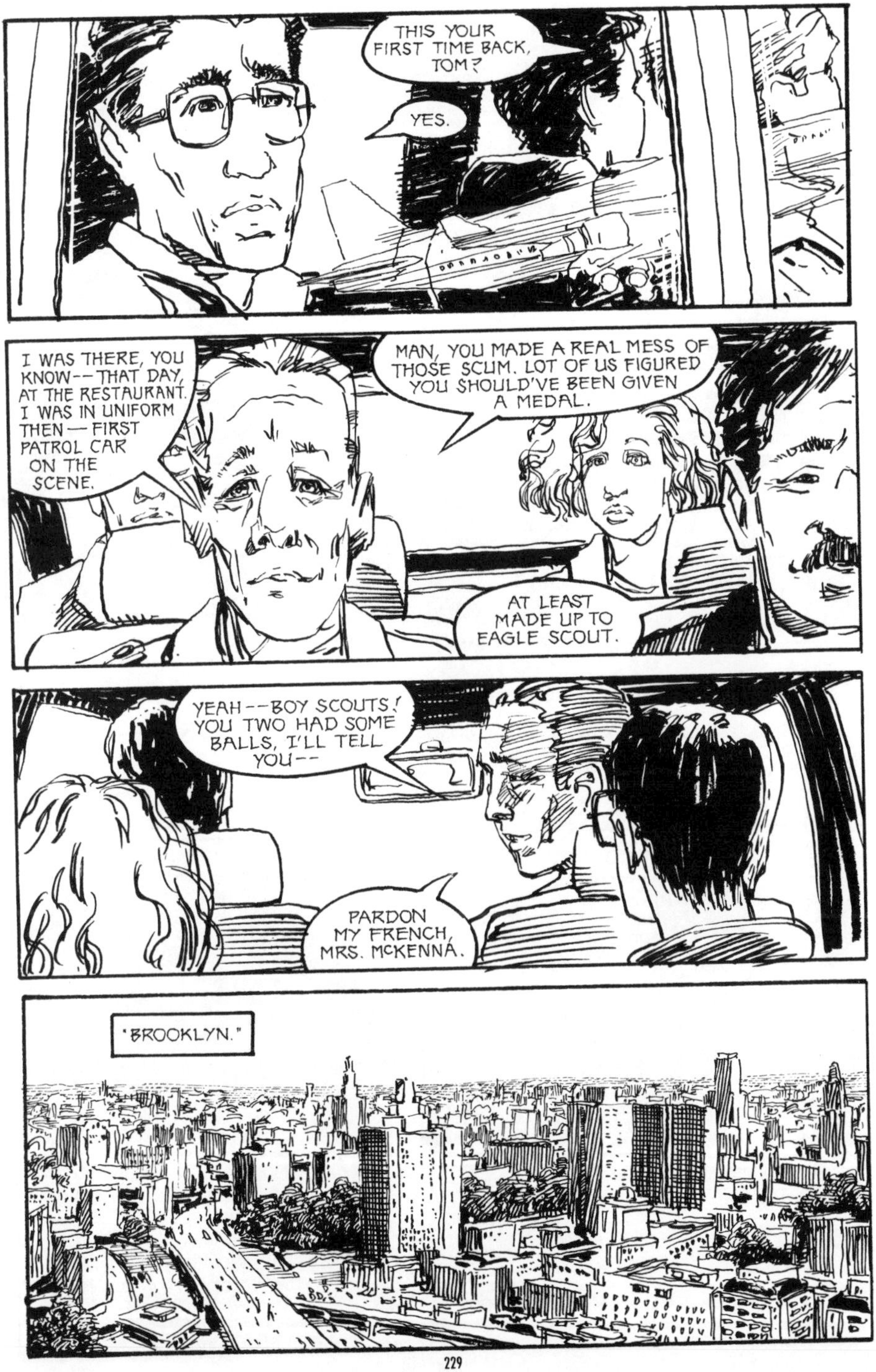
THIS YOUR FIRST TIME BACK, TOM?
YES.
I WAS THERE, YOU KNOW-- THAT DAY, AT THE RESTAURANT. I WAS IN UNIFORM THEN— FIRST PATROL CAR ON THE SCENE.
MAN, YOU MADE A REAL MESS OF THOSE SCUM. LOT OF US FIGURED YOU SHOULD'VE BEEN GIVEN A MEDAL.
AT LEAST MADE UP TO EAGLE SCOUT.
YEAH--BOY SCOUTS! YOU TWO HAD SOME BALLS, I'LL TELL YOU--
PARDON MY FRENCH, MRS. McKENNA.
"BROOKLYN."

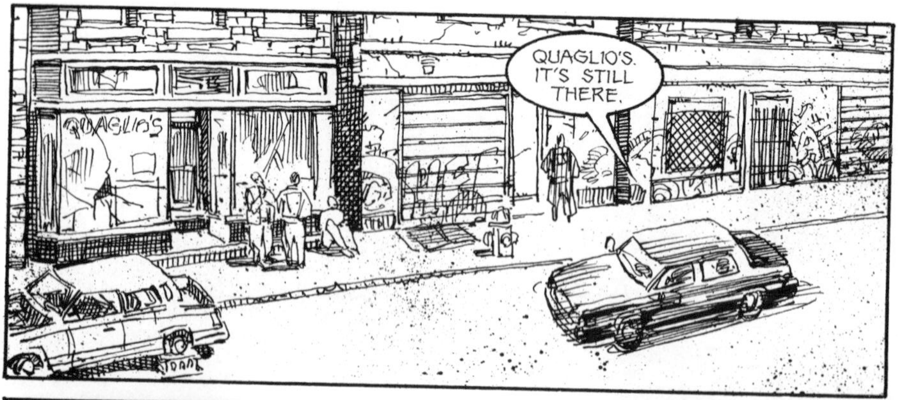
QUAGLIO'S. IT'S STILL THERE.

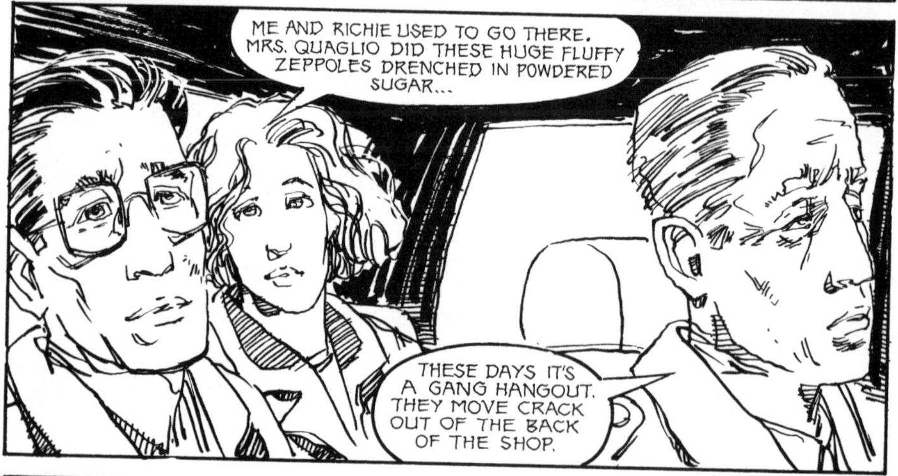
ME AND RICHIE USED TO GO THERE. MRS. QUAGLIO DID THESE HUGE FLUFFY ZEPPOLES DRENCHED IN POWDERED SUGAR...
THESE DAYS IT'S A GANG HANGOUT. THEY MOVE CRACK OUT OF THE BACK OF THE SHOP.

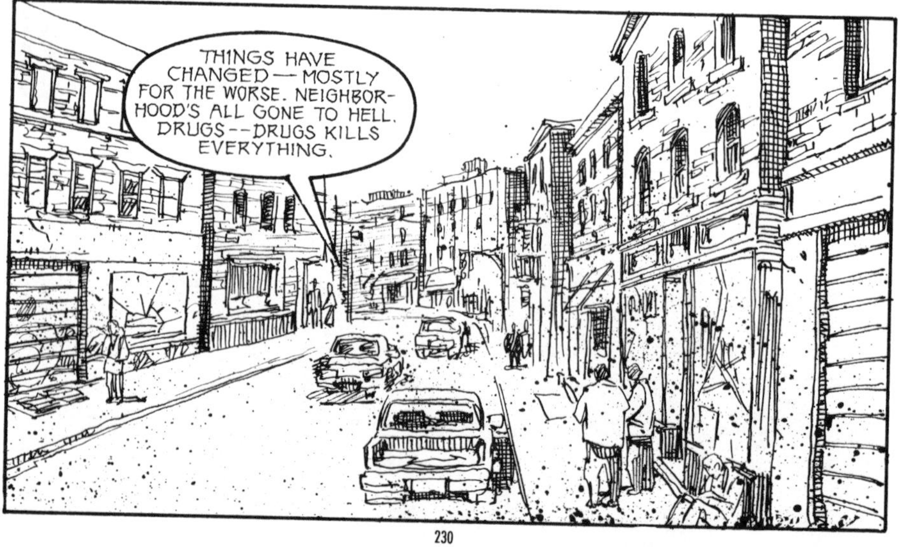
THINGS HAVE CHANGED—MOSTLY FOR THE WORSE. NEIGHBORHOOD'S ALL GONE TO HELL. DRUGS--DRUGS KILLS EVERYTHING.

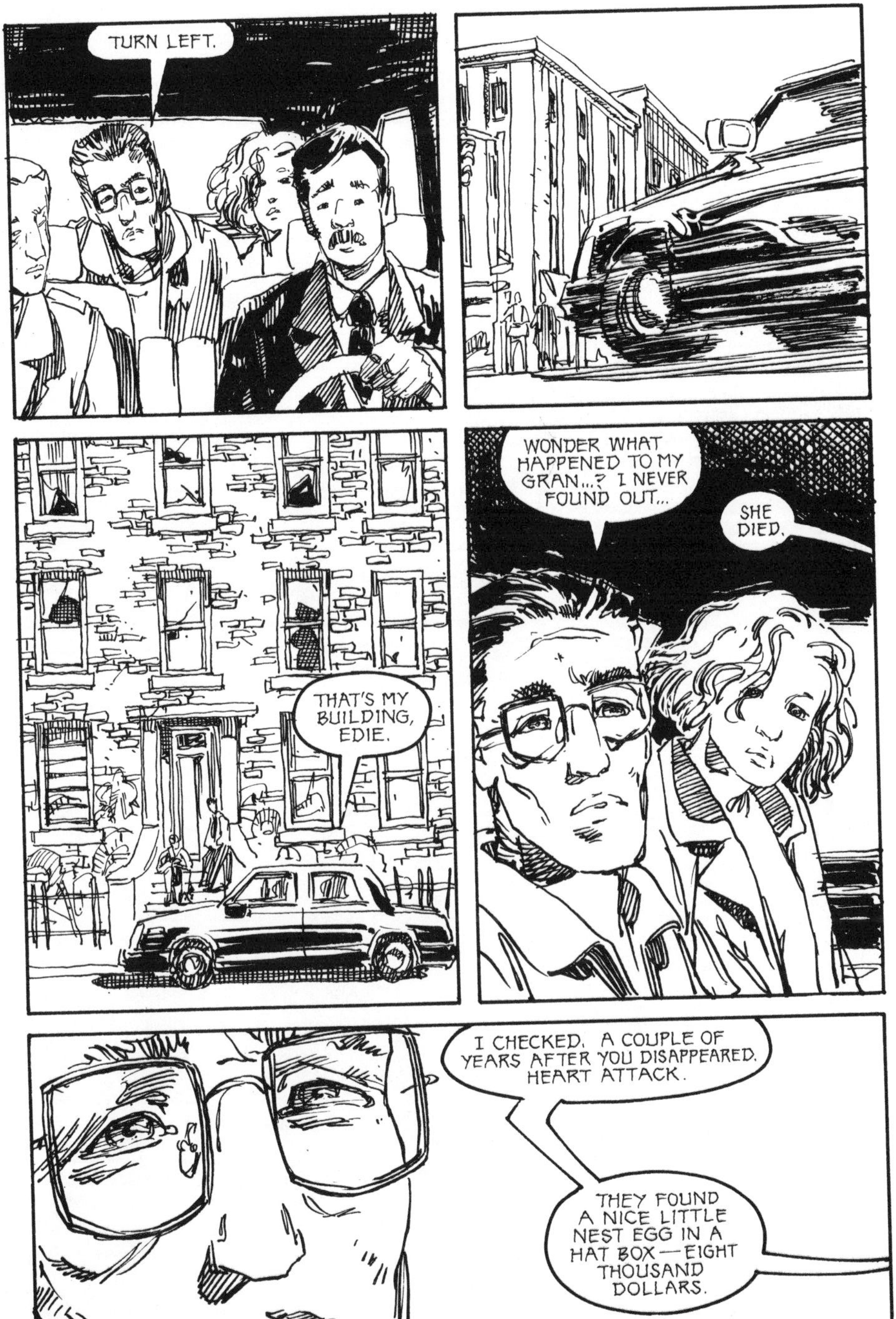
TURN LEFT.
THAT'S MY BUILDING, EDIE.
WONDER WHAT HAPPENED TO MY GRAN...? I NEVER FOUND OUT...
SHE DIED.
I CHECKED. A COUPLE OF YEARS AFTER YOU DISAPPEARED. HEART ATTACK.
THEY FOUND A NICE LITTLE NEST EGG IN A HAT BOX — EIGHT THOUSAND DOLLARS.

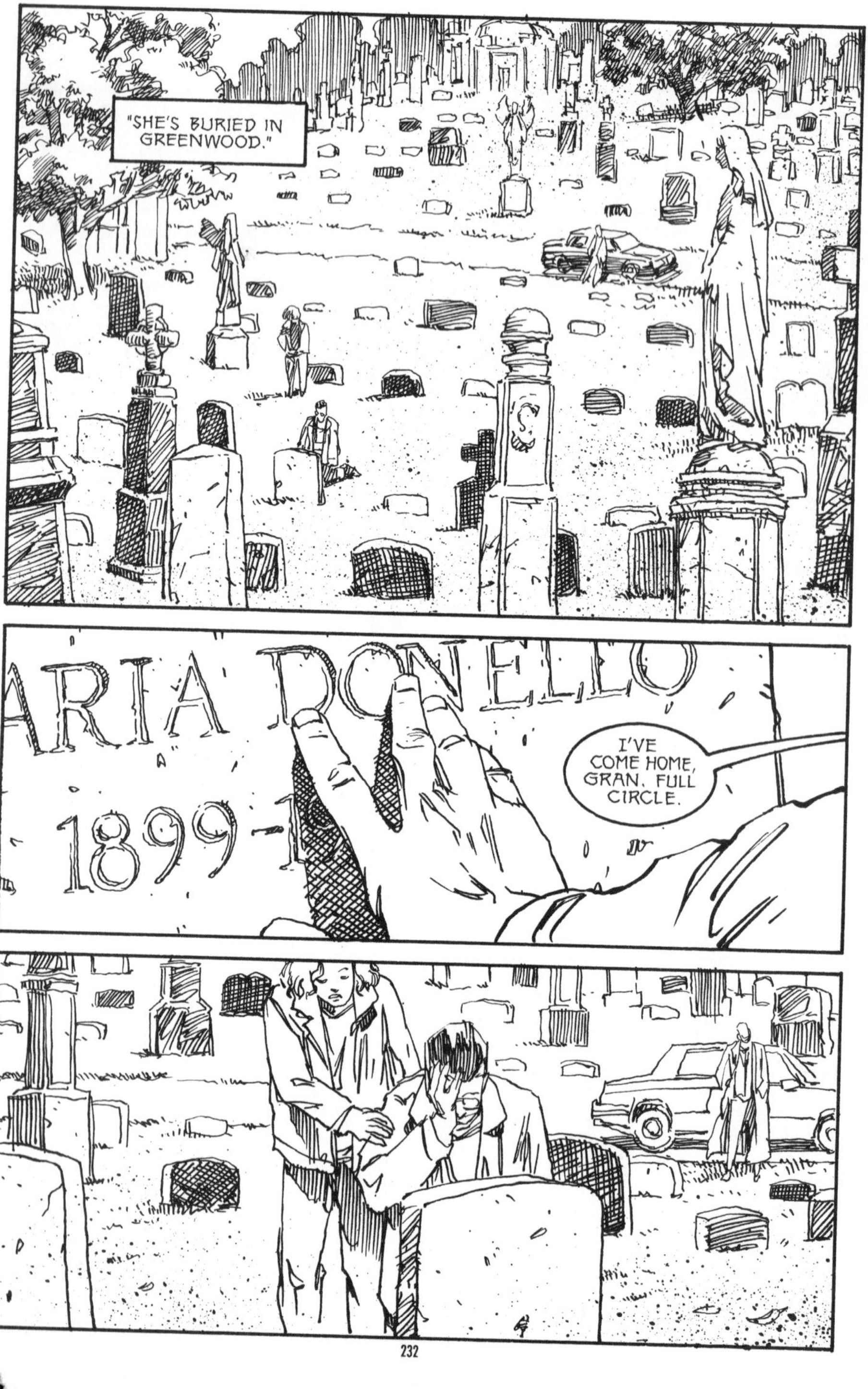
"SHE'S BURIED IN GREENWOOD."
I'VE COME HOME, GRAN. FULL CIRCLE.

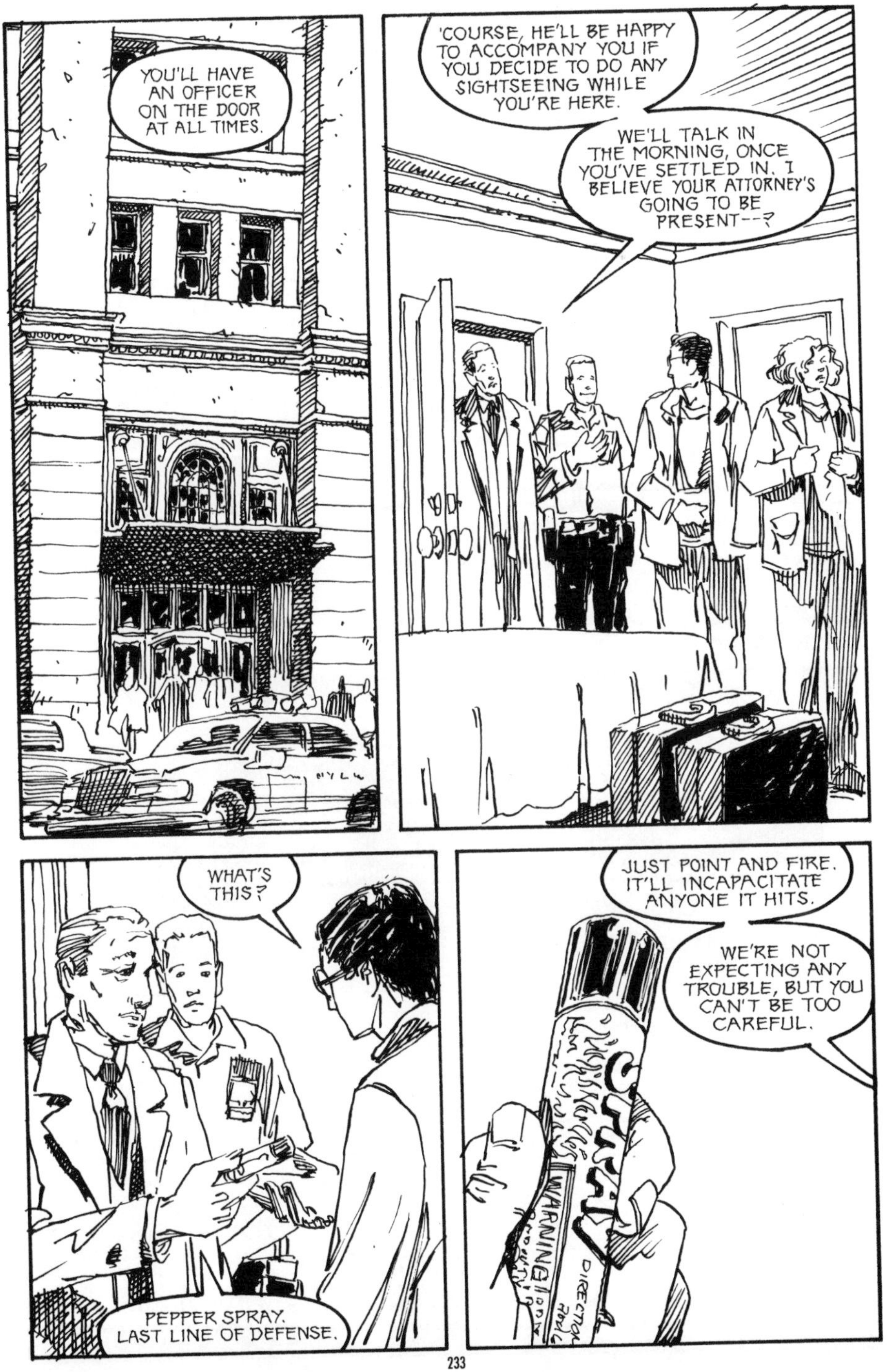

YOU'LL HAVE AN OFFICER ON THE DOOR AT ALL TIMES.
'COURSE, HE'LL BE HAPPY TO ACCOMPANY YOU IF YOU DECIDE TO DO ANY SIGHTSEEING WHILE YOU'RE HERE.
WE'LL TALK IN THE MORNING, ONCE YOU'VE SETTLED IN. I BELIEVE YOUR ATTORNEY'S GOING TO BE PRESENT--?
WHAT'S THIS?
PEPPER SPRAY. LAST LINE OF DEFENSE.
JUST POINT AND FIRE. IT'LL INCAPACITATE ANYONE IT HITS.
WE'RE NOT EXPECTING ANY TROUBLE, BUT YOU CAN'T BE TOO CAREFUL.
WARNING
DIRECTION

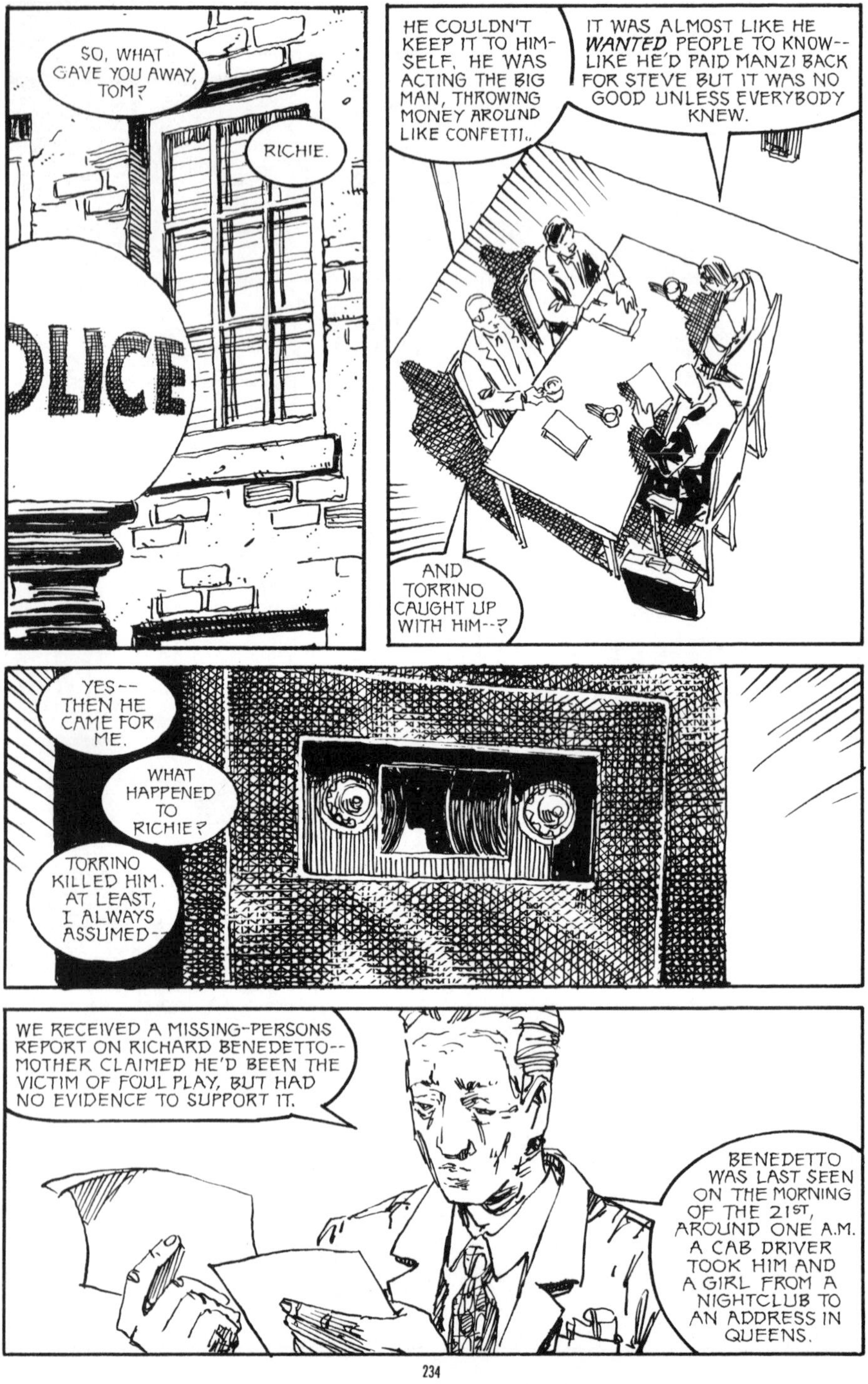
SO, WHAT GAVE YOU AWAY, TOM?
RICHIE.
OLICE
HE COULDN'T KEEP IT TO HIMSELF. HE WAS ACTING THE BIG MAN, THROWING MONEY AROUND LIKE CONFETTI..
IT WAS ALMOST LIKE HE *WANTED* PEOPLE TO KNOW-- LIKE HE'D PAID MANZI BACK FOR STEVE BUT IT WAS NO GOOD UNLESS EVERYBODY KNEW.
AND TORRINO CAUGHT UP WITH HIM--?
YES-- THEN HE CAME FOR ME.
WHAT HAPPENED TO RICHIE?
TORRINO KILLED HIM. AT LEAST, I ALWAYS ASSUMED--
WE RECEIVED A MISSING-PERSONS REPORT ON RICHARD BENEDETTO-- MOTHER CLAIMED HE'D BEEN THE VICTIM OF FOUL PLAY, BUT HAD NO EVIDENCE TO SUPPORT IT.
BENEDETTO WAS LAST SEEN ON THE MORNING OF THE 21ST, AROUND ONE A.M. A CAB DRIVER TOOK HIM AND A GIRL FROM A NIGHTCLUB TO AN ADDRESS IN QUEENS.

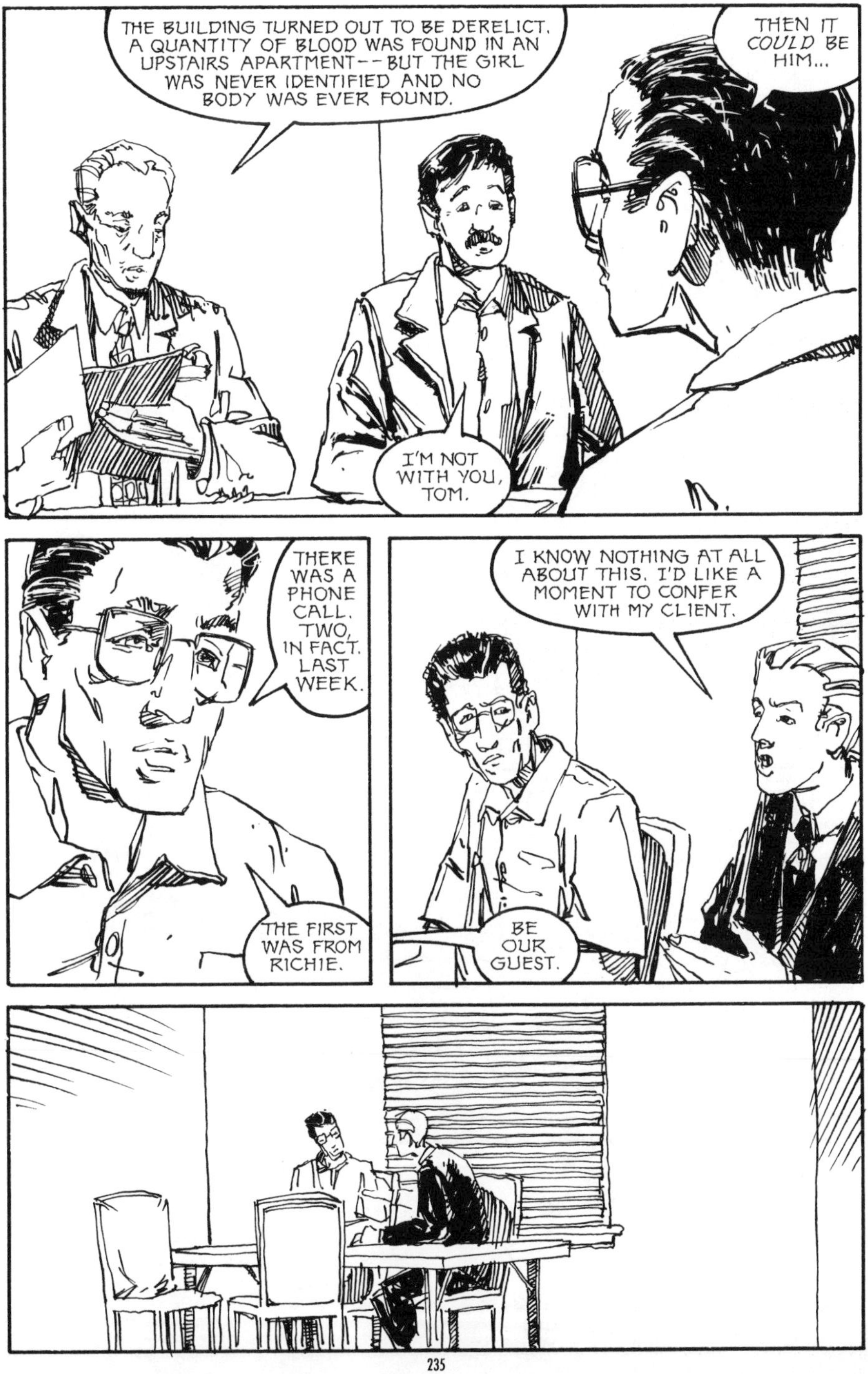
THE BUILDING TURNED OUT TO BE DERELICT. A QUANTITY OF BLOOD WAS FOUND IN AN UPSTAIRS APARTMENT--BUT THE GIRL WAS NEVER IDENTIFIED AND NO BODY WAS EVER FOUND.
THEN IT *COULD* BE HIM...
I'M NOT WITH YOU, TOM.
THERE WAS A PHONE CALL. TWO, IN FACT. LAST WEEK.
THE FIRST WAS FROM RICHIE.
I KNOW NOTHING AT ALL ABOUT THIS. I'D LIKE A MOMENT TO CONFER WITH MY CLIENT.
BE OUR GUEST.

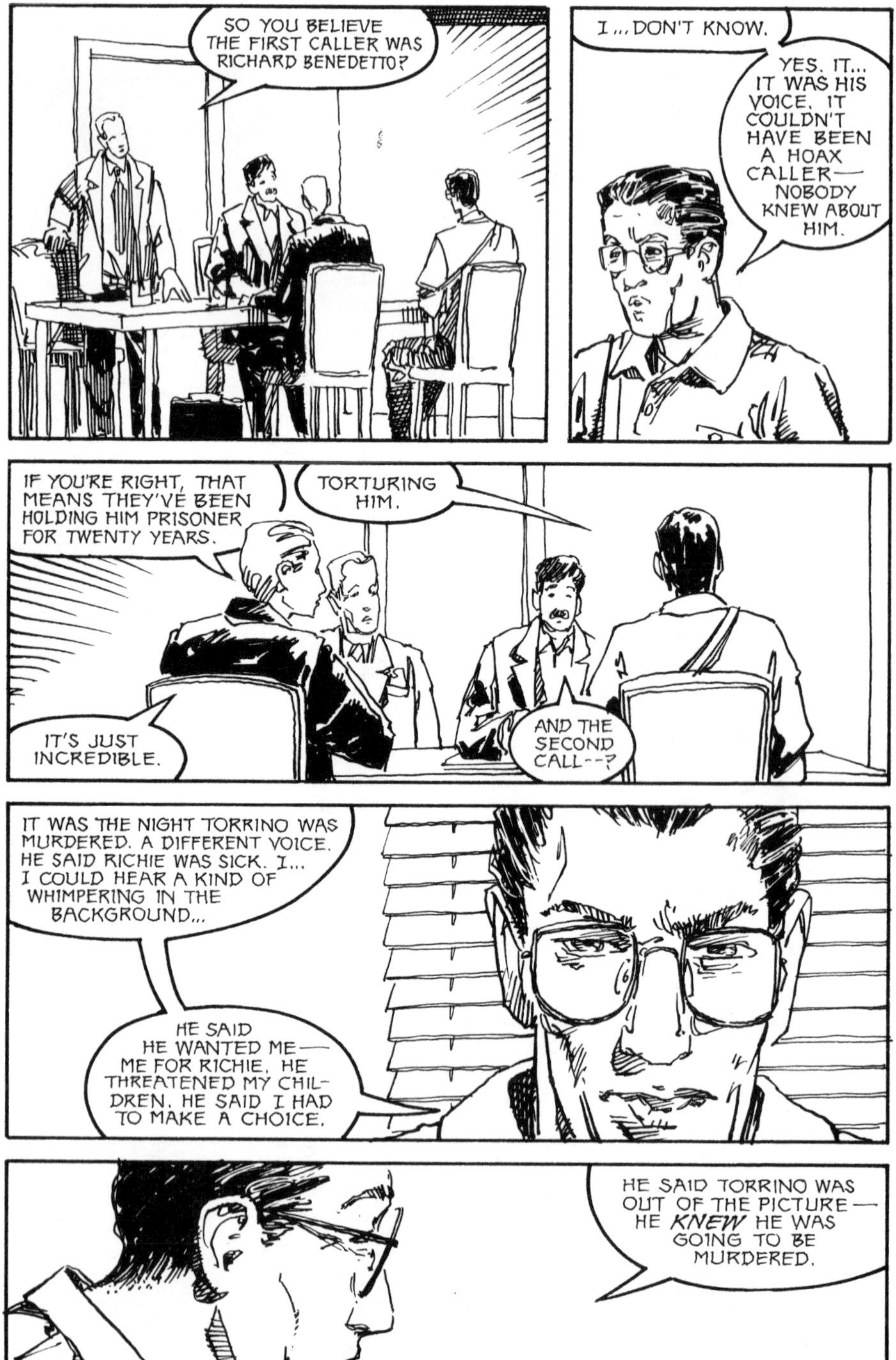
SO YOU BELIEVE THE FIRST CALLER WAS RICHARD BENEDETTO?
I ... DON'T KNOW.
YES. IT... IT WAS HIS VOICE. IT COULDN'T HAVE BEEN A HOAX CALLER— NOBODY KNEW ABOUT HIM.
IF YOU'RE RIGHT, THAT MEANS THEY'VE BEEN HOLDING HIM PRISONER FOR TWENTY YEARS.
TORTURING HIM.
IT'S JUST INCREDIBLE.
AND THE SECOND CALL--?
IT WAS THE NIGHT TORRINO WAS MURDERED. A DIFFERENT VOICE. HE SAID RICHIE WAS SICK. I... I COULD HEAR A KIND OF WHIMPERING IN THE BACKGROUND...
HE SAID HE WANTED ME— ME FOR RICHIE. HE THREATENED MY CHILDREN. HE SAID I HAD TO MAKE A CHOICE.
HE SAID TORRINO WAS OUT OF THE PICTURE— HE *KNEW* HE WAS GOING TO BE MURDERED.

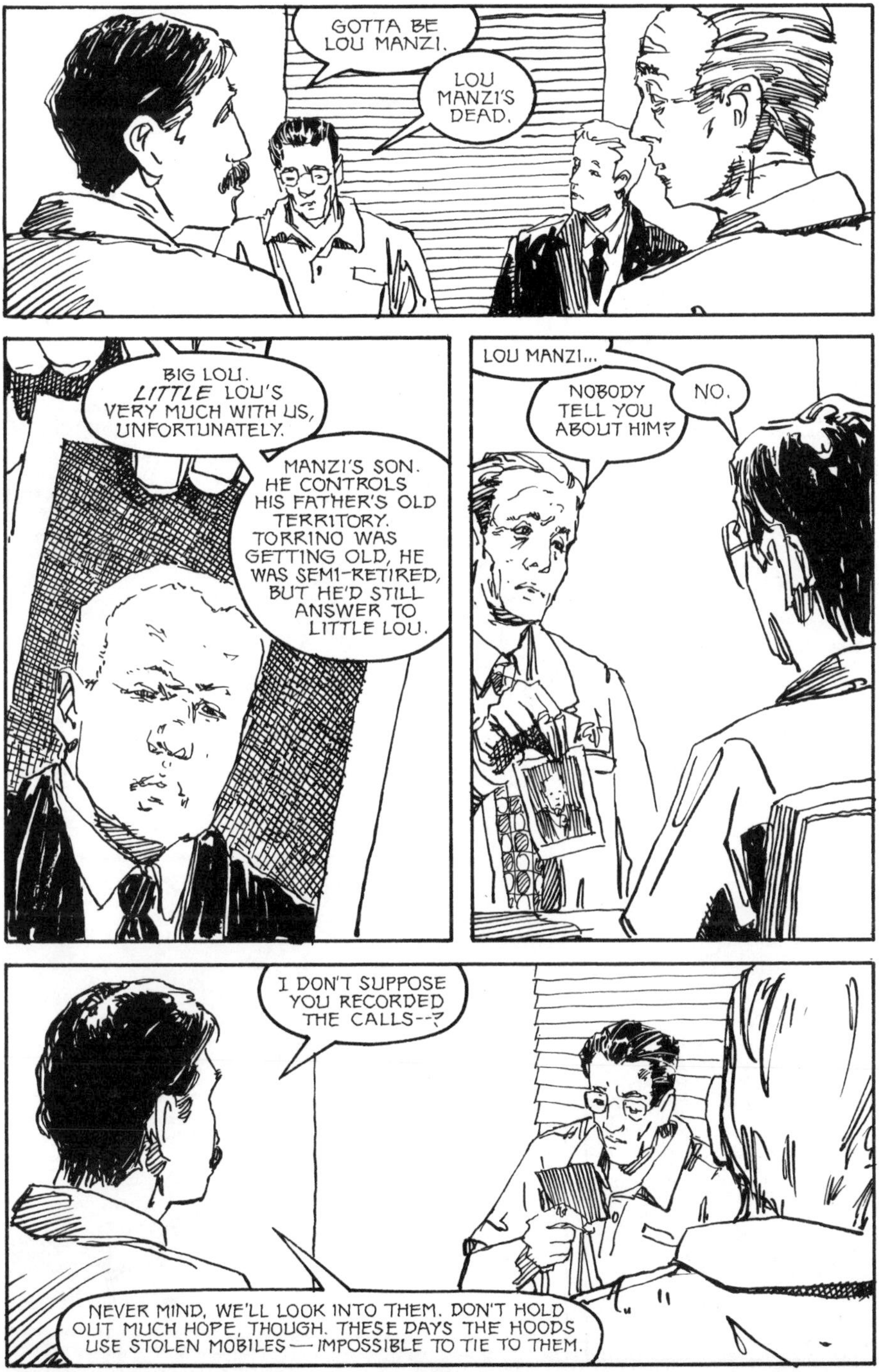
GOTTA BE LOU MANZI.
LOU MANZI'S DEAD.
BIG LOU. *LITTLE* LOU'S VERY MUCH WITH US, UNFORTUNATELY.
MANZI'S SON. HE CONTROLS HIS FATHER'S OLD TERRITORY. TORRINO WAS GETTING OLD, HE WAS SEMI-RETIRED, BUT HE'D STILL ANSWER TO LITTLE LOU.
LOU MANZI...
NOBODY TELL YOU ABOUT HIM?
NO.
I DON'T SUPPOSE YOU RECORDED THE CALLS--?
NEVER MIND, WE'LL LOOK INTO THEM. DON'T HOLD OUT MUCH HOPE, THOUGH. THESE DAYS THE HOODS USE STOLEN MOBILES— IMPOSSIBLE TO TIE TO THEM.

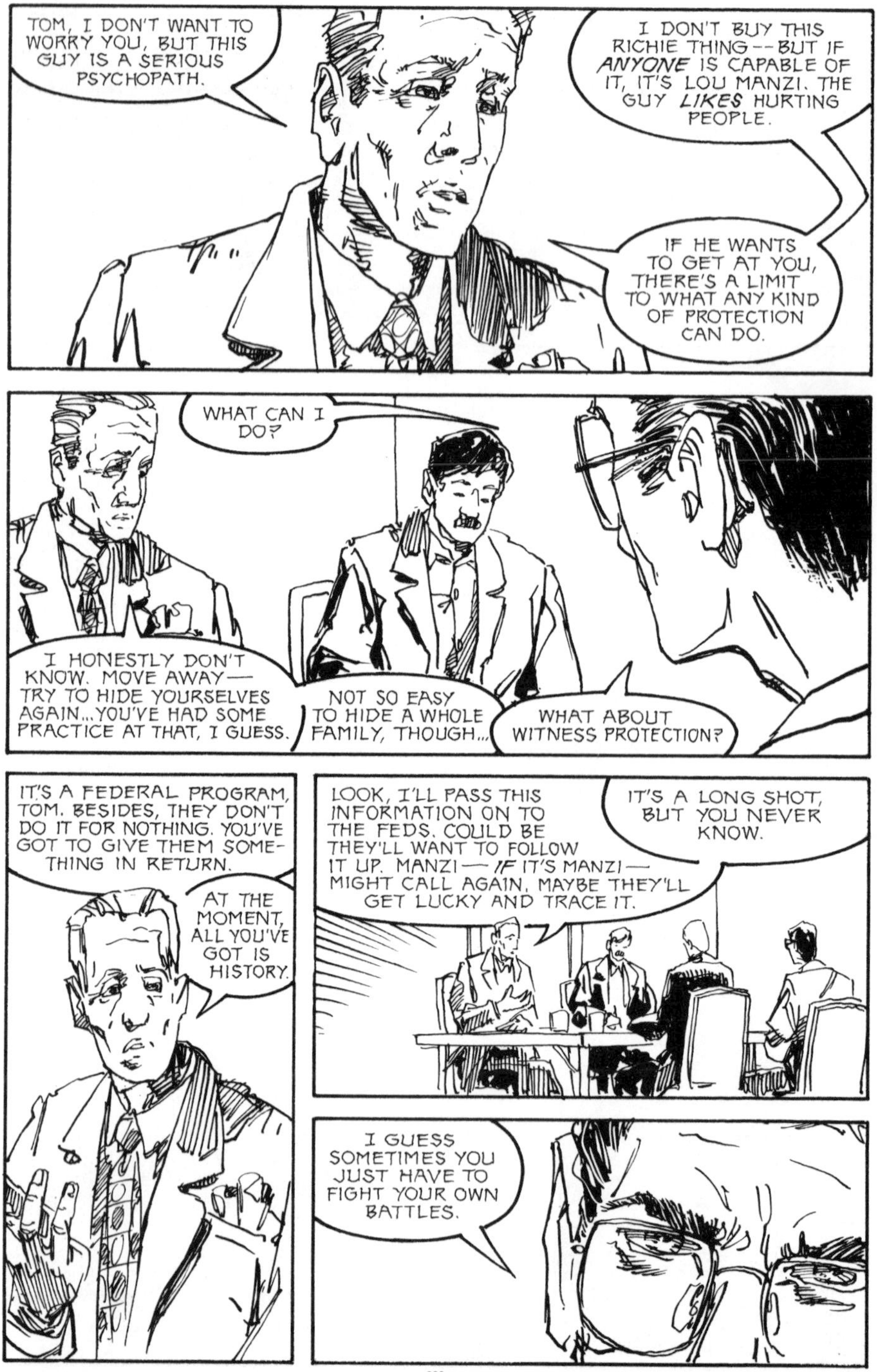
TOM, I DON'T WANT TO WORRY YOU, BUT THIS GUY IS A SERIOUS PSYCHOPATH.
I DON'T BUY THIS RICHIE THING--BUT IF *ANYONE* IS CAPABLE OF IT, IT'S LOU MANZI. THE GUY *LIKES* HURTING PEOPLE.
IF HE WANTS TO GET AT YOU, THERE'S A LIMIT TO WHAT ANY KIND OF PROTECTION CAN DO.
WHAT CAN I DO?
I HONESTLY DON'T KNOW. MOVE AWAY— TRY TO HIDE YOURSELVES AGAIN... YOU'VE HAD SOME PRACTICE AT THAT, I GUESS.
NOT SO EASY TO HIDE A WHOLE FAMILY, THOUGH...
WHAT ABOUT WITNESS PROTECTION?
IT'S A FEDERAL PROGRAM, TOM. BESIDES, THEY DON'T DO IT FOR NOTHING. YOU'VE GOT TO GIVE THEM SOMETHING IN RETURN.
AT THE MOMENT, ALL YOU'VE GOT IS HISTORY.
LOOK, I'LL PASS THIS INFORMATION ON TO THE FEDS. COULD BE THEY'LL WANT TO FOLLOW IT UP. MANZI— *IF* IT'S MANZI— MIGHT CALL AGAIN, MAYBE THEY'LL GET LUCKY AND TRACE IT.
IT'S A LONG SHOT, BUT YOU NEVER KNOW.
I GUESS SOMETIMES YOU JUST HAVE TO FIGHT YOUR OWN BATTLES.

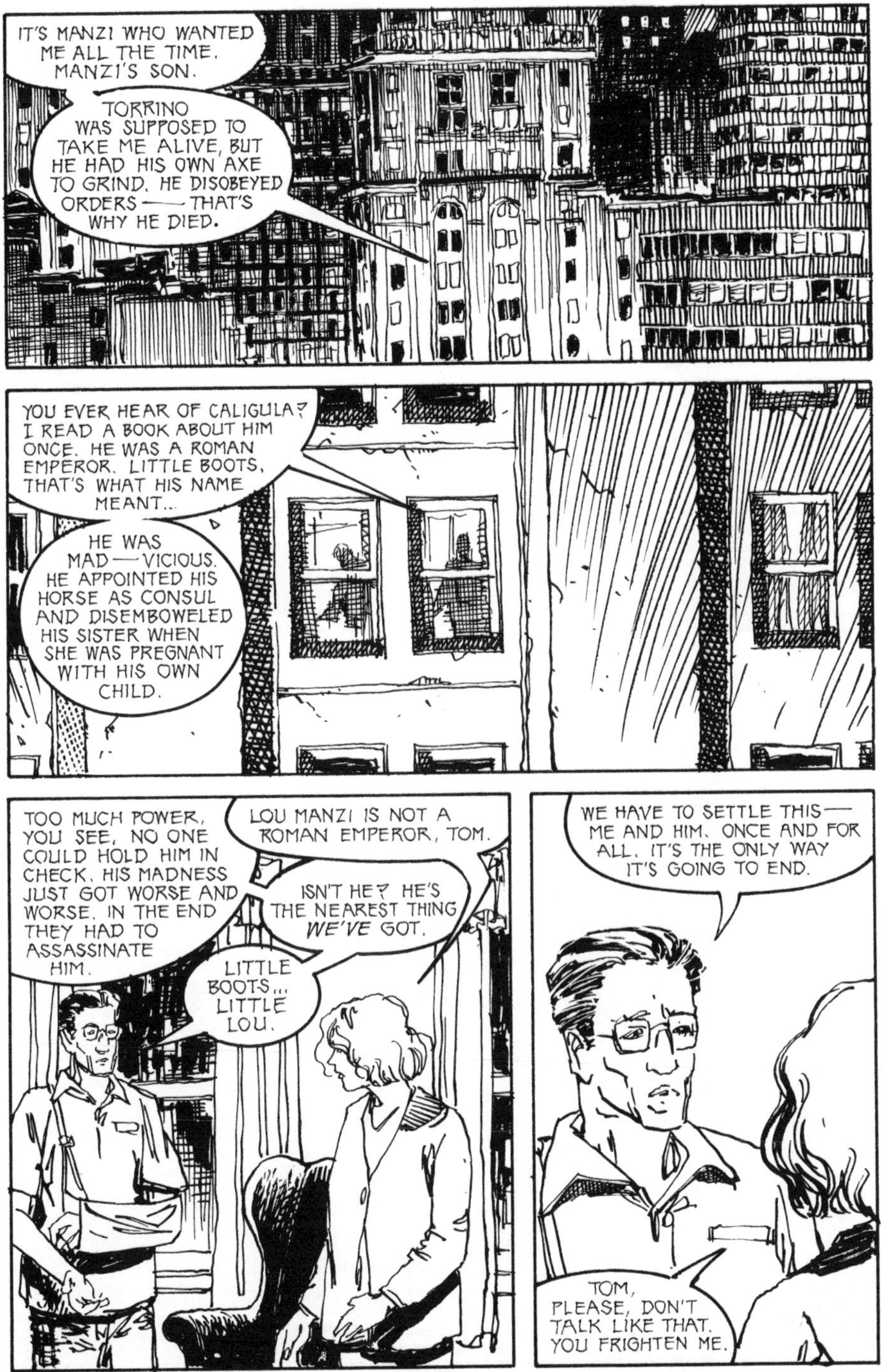
IT'S MANZI WHO WANTED ME ALL THE TIME. MANZI'S SON.
TORRINO WAS SUPPOSED TO TAKE ME ALIVE, BUT HE HAD HIS OWN AXE TO GRIND. HE DISOBEYED ORDERS — THAT'S WHY HE DIED.
YOU EVER HEAR OF CALIGULA? I READ A BOOK ABOUT HIM ONCE. HE WAS A ROMAN EMPEROR. LITTLE BOOTS, THAT'S WHAT HIS NAME MEANT...
HE WAS MAD — VICIOUS. HE APPOINTED HIS HORSE AS CONSUL AND DISEMBOWELED HIS SISTER WHEN SHE WAS PREGNANT WITH HIS OWN CHILD.
TOO MUCH POWER, YOU SEE. NO ONE COULD HOLD HIM IN CHECK. HIS MADNESS JUST GOT WORSE AND WORSE. IN THE END THEY HAD TO ASSASSINATE HIM.
LOU MANZI IS NOT A ROMAN EMPEROR, TOM.
ISN'T HE? HE'S THE NEAREST THING *WE'VE* GOT.
LITTLE BOOTS... LITTLE LOU.
WE HAVE TO SETTLE THIS — ME AND HIM. ONCE AND FOR ALL. IT'S THE ONLY WAY IT'S GOING TO END.
TOM, PLEASE, DON'T TALK LIKE THAT. YOU FRIGHTEN ME.

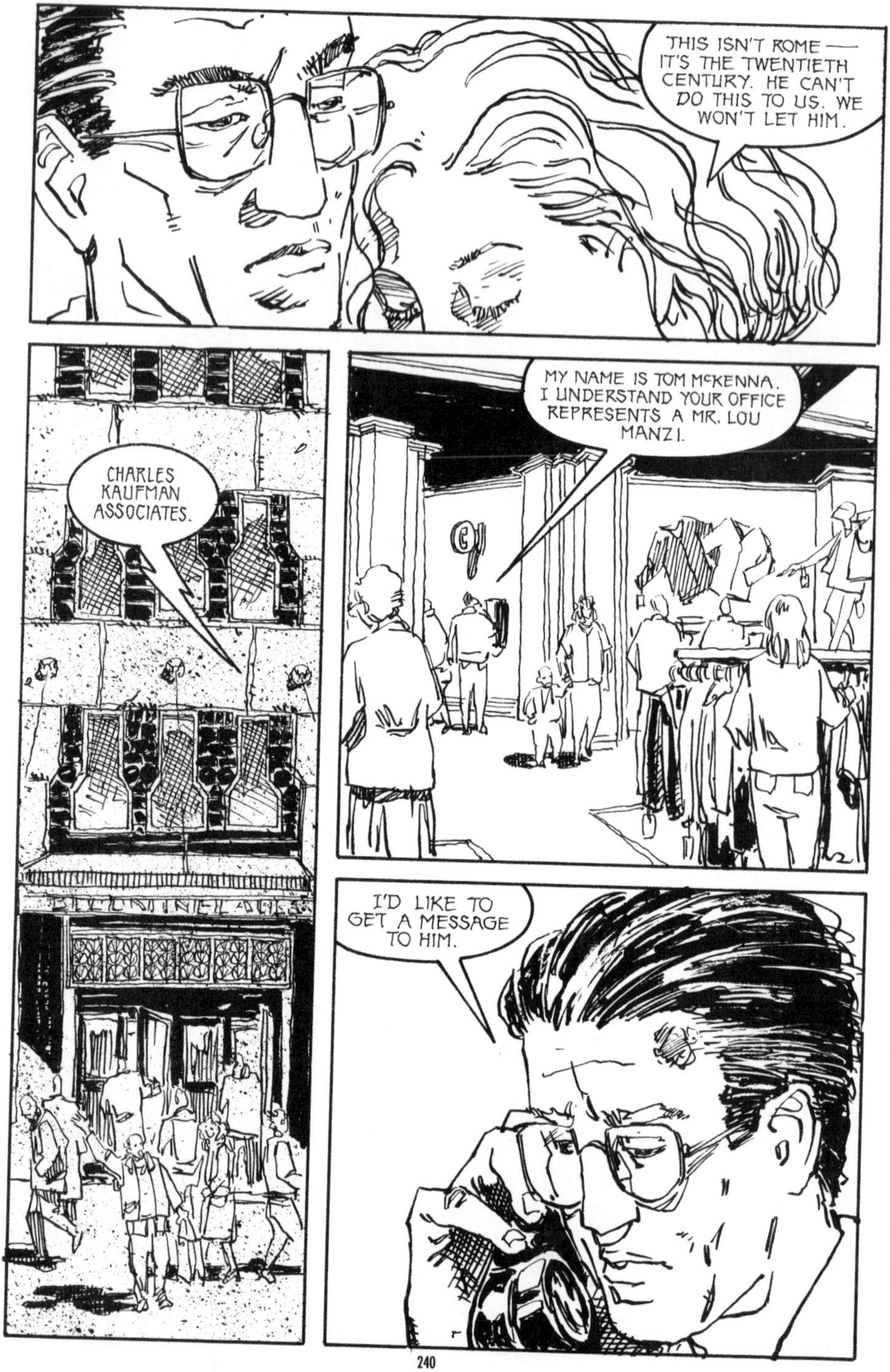
THIS ISN'T ROME — IT'S THE TWENTIETH CENTURY. HE CAN'T DO THIS TO US. WE WON'T LET HIM.
CHARLES KAUFMAN ASSOCIATES.
MY NAME IS TOM McKENNA. I UNDERSTAND YOUR OFFICE REPRESENTS A MR. LOU MANZI.
I'D LIKE TO GET A MESSAGE TO HIM.

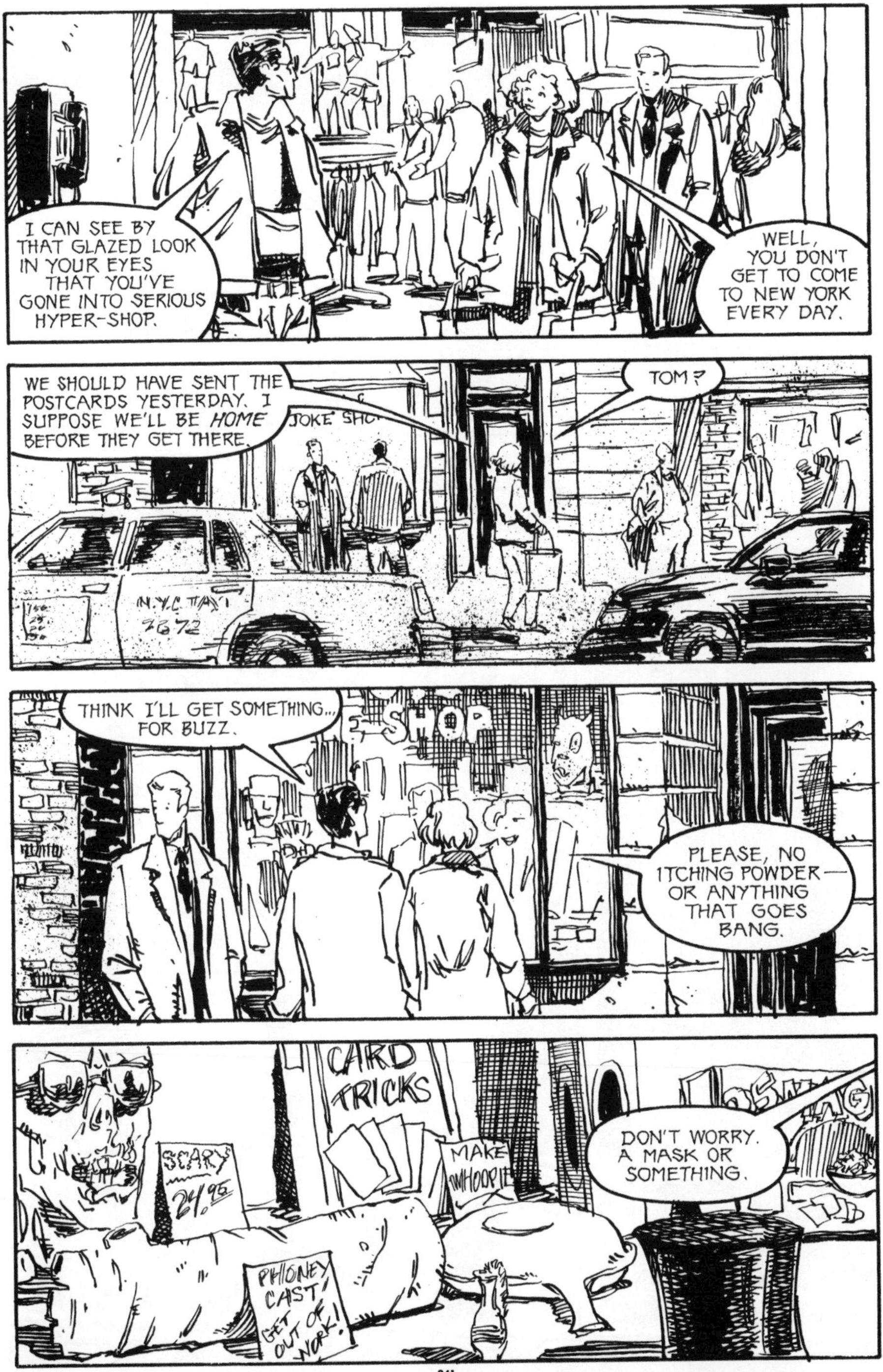
I CAN SEE BY THAT GLAZED LOOK IN YOUR EYES THAT YOU'VE GONE INTO SERIOUS HYPER-SHOP.
WELL, YOU DON'T GET TO COME TO NEW YORK EVERY DAY.
WE SHOULD HAVE SENT THE POSTCARDS YESTERDAY. I SUPPOSE WE'LL BE *HOME* BEFORE THEY GET THERE.
TOM?
JOKE SHO
N.Y.C TAXI
2672
THINK I'LL GET SOMETHING... FOR BUZZ.
SHOP
PLEASE, NO ITCHING POWDER— OR ANYTHING THAT GOES BANG.
CARD TRICKS
SCARY
24.95
MAKE WHOOPI
PHONEY CAST! GET OUT OF WORK!
DON'T WORRY. A MASK OR SOMETHING.

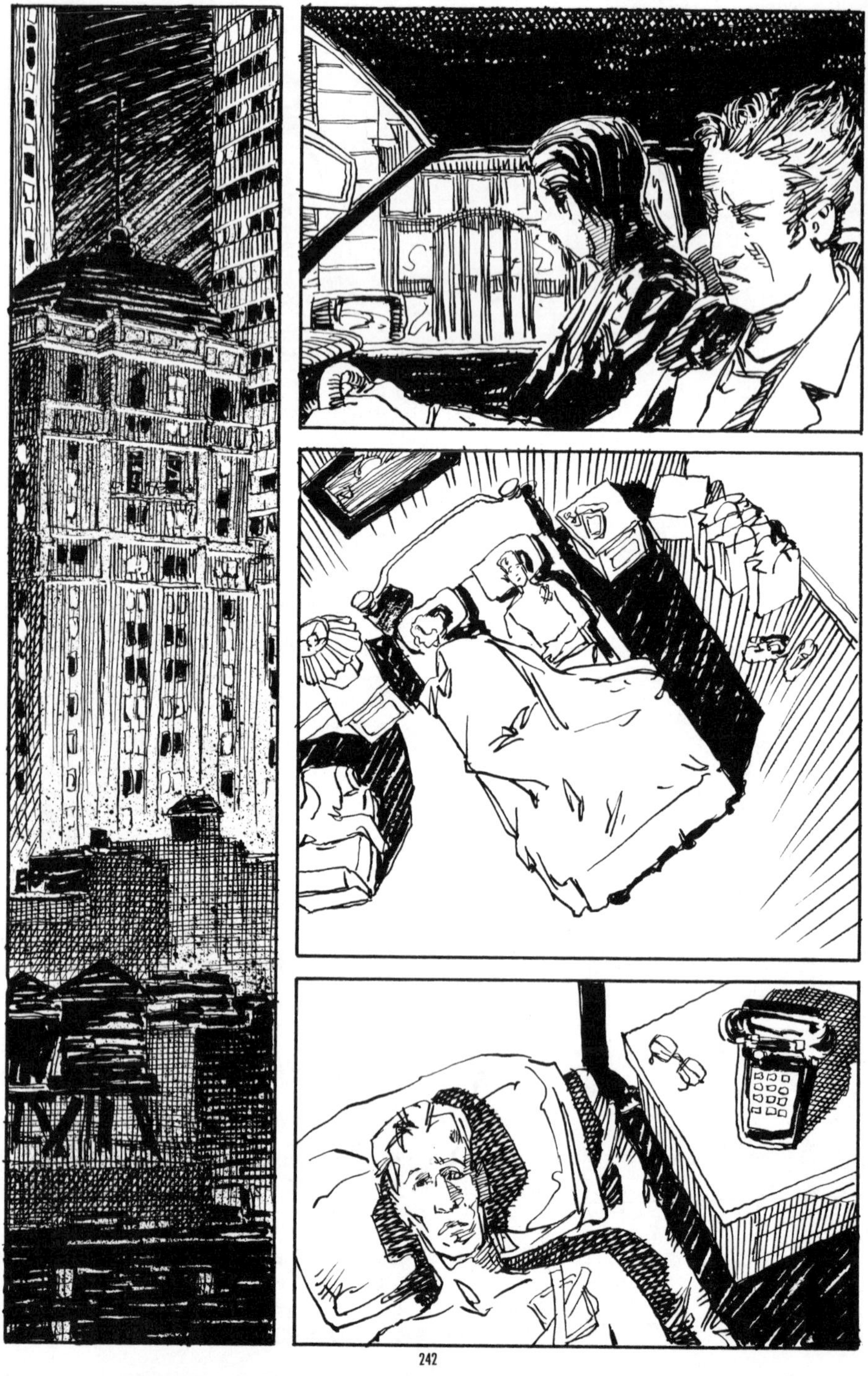

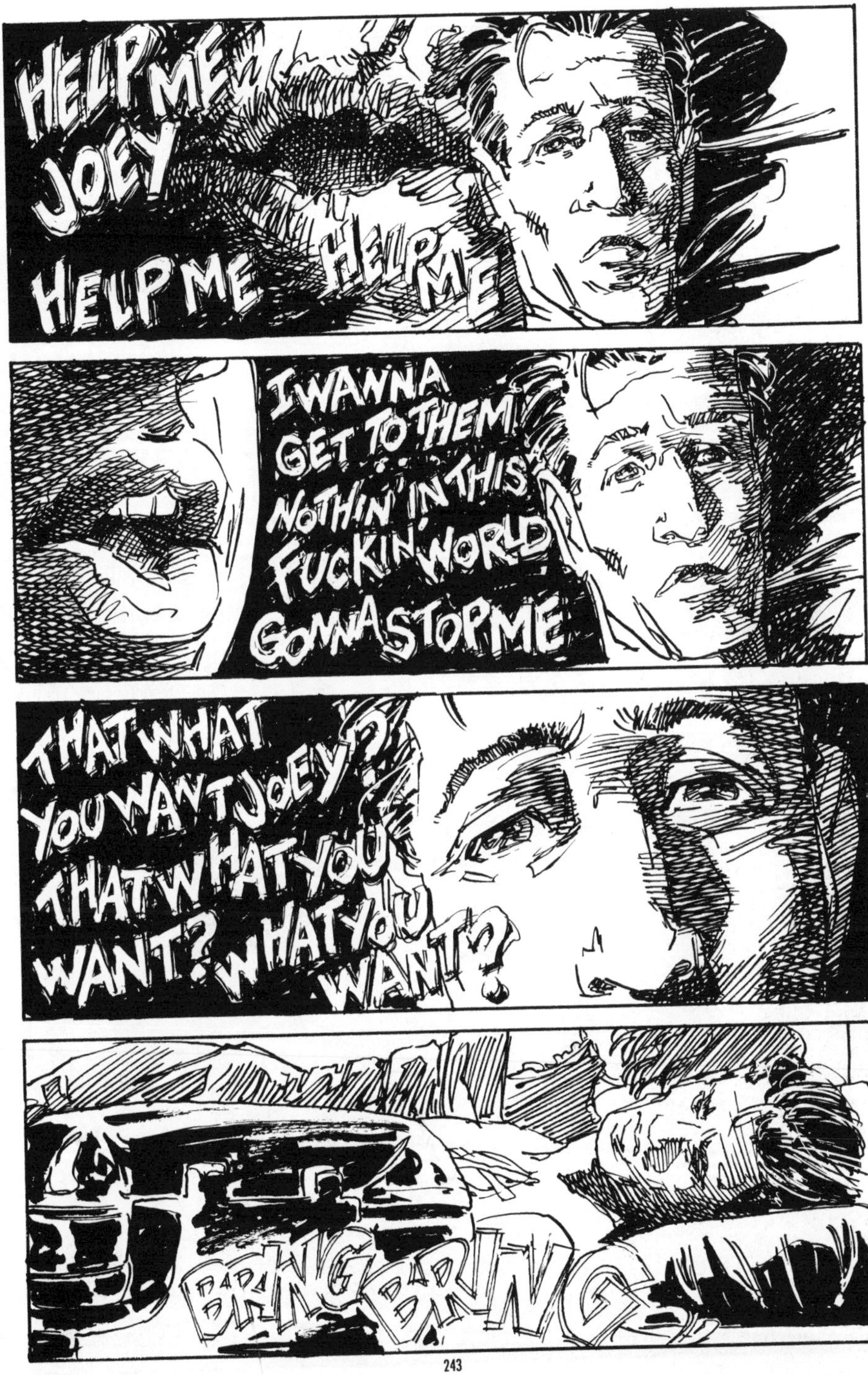
HELP ME, JOEY
HELP ME HELP ME
I WANNA GET TO THEM!
NOTHIN' IN THIS FUCKIN' WORLD GONNA STOP ME
THAT WHAT YOU WANT JOEY?
THAT WHAT YOU WANT? WHAT YOU WANT?
BRING BRING

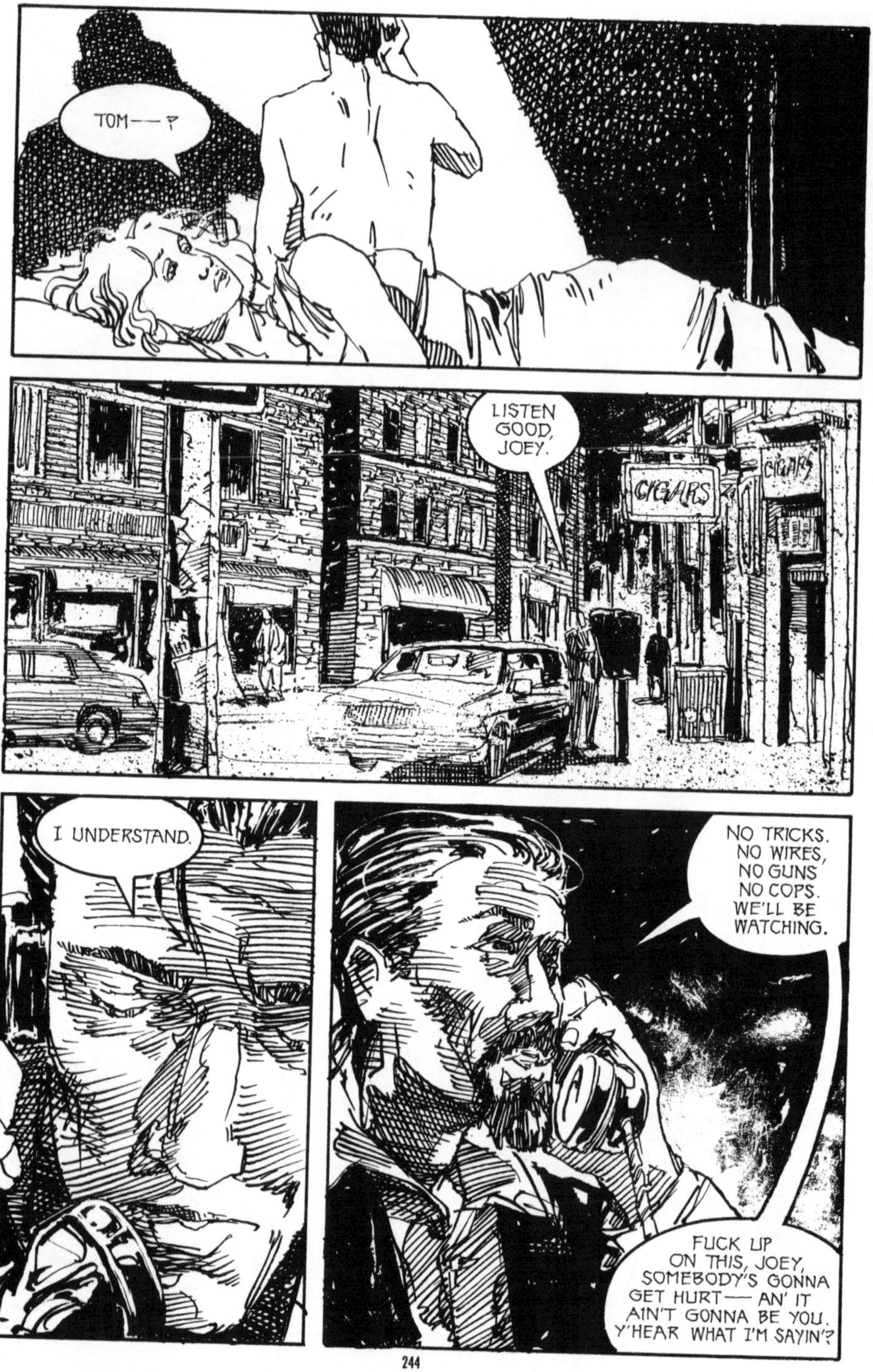

TOM——?
LISTEN GOOD, JOEY.
CIGARS
CIGARS
I UNDERSTAND.
NO TRICKS. NO WIRES, NO GUNS NO COPS. WE'LL BE WATCHING.
FUCK UP ON THIS, JOEY, SOMEBODY'S GONNA GET HURT—— AN' IT AIN'T GONNA BE YOU. Y'HEAR WHAT I'M SAYIN'?

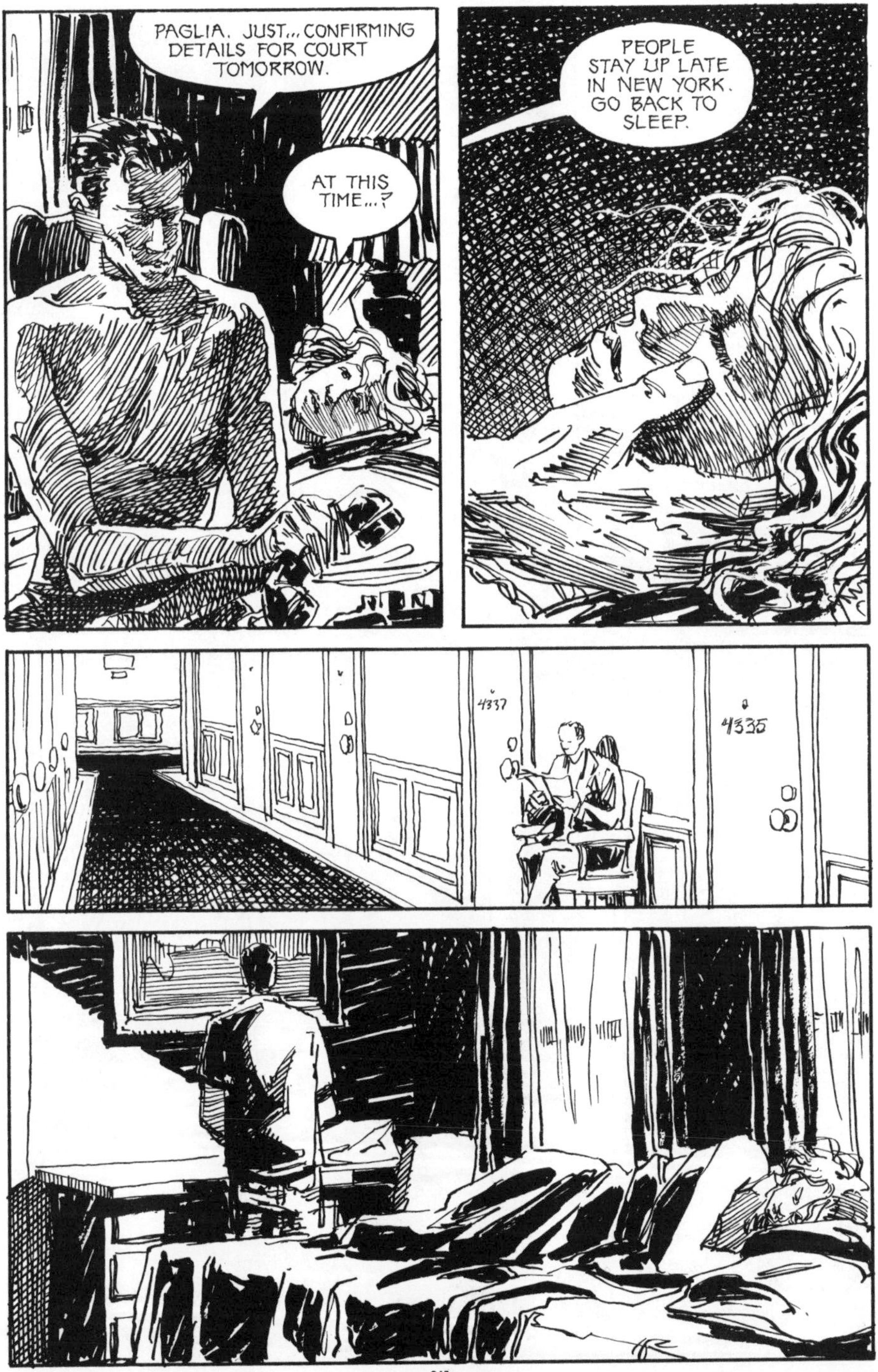
PAGLIA. JUST... CONFIRMING DETAILS FOR COURT TOMORROW.
AT THIS TIME...?
PEOPLE STAY UP LATE IN NEW YORK. GO BACK TO SLEEP.
4337
4335

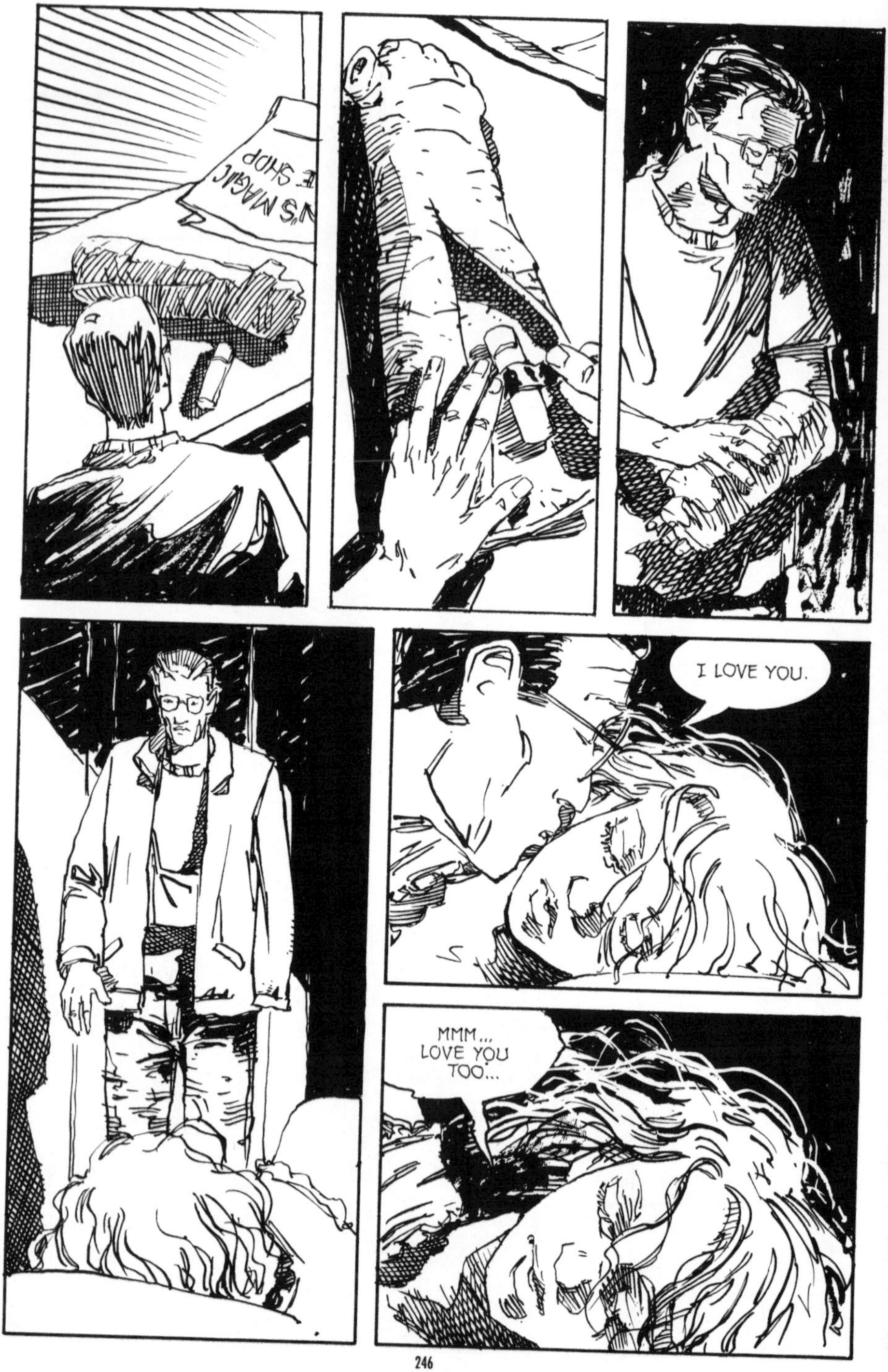
I LOVE YOU.
MMM... LOVE YOU TOO...

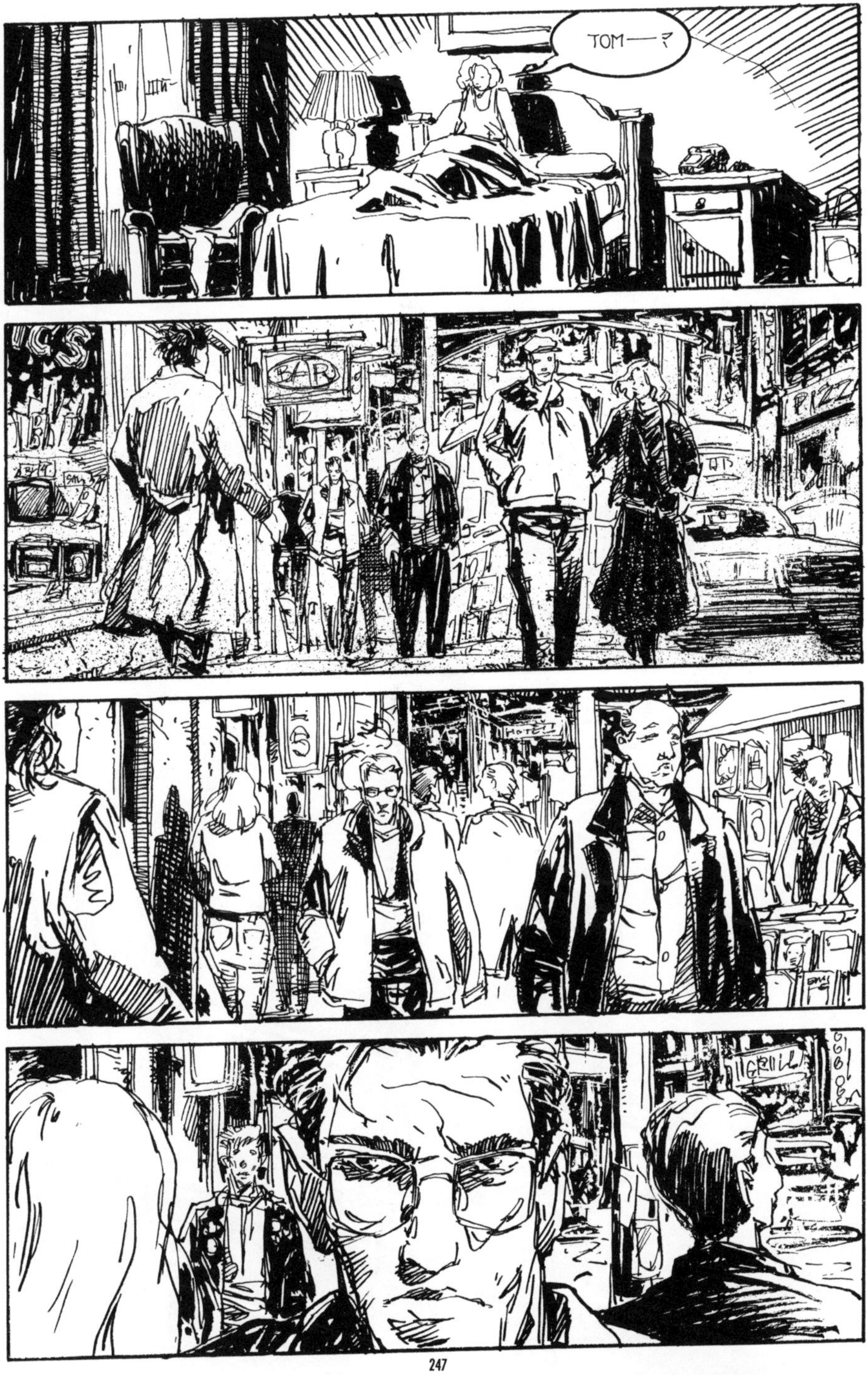
TOM—?
BAR
PIZZ
GRILL

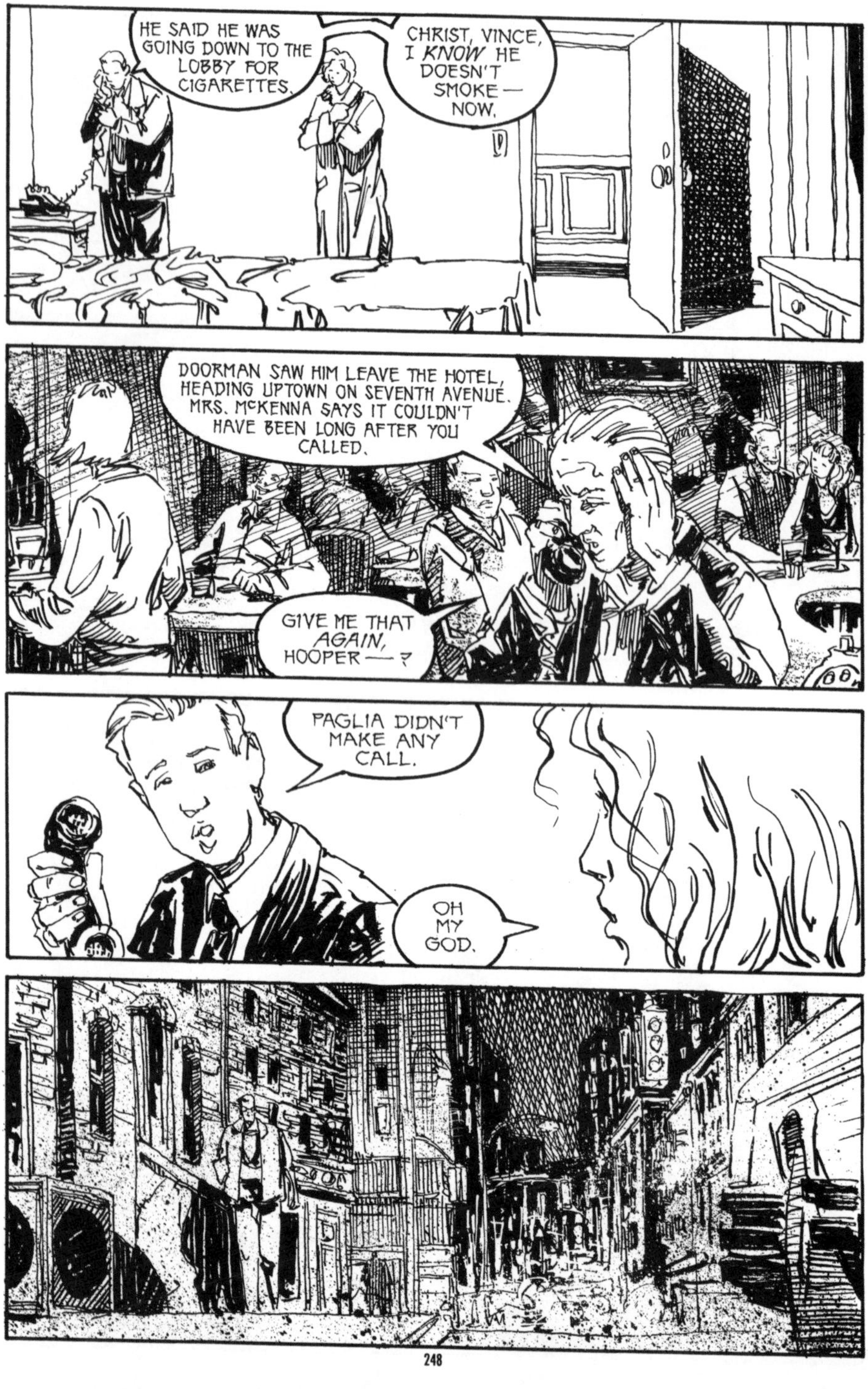
HE SAID HE WAS GOING DOWN TO THE LOBBY FOR CIGARETTES.
CHRIST, VINCE, I *KNOW* HE DOESN'T SMOKE— NOW.
DOORMAN SAW HIM LEAVE THE HOTEL, HEADING UPTOWN ON SEVENTH AVENUE. MRS. McKENNA SAYS IT COULDN'T HAVE BEEN LONG AFTER YOU CALLED.
GIVE ME THAT *AGAIN,* HOOPER—?
PAGLIA DIDN'T MAKE ANY CALL.
OH MY GOD.

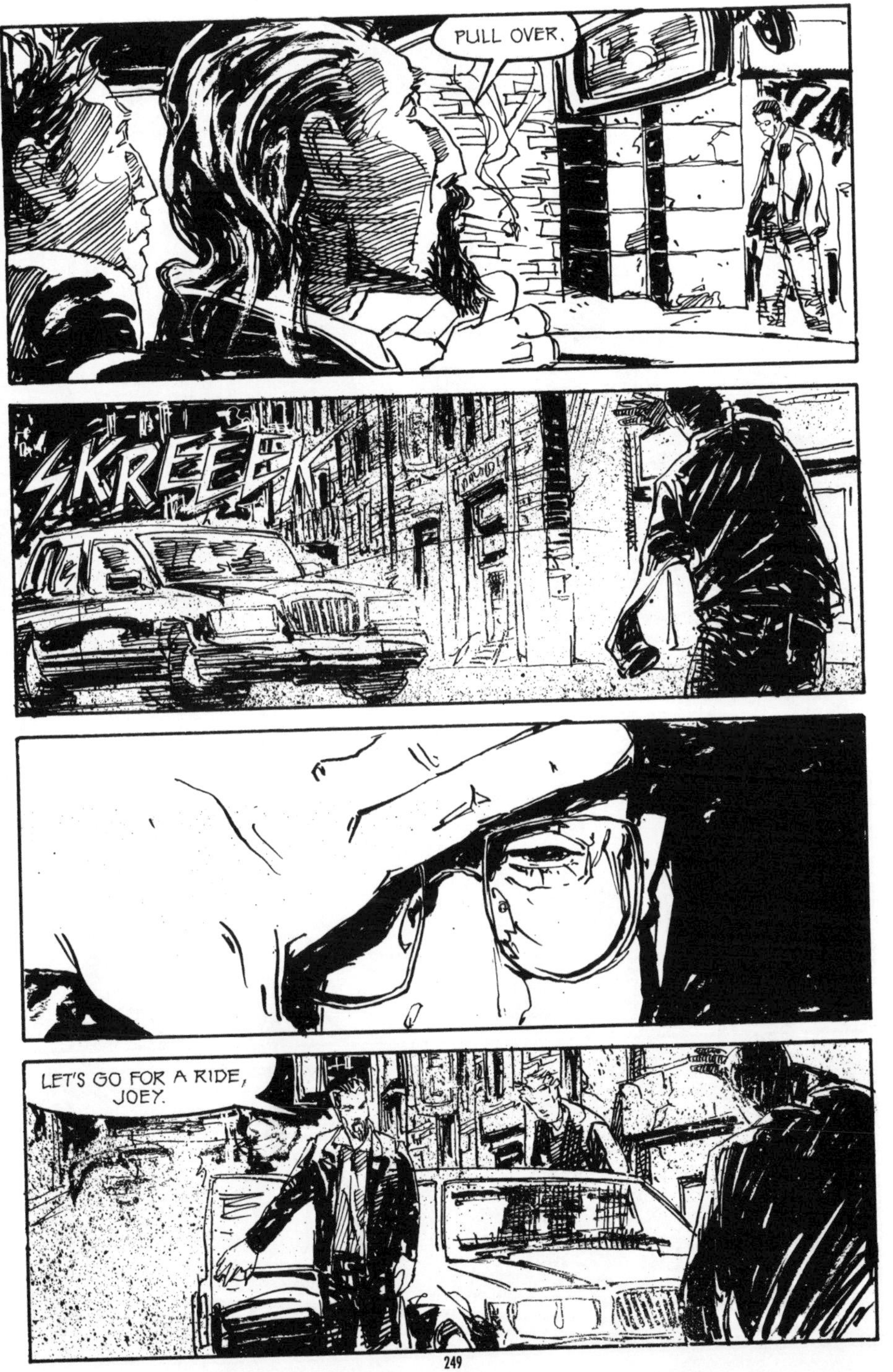
PULL OVER.
SKREEEK
LET'S GO FOR A RIDE, JOEY.

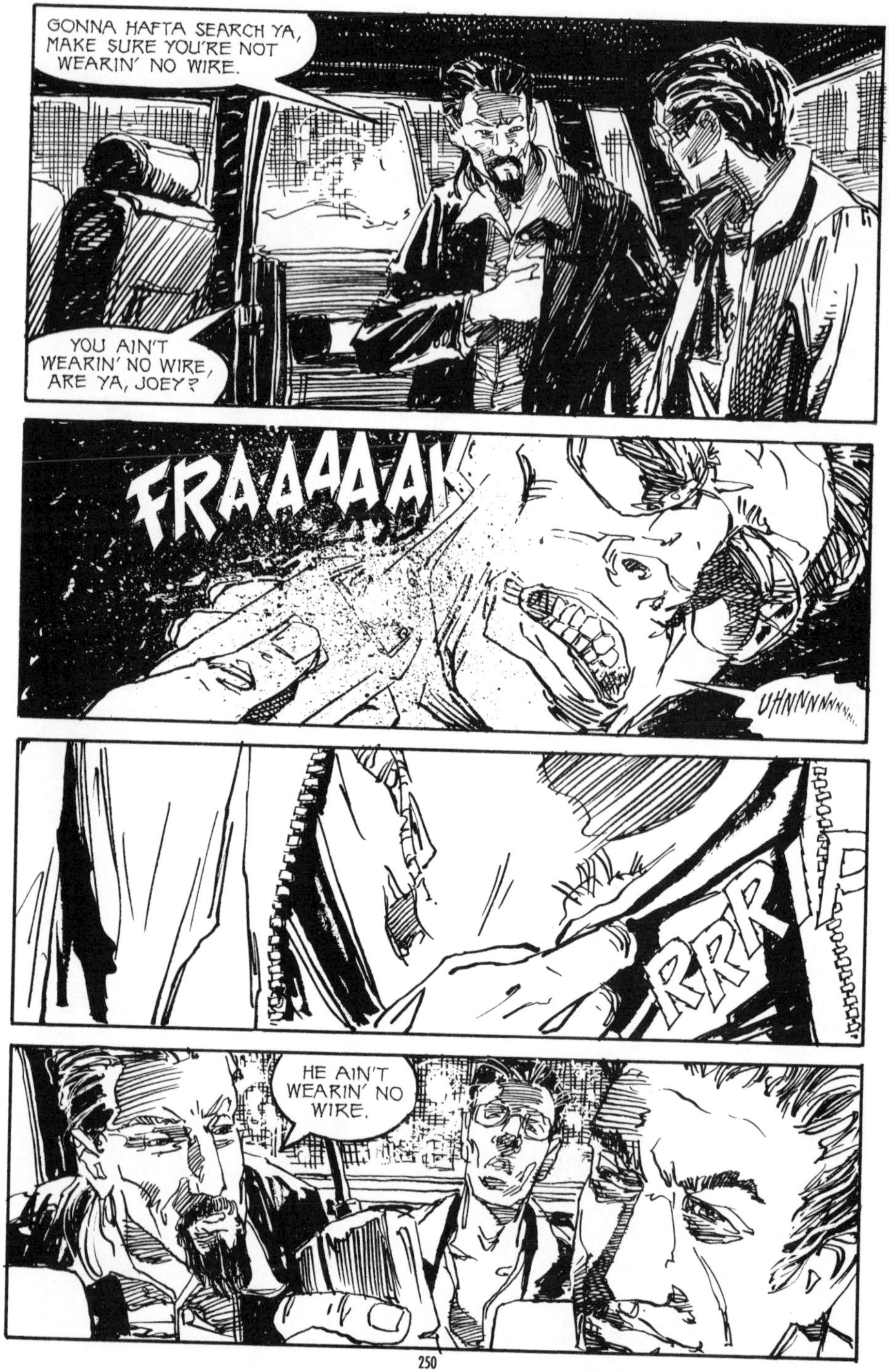
GONNA HAFTA SEARCH YA, MAKE SURE YOU'RE NOT WEARIN' NO WIRE.
YOU AIN'T WEARIN' NO WIRE, ARE YA, JOEY?
FRAAAAAK
UHNNNNNNNN...
RRRIP
HE AIN'T WEARIN' NO WIRE.

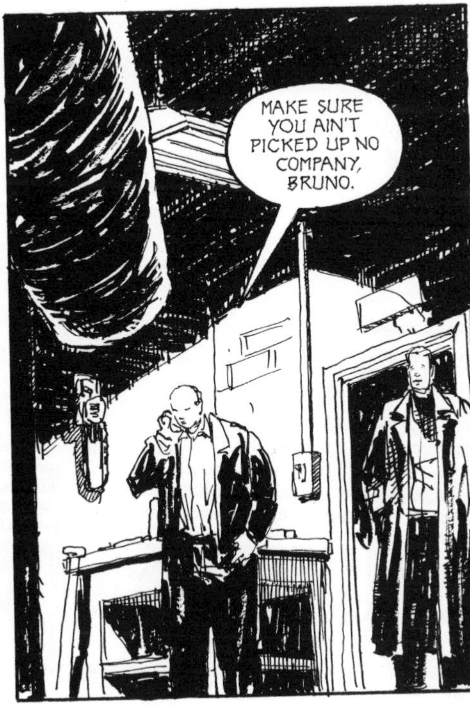
MAKE SURE YOU AIN'T PICKED UP NO COMPANY, BRUNO.

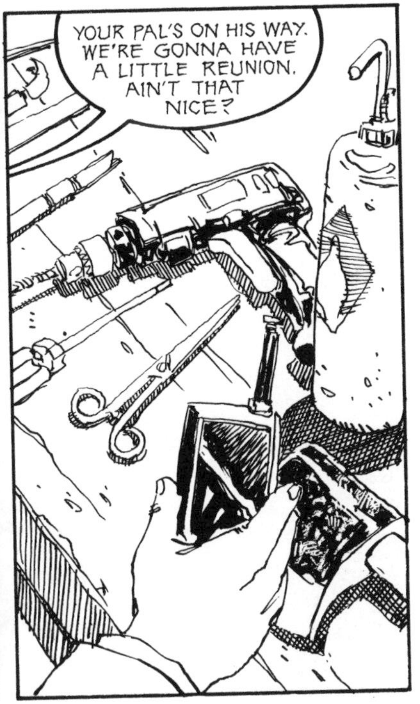
YOUR PAL'S ON HIS WAY. WE'RE GONNA HAVE A LITTLE REUNION. AIN'T THAT NICE?

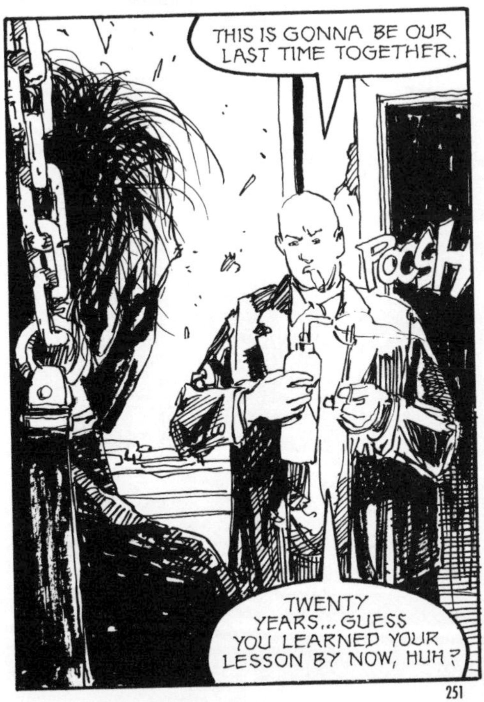
THIS IS GONNA BE OUR LAST TIME TOGETHER.
POOSH
TWENTY YEARS... GUESS YOU LEARNED YOUR LESSON BY NOW, HUH?

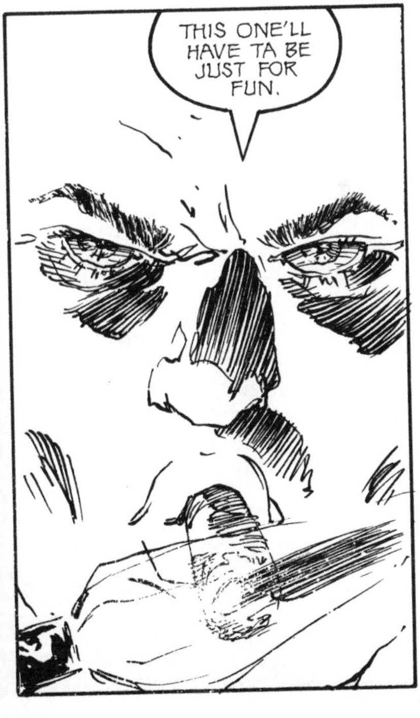
THIS ONE'LL HAVE TA BE JUST FOR FUN.

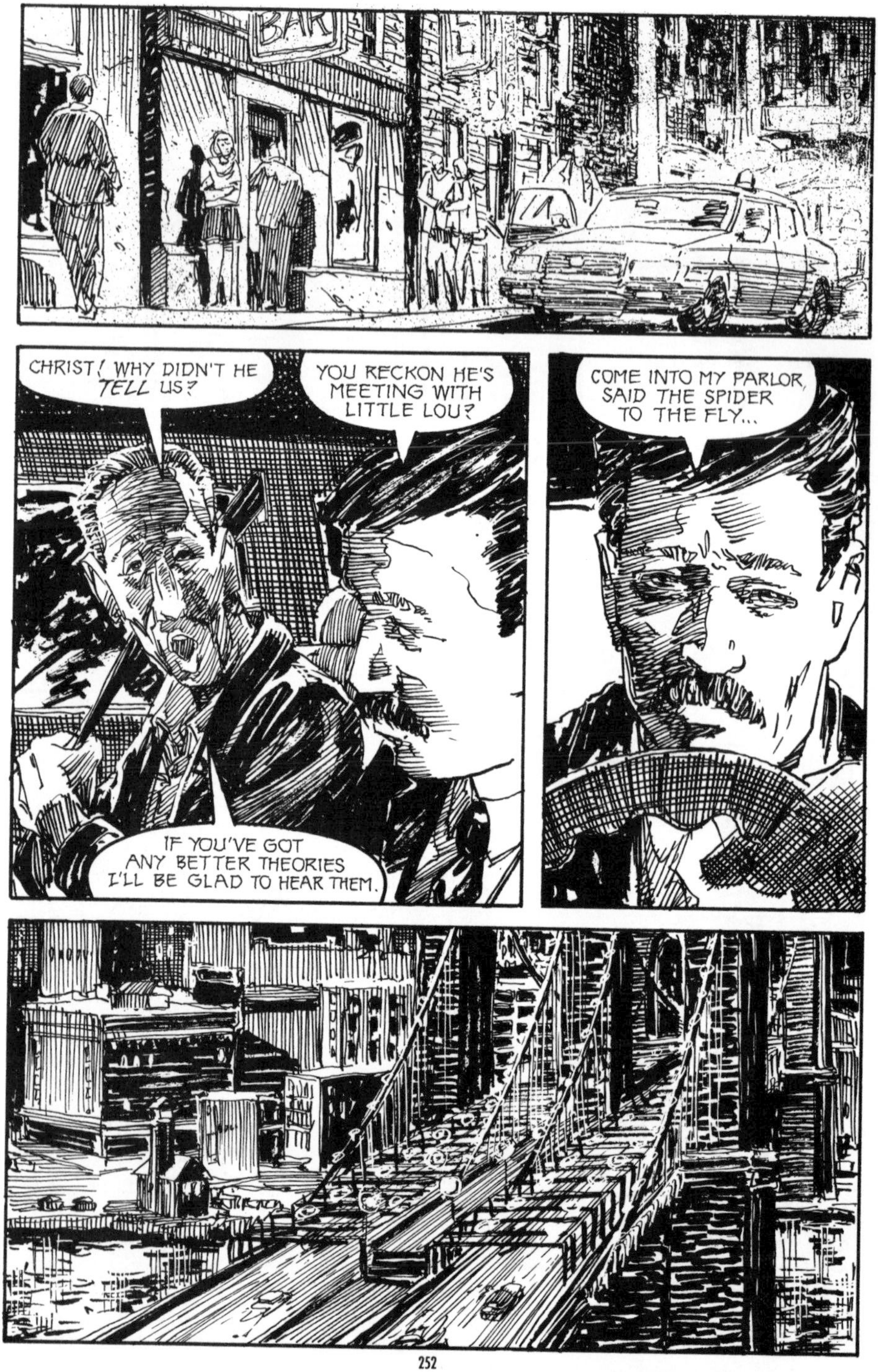

CHRIST! WHY DIDN'T HE TELL US?
YOU RECKON HE'S MEETING WITH LITTLE LOU?
IF YOU'VE GOT ANY BETTER THEORIES I'LL BE GLAD TO HEAR THEM.
COME INTO MY PARLOR, SAID THE SPIDER TO THE FLY...

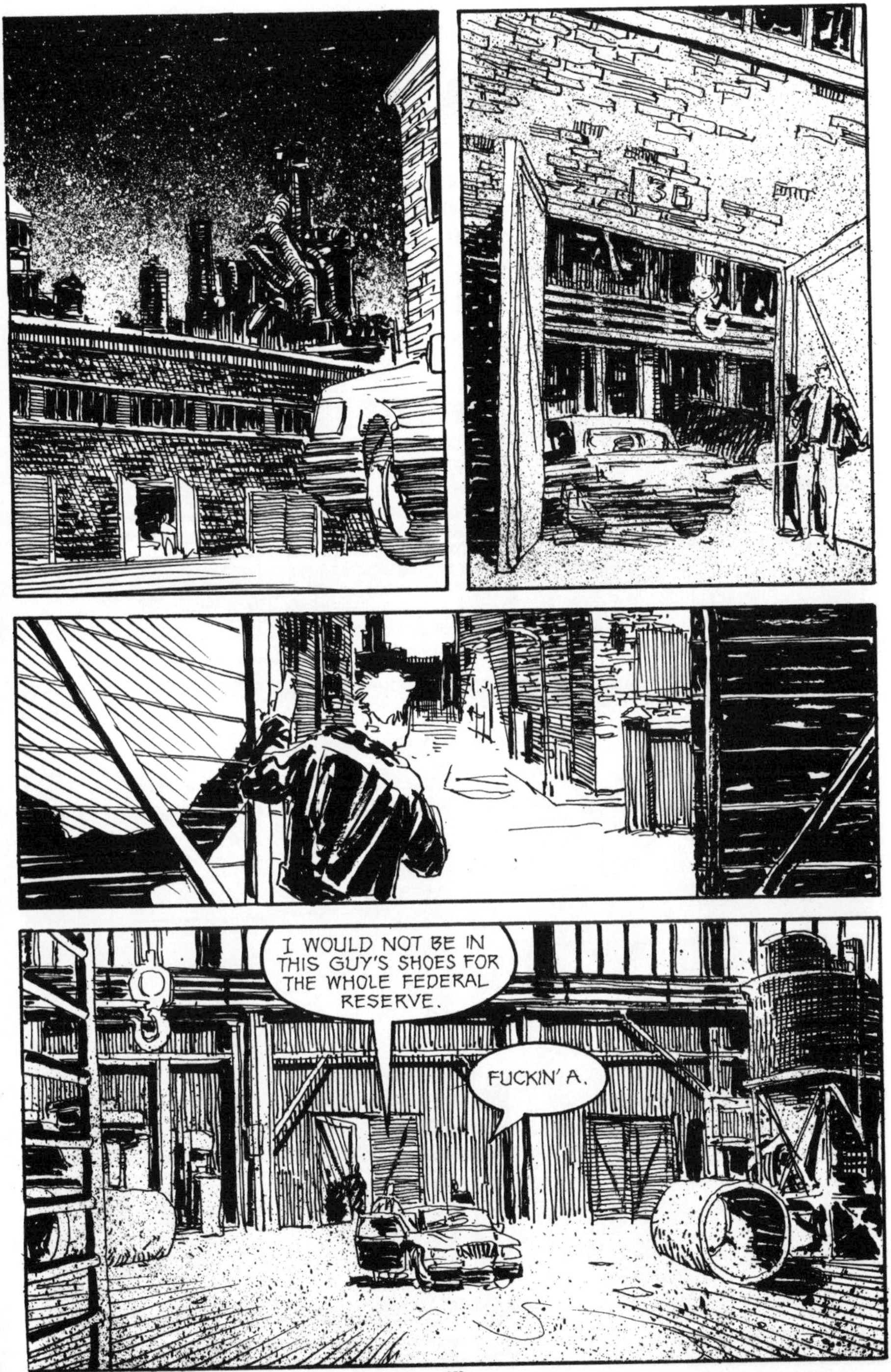
I WOULD NOT BE IN THIS GUY'S SHOES FOR THE WHOLE FEDERAL RESERVE.
FUCKIN' A.

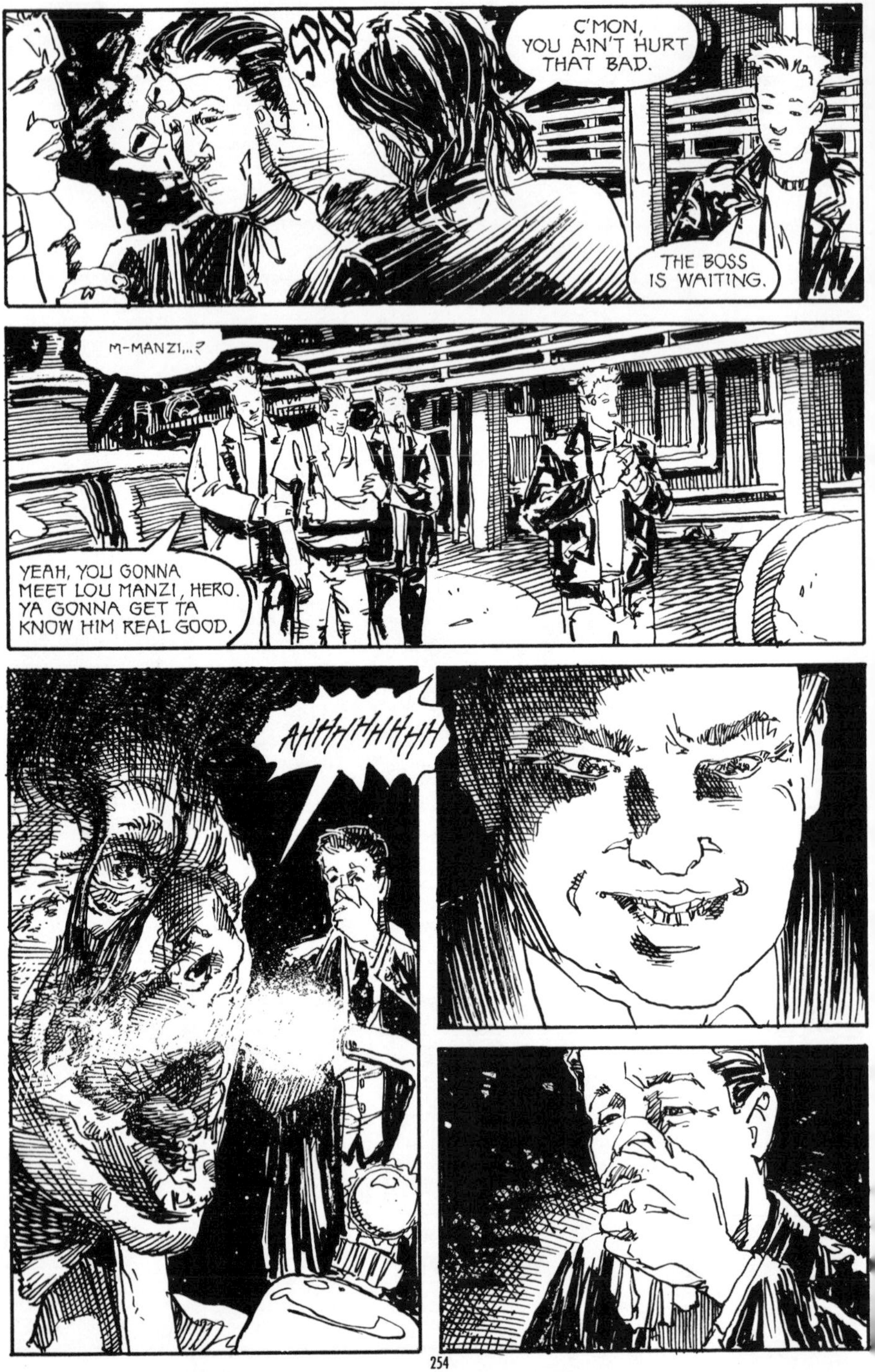
SPAP
C'MON, YOU AIN'T HURT THAT BAD.
THE BOSS IS WAITING.
M-MANZI...?
YEAH, YOU GONNA MEET LOU MANZI, HERO. YA GONNA GET TA KNOW HIM REAL GOOD.
AHHHHHHHH

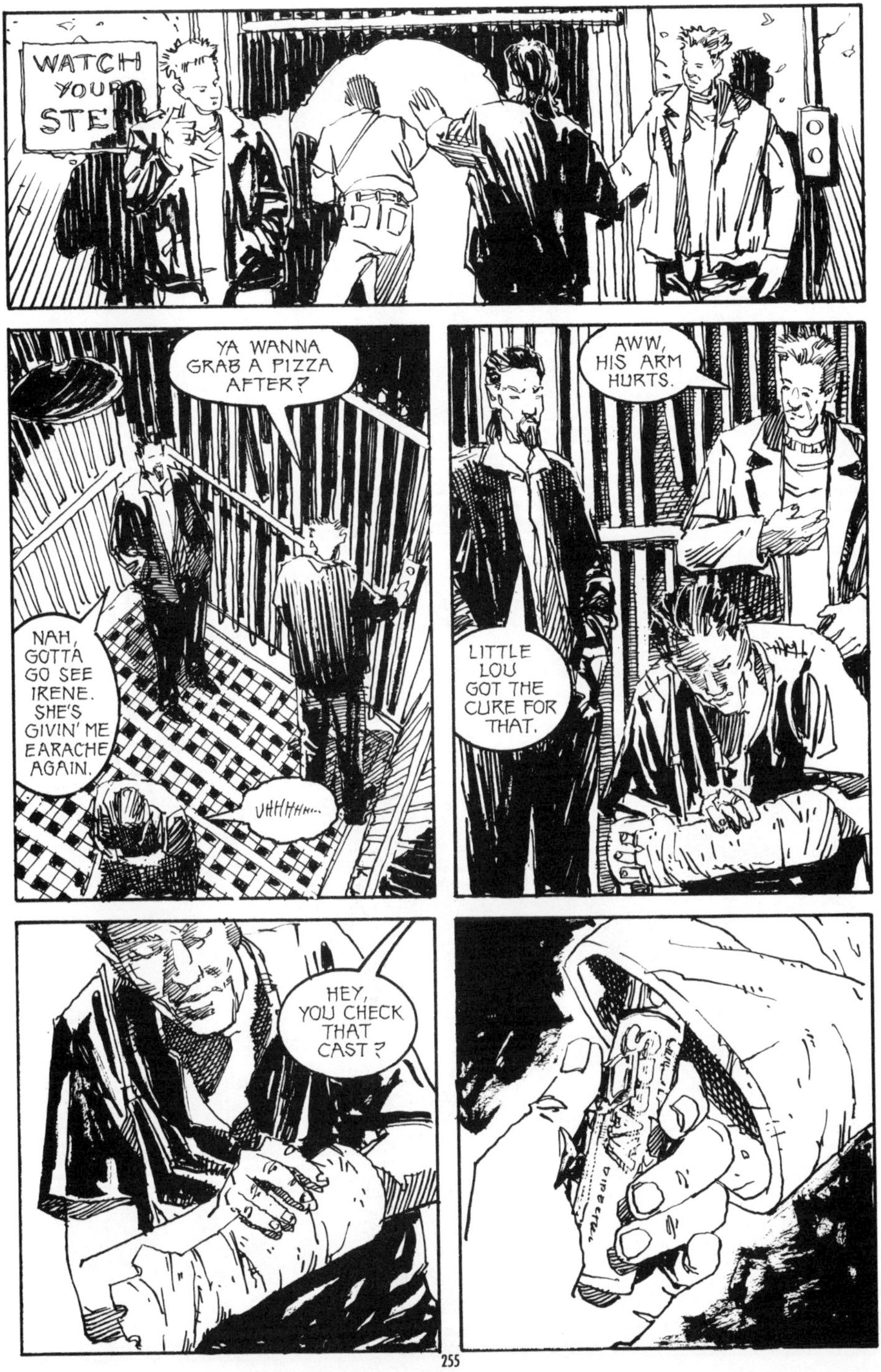
WATCH YOUR STE
YA WANNA GRAB A PIZZA AFTER?
NAH, GOTTA GO SEE IRENE. SHE'S GIVIN' ME EARACHE AGAIN.
UHHHHH...
AWW, HIS ARM HURTS.
LITTLE LOU GOT THE CURE FOR THAT.
HEY, YOU CHECK THAT CAST?

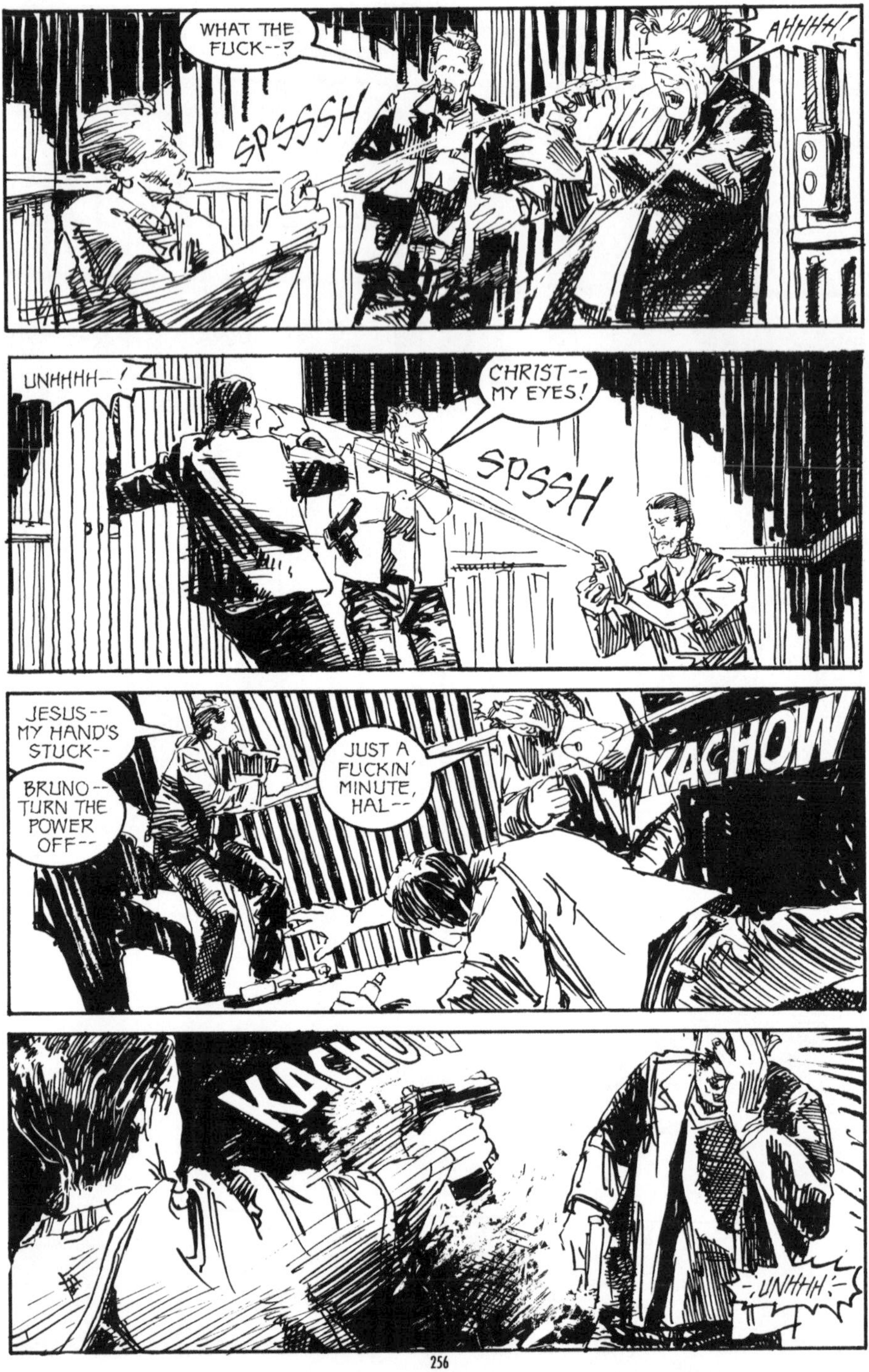
WHAT THE FUCK--?
AHHHH!
SPSSSH
UNHHHH--!
CHRIST-- MY EYES!
SPSSSH
JESUS-- MY HAND'S STUCK--
BRUNO-- TURN THE POWER OFF--
JUST A FUCKIN' MINUTE, HAL--
KACHOW
KACHOW
UNHHH!

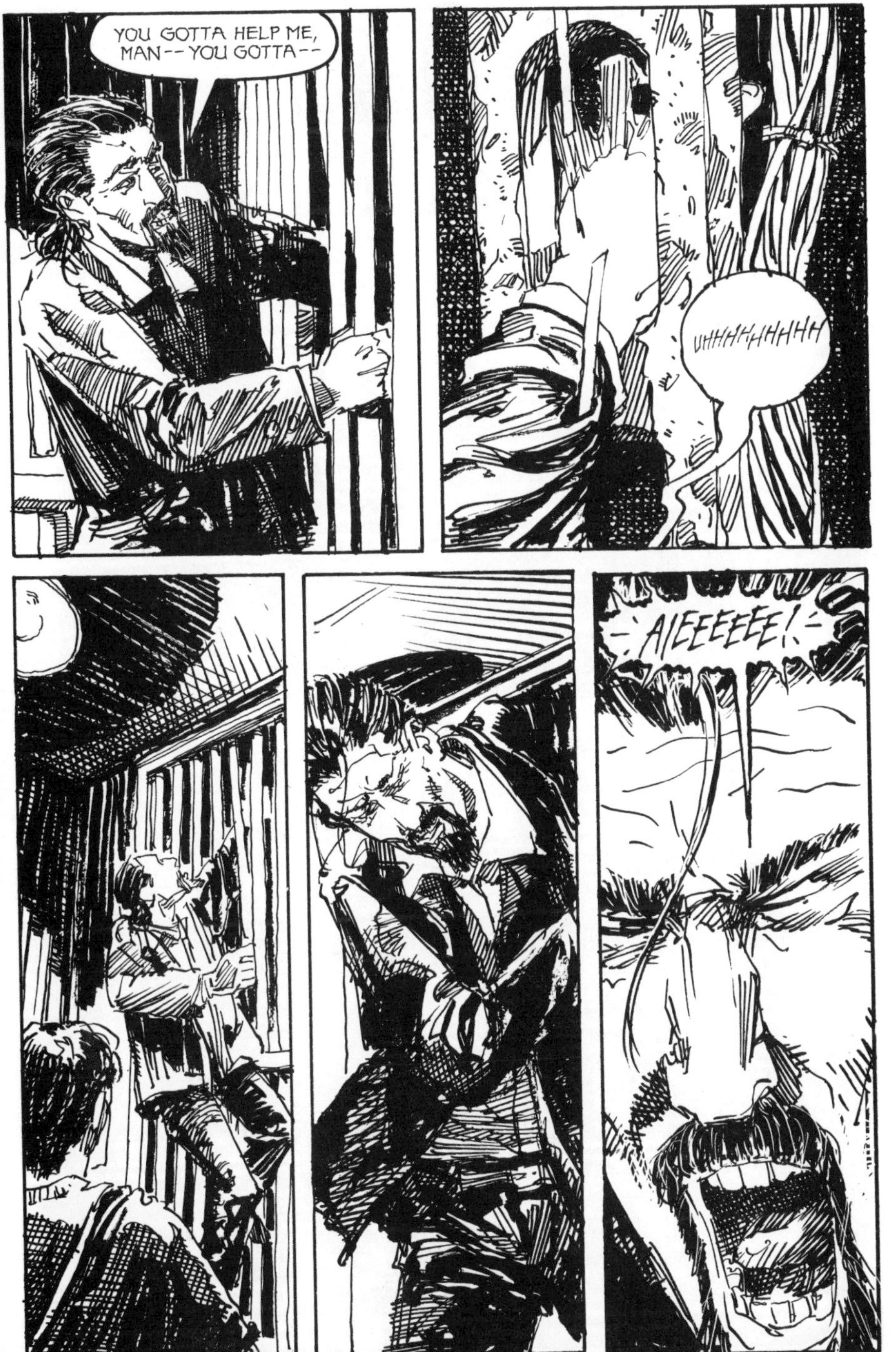
YOU GOTTA HELP ME, MAN--YOU GOTTA--
UHHHHHHHHH
AIEEEEEE!

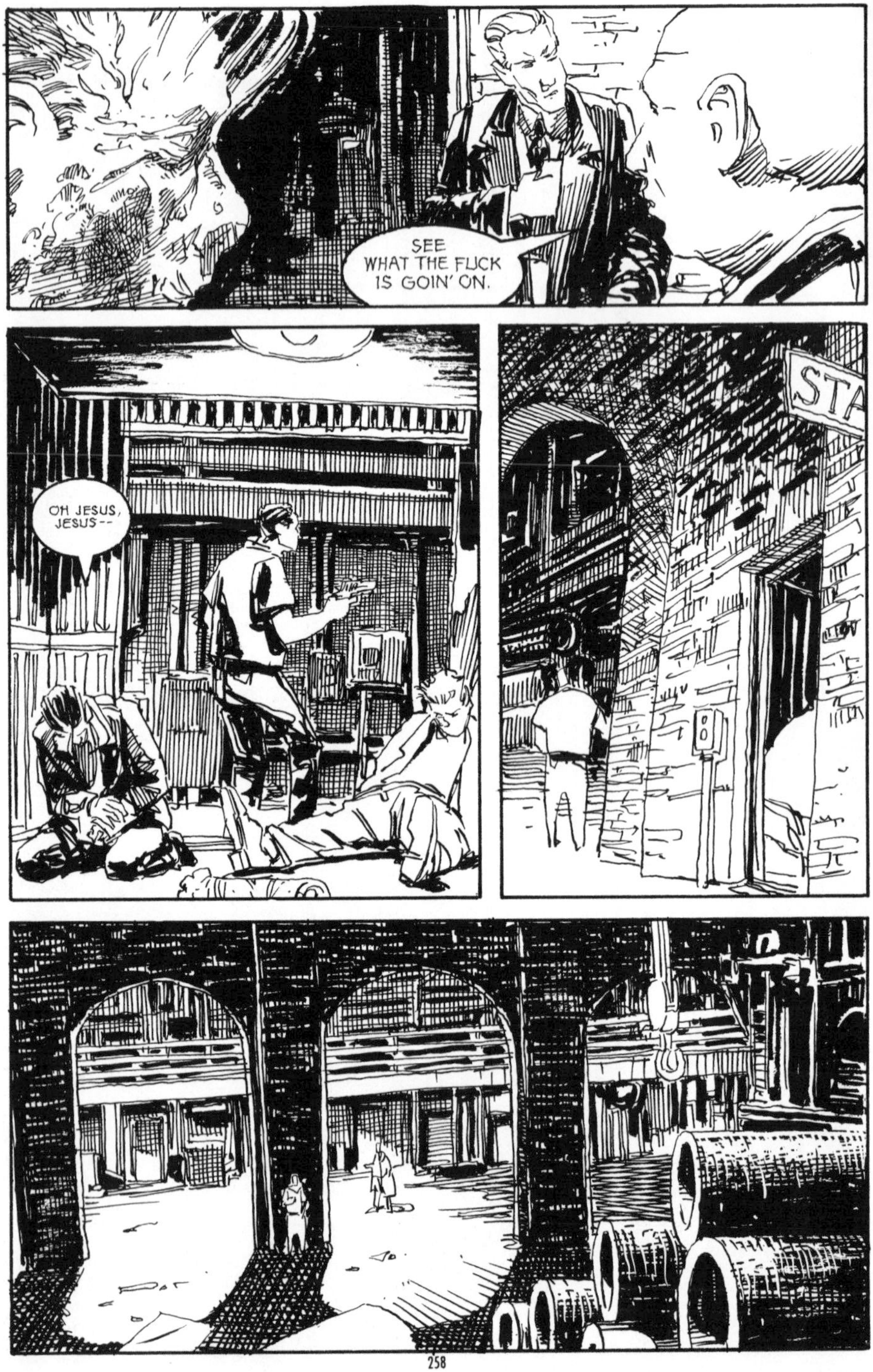
SEE WHAT THE FUCK IS GOIN' ON.
OH JESUS, JESUS--
STA

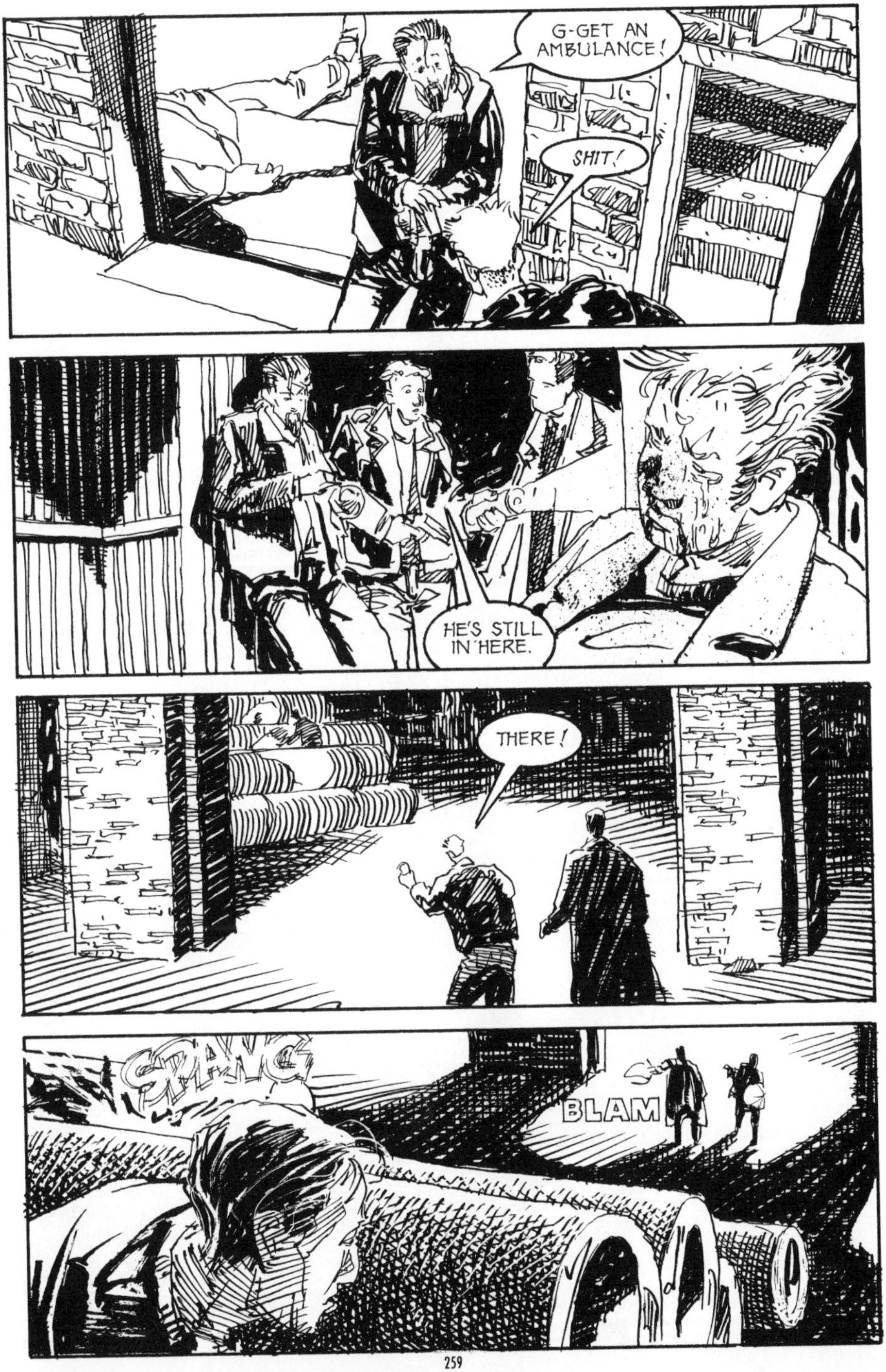
G-GET AN AMBULANCE!
SHIT!
HE'S STILL IN HERE.
THERE!
SPANG
BLAM

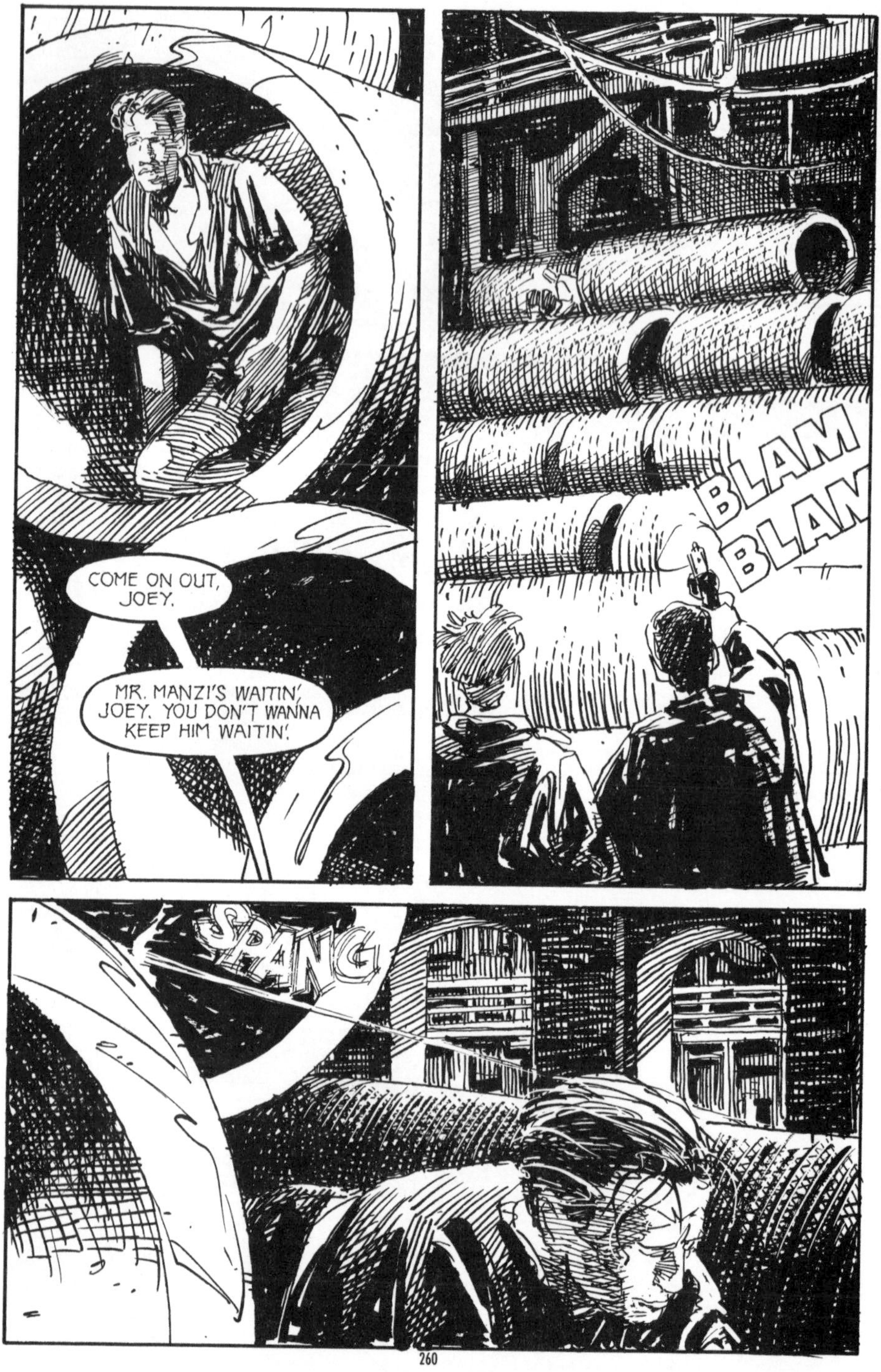
COME ON OUT, JOEY.
MR. MANZI'S WAITIN', JOEY. YOU DON'T WANNA KEEP HIM WAITIN'.
BLAM
BLAM
SPANG

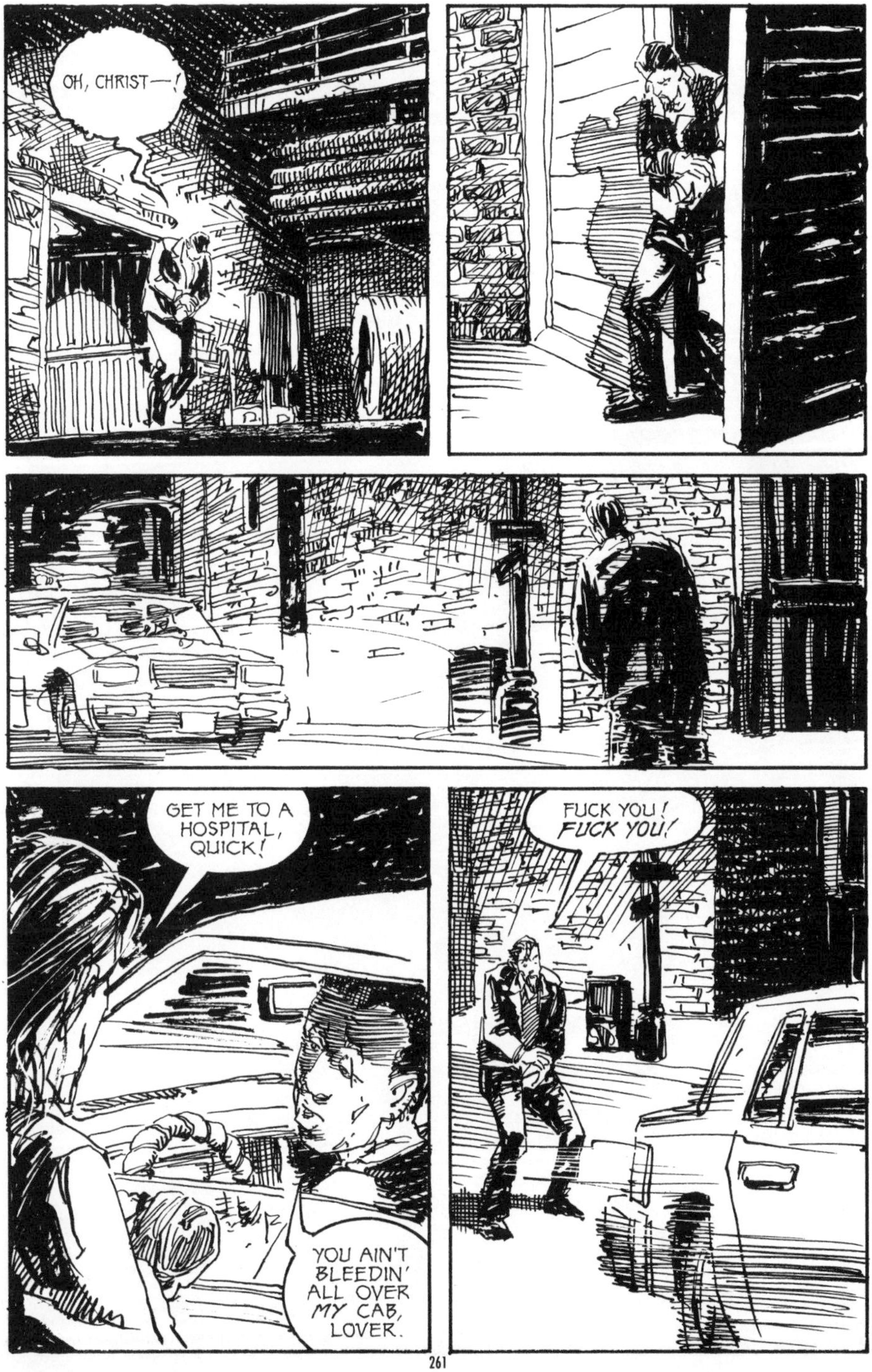
OH, CHRIST—!
GET ME TO A HOSPITAL, QUICK!
YOU AIN'T BLEEDIN' ALL OVER *MY* CAB, LOVER.
FUCK YOU! *FUCK YOU!*

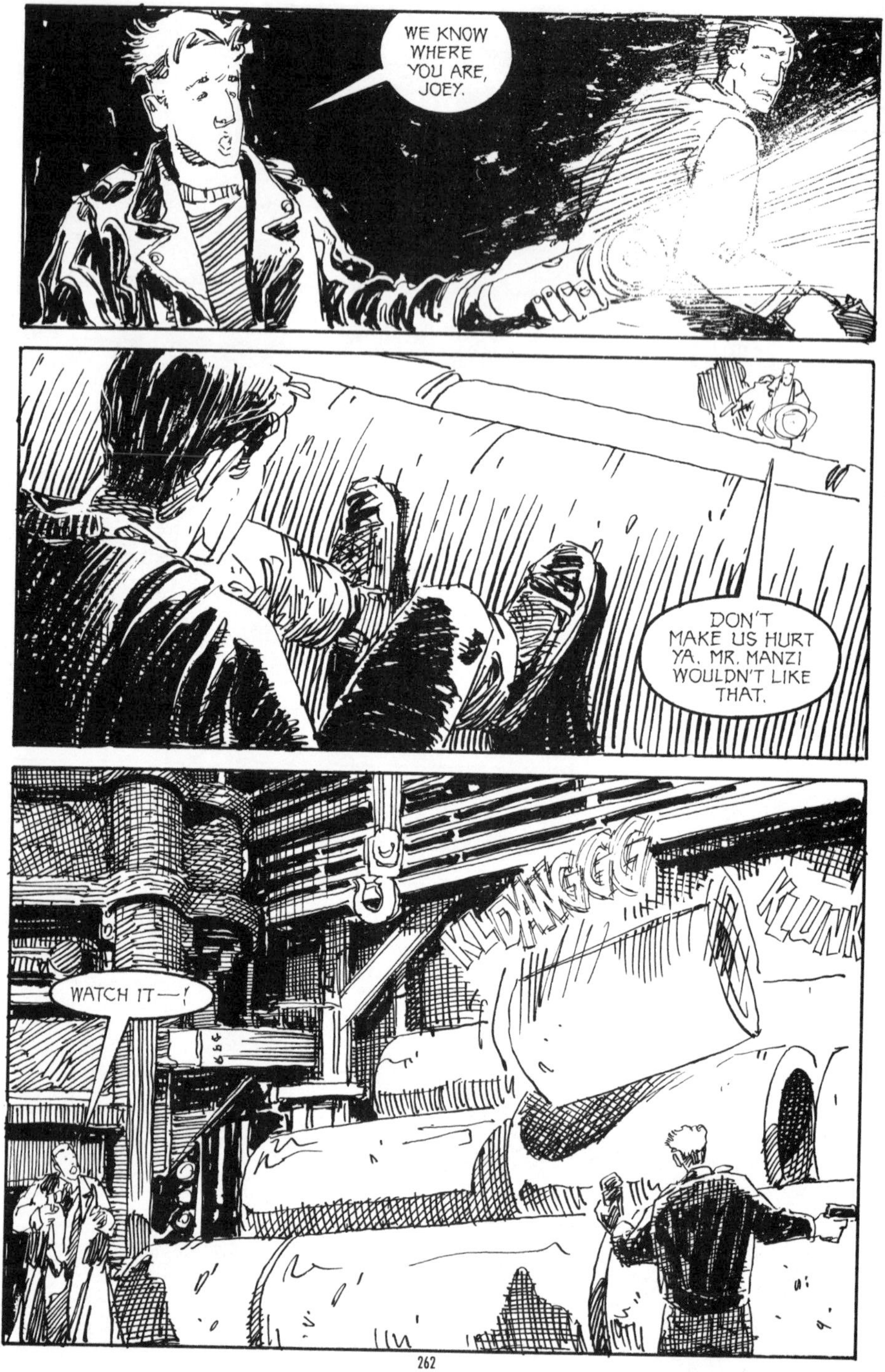
WE KNOW WHERE YOU ARE, JOEY.
DON'T MAKE US HURT YA. MR. MANZI WOULDN'T LIKE THAT.
KLDANGGG
KLUNK
WATCH IT—!

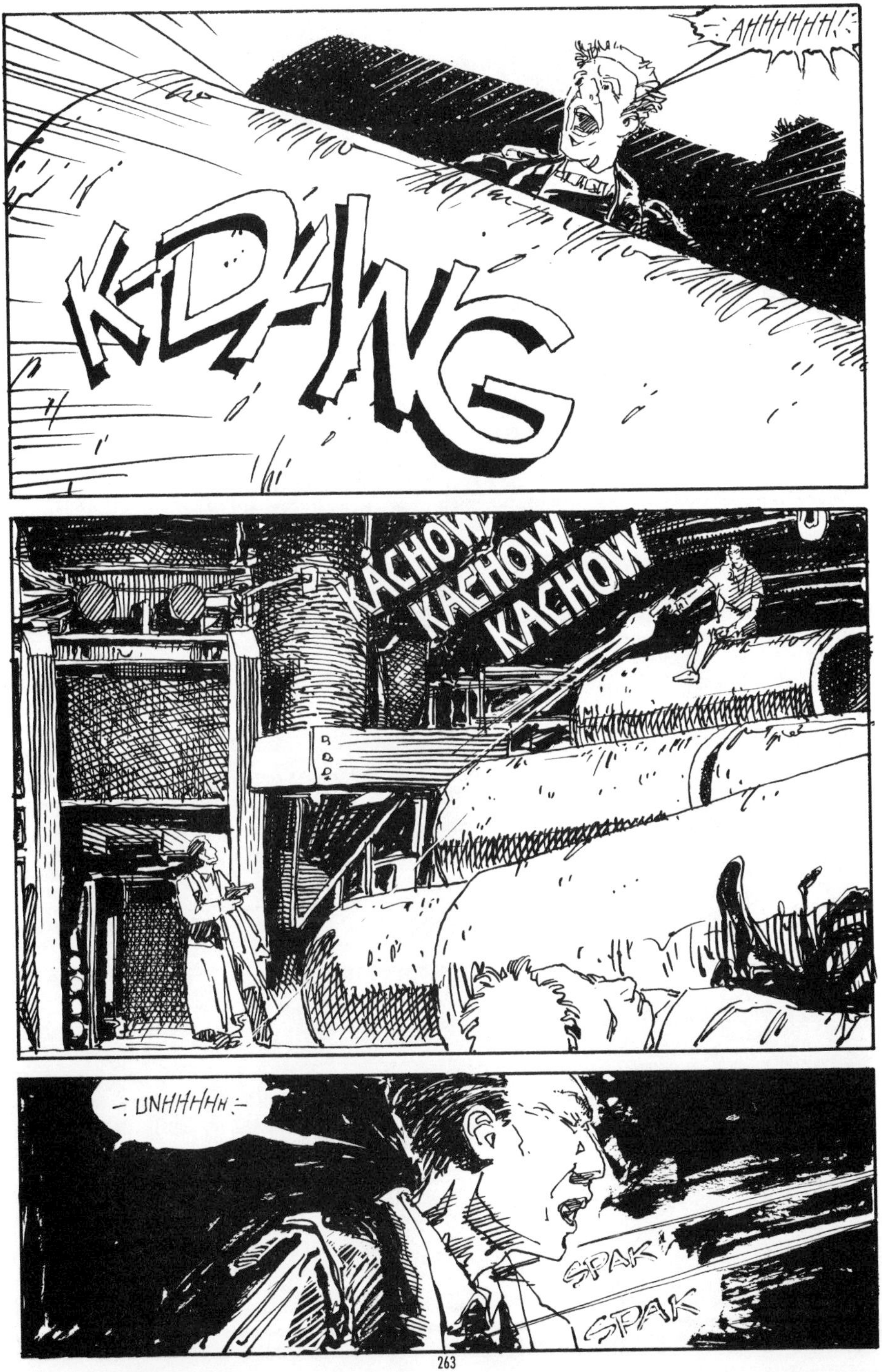
AHHHHHH!
K-DANG
KACHOW
KACHOW
KACHOW
UNHHHHH
SPAK!
SPAK

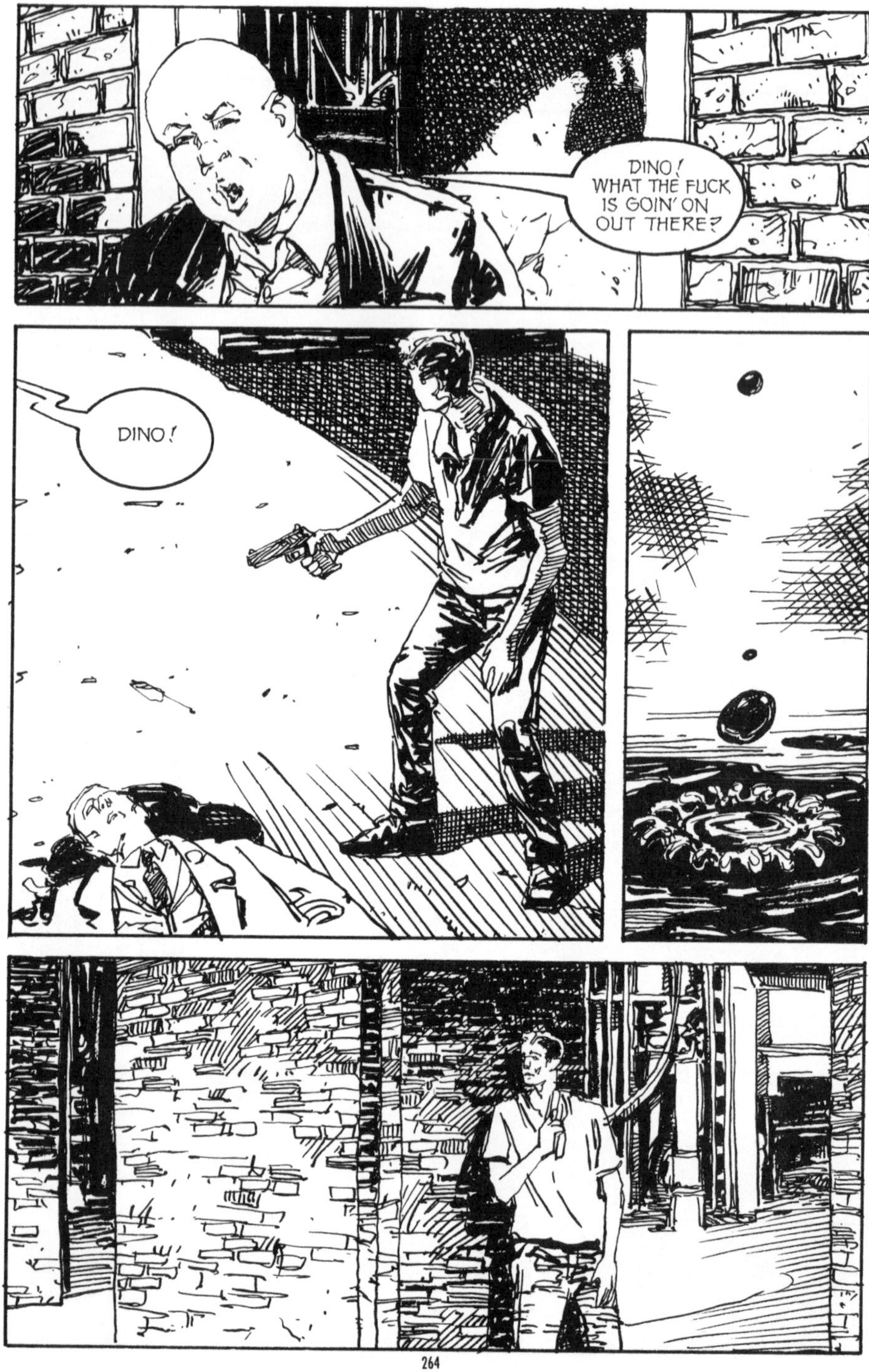
DINO! WHAT THE FUCK IS GOIN' ON OUT THERE?
DINO!

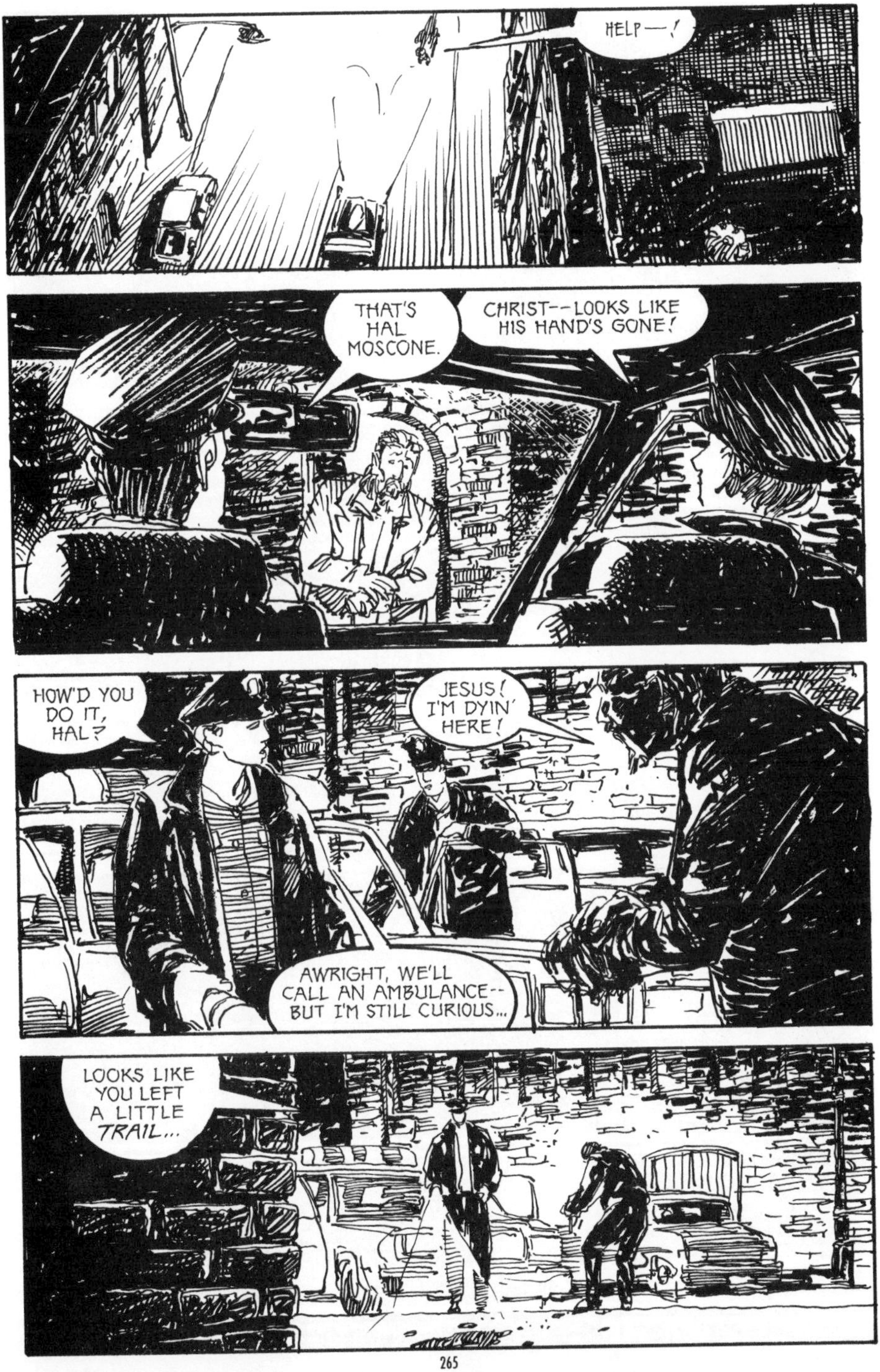
HELP—!
THAT'S HAL MOSCONE.
CHRIST--LOOKS LIKE HIS HAND'S GONE!
HOW'D YOU DO IT, HAL?
JESUS! I'M DYIN' HERE!
AWRIGHT, WE'LL CALL AN AMBULANCE-- BUT I'M STILL CURIOUS...
LOOKS LIKE YOU LEFT A LITTLE *TRAIL*...

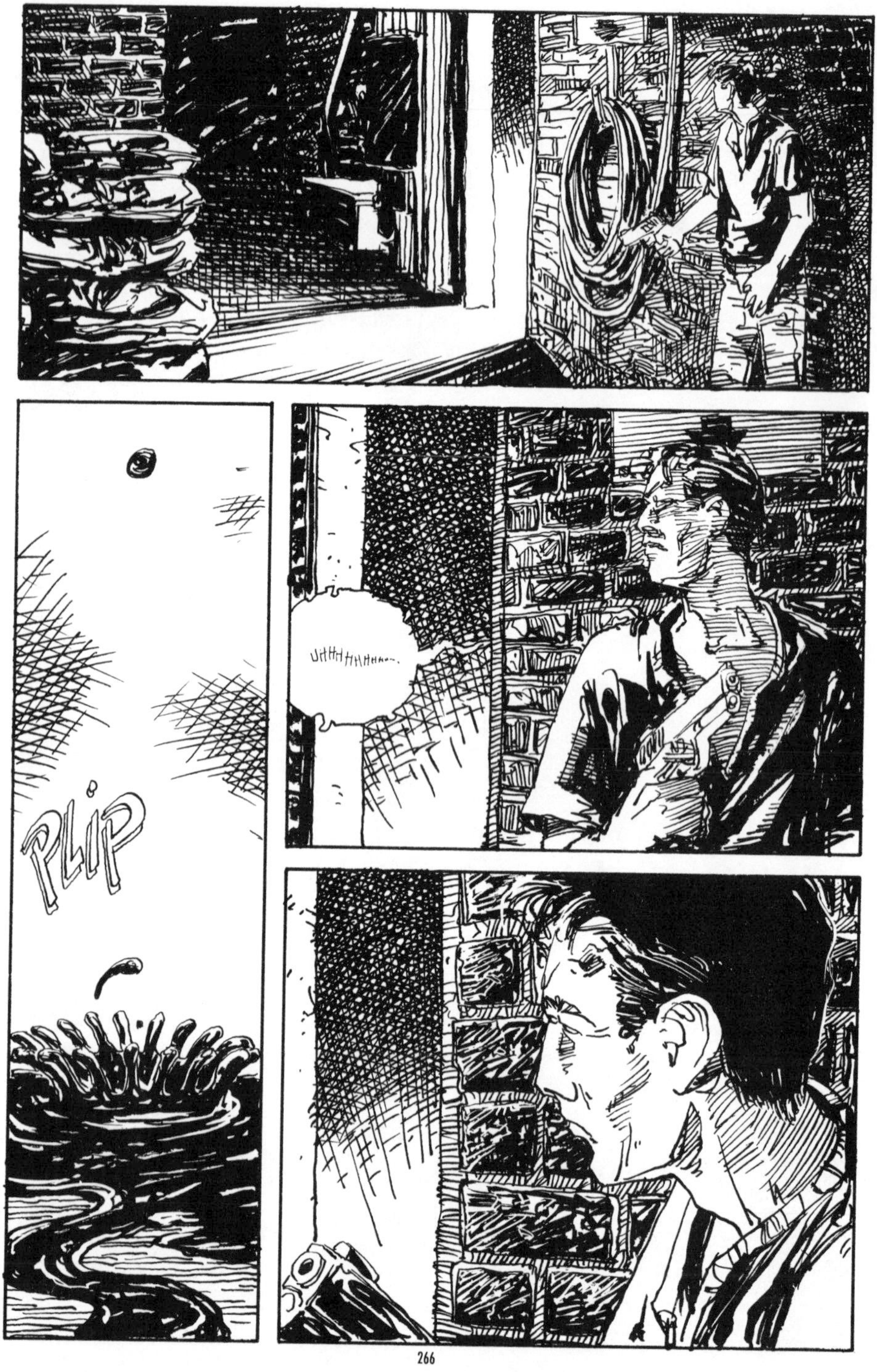
PLIP
UHHHHHHHHH...

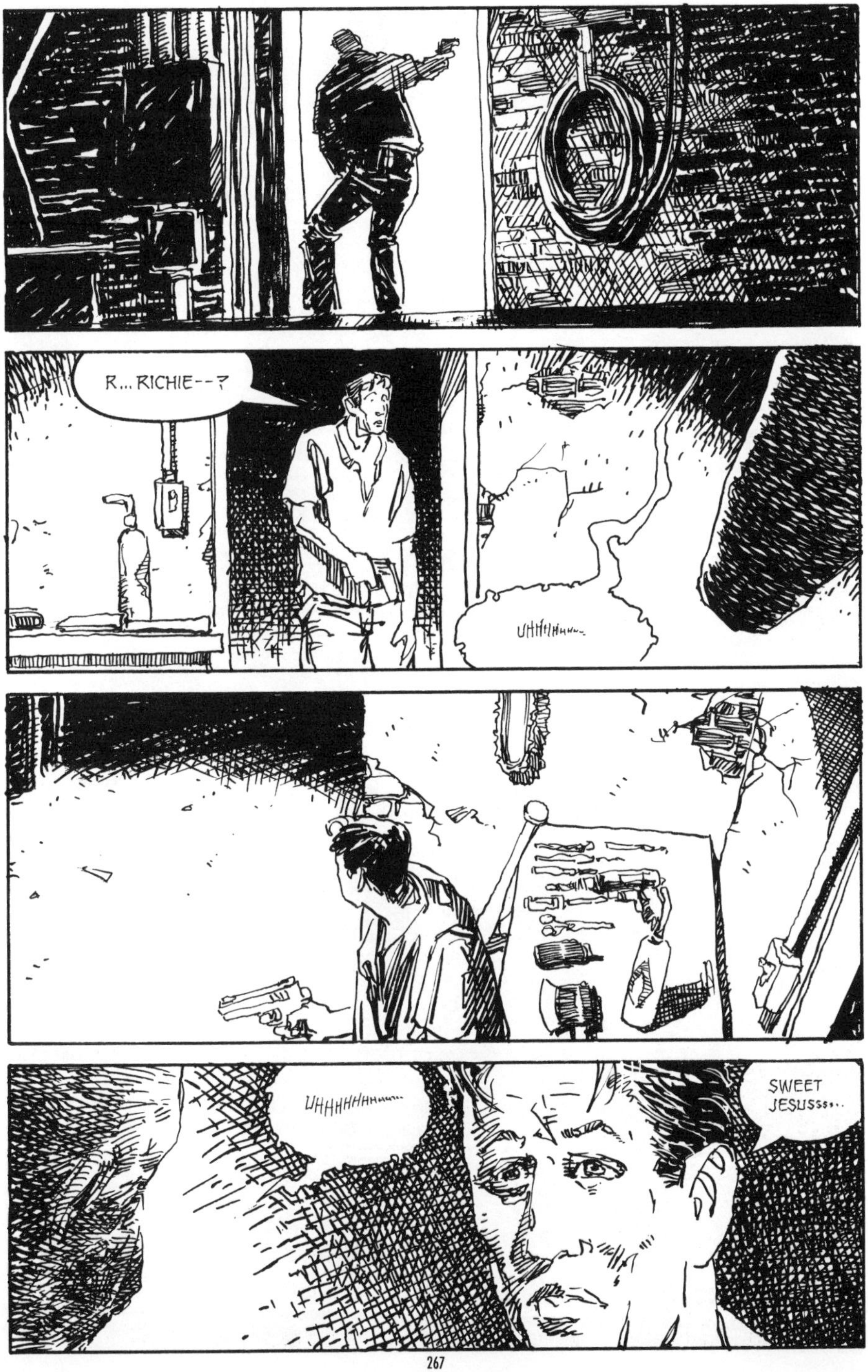
R... RICHIE--?
UHHHHhhhh...
UHHHHHHHhhhhh...
SWEET JESUSsss...

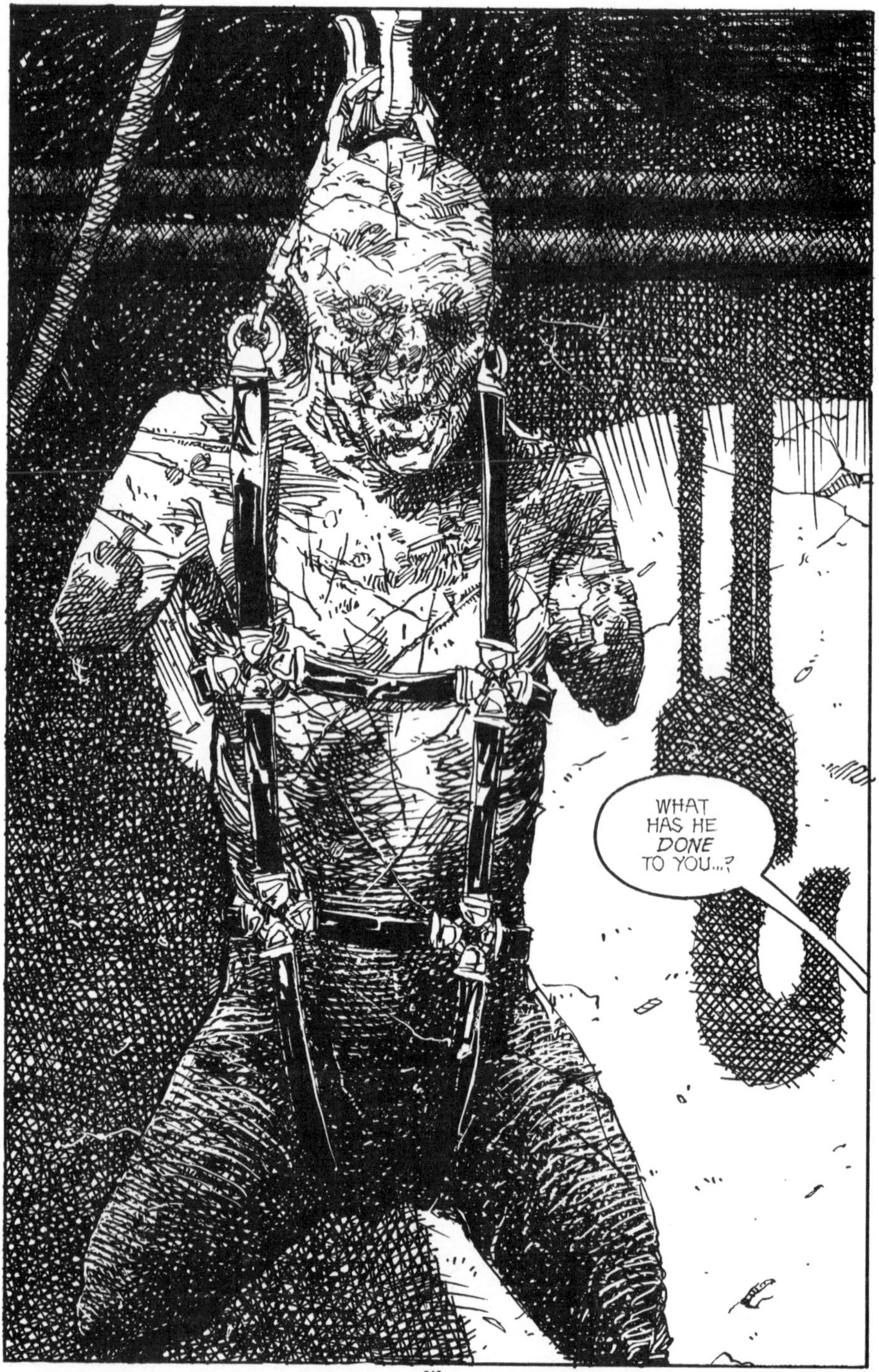
WHAT HAS HE DONE TO YOU...?

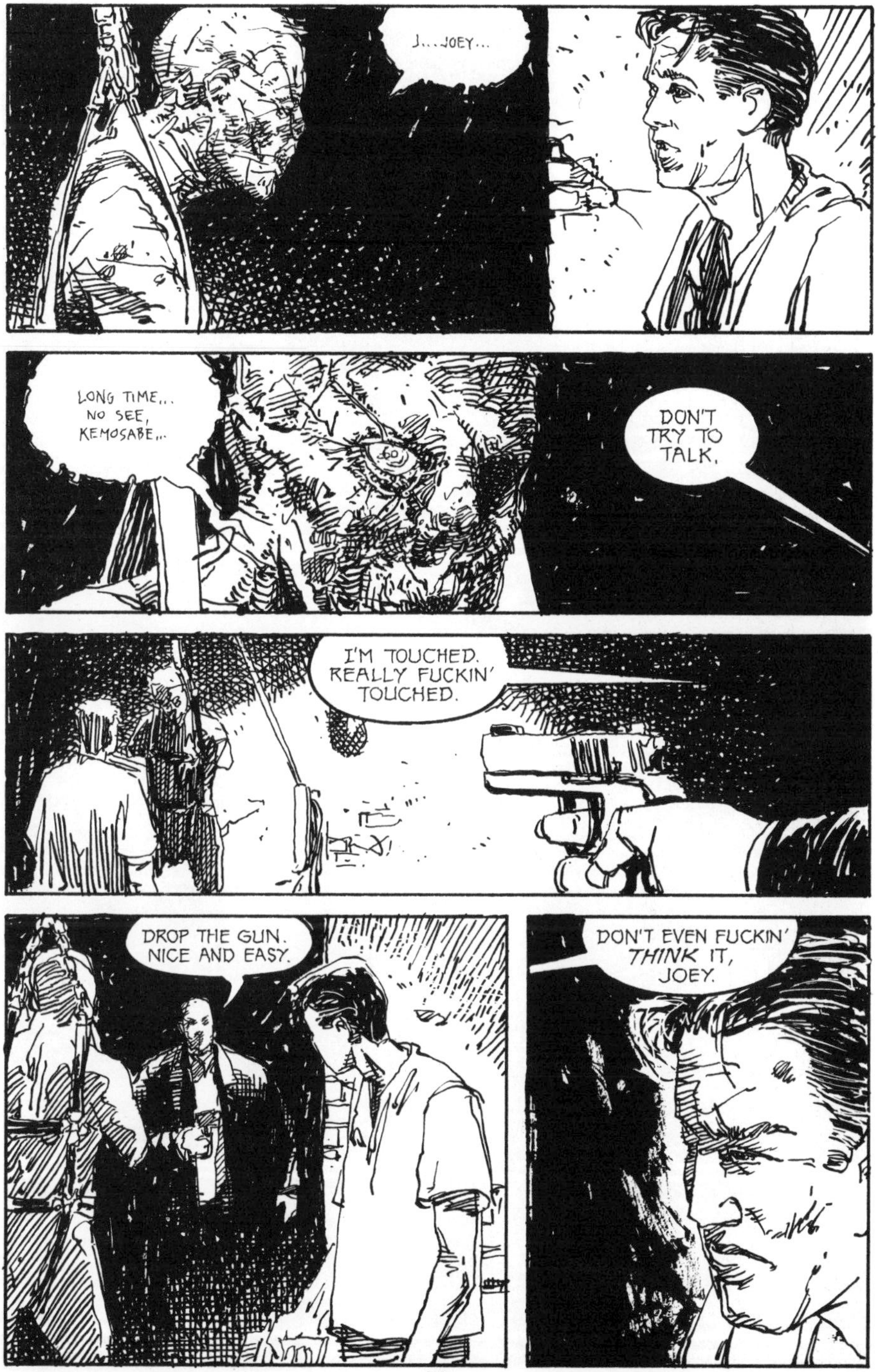
J... JOEY...
LONG TIME... NO SEE, KEMOSABE...
DON'T TRY TO TALK.
I'M TOUCHED. REALLY FUCKIN' TOUCHED.
DROP THE GUN. NICE AND EASY.
DON'T EVEN FUCKIN' *THINK* IT, JOEY.

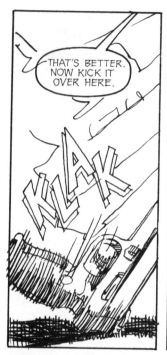

THAT'S BETTER. NOW KICK IT OVER HERE.

KLAK

ATTABOY.

CHRIST, YOU DON'T LOOK LIKE MUCH.

YOU THE SAME GUY MADE A MONKEY OUTTA *JOHN TORRINO?* HARD TA FUCKIN' BELIEVE.

UNGGG!

HARD TA FUCKIN' BELIEVE!

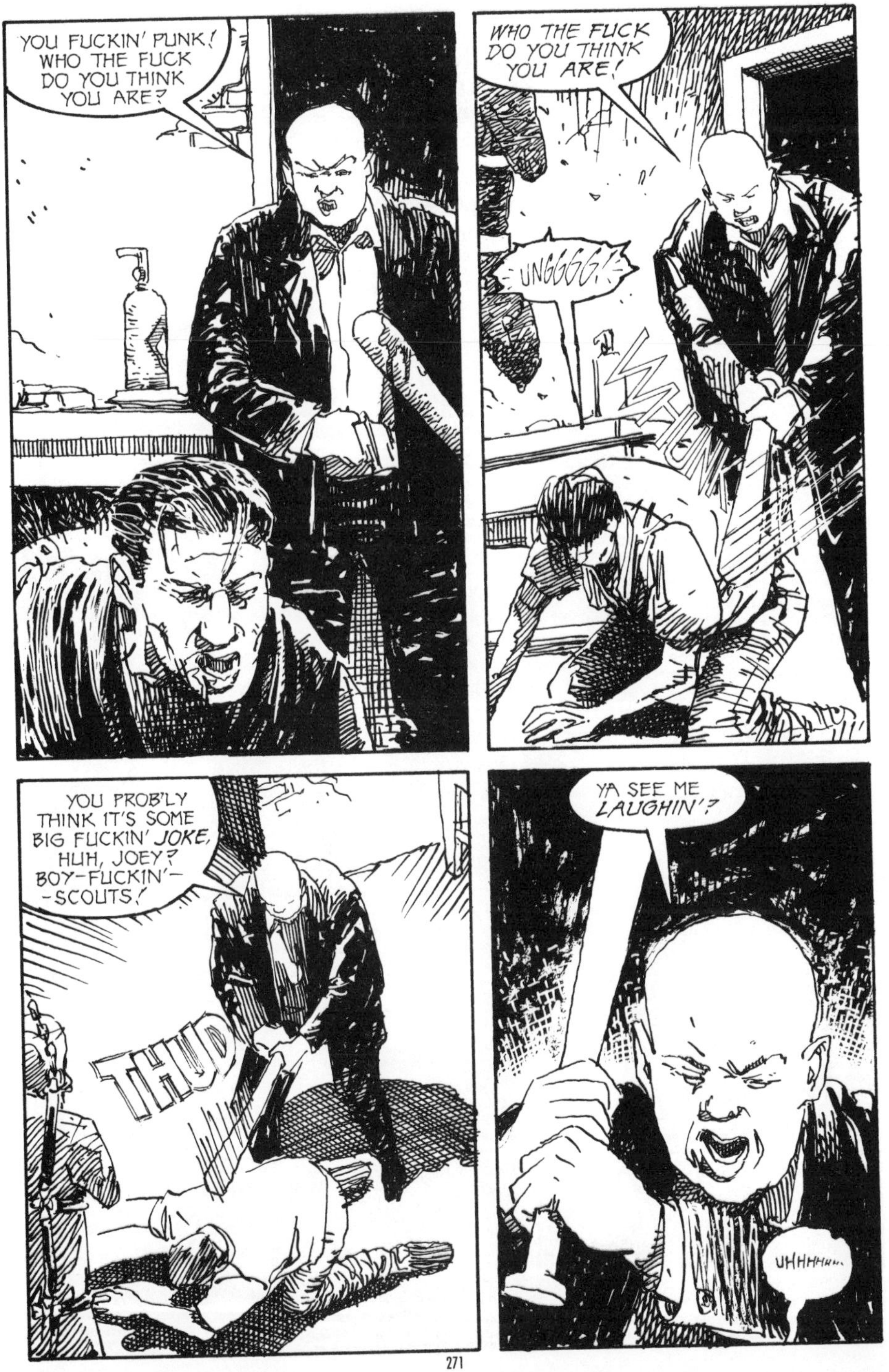
YOU FUCKIN' PUNK! WHO THE FUCK DO YOU THINK YOU ARE?
WHO THE FUCK DO YOU THINK YOU ARE!
UNGGGG!
WHUNK
YOU PROB'LY THINK IT'S SOME BIG FUCKIN' JOKE, HUH, JOEY? BOY-FUCKIN'- -SCOUTS!
THUD
YA SEE ME LAUGHIN'?
UHHHH...

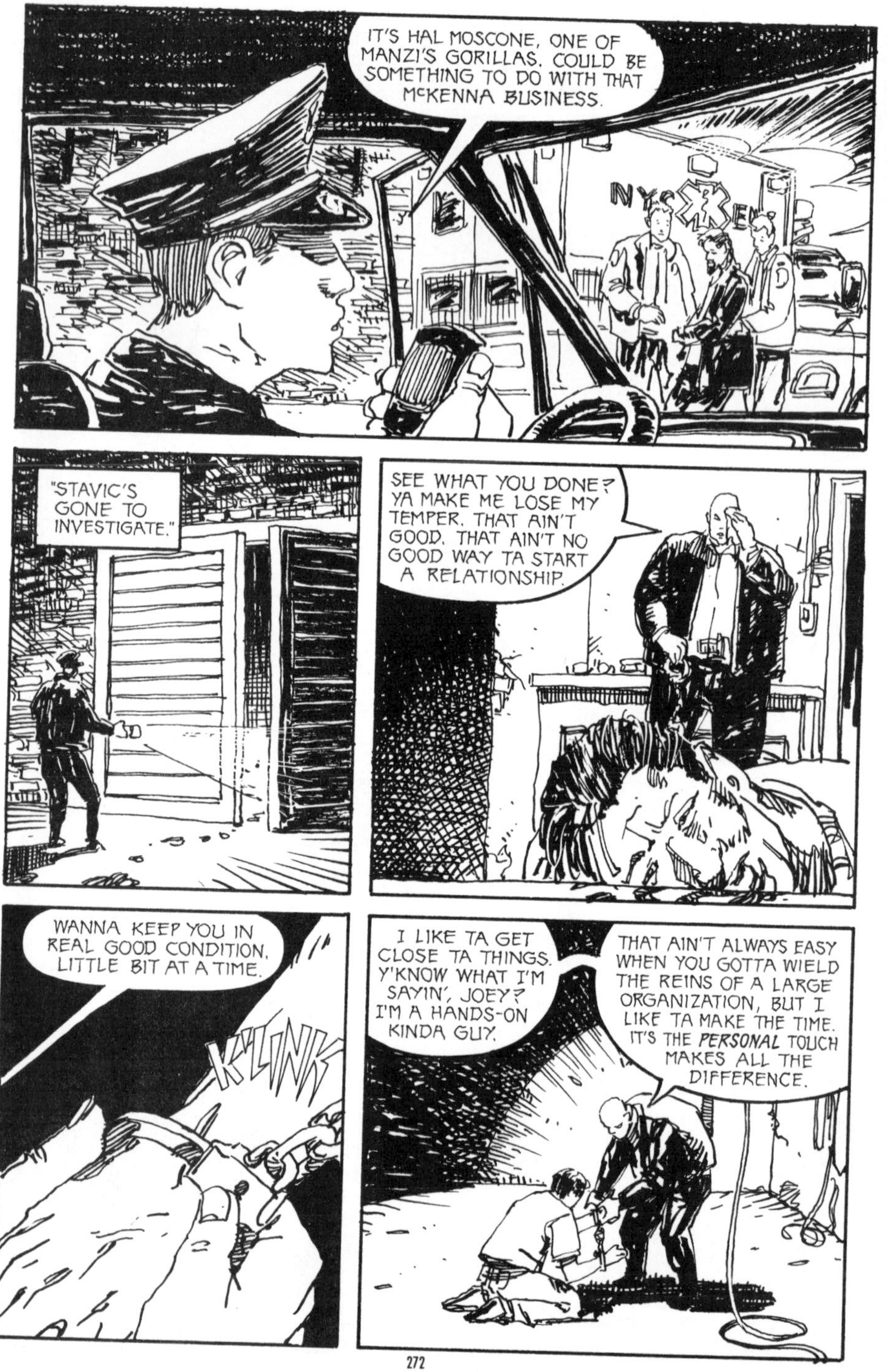
IT'S HAL MOSCONE, ONE OF MANZI'S GORILLAS. COULD BE SOMETHING TO DO WITH THAT McKENNA BUSINESS.
NY
"STAVIC'S GONE TO INVESTIGATE."
SEE WHAT YOU DONE? YA MAKE ME LOSE MY TEMPER. THAT AIN'T GOOD. THAT AIN'T NO GOOD WAY TA START A RELATIONSHIP.
WANNA KEEP YOU IN REAL GOOD CONDITION. LITTLE BIT AT A TIME.
K'CLINK
I LIKE TA GET CLOSE TA THINGS. Y'KNOW WHAT I'M SAYIN', JOEY? I'M A HANDS-ON KINDA GUY.
THAT AIN'T ALWAYS EASY WHEN YOU GOTTA WIELD THE REINS OF A LARGE ORGANIZATION, BUT I LIKE TA MAKE THE TIME. IT'S THE *PERSONAL* TOUCH MAKES ALL THE DIFFERENCE.

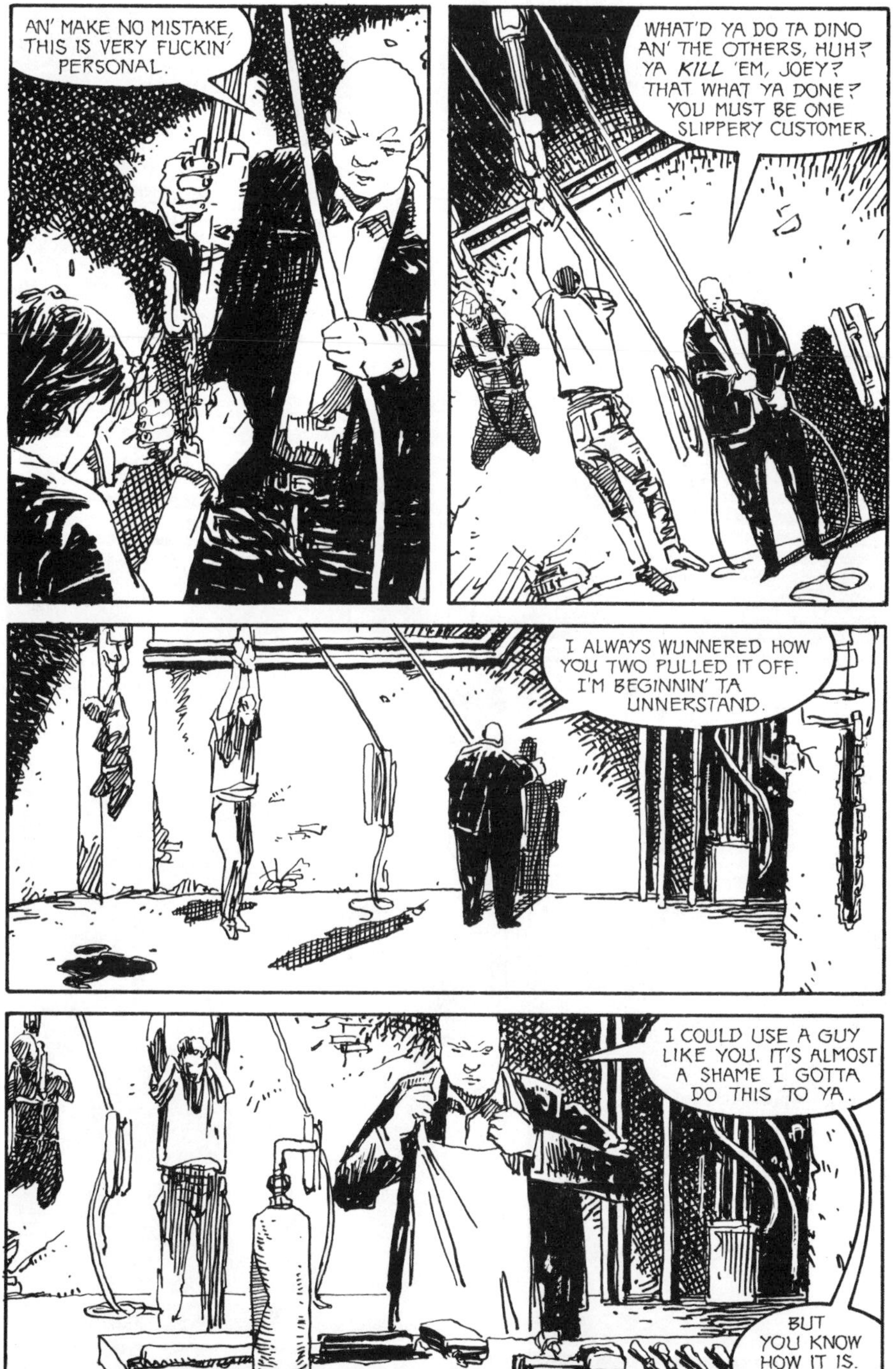

AN' MAKE NO MISTAKE, THIS IS VERY FUCKIN' PERSONAL.
WHAT'D YA DO TA DINO AN' THE OTHERS, HUH? YA KILL 'EM, JOEY? THAT WHAT YA DONE? YOU MUST BE ONE SLIPPERY CUSTOMER.
I ALWAYS WUNNERED HOW YOU TWO PULLED IT OFF. I'M BEGINNIN' TA UNNERSTAND.
I COULD USE A GUY LIKE YOU. IT'S ALMOST A SHAME I GOTTA DO THIS TO YA.
BUT YOU KNOW HOW IT IS.

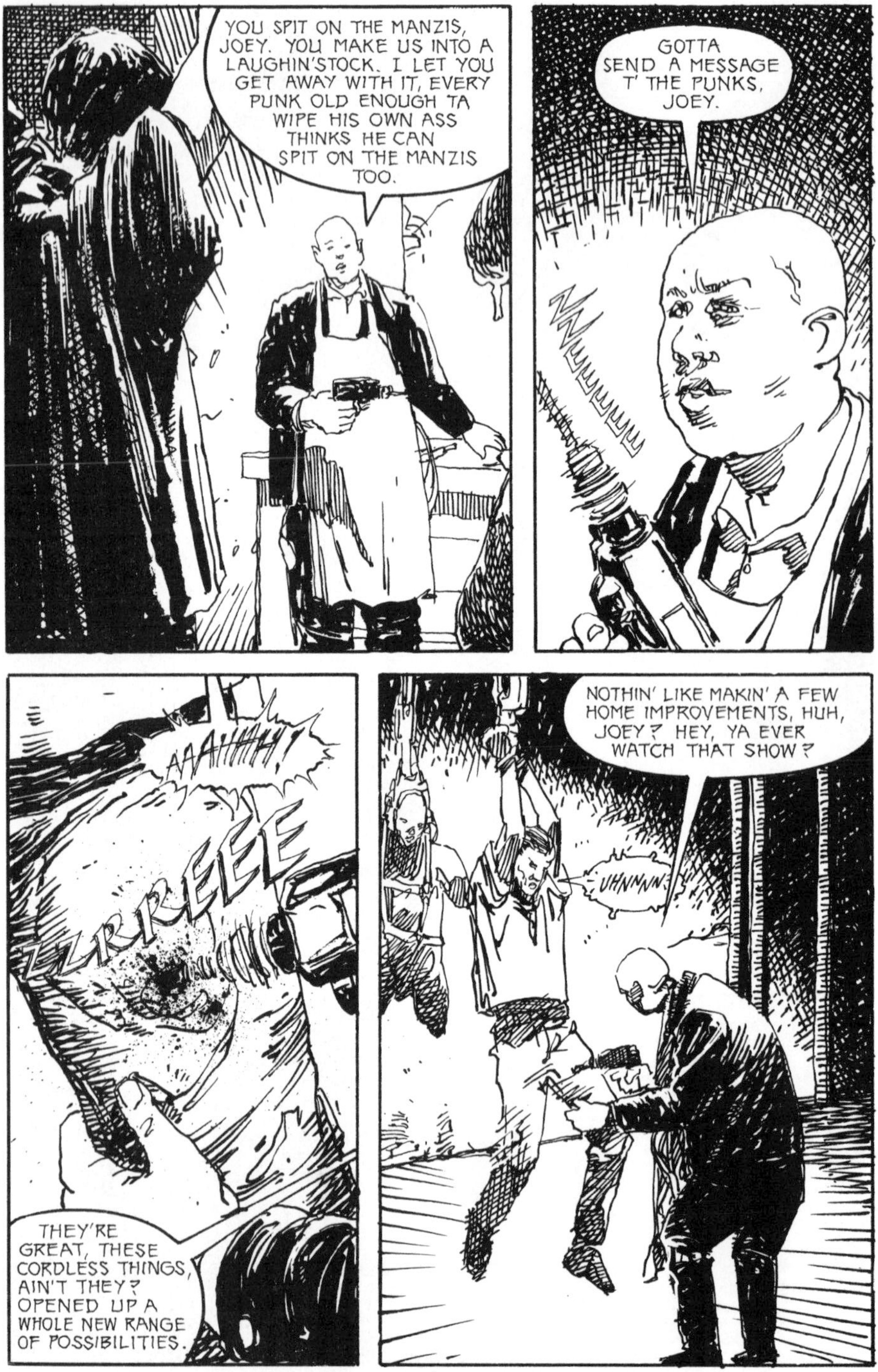
YOU SPIT ON THE MANZIS, JOEY. YOU MAKE US INTO A LAUGHIN'STOCK. I LET YOU GET AWAY WITH IT, EVERY PUNK OLD ENOUGH TA WIPE HIS OWN ASS THINKS HE CAN SPIT ON THE MANZIS TOO.
GOTTA SEND A MESSAGE T' THE PUNKS, JOEY.
ZZRREEE
THEY'RE GREAT, THESE CORDLESS THINGS, AIN'T THEY? OPENED UP A WHOLE NEW RANGE OF POSSIBILITIES.
NOTHIN' LIKE MAKIN' A FEW HOME IMPROVEMENTS, HUH, JOEY? HEY, YA EVER WATCH THAT SHOW?
UHNNNN

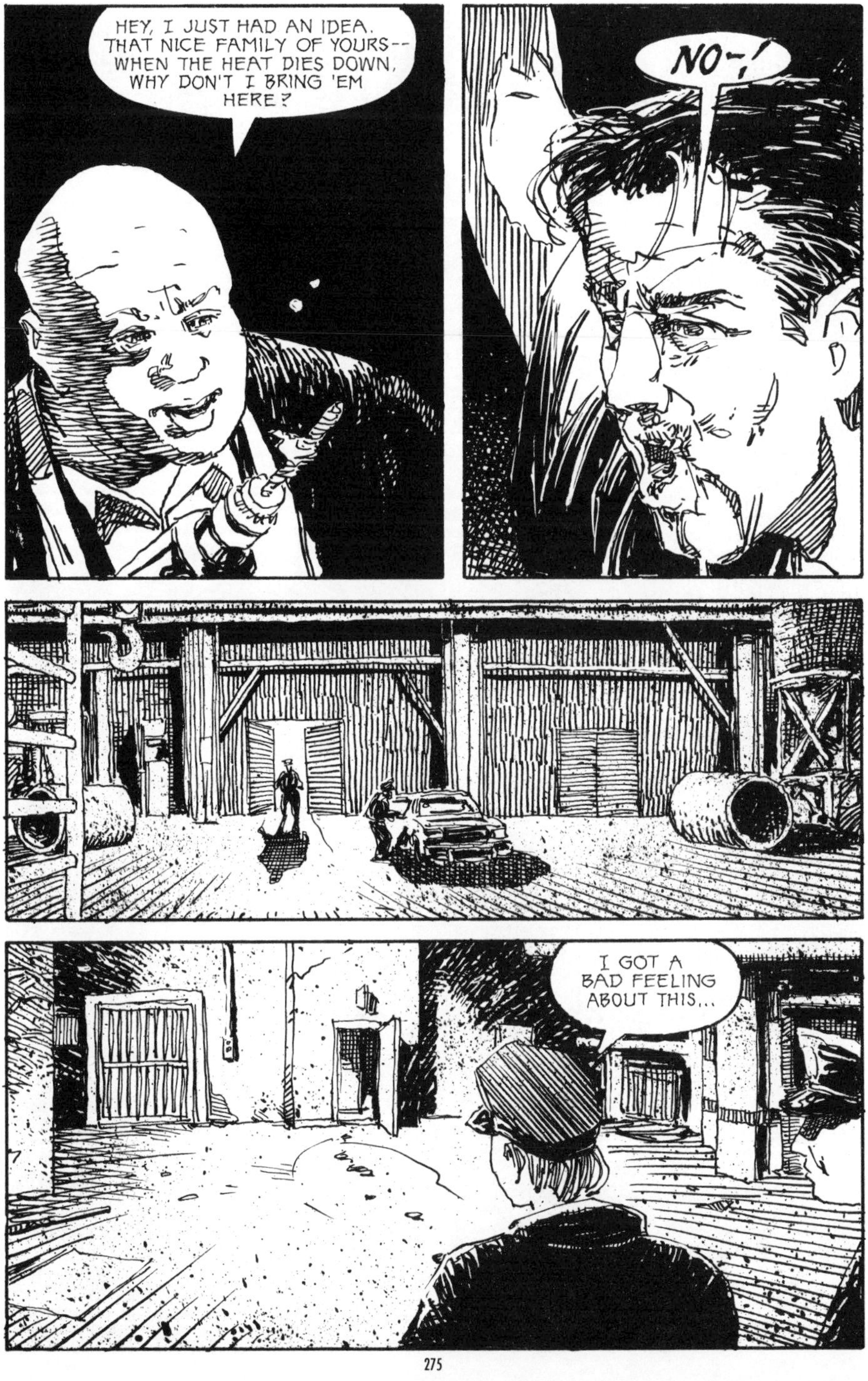

HEY, I JUST HAD AN IDEA. THAT NICE FAMILY OF YOURS-- WHEN THE HEAT DIES DOWN, WHY DON'T I BRING 'EM HERE?
NO-!
I GOT A BAD FEELING ABOUT THIS...

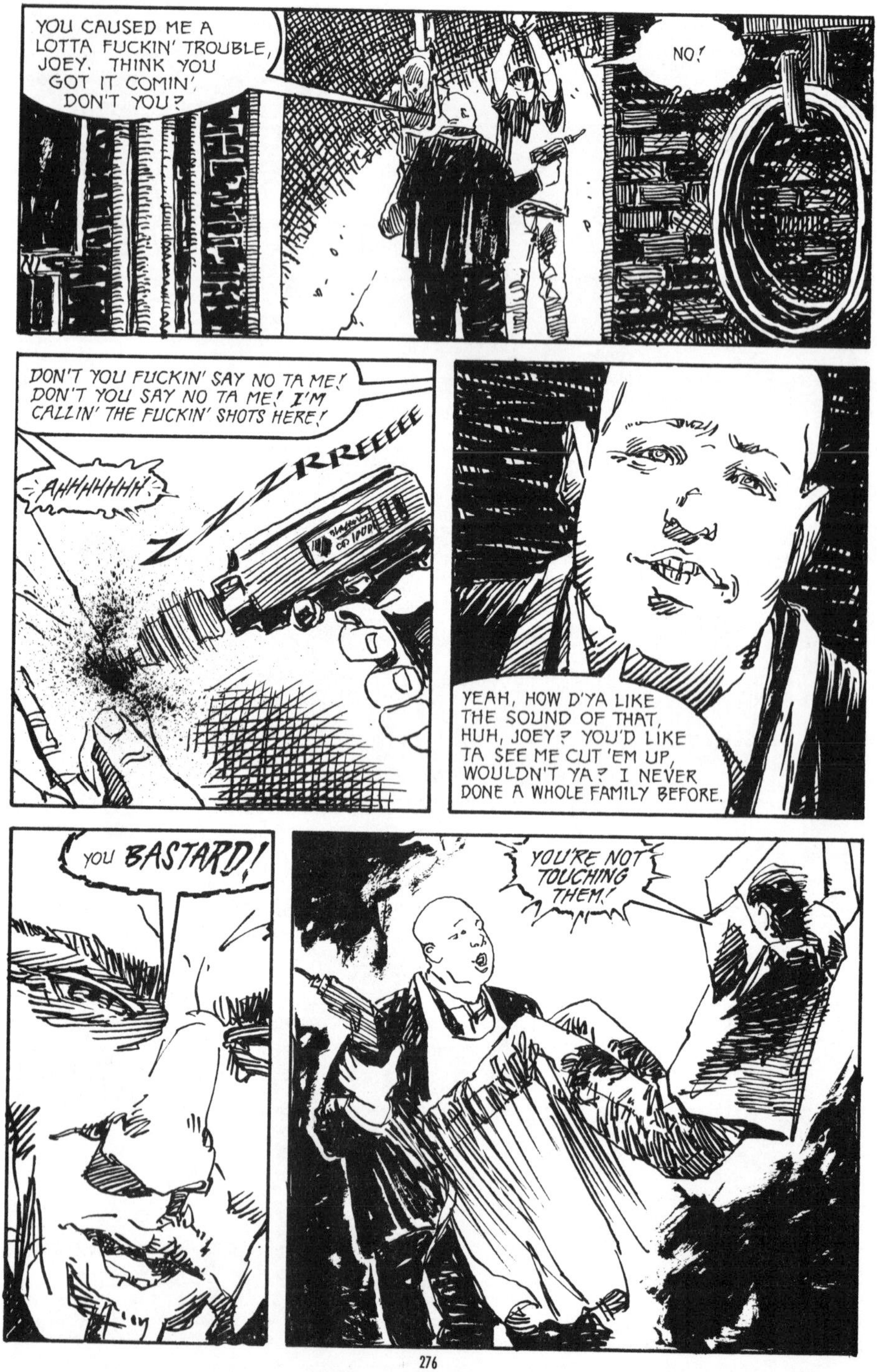
YOU CAUSED ME A LOTTA FUCKIN' TROUBLE, JOEY. THINK YOU GOT IT COMIN' DON'T YOU?
NO!
DON'T YOU FUCKIN' SAY NO TA ME! DON'T YOU SAY NO TA ME! I'M CALLIN' THE FUCKIN' SHOTS HERE!
ZZZRREEEEE
AHHHHHHH
YEAH, HOW D'YA LIKE THE SOUND OF THAT, HUH, JOEY? YOU'D LIKE TA SEE ME CUT 'EM UP, WOULDN'T YA? I NEVER DONE A WHOLE FAMILY BEFORE.
YOU BASTARD!
YOU'RE NOT TOUCHING THEM!

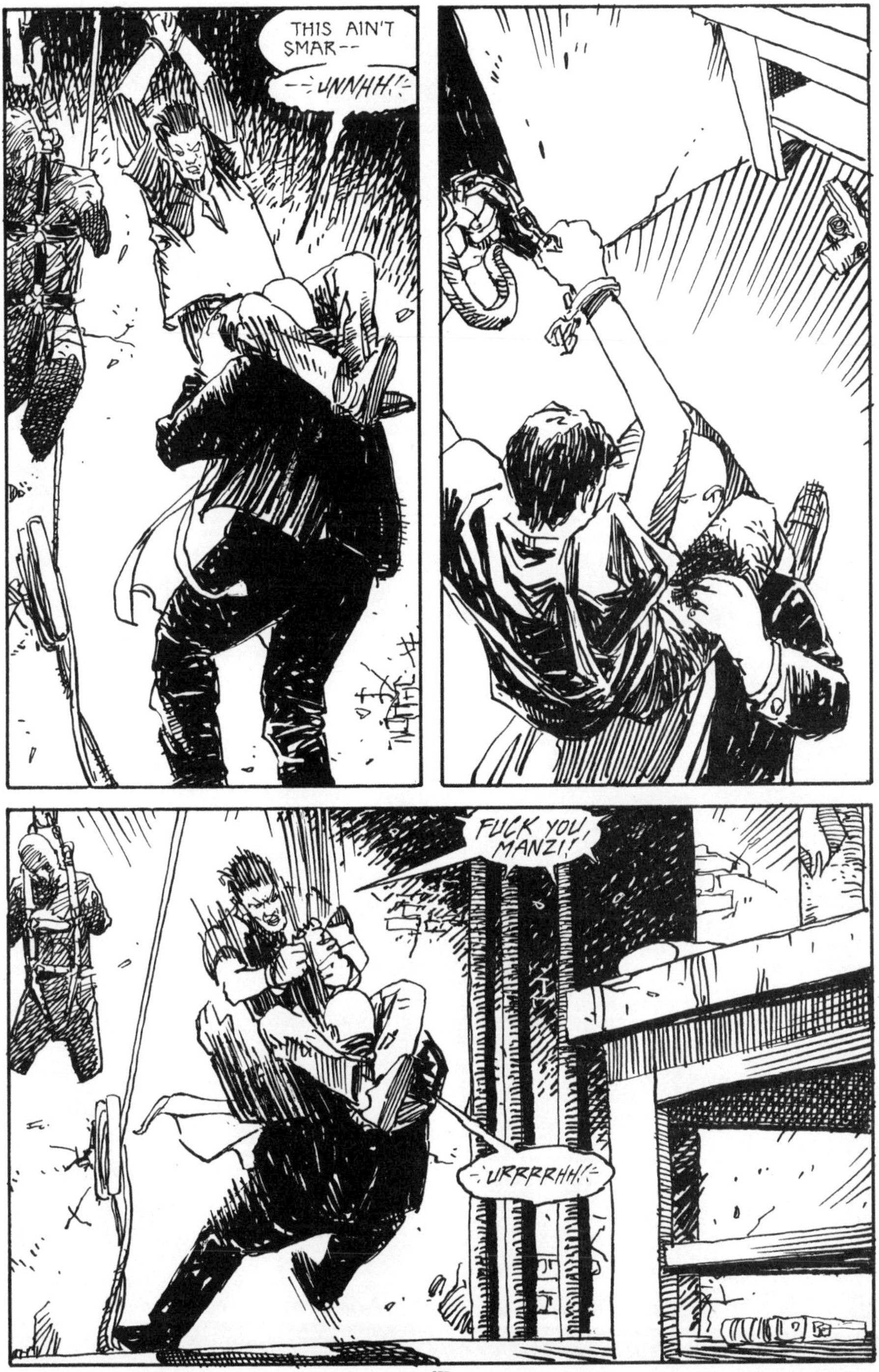

THIS AIN'T SMAR--
--UNNHH!
FUCK YOU, MANZI!
URRRRHH!

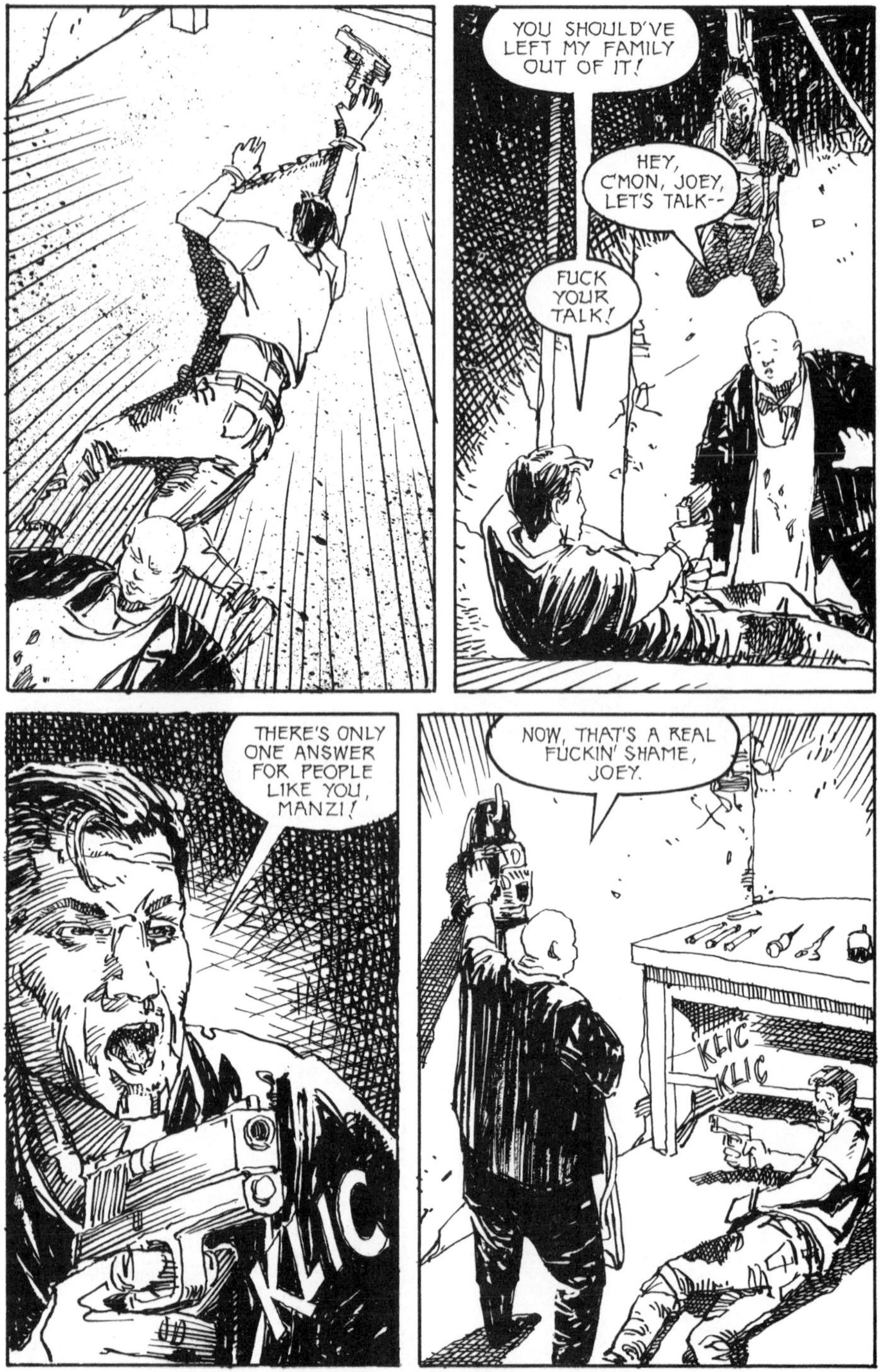

YOU SHOULD'VE LEFT MY FAMILY OUT OF IT!
HEY, C'MON, JOEY, LET'S TALK--
FUCK YOUR TALK!
THERE'S ONLY ONE ANSWER FOR PEOPLE LIKE YOU, MANZI!
KLIC
NOW, THAT'S A REAL FUCKIN' SHAME, JOEY.
KLIC
KLIC

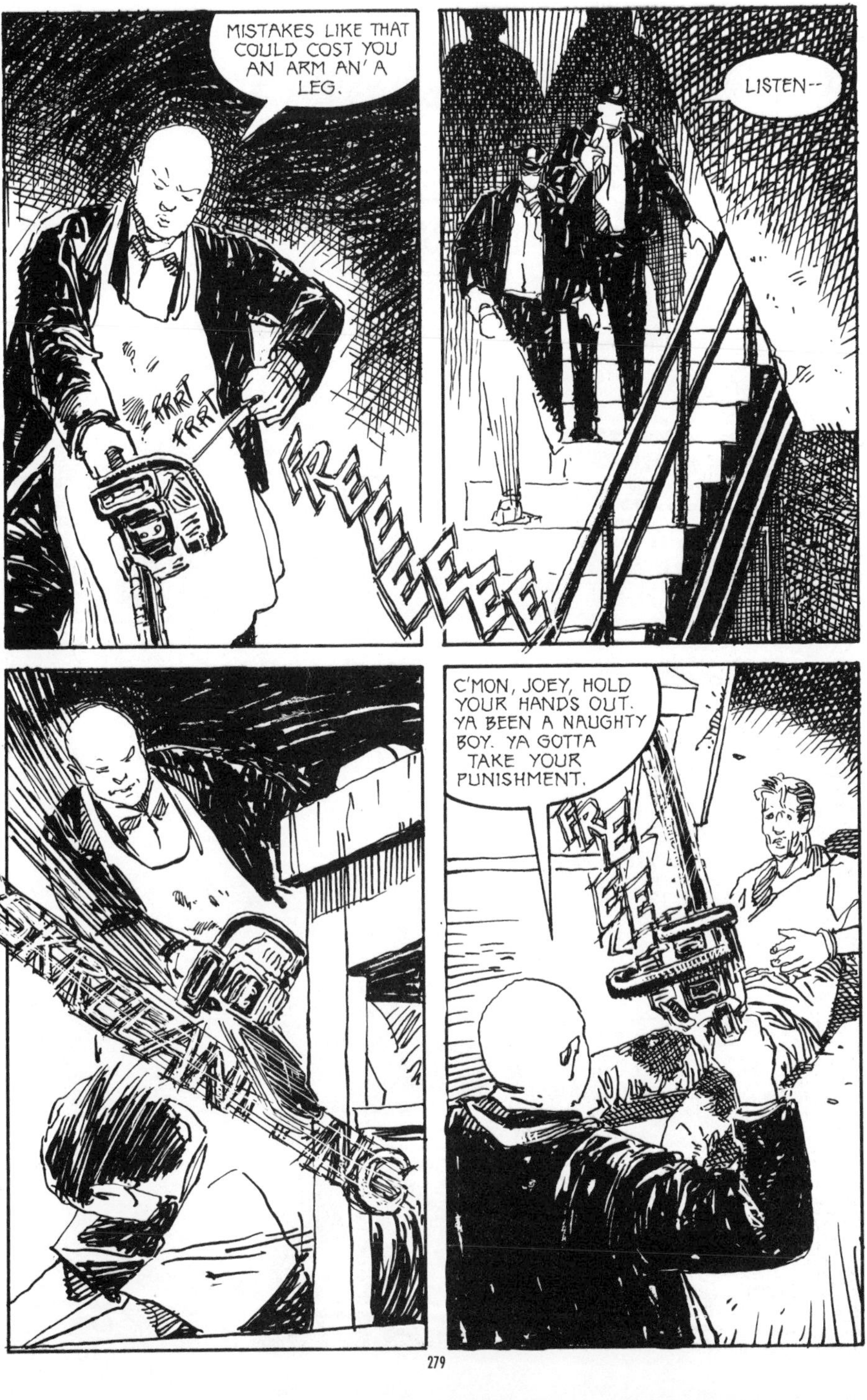
MISTAKES LIKE THAT COULD COST YOU AN ARM AN' A LEG.
FRRT FRRT
LISTEN--
C'MON, JOEY, HOLD YOUR HANDS OUT. YA BEEN A NAUGHTY BOY. YA GOTTA TAKE YOUR PUNISHMENT.

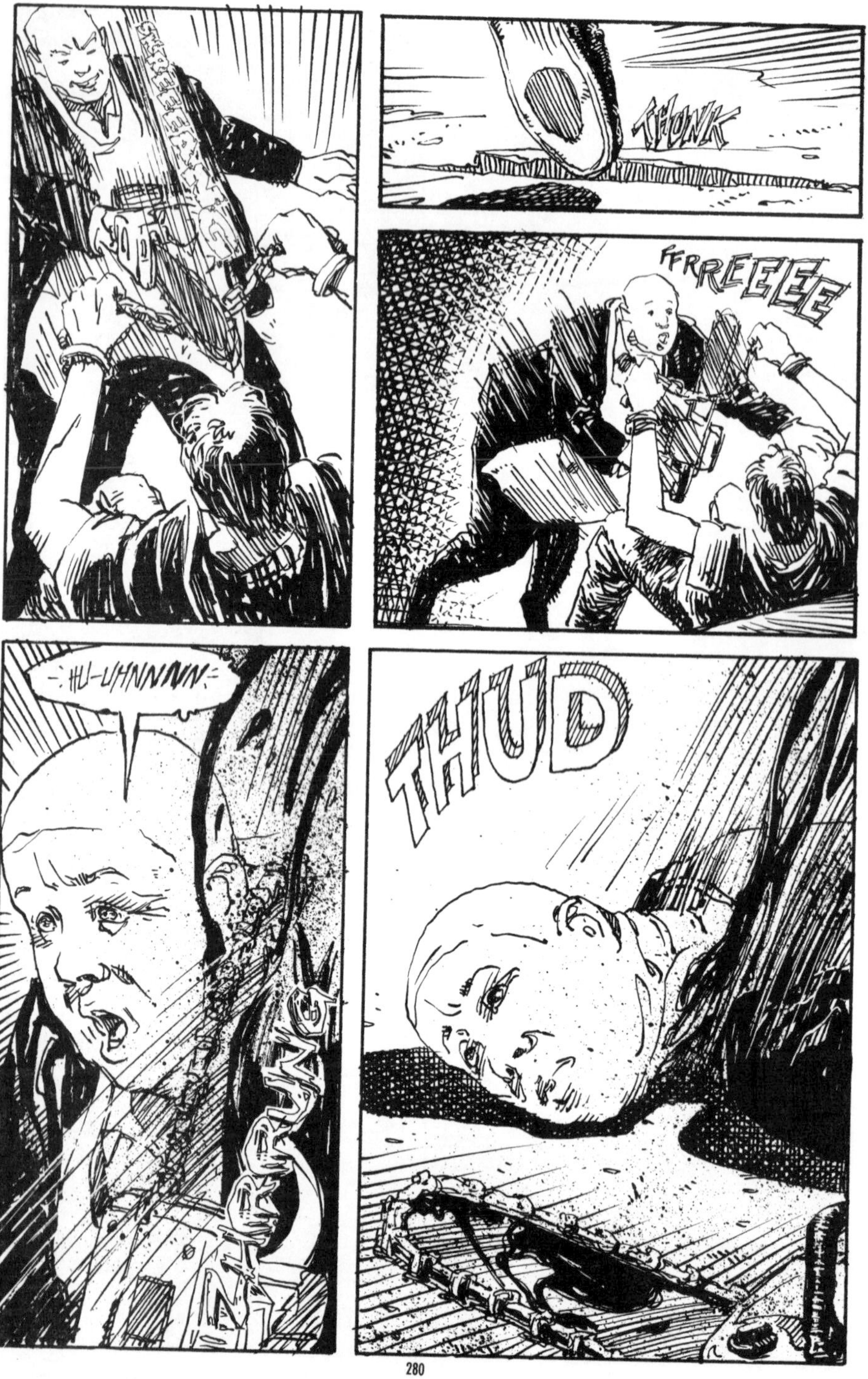
THONK
FFRREEEEE
HU-UHNNNNN
THUD

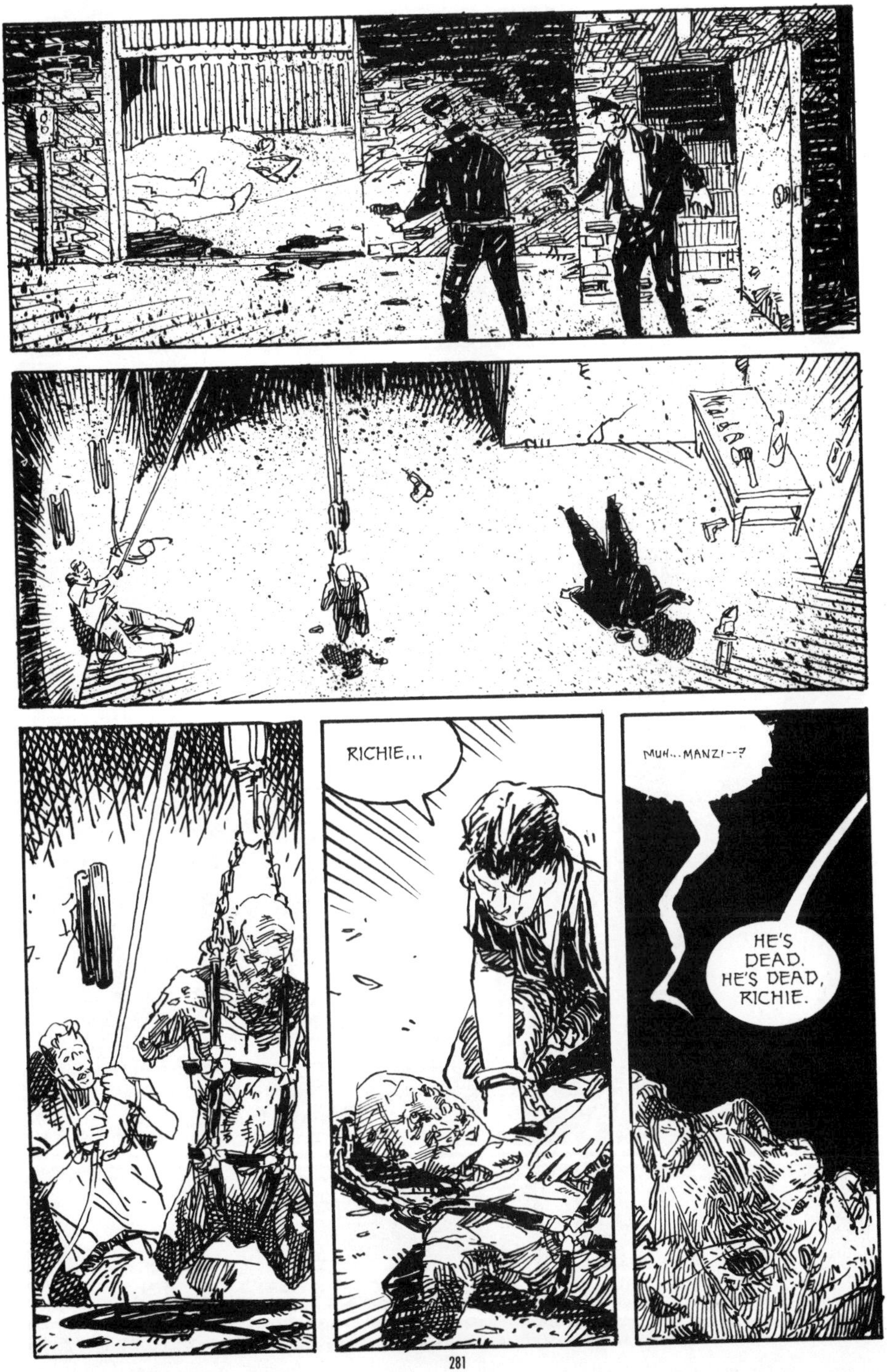
RICHIE...
MUH... MANZI--?
HE'S DEAD. HE'S DEAD, RICHIE.

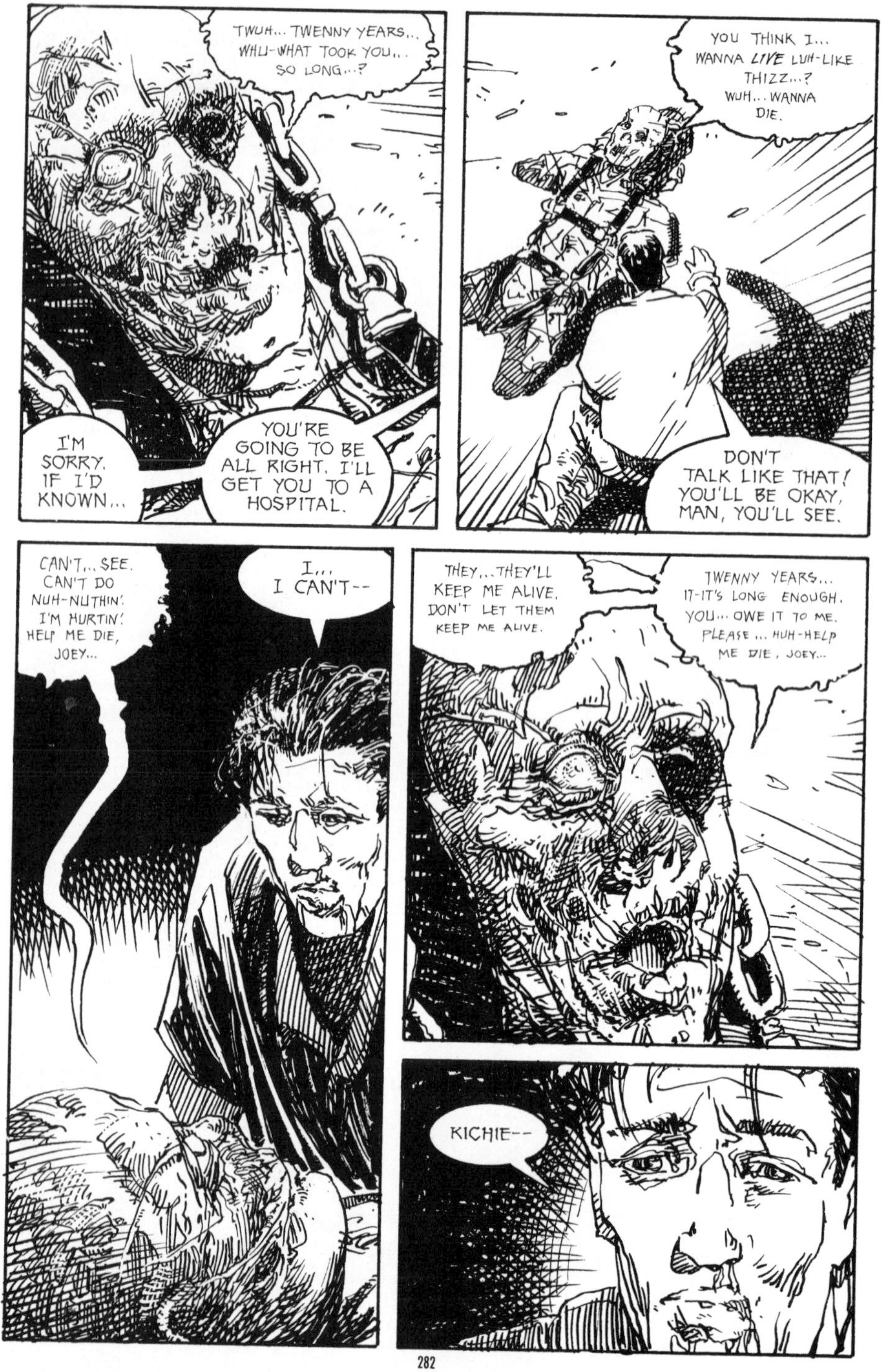
TWUH... TWENNY YEARS... WHU-WHAT TOOK YOU... SO LONG...?
I'M SORRY. IF I'D KNOWN...
YOU'RE GOING TO BE ALL RIGHT. I'LL GET YOU TO A HOSPITAL.
YOU THINK I... WANNA *LIVE* LUH-LIKE THIZZ...? WUH... WANNA DIE.
DON'T TALK LIKE THAT! YOU'LL BE OKAY, MAN, YOU'LL SEE.
CAN'T... SEE. CAN'T DO NUH-NUTHIN'. I'M HURTIN'. HELP ME DIE, JOEY...
I... I CAN'T--
THEY... THEY'LL KEEP ME ALIVE. DON'T LET THEM KEEP ME ALIVE.
TWENNY YEARS... IT-IT'S LONG ENOUGH. YOU... OWE IT TO ME. PLEASE... HUH-HELP ME DIE, JOEY...
KICHIE--

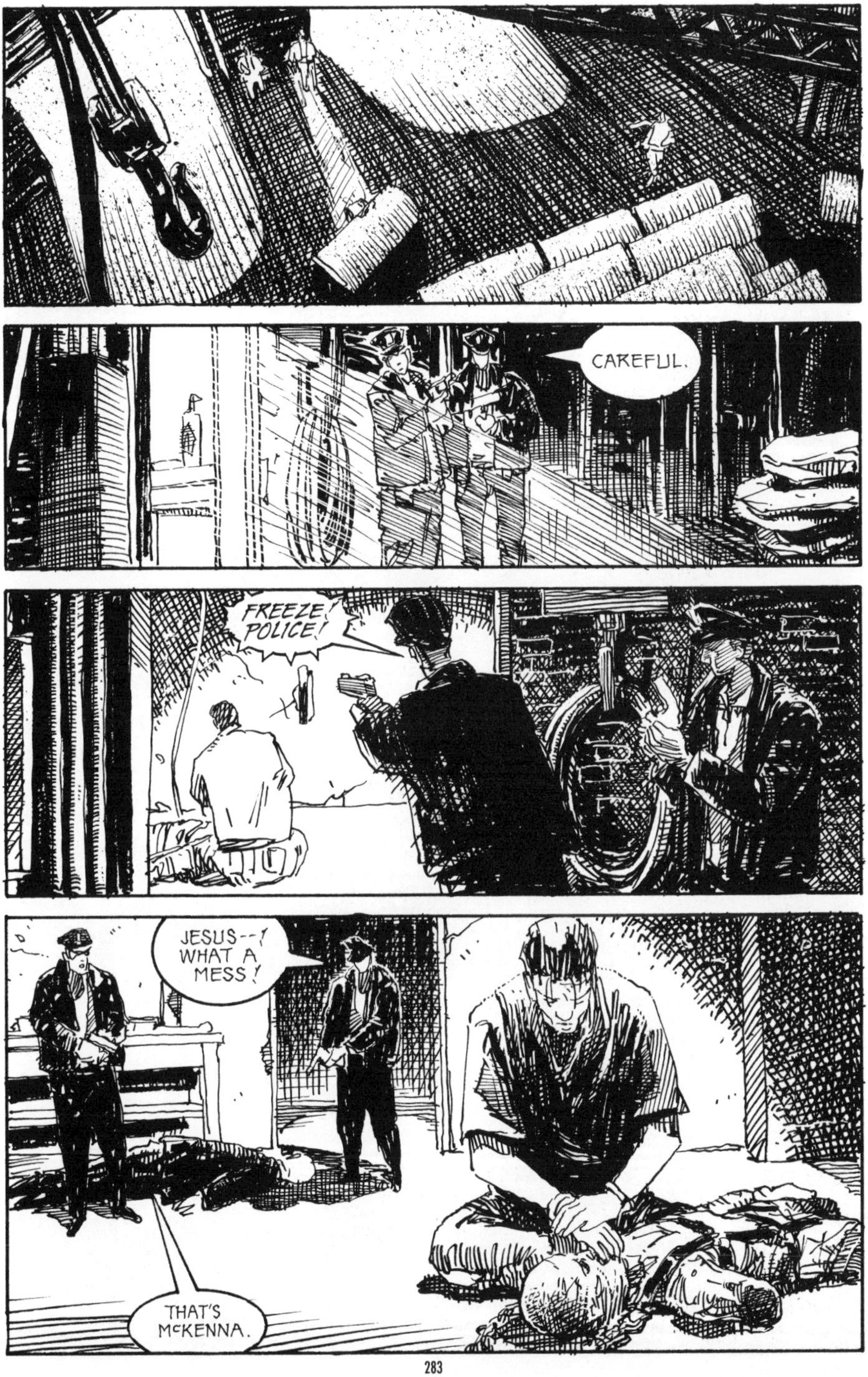
CAREFUL.
FREEZE! POLICE!
JESUS--! WHAT A MESS!
THAT'S McKENNA.

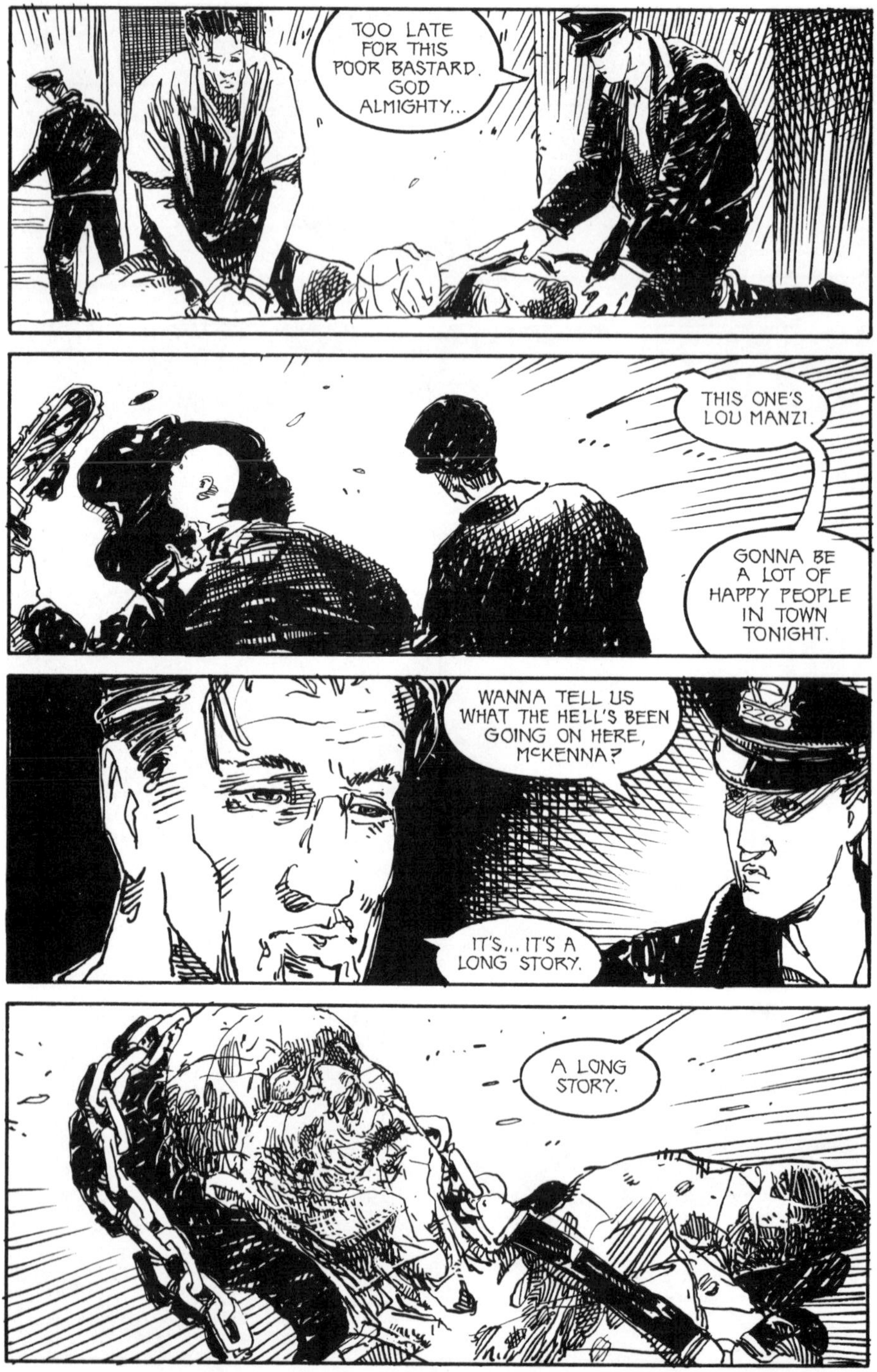
TOO LATE FOR THIS POOR BASTARD. GOD ALMIGHTY...
THIS ONE'S LOU MANZI.
GONNA BE A LOT OF HAPPY PEOPLE IN TOWN TONIGHT.
WANNA TELL US WHAT THE HELL'S BEEN GOING ON HERE, McKENNA?
2206
IT'S... IT'S A LONG STORY.
A LONG STORY.

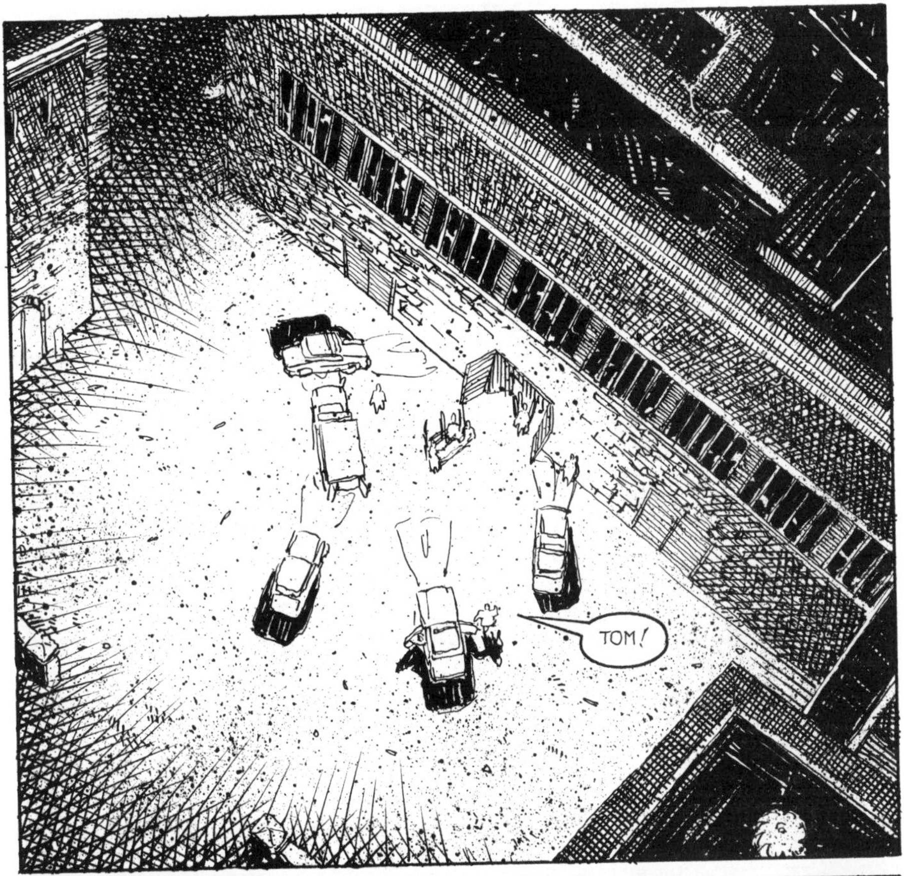
TOM!

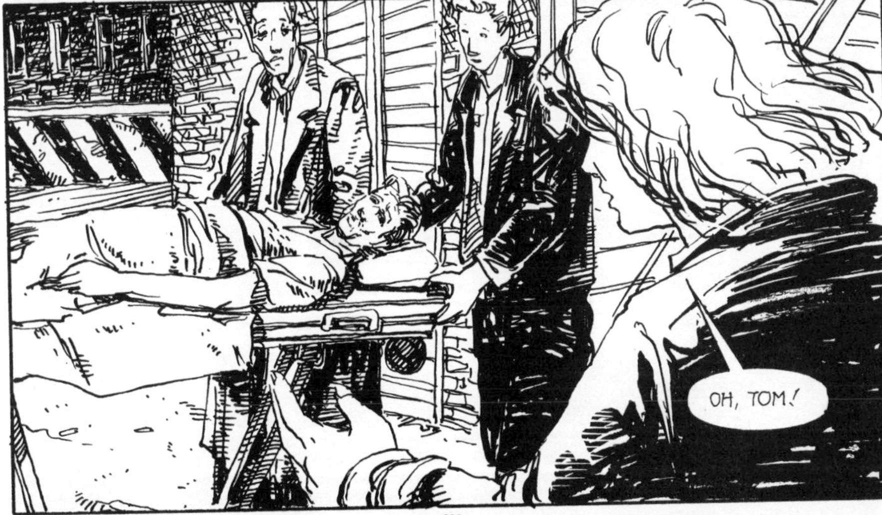
OH, TOM!

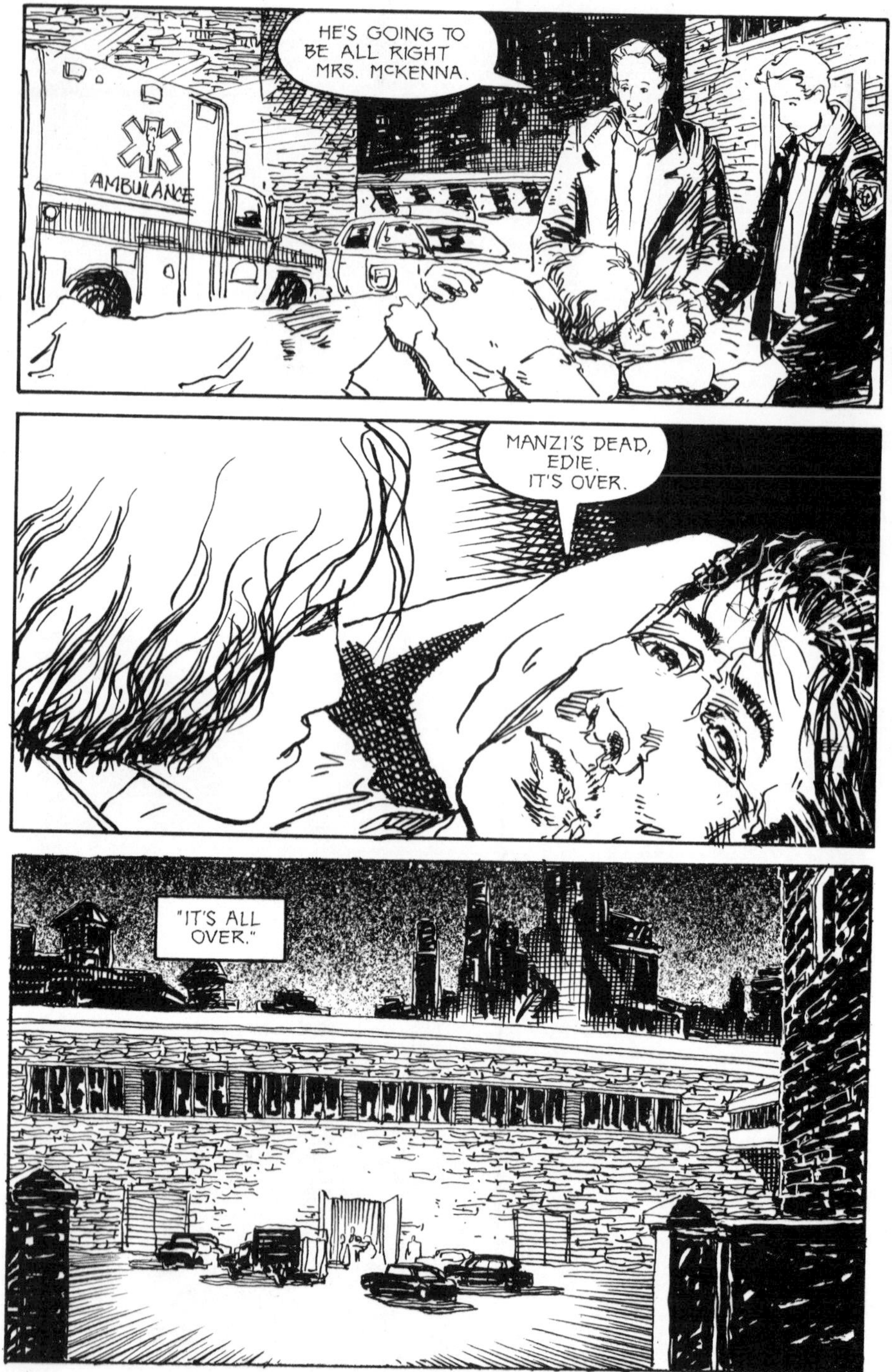
HE'S GOING TO BE ALL RIGHT MRS. McKENNA.
AMBULANCE
MANZI'S DEAD, EDIE. IT'S OVER.
"IT'S ALL OVER."